Medical Perspectives
in
VOCATIONAL ASSESSMENT
OF
IMPAIRED WORKERS

Edited by
Steven J. Scheer, MD
Associate Professor and Director
Department of Physical Medicine and Rehabilitation
University of Cincinnati Medical Center
Cincinnati, Ohio

AN ASPEN PUBLICATION ®
Aspen Publishers, Inc.
Gaithersburg, Maryland
1991

Library of Congress Cataloging-in-Publication Data

Medical perspectives in vocational assessment
of impaired workers /
edited by Steven J. Scheer.
p. cm.
Includes bibliographical references.
Includes index.
ISBN: 0-8342-0179-8
1. Disability evaluation. 2. Work capacity evaluation.
I. Scheer, Steven J.
[DNLM: 1. Disability Evaluation. 2. Rehabilitation, Vocational.
3. Work Capacity Evaluation. HD 7255 M489]
RC963.4.M43 1991
617.1'03 — dc20
DNLM/DLC
for Library of Congress
90-1093
CIP

The authors have made every effort to ensure the accuracy of the
information herein, particularly with regard to technique, procedure,
drug selection, and dose. However, appropriate information sources
should be consulted, especially for new or unfamiliar drugs or procedures.
It is the responsibility of every practitioner to evaluate the appropriateness of a particular opinion in the context of actual clinical situations and
with due consideration to new developments. Authors, editors, and the
publisher cannot be held responsible for any typographical or other errors
found in this book.

Editorial Services: Lorna Perkins

Library of Congress Catalog Card Number: 90-1093
ISBN: 0-8342-0179-8

Printed in the United States of America

1 2 3 4 5

To
Aviva, Jennifer, Rachel, and Erica,
who have put up with me
throughout this long ordeal . . .

Table of Contents

Contributors

William Anthony, PhD
Executive Director
Center for Psychiatric Rehabilitation
Boston University
Boston, Massachusetts

John M. Bednar, MD
Assistant Professor of Orthopaedic and Hand
  Surgery
Hospital of the University of Pennsylvania
Philadelphia, Pennsylvania

Brian Boehlecke, MD, MSPH
Associate Professor of Medicine
Department of Medicine
Division of Pulmonary Diseases
University of North Carolina at Chapel Hill
Chapel Hill, North Carolina

Pamela Brown, MD
Assistant Professor of Rehabilitation Medicine
University of Arkansas for Medical Sciences
Little Rock, Arkansas

Bruce Caplan, PhD
Associate Professor and Chief Psychologist
Department of Rehabilitation Medicine
Thomas Jefferson University Hospital
Philadelphia, Pennsylvania

Karen Danley, PhD
Director, Career Achievement Services
Center for Psychiatric Rehabilitation
Sargent College of Allied Health Professions
Boston University
Boston, Massachusetts

Charles A. Dennis, MD, FACC
Director of Cardiac Rehabilitation
Scripps Clinic and Research Foundation
La Jolla, California

Theodora Fine, MA
Principal
Fine Wordcrafters
Columbia, Maryland

William Frankenstein, PhD
Assistant Professor
Center for Alcohol Studies
Rutgers University
Piscataway, New Jersey

Richard Gray, MD
Assistant Professor
Division of Rehabilitation Medicine
University of Arkansas for Medical Sciences
Little Rock, Arkansas
Staff Physiatrist
John L. McClellan VA Medical Center
North Little Rock, Arkansas

M. Drue Lehmann, MA, CCC-SLP
Field Service Associate Professor
Department of Physical Medicine and
  Rehabilitation
University of Cincinnati College of Medicine
Cincinnati, Ohio

F. Patrick Maloney, MD
Professor and Head
Division of Rehabilitation Medicine
College of Medicine
University of Arkansas for Medical Sciences
Little Rock, Arkansas

Arthur T. Meyerson, MD
Professor and Chairman
Department of Mental Health Sciences
Hahnemann University
Philadelphia, Pennsylvania

Anne M.B. Moscony, MA, OTR/L
Hand Therapist
Sports Physical Therapists, Inc.
Cherry Hill, New Jersey

John J. Nicholas, MD
Professor and Acting Chairman
Department of Physical Medicine and
   Rehabilitation
Rush Medical College
Rush University
Chicago, Illinois

A. Lee Osterman, MD
Associate Professor of Orthopaedic and Hand
   Surgery
Hospital of the University of Pennsylvania
Philadelphia, Pennsylvania

Dianne M. Parrotte, MD
Chief, Occupational Health
Bath Iron Works
Bath, Maine

Michael D. Privitera, MD
Assistant Professor
Department of Neurology
University of Cincinnati Medical Center
Cincinnati, Ohio

John B. Redford, MD
Professor and Chair
Department of Rehabilitation Medicine

University of Kansas Medical Center
Kansas City, Kansas

Mark A. Rothstein, JD
Professor of Law
Director, Health Law and Policy Institute
University of Houston Law Center
Houston, Texas

Steven J. Scheer, MD
Associate Professor and Director
Department of Physical Medicine and
   Rehabilitation
University of Cincinnati Medical Center
Cincinnati, Ohio

**Melanie A. Schleicher, MS,
   CCC-SLP**
Clinical Speech-Language Pathologist
Department of Physical Medicine and
   Rehabilitation
University of Cincinnati College of Medicine
Cincinnati, Ohio

Judith A. Shechter, PhD
Department of Neurology
Lankenau Hospital
Philadelphia, Pennsylvania

Terri Skirven, OTR/L
Program Director
Hand Therapy
Department of Occupational Therapy
Hospital of the University of Pennsylvania
Philadelphia, Pennsylvania

Richard J. Wickstrom, PT
President
Disability Control, Inc.
Cincinnati, Ohio

Preface

The human being is a mean machine. Its exquisite complexity makes easily understandable the number of potential human system malfunctions. Yet the equally impressive capacity to compensate for bodily impairment is testimony to the power of the human spirit, the grease of this mean machine.

In the workplace, injury or disease can alter performance in many ways. Specific impairment chapters in these two volumes bring to mind many human vulnerabilities with occupational ramifications. The 1980 census showed that just under 9% of working-age Americans (over 12 million) have one or more disabling conditions. But for some individuals, having a particular impairment is insufficient reason to not work. What is disabling for one is merely a barrier to overcome for another. And of those not working due to disability, a recent survey showed that two thirds would prefer to work if offered a job.

These two texts, *Multidisciplinary Perspectives in Vocational Assessment of Impaired Workers* and *Medical Perspectives in Vocational Assessment of Impaired Workers*, are thus dedicated to medical and vocational professionals who make decisions about work capacity. The intended audience includes physicians, allied health workers, rehabilitation counselors in training and practice, occupational nurses, employers, engineers, disability managers, and vocational rehabilitation agencies. The fact that the material is directed to so many in health care, the physical sciences, and industry suggests that all should be speaking a common language in effecting return to work of patients with injury or disease.

The texts address some extremely significant questions. While disease/injury states are often grouped by impairment types, and jobs are categorized by physical, social, or intellectual demand, it does not follow that a human being with a particular diagnosis will necessarily be incapable of performing a given job. A particular impairment may constitute vocational handicap in one person but not another, suggesting the need for an individualized assessment that matches the worker and the job requirements. The context-specific question is *what level of abilities constitutes sufficient capacity for a person with a given impairment to function at a particular type of work?*

Each chapter author was invited to describe state-of-the-art methods of assessment. However, as one might expect, the capacity to measure skills objectively, particularly work abilities, varies greatly across the spectrum of impairments. Also, simulating a work environment can only be, at best, a contrived attempt to imitate the actual work surroundings. Nevertheless, certain functional limitations are fairly easily demonstrated, and others are not. *Which impairments can be objectively measured?*

The question of *who should be involved in job-related capacity determinations* is another important issue. While the physician continues to play a crucial and coordinating role, the efforts of vocational rehabilitation counselors, allied health care professionals, employers, union representatives, engineers, and family members are all extremely important. Examination of the chapter writers' credentials confirms this fact: fourteen are physicians; seven, vocational counselors; six, psychologists; three, physical and occupational therapists; two, speech pathologists; and one each, rehabilitation engineer and legal expert.

The focus is on evaluating ability to work in spite of impairment, rather than on quantification of disability. It has been difficult to separate these two notions for many health care professionals. The difficulty is fostered in part by directed requests from third-party payers, attorneys, and patients themselves to focus on limitations so as to assist in monetarily compensating the worker. This legalistic disability evaluation does serve a function. Financial subsidy is, after all, an earned right of every disabled citizen in our society. However, it is not the purpose of *Multidisciplinary Perspectives in Vocational Assessment of Impaired Workers* and *Medical Perspectives in Vocational Assessment of Impaired Workers* to dwell on disability evaluation. Compared to quantification of disability, recognizing ability and identifying ways to compensate for its lack are nobler societal goals.

During the period that these books were in preparation, our nation experienced the awakening of "deaf power" when the student body of Gallaudet University rose up to protest the trustees' choice of a hearing person for the university's seventh president. The experience, initially of intense national concern, quickly faded from the memories of most hearing persons. But the crucial issue will remain: Why should this position, president of a university, be considered an unreasonable pursuit for a deaf person? In this book, and it is hoped others that follow it, the undeniable message is that through assessment of vocational capacity, a full recognition of ability will allow persons, though otherwise impaired, to become maximally productive in our society.

Acknowledgments

I am personally indebted to my many teachers—before, during, and since medical training—for their guidance in helping to shape my professional development. It was an extreme honor to be able to count myself among those trained by Frederic J. Kottke, MD, PhD, at the University of Minnesota. I have fond recollections of my formative years in medical and specialty training, where I encountered such lofty role models as Joel Rosen, MD; Franz Steinberg, MD; Henry B. Betts, MD; Theodore Cole, MD; Glenn Gullickson, MD, PhD; Tom Anderson, MD; Keith Sperling, MD; Dan Halpern, MD; Esam Awad, MD, PhD; Rita Bistevins, MD; and Jesse Easton, MD. To all of them goes my gratitude.

Like the interdisciplinary teamwork frequently ascribed to herein, this book and its accompanying volume, *Multidisciplinary Perspectives in Vocational Assessment of Impaired Workers*, would not have been possible without the concerted efforts of many individuals. The secretarial talents of Terri Chiatkowski (New England Rehabilitation Hospital); Pat Walk, Marilyn Weinheimer, and Carol Dupps (University of Cincinnati College of Medicine); and Marilyn Gloss were most appreciated, as well as the library services of Carol Spencer and Cathy J. Hansen (Lahey Clinic, Boston). Many others who worked with individual chapter writers could not be mentioned, but their efforts are no less appreciated.

I owe many thanks to Aspen Publishers, Inc., in Gaithersburg, Maryland. I am grateful for the editorial assistance of Nancy Smith, Martha Sasser, and Bill Burgower, and most particularly to Margaret Quinlin for their continued efforts to help put this book to bed. Thanks to Margaret, I learned about the extraordinary copy editing skills of Gail Martin, who provided the manuscript with consistency, clarity, and succinctness—all done in a most reassuring and professional manner. I am most grateful to her.

Finally, I am mindful of the many sacrifices endured by my family, who suffered through the long periods of Dad-in-the-study-working-on-his-book. Without their forbearance and support, I would not have garnered the fortitude and psychic energy necessary to persevere with this onerous task.

chapter 1

The Physician's Responsibility in Assessing Vocational Capacity

Steven J. Scheer

"Society reaps at this moment but a small fraction of the advantage which current knowledge has the power to confer."

Abraham Flexner[1]

Many physicians consider themselves scientifically driven to pursue objectivity and consistency in decision making. Yet, professional idiosyncracies and the phenomenon of iatrogenic medical injury have been the subject of much debate in the recent past, from both outside and inside the field.[2–4] In most situations that call for their involvement, physicians use their knowledge to perform medical functions admirably. One area, however, in which physicians fail to measure up consistently to societal expectations is the medical assessment of work potential.

CIRCUMSTANCES OF WORK-RELATED DECISIONS BY PHYSICIANS

The circumstances under which a physician sees a patient to determine the extent of work-limiting impairment vary greatly. In some instances, the normal physician-patient relationship holds. In others, an occupational physician representing a company is asked to render an opinion. In still others, an objective third-party physician is involved. In addition, there are several levels of formality for decisions about medical fitness to work: (1) pre-employment screening or physical examination; (2) return-to-work letter, requested by the patient or employer after illness/injury; (3) evaluation and treatment plan implementation; (4) impairment rating; (5) Social Security disability evaluation; and (6) the impartial medical evaluation (IME).

Pre-Employment Examination

Many companies require a pre-employment health screening and physical examination. Sometimes, such an examination includes a functional capacity assessment, generally one that is relevant to the physical demands of the work. It may also involve anthropometric measurements of height, weight, reach, or other parameters to obtain further job-relevant information. Depending on the degree of job specificity required, a pre-employment screening and physical examination may be performed by the individual's personal physician or by a company physician.

Return-to-Work Letter after Short-Lived Illness/Injury

Patients and employers commonly call upon physicians to substantiate a worker's ability to return to work after a brief ailment or self-limited injury. Generally, these decisions can be made after a physical examination alone, which is occasionally supplemented by laboratory testing.

Evaluation and Treatment Plan Implementation

When the worker has an impairment that has resulted in work disability, the family or company physician evaluates the history, symptoms, and signs; performs appropriate laboratory studies; and determines a specific diagnosis. If treatment is necessary, the physician makes recommendations, and the treatment success and the proper time for work return can be readily determined, at times utilizing a functional capacity assessment (see Chapter 2, this volume; Chapter 6, accompanying volume).

Circumstances are more ill defined, however, when psychosocial variables complicate a seemingly simple injury. Physicians who treat injured workers must be sensitive to the pathologic impairment-functional disability interface.

Treatment should be as job-specific as possible, with successes, especially in more chronic cases, measured objectively by means of a functional capacity assessment. Ideally, a decision to involve a rehabilitation specialist and the allied health care team should not be made before the patient has begun to believe that he or she will never heal, a perception that can become a self-fulfilling prophecy. The sooner a definitive return-to-work rehabilitation program can be initiated, the better.

Impairment Rating

Developed to compensate workers for anatomic dysfunction, a medical impairment rating is generally determined by specialists in the medical field of the specific impairment. The most commonly used system of rating impairment among American physicians is found in the *Guides to the Evaluation of Permanent Impairment (GEPI)*, produced by the American Medical Association specialty panels.[5] This book contains more than 200 pages of charts, graphs, and descriptive material divided into the major areas of diagnosis-related impairment. It purports to assist physicians in enumerating the degree of impairment that a particular disorder represents, but leaves the determination of disability to a so-called administrative or legal system. It defines the term "impairment" as "an alteration of health status assessed by medical means," whereas "disability" is defined as "an alteration of the patient's capacity to meet the personal, social, or occupational demands or to meet statutory or regulatory requirements, which is assessed by nonmedical means."[5]

The impairment rating system is supposed to allow a physician to measure permanent-and-partial or permanent-and-total impairments in a way that can help a patient to receive a monetary settlement for an injury. For example, after a serious back injury that requires a patient to have a surgical fusion of three lumbar spine segments in the fully extended (neutral) position, the listed impairment is 6%-of-whole-body. Amputation of the right arm at the shoulder is listed as a 60%-of-whole-body impairment. These percentages may be multiplied by the injured person's annual wages for the number of years before retirement to come up with a financial worth of the claim.

There are several operational problems in using the system described in the *GEPI*. The writers specifically request that physicians define a disorder only by arbitrary and, at times, irrelevant categories of affected functions. In the chapter on musculoskeletal impairment, for example, altered range of joint motion and fusion of a joint are the only two considerations for degrees of impairment, even though joint immobility can frequently be accommodated without limiting function. Furthermore, there is no way of assessing the validity of any impairment rating because age, occupation, background, and locality (work availability) are not to be taken into account in the determination. Physicians are to focus on medical issues of organ- or physiology-specific limitations while ignoring the context of the person's life. The *GEPI's* stated denial of the physician's role in determining the social or personal implications of illness or injury is curious, since this proscription leaves important quality-of-life considerations to the "administrative system," usually a veiled euphemism for two or three attorneys and/or a judge.[5–7] Thus, the administrative body that makes the ultimate decision of disability may be neither medically informed nor sophisticated in vocational or societal handicaps.

In actual practice, some physicians do consider social and vocational variables in determining impairment ratings,[8] but they do so with great inter-rater inconsistencies. In an attempt to establish the inter-rater reliability and validity of the *GEPI*, Gloss and Wardle compared the *GEPI*-derived impairment with a summation of psychomotor gripping and finger dexterity tests in 118 patients with hand injuries.[9] Although the inter-rater reliability was satisfactory in assessing simple impairments, the reliability was attenuated in assessing multiple impairments: "The AMA's *Guide* provided ambiguous guidelines that could and often did lead to large differences between raters."[9] In addition, although the authors claimed to have shown the validity of the *GEPI* by correlating the psychomotor tests in each case with the ratings by physicians, there was no evidence that any of these psychomotor tests were really meaningful for the jobs or everyday activities of any of these 118 individuals tested. The authors thus failed to satisfy criteria for content or construct validity.[10]

Another issue of great concern is the potential prostitution of the medical profession by the use of impairment ratings for financial settlements. An adversarial situation may arise in which two physicians, one selected by the employer or insurance company paying the disability benefits and the other by the patient's lawyer, examine the patient and rate the impairment. The two physicians often arrive at totally different ratings, reflecting either their preconceived biases, a desire to continue to draw attorney business, or inconsistencies in the information transmitted to them by referring parties.[11] In the state of New Jersey in 1986, for example, a highly adversarial system resulted in 67% of claimant orthopedic ratings of 30%-of-whole-body impairment or more, whereas 95% of respondent orthopedic ratings in the same cases were 15%-of-whole-body impairment or less. The judge generally settles on a compromised rating, recognizing that the two expert determinations are biased.[11] Thus, this impairment rating system, which is often vocationally and socially irrelevant, may serve to manipulate physicians to meet the financial self-interests of attorneys and their clients.

Several medical and legal sources have reflected on this adversarial system for determining degree of impairment. Carey and Hadler suggested reconstructing the disability schedules to make them comprehensive and yet predictive in validity.[6,7] Richman, defending the adversarial system while recognizing its limitations, felt that under the best of circumstances, there is no better way of determining the truth of causality and degree of dysfunction.[12] He further challenged critics of the adversarial system to suggest reasonable alternative systems.

Both critics and proponents of impairment ratings are certainly aware that multiple medical evaluations can become an obstacle to work return by increasing the amount of time lost and the magnitude of the chronicity syndrome.[11] It is important to recognize that impairment ratings are not evaluations of employability, vocational capacity, or return-to-work potential. Yet, the results of ratings are used generally to determine the amount of compensation due a worker for not being able to work. A system that rewards for work incapacity ought to measure that specific capacity, rather than some vaguely connected anatomic abnormalities.

Social Security Disability Evaluation

Social Security Disability Insurance (SSDI) was first established in 1954 during the Eisenhower administration. In the summer of 1979, the Social Security Administration produced a handbook to clarify the procedures that physicians should follow in conducting examinations to determine eligibility for Title II (SSDI) and Title XVI (Supplemental Security Income) benefits.[13] The Social Security Disability Amendments were then introduced, which provide work return incentives to beneficiaries.

With monies collected through payroll taxes, the system establishes a trust fund to ensure just compensation for persons unable to work. In order to qualify for SSDI, an individual must be unable "to engage in *any* substantial gainful activity by reason of a medically determinable physical or mental impairment which can be expected to result in death or has lasted or can be expected to last for a continuous period of not less than 12 months."[13] The consulted physician must determine if the patient's condition meets the eligibility criteria established by the Social Security Administration. If so, a lengthy process entailing several steps then ensues, requiring a minimum of 5 months but often more than a year if appeals are necessary.[7] During the mandatory 5 months' waiting period, many disabled workers lose motivation for medical treatment and avoid seeking vocational rehabilitation.

Carey and Hadler[6] suggested reorganizing the system to remove the district variability in granting the insurance and to improve the accuracy of the determination of deservedness. Although these measures would be helpful, modifications of the lengthy application process, which seemingly dares applicants to prove a disability and thus helps them to internalize it, and mandated vocational rehabilitation early in the treatment course may lessen the number of those who need long-term disability insurance benefits.[14]

Certainly, there are those who, by virtue of their disablement, must exercise their earned rights to claim the insurance benefits. There is evidence, however, that many who receive SSDI have arrived at the point where they need to apply for these benefits as a result of shortcomings in our system. For more on the topic of SSDI, refer to Chapters 1 and 13 of the accompanying volume.

Impartial Medical Evaluation

The physician who has been asked to make an impartial medical evaluation (IME), sometimes called an independent medical examination, generally files a formal report. Occasionally, such reports must be defended in legal depositions or even in the courtroom. These evaluations may require a higher degree of sophistication and thoroughness than can be accomplished within the physician's office. In all instances, the helpfulness of the examination is in direct proportion to the degree of specificity of the information requested by the company or attorney.

Doing IMEs can produce a moderate income for physicians. Because IMEs are frequently used in adversarial circumstances, attorneys have learned which physicians are likely to provide the opinion that they seek as to the presence and extent of a disability.[11] Organizations created to restore unbiased objectivity to IMEs have begun to merge, however. In Boston, for example, a partnership of industrial nurses has recently organized a consortium of 500 specially chosen physicians who represent 53 specialties (Ormont S, personal communication). Together, the physicians perform in excess of 2,100 IMEs per year at a cost of $350 each. In the first year of this consortium's existence, inconsistencies were found in the content of participating physicians' reports, and such important information as medications required, daily activities performed while on disability, and job demands was noticeably absent in many reports. An education process has improved consistency by structuring the content in all reports.

Because these evaluations, at all levels of formality, are extremely important in the working lives of involved patients, an educational process should be undertaken nationwide not only to expose physicians in training to those assessments but also to acquaint them with the limitations of office examination in demonstrating functional capacity or disability.

DEFINING A PHYSICIAN'S RESPONSIBILITIES IN WORK CAPACITY ASSESSMENT

More than three fourths of the U.S. work force is employed by small companies that may not have on-site health services.[15] Thus, the family physician is commonly called upon to serve as an occupational health physician and to assess vocational capacity.[16] Such an assessment may be straightforward, requiring only the knowledge base of a medical model, but there may be complications that require additional expertise.

The philosophic traditions of the medical model render patients' health the first priority of physicians. In medical training, physicians learn to analyze symptoms, diagnose new disease, and determine the extent of previous impairment. The patient has the right to full disclosure of the nature and implications of a diagnosis. The medical model further establishes that physicians prescribe a course of treatment, monitor the patient's response, and follow the patient for any alterations in health status that require additional treatment. Throughout the process, physicians continue to keep patients and families fully informed. Clinicians in active practice have come to accept this modus operandi as a matter of course.

In addition, within the usual physician-patient relationship, a patient engages knowingly in a sacred trust with the physician. The patient reveals the intimate details of his or her health, social, and emotional status with every expectation that the physician will keep this information in confidence. Like the concepts of the medical model, the confidentiality doctrine is fundamental to the Hippocratic oath: "I will practice my profession with conscience and dignity; the health of my patients will be my first consideration; I will respect the secrets which are confided in me."

In this traditional physician-patient relationship, the two partners have the common goal of promoting health. There are special considerations for the physician involved in vocational assessment that complicate this traditional relationship: establishment of causality, specialized medical evaluation, and medical advocacy to the employer.

Causality

The question of work-relatedness is posed to the physician first in order to establish which insurance—workers' compensation or personal health—will cover evaluation and treatment expenses. Because state workers' compensation systems require claimants' proof both of the presence and of the work-relatedness of a disabling injury, patients often seek legal representation to protect them in causality disputes. The claims may pit worker against employer, and the physician evaluator then becomes a central focus of the dispute. The more adversarial the situation becomes, the greater the injured worker's investment in building a case for work-related disability, rather than in seeking vocational rehabilitation.

In many cases, the cause of the disability is obvious to physicians, but occasionally there are added degrees of difficulty in determining it precisely. For example, the courts have recently been establishing legal precedent for the work-relatedness of cardiac illness and psychologic stress.[17] Previously, these conditions were difficult to connect directly to work. Thus, causality issues can at times be thorny, and treatment may be delayed.

Specialized Medical Occupational Assessment

Once the causality issue has been resolved, the physician faces even greater difficulties in the objective medical assessment of a worker's capacity to do his or her job. Several causes—cognitive, psychomotor, and attitudinal—are potentially responsible for these difficulties. Problems of objectivity are due in part to the limitations of the medical model.

Cognitive Barriers

The basic medical training of physicians in the United States consists of 4 years of medical or osteopathic school. In the medical model, the curriculum of most training programs pays scant attention, if any, to the assessment of ability and the restoration of function.[18] Graduates of medical schools have not commonly received didactic instruction to explore functional problems of mobility, self-care, or safety. Even rarer is any mention during training of vocational issues, such as suspected hazards in the work environment, protective measures used by employees to prevent exposure, patterns of symptoms among fellow workers, and the effects of medical problems on work performance.[15,16]

Although basic medical training gives short shrift to occupational issues, few medical specialties have been especially oriented to the measurement and restoration of function, including work capacity. Physicial medicine and rehabilitation (PM&R) training involves considerable exposure to the skills needed for daily living, leisure, and working in the face of varying impairments. Restoring function in the athlete and the working person is an emphasis in orthopedic surgery training. Training in occupational medicine specifically addresses vocational issues. Individuals in these specialties are commonly called upon to make work capacity decisions. Training in other specialties, however, often does not include sufficient exposure to the needs of disabled workers (Scheer S, unpublished data).

When Brewerton and Daniel interviewed 77 patients with brachial plexus injuries, they found that only 24 of the 77 were using their injured limbs 8 years after the injury.[19] Issues of the patients' background, personality, adjustment to amputation, handedness, altered self-perception, compensation status, and job requirements all played a part in prolonging their recovery and delaying their return to work. The patients felt that their physicians had not given them knowledgeable vocational guidance. Many patients had to find out themselves where to go for vocational advice, rehabilitation training, and ultimate resettlement. The authors concluded that physicians involved with cases of this nature must assume more responsibility for their vocational disposition. The physician knows the patient, the disease, the course of treatment, and the prognosis, and it is an error to separate rehabilitation from acute and subacute medical care. Because of the lack of vocational rehabilitation content in basic and specialty medical training, however, physicians asked to deal with occupational health issues must know their own limits and must refer patients for specialized vocational guidance.

Psychomotor Barriers: Those Relating to a Learned Physical Skill

Work capacity assessment requires technical skills not commonly taught in basic medical or specialization training. The standard history and physical examination (H&P) performed in the physician's office may be sufficient for some preemployment considerations or for a return-to-work decision in a patient with short-lived illness or injury.[20] If the patient needs a long time to recover from an illness or undergoes a profound physical or intellectual change, however, a more functionally relevant assessment than can be obtained in the H&P format may be necessary. Quantification of function falls outside the traditional medical model of pathology/diagnosis/acute treatment.[21,22]

The one type of functional testing commonly performed by physicians is the graded treadmill or bicycle ergometer test. This procedure has become a widely practiced part of general internal medicine, cardiology, and pulmonary clinical assessment. It provides useful information on the patient's cardiac capacity and cardiac or pulmonary prognosis. In the laboratory setting, however, assessment of the worker's concomitant performance of actual job tasks is often omitted. This omission is unfortunate, because, for certain patients, measurement of physiologic parameters during the performance of actual work tasks is a more valid indicator of vocational capacity.[23] Thus, functional testing is typically not within the technical skills of most physicians. Here, once again, physicians must be cognizant of their own knowledge and experiential limitations, and they must refer patients to specialists who are more qualified to do functional capacity testing.

Functional capacity testing is now provided by specially trained physical and occupational therapists,[23,24] specialized vocational evaluators, and rehabilitation engineers. For example, therapists in industrial injury clinics nationwide measure the lifting, reaching, and other capacities of industrial workers who are recovering from musculoskeletal trauma to determine their work readiness.[24] Many such functional assessments use tasks specifically required for the job. The reader may refer to Chapter 6 in the first volume, or to Chapers 2 and 3 in this volume for further information on this topic.

Attitudinal Factors

The naive physician may misinterpret changes in the physician-patient relationship if the patient's recovery takes longer than anticipated. When the low back strain that was expected to have healed by 8 weeks continues to be a source of patient-imposed activity restriction and work disability, the physician's traditional explanation has been that the patient is malingering. In reality, most patients do not consciously manipulate their responses to evaluation and treatment. Therefore, such a situation ought to prompt the physician first to re-examine the patient in order to make certain that a more serious condition was not overlooked weeks earlier. Second, the physician must consider a host of possible nonmedical explanations for the delayed recovery:

- psychosocial stressors (anxiety over possible reinjury, marital problems, or child-related concerns at home)

- socially unacceptable disabilities in disguise (substance abuse crisis behind a low back pain ruse)
- vocational dissatisfaction (underlying desire to find a different job)
- employer and labor relations issues (desire to punish the boss)
- legal issues (ongoing causality dispute or a desire for cash compensation)

The physician who has established a genuine rapport with the patient may ferret out the patient's motivations underlying what appears to be a malingering attitude. If successful, both physician and patient may benefit, and the relationship is undamaged. The solution may require medical advice, referral to a vocational counselor or psychologist, or merely reassurance from the physician or the employer. If the physician lacks the patience, intuitive concern, or the desire to understand the patient fully, however, and insists on an immediate return to work because there are no objective signs of continued back injury, the physician-patient relationship may take a serious turn. A confrontation by the physician, someone who was trusted and admired in the past, may cause the patient not only to re-examine their relationship but also to rationalize the actual underlying motivation for delay. A desire to seek a big financial settlement becomes, "My doctor doesn't believe how much I've been physically hurt every day on that job! He doesn't care about me as much as my lawyer does!"

As time continues to pass, a further subtle transition occurs. After 6 months, the underlying physical nature of the patient's back strain may have stabilized, but the psychologic context has undergone a significant transformation: the chronicity syndrome has arisen.[25,26] Often perceived erroneously by the physician as malingering, the chronicity syndrome is in actuality a change in the psychologic nature of the patient, who begins to view him- or herself more and more as an invalid. General practice physicians and specialists have all witnessed this phenomenon. According to Strang,[25] the chronicity syndrome has five features:

1. 6 months consecutively out of work, with disability claim for compensation
2. subjective complaints that are disproportionate to objective ones
3. psychologic findings, underlying complaints, and disability perceptions
4. lack of motivation to recover and negative attitude to work return
5. persistence of the above for 6 months without an intervening secondary medical or psychologic condition

A strong physician-patient relationship can prevent the development of distrust and apprehension, but the slow onset of a chronicity syndrome inevitably strains this relationship. Once the chronicity syndrome has evolved, the chance of the patient's ever returning to work is diminished. McGill noted that only 50% of those out of work more than 6 months with low back pain were able to work again, and only 25% of those out more than a year were able to return to work.[27]

The best approach, of course, is to attempt to prevent the development of the chronicity syndrome early in recovery. Eager pursuit of the patient's feelings about returning to work, preferably as soon as the very acute medical aspects have been rendered stable, is generally perceived as a sign that the physician wishes to restore vocational normalcy. A delay in discussing the patient's return to work and in implementing a proper rehabilitation program thus jeopardizes a successful work return.[28]

Overcoming Barriers to Effective Assessment

Although society is accustomed to putting physicians in decision-making roles for assessing work readiness, most physicians, working alone, can provide only broad medical guidelines for return to work. If medical constraints are the sole or major concern, the primary care physician who knows the patient's job description can determine when medical recovery is sufficient for a return to work. Some cases are complex, however, and require management of additional issues, including the following:

- medical/interdisciplinary team coordination
- employer liaison
- job description procurement, analysis, and compartmentalization
- job-relevant functional testing
- consideration of job reinjury potential

The general physician may not feel qualified to assume these additional responsibilities. Simply knowing the job description is insufficient in these cases. Any needed functional capacity testing based on that job description generally involves one or more allied health care specialists. Also, a vocational counselor (state or private) should be involved in any cases that require vocational evaluation, job resettlement, or discrete handling of delicate employee-employer/union relations problems. Furthermore, an ergonomics specialist may be required to modify the worker's job, with the employer's approval, to reduce the risk of reinjury.

Thus, physicians who are inexperienced in coordinating the activities of multiple health care team members are advised to refer their complicated worker return cases to a physiatrist (ie, a specialist in physical medicine and rehabilitation), or to the employer's occupational physician, if one exists. These medical specialists generally possess the training and experience to ensure the successful and safe return of the worker to productive employment.

Medical Advocacy to Employer

In our increasingly litigious age, the questions of what to say and to whom to say it are increasingly complex and potentially expensive. Few general physicians have read the most recent guide of the Occupational Safety and Health Administration (OSHA) and know in detail the standards of industrial safety compliance legislated by the federal government. Even those who have read the guide may find the text difficult to interpret. The regulations have been written to allow the physician maximum discretion for problem identification and to leave for the employer the responsibility for the correction of safety and health problems and for the actions of company physicians.

In an established physician-patient relationship, a physician who concludes that a work environment is dangerous or otherwise unsafe is obligated to communicate these concerns to the patient. Furthermore, the physician should express the same concerns to the employer, both verbally and in writing. Generally, the safety manager or occupational health personnel appreciate receiving the information and promptly initiate action to correct the problems. The local Chamber of Commerce, state industrial commission, or other organizations that promote occupational health safety may agree to visit a worksite at no risk to an employer. If the company takes no corrective action, the threat of a call to OSHA may encourage employer compliance.

More common than situations of gross medical abuse to workers are those involving innocently repeated toxicant exposure or cumulative repetitive trauma.[29] Here again, a physician may rightly feel a responsibility to report an apparent hazard to an employer, as well as to inform the returning worker of the problem in the environment. Some employers may correct the problem out of concern for their workers. Self-insured employers may realize a direct cost savings from preventing injuries and toxic work exposures. In these cases, the physician's informed communication is important.

Medical advocacy to the employer also has legal and ethical dimensions. What are the possibilities that this patient's return to work may jeopardize the health and safety of co-workers? The physician may expect a patient to discuss with the employer a newly developed seizure disorder, for example. Because the safety of both the epileptic worker and surrounding co-workers could be in jeopardy, a letter to the employer is advisable. Only if worker and co-worker safety is at risk can such a letter be justified, however. In all such cases, it is extremely important to inform the patient that a letter must be sent. It may also be advisable to allow the patient to review the letter before it is mailed to the employer. The physician may already have an established relationship with this patient and must respect the patient's rights to limited disclosure of sensitive information.

The situation is more difficult when a worker's return to the job jeopardizes only co-workers' safety. In this case, the returning worker may have less motivation to report the problem to the employer. For example, there are no known instances in which acquired immunodeficiency syndrome (AIDS) has spread through normal work settings, but there is great fear that it may yet occur.[30] As a result, some employers may feel a moral obligation to inform other employees that a worker has AIDS; however, present law favors the rights of the infected worker to remain at work unless job performance is affected.[30] Therefore, attorneys who specialize in workplace policies toward AIDS patients recommend that employers and physicians maintain strict confidentiality of medical records. Recent court law, however, requires physicians to inform unknowing sexual partners of potential AIDS exposure.[31] Undoubtedly, the issue of employees' rights to be informed of a co-worker's illness will be raised increasingly in the future, and AIDS patients' physicians will clearly be involved in this controversy.

To appreciate more fully the legal doctrine of medical advocacy for the disabled worker, physicians should become familiar with the Rehabilitation Act of 1973. This landmark legislation, which prohibits discrimination against persons with functional disabilities by certain businesses, universities, and federal agencies, greatly expanded the opportunities available to disabled workers. (Griest, American Board of Preventive Medicine, personal communication). Physicians may feel obliged to refer their patients for legal advice in questions of prejudicial treatment by employers. A more comprehensive summary of the Rehabilitation Act is found in Chapter 14.

PHYSICIANS IN OCCUPATIONAL MEDICINE

By 1983, approximately 2,000 physicians were practicing occupational medicine on a full-time basis, and another 8,000 to 13,000 were practicing part-time.[17] Specific training is frequently not a pre-employment requirement for these physicians, however. As of 1988, only 1,257 physicians had been certified in occupational medicine by the American Board of Preventive Medicine (Griest J, personal communication). Apparently, most physicians obtain their training in the practice of occupational medicine while on the job.

All corporate physicians must resolve some very telling conflict-of-interest problems inherent in the practice of occupational medicine. In recognition of these conflicts, the board of the American Occupational Medicine Association engaged in lengthy deliberations before arriving at a Code of Ethical Conduct for Physicians Providing Occupational Medical Services. The code, published in 1976, establishes a moral basis for practice in the field of occupational medicine:[32]

> These principles are intended to aid physicians in maintaining ethical conduct in providing occupational medical service. They are standards to guide physicians in their relationships with the individuals they serve,

with employers and workers' representatives, with colleagues in the health professions, and with the public. Physicians should:

1. accord highest priority to the health and safety of the individual in the workplace
2. practice on a scientific basis with objectivity and integrity
3. make or endorse only statements which reflect their observations or honest opinion
4. actively oppose and strive to correct unethical conduct in relation to occupational health service
5. avoid allowing their medical judgment to be influenced by any conflict of interest
6. strive conscientiously to become familiar with the medical fitness requirements, the environment, and the hazards of the work done by those they serve, and with the health and safety aspects of the products and operations involved
7. treat as confidential whatever is learned about individuals served, releasing information only when required by law or by over-riding public health considerations, or to other physicians at the request of the individual according to traditional medical ethical practice; and should recognize that employers are entitled to counsel about the medical fitness of individuals in relation to work, but are not entitled to diagnoses or details of a specific nature
8. strive continually to improve medical knowledge, and should communicate information about health hazards in timely and effective fashion to individuals or groups potentially affected, and make appropriate reports to the scientific community
9. communicate understandably to those they serve any significant observations about their health, recommending further study, counsel, or treatment when indicated
10. seek consultation concerning the individual or the workplace whenever indicated
11. cooperate with governmental health personnel and agencies, and foster and maintain sound ethical relationships with other members of the health professions
12. avoid solicitation of the use of their services by making claims, offering testimonials, or implying results which may not be achieved, but they may appropriately advise colleagues and others of services available

The ultimate question for occupational physicians to resolve is, Where is my first loyalty—to worker protection or to company profits and promotion?

A NEW SYSTEMATIC WAY OF THINKING ABOUT
IMPAIRMENT, DISABILITY, AND HANDICAP

In 1980, the Geneva-based World Health Organization (WHO) commissioned Dr. Phillip H.N. Wood, of Manchester, to collate previous functional assessment techniques into a system of classification for disease consequences. The system was to be modeled initially after the International Classification of Diseases (ICD) system. Limitations had long been noted in the medical model of illness, which deals effectively with short-lived or preventable conditions, but fails to address fully the chronic sequelae of many diseases or injuries. With much input from around the world, Dr. Wood arrived at a system that departed somewhat from the ICD taxonomic principles. A book entitled *The International Classifications of Impairment, Disabilities, and Handicaps* [21] has popularized the concepts of the ICIDH system, which has defined three categories of disease sequelae:

1. impairment: an exteriorized defect at the "organ" level; abnormality of structure, appearance, and/or function
2. disability: an objectified defect at the level of the person, causing dysfunctional ability to perform an activity
3. handicap: a socialized defect at the environmental level, reflecting societal disadvantage experienced by the individual trying to fulfill a role

In such a system, impairment becomes a yes-no phenomenon, depending on the diagnosis. Disability is the degree of dysfunction and can be measured in percentage or levels of incapacity. Handicap, used rather nonspecifically in the past, becomes a culture-specific phenomenon defined in terms of the environmental surroundings of the disabled person. For example, a 30-year-old laborer with low back pain (impairment) is unable to lift more than 25 lb or to walk longer than 10 minutes (disabilities) before experiencing back pain. He is thus unable to perform his job (handicap), because there is no lifting equipment available, and there is no opportunity for frequent position changes (eg, from standing to sitting) at the job.

An individual can be impaired without being disabled or handicapped. A business executive who requires a bottle of nitroglycerin tablets at his desk for the pain of angina pectoris may continue to work at full capacity. An individual can have an impairment and a related disability, but not be incapacitated at work. For example, a secretary recently rendered paraplegic may have lost her company job because she could not reach a second-floor office; however, her boss arranged for a ramped building entryway and moved her office to a first floor location where steps were unnecessary. The possibility of handicap at this job site was overcome by an accommodating employer.

A system of semantic distinctions, such as the ICIDH system, becomes important if its creation can promote practical benefits. What does, indeed, follow from the use of this system is a better appreciation for life quality as opposed to mere survival. Granger has shown from a study of 307 subjects in five impairment groups that the degree of a patient's activity restrictions was a predictor in societal outcome for job, habitat, and social integration.[33] The diagnosis, however, revealed little about any of the ultimate societal handicaps. Similar impairments in two individuals resulted in a wide range of disabilities and handicaps, depending on the avalability of treatment, the occupation, the amount of family support, cultural variations, the degree of patient social acceptance at work or leisure, and other factors. These studies show physicians the limitations of merely listing a diagnosis and the need for a functional assessment to characterize life quality and job-specific capacity.

The ICIDH system is also useful at the federal government level. Although rehabilitation professionals have long appreciated quality-of-life issues and the failure of a strictly medical model to address function, attempts to classify functional capacities have thus far not resulted in a systematic examination of societal responsibilities and shortcomings. The ICIDH system may assist certain governmental bodies in focusing attention on eliminating handicap in the face of disability—through legislation, through attack on architectural barriers, and even through changes in attitudes.

Table 1-1 Seven Principles for the Physician Involved in Assessing Vocational Capacity

1. *Objectivity*. Be precise and thorough in diagnostic assessment; admit to uncertainty. Distinguish among what is known, observed, stated, or perceived.
2. *Communication*. Describe diagnostic opinions to patients. Inquire about patients' concerns for work return. Convey these concerns to others involved. Project confidence of treatment success.
3. *Job Relevancy*. Consider job-injury/disease relationship. Where possible, obtain testing and treatment that are valid and meaningful to the job and life of this individual. Distinguish among medical impairment, functional disability, and job handicap.
4. *Empathy*. Be sensitive, as physician concern abets patient cooperation in treatment. Know the psychosocial confounders of worker motivation that may interfere with measurement.
5. *Humility*. Know the limitations of medical assessment to determine disability and the common need for information from other allied health care sources. Be prepared to refer when a more thorough job-relevant examination can be done elsewhere.
6. *Prevention*. Consider prognosis and the predictability of recurrence. Know the job situation to which a patient returns. Be alert to dangers. Arm the worker with knowledge. Advocate for cooperation from the employer.
7. *Expeditiousness*. Be aware that chronicity is always around the corner! Return reports quickly. Make recommendations, initiate treatment, and follow up eagerly with needed program modifications. Urge patients to comply. Set dates consistently for goal achievement and return to work.

RECAPITULATION

We can thus characterize the important responsibilities of physicians involved in assessing work capacity (Table 1-1). The formidable task for our centers of medical learning is to educate physicians—those in training and those already practicing—to appreciate and uphold these principles so as to promote the ideal molding of workers with jobs they can perform safely and in a fulfilling manner.

The credibility of physicians asked to render these important decisions will thus be deservedly enhanced and all involved parties—workers and their families, employers, unions, and awaiting consumers—will benefit.

REFERENCES

1. Flexner A. *Medical Education in the US and Canada*. Bulletin no. 4. New York: Carnegie Foundation for Advancement of Teaching; 1910.

2. Illich I. *Medical Nemesis—The Expropriation of Health*. New York: Random House, Inc; 13–38.

3. Starr P. *The Social Transformation of American Medicine*. New York: Basic Books; 1982:379–419.

4. Cape R. *Aging—Its Complex Management*. Hagerstown, MD: Harper & Row; 1978.

5. *Guides to the Evaluation of Permanent Impairment*, 2nd ed. Chicago: American Medical Association; 1984.

6. Carey TS, Hadler NM. The role of the primary physician in disability determination for social security insurance and workers compensation. *Ann Intern Med*. 1986;104:706–710.

7. Hadler NM. Who should determine disability? *Semin Arthritis Rheum*. 1984;4:45–51.

8. Brand RA, Lehman TH. Low-back impairment rating practices of orthopedic surgeons. *Spine*. 1983;8:75–78.

9. Gloss DS, Wardle MG. Reliability and validity of AMA's guides to rating of impairment. *JAMA*. 1982;248:2292–2296.

10. Feinstein AR, et al. Scientific and clinical problems in indexes of functional disability. *Ann Intern Med*. 1986;105:413–420.

11. Use of medical evidence—low back permanent partial disability claims in New Jersey. WCRI Research Brief. 1987;3:10.

12. Richman SI. Why change? A look at the current system of disability determination and worker's compensation for occupational lung disease. *Ann Intern Med*. 1982;97:908–914.

13. *Disability Evaluation under Social Security, August, 1979*. US Dept of HEW, SSA No. 79-10089. Washington, DC, 1980.

14. Hester EJ. Disability and disincentives: prospective models for change. In: Scheer SJ, ed. *Multidisciplinary Perspectives in Vocational Assessment of Impaired Workers*, Rockville, MD: Aspen Publishers; 1990:205–218.

15. Rothstein MA. Role of occupational medicine. In: *Medical Screening of Workers*. Washington, DC; Bureau of National Affairs; 1984:1–13.

16. Rosenstock L. Occupational medicine—too long neglected. *Ann Intern Med*. 1981;95:774–776.

17. *Battista v Chrysler Corp.*, Super. Court of Delaware, 7-21-86; and *Nix v City of Houma*, Sup. Court of Louisiana, 5-20-86.

18. Symington DC. Vocational rehabilitation—how everybody benefits. *Rehab Digest.* 1984;15:2–3.

19. Brewerton DA, Daniel JW. Factors influencing return to work. *Br Med J.* 1971;4:277–281.

20. Chaffin DB, Andersson GBJ. Worker selection and training criteria. In: Chaffin DB, Andersson GBJ, eds. *Occupational Biomechanics.* New York: Wiley & Sons; 1984:389–410.

21. *International Classification of Impairments, Disabilities and Handicaps.* Geneva, Switzerland: World Health Organization; 1980.

22. Carbine ME, Schwartz G. *Strategies for Managing Disability Costs.* Washington, DC. Washington Business Group on Health; 1987.

23. Wilke NA, Sheldahl LM. Use of simulated work testing in cardiac rehabilitation. *Am J Occup Ther.* 1985;39:327–330.

24. Battencourt CM, et al. Using work simulation to treat adults with back injuries. *Am J Occup Ther.* 1986;40:12–18.

25. Strang JP. The chronic disability syndrome. In: Aronoff GM, ed *Evaluation and Treatment of Chronic Pain.* Baltimore: Urban & Schwartzenberg; 1985:603–623.

26. Nachemson A. Work for all—For those with low back pain as well. *Clin Orthop.* 1983;179:77.

27. McGill CM. Industrial back problems. A control program. *J Occup Med.* 1968;10:174–178.

28. Leavitt SS, et al: The process of recovery—Patterns in industrial back injury, Parts 3 and 4. *Indust Med.* 1972;41:7–11, 41:5–9.

29. Armstrong TJ. Ergonomics and cumulative trauma disorders. *Hand Clin.* 1986;2:553–565.

30. Friddle J, et al. How companies can ease the burden of AIDS at work. *Occup Health & Safety.* 1988;57:12–19, 31.

31. American Medical Association. *American Medical News.* 1988:4.

32. Code of Ethical Conduct for Physicians Providing Occupational Medical Services. *J Occup Med.* 1976;18.

33. Granger CV. Outcome of comprehensive medical rehabilitation: An analysis based upon the impairment, disability, handicaps model. *Int Rehab Med.* 1985;7:45–50.

chapter 2

Vocational Capacity with Low Back Pain Impairment

Steven J. Scheer and Richard J. Wickstrom

Of all the conditions that affect the productivity of workers, low back pain (LBP) is easily the most common and the most costly. Hundreds of articles on the subject appear annually in medical, business, and lay journals, attesting to its importance as a public health issue. Studies have shown that 50% to 80% of the population will experience significant back pain at some point in their lives.[1-5] At any given moment in time, between 12% and 35% of people will admit to recent LBP.[4-8] According to information released by the National Safety Council, 2% of all employees each year have compensable back injuries.[9]

The ailing back is responsible for many early retirements, temporary disabilities, and permanent disability pensions. Impairment in the low back is the most frequent cause of activity limitation in people younger than 45 years of age. It accounts for one sixth of all occupational injuries.[9] McGill's often-quoted study demonstrated that, the longer the duration of work disability, the less likely a successful restoration of function.[10] Patients out of work for more than 6 months had only a 50% chance of returning to work; at 2 years, patients had a negligible chance of ever returning to work.

Although occupational back pain is common, it is difficult to determine its exact incidence and prevalence in the workplace for several reasons:

- LBP is often not included in company health statistics when work is not missed.
- The natural history of LBP is that of recurring disease.[11]
- Diagnosis is often imprecise; the differential diagnosis of LBP may include mechanical, vascular, or urologic impairments.[12]
- The causation of LBP is often multifactorial, with job- and leisure-related risk factors mechanistically combined.[2,13,14]
- Individuals often have poor recall of previous LBP, even for back pain severe enough to necessitate sick leave.[5,15]

Because of its frequency and its disabling potential, LBP results in considerable expense to society. In the United States, the annual medical and lost wage costs attributed to LBP are in excess of $10 billion.[16] When Snook and Jensen reviewed insurance claim data in several states, they estimated the average cost per industrial LBP claim to be $6,000.[17] Klein and associates reported that "dislocated backs" resulted in the highest disability costs—almost $20,000 per case.[18]

The average per case cost data are misleading, however. In 85% to 90% of the cases, workers with LBP make a vocational recovery by 6 to 12 weeks.[19,20] The remaining 10% to 15% (ie, those who have a persistent work disability after 3 months) account for the majority of costs. In studying more than 30,000 workers at Boeing, Spengler and associates found that 10% of low back claims accounted for almost 80% of all the LBP dollars spent.[21] Leavitt and colleagues reported that 24 of 100 randomly selected LBP cases in California accounted for 87% of the costs.[22]

Although LBP will continue to be the legacy of human posture, its considerable cost to society may be lessened by cost-effective injury prevention and disability management.

MEDICAL IMPAIRMENT EVALUATION

Under the World Health Organization's classification system of impairment, disability, and handicap, an impairment is an anatomic defect at the level of the organ system.[23] The role of the physician in labeling the medical impairment is to hear the patient's perception of the problem, to probe for its pathophysiologic ramifications, and to observe confirming or conflicting presenting evidence. However, the anatomic impairment associated with LBP is frequently ill defined. Rather than confidently diagnosing a distinct condition, the physician must frequently infer and surmise uncertainly; examination and laboratory techniques for the identification of a low back impairment are still imperfect.

Uncertain pathologic etiology may lead to questions of the work-relatedness of a claim, which may delay the start of workers' compensation payments. That delay tends to initiate a rift between the worker and the employer, the company physician, and the insurance company. Injured workers with challenged claims have longer work absences, more expensive claims, and a greater tendency to seek legal redress.[24]

Even in some cases of unequivocal pathophysiology, it may be difficult to predict the functional outcome. In these circumstances, psychosocial and vocational factors may render the anatomic impairment less important for work prognosis. Ever mindful of these disclaimers, the physician should attempt to identify medical impairment, using input from the worker and the employer, the health history, and the health care team.

Anatomy and Pathophysiology

Much of what is known regarding LBP pathophysiology relates to the intervertebral disc and the degenerative cascade. The young intervertebral disc is highly resilient to compressive loads, being fibrous outside and viscous fluid-filled inside. Exposure to heavy or high compression loads will fracture the vertebral end-plate before damaging the healthy disc.[25,26] The extensive intradiscal pressure studies (Fig. 2-1) that Nachemson performed at the Sahlgren Hospital in Gothenberg, Sweden have supported empiric observations that LBP during different postures and activities correlates with elevated intradiscal pressures.[27] The fact that LBP coincides with elevated intradiscal pressure does not isolate the pathologic cause of the pain to the disc space, however.

After spinal maturity, degenerative changes occur in the disc (Fig. 2-2).[26,28] Farfan, Hoberdeao, and Dubow suggested that torsional stress plays a major role in degenerative change.[26] The initial injury in torsion may be at the facet joint or posterior ligamentous system. Although the facet joints ordinarily pick up only 10% to 15% of the weight in spinal loading, a hyperlordotic (back arched) posture increases weight distribution posteriorly, suggesting that frequent overhead lifting is a mechanism of early facet degeneration.[25] Subsequent discal migration then leads to annular degeneration.[25,29] Nuclear damage and end-plate disruption generally occur still later.[28] In those who regularly lift heavy weights, the additive

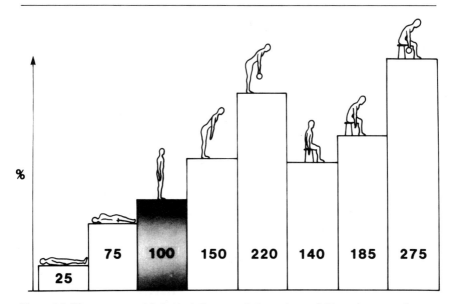

Figure 2-1 Disc pressures at L3 (in vivo) disc space during various activities and postures. *Source:* Reprinted with permission from *Spine* (1976;1:59), Copyright © 1976, JB Lippincott Co.

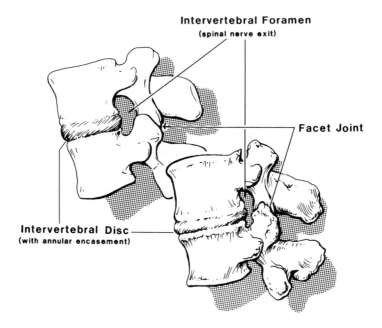

Figure 2-2 Progressive degeneration of a lumbar disc. *Top*, disc is intact and shows no evidence of collapse. *Bottom*, as the degenerative process progresses, disc height decreases, the annulus frays, and the posterior facet joints show osteophytic overgrowth that impinges on the intervertebral foramen. *Source:* Reprinted from *The Intervertebral Disc* (p 77) by AF DePalma and RH Rothman with permission of WB Saunders Co, © 1970.

effects of decreased disc height secondary to fluid shift may promote further degeneration, both of the disc and of the bony structure.

Of all the factors associated with disc degeneration, age is the most well established.[30,31] Age-related degenerative changes are seen in virtually all spines by 60 years of age.[29] Generally, the more physically heavy the person's work, the greater the disc degeneration.[4,32–34] Although LBP is common in those with severe degenerative changes in several discs,[33] unilevel or otherwise moderate degenerative changes have not been associated with increased LBP.[34–37] Although degeneration continues with age, there is a *decline* in the incidence of initial LBP in men after the age of 55 years.[9] This decline in the incidence of first-time LBP, along with the inevitably increasing spinal degenerative changes as observed on roentgenograms, is one of the curious enigmas faced by back pain researchers.

In their efforts to establish possible causes of LBP, some investigators have used laboratory models of spine trauma. Adams and Hutton were able to reproduce such spinal injuries as prolapsed disc, radial disc rupture, vertebral fracture, facet and capsoligament damage, and longitudinal ligamentous sprain by applying loads to lumbar spines in cadavers.[25] From such in vitro models, possible mechanisms of pathoanatomic events can be inferred.

The occurrence of pain, although often abrupt, is difficult to associate unequivocally with a pathoanatomic event. Because early disc degeneration is a physically painless process, the time of the initial lesion in discogenic LBP cannot be recorded. Certain annular fibers are pain-sensitive, however, and disc bulging may be painful even if the disc does not actually penetrate the annulus (Fig. 2-3).[38,39] After continued annular degeneration, herniation of the disc nucleus may occur, followed by symptoms associated with penetration of the annulus, impingement on the pain-sensitive posterior longitudinal ligament, or traction on the nerve root.[28,38,40,41] Nerve root scarring may result in the continuation of back and leg pain even after relocation or surgical removal of a disc.[38]

With so many potential pain-sensitive structures, a decision on the exact cause of acute or chronic LBP is quite often speculative. There are also a variety of explanations for pain referred into the leg (sciatica): nerve root irritation after a herniated nucleus pulposus, facet irritation, spinal stenosis, and even muscle strain or spasm.[42,43] Clearly, although much is known of the possible pathophysiology of back pain, there is much uncertainty in linking an event or a physical presentation to a single pathologic diagnosis.

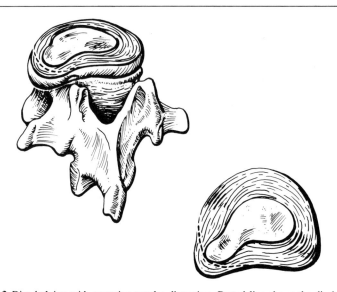

Figure 2-3 Disc bulging with posterior annular disruption. Dotted line shows the disc's original contour. Nerve root irritation may result from annular deformation of this degree. *Source:* Reprinted from *The Clinical Biomechanics of the Spine* (p 287) by AA White and MM Panjabi with permission of JB Lippincott Co, © 1978.

Pathologic Diagnoses

Recognizing the frequently multifactorial and nonspecific nature of LBP, some back pain experts have given up trying to label it.[12,20,42] These difficulties notwithstanding, Frymoyer and Howe have generated the following 10 categories of pathologies to be considered in work-related LBP.[42]

1. Idiopathic Low Back Pain

Frymoyer and associates,[44] as well as White and Gordon,[20] suggested that 85% of acute LBP cases in the general population lack a specific anatomically designated cause. Only 10% to 15% of those who suffer acute LBP have not improved through spontaneous restoration over 3 months.[19,20,45] Of those 10% to 15% of patients whose LBP has not improved after 2 to 3 months, a distinct structural diagnosis can be made in approximately 50% of cases.[12] The idiopathic causes probably relate to injured muscle or ligament,[25,46] end-plate microfractures,[25] ruptured or torn annulus,[28] pressure on the posterior longitudinal ligament, bloodletting into the canal by a bulging disc,[24,25] or facet irritation[28] (Fig. 2-4). These "diagnoses" cannot be made with certainty, however, because it has not been possible to visualize the damaged anatomic part in the past.[42] Magnetic resonance imaging may now improve visualization, but its present cost does not justify its use for those who recover readily from LBP.

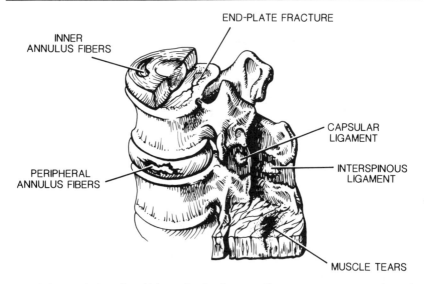

Figure 2-4 Acute back strain, which may involve damage to ligamentous structure, muscle, or the vertebral end-plate. *Source:* Reprinted from *The Clinical Biomechanics of the Spine* (p 286) by AA White and MM Panjabi with permission of JB Lippincott Co, © 1978.

2. Degenerative Disc Disease

Many studies have shown increasing degenerative disc disease, as evidenced by disc space narrowing and osteophytosis (see Fig. 2-2) that begins in the patient's twenties and increases with age.[33,47–50] The greatest degenerative changes are found at L4-5 and L5-S1, presumably secondary to the amount of stress, load-bearing, and degree of lordosis at these points. No consistent relationship has been established between moderate amounts of disc degeneration and pain or radiculopathy. The mere presence of numerous osteophytes is also of little significance.[32]

It appears that LBP is more common in those with severe degenerative changes at several disc spaces.[33,35,51] At Eastman Kodak, Rowe found that the majority of preretirement workers with severe degenerative disc disease that can be seen on roentgenograms admitted to previous LBP that required work absences; a minority of workers with similar radiologic findings had no LBP history.[34,52] The exact mechanism of pain in degenerative disc disease is speculative and probably multifactorial.

3. Prolapsed or Herniated Disc

After acute or chronic/repetitive trauma, the inner nucleus pulposus of a disc may pass through an attenuated annulus, damage nerve roots, and thus cause neurologic changes (Fig. 2-5).[53] The resultant symptoms of sensory change and radicular pain below the knee, together with such examination findings as a positive straight-leg raising test (flexing the straight leg at the hip causes pain/numbness below the knee), reflex asymmetry, isolated muscle weakness, and nerve root tension signs,[41] make up the clinical syndrome of a herniated nucleus pulposus.[53] These symptoms are believed to be due to secondary pathoanatomic changes, such as nerve root inflammation, rather than the disc protrusion per se.[54] As mentioned earlier, disc bulging without herniation may also be symptomatic.[29] Central herniation is more likely to compromise multiple roots, as in the cauda equina syndrome (see Fig. 2-5).

The L5-S1 disc herniation has its peak incidence at age 30 years, whereas the L4-5 herniation increases with age.[53] The true incidence of herniated disc is difficult to characterize, however, because the symptoms frequently resolve before a definitive diagnosis can be made by radiographic means. Even the "acid test"—myelographic identification—has been challenged. Hiteselberger and Witten found that a sizable percentage of patients with an abnormal myelogram had no LBP symptoms or associated signs.[55]

It is not always necessary to refer patients with symptomatic herniated disc for surgical treatment. In fact, a majority of these cases will probably remit spontaneously with minimal functional detriment.[42] The healing time for a symp-

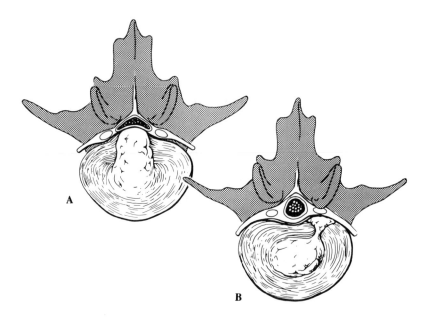

Figure 2-5 Herniated nucleus pulposus. (**A**) Massive extrusion of disc material, almost obliterating the spinal canal completely. (**B**) Large sequestrated disc fragment that has migrated into the foramen and severely compressed the nerve root. *Source:* Reprinted from *The Intervertebral Disc* (pp 63–65) by AF DePalma and RH Rothman with permission of WB Saunders Co, © 1970.

---

tomatic and well-documented herniation, however, is probably longer than that required for the idiopathic LBP without sciatica. Restricted activity after a documented disc herniation generally exceeds 2 weeks; for idiopathic LBP, 3 to 4 days.[56–57]

4. Spinal Stenosis

Both lateral recess and central spinal stenosis are now increasingly associated with LBP (Fig. 2-6). In one study, such cases made up one fifth of those in which initial conservative treatment failed.[52] Lateral recess stenosis commonly occurs as a result of facet joint hypertrophy;[42] central spinal stenosis can be congenital or degenerative. The more common degenerative type is associated with the insidious onset of nonradicular LBP, which is aggravated by changes in posture and exertion. In a narrowed spinal canal, even small disc herniations may be associated with nerve entrapment that results in radicular pain. There is controversy over the extent to which facet arthopathy, in the absence of lateral recess stenosis, may cause LBP. The fact that facet anesthetic blocks may relieve LBP and its accom-

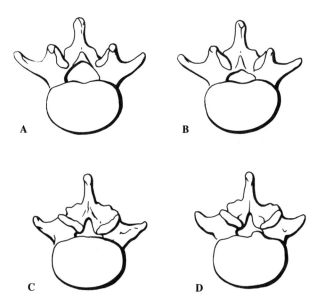

Figure 2-6 Types of lumbar spinal stenosis. (**A**) Normal canal. (**B**) Congenital developmental stenosis. (**C**) Degenerative stenosis, as from facet hypertrophy. (**D**) Degenerative stenosis with disc herniation. *Source:* Reprinted with permission from *Spine* (1976;1:4–6), Copyright © 1986, JB Lippincott Co.

panied thigh referral suggests a true association,[43] but it is not always clear what such a procedure blocks anatomically.

5. Segmental Instability

Otherwise known as degenerative spondylolisthesis, segmental instability is a rather controversial entity. The diagnosis is made when lateral spinal films show that displacements or angulations occur with normal motion. Patients with this condition frequently have had recurrent episodes of acute LBP.[58]

6. Congenital Spinal Disorders

Unfortunately, some individuals have been eliminated from consideration for a job because of the radiologic demonstration of certain congenital anomalies that are now known to occur equally often in those with and those without LBP.[10,52,59,60] Such anomalies include spina bifida occulta, spinal segmentation abnormalities (eg, sacralization, lumbarization, transitional hemivertebra), spondylolysis, idiopathic scoliosis (of less than 80°), and Scheuermann's disease.

Spondylolisthesis is a congenital or acquired spinal disorder that most investigators have shown to be associated with an increased incidence of LBP

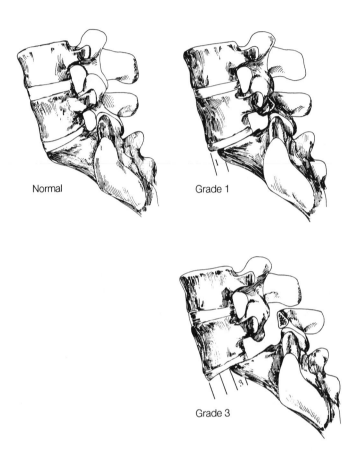

Normal

Grade 1

Grade 3

Figure 2-7 Spondylolisthesis. Spinal slippage, usually of L5 on S1 (as shown here) or of L4 on L5 is measured in degrees: grade 1, less than 25% of vertebral width; grade 2, less than 50%; grade 3, less than 75%; grade 4, more than 75%. *Source:* Adapted from *The Intervertebral Disc* (p 254) by AF DePalma and RH Rothman with permission of WB Saunders Co, © 1970.

(Fig. 2-7).[4,42,50,61] Some investigators, however, have found no such association.[59,62] A spondylolytic defect predisposes those affected to a fatigue fracture in the pars interarticularis. The repetitive stresses of such competitive sports as gymnastics, javelin throwing, and football (interior linemen) apparently increase the likelihood that a pars defect will lead to a fatigue fracture.[42] As a result of the fracture, the overlying vertebral bodies slip forward. Nachemson and Wiltse have challenged the notion that backache is an indication for fusion of the spine with spondylolisthesis—unless the degree of slippage is greater than 50% (grades 3 and 4) of vertebral diameter.[63]

7. Spinal Fractures

The bony elements of the spine are susceptible to acute mechanical perturbation with these resultant types of fracture:

- vertebral body fracture/dislocation: The most frequent victim of a vertebral body fracture is a man in his twenties. Of those fractures that involve the lumbar or thoracolumbar spine, 4% are associated with neurologic sequelae. In these cases, rotation during the injury process disrupts the posterior ligament complex and renders the spine neurologically unstable. The motor vehicle accident is the most common traumatic cause of vertebral fracture, followed by falls, gunshot wounds, and recreational activities.[51]
- end-plate fracture: Superincumbent weight, often chronically applied, is a frequent cause of end-plate fractures. These fractures, which may be microscopic, are a much more common cause of LBP than was formerly believed.[29]
- posterior element fracture: According to Frymoyer and Howe,[42] posterior element fractures commonly occur in mining and quarrying occupations when a blow is sustained from behind the back.

8. Inflammatory Cause

Approximately 0.5% of patients who have had a disc excision develop a postoperative disc space infection.[53] Usually, these patients have an underlying disease, such as diabetes. The back pain that results from such an infection is severe and unrelenting, unaffected by a position change, and associated with ongoing radiologic changes in the disc space over a relatively short period.

Spondyloarthropathy (eg, ankylosing spondylitis, arthritis of ulcerative colitis, psoriatic arthritis, and Reiter's syndrome) not only may cause ongoing LBP but also may limit motion. Ankylosing spondylitis has a tendency to cause spinal flexion deformity; thus, patients with this condition are frequently unable to perform work that requires spinal flexibility.

9. Metabolic Spinal Disease

Osteoporosis is the single most important metabolic cause of LBP. Its prevalence is high among women in their forties and older.[42] In one study, the lifetime incidence of LBP associated with osteoporosis rose from 62% in earlier adulthood to 81% by the seventh decade in women; it remained approximately 68% across all age groups in men.[63] Of course, if associated with vertebral body fracture, osteoporosis can be quite painful. More commonly, it is not greatly discomfiting and thus proceeds relatively silently. Iskrant and Smith[64] showed that 50% of women they studied over the age of 45 years had radiologic evidence of osteoporosis; of this number, 60% were symptomatic. Women with such evidence of osteoporosis should not lift heavy materials, particularly in a flexed posture. Unfortunately, it is difficult to quantify the limits of safe lifting to prevent osteoporotic fracture.

10. Spinal Tumor

Metastatic cancer to the spine, primary spinal tumor, or multiple myeloma are infrequent causes of LBP in the working population.

History, Physical Examination, and Laboratory Measures

Although, as mentioned earlier, the exact cause of a given case of LBP is quite often speculative, certain historical and physical examination findings can be prognostically useful.

History

Observer error in recording histories of LBP patients is high.[65] Many authors have documented patients' common failure to recall LBP, even when it has been severe.[2,5,50] According to Waddell and associates,[66] clinical information sought from LBP patients must be discriminating, reproducible, valid, easily accessible, and cost effective. Unfortunately, few studies to date have addressed ways to improve data collection, and the disconcerting fact remains that the reproducibility of historical data in back pain histories is frequently less than 70%.[66,67]

Nevertheless, the physician and other team members should attempt to obtain complete historical information. The inquiry should delve into the present episode of LBP, as well as into any previous work injuries. The following areas should be included:

- the nature of the pain—its onset and believed causation, duration, affecting postures and work associations, locations, and radiation
- associated medical problems—sphincteric, sexual, radicular motor problems, and other joint effects
- the results of diagnostic tests performed
- the types of pharmacologic, physical, and surgical treatments and their effects
- the extent of functional disability—average day described, activity and lifting tolerances at different work heights, and awareness of proper lifting mechanics

- complete history of previous work injuries, treatment(s) required, and length of recovery
- psychosocial stressors—pain-promoting circumstances at home
- vocational issues—job description, desirability, and satisfaction with employer

The patient's perception of causation is often subject to bias, either positive or negative. Epidemiologic evidence of an association between LBP and certain occupations is plentiful,[1,42] but there is also evidence that many individuals have LBP without ready anatomic explanations.[20,44] If the alleged incident or series of incidents can be associated with the workplace, compensation is automatically ensured for most workers in the United States. It is conceivable that Monday's well-documented fall on a slippery workroom surface had little to do with worsening pain in the already abused back of the fixated weekend golf enthusiast, but there is no way to prove that the work is unassociated with the back pain. Furthermore, the worker has no financial incentive to claim that the golf game is the real problem. Even in the case of pain that develops gradually without a distinct causative event, the worker is generally looking for ways to implicate the job for purposes of compensation. Both society and the workplace culture sanction this course of events.

To the extent possible, the nature of the referred pain should be assessed. The analysis can be diagnostically helpful (speculatively) and serves as a benchmark of therapeutic progress.[14] Back pain referred from an intrapelvic, urologic, or vascular source may be baffling; a high index of suspicion should prompt further workup. Associated pathophysiologic effects should always be sought, but are commonly neglected. In their multivocational series of 400 LBP sufferers, Magora and Taustein found that physicians generally failed to inquire about sphincter tone and erectile capacity.[8] Clearly, any evidence of neurogenicity should be evaluated thoroughly. Neurologic worsening may warrant consideration of surgery.

In acute LBP, there is generally little doubt about activity limitations. The physician should ask about the patient's tolerances for walking, sitting, driving, and bending. The greater these tolerances, the better the patient's functional capacity. Similar questioning is of considerable importance in assessing the capacities of chronically disabled workers who may have altered their self-images sufficiently to have a false notion of their abilities. Nevertheless, it is useful to hear them recount their view of their limits.

A history of previous work injuries, especially of those that required lengthy recovery periods, is an especially bad prognostic sign. Troup, Martin, and Lloyd found that coal miners who had experienced more than two episodes of LBP were likely to need more than 5 weeks to recover from a subsequent episode of LBP.[14] There was also a greater likelihood that these workers would have a recurrence of

LBP with lengthy recovery within the year. Chaffin and Andersson suggested that possibly the single most useful question for pre-employment hiring decisions is, "Can you describe any previous work injuries?"[68]

Psychosocial factors, especially in chronic cases, are associated with a refractory treatment response and a prolonged recovery period before return to work.[69,70] Numerous investigators have studied the negative influences of depression, alcoholism, divorce, and personality disorders on recovery from LBP and return to work.[27,69,71] The history-taking should include questions of the home arrangements before and after the onset of LBP, the typical day's responsibilities, and family attitudes toward the worker.

Other investigators have focused on the effects of vocational factors (eg, job desirability, autonomy of job functions, relationship with employer) on recovery rates.[24,69,70,72–74] It is important to ask these simple questions: "How do you like your work?" and "Are you planning to go back to work?" The manner of the worker's response is often highly informative. The physician should also ask about the nature of the job, both from the worker's and from the employer's perspective. A useful way to close the history is to ask when the worker expects to return to work and what the worker hopes to learn from this evaluation. Here, once again, the nature of the answers may reveal much about the patient's attitude toward returning to work, and that attitude has a powerful influence on the subsequent course of events.

Physical Examination

There is no clear-cut relationship between LBP and various anthropometric features, such as height, weight, and body build.[1,4,52] Similarly, hyperlordosis and kyphoscoliosis (unless severe) are not associated with LBP.[4,37,52,75] In fact, the lack of physical findings characteristic of particular LBP presentations makes it difficult to validate that the LBP is due to pathology at any particular site.[66,76,77]

Some experts find traditional examination techniques to have limited interobserver agreement.[65,76] To resolve this problem, the National Institute for Occupational Safety and Health (NIOSH) has recently published an atlas on those physical examination techniques that a panel of respected back researchers found to be consistently reproducible.[78] No attempt has been made, however, to determine which signs are truly valid for back pathology. The clinical examination is thus of limited value in ruling in or ruling out a definitive pathologic causation. The physician may be wise to take Deyo's advice and be satisfied with the answers to just three basic questions[77]:

1. Is there a systemic or visceral cause of LBP?
2. Is there neurologic compromise suggesting the need for surgery?
3. Do findings on examination affect the choice of treatment?

Suggestive historical information, failure to respond to traditional acute therapy, and an index of suspicion, should prompt a search for nonmechanical or systemic causation. For example, the initial presentation of LBP in an elderly person suggests a vascular, neoplastic, or other causation because of the typically younger age at which most nonmalignant LBP first occurs. Low back pain associated with urinary burning may relate to cystitis or even pyelonephritis. Other organ-specific causes include urinary calculus, Paget's disease, or abdominal aortic aneurysm.

In the most common acute LBP presentations, the neurologic findings are normal.[8,75] A limited degree of neurologic compromise is not uncommon, however. Diminished tendon reflex, focal motor weakness, or dermatomal hypesthesia generally follow a distinct radicular pattern. For example, almost 90% of patients with proved L5-S1 disc hernia have a diminished ankle reflex.[53,77] Disc impingement on the L5 root can cause weak ankle and big toe dorsiflexion, lead to hypesthesia along the lateral calf, and/or eliminate the hamstring reflex. Following conservative treatment, recovery may be associated with full or partial improvement in any of these findings. A more serious neurologic picture may warrant a more aggressive surgical approach. Physical examination findings of multiple root compromise, progressive neurologic deterioration, or evidence of sphincter dysfunction should prompt immediate testing.

Several studies have described the usefulness of the straight-leg raising (SLR) test.[45,75,77] In this test, the straightened leg of the supine patient is flexed at the hip by the examiner; by convention, a positive test occurs when pain or numbness is referred down the leg. This referred pain is caused primarily by root tension.[41] Unfortunately, many reports lack not only a clear definition of the angle of hip bending beyond which positivity ends but also a clear indication of whether induced LBP without radiation below the knee is considered a positive test. Magora found that, of 120 LBP patients with positive findings on an SLR test (undefined), only 51 had other neurologic signs, eg, decreased reflexes or strength, hypesthesia, decreased sphincter tone.[75] He concluded that the findings of an SLR test alone may not be very discriminating as a neurologic sign. Referred pain may be due to stretching of other involved tissue, rather than to root irritation.[42,75] Deyo agreed that the SLR test lacks specificity, but added that, because 95% of patients with proved disc hernia do demonstrate positive findings, the test must be considered sensitive.[53,77] Negative findings on an SLR test almost always rule out disc herniation.

Investigators have commonly described limitation of motion, especially spinal flexion, in acute LBP sufferers.[42,70,75,79,80] Two studies have found the greatest spinal limitations in those with recurrent LBP.[2,79,81] Interestingly, Biering-Sorensen found hypermobility in men to be a risk factor for future LBP.[82] McKenzie noted a gradual loss of lumbar extension in chronic LBP sufferers.[83]

In a study of 100 patients with a trunkal list (leaning), Porter and Miller found that, contrary to popular opinion, the list did not correlate to the side of root traction.[84] The significance of a list was that, in those patients who had one associated with certain other neurologic evidence for discal hernia, conservative therapy was much more likely to fail by the criteria of success established by Porter and Miller.

Wadell and associates popularized five physical signs of hysterical symptom exaggeration in chronic back pain sufferers.[85] The five signs included tests for

1. nonanatomic or superficial tenderness
2. pain with simulated loading or rotation
3. inconsistency on distracted retesting
4. regional strength/sensation peculiarities
5. observed overreaction to examination

Patients with three or more of these Waddell signs benefit more from a multidisciplinary psychobehavioral approach than from surgery. Such patients are not truly malingering; their hysterical features are rarely conscious and premeditated. Identifying those patients who require behavior modification is essential in designing proper treatment.

Laboratory Measures

The use of laboratory measures may help to solve diagnostic dilemmas and confirm clinical impressions from the physical examination. The most worldrenowned back pain diagnosticians have maintained a humble perspective, however. As Frymoyer noted, ''The precise cause of LBP is unclear in at least 50% of patients who have undergone extensive radiographic and laboratory evaluations.''[42]

For the great majority of patients with acute LBP, workup need include only a good physical assessment in the physician's office.[45,77,86] Extensive laboratory testing in this population without reasonable justification supplied by the office examination is unlikely to be revealing.[27,45,59,77,86] In patients who do undergo laboratory studies, the relationship between pain complaints and diagnostic testing results is only presumptive.

Spinal Radiography. Although widely used, lumbar spine films in most acute LBP sufferers are at best of questionable value and at worst a source of unnecessary radiation exposure. Hall claimed that the three-view spinal radiographic examination irradiates the patient equivalent to daily chest roentgenograms for 6 years.[59] The fact that such radiographic findings as disc space narrowing, spondylosis, sacralization and lumbarization, Schmorl's nodes, spina bifida, and mild scoliosis are equally prevalent in symptomatic and asymptomatic individuals suggests that little change in treatment or prognosis is likely to occur with any of these radiologic findings.[27,42,59,77] There are, however, certain indications for spinal radiography[45,77,86]:

- In the very acute phase
  1. presumption of spinal fracture (eg, osteoporosis, history of trauma)
  2. known predisposing disease or treatment (eg, steroid use, rheumatoid arthritis)
  3. directing examination finding (eg, absent femoral pulses with abdominal mass)
  4. severe neurologic compromise
  5. history of LBP recurrences with increased frequency or intensity (eg, spondylolisthesis or segmental instability)
- After 2 to 3 weeks of unsuccessful conservative treatment
  1. age over 50 years (eg, possibility of occult malignancy)
  2. history of cancer or unexplained recent weight loss
  3. known drug/alcohol abuse (predisposing to osteomyelitis or trauma)
  4. unexplained fever or night sweats (eg, epidural abscess, Pott's disease, osteomyelitis)
  5. medicolegal issues
- After 6 weeks of unsuccessful conservative treatment

Blood Studies. Suspicion of infection, neoplasm, or spondyloarthropathy may be cause for obtaining confirmatory tests (eg, determinations of HLA-B27, erythrocyte sedimentation rate (ESR), and alkaline or acid phosphatase levels).

Computed Tomography. Although it introduces significant radiation exposure, computed tomography (CT) has become a commonly employed noninvasive screening test for the early evaluation of clinical disc disease.[45] It is highly sensitive and rarely fails to reveal disc herniations that are later surgically proved.[77] The test is not highly specific, however. Wiesel and associates found that 20% of asymptomatic men under 40 years of age showed an apparent disc herniation on CT scan and 50% of those over 40 appeared to have disc protrusion, though without symptoms.[87] In addition to simple axial tomography, a reformatted CT scan with extensive multiplaner reconstruction and three-dimensional imaging can add immeasurably to the diagnostic precision. After the failure of conservative therapy or sooner if clinical suspicion warrants noninvasive radiographic scrutiny, CT scan is useful for detecting spinal stenosis, disc herniation, or possible facet arthropathy.[45] The test is not helpful in the detection of intrathecal tumors, however.[88]

Electromyography. If performed more than 2 weeks after the onset of LBP, electromyography and the determination of nerve conduction velocities can be useful extensions of the physical examination. In the paraspinal muscles, nerve injury potentials (called fibrillations) from disc impingement may be picked up even before 2 weeks. These studies confirm nerve root irritation of a particular radicular pattern and help to localize injury along the motor unit. Chronic disuse atrophy can easily be distinguished from neurogenic atrophy.

Bone Scan. When LBP is associated with clinical evidence of infection or neoplasm, or when it is necessary to confirm acute inflammatory changes of the facet joints, radionuclide scanning is a reasonable procedure.[45]

Myelography. A lumbar myelogram is no longer commonly performed in the diagnostic and presurgical workup of an LBP patient. Intrathecal and conus tumors can now be more easily detected with magnetic resonance imaging.[88] The potential morbidity associated with myelography (eg, later development of arachnoiditis) and the unpleasantness of the procedure have relegated it to more limited use.

Magnetic Resonance Imaging. Physicians are using magnetic resonance imaging (MRI) more and more frequently to evaluate LBP, especially when they presume involvement of the soft tissue or when they need to analyze the intrathecal contents for a possible tumor. This study has the advantage of avoiding hazardous radiation exposure. Furthermore, because MRI is not invasive, it is relatively painless and eliminates the risk of arachnoiditis. It can be hoped that its limitations, such as the inability to obtain thinner transverse cuts or to produce an image of cortical bone, will be overcome.[88]

Treatment and Its Implications

Spontaneous healing occurs after most cases of acute LBP. Patients who experience all but the most short-lived episodes generally seek treatment, however. There are four generic categories of treatment: (1) the conservative approach, (2) surgery, (3) a chronic behavioral approach, and (4) specific work reconditioning. Any attempt to evaluate the worker's functional disability after LBP should take into consideration the nature of and response to treatment.

After an initial period of bedrest, the conservative approach is chosen in nearly all cases of LBP. Even a majority of patients with disc herniation can improve without surgery. Physical therapists who see workers with acute LBP generally take a cautious, but direct, approach. This treatment will increase comfort, but probably has little effect on healing. Patients first learn to relieve their pain by proper rest postures, body mechanics, and a palliative modality (ie, penetrating heat or ice massage). Next, flexibility and trunk strengthening exercises are added gradually and later intensified. Emphasis is placed on aerobic fitness, even for those with acute LBP. To ensure work readiness at the conclusion of the program, most of these workers should undergo functional capacity testing.

Surgery is generally not even considered for acute LBP, except in patients who have the cauda equina syndrome with bowel and bladder neurogenicity or unstable spinal fractures.[72] When a conservative treatment approach has been unsuccessful for over 2 to 3 months, surgery is a reasonable approach if a clear-cut case can be made for disc herniation with progressive or persistent and nagging radiculopathy; for compromising central or lateral spinal stenosis; or for spondylolisthesis, grades 3 or 4 (or selectively in lesser grades). Surgical referral for cases of segmental instability, a controversial condition, may also be necessary.[42,77]

The particular job-relatedness of symptoms may influence a decision to consider surgery, especially if a job switch is unlikely. For example, a worker with mild spondylolisthesis and recurrent LBP may be more inclined to consider a spinal fusion if the only work he or she can do requires heavy lifting, impact, or bending, potential sources of spinal slippage. Postoperatively, some of these patients may continue to have medical impairment by virtue of their presurgical conditions and their surgically altered anatomies, however.

The length of time that patients are off work after surgery varies greatly and relates to the intensity of job demands and the availability of light-duty work. In Rowe's study of postlaminectomy patients, the total time away from work averaged 14 weeks.[34] Using microsurgical techniques, Camp reduced the postoperative recovery time to an average of only 38 days.[88] Following surgery, a conservative rehabilitation program is concluded by work reconditioning. Functional capacity evaluation is essential and often must be repeated in those with lengthier recovery periods.

The approach to management of chronic back pain is of considerable consequence, as it greatly affects the cost of health care within self-insured companies. Moreover, the 10% to 15% of back-injured workers who do not return to work by 3 months may develop the chronicity syndrome. The majority of these workers had not entered treatment with intentions of manipulating recovery, but circumstances, at times anatomic and at times context-specific, have prevented a more prompt recovery. Interestingly, those chronically out of work are no more likely to demonstrate serious neurologic compromise than the earlier returning group.[8,74,89] Commonly, the chronic pain patient exhibits low self-esteem, depression, dependency on others, hopelessness, and psychosomatic focus.[89] The longer the individual remains dysfunctional, the worse these feelings become. Narcotic addiction may accompany the other psychologic problems. Physical deconditioning is also inevitable.

Numerous programs have sprung up nationwide to help patients with chronic pain. These programs generally adopt a multidimensional and behavioral—rather than strictly medical—methodology. Drug detoxification, incremental functional restoration, pain behavior modification, and regained self-confidence to return to productive life are all the results of successful treatment.[89] The treatment team consists of physician(s), nurse, physical and/or occupational therapists, psychologist (psychiatrist), and, typically, a vocational counselor. Treatment can be on an inpatient or outpatient basis.

Work reconditioning is a directed and goal-oriented program of rehabilitation.[90] It may occur in the hospital setting, in a remote warehouse, or in the natural work environment. The physical or occupational therapist attempts to rebuild a worker's capacity to perform the specific tasks of a normal work day. A work reconditioning approach requires job site simulation and graduated accommodation to work stress.[91] Success in this program is readily measured by means of functional capacity testing.

Any given worker with LBP often requires elements of all these treatment approaches. Functionally relevant reconditioning is frequently appropriate, even for the patient with acute LBP. A premorbid history of low self-esteem and dependency in any worker with LBP may necessitate counseling and positive reinforcement early in rehabilitation. Even chronic LBP sufferers may benefit from initial application of soothing modalities, akin to the treatment of acute LBP. Thus, in the most successful back rehabilitation programs, therapists employ a breadth of approaches. Effective treatment requires flexibility and the capacity to tailor a program to fit the patient's individual characteristics and job demands.

Natural History and Prognosis

A significant number of LBP sufferers have their first attack before the age of 30 years.[1,4,70,74] For women, the 1-year incidence and prevalence increase with age into the sixties, presumably secondary to increasing osteoporosis.[63] For men, the peak annual incidence of back pain is at age 40 years.[20]

Several industrial studies have shown that the natural history of work disability after a single bout of LBP is fairly constant: 40% to 50% of workers who stayed home have returned to work by 2 weeks after the first sick day; 60% to 80% of workers, by 4 weeks; and 85% to 90% of workers, by 12 weeks.[14,19,70] These incidences of work return are found regardless of the treatment. When conservative treatment is employed, it principally accomplishes three objectives for the worker: some degree of comfort during healing, re-establishment of job-specific conditioning, and education in proper body mechanics for performing his or her work.

Unfortunately, the long-term prognosis for many industrial back pain sufferers is not entirely rosy, as LBP commonly recurs.[4,13,14] Troup, Martin, and Lloyd described two common patterns for recurrent symptoms.[14] In the first, a degenerative type of LBP causes symptoms intermittently, but the individual functions normally during the symptom-free intervals. In the second pattern, the individual recovers from the initial injury gradually over 1 to 2 years, during which time he or she is never quite symptom-free and remains sensitive to exacerbations. In addition, there are limits to the efficacy of worker back education programs. Some investigators have shown how short-lived are the ability and willingness of workers to practice back injury prevention skills taught to them.[92] Thus, many workers with recurrent LBP may be exacerbating their own problems by work practices that they themselves know to be injudicious.

Some neurologic signs, such as a lost ankle reflex, hypesthesia, or even focal muscle weakness, are not of prognostic value in indicating those patients likely to have recurrent back problems.[14,86] On the other hand, several studies have shown that persistent pain referred into the legs is of great prognostic significance.[2,14,93] For example, Troup, Martin, and Lloyd found that coal miners who returned to work with back pain alone had a 26% chance of being absent from work for 5 weeks in the following year. When the workers returned with sciatica, with or without back pain, their chance of requiring 5 weeks off was 39% in the first year and 24% in the second year.[14]

In the same study, Troup and associates identified five physical signs that were consistently helpful in predicting which LBP patients were likely to require ongoing care and absence from work in the subsequent 2 years:

1. SLR restriction (ie, positive within 45° on one side or a 15° difference between the two sides)
2. abnormal nerve root tension tests (pain reproduced on SLR by cervical flexion, medial hip rotation, or ankle dorsiflexion)
3. dynamic flexor trunk muscle weakness (while doing sit-ups)
4. pain or weakness on resisted hip flexion while seated
5. back pain on prone-lying knee flexion

If four or five of these physical signs were present when the coal miners wished to return to their normal work, the chance of their developing LBP sufficient to keep them out of work 5 weeks or more in the subsequent year was nearly 50%, compared to 25% for patients with one or two positive signs. It seems ill-advised to permit a worker to return to a former job without modification when the chance of a severely disabling LBP recurrence is as high as 50%.

It is dangerous to apply one clinical researcher's statistics to another setting, but similar physical findings in a worker who wants to return to a vigorous job ought at least to give the examining physician pause. Further useful information regarding the readiness of an injured worker to return to work can be obtained through functional capacity testing. The physician and collaborating therapist must compare this information with known job demands to make a truly objective decision on the patient's ability to return to work safely.

Although some factors that affect chronicity are uncontrollable and are pre-determined at the time of treatment, others may be modified or preventable, thus improving the natural history and prognosis for work. For example, both the nature of onset and the type of work influence the length of work absence. According to several sources, a rapid recovery is less likely if the onset of LBP is gradual.[7,24,70,80] Other investigators have shown that the prognosis is worse with an acute onset from falls.[14,94] Lloyd, Gould, and Soutor found that the prevalence of LBP in the administrators in the Scottish mines was the same as that in the miners themselves, but the administrators tended to miss less work because of the LBP.[95] Youth and a high level of education are also associated with faster recovery.[74,89] None of these factors is controllable, however.

In contrast, certain contextual factors that are subject to external control play a great role in the natural history of LBP. Health care teams that assess the condition of patients with LBP are increasingly sensitive to such psychosocial variables as substance abuse, marital or childrearing issues, and other personal confounders. Workplace issues, such as job dissatisfaction and employer-employee relations problems, can also complicate a patient's recovery from a mechanical back disruption that had originally appeared to be of modest consequence. Proper care management sometimes resolves these issues and avoids chronic scenarios. Direction may be provided from within the company by proactive occupational health nurses or from outside the company through an insurance or private rehabilitation specialist. Exerting control at this stage is more effective than any efforts to handle a worker with the chronicity syndrome. It is difficult to return such a worker to the job.[10,86]

Impairment Rating

Physicians are often called upon to determine both the point at which reasonable progress during recovery has reached a plateau and the extent of residual impairment. Although some degree of tissue healing may continue for up to 2 years after disc herniation, the major portion of recovery occurs within 6 months post-injury.[96,97] Nondiscogenic mechanical back pain usually has undergone major healing even sooner. To assess residual back impairment, the physician can use one of several rating systems that have been developed in order to distribute financial settlements for low back disability fairly.[25,98–100] Unfortunately, not all the premises underlying these systems are sound ones. Although there are known to be anatomic markers of back motion, they could not be reliably and reproducibly measured until recently. Furthermore, no one has shown that limitations of motion are similarly meaningful from one subject to another.

The practices of physicians who evaluate low back impairment have been studied in two retrospective surveys, one of Iowa orthopedists in 1980[101] and a second of West Virginia orthopedic and neurosurgeons in 1983.[102] In both studies, the investigators noted physicians' tendencies to include their own perceptions of patients' disabilities in the impairment ratings. These perceptions can be colored by preconceived biases of those who seek the impairment rating, the physician-patient rapport, and other intangible factors. The resultant lack of inter-rater reliability has prompted much concern.

One of the rating systems involves the use of an inclinometer to make back motion measurements more reproducible between testers.[6] Improving test objectivity does not, however, lead unalterably to consistent back impairment ratings among evaluators. Physicians know that their ratings are used to compensate for permanent impairment, still frequently translated to mean "permanent work disability." Perception biases may thus continue to taint the rating decisions of physicians who assess their patients' back impairments.

The total elimination of physician subjectivity would not improve the validity of these ratings as predictors of present or future employability. The latter determination requires job-relevant functional capacity testing and vocational expertise, as well as a medical statement of prognosis. The low back impairment rating as an arbitrary assessment of anatomic relevance is invalid as an indicator of work capacity.

Uncertain Anatomic Impairment

When a full diagnostic workup does not demonstrate fully a relevant pathology, as frequently happens, the physician has difficulty in assessing impairment. The consequences may be severe. In addition to the professional dismay and embarrassment of diagnostic uncertainties, physicians often incur patients' anxiety and loss of confidence when this uncertainty is admitted. As a result, several treatment approaches, some highly unscientific, may be tried by patients.

When diagnosis is uncertain, it is better for the physician to acknowledge this to patients and to assert the conditions ruled out by the workup (eg, surgical back problems and pain referred from other organs). In these cases, the patient's functional limitations are addressed more readily while the label of medical impairment remains uncertain. The range of possible functional outcomes is quite disparate, even in cases of clearly identifiable pathology. Readiness for work return is not inferred from the label of a medical impairment as the functional disability of LBP is equally or more dependent on other factors. Evaluating capacity to work in LBP patients includes behavioral as well as biomechanical issues in the workplace.

FUNCTIONAL CAPACITY EVALUATION

The American Medical Association has suggested that physicians limit their role to assessing medical impairment.[98] Much of the information needed to explore the safety of available return-to-work options is not directly measured during the physician's traditional clinical evaluation of the employee's health status and impairment. Except after short-lived illness or injury, an office examination does not provide all the information necessary for a physician to make a reliable prediction of a worker's functional capacity.

Objective functional capacity measures are often necessary to substantiate the medical impairment, disability, and job handicap of the worker with LBP. The questions to be answered by the functional capacity evaluation (FCE) usually dictate the composition and duration of the testing battery, which is typically administered by physical and occupational therapists. In any FCE testing battery, the choice of measures to be included should be determined by their safety, reliability, practicality, limitations, and relevance to the stated purpose.[40]

General Physical Screening for Safe Placement

As a "bridge" between health care and the workplace, the general physical screening battery assists the rehabilitation team in identifying job placement options that reduce the risk of cumulative trauma and overexertion.[90] After some back injuries, the judicious use of a screening battery may allow the worker to remain productive even while undergoing treatment, as the screening defines safe light-duty placement. The worker progresses gradually to a permanent job position when maximum recovery and acclimation to job demands have occurred. This human-centered approach can effectively improve the injured employee's morale while reducing the high costs of chronic disability, litigation, and replacement of valuable employees.

The job analysis approach developed by the Department of Labor has been used widely to survey the functional demands of jobs.[103] Smith, Cunningham, and Weinberg used a general FCE in conjunction with the physical demands and environmental conditions specified by the U.S. Department of Labor system to evaluate workers' abilities to return to work, for example.[104] To enhance safe placement of low back-injured workers further, more specific anthropometric, strength, and aerobic endurance measurements are frequently included in the FCE and job analysis. This additional information assists the team in balancing potential labor relations ramifications, costs for training and job modifications, safety, and productivity.

Tests of Manual Materials Handling

The assessment of lifting capacity is critical to the safe placement of workers with a history of LBP. Direct dynamic testing of lift and carry strength is recommended over indirect static or isokinetic testing, because dynamic testing is more similar to the actual demands of the job. The lifting protocols developed by Snook and Irvine,[105,106] by Snook,[107] and by Mayer and associates[108,109] are simple, inexpensive, and portable. Suggestions for modification to improve the safety and reliability of psychophysical testing protocols include graduated progression of weights,[108] use of ratings of perceived exertion to establish the psychophysical end-point,[110–112] heart rate monitoring to establish the cardiovascular end-point,[108,109] controlled lifting postures to reduce variability of spinal stress,[113] and evaluator judgment of the kinesiophysical end-point.[91]

Tests of Aerobic Capacity

Because of the deconditioning associated with chronic LBP, aerobic capacity testing is relevant when evaluating a client's cardiorespiratory fitness for metabolically demanding job options.[114,115] Information on the client's exercise tolerance level may be directly compared to the estimated metabolic energy expenditure rate of potential jobs to predict the maximum intensity at which the client can perform job tasks continuously without excessive cardiorespiratory fatigue.[116] The most practical submaximal aerobic testing protocols to assess patients with LBP impairment involve a bicycle ergometer or step test.

Tests of Posture Tolerance and Mobility

Activity tolerances can often be estimated by means of a simple obstacle course, performance on standardized work samples, and self-report questionnaires. Safe placement requires a knowledge of the client's tolerance for standing, walking, sitting, bending/stooping, squatting/crouching, climbing, twisting, reaching, and operating of foot controls.

Anthropometric Measures

The low back-injured worker may have limitations in bending, squatting, or standing on tiptoe because of restricted spinal flexion or extension. It is essential to document these anthropometric data, along with measurements of the client's acceptable forward and vertical reaches. Given this information, the ergonomist may implement reasonable workplace accommodations that allow the disabled worker to maximize his or her abilities without reaggravating the existing injury.

For example, the range of acceptable heights of shelves in the workplace may have to be raised to accommodate the low back-injured worker who is unable to squat comfortably.

Job-Specific Work Tolerance Testing

When the exact job to which the worker with LBP will return is known, a more precise FCE can be undertaken to determine the worker's tolerance for that job. Before this evaluation, a general FCE may have already identified functional limitations and anthropometric characteristics that must be tested further. In drawing conclusions from the work tolerance screening, the clinician should take into consideration job stress factors and personal risk factors for LBP (eg, gender, age, experience/training, attitude, body mechanics, and strength). The ideal setting for work tolerance testing is the actual job.

Results from this work simulation help establish accommodations needed because of the employee's job handicap, if there is one. If accommodations cannot be made, other light-duty options that are consistent with the client's work capacity should be explored. When light-duty work is not available, work tolerance screening is often conducted within a work hardening program.

Work hardening is a highly structured, productivity-oriented evaluation and treatment program in which work simulation tasks and employer-donated materials are used to decrease impairment, functional limitations, disability, and vocational handicap.[90] The potential benefits of this supervised work simulation include worker education in pacing and body mechanics and identification of any reasonable workplace accommodations or reassignment needed to enhance worker safety and productivity at the identified job.

Testing to Substantiate Disability

When the patient's subjective self-report of disability appears to be out of proportion with more objective signs of physical impairment, the FCE can be used to substantiate disability. Potential causes of magnified illness behavior include (1) unrecognized severity of the patient's pathologic condition; (2) psychologic distress related to the duration, nature, and/or failure of treatment or dislike of the job or employer; and (3) voluntary exaggeration to influence medicolegal proceedings. Most workers are not malingerers. Waddell and associates characterized the majority of patients with chronic LBP as not "personality deficient, neurotic, hypochondriac, hysterical, or mad but simply distressed by their physical problem."[117] This distress causes many workers to alter their self-perception, however, which may in turn alter their behavior.

Several objective testing procedures (eg, static strength testing and isokinetic testing) may be useful in substantiating the level of low back functional disability. Comparison of the results obtained in these tests with relevant self-report measures can provide valuable insight into the psychosocial and behavioral aspects of disability associated with LBP.[118] This information is important both to develop a holistic treatment plan for patients with LBP complicated by pain behavior and to distribute compensation awards fairly.

Static Strength Testing

Not only has static strength testing been shown to be safe, reliable, and somewhat predictive of injury or treatment outcome in unimpaired workers[119] but it also has the practical advantages of low cost, portability, anatomic stabilization, and control over speed/acceleration variables. However, questions about the value of static strength test results in predicting performance on dynamic "real-life" activities make such a test more useful in substantiating disability than in assessing true work capacity.

There has been some concern about applying to chronically disabled workers the same strength assessment procedures that are applied to healthy, unimpaired workers.[58,120,121] Instructions for these studies often call for the exertion of a maximum voluntary effort (MVE). Although they seek to employ reliable methods, testers must avoid further injury to the low back during testing. Thus, the exertion of an MVE, although an appropriate end-point in normal healthy workers, is problematic in back-impaired workers because of liability and safety issues. To lessen these concerns, Matheson[90] suggested that measures of MVE should

- not require a cardiovascular effort that exceeds 65% of the predicted maximal heart rate
- not directly involve an impaired component of the biomechanical system
- have low error variance
- be controlled by the evaluee
- have high inherent consistency
- allow short-term (brief rest) replication
- give the evaluee minimal visual or proprioceptive feedback about the results of his or her effort

Testing devices that fulfill these criteria for workers with LBP impairments include the BTE Work Simulator, Jamar Hand Dynamometer, arm static strength testing device, and the WEST 2 upper extremity strength and fatigue tolerance test system. Both the torso and squat static strength tests may be more important measures of rehabilitation progress than of effort because of the potentially high compression loading on L3, as determined by biomechanical analysis.[122] The potential damage and stress to the site of low back impairment cause concern about the consistent use of these measures in back-disabled persons as an assessment of effort. The usefulness of the Jamar Hand Dynamometer is in detecting sincerity of effort when measuring grip strength, as detailed by Mathiowetz and associates.[123] Niebuhr and Marion,[124] Stokes,[125] and Gilbert and Knowlton.[126] The hand grip strength of the LBP patient may be compared to that of others who are the same age and sex to help substantiate sincerity of effort on other tests.[123]

Isokinetic Tests

Some authorities have advocated the use of isokinetic testing of strength at constant speeds in the assessment of rehabilitation progress and of joint motion coordination following industrial and sports injuries. The chief advantage of this technique over static strength testing lies in the fact that it permits an evaluation of strength over the entire range of joint motion at assigned speeds. Improved anatomic stabilization, the accommodation of resistance to enhance safety, and the ability to set alternate speeds during testing are clear advantages of this technique over simple, dynamic testing methods for the scientific assessment of lifting and joint performance. Its chief limitations are equipment expense, lack of portability, and controversy about its predictive validity—the relationship of isokinetic testing results to a patient's actual functional capability.

It has been proposed that isokinetic measures of trunk and lifting strength can be used to substantiate consistency of effort, as maximal effort can be differentiated from submaximal effort by comparing the forces of torque during repeated efforts.[108,109] Hazard and associates tested this concept on a random sample of 30 unimpaired subjects, using the Cybex Trunk Extension/Flexion and Cybex Lift Test to measure maximal (100%) and submaximal (50%) efforts.[127] They concluded that the use of measurement models to compare the exertions of force over time was clearly more accurate than was the use of subjective visual assessment scales of curve variability.

At present, there are no controlled studies that demonstrate the ability of isokinetic testing devices to differentiate between various causes of submaximal effort. The clinical experience of the therapist, other testing procedures, and input from other team members may be necessary to determine if the submaximal effort is due to depression, fear of injury, pain, or malingering. Therapists have used consistency of performance in the same or related tasks to interpret testing results, but many factors can affect reproducibility. Before concluding that the problem is mental rather than physical, one should also consider poor inherent reproducibility of the test due to motor learning, which may cause a gradual improvement in performance; fatigue, which may cause a gradual decay in performance; a problem in communication/perception; and of course, unstable irritation/injury.

JOB EVALUATION

Return to work, even when fully healed, may expose some workers to the same job site hazards that brought about the back injury in the first place. If a trend of LBP is identified at a particular site, a job evaluation should be conducted to determine whether job site modifications are necessary. Although most job evaluations focus solely on identifying physical work factors, such as posture, lifting, pulling, pushing, and cyclic loading, it is important not to overlook the individual and work situation stress factors that contribute to injury and disability.

An injured worker may find reasons and ways not to rush back to the job site when work is unenjoyable and uninspiring. Bigos and associates found that workers who take longer to return to work after a back injury than did others had poorer appraisal ratings by their supervisors.[69] Two key factors in an impaired worker's decision to apply for long-term disability are limited autonomy and the employer's inability or unwillingness to make job modifications.[73] According to Vallfors, Swedish auto workers considered the working environment to be the major factor in causing the initial injury and in preventing work return; those who were satisfied with their jobs and had freedom to move about from one task to another returned to work sooner after a back injury than did others who experienced the same type of back injury.[74]

If the job site problem appears to be an individual one, reasonable accommodations for the worker at the workplace or light-duty placement in a job consistent with the worker's functional capabilities should be considered. If the worker is representative of a larger group, such as older workers, job demand-worker capacity mismatches should be dealt with as a job site problem. If the problem is due to work situational factors, such as supervisory style, production pressures, management policies, or other psychosocial issues, interventions should be targeted toward this important area.

Physical Work Associations

A number of epidemiologic studies of lifting have shown that the rates of musculoskeletal injury and the severity of those injuries increase from exposure to heavy or frequent lifting. The six most important vocational factors, as cited by Andersson, are shown in Figure 2-8. To this list, Magora and Taustein have added sudden unexpected movement.[8,37] Some or all of the risk factors are encountered by truck drivers, materials handlers, and nurses—the three occupational groups that have the highest risk of LBP.[8,31,107] More than 30% of the U.S. work force are employed in jobs that require daily lifting of weights in excess of 20 kg (44 lb), and more than 60% of LBP patients claim that overexertion is the cause of their injuries.[40] Lifting bulky objects, lifting from the floor, or lifting even light loads

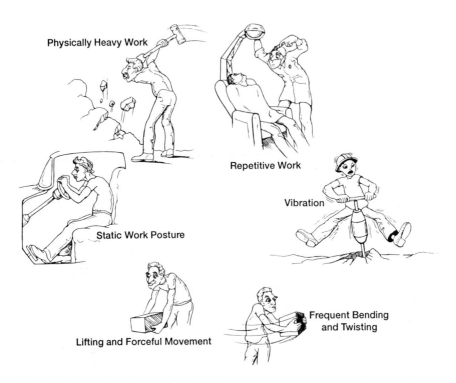

Figure 2-8 Six vocational factors associated with absence from work due to lower back pain. *Source:* Reprinted with permission from *Spine* (1981;6[1]:53–60), Copyright © 1981, JB Lippincott Co.

with awkward body postures can place a great deal of biomechanical stress on the low back.[40]

The relationship between worker strength and job demands can also have an important effect on injury and reinjury rates. Magora and Taustein found that more than 20% of workers who perform heavy lifting versus 10% of bank workers had experienced recent LBP.[8] Gyntelberg found that 34% of workers doing heavy lifting versus 23% of sedentary workers had back pain during a 1-year period.[7] Liles and associates found an increase in musculoskeletal injury rates and costs as the percentage of workers who overexert themselves in their job increases.[128] Finally, Keyserling and associates demonstrated that the incidence of LBP in employees selected with the use of strength tests was approximately one third that of LBP in employees screened by traditional medical criteria.[129]

Sitting may predispose and perpetuate back complaints. For example, Kelsey and Hardy have shown that workers in sitting occupations have a higher risk of disc prolapse.[30,51] Nachemson found that sitting, particularly if unsupported, is associated with elevated intradiscal pressures[27] (see Fig. 2-1), although these elevated pressures do not necessarily produce radiographic changes in the discs. After observing primitive Indian tribes and obtaining roentgenograms of their members, Fahrni speculated that their willingness to squat and lack of chair sitting were responsible for the low incidence of degenerative disc disease in these groups.[130]

Frymoyer and colleagues suggested that the 5-Hz resonance frequency of the intervertebral disc may be produced by many tools, including the chainsaw and jackhammer, and that this vibration may be a mechanism by which energy absorption can lead to degenerative disc disease.[3] Driving combines the risk factors of a relatively poor position (ie, sitting) with exposure to vibration. The result is predictable. According to Kelsey,[30] men who drive during 50% or more of their working hours have a fourfold increased risk of disc herniation. Moreover, commuters who drive more than 20 miles per day have two to four times the number of back complaints and twice the incidence of herniated nucleus pulposus than do people who drive less frequently.

These work associations with LBP underscore the importance of identifying and reducing risk factors for LBP. An ergonomic approach of matching worker capabilities to job demands to reduce cumulative trauma also shows a great deal of promise in promoting healthful work.

Work Practice Guidelines

According to the *NIOSH Work Practices Guide for Manual Lifting*,[40] administrative or engineering controls are necessary to prevent injury in unimpaired worker populations that handle manual materials (ie, weight lifted by hand). In other words, it is as important to treat the workplace as the worker. Using the *NIOSH Guide*, companies can consider such variables as the object weight, horizontal location of the hands, vertical location of the hands, vertical travel distance, frequency of lifting, and duration of lifting. When quantitated, these variables can be used to calculate an action limit within the strength capabilities of 75% of women and 99% of men. Unfortunately, this guide has been developed using data collection from healthy populations, and caution is warranted when applying this simplistic approach to workers with low back impairments.

INTEGRATION OF FINDINGS

LBP is a common, yet enigmatic ailment. Except for the rapidly healing LBP that involves little or no time off from work, occupational back pain often requires a multidisciplinary and vocationally oriented assessment. Matheson described the vocational capacity evaluation team as a "well-integrated, cohesive, multi-facet-ed unit that is responsible for the holistic care of the evaluee.''[90] The case manager of such a team can be a medical or a vocational professional. The team participants include (1) a physician who assesses the medical impairment and prognosis, recognizes the potential vocational implications, and mobilizes the assessment team; (2) a physical and/or occupational therapist who treats in the recovery period, improves faulty body mechanics, measures functional capacity objectively, performs functional job site analyses, and occasionally works with ergonomic engineers who provide necessary tool or job modifications; (3) a vocational counselor who, when return to the original job is unlikely, assesses work skills that can be transferred to another job and assists in the job search; and (4) a psychologist who evaluates psychosocial stressors and their subsequent effect on work output.

The following 10 scenarios are commonly encountered by the vocational evaluation team involved in LBP assessment.

Case 1

> A 46-year-old male truck driver with initial LBP 5 days ago; 3 days at bedrest and already improving. Job includes loading/unloading 50- to 80-lb variably shaped boxes and driving more than 4 hours daily.

Nearly all acute LBP improves readily. Nevertheless, a thorough history and physical examination by the physician on the team are important in every case. The history should include the worker's description of the worksite and, if possible, a written job description from the employer. The physical examination should at least establish the presence or absence of neurologic compromise.

Although this truck driver is apparently on the mend, he will undoubtedly be at risk for reinjury when he returns to the job. Because the lifting demands imposed on truck drivers exceed the NIOSH-recommended action limit for engineering or administrative controls,[40] this worker should undergo a general FCE to ensure his safe return to work. The results should be compared with the results of a physical stress job analysis to determine the most cost-effective job modification options. Someone on the team, generally the ergonomically oriented therapist, should instruct this truck driver on proper body mechanics for lifting. Those in the driving professions should be advised to take mini-exercise breaks during long drives.

Unfortunately, many patients forget back school concepts, unless they are frequently reinforced, in the heat of the working environment. For this reason, the ultimate goal of industry ought to be job redesign and site modification. For this truck driver, truck-to-ground unloading stress can be alleviated by a two-wheel dolly and a pull-out ramp.

Case 2

A 57-year-old male hospital orderly with nonradiating LBP; referred to clinic 4 to 6 weeks after onset without improvement.

If an LBP patient is still unimproved after 4 weeks, the newly involved physician should review the history thoroughly and perform another physical examination carefully. An attempt to establish consistent pain patterns by postural provocative maneuvers may implicate a mechanical cause. Any evidence of neurologic involvement should be studied carefully. Nonmechanical causes of LBP, including other system problems (eg, hypernephroma, aortic aneurysm) should be considered. By 4 to 6 weeks after the onset of LBP, even without clinical evidence of neurologic worsening, the physician may wish to pursue laboratory and radiographic testing.

If further workup reveals no clear-cut anatomic causation of the LBP and if improvements appear to lag behind reasonable recovery expectations, treatment adequacy and worker motivation must be considered. The use of a modality-dominated approach (ie, hot packs and massage alone) after 2 to 3 weeks is, for example, inappropriate. Even more important is the underlying agenda of the worker. Is this hospital orderly's job appealing? Does it pay well? Are there indications of a hospital layoff soon? Does he like the head nurse, his co-workers, and his immediate supervisors? How stressful (or cozy) is life at home now? Is his wife working? Are there children to care for at home? How many beers or highballs does he consume in an average day? Although these questions may evoke evasive answers, they are often useful and revealing. If psychosocial or vocational stressors can be identified at this juncture, corrective action by team members is more likely to result in a return to work.

For this hospital orderly with unremitting symptoms but an unrevealing physical examination and laboratory study, an FCE can help clarify the major issues and provide the necessary documentation of the worker's inability to return to the previous position. There are, then, three alternatives: job restructuring, reassignment consistent with the worker's physical capacity, or a renewed work reconditioning program. Complete cessation of pain is unnecessary before return to work.[86]

Case 3

A 32-year-old female office secretary who types, answers phone, and files has LBP with sciatica and foot drop; also has a strong desire to continue working.

When the need to work is great, the job desirable, and/or the work ethic strong, this situation can arise. If the secretarial job is to continue unchanged, there must be an active and ongoing dialogue between the secretary and her physician in order to ensure rapid treatment should symptoms increase. One question that must be addressed is the extent to which her medical impairment will impair the patient's performance on the job now and in the future.

Before considering surgery for this sedentary worker, the physician should exhaust conservative treatment and job modification options. For example, trunk muscle strengthening in a neutral back position is beneficial as prophylaxis against recurrent back injury.[2,131,132] A program of low-impact aerobic exercise also appears to be beneficial (Cady LD, personal communication). A switch to a less stressful office situation, modification of the order of daily tasks, or a more ergonomically positioned work station may make this secretary's job easier. Occasionally, the temporary reinforcement provided by an abdominal binder can be helpful. The therapist should perform an FCE and a job site assessment, both crucial to reassure all parties that the secretarial position is likely to be tolerable.

In theory, most sedentary jobs can be modified to accommodate even the most physically disabled workers. If it becomes clear that this particular job site is unalterable or that this secretary's physical capacity cannot be improved sufficiently while she is working, the choices narrow to consideration of further rehabilitation while she does not work, a job switch, or an investigation of a possible vocational or psychosocial disturbance that the secretary is reluctant to acknowledge. The entire team, including the vocational counselor, the employer, and the union representatives, need to confer before such problems can be resolved.

Case 4

> A 44-year-old male bus mechanic who experiences sharp central LBP, immediately after an awkward fall; notices tingling around anus, foot drop, and knee buckling a few hours later; awakens the next morning with an incontinent stool.

This case is clearly a neurosurgical emergency. Evidence of severe neurologic worsening, including bowel/bladder/sexual dysfunction, foot drop, and perineal sensory dysfunction, should prompt consideration of a surgical solution. In fact, the sooner referral can be made, the better. A central disc herniation involving multiple nerve roots frequently has a constellation of sensory, motor, and autonomic disturbances. These signs and symptoms may develop quickly or over days or weeks. Once the progression is noted, too long a delay in surgical decompression can result in irreversible, disabling neurologic impairment, even after treatment.

Case 5

> A 31-year-old male truck driver with several work-affecting episodes of
> LBP in the past 3 years, most recently 4 weeks ago.

As Troup, Martin, and Lloyd noted,[14] recurrent LBP is fairly common in those
who do menial work and may reflect ongoing, repeated disc abuse. The physician
should rule out segmental instability, spinal stenosis, spondylolisthesis, or other
more unusual LBP etiology (ie, inflammatory spondyloarthropathy).

Once again, the evaluating physician and other team members should establish
the worker's functional capacity and uncover any hidden psychosocial problems,
such as marital discord, alcoholism, or other substance abuse, that may hide
behind the more socially acceptable LBP. Finally, job dissatisfaction, even in a
worker who returns to work as often as this one, is fairly common and should be
considered. The ultimate return to work is often a labor relations issue.

If the physical nature of the work is taking its toll, the physician must consider
recommending a job change or at least a job modification for the truck driver. Job
modification within the same company is ideal, as the worker is familiar with that
context and has already established relationships in that company. Capacity to
perform the less stressful job can again be determined through an FCE.

Case 6

> A 41-year-old female assembly line worker required to reach forward,
> bend, and twist long hours each day; out of work 15 months with LBP,
> but no objective physical findings.

It is commonly believed that the chronic pain patient is the source of his or her
own problems and willfully abuses the compensation system. In most cases,
however, malingering is too simplistic an explanation. At the onset of LBP,
patients become victims of a cumbersome, confusing, or unyielding system of
case management far more often than they become conscious manipulators of the
system. Leavitt, Johnston, and Beyer showed that the underlying problem with
many expensive (ie, prolonged) back claims is excessive and unnecessary lag
time, sometimes caused by employer or insurance carrier ambivalence and sometimes caused by delay in a physician's diagnosis or treatment.[22]

This assembly line worker may have been the victim of poor case management,
inadequate medical assessment, ineffective rehabilitation, a poorly designed work
site, and/or an indifferent employer. The difficulties of sorting out the possible
contributing factors have led some larger organizations to develop an algorithmic

system for dealing with the LBP problem in their workers. For example, a standardized LBP management system for nearly 20,000 utility and federal workers was developed in the Washington, D.C., area by consolidating data from successfully and unsuccessfully treated cases of LBP.[133] The algorithm allowed participating physicians in the community to make decisions in LBP management by well-defined rules, rather than by intuition and self-interest (Fig. 2-9). Intervention from orthopedic experts was immediately available at any point if a patient's course deviated from the protocol. If this assembly line worker had been handled in such a manner, she might have returned to work more readily.

A further cause of concern, however, is often the nature of the work to which the worker returns. In such situations as an assembly line in which cumulative repetitive strain is common, the most important part of the rehabilitation is removing the worker from the site of repetitive strain. If the employer chooses to ignore the advice of the treatment team to change the physical demands and repetitiveness of her job, any attempt by this woman to return to her job is likely to cause a recurrence of symptoms. Thus, a flexible employer is often important in resolving a worker's lengthy work absence problem.

Finally, many workers, on questioning, will admit to disliking their jobs. A situation of job dissatisfaction, promoted by an indifferent employer with an unwillingness to change the job, can lead to situations such as this one. Yelin[134] studied those who had attempted to apply for Social Security disability benefits as compared to those with similar disabilities who continued to work. The factors most predictive of a decision to seek benefits by these patients were poor match of worker with job demands, low degree of job autonomy, and a low level of commitment to work. Perhaps this woman has harbored resentment toward her job for a long time. Proper case management might have revealed this potential impasse sooner; feelings about the job are often of central concern.

It is a mistake simply to recommend that this woman return to work because there are no "objective findings" of disability. Owing to deconditioning, this worker may not be in any shape to return to the assembly line. Even sedentary work as a light-duty return alternative may require a rebuilding of sitting tolerance, walking capacity, or other job-related activities. A rehabilitation program that specializes in chronic pain problems is needed. Even the best of rehabilitation programs may have only limited success in returning workers with chronic pain to the job, however.

If there are no physical reasons to prevent an immediate work return, the woman can be reassured that the symptoms of LBP do generally subside with time, especially if the affected individual is occupied at work.[86] Also, there is no evidence that neurologic injury occurs more commonly in chronic cases than in acute cases or that the work return will exacerbate the injury, so long as reasonable precautions are taken.[74–86]

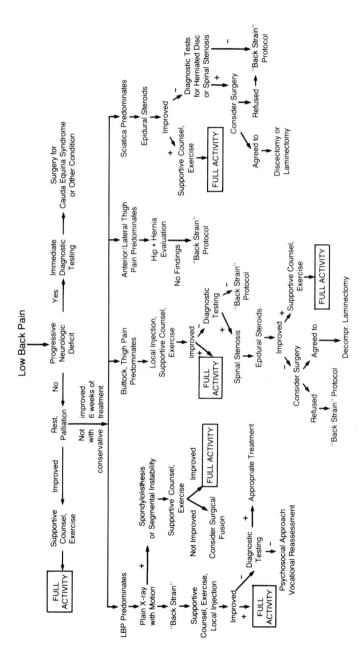

Figure 2-9 Algorithm for low back pain management. (System devised by Wiesel et al to assist low back pain case management.) *Source:* Adapted with permission from *Spine* (1984;9:199–203), Copyright © 1984, JB Lippincott Co.

Supportive Counsel = Back school, body mechanics, pacing skills, and functional capacity evaluation.

Diagnostic Testing = CAT scan, EMG, MRI, bone scan, and/or myelogram in select cases.

"Back Strain" Protocol = Supportive counsel, exercise, vocational assessment, and optional light-duty work return.

Case 7

> The fourth worker from a particular plant work station to report to the plant physician for LBP.

In this situation, there may be a biomechanically deleterious work station that requires cumulative repetitive strain or an employer-union-worker relations problem masquerading as an injury epidemic. Collaboration of physician, ergonomic engineer or therapist, and a work site representative is essential to decipher the cause of the back "flu."

Case 8

> The potential employee with newly discovered congenital spine abnormality.

Most congenital spinal defects do not increase the affected individual's risk of LBP.[1,27,59] The American College of Surgeons does not recommend screening roentgenograms because of the associated radiologic exposure and because of their limited efficacy in identifying likely LBP sufferers.[61] Only spondylolisthesis appears to predispose to LBP.[4,50] It is a prospective worker's legal right to take a job despite the presence of radiologic abnormalities *unless* the safety of the worker or other employees could be jeopardized by his or her employment.

Case 9

> A male worker recovering from a lengthy non-low back disability who reports to work deconditioned.

It is advisable to recommend an aerobic reconditioning program for any worker returning to vigorous work after a lengthy absence. Fitness prevents LBP, as Cady and associates showed so well in their prospective study of Los Angeles firefighters who applied for work.[135] Those who were most fit had the fewest episodes of LBP in a 3-year prospective period, and those who were least fit had the most claims. Also, of those with previous LBP, the firemen most aerobically fit had a lower rate of LBP recurrence in the follow-up period than did those who were unfit (Cady LD, personal communication). This worker should be gradually eased into his full work duties.

Case 10

> A 41-year-old male worker with two previous laminectomies, the last performed 6 months ago, who reports to a new company for work as a machinist.

This significant past history of back problems does not augur well for the future.[68] In this situation, pre-employment functional capacity testing, universally applied to all new workers, can screen out those who are physically incapable of performing the work. If this worker is found to be physically capable, he cannot legally be discriminated against simply because he has had laminectomies in the past. The worker who fails a job-relevant functional assessment—one that is given to all workers applying for this position—can be legally eliminated from consideration for the position, however.

In the event he does not pass the physical assessment, an individual with this type of history is best served by guidance from a vocational counselor about more appropriate work situations.

SUMMARY

Although low back pain will continue to affect workers adversely, an interdisciplinary team, working in concert with the involved employer, can sort out the relative contributions of individual and work-related risk factors that affect disability. The use of functional capacity assessment and job analysis can help considerably to define the extent of job handicap.

The most important factors that increase the back-injured worker's chance of rapid return to work are performing work that is less physical, employer willingness to adapt the job, and job desirability. These positive prognosticating influences are counteracted, however, by important negative influences: history of multiple LBP occurrences, previous episodes of lengthy sickness absence, predisposing psychosocial problems, job dissatisfaction, and poor case management practices.

Low back pain is an enigmatic impairment that is often not clearly identified. Any associated functional disability is best dealt with by an experienced treatment team. The ideal result, with minimal job handicap for the affected worker, is most likely to occur in the context of an adaptable employer and desirable job.

REFERENCES

1. Andersson GBJ. Epidemiologic aspects of low back pain in industry. *Spine*. 1981;6:53–60.

2. Biering-Sorensen F. A prospective study of LBP in a general population: I. occurrence, recurrence, etiology. *Scand J Rehabil Med*. 1983;15:71–79.

3. Frymoyer JW, Pope MH, Clements JH, et al. Risk factors for low back pain. *J Bone Joint Surg*. 1983;65A:213–218.

4. Hult L. Cervical, dorsal and lumbar spinal pain syndromes. *Acta Orthop Scand*. 1954; 118(suppl):1–109.

5. Svensson HO, Andersson GBJ. Low back pain in forty to forty-seven year old men: work history and work environmental factors. *Spine*. 1983;8:272–276.

6. Engelberg A, ed. *AMA Guides*, 3rd ed. Chicago: American Medical Association; 1988.

7. Gyntelberg F. One year incidence of low back pain among male residents of Copenhagen aged 40–59. *Dan Med Bull*. 1974;21:30–36.

8. Magora A, Taustein I. An investigation of the problem of sick-leave in the patient suffering from low back pain. *Indust Med Surg*. 1969;38:398–408.

9. Kelsey J, White AA, Pastides H, et al. The impact of musculoskeletal disorders on the population of the United States, October 1979. *J Bone Joint Surg*. 1979;61A:959–964.

10. McGill CM. Industrial back problems: a control program. *J Occup Med*. 1968;10:174–178.

11. Troup JD. Causes, prediction and prevention of back pain at work. *Scand J Work Environ Health*. 1984;10:419–428.

12. Pope MH, Bevins T, Wilder DG, et al. Biomechanical testing as an aid to the decision making in low-back pain patients. *Spine*. 1979;4:135–140.

13. Chaffin DB, Spark KS. A longitudinal study of low back pain as associated with occupational weight lifting factors. *Amer Indust Hygiene Assoc J*. 1973;34:513–525.

14. Troup JD, Martin JW, Lloyd DC. Back pain in industry: a prospective study. *Spine*. 1981; 6:61–69.

15. Biering-Sorensen F, Hilden J. Reproducibility of the history of low-back trouble. *Spine*. 1984; 9:280–286.

16. Snook SH. The costs of back pain in industry. In: Deyo RA, ed. *Occupational Back Pain*. Philadelphia: Hanley & Belfus; 1987:1–5.

17. Snook SH, Jensen RC. Cost. In: Pope MH, Frymoyer JW, Andersson GBJ, eds. *Occupational Low Back Pain*. New York: Praeger; 1984:115–121.

18. Klein BP, Jensen RC, Sanderson LM. Assessment of workers' compensation claims for back strains/sprains. In: Snook SH, Jensen, RC, Cost. In: Pope MH, Frymoyer JW, Andersson GBJ, eds. *Occupational Low Back Pain*. New York: Praeger; 1984:115–121.

19. Andersson GBJ, Svensson O, Oden A. The intensity of work recovery in low back pain. *Spine*. 1983;8:880–884.

20. White AA III, Gordon SL. Synopsis—workshop on idiopathic LBP. *Spine*. 1982;7:141–149.

21. Spengler DM, Bigos SJ, Martin NA, et al. Back injuries in industry: a retrospective study. I. overview and cost analysis. *Spine*. 1986;11:241–245.

22. Leavitt SS, Johnston TL, Beyer RD. The process of recovery patterns in industrial back injury. Part I (costs) and Part IV (mapping the health-care process). *Indust Med Surg*. 1971;40:7–12; 1972; 41:5–9.

23. World Health Organization. *International Classification of Impairments, Disabilities and Handicaps*. Geneva: WHO; 1980.

24. Leavitt SS, Beyer RD, Johnston TL. Monitoring the recovery process. *Industrial Med Surg*. 1972;41:25–30.

25. Adams M, Hutton W. Mechanical factors in the etiology of LBP. *Orthopedics*. 1982; 5:1461–1466.

26. Farfan H, Hoberdeao R, Dubow H. Lumbar intervertebral disc degeneration. *J Bone Joint Surg*. 1972;54A:495–510.

27. Nachemson A. The lumbar spine: an orthopaedic challenge. *Spine*. 1976;1:59–71.

28. Farfan H, Cossette J, Robertson G, et al. The effects of torsion on the lumbar intervertebral joints: the role of torsion in the production of disc degeneration. *J Bone Joint Surg*. 1970; 52A:468–497.

29. Frymoyer J, Pope M. The role of trauma in low back pain: a review. *J Trauma*. 1978; 18:628–634.

30. Kelsey J. Herniated lumbar intervertebral disc. *Rheumatol Rehabil*. 1975;14:144–159.

31. Kelsey JL, White AA. Epidemiology and impact of low back pain. *Spine*. 1980;5:133–142.

32. Kellgren JH, Lawrence JS. Osteo-arthrosis and disc degeneration in an urban population. *Ann Rheum Dis*. 1958;17:338–396.

33. Lawrence JS. Disc degeneration. Its frequency and relationship to symptoms. *Ann Rheum Dis*. 1969;28:121–137.

34. Rowe ML. Low back pain in industry. *J Occup Med*. 1969;2:161–169.

35. Caplan P, Freedman L, Connelly T. Degenerative joint disease of the lumbar spine in coal miners—a clinical and x-ray study. *Arthritis Rheum*. 1966;9:693–701.

36. Torgerson W, Dotter W. Comparative roentgenographic study of the asymptomatic and symptomatic lumbar spine. *J Bone Joint Surg*. 1976;58A:850–853.

37. Magora A. Investigation of the relationship between low back pain and occupation. *Scand J Rehabil Med*. 1973;5:186–90.

38. Loeser JD. Low back pain. In Bonica J, ed. *Pain*. New York: Raven Press; 1980:363–376.

39. White AA III, Panjabi MM, eds. *Clinical Biomechanics of the Spine*. Philadelphia: JB Lippincott; 1978.

40. National Institute for Occupational Safety and Health. *Work Practices Guide for Manual Lifting*. Washington, DC: US Department of Health and Human Services, National Technical Information Service; 1981. PB82:178-948.

41. Breig A, Troup JDG. Biomechanical considerations in the straight-leg raising test. *Spine*. 1979;4:242–250.

42. Frymoyer J, Howe J. Clinical classification. In: Pope MH, Frymoyer JW, Andersson GBJ, eds. *Occupational Low Back Pain*. New York: Praeger; 1984:71–98.

43. Lippitt AB. The facet joint and its role in spine pain. *Spine*. 1984;9:746–750.

44. Frymoyer J, et al. Epidemiologic studies of LBP. *Spine*. 1980;5:419–423.

45. Frymoyer J, Milhous R. Evaluation of the worker with LBP. In: Pope MH, Frymoyer JW, Andersson GBJ, eds. *Occupational Low Back Pain*. New York: Praeger; 1984:157–184.

46. Andersson GBJ, Ortengren R, Nachemson A. Quantitative studies of back loads in lifting. *Spine*. 1976;1:178–185.

47. Levin T. Osteoarthritis in lumbar synovial joints: a morphological study. *Acta Orthop Scand*. 1964;73(suppl):1.

48. Hussar A, Goller E. Correlation of pain and the roentgenographic findings of spondylosis of the cervical and lumbar spine. *Am J Med Sci*. 1956;518–527.

49. Rothman R. The pathophysiology of disc degeneration. *Clin Neurosurg*. 1973;20:174–182.

50. Horal J. The clinical appearance of low back disorders in the city of Gothenburg, Sweden. *Acta Orthop Scand*. 1969;118(suppl):15–57.

51. Kelsey J, Hardy R. Driving of motor vehicles as a risk factor for acute herniated lumbar intervertebral disc. *Am J Epidemiol*. 1975;102:63–73.

52. Rowe ML. Low back disability in industry: updated position. *J Occup Med.* 1971; 13:476–478.

53. Spangfort E. The lumbar disc herniation. A computer aided analysis of 2504 operations. *Acta Orthop Scand.* 1972;142(suppl):1–95.

54. Berg A. Clinical and myelographic studies of conservatively treated lumbar disc protrusion. *Acta Chir Scand.* 1953;104:124.

55. Hiteselberger WE, Witten R. Abnormal myelograms in asymptomatic patients. *J Neurosurg.* 1968;28:204–206.

56. Pearce J, Moll JM. Conservative treatment and natural history of acute lumbar disc lesions. *J Neurol Neurosurg Psychiatry.* 1967;30:13–17.

57. Deyo RA, Diehl AK, Rosenthal M. How many days of bedrest for acute LBP? A randomized clinical trial. *N Engl J Med.* 1986;315:1064–1070.

58. Kirkeldy-Willis WH, Farfan FH. Instability of the lumbar spine. *Clin Orthop.* 1982; 165:110–125.

59. Hall FM. Over-utilization of radiological examinations. *Radiology.* 1976;120:443–448.

60. Montgomery CH. Preemployment back x-rays. *J Occup Med.* 1976;18:495–497.

61. Rowe ML. Are routine spine films on workers in industry cost- or risk-benefit effective? *J Occup Med.* 1982;24:41–43.

62. Splithoff C. Lumbosacral junction—roentgenographic comparison of patients with and without backaches. *JAMA.* 1953;1610–1613.

63. Nachemson A, Wiltse LL. Editorial comment—spondylolisthesis. *Clin Orthop Rel Res.* 1976; 117:2–3.

64. Iskrant AP, Smith RW. Osteoporosis in women 45 years and over related to subsequent fractures. *Public Health Rep.* 1969;84:33–38.

65. Nelson M, Allen P, Clamp S, et al. Reliability and reproducibility of clinical findings in low-back pain. *Spine.* 1979;4:97–101.

66. Waddell G, Main C, Morris E, et al. Normality and reliability in the clinical assessment of backache. *Br Med J.* 1982;284:1519.

67. Million R, et al. Assessment of the progress of the back pain patient. *Spine.* 1980;7:204–212.

68. Chaffin DB, Andersson G. *Occupational Biomechanics.* New York: John Wiley & Sons; 1984.

69. Bigos SJ, Spengler DM, Martin NA, et al. Back injuries in industry: A retrospective study— III. employee-related factors. *Spine.* 1986;11:252–256.

70. Bergquist-Ullman M, Larsson U. Acute LBP in industry. *Acta Orthop Scand.* 1977; 170(suppl):1–113.

71. Gatchel RJ, et al. Quantification of lumbar function: VI. use of psychological measures in guiding physical functional restoration. *Spine.* 1986;11:36–42.

72. Lehmann TR, Frymoyer J, Milhous R. Treatment, education and rehabilitation. In: Pope MH, Frymoyer JW, Andersson GBG, eds. *Occupational Low Back Pain.* New York: Praeger; 1984: 185–209.

73. Yelin EH, Henke CJ, Epstein WV. Work disability among persons with musculoskeletal conditions. *Arthritis Rheum.* 1986;29:1322–1333.

74. Vallfors B. Acute, sub-acute and chronic LBP—clinical symptoms, absenteeism and working environment. *Scand J Rehabil Med.* 1985;11(suppl):1–98.

75. Magora A. Investigation of the relation between low back pain and occupation. *Scand J Rehabil Med.* 1975;7:146–151.

76. Partridge R, Duthie J. Rheumatism in dockers and civil servants: a comparison of heavy manual and sedentary workers. *Ann Rheum Dis*. 1968;27:559.

77. Deyo RA. The role of the primary care physician in reducing work absenteeism and costs due to back pain. In: Deyo RA, ed. *Occupational Back Pain*. Philadelphia: Hanley & Belfus; 1987:17–30.

78. National Institute for Occupational Safety and Health. *NIOSH Low Back Atlas*. Morgantown, WV: NIOSH; 1988.

79. Vanharanta H, Korpi J, Heliovaara M, et al. Radiographic measurements of lumbar spinal canal size and their relation to back mobility. *Spine*. 1985;10:461–466.

80. Biering-Sorensen F. A prospective study of LBP in a general population: II. location, character, aggravating and relieving factors. *Scand J Rehabil Med*. 1983;15:81–88.

81. Biering-Sorensen F, Thomsen C. Medical, social and occupational history as risk indicators for low-back trouble in a general population. *Spine*. 1986;11:720–725.

82. Biering-Sorensen F. Physical measurements as risk indicators for low back trouble over a one-year period. *Spine*. 1984;9:106–118.

83. McKenzie RA. *The Lumbar Spine—Mechanical Diagnoses and Therapy*. New Zealand: Spinal Public; 1983.

84. Porter RW, Miller C. Back pain and trunk list. *Spine*. 1986;11:596–600.

85. Waddell G, McCullough JA, Kummel EG, et al. Non-organic physical signs in low back pain. *Spine*. 1980;5:117–125.

86. Nachemson A. Work for all—for those with LBP as well. *Clin Orthop*. 1983;179:77–85.

87. Wiesel SW, et al. A study of computed-assisted tomography: I. incidence of positive CAT scans in an asymptomatic group. *Spine*. 1984;9:549–552.

88. Camp P. Invasive procedures for treating herniated discs—clinical and cost considerations. In Deyo RA, ed. *Occupational Back Pain*. Philadelphia: Hanley & Belfus; 1987:75–90.

89. Aronoff FM, et al. Pain treatment programs—do they return workers to the workplace? In: Deyo RA, ed. *Occupational Back Pain*. Philadelphia: Hanley & Belfus; 1987:123–136.

90. Matheson LN. *Work Capacity Evaluation: Interdisciplinary Approach to Industrial Rehabilitation*, Anaheim, CA: Employment and Rehabilitation Institute of California (ERIC), 1984.

91. Isernhagen S. *Functional Capacity Evaluation. Work Injury: Management and Prevention*, Rockville, MD: Aspen Publishers; 1988.

92. Snook SH, Campanelli RA, Hart JW. A study of three preventive approaches to low back injury. *J Occup Med*. 1978;20:478–481.

93. Pedersen PA. Prognostic indicators in LBP. *J Roy Coll Gen Pract*. 1981;31:209–216.

94. Bigos SJ, Spengler DM, Martin NA, et al. Back injuries in industry: a retrospective study, II. injury factors. *Spine*. 1986;11:246–251.

95. Lloyd MH, Gould S, Soutor CA. Epidemiologic study of back pain in miners and office workers. *Spine*. 1986;2:136–140.

96. Weber H. Lumbar disc herniation: a prospective study of prognostic factors including a controlled trial. I. *Oslo City Hosp*. 1978;28:33–61.

97. Weber H. Lumbar disc herniation: a prospective study of prognostic factors including a controlled trial. II. *Oslo City Hosp*. 1978;28:89–113.

98. American Medical Association Committee on Rating of Mental and Physical Impairment. *Guides to the Evaluation of Permanent Impairment*, 1st ed. Chicago: AMA; 1971.

99. Kessler HH. *Disability Determination and Evaluation*. Philadelphia: Lea & Febiger; 1970.

100. McBride E. *Disability Evaluation*. Philadelphia: JB Lippincott; 1963.

101. Brand RA, Lehmann TR. Low back impairment rating practices of orthopedic surgeons. *Spine*. 1983;8:75–78.

102. Greenwood JH. Low back impairment rating practices of orthopaedic surgeons and neurosurgeons in West Virginia. *Spine*. 1985;10:773–776.

103. US Department of Labor, Employment and Training Administration. *Dictionary of Occupational Titles*, 4th ed. Washington DC: US Government Printing Office; 1977.

104. Smith SL, Cunningham S, Weinberg R. The predictive validity of the functional capacities evaluation. *Am J Occup Ther*. 1986;40:564–567.

105. Snook SH, Irvine CH. Maximum acceptable weight of lift. *Am Indust Hyg Assoc J*. 1967; 28:322–329.

106. Snook SH, Irvine CH. Maximum frequency of lift acceptable to male industrial workers. *Am Indust Hyg Assoc J*. 1968;29:532–536.

107. Snook SH. The design of manual handling tasks: the ergonomics society lecture. *Ergonomics*. 1978;21:963–985.

108. Mayer TG, Barnes D, Kishino ND, et al. Progressive isoinertial lifting evaluation. I. a standardized protocol and normal database. *Spine*. 1988;13:993–997.

109. Mayer TG, Barnes D, Kishino ND, et al. Progressive isoinertial lifting evaluation. II. a comparison with isokinetic lifting in a disabled chronic low back pain industrial population. *Spine*. 1988;13:998–1002.

110. Borg GAV. *Physical Performance and Perceived Exertion*. Lund, Sweden: Gleerups; 1962.

111. Borg GAV. Perceived exertion as an indicator of somatic stress. *Scand J Rehabil Med*. 1970; 2:92–98.

112. Borg GAV. *A category scale with ratio properties for intermodal and interindividual comparisons*. Presented at the International Congress of Psychology, Leibig, West Germany; 1980.

113. Hart DL, Stobbe TJ, Jaraiedi M. Effect of lumbar posture on lifting. *Spine*. 1987;12:138–145.

114. Anderson CK, Catteral MJ. The impact of physical ability testing on incidence rate, severity rate, and productivity. In: Asfour SS, ed. *Trends in Ergonomics/Human Factors IV*. New York: North Holland/Elsevier Science Publishers; 1987:577–584.

115. Caple GE. Energy expenditure modeling in the return-to-work decision process. *Appl Ind Hyg Assoc J*. 1988;3:348–352.

116. Garg A, Chaffin DB, Herrin GD. Prediction of metabolic rate for manual materials handling jobs. *Am Ind Hyg Assoc J*. 1978;39:661–674.

117. Waddell G, Main CJ, Morris EW, et al. Chronic low-back pain, psychological distress, and illness behavior. *Spine*. 1984;9:209–213.

118. Deyo RA. Measuring the functional status of patients with low back pain. *Arch Phys Med Rehabil*. 1988;69:1044–1053.

119. Chaffin DB, Herrin GD, Keyserling WM. Pre-employment strength testing: an updated position. *J Occup Med*. 1978;20:403–408.

120. Zeh J, Hansson T, Bigos S, et al. Isometric strength testing: recommendations based on a statistical analysis of the procedure. *Spine*. 1986;11:43–46, 1986.

121. Chaffin DB. Ergonomics guide for the assessment of human static strength. *Am Ind Hyg Assoc J*. 1975;36:505–510.

122. Hansson TH, et al. The load on the lumbar spine during isometric strength testing. *Spine*. 1984;9:887–884.

123. Mathiowetz V, Weber K, Volland G, et al. Reliability and validity of grip and strength evaluations. *J Hand Surg*. 1984;9:222–226.

124. Niebuhr BR, Marion R. Detecting sincerity of effort when measuring grip strength. (five position hand grip test). *Am J Phys Med*. 1987;66:16–23.

125. Stokes HM. The seriously injured hand: weakness of grip. *J Occup Med*. 1983;25:683–684.

126. Gilbert JC, Knowlton RG. Simple method to determine sincerity of effort during a maximal isometric test of grip strength. *Am J Phys Med*. 1983;62:135–144.

127. Hazard RG, Reid A, Fenwick J, et al. Isokinetic trunk and lifting strength measurements: variability as an indicator of effort. *Spine*. 1988;13:54–57.

128. Liles DH, Deivanayagam S, Ayoub MM, et al. A job severity index for the evaluation and control of lifting injury. *Hum Factors*. 1984;26:683–693.

129. Keyserling WM, Herrin GD, Chaffin DB. Isometric strength testing as a means of controlling medical incidents on strenuous jobs. *J Occup Med*. 1980;22:332–336.

130. Fahrni W. Conservative treatment of lumbar disc degeneration: our primary responsibility. *Orthop Clin North Am*. 1975;6:93–103.

131. Jorgensen K, Poulsen E. Physiological problems in repetitive lifting with special reference to tolerance limits to the maximum lifting frequency. *Ergonomics*. 1974;17:31–39.

132. Pedersen OF, Petersen R, Staffeldt ES. Back pain and isometric back muscle strength of workers in a Danish factory. *Scand J Rehabil Med*. 1975;7:125–128.

133. Wiesel SW, Feffer H, Rothman R. Industrial LBP—prospective evaluation of a standardized diagnostic and treatment protocol. *Spine*. 1984;9:199–204.

134. Yelin EH, Henke CJ, Epstein WV. Work disability among persons with musculoskeletal conditions. *Arthr. and Rheum*. 1986;29:1322–1333.

135. Cady LD, Bischoff DB, et al. Strength and fitness and subsequent back injuries in firefighters. *J Occup Med*. 1979;21:269–272.

chapter 3

Vocational Capacity and Physical Impairment in the Upper Extremity

A. Lee Osterman, John M. Bednar, Terri Skirven, and Anne M.B. Moscony

The upper extremity is vitally important for most activities of work and daily living. Because of its high rate of use, the chance of injury to the upper extremity is significant. In a survey of the frequency and cost of upper extremity disorders in the United States, Kelsey and associates found that such injuries result in 16 million work days lost and 90 million days of restricted activity each year.[1] They also noted that 3 million consumer product injuries and one third of all disabling industrial injuries each year involve the upper extremity. These injuries necessitate 12 million annual visits to physicians. The treating physician must be knowledgeable not only in the immediate care of these injuries but also in the rehabilitation and evaluation of long-term impairment.

The loss of function resulting from anatomic hand injury may have both economic and psychosocial ramifications. It may threaten economic security and limit independence in self-care, homemaking, communication, and the pursuit of avocational interests. Hand impairment may limit career options and may even hamper acceptance in certain social circles.

Traditionally, physicians have been required to determine when the injured worker has recovered the physical ability and psychologic status to resume work tasks safely. The legal and ethical implications of this decision make it a difficult one for the physician. The patient who is sent back to work too early may "ping-pong" in and out of a worksite because of exacerbations or reinjury. If the decision is delayed too long, however, the patient may not return to work at all, as psychologic impairment or secondary gain factors may arise.

CONCEPTS OF INDUSTRIAL HAND INJURY EVALUATION

As early as the seventeenth century, Ramazzini recognized and outlined the problem of workers in his treatise, *Diseases of Workers*.[2] The advent of the

Industrial Revolution dramatically increased the number of work-related injuries. Initially, English law held the employer responsible for injuries to employees under a tort system that proved both inequitable and expensive.

The social impact of the increased incidence of workplace injury led, first in Germany in 1884 and subsequently in other Western countries, to the adoption of a no-fault workers' compensation system. The determination of the disability and the associated payment remains a legal matter, but the determination of the degree of impairment, the timing of the release to work, and the type of work to which the patient is released remain primarily medical judgments based on an ever-evolving evaluation system that attempts to take into account and correlate all aspects of the injury.

To determine whether the patient can return safely to his or her previous level of employment requires an approach that includes not only the traditional physical examination but also an assessment of the impairment, an evaluation of the patient's functional capacity, and an investigation of the functional demands of the job. Information provided by the physician, occupational therapist, physical therapist, and rehabilitation counselor must be integrated. Therefore, treatment and assessment of the patient require a team approach and a cohesive rehabilitation plan.

FACTUAL AND SYMPTOMATIC HISTORY

Information in the factual and symptomatic history should include not only vital statistics but also the hand dominance, any history of previous difficulty in the extremity, and any general condition that influences the patient's recovery. If a work-related injury is involved, the date, location, and mechanism of the injury should be recorded. It is also useful to hear the patient describe the job requirements in some detail and the particular aspects that he or she cannot perform. Specific questions should also address the ability to perform activities of daily living (ADL) and avocational activities.

After this, a thorough description of the patient's symptomatic complaints should be elicited. It is often useful to record these complaints in the patient's own words. If there is any pain, the location of the pain and any radiation should be recorded. The exact nature of the pain (eg, toothache-like or sharp), the effect of activity and rest, and the temporal relationship of the pain should be noted. Occasionally, it is useful to have the patient rate the intensity of pain on a scale from 1 to 10. A further question should address the response of the pain or symptoms to previous treatments and medications.

After the history taking and recording of the subjective complaints, the examiner is ready to begin the anatomic evaluation.

METHODS OF ANATOMIC EVALUATION

In an anatomic evaluation of hand impairment, all the structural components of the upper extremity—the skin, nail bed, neurovascular structures, tendons, ligaments, bones, and joints—must be inspected carefully to determine abnormalities. Because the hand can function normally only when placed in the proper position in space, the evaluation of hand impairment must also include an evaluation of the wrist, elbow, and shoulder. It is extremely important to quantitate the physical examination where possible. Swelling, for example, can be measured accurately by volumetric displacement. Joint range of motion (ROM) is quantified through goniometric measurement. Muscle atrophy can be calculated by circumferential arm measurements. Measurement of pinch and grip strength, muscle strength testing, and full sensory evaluation complete the quantitative physical examination. Radiographs may be obtained to define structural loss, the presence of arthritic change, or any bony demineralization.

Topographic Evaluation

The texture of the skin, its adherence to deep structures, and any loss of subcutaneous substance should be observed. All scars should be measured and their position recorded. The temperature, color, location, and degree of swelling should be noted. Swelling can be quantified by circumferential tape measurement or by water displacement with the use of a volumeter (Figs. 3-1A & B). The nails are examined for deformities and defects in the matrix, nail bed, or eponychial fold.

Range of Motion

The goniometric method for measuring joint position and motion has become the accepted standard (Fig. 3-2). This method and the accepted ''normal'' ROM for all joints are described in the *Guides to the Evaluation of Permanent Impairment* by the American Medical Association[3] and the *Manual for Orthopaedic Surgeons in Evaluating Permanent Physical Impairment* by the American Academy of Orthopaedic Surgeons.[4] In these texts, zero equals the starting, or neutral, position for all motions. The extended anatomic position is accepted as the neutral position.

Measurement of the hand's range of motion is a systematic process. Techniques of measurement and methods of recording should be standard and uniform; it is preferable to follow recommended techniques, such as those established by the American Society of Hand Therapists, the American Society for Surgery of the

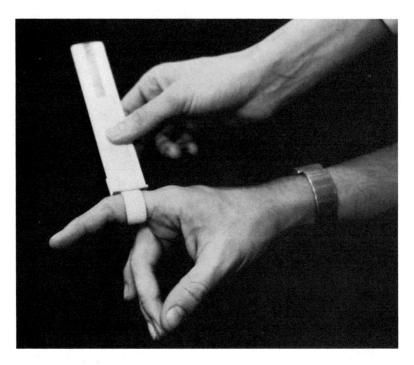

Figure 3-1 (A) Circumferential tape measurement of swelling in a finger.

Hand, or the American Academy of Orthopaedic Surgeons. Individual joint motion measurements are taken using a goniometer. Measurement is done with the wrist and proximal joints stabilized and in neutral or in the position that minimizes the tenodesis effect of the extrinsic musculotendinous units. Both active joint motion (ie, that accomplished by the patient's muscle power) and passive joint motion (ie, that determined by the examiner's movement of the joint) are evaluated. Deficits in active motion that exceed deficits in passive motion reflect muscle weakness or disruption in tendon function, such as tendon adherence, attenuation, bowstringing, or inflammation. Deficits in passive motion reflect joint contractures as a result of ligament or capsular shortening.

In addition to recording individual joint motion measurements, the examiner can calculate the total action motion (TAM) and total passive motion (TPM) values of the digit. The total motion value equals the sum of joint flexion measurements, taken with the digits in a fisted position, minus the sum of joint extension deficits. (Hyperextension is considered to be a negative value or deficit.) The use of total motion values facilitates the comparison of data. Deficits in total motion can result from tendon tightness or adherence. For example, extrinsic extensor

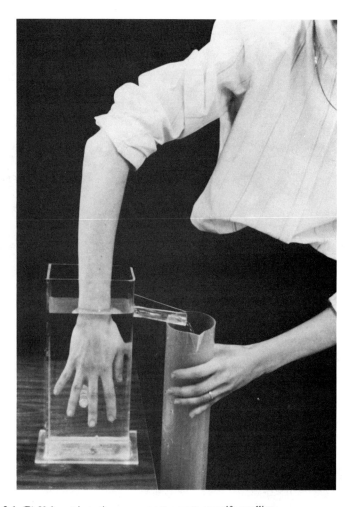

Figure 3-1 (B) Volumetric testing, an accurate way to quantify swelling.

tightness precludes full simultaneous flexion of all joints of the digit. The test for extensor tendon tightness involves measuring proximal interphalangeal (PIP) flexion first with the metacarpophalangeal (MCP) joint in extension and then with the MCP joint in flexion. If PIP flexion is greater with the MCP joint in extension, the extensor tendon is tight. PIP flexion that is greater with the MCP flexed than with the MCP extended indicates intrinsic tightness.

The method of Boyes for evaluating finger flexion by measuring the distance from pulp to distal palmar crease with the digit in maximal flexion should be in-

Figure 3-2 Measurement of motion in the metacarpophalangeal joint.

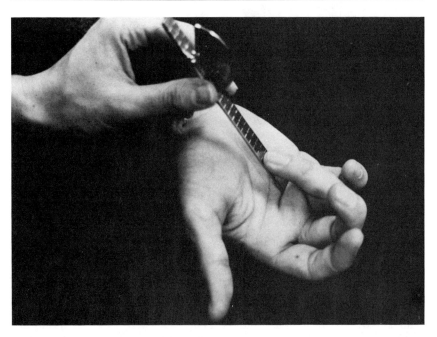

Figure 3-3 Two centimeter lack of full flexion in the active range of motion in this finger, representing a 30% involvement of finger flexion.

cluded (Fig. 3-3).[5] This single number represents a value for total digital motion that has more functional significance than does individual joint motion.

The determination of the range of motion at the thumb should include measurements not only of flexion and extension for each joint but also of radial abduction, palmar abduction, adduction, and opposition. The web span of the thumb is measured in centimeters from the distal palmar crease to the interphalangeal joint of the thumb, both with the thumb in extension and with the thumb in palmar abduction (Fig. 3-4). Finger spread or span can also be measured in centimeters.

Motion of the wrist is recorded in extension, palmar flexion, and radial and ulnar deviation. Elbow motion measures extension, with full extension being 0; flexion; pronation; and supination. Shoulder motion should be recorded in flexion, extension, and abduction. Internal and external rotation is measured at 0° and 90° of abduction.

Each joint should be inspected for degree of synovitis, ligamentous instability, subluxation, ankylosis, contracture, or rotational abnormality. The tendon system should be inspected carefully for rupture, adhesion, tenosynovitis, or subluxation.

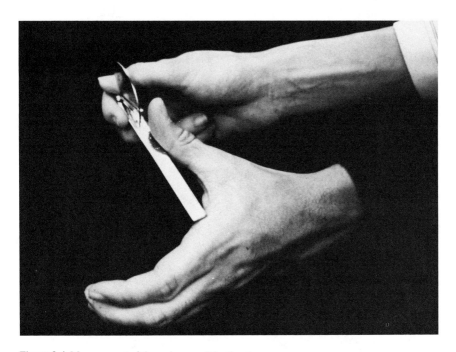

Figure 3-4 Measurement of the web span of the thumb.

Grip and Pinch Strength

Measurements of grip and pinch strength can be compared to those obtained from the opposite uninjured extremity or from an average extremity.[6] Grip strength, which normally changes with the size of the object being grasped, can be measured with a commercially available instrument called the Jamar Dynamometer (Fig. 3-5). Because this method has been shown to give a reliable measure of grip strength, the American Society for Surgery of the Hand and the American Society of Hand Therapists have accepted it as a standard measurement method.[7,8] The instrument is a hydraulic dynamometer with a handle that can be adjusted to five positions; maximum grip readings occur most frequently at the second and third handle positions.

Figure 3-5 Jamar Dynamometer for measuring grip strength.

Both the American Society for Surgery of the Hand and the American Society of Hand Therapists have recommended that the second handle position be used in determining grip strength. Because the position of the upper extremity influences grip measurements, it is further recommended that the subject be seated with the shoulder adducted and neutrally rotated, the elbow flexed at 90°, and the forearm and wrist in neutral.

Grip readings may also be taken at each consecutive handle position of the Jamar. When recorded on a graph, the readings will produce a bell-shaped curve, with the lower readings obtained at the extremes of the handle position and the highest reading obtained at the midposition.[9] This occurs because the intrinsic and extrinsic muscles of the hand function fully at this midposition. When the patient is not putting forth a consistent maximal effort or is attempting to feign weakness of grip, the readings may produce a straight or regular line on the graph. Pain produces the normal bell-shaped pattern, although absolute values are decreased. Hand fatigue can be eliminated as the cause of inconsistent results if a 5-minute rest period is provided between measurements at each handle position.

Pinch strength is also measured with a commercially available pinch meter (Fig. 3-6). Three types of measurements are made:

1. lateral pinch or key pinch: prehension of the thumb pulp to the lateral aspect of the index finger

Figure 3-6 Use of pinch gauge meter.

2. three-jaw chuck pinch: prehension of the pulp of the thumb to the pulp of the index and long finger
3. tip-to-tip pinch: prehension of the tip of the thumb to the tip of the index finger

The mean of three trials is compared with that obtained from the opposite extremity.

In measuring grip and pinch strength, the examiner should exclude as many variables as possible in order to ensure the reliability of repeated tests. Measurements should be taken at the same time of day and with the same instrument used for successive tasks. Both grip and pinch meters should be checked regularly for the accuracy of calibration. Mathiowetz and colleagues have published clinical norms for the grip and pinch strength of adults according to age, sex, and hand dominance.[10]

When hand impairment results from peripheral nerve involvement that has led to muscle paresis or paralysis, a specific manual muscle test is done to document the degree of muscle weakness.[11] Strength is graded on a rating system ranging from 0 to 5 or zero to normal:

- zero: no muscle activity
- trace: palpable muscle contraction, but no joint motion
- fair: range of motion against gravity with no resistance
- good: complete range of motion against gravity with some resistance
- normal: motion against gravity with full resistance

These findings can then be recorded on a master sheet (Fig. 3-7). Bilateral circumferential measurements of the arm and forearm also provide information relative to extrinsic muscle atrophy. Dominant arm measurements are generally 0.5 to 1 cm larger.

Sensibility Evaluation

The hand's sensibility is a complex function, and its evaluation is an equally complex process. By its very nature, such an evaluation is subjective, requiring a reponse from the patient. Usually, it is necessary to administer a battery of tests to assess fully the degree of sensory involvement. Callahan classified the most commonly used sensibility tests into three categories: modality tests, functional tests, and objective tests.[12]

Muscular Action	Prime Movers	Spinal Cord Level	Peripheral Nerve	Muscle Power								
				Left			Date			Right		
SCAPULA abduction and upward rotation	serratus anterior	C5-7	long thoracic									
adduction and downward rotation	mid. trapezius rhomboids	C2-5 C5	spinal accessory dorsal scapular									
elevation	levator scapulae upper trapezius	C3, 4 C2-4	dorsal scapular spinal accessory									
depression	lower trapezius	C2-4	spinal accessory									

Figure 3-7 Chart on which manual muscle strength measurements can be recorded.

Modality Tests

Among the modality tests are those for the classic cutaneous functions of pain, heat, cold, and touch pressure. Pain is tested by asking the subject to discriminate blindly between the sharp and dull sides of a safety pin. Temperature is tested by touching the subject with test tubes filled with hot and cold liquid. The subject's touch pressure threshold is tested with the Semmes-Weinstein Pressure Aesthesiometer (Fig. 3-8).[13] This instrument has a series of 20 probes, each consisting of a nylon monofilament attached to a lucite rod. The monofilaments, which range from very fine to thick, are graded for the amount of force required to bow the monofilament when it is applied at a perpendicular angle to the skin. The subject must indicate the perception of touch. Results are recorded on a chart that has the outline of the hand divided into zones. A scale of interpretation is available to assess the results of this test (Table 3-1).

Functional Tests

Functional sensibility tests include two-point discrimination and moving two-point discrimination.[14,15] The subject is required not only to detect the stimulus but also to interpret it. Two-point discrimination is evaluated with a blunt instrument, such as a Boley gauge or the DeMayo two-point discrimination device. The subject must discriminate between stimulation with one point and stimulation with two points applied to the volar surface of the fingertip. Seven or more correct responses out of 10 trials are required. Norms have been established by the American Society for Surgery of the Hand (Table 3-2). Normal two-point discrimination is between 3 and 5 mm.

Figure 3-8 Semmes-Weinstein monofilament test. In the lower portion of the photograph is a Boley gauge for measuring two-point discrimination.

Table 3-1 Interpretation Scale for Semmes-Weinstein Pressure Aesthesiometer

	Norms
	Semmes-Weinstein
Level	Filaments
Normal	2.36–2.83
Diminished light touch	3.22–3.61
Diminished protective sensation	3.84–4.31
Loss of protective sensation	4.56–6.65
Anesthetic	Unresponsive to 6.65

Dellon introduced the moving two-point discrimination test on the theory that fingertip sensibility depends on motion; therefore, according to Dellon, the stimulus for discrimination should be moving.[16] The testing instrument is moved proximally to distally on the fingertip parallel to the long axis of the fingertip. Again, 7 correct responses out of 10 are required. Normal moving two-point discrimination is 2 to 4 mm.

The Moberg pickup test is a timed test that requires motor participation.[17] The subject must pick up a series of small, everyday objects from the table surface and

Table 3-2 Two-Point Discrimination Norms

Level	Measurement
Normal	Less than 6 mm
Fair	6–10 mm
Poor	11–15 mm
Protective	One point perceived
Anesthetic	No points perceived

place them in a container; both the involved and the uninvolved hands are tested individually, first with the eyes open and then with the eyes closed. The examiner records the time, as well as observations related to the performance. The value of this test lies in the observations. For example, when picking up objects with the eyes closed, the subject tends not to use the digits with poor sensibility. This test can be used to validate the results of the other tests, such as a Semmes-Weinstein or the two-point discrimination.

A quick version of the Moberg pickup test is the Seddon coin test.[18] In this test, the examiner places a smooth-edged coin or a milled-edge coin in the patient's hand and asks him or her to determine whether it is the smooth or the milled coin.

Objective Tests

The Ninhydrin sweat test and the wrinkle test are both objective tests of intact sympathetic nervous innervation of the skin. They do not require subjective interpretation of a stimulus.[17,19] When the peripheral nerves have been injured, the denervated skin does not produce a sweat reaction. The Ninhydrin sweat test identifies such areas of diminished or lost sweat secretion because Ninhydrin stains purple the amino acid components of sweat. The subject makes a hand print, which is then treated with Ninhydrin to reflect the sweating function. The wrinkle test involves soaking the hand in warm water for 30 minutes. The denervated skin does not wrinkle secondary to sympathetic nerve fiber involvement.

IMPAIRMENT EVALUATION

After completing the traditional physical examination and other anatomic assessments, the examiner is ready to apply the data obtained to an impairment evaluation. The most common method of determining the level of impairment is to compare the loss of function with that resulting from an amputation. The upper limb is considered a unit of the whole person, which is subdivided into shoulder, elbow, wrist, hand, and fingers. Total loss of motion, sensation, or severe malposition that renders the part useless is considered equivalent to an amputation, even when the part is retained.

Amputation Impairment

Amputation of the entire upper extremity is obviously 100% loss of the extremity. According to the AMA's *Guides to the Evaluation of Permanent Impairment*, it is also 60% loss of the whole person (Fig. 3-9).[3] Amputation at levels distal to the biceps insertion but proximal to the metacarpophalangeal joint represents 95% loss of the limb (Fig. 3-10). Loss of all fingers represents 90% loss of the limb.

Hand function is divided such that the thumb represents 40% of the hand; index and long finger, each 20% of the hand; and ring and little finger, each 10% of the

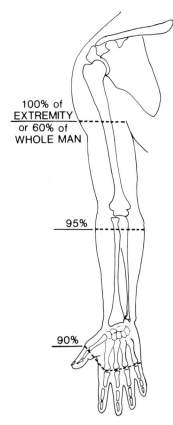

100% of
EXTREMITY
or 60% of
WHOLE MAN

95%

90%

Figure 3-9 Amputation impairment percentages as related to the whole person and the extremity. *Source:* Reprinted with permission from AB Swanson et al., "Evaluation of Impairment of Hand Function" in *Journal of Hand Surgery* (1983;8[5]:709–722), Copyright © 1983, CV Mosby Co.

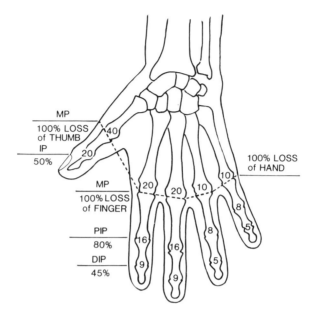

Figure 3-10 Amputation impairment percentages as related to the hand. *Source:* Reprinted with permission from AB Swanson et al., "Evaluation of Impairment of Hand Function" in *Journal of Hand Surgery* (1983; 8[5]: 709–722), Copyright © 1983, CV Mosby Co.

MP = Metacarpophalangeal; PIP = proximal interphalangeal; DIP = distal interphalangeal.

hand (see Fig. 3-10). Each digit is also evaluated as a unit, with partial loss being calculated as a percent loss of the unit value of the digit (Fig. 3-11). Multiple digit losses are calculated as a percent loss of each digit, and then summed to determine the total impairment to the whole hand.

Range-of-Motion Impairment

The most widely used system for evaluating impaired joint motion is that developed by Swanson and associates,[6,20] who refined the system presented in the first chapter of the AMA's *Guides to the Evaluation of Permanent Impairment*[3]. Swanson's system involves measuring the restriction of flexion and extension, or the degree of ankylosis, present at each joint and calculating a percent impairment based on the sum of individual impairments for each component of lost motion.

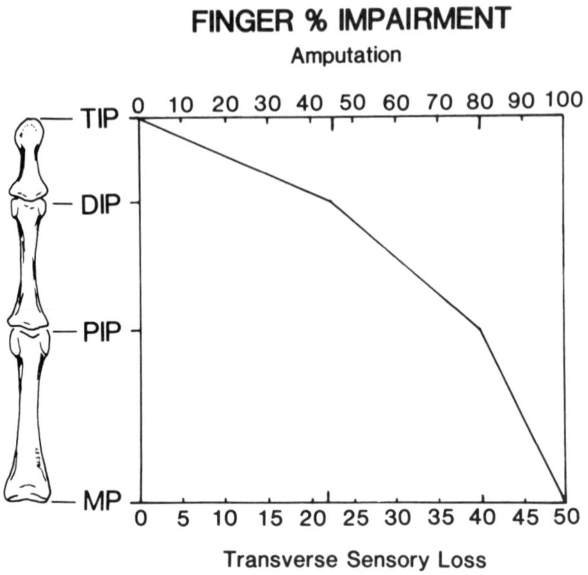

FINGER % IMPAIRMENT
Amputation

Transverse Sensory Loss

Figure 3-11 Amputation impairment percentages as related to the individual finger. Complete transverse sensory loss of a finger equates to that of one half the percentage of amputation. *Source:* Reprinted with permission from AB Swanson et al, "Evaluation of Impairment in Upper Extremity" in *Journal of Hand Surgery* (1987;12A(5):896–926), Copyright © 1987, CV Mosby Co.

MP = metacarpophalangeal; PIP = proximal interphalangeal; DIP = distal interphalangeal.

Thumb Impairment

In evaluating loss of motion, the thumb is considered three separate functional units: (1) flexion and extension of the metacarpophalangeal and interphalangeal joints, (2) adduction and abduction, and (3) opposition. These three units contribute to thumb function unequally. Flexion and extension represent 20% of function; adduction and abduction represent 20%, and opposition represents 60% of function.

Palmar abduction is measured in centimeters from the flex or crease of the thumb interphalangeal joint to the distal palmar crease at the MCP joint of the index finger with attempted palmar abduction. This measure must be multiplied by 20% to determine a percent impairment, which contributes to total thumb impairment (Fig. 3-12).

Limitation of opposition is recorded as the distance between the tip of the thumb and the tip of the small finger on attempted thumb-small finger pinch. This measure is related to a percent impairment, which is then multiplied by 60% to determine its contribution to total thumb impairment (Fig. 3-13).

THUMB ADDUCTION IMPAIRMENT %

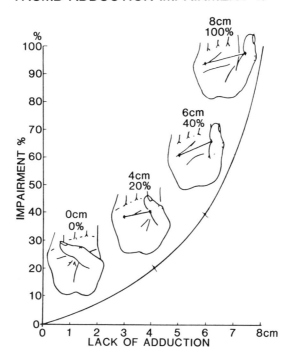

Figure 3-12 Linear measurement from the little finger to the interphalangeal joint of the thumb. *Source:* Reprinted with permission from AB Swanson et al, "Evaluation of Impairment in Upper Extremity" in *Journal of Hand Surgery* (1987;12A(5):896–926), Copyright © 1987, CV Mosby Co.

If the subject has some impairment in each of these units, the percent impairment for each is determined. Then, the three are added numerically to derive the total thumb impairment.

Wrist, Elbow, and Shoulder Impairment

Because of the importance of the arm in placing the hand in space, the wrist, elbow, and shoulder must be included in any impairment evaluation of the upper extremity. Loss of motion at the wrist is considered a 60% impairment of the total extremity; the elbow, 70%; and the shoulder segment, 60%. As is impairment in the finger joints, impairment of the wrist is determined in terms of motion loss or ankylosis. Two components of wrist motion are considered: dorsal and palmar flexion, which represent 70% of wrist function, and radial/ulnar deviation, which represents 30%.

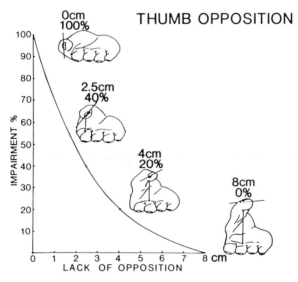

Figure 3-13 Linear measurement from the long finger to the interphalangeal joint of the thumb which accounts for 60% of functional thumb motion. *Source:* Reprinted with permission from AB Swanson et al, ''Evaluation of Impairment in Upper Extremity'' in *Journal of Hand Surgery* (1987;12A(5):896–926), Copyright © 1987, CV Mosby Co.

Elbow joint impairment is evaluated in terms of flexion, which is worth 60% of the elbow function, and rotation, which is worth 40%. For the shoulder, flexion (arm raised forward) is considered 50% of function; abduction (arm out to side), 20%; extension (flexed arm brought down), 10%; internal rotation, 10%; and external rotation, 10%. Loss of motion in the shoulder segment is equivalent to loss of 60% of the extremity.

Sensory Impairment

The impairment rating for loss of sensation in the upper extremity varies according to the location of the deficit. Loss of sensation on the dorsum of the fingers is not considered disabling, but loss of sensation on the opposing surfaces of the thumb and index finger is disabling. Complete transverse loss of palmar sensation of a digit is considered a 50% loss of the functional capacity of the finger and therefore is an impairment of 50% of that assigned for amputation of an equivalent digit (Fig. 3-14).

The calculation of the impairment caused by longitudinal sensory loss is based on the functional importance of the side of the digit involved. Sensory loss on the radial side of the thumb, which is less critical in pinch activity, represents a 40% loss of thumb sensory function (8% of hand impairment), as opposed to 60% loss (12% of hand impairment) if the ulnar side is involved. Radial sensation in the

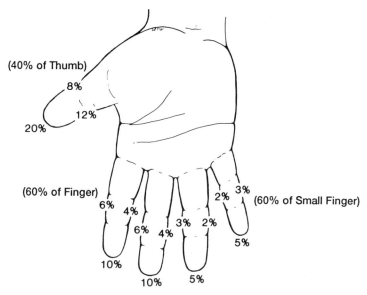

Figure 3-14 Sensory impairment, longitudinal loss. Rating includes the relative importance of the digital nerve for functional use, expressed as a percentage impairment of the hand and in parentheses of the finger. *Source:* Reprinted with permission from AB Swanson et al, "Evaluation of Impairment in Upper Extremity" in *Journal of Hand Surgery* (1987;12A(5):896–926), Copyright © 1987, CV Mosby Co.

fingers is more important than ulnar sensation with the exception of the small finger. Loss of the radial sensation therefore represents a 60% loss in the fingers. Loss on the ulnar side of the little finger is assigned a 60% value because of the exposed border position of this finger and its importance to hand function (see Fig. 3-14).

Cosmetic Impairment

There are two components to a cosmetic impairment: a passive and an active component. The passive aspect refers to the static appearance of the upper extremity. A problem in this area can reasonably be overcome by the use of prostheses, some of which are difficult to distinguish from uninjured extremities. The active component refers to the loss of normal movements, aside from actual functional tasks. This aspect is more difficult to overcome, as most prostheses lack this subtle dynamic component. Swanson and associates have described a point system for evaluating cosmetic impairment; their system takes into account both active and passive components, as well as the patient's perception of his or her own cosmetic result.[6,20] The combined index finger impairment for the whole man or woman is 60% of 14%, or 8%.

Combination of Multiple Impairment Estimates

Each segment of the upper extremity is evaluated to determine not only loss due to impairment but also the effect of decreased motion and altered sensation on the remaining parts. The sum of these impairments, as related to the entire extremity, produces the total impairment.

An impairment does not act on the whole extremity. Impairment acts on the unit considered, which then acts on the next proximal unit. When more than one impairment is acting on a given unit, these impairments must be combined before their impact on the larger unit is calculated. Impairments are combined by means of the following formula:

$$a\% + b\% (100\% - a\%) = \text{Combined effect of } a\% + b\%$$

If three or more values are to be combined, the combined effect of two is calculated first. This value is then added to the third value in the same formula. This combined impairment is then used to calculate the impairment of the proximal units by multiplying the figure by its representative percentage repeatedly until the impairment for the whole person has been determined (see Fig. 3-9). Consider this case example.

> The subject has an index finger with an amputation through the distal interphalangeal joint, flexion loss of the proximal interphalangeal joint of 30°, and a loss of sensation of the radial side of the finger from the MCP joint distally. With Swanson's methods, amputation through the distal interphalangeal represents a 45% impairment of the finger (see Fig. 3-11). Flexion loss of the proximal interphalangeal joint of 30° represents an 18% impairment, as calculated from the AMA tables.[3] Sensory loss of the radial digital nerve of the index finger represents a 60% impairment (6% out of 10% for that finger—see Fig. 3-14). These are combined in the formula:
>
> $$45\% + 18\% (100\% - 45\%) = 55\%$$
> $$55\% + 60\% (100\% - 55\%) = 82\%$$

Impairment of the index finger is 82%. Because the index finger is 20% of the hand (see Fig. 3-10), this impairment (82%) represents a 16% impairment of the hand. The hand is 90% of the upper extremity. This combined impairment therefore is a 16% of 90%, or 14%, impairment to the upper extremity.

Assessment of Pain

Although pain is an important component of disability, it is difficult to measure; therefore, it is often omitted from impairment rating methods. An effort should be made, however, to quantitate the effect of pain on the functional use of the extremity. Swanson and associates have assigned percentages to four levels of pain and have described these levels as (1) minimal pain, which is primarily annoying (0% to 25%); (2) slight pain, which interferes with activity (26% to 50%); (3) moderate pain, which prevents activity (51% to 75%); and (4) severe pain, which prevents activity and causes distress that requires medication (76% to 100%).[6] These percentages are then used in a formula similar to that used for sensory loss to calculate the percentage of impairment of the part.

There are no valid reproducible methods to quantitate pain. Taken together with the problems inherent in evaluating the conditions of patients involved in litigation, the inability to measure pain makes it increasingly difficult for an examiner to rate pain in a fair manner. The classic example of such difficulty is that of two patients who sustained a similar digital nerve injury. Both showed sensory loss in the recognized distribution of the nerve; both had an objective impairment of 25% of the digit. One patient, however, had minimal complaints and lost no time from work, whereas the other patient was completely crippled by the pain and the inability to use not only the finger, but the whole extremity. From a practical point of view, the rating examiner who is convinced that pain is present and is by itself a permanent impairing factor may use the pain modifiers to upgrade the final impairment rating.

FUNCTIONAL TESTING

A reliable anatomic rating of hand impairment should correlate with the subject's ability to use the hand. The previously described measurements of structural damage are inadequate for assessing the functional defects that such abnormalities reflect, however. A recent study suggests that impairment ratings based on the AMA *Guides to the Evaluation of Permanent Impairment* do correlate substantially with the various tests of hand functions.[21] Such tests may be standardized tests or observations of the subject's performance of selected tasks.

Standardized Dexterity or Psychomotor Tests

A number of standardized dexterity or psychomotor tests are available to assess function, but none was designed specifically to address hand impairment. Rather, they were designed to address motor performance skills. Methods of test administration are precisely described, and the majority are time-measured.

Dexterity evaluations include the Minnesota Rate of Manipulation Test,[22] the O'Connor Finger Dexterity Tests, the Purdue Pegboard Test,[23,24] and the Crawford Small Parts Dexterity Test. These tests were developed as tools to be used in the selection of efficient employees for industrial activities. Norms therefore are correlated to such groups as electric shaver repairmen, sewing machine operators, general factory workers, vocational school students, and National Guard contestants in a rifle assembly competition. Several tests have produced normative data for hand dominance, sex, and age. Only the Minnesota Rate of Manipulation Test and the O'Connor Finger Dexterity Test have been studied specifically in relationship to hand impairment, however.[21]

Based on time and cost constraints, the O'Connor Finger Dexterity Test or the Purdue Pegboard Test is recommended for the assessment of fine prehension and the Minnesota Rate of Manipulation Test for the assessment of motor function. The O'Connor Finger Dexterity Test has been used as a predictor of function whenever rapid manipulation of objects, such as pickup and placement of a small object, is important. It measures fine prehensile activities of the thumb and fingers. The subject sits in front of a board measuring 11 × 5.5 inches with a molded shallow well. On the board are 100 holes arranged in 10 rows of 10 holes each. In the well are 300 pins, each approximately 1 inch long. As many as three pins can be inserted in each hole. Following a practice round in which the subject places 30 pins, 3 in each of the top 10 holes, he or she is allowed to rest. During the actual test, the examiner uses a stopwatch to record the time that the subject takes to fill the first 50 holes with three pins each and then the time for the second 50 holes. Performance time usually varies between 8 and 16 minutes.

The Purdue Pegboard Test can be used to measure dexterity both unilaterally and bilaterally (Fig. 3-15). It measures dexterity for two types of activities, one involving gross movements of the arm, hands, and fingers and the other involving fingertip dexterity. It has been standardized not only on men and women but also on schoolchildren. Like the O'Connor Finger Dexterity Test, the Purdue Pegboard Test uses a board with rows of holes. On one side of the board are wells that contain pegs, collars, and washers that fit over the pegs. Four subtests are administered: a right-hand peg test, a left-hand peg test, a peg test with both hands, and an assembly test. The right- and left-hand tests involve picking up pins, one at a time, from a cup at the top of the board and placing them in the holes. A similar test involves forming assemblies of pins, collars, and two washers with both hands. The entire test takes approximately 10 to 15 minutes. The Purdue Pegboard Test provides a more sophisticated measurement and has a larger normative data base than does the O'Connor Finger Dexterity Test.

For measurement of gross manipulation and coordination over a broad range of upper extremity positioning, the Minnesota Rate of Manipulation Test is most suitable (Fig. 3-16). The test involves a board and round disks. There are five subtests: (1) the placing test, (2) the turning test, (3) the displacing test, (4) the one-

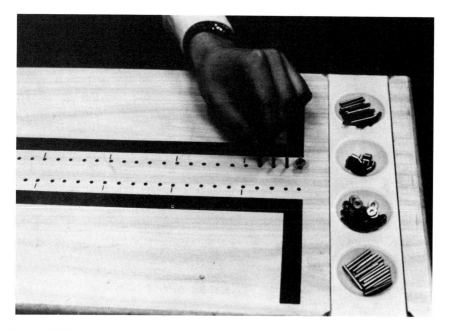

Figure 3-15 Purdue Pegboard Extremity Test.

Figure 3-16 Minnesota Rate of Manipulation Test.

hand turning and placing test, and (5) the two-hand turning and placing test. These tests involve moving the disks from one place to another by arm movement alone or by combining arm and trunk motion. A broad range of shoulder motion is required. Usually one trial of these tests is insufficient. The reliability is higher with two trials and highest with four trials. Each trial requires 10 minutes or less. It is usually unnecessary to administer all five subtests, because they correlate closely with each other. Scores can be reported as a percentile of the sampled population, as well as a number of standard deviations from the mean. The use of several trials also indicates endurance.

Activities of Daily Living Tests

Among the tests that measure the subject's abilities to perform activities of daily living (ADL) are the Jebsen Test of Hand Function,[25] the Smith Hand Function Evaluation,[26] the Simulated Activities of Daily Living Examination (SADLE),[27] and the Nine Hole Peg Test.[28] Originally used in the care of neuromuscular system-impaired and rheumatoid patients, the ADL tests indicate both the patient's functional capability and the response to treatment. Many of these tests (eg, the SADLE, the Smith Hand Function Evaluation) have homemade components and thus lack the rigid standardization of the prefabricated industrial tests. In other tests, specially designed blocks or pegs are used (eg, Nine Hole Peg). Most ADL are based on time measures. Norms are generally available; however, the numbers of those tested are often small, and comparability to patient populations is questionable. Norms are also listed by hand dominance, sex, and age in several of the tests (eg, Jebsen, Smith). All tests emphasize an observational component—not only that the coin was picked up in 1 second, for example, but also with which fingers. No correlations to impairment ratings have been done other than a preliminary testing by Carroll, who found that the rated ADL impairment for subjects with hand amputations was generally less than that assessed according to criteria in the AMA *Guide*.[29]

At the University of Pennsylvania Hand Center, the Jebsen test is used (Fig. 3-17). Seven subtests measure major aspects of hand function. These include (1) writing, (2) simulated page turning, (3) picking up small common objects, (4) simulated feeding, (5) stacking checkers, (6) picking up large light objects, and (7) picking up large heavy objects.

An appraisal of the loss of function in relation to actual ADL is the final component of this segment of the impairment evaluation. Through a combination of an interview, questionnaires, and observed performance on selected tasks, the examiner assesses the subject's ability to perform self-care tasks, to handle household responsibilities, to pursue leisure activities, and to perform job tasks. Where possible, the subject should be asked to perform sample tasks in addition to filling out the questionnaire, as the subject's level of satisfaction with a new,

Figure 3-17 Placing beans in a can as part of the Jebsen Simulation of Utensil Use.

adapted method of performance may influence the responses to a questionnaire. Motivational factors play a role here as well. There is a wide range of response to altered ability. Some individuals learn to adapt methods and accomplish tasks, whereas others can only dwell on the loss of function and become dependent on others.

It takes between 15 and 30 minutes to administer all of the self-care tests. Each focuses on composite measures of motion, strength, sensibility, coordination, mental state, and other relevant factors. In this regard, functional testing relates more directly to actual use than does any individual anatomic measurement. In cases of symptom exaggeration or malingering, functional testing can serve as a reference with which to compare other components of the evaluation. For many reasons, functional testing is an extremely important part of the overall hand impairment evaluation.

RETURN-TO-WORK EVALUATION

Because two persons with the same diagnosis and the same medically determined level of impairment do not have the same degree of occupational limitation, the anatomic impairment rating alone is not sufficient to determine work capacity.

Other factors to consider include psychologic factors (eg, behavioral motivation), socioeconomic factors (eg, local economic and employment conditions), cultural factors (eg, the value placed on work) and individual situational factors (eg, age, amount of therapy received, and education).[30] A hand surgeon is unlikely to have the time to assess these factors adequately; therefore, many physicians have begun to rely on the report of the hand therapist, who has often worked closely with the patient, to make recommendations about the patient's capacity to return to work. As a result, once the hand-injured patient's medical condition has stabilized and there are no other medical contraindications, the patient may be sent to the hand therapist for a return-to-work evaluation.

The experienced hand therapist can evaluate the patient's ability to make a sustained work effort, analyze work demands, and identify biomechanically unsafe tasks that are likely to exacerbate the patient's condition. Often working closely with vocational evaluators, the hand therapist can evaluate the transferability of skills for a newly available job and recognize those factors that may preclude the patient from gainful employment (eg, litigation or application for Social Security Disability Insurance). In addition, the hand therapist can offer recommendations to improve the patient's capacity for work, such as the use of splints, task modifications, further therapy, or environmental adaptions.[31-33] Finally, the therapist can assist the subject to improve physical tolerances so as to promote work readiness, or to clarify limiting factors for a return to work.

There are excellent return-to-work evaluations for the hand-injured population.[34,35] The common components of these evaluations are the intake interview, a job analysis, an individualized evaluation plan, assessment of sustained work performance, a Validity Profile, and a final report with recommendations.

Intake Interview

During the intake interview, the therapist should obtain all identifying information, a statement of the evaluation objective, all pertinent disability information, and background history. This may be the therapist's first meeting with the patient. Because most of the tests require optimal cooperation from the patient to ensure the accuracy of the data, the patient should be informed about the purpose, the procedures, the time frame, and the expected outcome of the evaluation. Emphasis should be on the evaluation of "enablement," not disablement.

Identifying information that should be obtained includes age, dominance of hand, referral source, occupation, date last worked, any pending litigation, and insurance information. The evaluation request should identify the referral purpose and should indicate whether there is a specific job to which the patient may return or whether the patient is to obtain a general assessment of work tolerances. The referral information should also include the diagnosis, date of injury, mechanism of injury, treatment to date, a self-assessment of physical tolerances and self-care status, and any current precautions and/or work restrictions. The background history should cover work history; medical history (ie, a gross overview of all body systems); a social history (eg, marital status, education level, community and family obligations or duties); and an avocational history, including identification of leisure activities in which the patient no longer participates because of the injury.

Job Analysis

A detailed biomechanical analysis of the job to which the patient is to return should identify and describe work tasks, the results of the work (ie, goods produced), and the worker characteristics and skills required to perform the job. A formal job description is often available through the patient's supervisor or through the employer's medical department or personnel department. This description is a legal document that should outline duties, shifts available, machinery used, expertise required, environmental hazards, productivity quotients, and weight limits for material handling. The quality of the job descriptions varies greatly, however.

If a formal job description is not available or requires augmentation, the therapist may do an on-site evaluation to acquire the necessary information. Before proceeding, however, the therapist must obtain permission for the visit from all concerned parties: the physician, the patient, the insurance company, and the employer. It is helpful for the therapist to carry a kit containing a pen, paper, a scale, a tape measure, and a camera for recording such things as weight limits for material handling, machinery used, and prehension patterns required.

If a job site evaluation is not possible, the therapist may do an informal job analysis (Fig. 3-18). In this situation, information about the job comes primarily from the patient and should be verified with the patient's acting supervisor. Discrepancies often occur; it is helpful in this instance to seek the help of a vocational rehabilitation specialist to resolve the difference(s) or to negotiate with the patient and employer an informal written job description that lists general job demands, including maximum and repetitive weight-handling demands, and acknowledges those job description difference(s) noted by each party.

A job can also be analyzed by using the *Dictionary of Occupational Titles (DOT)*, a 1977 Department of Labor publication that defines thousands of jobs; lists the worker traits required; and identifies the environment, the hazards associated with the job, and the general physical demands of the job.[36] The *DOT* identifies the following physical demand categories or work factors:

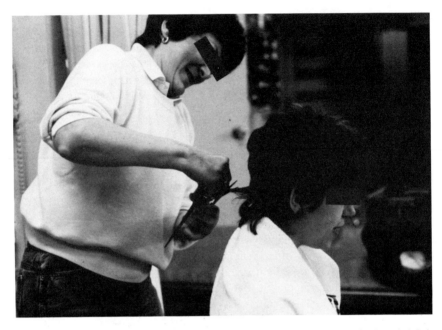

Figure 3-18 Hand-injured hairdresser recreating the demands of her job by cutting the therapist's hair.

- strength, determined by the worker's involvement with one or more of the following: standing, walking, sitting, lifting, carrying, pulling, and pushing. This factor is expressed in terms of intensity of load (or weight to be moved) and frequency and/or duration required by further dividing the strength category into five levels or degrees: sedentary, light, medium, heavy, and very heavy
- climbing/balancing
- stooping, kneeling, crouching, crawling
- reaching, handling, fingering, feeling
- talking/hearing
- seeing

The *DOT* has been the accepted standard for defining physical demand categories for many years. It is an excellent reference source, but its information still requires verification by the patient and/or employer. It may be incomplete or inaccurate in some job descriptions, as it has not been recently revised. Furthermore, it fails to define the strength requirements for torquing.

Individualized Evaluation Plan

The purpose of the individualized evaluation plan is to assess the patient's current maximum performance level and to identify those critical job demands that produce symptoms. The patient's performance level is then compared to that required for a return to work and discrepancies are noted. The therapist assesses the patient's ability to meet all the physical demands of the job, as defined by the job analysis. If the patient is required to perform under load, for example, the therapist determines the maximum load that the patient can tolerate. For each tested job demand, the therapist carefully monitors and records the patient's response, including facial expression, timing, effort, attitude, posturing, and somatic response.

If no specific job is mentioned in the evaluation objective and the patient has been referred for a general assessment of work tolerances, the patient is tested for the maximum capacity tolerated for each of the *DOT* physical demand factors.

Sustained Work Performance Evaluation

In order to determine the patient's ability to tolerate work continuously over a period of time, the therapist conducts a sustained work performance evaluation. During the test, the therapist monitors symptom response to those job tasks that had already produced symptoms when the patient was required to work under maximum load or tasks that may be suspect by virtue of the patient's diagnosis and symptom history (Fig. 3-19). Putting the patient through a circuit endurance evaluation that may last several hours to several work days makes it possible to determine the effect of the accumulated stress on the injured extremity. This circuit evaluation should consist of various work tasks performed in a circuit with the duration, speed, and frequency of performance required in the actual job situation. The patient should be allowed to adjust all tasks requiring load to a level that he or she considers to be reasonably manageable. Symptom response and performance levels are then recorded.

If a specific job has not been identified for the patient, endurance can be assessed by means of standardized work samples, such as the Bennett Hand Tool Dexterity Test, the Pennsylvania Bimanual Work Sample, the Valpar Component Work Samples, or the WEST (Work Evaluation Systems Technology) Work Sample Series. The Bennett Hand Tool Dexterity Test was constructed to provide a measure of the patient's proficiency in using ordinary mechanics' tools.[37] It is intended to measure manipulative skills independent of intellectual factors. The test requires the patient to disassemble and assemble units of 12 various-sized nuts, bolts, and washers with a crescent wrench, two box wrenches, and a screwdriver.

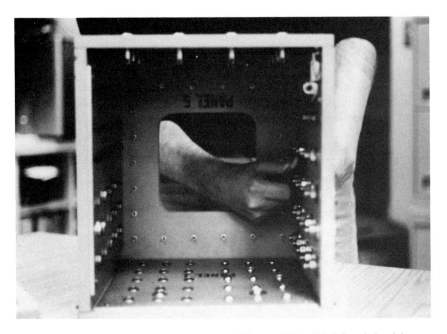

Figure 3-19 Objective measurement of a patient's ability on a Valpar Work Sample involving non-visual manipulation.

The patient stands and uses both hands, although one-handed patients can successfully complete this test. It is standardized for normal adults, injured workers, and mentally handicapped students (aged 16 to 21).

The Pennsylvania Bimanual Work Sample was designed to show a patient's ability to integrate several motor tasks into a well-organized and smooth-working pattern of performance. It encompasses bilateral finger dexterity, eye-hand coordination, and bimanual coordination. The patient grasps a nut with one hand and a bolt with the other hand, places the bolt through a hole in the board, and spins the nut onto the bolt. Assembly and disassembly are timed separately, yielding two scores. Available norms are for men and women, and for blind and partially blind adults.

The Valpar Component Work Samples (see Fig. 3-19) are 16 standardized tests involving nonmedical measurements of the agility of a patient's gross movements of the trunk, legs, arms, hands and fingers, as these movements relate to finer manual dexterity in different job tasks.[38] For example, the Whole Body Range of Motion Work Sample allows the therapist to assess the effect of reaching overhead and of crouching on the patient's ability to manipulate small objects, and the Eye-Hand-Foot Coordination Work Sample makes it possible to assess the patient's ability to coordinate the use of the hands and feet simultaneously. Unlike many other work samples, the Valpar samples have standardized work positions, including crouching, sitting, standing, and reaching overhead, and all correspond to various physical demand levels described in the *DOT*. Furthermore, they provide a format for evaluating salient psychosocial factors (eg, ability to follow directions, perseverance, frustration tolerance). Norms are available for employed workers, and the test can be administered to persons with varying degrees of work experience.

The WEST (Work Evaluation Systems Technology) Work Sample series consists of several structured, graded evaluation devices that measure an individual's response to various physical work demands.[39] The WEST 1 measures whole body range of motion (from 0 to 78 inches above the floor) in a lengthy assembly/disassembly task. The WEST 2 measures upper extremity endurance and, when combined with the WEST Comprehensive Weight System, can indicate whole body range of motion under load. Loads can be adjusted from 5 to 90 lb in 5-lb increments. The WEST 4 measures strength and endurance in torquing tasks against resistance. Torque resistance values can be calibrated to range from 12 to 50 inch/lb. The WEST 7 measures speed and dexterity for the assembly and disassembly of a bus bench. These tests are designed for people with industrial injuries who have the potential for competitive employment. Each sample has norms based on the performance of a selection of people in a regional occupational center.

An additional state-of-the-art tool for assessing work capacity is the BTE Work Simulator (Figs. 3-20A, B, and C).[40] John Engalitcheff, Jr., designed the machine in 1979, and the Baltimore Therapeutic Company modified and refined it; the first commercial models were distributed in January 1982. The BTE Work Simulator consists of two primary components mounted on a pedestal base. One is a passive variable resistance assembly from which a shaft protrudes. This assembly can be set in any one of five vertical-to-horizontal positions, depending on the desired task simulation. By slipping one of the many different attachments or "tool" handles onto the shaft and adjusting the resistance, the therapist can simulate an actual work task at a controlled effort level. The other primary component is the control panel, at which the therapist can program the resistance level and receive a hard copy record of the patient's performance: time elapsed, distance or degrees the tool has moved, force output in inch/lb, and power output. Job simulation can also be used to assess work tolerance by asking patients to perform repetitive lifting, carrying, or other weighted activities similar to the loads required by their job. At this time, however, there are no norms available for using the BTE Work Simulator to assess work capacity.

Figure 3-20 Graded exercises in a BTE Work Simulator. (**A**) Use of pliers. (**B**) Use of a rotation knob to simulate torque or twisting jobs.

C

Figure 3-20 (C) Use of a steering wheel to simulate driving.

Validity Profile

The validity of the testing methods used in this evaluation assumes that the patient is motivated to accurately represent his or her true abilities and puts forth a maximum voluntary effort in each of the tasks required. Therefore, a Validity Profile is developed based upon a combination of nonstandardized tests and the therapist's observations of inter- and intratest inconsistencies. For example, the West Tool Sort is an evaluation of an individual's perception of his or her ability to perform a variety of work tasks.[41] The patient is shown 65 cards, each of which portrays a work tool. The patient is required to place the card into one of the following categories of perceived ability:

A. I would have no change in the speed at which I work.
B. I would have a decrease in the speed at which I work.
C. I would be unable to continue work without an extra break.
D. I don't know whether or not I could use this tool.

Many of the tools require similar hand positions and motions, and three tools are duplicated within the card series. It is during the debriefing session when the therapist reviews the responses with the patient that "work function" themes are revealed. These are the unconscious rules by which the patient guides his or her participation in work activities. A patient's work function theme could suggest that the grasp of any heavy object will cause pain or that fine finger pinch is perceived as difficult.

The therapist looks for inconsistencies in the placement of the three duplicate cards or of tools requiring similar motions. The therapist also assesses congruency between observed and actual performance and the patient's reported capacity. These inconsistencies may be related to efforts on the patient's part to confound the results of the evaluation and can be used to support other observations related to the patient's accurate representation of his or her ability.

Other nonstandardized methods for identifying those who may not be exerting themselves fully on the work capacity tests include the use of a pain and sensation drawing and the use of a Jamar Dynamometer. In using a pain and sensation drawing, the therapist asks the patient to indicate on a drawing of a human figure the location and intensity of pain, as well as the specific factors that increase and decrease symptoms. Diffuse, nonorganic patterns of pain and an inability to identify factors that increase or decrease pain suggest that the patient is not performing the tests to the best of his or her ability. Use of the Jamar Dynamometer to detect a less-than-maximum effort is described earlier in the chapter. Interpretation of these test results as signs of a patient's malingering or magnifying symptoms may, however, be grossly inaccurate. Matheson and co-workers have pointed out that poor effort may be indicative of an underlying unidentified pathology and/or a fear of tests or reinjury.[42]

Recommendations

After a comprehensive return-to-work evaluation for the hand-injured patient, the therapist may recommend

- a return to work with no modifications or additional therapy
- job modification (including light duty if available), tool modification, and/or for the use of supports or splints to use on the job with specific tasks
- work hardening

CONCLUSION

Evaluating the work capacity of an upper extremity-injured patient by addressing the patient's ability to perform the physical demands of the job permits an appropriate return to work in terms of maximal medical recovery. Additional work is needed to increase the correlations between the anatomic impairment evaluations and the various functional tests that are currently used, thereby improving rehabilitation regimens for the worker with an injured upper extremity.

REFERENCES

1. Kelsey J, Postides H, Kueger N, et al. *Upper Extremity Disorders—A Survey of Their Frequency and Cost in the United States*. St Louis: CV Mosby; 1980:1–70.

2. Ramazzini B, Wright WC, trans. *De Mortis Ortifican (Disease of Workers)*. Chicago: University of Chicago Press; 1940:13.

3. American Medical Association. *Guides to the Evaluation of Permanent Impairment*, 2nd ed. Chicago: AMA; 1984.

4. American Academy of Orthopaedic Surgeons. *Manual for Orthopaedic Surgeons in Evaluating Permanent Physical Impairment*. Chicago: American Academy of Orthopaedic Surgeons; 1968.

5. Boyes JH. *Bunell's Surgery of the Hand*, 5th ed. Philadelphia: JB Lippincott; 1970.

6. Swanson AB, Hagert CG, Swanson G. Evaluation of impairment in the upper extremity. *J Hand Surg*. 1987;12A: 896–926.

7. Kirkpatrick J. Evaluation of grip loss. *Calif. Med*. 1958;85:314.

8. Bechtol CD. Grip test: use of a Dynamometer with adjustable handle spacing. *J Bone Joint Surg*. 1954;36-A:820.

9. Fess E. The effects of Jamar Dynamometer position and test protocol on normal grip strength. *J Hand Surg*. 1982;7:308.

10. Mathiowetz V, Kashman N, Volland G, et al. Grip and pinch strength: normative data for adults. *Arch Phys Med Rehabil*. 1985;72:66–69.

11. Kendall H, Kendall F, Wadsworth G. *Muscle Testing and Function*. Baltimore: Williams & Wilkins; 1971.

12. Callahan A. Sensibility testing: clinical methods. In: Hunter J, Schneider L, Mackin E, et al., eds. *Rehabilitation of the Hand*. St Louis: CV Mosby; 1984:407–431.

13. Levin S, Pearsall G, Ruderman R. Von Frey's method of measuring pressure sensibility in the hand: an engineering analysis of the Weinstein-Semmes pressure anesthesiometer. *J Hand Surg*. 1978;3:211.

14. Weber E. Weber den tastsinn. *Aish Anat Physiol, Weissen Med Muller's Archives*. 1835;1:152.

15. Bell J. *Symposium: Assessment of Levels of Cutaneous Sensibility*. Carville, LA: US Public Health Services Hospital; 1980.

16. Dellon AL. The moving Two Point Discrimination Test: clinical evaluation of the Quickly-Adapting Fiber/Receptor System. *J Hand Surg*. 1978;3:474.

17. Moberg E. Objective methods of determining the functional value of sensibility in the hand. *J Bone Joint Surg*. 1958;40-B:454.

18. Seddon H. *Surgical Disorders of the Peripheral Nerves*, 2nd ed. New York: Churchill Livingstone; 1975.

19. O'Rain S. New and simple test for nerve function in the hand. *Br Med J*. 1975;3:615.

20. Swanson AB, Boran-Hagert C, Swanson G. Evaluation of impairment of hand function. In: Hunter J, Schneider L, Macklin E, et al., eds. *Rehabilitation of the Hand*. St Louis: CV Mosby; 1984:101–132.

21. Gloss DP, Wardle M. Reliability and validity of *AMA Guide to Ratings of Permanent Impairment*. *JAMA* 1982;248–292.

22. Lafayette Instrument Co. *Instructions for 32023 Minnesota Manual Dexterity Test*. Lafayette, IN: Sagamore; 1969.

23. Tiffin J. *Purdue Pegboard Examiner Manual*. Chicago: Scientific Research Associates; 1968.

24. Tiffin J, Asher EJ. The Purdue Pegboard: norms and studies of reliability and validity. *J Appl Psychol.* 1948;32:234–247.

25. Jebsen RH. An objective and standardized test of hand function. *Arch Phys Med Rehabil.* 1969; 50:311–319.

26. Smith H. Smith Hand Function Evaluation. *Am J Occup Ther.* 1975;27:244–251.

27. Potvin AR, et al. Simulated activities of daily living examination. *Arch Phys Med Rehabil.* 1972;53:476–486.

28. Mathiowetz V. Adult norms for the Nine Hole Peg Test of Finger Dexterity. *Occup J Res.* 1985;5:24–38.

29. Carroll D. A quantitative test of upper extremity function. *J Chronic Dis.* 1965;18:479.

30. Bear-Lehman J. Factors affecting return to work after hand injury. *Am J Occup Ther.* 1983; 37:189–194.

31. Holmes D. The role of the occupational therapist-work evaluator. *Am J Occup Ther.* 1985;39: 308–313.

32. Hightower-Vandamm M. The role of occupational therapy in vocational evaluation—part 1. *Am J Occup Ther.* 1981;46:563–565.

33. DeMaio-Feldman D. The occupational therapist as an expert witness. *Am J Occup Ther.* 1987; 41:590–594.

34. Ziporyn T. Disability evaluation: a fledgling science. *JAMA.* 1983;7:873–881.

35. Matheson L, Ogden L. *Work Tolerance Screening.* Trabuco Canyon, CA: Rehabilitation Institute of Southern California; 1983.

36. US Department of Labor. *Dictionary of Occupational Titles,* 4th ed. Washington, DC: US Government Printing Office; 1977.

37. Bennett GK. *Hand Tool Dexterity Test Manual.* Cleveland: Harcourt, Brace, Jovanovich; 1981.

38. Valpar Corp, 3801 East 34th St, Tucson, Arizona; 1984.

39. *Work Evaluation Systems Technology.* Huntington Beach, CA: Work Evaluation Systems Technology; 1986.

40. Curtis RM, Clark G, Snyder R. The work simulator. In: Hunter J, Schneider L, Macklin E, et al., eds. *Rehabilitation of the Hand.* St Louis: CV Mosby; 1984:905.

41. *West Tool Sort.* Huntington Beach, CA: Work Evaluation Systems Technology; 1983.

42. Matheson L, Ogden L, Violette K, et al. Work hardening: occupational therapy in industrial rehabilitation. *Am J Occup Ther.* 1985;39:314–321.

chapter 4

Vocational Capacity
with Arthritis

John J. Nicholas

The outlook for continued employment among persons who develop peripheral arthritis is not generally optimistic.[1] Arthritis impairs the mobility and dexterity of patients; it leaves their minds free of organic disease, but it depresses their spirits. The methods commonly used to assess the functional and physical capabilities of these patients generally focus on what the patient *cannot* do. As time passes, these assessments do reveal more and more things that the patients cannot do. It behooves the interested and compassionate physician, working with allied health care professionals, to discover what each arthritic patient *can* do and to match the individual with an occupation that is within his or her grasp.

The conditions that cause the greater part of disability due to peripheral arthritis are rheumatoid arthritis, osteoarthritis, and the spondyloarthropathies (a group of diseases often classified as seronegative rheumatoid arthritis). The spondyloarthropathies include Reiter's disease, psoriatic arthritis, ankylosing spondylitis, and, to a lesser degree, the arthritis associated with inflammatory bowel disease and Whipple's disease.

It is likely that the national economic loss caused by these diseases would be much lower if affected individuals were specifically trained and allowed the first opportunity of employment in joint-sparing occupations. This approach would improve the disrupted social, economic, and personal lives of multitudes of arthritic patients.

INCIDENCE AND PREVALENCE

Rheumatoid arthritis is second to osteoarthritis in incidence and prevalence, but it is more likely to affect working-aged persons. Zvaifler and Allander estimated

Note: The author wishes to acknowledge the contributions of Mrs. Ruth Reilly, MA, in the writing of this chapter.

the incidence of rheumatoid arthritis to be 1% to 2% of most white populations.[2,3] The disease is universal, with no geographic or racial preference, but two to three times as many women as men have the disease. Harris noted that the prevalence of rheumatoid arthritis in the United States as of 1984 was 4 to 6 million cases.[4] Hochberg estimated a prevalence rate of 1% for definite rheumatoid arthritis among whites (approximately 2 million people).[5]

Kelsey pointed out that osteoarthritis is the most common joint disorder. Because it manifests symptoms in an older population, however, it affects the work force somewhat less than do other joint disorders.[6] Moskowitz described two common misconceptions.[7] The first is that osteoarthritis is a specific, inevitable disease of aging. In fact, osteoarthritis begins as a joint process at a very early age. In one study, almost all persons over the age of 40 had roentgenographic evidence of arthritis of a weight-bearing joint.[7] Another study of patients aged 55 to 64 showed radiographic evidence of osteoarthritis in at least one joint in 63% of men and 75% of women.[8] The second misconception is that osteoarthritis is a benign condition that infrequently leads to crippling. Although many individuals are asymptomatic, a severe and crippling degree of osteoarthritis does occur; however, it probably occurs in only a small percentage of all those with the disorder.

There seems to be a predilection for osteoarthritis of the hands in women and of the hips in men. There is conflicting evidence that race, obesity, and overuse cause an increased incidence of osteoarthritis, although there is probably an increased incidence of the disease in the knees of obese women.[9]

The prevalence of the spondyloarthropathies is very difficult to estimate, as recent genetic investigations have demonstrated many subclinical cases. It was once thought that Reiter's disease and ankylosing spondylitis were solely diseases of young men, but genetic tissue typing in patients with rheumatic diseases has demonstrated an increased incidence of the cell surface antigen HLA-B27 in patients with ankylosing spondylitis (95%) and Reiter's disease (80%). Population surveys have demonstrated that 8% to 14% of the healthy white population possesses this antigen, whereas only 3% to 4% of both African and American blacks possess it. The Haida Indians of British Columbia and the Pima Indians of the United States possess the antigen in 50% and 18% of their populations, respectively.[10] Approximately 20% of those who possess this antigen develop one of the spondyloarthropathies. It is estimated that fewer than 1 in 1,000 persons in the United States has a form of the spondyloarthropathies, although many more are predisposed to develop one of these diseases because of their genetic characteristics.[11]

COST

Liang and Daltroy reported that the musculoskeletal diseases are second only to circulatory disorders in their annual cost to society and in the earnings lost.[12] They estimated a loss of $20 billion each year in time off from work. The same investigators estimated the cost of rheumatoid arthritis to be 2.2 million lost work days annually.[12] Straszheim calculated that rheumatoid arthritis accounted for 20% of all costs of arthritis and rheumatism generally.[13] Meenan and associates reported a 50% loss of predicted income in 245 rheumatoid arthritis patients.[14]

The direct medical costs of patients with rheumatoid arthritis in the studies conducted by Liang and Daltroy were three times the national per capita average costs for health care.[12] In another study, Liang and associates examined the total annual medical costs for 99 patients with rheumatoid arthritis and 49 patients with osteoarthritis of the hip and knee.[15] Of these patients, 47% had annual incomes less than $10,000, and 22% had incomes of $20,000 or more. The monthly outpatient costs for patients with rheumatoid arthritis averaged $22 in 1979 dollars; the costs for patients with osteoarthritis averaged $8. The total per patient annual direct costs for both groups, which included outpatient visits, purchases, hospital visits, and physician fees, were $682; the patients themselves paid $136 of this amount.

In 1981, Lubeck and associates surveyed 940 patients with rheumatoid arthritis in the northwestern part of the United States through mailed self-administered questionnaires.[16] These patients recorded annual expenditures of $2,533, including third-party expenditures for hospital care physicians; expenditures for visits to other health care professionals; and expenditures for laboratory tests, radiographs, assistive devices, and nontraditional therapies. The investigators noted that the expenditures of their patients were twice the per capita health care expenditures of the general population over 19 years of age in 1981.

No data are currently available to assess the costs to the economy of the osteoarthritis or the spondyloarthropathies.

PATHOLOGY AND PATHOGENESIS

Rheumatoid Arthritis

As Harris described it, rheumatoid arthritis is an inflammation of the tissues that line the joints (synovial tissues).[17] These tissues become swollen with increased blood vessels, round cells (ie, lymphocytes, plasma cells, and macrophages), edema fluid, and fibrin. The pathology is represented clinically by swollen joints, which hurt both at rest and with use. As a result, the range of motion at these joints is limited, and strength is diminished because of disuse.

As the disease progresses to a subacute or chronic stage, the synovial proliferation leads to the formation of pannus, an inflammatory tissue that covers the joint cartilage. Further, certain osteoclastic factors and collagenase are produced that destroy the cartilage and the underlying bone (Fig. 4-1). Thus, while the tissues of the joints become stiff with inflammatory tissue, the joints themselves are struc-

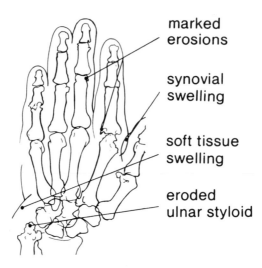

marked
erosions

synovial
swelling

soft tissue
swelling

eroded
ulnar styloid

Figure 4-1 Radiographic abnormalities in rheumatoid arthritis. Persistent use of hands with these abnormalities causes deformities.

turally weakened and become unstable because there is no longer a snug fit of opposing surfaces. Pain on use, incoordination, loss of strength and endurance, and loss of dexterity ensue. Because of both the fusion (ankylosis) of joints and the great laxity and loss of stability in the joints, rheumatoid arthritis can produce a major physical impairment.

Physical examination identifies joint laxity or clinical deformity (Fig. 4-2). These findings are not compatible with the ability to functionally utilize the hands. Even patients with severe hand deformities, such as boutonniere, swan's neck, and metacarpophalangeal subluxation, are often able to perform a surprising array of vocational tasks and activities of daily living (ADL). The boutonniere deformity is characterized by hyperflexion of the proximal interphalangeal joint and hyperextension of the distal interphalangeal joint; the swan's neck deformity is the reverse, with proximal interphalangeal joint hyperextension and distal interphalangeal joint hyperflexion. In subluxation of the metacarpophalangeal joint, the proximal phalanx rides down under the distal end of the metacarpal bone and angles off toward the ulnar aspect of the hand. The healthy wrist functions much like a pulley, but these deformities result in unstable joints that do not function well and will not efficiently assist the bones of the forearm and hand in completing normal motions or exerting normal pressures. The joints may become stiff, either flexed or extended, and interfere with the proximal and distal interphalangeal joint flexion and extension that are essential for fine manipulation.

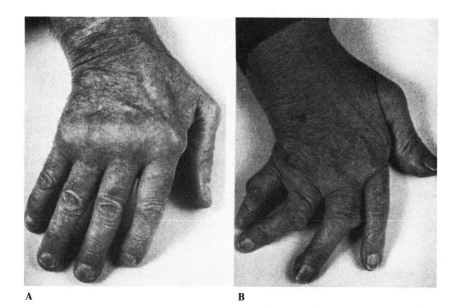

A   **B**

Figure 4-2 Clinical deformities caused by rheumatoid arthritis. (**A**) Partially dislocated, enlarged (metacarpophalangeal) joints and deviation of fingers to the little finger side (ulnar deviation). (**B**) More severe deformity that may interfere with function. *Source:* Reprinted from ''Rheumatoid Arthritis of the Hands and Feet'' in Slide Atlas of Rheumatology (p. 4.10) by PA Dieppe, PA Bacon, AN Bamji, and I Watt with permission of Gower Medical Publishing Ltd, © 1985.

Some manifestations of rheumatoid arthritis are extra-articular. The most common and least disabling is the development of subcutaneous nodules at points of repeated bumping, such as the extensor surfaces of the elbows, the knuckles, and the knees. Although relatively rare, uveitis (inflammation of ocular tissues) may occur, threatening the patient's sight. Peripheral neuropathies may damage neurologic function. Lung disease may cause shortness of breath. Destruction of white cells (Felty's syndrome) may result in frequent infections. Immunoglobulin infiltration of lymph glands (Sjogren's syndrome) may cause painful dryness of the eyes, vagina, and lungs, as well as dysfunction of the liver and kidneys.

The course of rheumatoid arthritis is variable; 15% of patients experience a spontaneous remission, 25% have mild symptoms and little loss of function, 50% or more are disabled eventually, and 10% have a relentless destructive disease that quickly leads to disability.[18] Poor prognostic features include early and marked development of nodules, bony erosions, and a high rheumatoid factor titer (as determined by a serologic test), and extra-articular manifestations and persistent activity in spite of vigorous treatment.[2]

Osteoarthritis

Unlike rheumatoid arthritis, osteoarthritis does not have systemic manifestations.[19] Both single joint and multiple joint involvement are common. Pain with use, loss of adjacent muscular strength from disuse, and joint instability characterize the physical impairment that results from osteoarthritis. The discomfort and joint laxity follow a distinct chain of events.

The initial pathologic findings are changes in the staining characteristics of the cartilage, indicating abnormalities in the ground substance or mucopolysaccharides. Next, white cells proliferate, which seems to be a body repair response; this attempt at repair fails, however, and the cartilage subsequently fibrillates, fissures, and thins (Fig. 4-3). Bony spurs or osteophytes then develop, apparently in an attempt to defend the joint against the loss of cartilage. Even so, the cartilage loss proceeds, causing pain and instability because, without the cartilage, the opposing surfaces of the joint no longer fit together snugly. On occasion, polymorphonuclear cells of inflammation appear in these joints, but the pathology and the synovial fluid generally reveal only bland, noninflammatory fluid. The severity of the radiographic changes is not always related to pain and impairment, as pointed out by Gresham and Rathey,[20] as well as by Cobbs and associates.[21] Minimal radiologic findings may accompany great pain, whereas considerable radiologic abnormality may correspond to few symptoms.

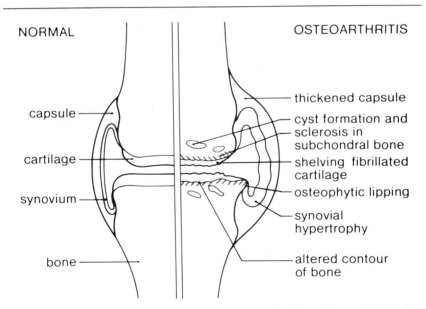

Figure 4-3 Pathologic features of osteoarthritis. *Source:* Reprinted from ''Osteoarthritis'' in *Slide Atlas of Rheumatology* (p. 15.2) by PA Dieppe, PA Bacon, AN Bamji, and I Watt with permission of Gower Medical Publishing Ltd, © 1985.

The Spondyloarthropathies

The pathology and pathogenesis of the spondyloarthropathies have two stages—inflammation and calcification.[22–24] The peripheral joint involvement and the pathogenesis of impairment are similar to rheumatoid arthritis. The basic difference is that in the spondyloarthropathies, not only the synovial tissue but also the tissue that fastens ligaments and muscular tendons to bones—the enthesis—becomes inflamed, and there is pain and tenderness at these sites. In addition, the inflammation of the enthesis is followed by calcification and ossification in the body's attempt at healing. The bony replacement to the enthesis eventually results in a rigid fusion of one bone to another. These changes are particularly evident at the sacroiliac joint, where they cause little impairment, and the spine, where they cause significant rigidity and loss of motion. The chronically involved spine in patients with ankylosing spondylitis, for example, is as rigid as a bamboo rod, which it resembles on a roentgenogram (Fig. 4-4). Because patients with psoriasis, Reiter's disease, and bowel disease have less complete inflammation and ossification of the enthesis, they have normal segments of the spine between involved segments; thus, spinal rigidity in these patients is much less severe.

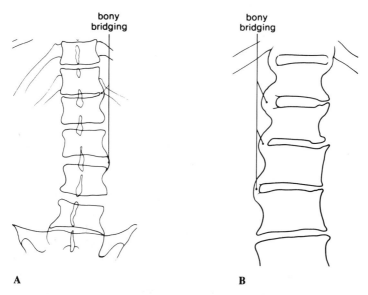

A   **B**

Figure 4-4 Bridges of bone that connect the vertebral body to its neighbor in a patient with ankylosing spondylitis. One bridge may not cause significant disability, but the presence of many bridges severely limits spinal motion. (**A**) Front view. (**B**) Lateral view. *Source:* Reprinted from "Seronegative Spondarthritis" in *Slide Atlas of Rheumatology* (p. 13.6) by PA Dieppe, PA Bacon, AN Bamji, and I Watt with permission of Gower Medical Publishing Ltd, © 1985.

DIAGNOSIS

Osteoarthritis is the most readily apparent of the arthritic conditions. Patients complain of the gradual onset of pain or swelling in one particular joint, which grows worse with use and eases somewhat with rest, but is progressive and continuous. The joint is rarely inflamed, and there may not be symmetrical involvement on both sides of the body. Joint destruction is, of course, the hallmark of osteoarthritis. In fact, it is impossible to confirm the diagnosis of osteoarthritis without radiologic evidence of joint damage. Arthroscopy may on occasion reveal joint damage even before a roentgenogram does. It has been demonstrated generally that osteoarthritis of the hands and feet is related to an increasing functional disability, but the radiograph may be of little help on an individual case basis.[25]

Rheumatoid arthritis, on the other hand, occurs in a much younger age group, although there is an unfortunate minority who note its onset after age 55. A symmetrical, persistent, inflammatory polyarthritis in a woman in her thirties or forties is in all likelihood due to rheumatoid arthritis, although systemic lupus erythematosus, sarcoidosis, and amyloidosis must be ruled out. In a few patients with very acute cases, rheumatoid arthritis may mimic serum sickness, rubella, infectious mononucleosis, and hepatitis. As time passes and the arthritis persists, however, it becomes clear that the disease is rheumatoid arthritis.

Although the spondyloarthropathies have the acute or gradual onset of inflammatory joint disease, the clinical signs are not symmetrical. A characteristic swelling of the tendon near the joint, as well as of the joint itself, produces a sausage-like swelling of a toe or finger, rather than a fusiform swelling of the joint alone as occurs in rheumatoid arthritis.

The result of a rheumatoid factor test for abnormal serum globulins is positive in approximately 80% of patients with rheumatoid arthritis some time during the first year of onset and is negative in patients with osteoarthritis or spondyloarthropathies. The HLA-B27 antigen, however, is present in a high proportion (90% to 95%) of those patients with ankylosing spondylitis and Reiter's syndrome and in a smaller proportion (25% to 50%) of those patients with the other spondyloarthropathies. Thus, the discovery of this antigen in a patient with monoarticular or polyarticular arthritis strongly suggests that the patient has a spondyloarthropathy. The sedimentation rate, which reflects the degree of inflammation, is elevated in patients with rheumatoid arthritis and spondyloarthropathies, but is not specific for diagnosis. Osteoarthritis is rarely responsible for an elevated sedimentation rate.

Radiologic findings are frequently normal during the early course of all of these conditions, except osteoarthritis in which abnormal findings often antedate the development of pain. Ultimately, radiographs disclose the extent of the loss of cartilage and bone destruction. The discovery of sacroiliitis on a roentgenogram is quite characteristic and nearly diagnostic for the spondyloarthropathies; it rarely occurs in rheumatoid arthritis. Degenerative sacroiliitis, which occurs in older patients, is generally asymptomatic and can be readily recognized by a radiologist.

Radionuclide bone scans are rarely helpful in these conditions other than as a screen to demonstrate both inflammatory and degenerative joint involvement without the use of a screening roentgenogram. There is much debate about the sensitivity of radionuclide bone scans for the detection of sacroiliitis prior to its appearance on roentgenograms in the patient with one of the spondylo-arthropathies.

TREATMENT

It is imperative that the physician who attempts to assess the employability of patients with the peripheral arthritides determine whether the treatment is appropriate, adequate, and comprehensive.

Rheumatoid Arthritis

The patient with rheumatoid arthritis should be treated with the maximal tolerable dosages of the nonsteroidal anti-inflammatory drugs (NSAID). The drugs prescribed may include aspirin alone or in conjunction with the now commonly employed newer NSAID. Aspirin is cheaper, and its absorption and patient compliance can be assessed by measuring the level of the drug in serum. In addition, the use of oral corticosteroids is appropriate for patients who are starting second-line drugs, which may not take action for 3 to 4 months. The prolonged use of steroids, however, frequently increases the destruction of joints and muscles, thus increasing the patient's disability. The patient may also require such pain medications as acetaminophen, propoxyphene, or, more rarely, pentazocine or oxycodone.

The patient should also be referred for evaluation and treatment to an occupational therapist and a physical therapist. Activities of daily living and vocational activities should be altered and a set of exercises taught so that the patient can maintain the range of motion of the involved joints, increase muscle strength, diminish stress on joints, and conserve body reserves of strength and energy. For most patients with rheumatoid arthritis, it requires several visits to the therapists, and even hospitalization in some instances, to obtain the needed information and to make the needed changes in lifestyle. Physician contact with all the allied health care professionals is essential for an informed and coordinated treatment.

If the rheumatoid arthritis is progressing, the second-line drugs (eg, gold, hydroxycholoroquine sulfate, D-penicillamine) should be tried adequately; they should not be stopped simply because the patient was not cured. Currently, methotrexate has been found to be highly effective in reducing the inflammation of patients with rheumatoid arthritis, although the inflammation promptly recurs when the patient stops taking it. After taking hydroxychloroquine, D-penicillamine, or gold, patients often experience a cessation of symptoms or remissions for variable, sometimes prolonged, periods of time.

Surgical procedures should be considered for joints that have lost their stability, have bone destruction that is demonstrable on a roentgenogram, and are quite painful. All these treatments should be applied to the patient. Certainly, no one form of therapy will enable the patient with rheumatoid arthritis to live and function pain-free at home or in the work setting.

Osteoarthritis and the Spondyloarthropathies

Osteoarthritis is more simply, but not necessarily more successfully, treated than is rheumatoid arthritis. The involved joints should be rested, NSAID should be taken to relieve pain, muscular strength around the joints should be maintained and increased by appropriate exercises, and surgical joint replacement (total joint arthroplasty) should be performed in severe cases with hip or knee arthritis. The use of canes and crutches helps the patient remain mobile prior to the total joint arthropathy. Loss of weight decreases the load, reduces pain, and possibly slows deterioration of osteoarthritic joints.

The treatment of the spondyloarthropathies is similar to that of rheumatoid arthritis. Local joint injections and NSAID are the backbone of treatment. The use of gold in Reiter's disease and psoriatic arthritis is often successful. The spine stiffness of ankylosing spondylitis, unfortunately, progresses unremittingly in spite of second-line drugs or the use of oral corticosteroids.

TESTS OF PHYSICAL WORK ATTRIBUTES

The degree of joint destruction is a factor in assessing the disability. Inflamed joints may be an overwhelming obstacle to employment in early rheumatoid arthritis, even before any gross evidence of joint destruction is apparent on physical or radiologic examination. Roentgenograms must be obtained, however, because joint destruction is established beyond a doubt when erosion and loss of cartilage space can be demonstrated. Minimal or mild degrees of joint destruction can usually be treated medically or with intra-articular steroids and do not usually mandate total joint replacement. Nevertheless, further heavy use of minimally involved joints is likely to hasten joint destruction. A prevocational trial of job tasks, performed under the observation of therapists or vocational evaluators, is necessary to determine how well the patient can perform work in the presence of mild or minimal joint damage. The effects of joint impairment on the patient's ability to move, strength and endurance, and motor control can be measured.

Ability To Move

Obviously, the ability to move and to change position is essential in any job situation. The 50-ft timed walk is a standard method of testing a patient's ability to move and determining his or her level of energy, strength, endurance, and cardiovascular fitness, as well as the integrity of the joints and the severity of pain in them. As in other tests that require patient cooperation, motivation and level of depression are also factors. The individual analysis of these factors by the therapists involved provides valuable information to the referring physician. Together, the team decides which problems contribute most to a decreased walk time and develop a treatment program.

It is simply not possible to determine if a patient can transfer from place to place without personally observing the activity. Even patients with remarkably diminished strength, including those in wheelchairs, can develop the ability to transfer when faced with the prospect of not returning home or of losing a job unless they can master transfers. One memorable woman was able to master transfers in spite of a girdlestone procedure (hip joint removal) on the right, a revised total hip replacement on the left, a flail knee on the left, and almost total destruction of the shoulders. Motivation can often induce remarkable motion when very little ability is apparent on physical examination.

Strength and Endurance

The methods currently employed by treating professionals to assess a patient's strength and endurance include measuring the time that the patient requires to walk 50 ft, with or without a walking aid; calculating the patient's hand grip strength; conducting a manual muscle strength test; and determining the patient's ability to persist at occupational and daily living tasks. The assessment reflects not only the patient's strength and endurance but also the amount of pain and destruction in the joints that the patient uses for each test. Hand grip tests correlate with some, but not all, functional tasks.[26] Isokinetic muscle testing equipment has been applied only in very mild cases.[27] Observation and trial reveal what the patient with an arthritic joint deformity that compromises power can accomplish with substitute movements.

The severity of the pain that an involved joint produces is critical to the function of the patient. Pain cannot be estimated by palpation or even by hand-held "dolorimeters." The patient who has an unstable, swollen, or contracted joint, but is relatively free of pain, may be able to perform surprisingly skillful tasks. The patient's strength and endurance will be markedly diminished, however, and the task will be completed at a higher energy cost.

Motor Control

The physician and therapists must watch a patient demonstrate skills at self-care or vocational tasks in order to assess motor control. Although it may be compromised from muscle weakness, abnormal tendon angulation, tendon rupture, and loss of joint alignment, motor control is rarely lost because of neuromuscular disease associated with rheumatoid arthritis, osteoarthritis, or the spondyloarthropathies.

INTANGIBLES THAT MAKE PHYSICAL ASSESSMENT DIFFICULT

Pain, stiffness, fatigue, and variable motivation are predictable concerns in the evaluation of arthritic conditions. Although these factors make assessment difficult, they must be addressed in the consideration of future employability.

Pain and Stiffness

Pain is a paramount characteristic of both inflammatory arthritis and osteoarthritis. The pain of rheumatoid arthritis occurs both at rest and with motion of the joints. It is not entirely related to the amount of inflammation and may be seen with minimal evidence of synovitis. Also, much inflammatory synovitis may be accompanied by little pain. Characteristically, the pain of an inflamed joint is more severe following a period of immobilization (eg, worse in the morning after a night's lack of use). The duration of morning pain and morning stiffness is often considered in estimating the severity of the inflammation. Patients often distinguish stiffness from pain.[28] The degree of stiffness is alarming to patients, and it is not uncommon for a patient to overuse joints in order to "keep going so my joints won't stiffen up and cripple me." This misinterpretation of the nature and cause of deformities in rheumatoid arthritis only exacerbates the problem of arthritis. Morning or other stiffness has never been implicated as a cause of flexion contractures or metacarpal subluxation, which are common deformities.

The pain of osteoarthritis occurs to a larger degree with use and less at rest. It occurs only in the affected joint and is not as widespread as that associated with rheumatoid arthritis.

The pain associated with the spondyloarthropathies is more or less limited to the specifically involved peripheral joint. The pain is so variable, however, that it is difficult to apply a general rule. If spondylitis is present, the spine inevitably becomes stiff as spinal joints are ossified. Bending, carrying, digging, and lifting become awkward and very nearly impossible for persons with this condition. In many cases peripheral joints (principally the hips and shoulders) are significantly painful, and these joints must not be subjected to overuse or even routine use but must be protected. The pain from the inflamed spinal enthesis and apophyseal joints responds remarkably well to nonsteroidal analgesics and is a less limiting factor in vocational tasks. The accompanying lack of spinal motion, however, is certainly a factor in choosing an occupation.

Fatigue

Patients with rheumatoid arthritis commonly experience fatigue. Although rheumatoid arthritis is a disease of the peripheral joints, all patients probably have at least a minimal degree of the extra-articular manifestations. They may feel ill, lack energy, and tire readily. Fatigue is present early in the course of rheumatoid arthritis; even before the results of laboratory tests become positive or erosions appear on a roentgenogram, the patient may be unable to perform vocational or self-care activities. At that point, it is possible to determine how long before fatigue sets in only by the patient's subjective estimate. Many patients make a heroic effort to carry on their normal activities in spite of feeling constantly sick and tired, whereas others give up almost immediately.

Patients with osteoarthritis suffer only the fatigue that results from walking with a mechanically disadvantaged hip or knee, a gluteus medius limp, an unstable varus or valgus knee, or a shortened femur. Because of these impairments, walking requires more energy than normal.

Although less often than do patients with rheumatoid arthritis, patients with the spondyloarthropathies may from time to time note a systemic and subjective sense of fatigue. A rigid spine or an ankylosis of the hip certainly increases the energy required for ambulation or working, thus causing the patient to become prematurely tired. These patients rarely experience the degree of fatigue that affects patients with rheumatoid arthritis, however, who may be tired before they exert any effort.

There is no direct measure of systemic fatigue, but there are several indirect ones. An elevated platelet count (in the absence of drug toxicity), an elevated sedimentation rate, and a decreased hematocrit may indicate increased systemic inflammation. It seems reasonable that fatigue is greatest when inflammation is marked. Stiffness, which can be measured by patient report, has been found to decrease with the time of day and effective treatment and to increase with inflammation. It may be correlated with fatigue.

Motivation

No prevocational assessment is complete without an attempt to evaluate motivation, the intangible characteristic that often determines whether a patient is willing to work in spite of many measurable physical deficits. Some patients with rheumatoid arthritis who have clear evidence of disease on a roentgenogram, a low hematocrit, and an increased sedimentation rate are able to work, whereas other patients with seemingly much less involvement are not.

If there are economic disincentives to return to work—for example, if the income from disability, compensation, or welfare is greater than that from the job—motivation may decrease. On the other hand, improvement in the patient's physical condition after medical or surgical treatment may increase motivation. Even in the absence of some of the inflammation markers, patients with rheumatoid arthritis may feel lousy, sick, or "hurt all over" most of the time. It is difficult for any but the most highly motivated patient to continue working under these circumstances. For some vigorous persons with a strong work ethic, the physician must determine whether the work will ultimately lead to greater joint destruction and counsel the patient accordingly while applauding the patient for high motivation. For others, the nature of the work and the degree of job satisfaction are more significant factors. Yellin and associates found that the level of commitment to a particular job, the relative capacity vis-à-vis the work requirements, and the job autonomy had a great deal to do with a worker's decision to seek disability status.[29]

VOCATIONAL ASSESSMENT

Skill and preference inventories can be administered during a vocational assessment. Examiners must be cognizant of individual differences in literacy and language skills when administering these tests. Patients with a rich endowment of intellectual capabilities and training, of course, have more applicable skills. Manual laborers may have fewer available or applicable skills. There are also individual tests or indexes of disease progression and its effect on the patient's physical, social, and personal life, but these tests do not provide an individual assessment of whether the patient can perform a particular job. In order to obtain this information, the patient must undergo job-specific testing.

According to Fries and associates, questionnaire assessments of patients with rheumatoid arthritis can provide applicable, repeatable, and comprehensive information on patients' function, social situation, and vocational experience.[30] In fact, they have suggested that many functional assessments of patients' physical skills and potential for work obtained by questionnaire are equal or superior to those obtained by interview, physical measurements, or laboratory tests. Other measures of the effects of peripheral arthritis are implied by the degree to which the patient varies from normal (eg, sedimentation rate, speed of the 50-ft walk, radiologic change, hand grip strength, or spinal motion). These parameters and those obtained by questionnaire are unlikely to estimate vocational capability unless hand grip, walking 50 ft, or buttoning buttons happen to be the specific vocational task required. Again, patients require testing with job-specific tasks. Questionnaires may provide information on tasks that fit particular jobs, but the occupational therapist must generally identify the exact tasks required of the patient and then attempt to simulate them.

If the appropriate equipment is available, the patient's performance in realistic work situations may be evaluated (eg, typing, computer operation, operation of lathes). Often, the limiting factor to the performance of a job is endurance. The patient may be able to perform several repetitions of a task, but a prolonged vocational assessment may disclose that the patient is unable to continue the task for a day's work. After observing the patient, the occupational therapist may supply aids and devices that enable the patient to perform an otherwise impossible task.

Many patients cannot successfully perform certain specific vocational tasks. In these cases, the British have led the way in job alteration. Such alterations have ranged from providing better access, a parking place, or fewer stairs to modified hand grips for wrenches or different angles for typewriter or computer keyboards. Occupational therapists are generally familiar with the modifications to the home, the use of ADL devices, and the joint protection and energy conservation techniques that are usually suggested to homemakers. These can be applied with equal success to the workplace. In one British study, employment of rheumatoid arthritis patients rose from 35% to 67% following vocational counseling and job modification and remained at 57% after 1 year.[31]

Governments attempting to cut social service expenditures do not generally support costly job alterations. In addition, when unemployment is high, employers find it to their financial advantage to hire those who can work without any job modifications. Environmental work adaptations need not necessarily be expensive, however.

If workers with rheumatoid arthritis are to remain employed, not only must their jobs be evaluated to determine the exact tasks involved—with special attention to those tasks that require forceful repetitious use of joints, unusual dexterity, or extra muscular effort—but also pace, control, transportation, and architectural barriers must be considered carefully. Yellin and associates performed a study by questionnaire and found that the ability to establish the pace of work and to exercise independent control over the location of the worksite were related to the patient's employment.[32] Thus, patients who had more control over their jobs and the work environment were more likely to continue working. In another study,

Yellin found that physical impairment seemed to decrease the likelihood of employment to a greater extent than did lack of motivation.[33] Rosenthal and associates demonstrated that many patients with rheumatoid arthritis are unable to use public buses and thus find transportation a barrier to work.[34]

When Sherrer and associates administered a questionnaire to patients with rheumatoid arthritis in the northwestern part of the United States, they found that gender, functional class, and radiologic stage were directly related to eventual unemployment.[35] Their 11.9-year follow-up study revealed that older women with a poor functional status at onset and radiographic progression in the first years after onset were most likely to have a work disability. Earlier, Robinson and Walters had reported that only 58% (55 of 94) of rheumatoid arthritis patients were re-employed after an inpatient rehabilitation program.[36] A higher level of education, a previous occupation, and an urban location tended to be associated with return to work.

The employability of patients with osteoarthritis is more easily assessed because they often have problems only in a single joint, such as the hip or the knee. These patients are able to perform their work if it can be modified so that it does not require the use of their legs or frequent or prolonged walking or climbing. If the job cannot be altered, the use of canes, crutches, or electric wheelchairs or scooters may maintain employability. The inability to do finger activities because of the pain of osteoarthritis may be partially overcome by intra-articular injections or surgical fusion; certainly, the pain of osteoarthritis does not limit the use of finger joints as often as the pain associated with rheumatoid arthritis does.

Patients with the spondyloarthropathies cannot perform jobs that require spinal mobility or strength (eg, jobs that involve lifting, bending, or digging), but they generally do not suffer stiffness, pain, and fatigue to as great an extent as do patients with rheumatoid arthritis. Therefore, patients with the spondyloarthropathies can more readily retain their previous jobs or find new jobs.

Patients with ankylosing spondylitis have a much higher rate of employment than do those with rheumatoid arthritis.[37] A British study showed that 51 of 60 such patients were employed, with 5 as manual laborers. The severity of spinal restriction was related to work disability, but 60% of those with severe lumbar spine involvement were employed. A further study revealed that 84 of 93 patients with ankylosing spondylitis who were of work age were employed in spite of many complications.[38] Of these, 22 were manual laborers.

The therapist or vocational counselor who is examining an arthritic patient's physical condition and observing the results of a vocational assessment should not forget the fact that most patients with a form of arthritis are generally better off performing tasks that require intellectual effort, rather than physical effort. Even a patient with osteoarthritis who has a single joint involved may benefit by being switched to a task that makes it possible to rest the joint frequently, rather than working at a task that makes it necessary to brace the joint or use a cane.

VOCATIONAL COUNSELING

In testing a patient, the vocational counselor should focus on the patient's *abilities*. Lost abilities may be addressed by modifications, but the counselor who seeks work for a client should have uppermost in his or her mind the skills—intellectual, personal, and physical—that the patient still has. Selective placement, the art of matching individual skills to particular job requirements, is essential.[39] Patient preference must also be considered.

The counselor may suggest that the patient apply for Social Security Disability Insurance (SSDI) in an effort to obtain financial support if the patient cannot return to the former job or find a new one immediately. Currently, SSDI initial requirements for disability include the physical findings of inflamed joints, a positive result on a serologic test for rheumatoid factor (RF), the presence of serum antinuclear antibodies, elevated sedimentation rate, and characteristic biopsy changes.[40] These criteria do not allow sufficiently for fatigue and weakness, which are more difficult to assess objectively, but are just as important in limiting the patient's ability to perform a job. Vocational experience, training, and inherent skills of patients who do not completely satisfy the entry criteria for disability are considered in the final determination of SSDI eligibility.[39,41] Once established SSDI pays for medical expenses and makes disability payments during a trial period while the patient seeks gainful employment.

Unless the vocational counselor is quite familiar with arthritic patients, the referring physician must maintain frequent face-to-face or telephone contacts in order to make sure that the counselor knows just what skills the patient has and just what tasks the patient can perform. The physician and counselor together should assess the match of patients to jobs. The physician has a clearer grasp of what patients can do, but the counselor has a greater knowledge of the jobs that are available.

REFERENCES

1. Pincus T, Callahan LF, Sale WG, et al. Severe functional declines, work disability, and increased mortality in seventy-five rheumatoid arthritis patients studied over nine years. *Arthritis Rheum.* 1984;27:864–872.

2. Zvaifler NJ. Rheumatoid arthritis: a clinical perspective. In: Lawrence RC, Shulman LE, eds. *Epidemiology of the Rheumatic Diseases.* New York: Gower Medical; 1984:107–119.

3. Allander E. The prevalance of rheumatoid arthritis: present knowledge of some future directions of research. In: Lawrence RC, Shulman LE, eds. *Epidemiology of the Rheumatic Diseases.* New York: Gower Medical; 1984:172–131.

4. Harris ED Jr. Rheumatoid arthritis: the clinical spectrum. In: Kelley WN, Harris ED Jr, Ruddy S, et al, eds. *Textbook of Rheumatology,* 2nd ed, Vol 1. Philadelphia: WB Saunders; 1985:915–950.

5. Hochberg MC. Adult and juvenile rheumatoid arthritis: current epidemiologic concepts. *Epidemiol Rev.* 1981;3:27–44.

6. Kelsey JL. Prevalence studies of the epidemiology of osteoarthritis. In: Lawrence RC, Shulman LE, eds. *Epidemiology of the Rheumatic Diseases*. New York: Gower Medical; 1984:282–288.

7. Moskowitz RW. Osteoarthritis: a clinical overview. In: Lawrence RC, Shulman LE, eds. *Epidemiology of the Rheumatic Diseases*. New York: Gower Medical; 1984:267–276.

8. National Center for Health Statistics. *Osteoarthritis in Adults by Selected Demographic Characteristics, United States 1960–1972*. Series 11 No. 20, 1976, cited by Kelsey JL. Prevalence studies of the epidemiology of osteoarthritis. In: Lawrence RC, Shulman LE, eds. *Epidemiology of the Rheumatic Diseases*. New York: Gower Medical; 1984:283.

9. Leach RE, Baumgard S, Broom J. Obesity: its relationship to osteoarthritis of the hip. *Clin Orthop*. 1973; 93:271–273.

10. Calin A. The epidemiology of ankylosing spondylitis: a clinician's point of view. In: Lawrence RC, Shulman LE, eds. *Epidemiology of the Rheumatic Diseases*. New York: Gower Medical; 1984:51–67.

11. Barrett-Connor E. The epidemiology of Reiter's syndrome, psoriatic arthritis and arthritis associated with inflammatory bowel disease. In: Lawrence RC, Shulman LE, eds. *Epidemiology of the Rheumatic Diseases*. New York: Gower Medical; 1984:81–88.

12. Liang MH, Daltroy LH. The impact of inflammatory arthritis on society and the individual: options for public health programs. In: Hadler NM, Gillings DB, eds. *Arthritis and Society: The Impact of Musculoskeletal Diseases*. Boston: Butterworths; 1985:5–16.

13. Straszheim M. Economic costs. In: Utsinger PD, Zvaifler NJ, Ehrlich GE, eds. *Rheumatoid Arthritis, Etiology, Diagnosis, Management*. Philadelphia: JB Lippincott; 1985:845–857.

14. Meenan RF, Yellin EH, Nevitt M, et al. The impact of chronic disease: a sociomedical profile of rheumatoid arthritis. *Arthritis Rheum*. 1981;24:544–549.

15. Liang MH, Larson M, Thompson M, et al. Costs and outcomes in rheumatoid arthritis and osteoarthritis. *Arthritis Rheum*. 1984;27:522–529.

16. Lubeck DP, Spits PW, Fries JF, et al. A multicenter study of annual health service utilization and costs in rheumatoid arthritis. *Arthritis Rheum*. 1986;29:488–493.

17. Harris ED Jr. Pathogenesis of rheumatoid arthritis. In: Kelley WN, Harris ED Jr, Ruddy S, et al, eds. *Textbook of Rheumatology*, 2nd ed. Philadelphia: WB Saunders; 1985;I:886–915.

18. Valkenburg HA. An epidemiologist's view of rheumatoid arthritis. In: Lawrence RC, Shulman LE, eds. *Epidemiology of the Rheumatic Diseases*. New York: Gower Medical; 1984:120–131.

19. Mankin HF. Clinical features of osteoarthritis. In: Kelley WN, Harris ED Jr, Ruddy S, et al, eds. *Textbook of Rheumatology*, 3rd ed. Philadelphia: WB Saunders; 1989:1480–1500.

20. Gresham GE, Rathey UK. Osteoarthritis in knees of aged persons: relationship between roentgenographic and clinical manifestations. *JAMA*. 1975;233:168–170.

21. Cobbs S, Merchant WR, Rubin TR. The relation of symptoms to osteoarthritis. *J Chron Dis*. 1957;5:197–204.

22. Calin A. Ankylosing spondylitis. In: Kelley WN, Harris ED Jr, Ruddy S, et al, eds. *Textbook of Rheumatology*, 2nd ed. Philadelphia: WB Saunders; 1985; II:993–1007.

23. Calin A. Reiter's syndrome. In: Kelley WN, Harris ED Jr, Ruddy S, et al, eds. *Textbook of Rheumatology*, 2nd ed. Philadelphia: WB Saunders; 1985:II:1007–1020.

24. Wright V. Psoriatic arthritis. In: Kelley WN, Harris ED Jr, Ruddy S, et al, eds. *Textbook of Rheumatology*, 2nd ed. Philadelphia: WB Saunders; 1985:II:1021–1031.

25. Acheson RM, Ginsburg GH. New Haven survey of joint diseases XVI. Impairment, disability and arthritis. *Br J Prev Soc Med*. 1973;27:168–176.

26. Sheehan NJ, Sheldon F, Marks D. Grip strength and torquometry in the assessment of hand function in patients with rheumatoid arthritis. *Br J Rheum*. 1983;22:158–164.

27. Hsieh LF, Didenko B, Schumacher HR, et al. Isokinetic and isometric testing of knee musculature in patients with rheumatoid arthritis with mild knee involvement. *Arch Phys Med Rehabil.* 1987;68:294–297.

28. Rhind VM, Unsworth A, Haslock I. Assessment of stiffness. *Br J Rheumatol.* 1987; 26:126–130.

29. Yellin EH, Henke C, Epstein W. Work disability among persons with musculoskeletal conditions. *Arthritis Rheum.* 1986;29:1322–1333.

30. Fries JF, Spits P, Kraines RG, et al. Measurement of patient outcome in arthritis. *Arthritis Rheum.* 1980;23:137–145.

31. Sheppeard H, Bulgen D, Ward DJ. Rheumatoid arthritis: returning patients to work. *Rheumatol Rehabil.* 1981;20:160–163.

32. Yellin E, Meenan R, Nevitt M, et al. Work disability in rheumatoid arthritis: effects of disease, social, and work factors. *Ann Intern Med.* 1980;93:551–556.

33. Yellin E, Henke C, Epstein W. The work dynamics of the person with rheumatoid arthritis. *Arthritis Rheum.* 1987;30:507–512.

34. Rosenthal D, Boblitz MH, Rao VR. Bus use by disabled arthritics: functional requirements. *Arch Phys Med Rehabil.* 1977;58:220–223.

35. Sherrer YS, Bloch DA, Mitchell DM, et al. The development of disability in rheumatoid arthritis. *Arthritis Rheum.* 1986;29:494–500.

36. Robinson HS, Walters K. Return to work after treatment of rheumatoid arthritis. *CMA Journal.* 1971;105:166–169.

37. McGuigan LE, Hart HH, Gow PJ, et al. Employment in ankylosing spondylitis. *Ann Rheum Dis.* 1984;43:604–606.

38. Wordsworth BP, Nowat AG. A review of 100 patients with ankylosing spondylitis with particular reference to socio-economic effects. *Br J Rheum.* 1986;25:175–180.

39. Goldman R. Finding jobs for arthritis patients. *J Rehabil.* 1959;25:21–23.

40. Meenan RF. Work disability in rheumatoid arthritis: an approach to the problem. In: Utsinger PD, Zvaifler NJ, Ehrlich GE, eds. *Rheumatoid Arthritis: Etiology, Diagnosis, Management.* Philadelphia: JB Lippincott; 1985:829–833.

chapter 5

Vocational Capacity with Amputation

John B. Redford

INCIDENCE AND CAUSES OF AMPUTATION

Despite advances in the medical-surgical management of cancer and arteriosclerotic disease, between 22,000 and 25,000 major amputations are performed in the United States each year. It is estimated that there are between 358,000 and 500,000 major amputees now living in the United States.[1]

In most reported series, the incidence of amputation in men is twice that in women, except in the very old. Lower extremity amputation is much more common than is upper extremity amputation, except in the case of congenital amputees. One study of child amputees showed that 60% had upper limb amputations; 30%, lower limb amputations; and 10%, combined upper and lower limb amputations.[2]

The causes of amputation generally fall into four major categories:

1. congenital condition
2. trauma (either direct or indirect result of severe fractures, burns, or other injuries)
3. neoplasm (almost always malignant)
4. disease (eg, peripheral vascular disease, severe infection, gangrene, severe edema), the vast majority of cases due to peripheral vascular disease

Disease accounts for the large majority of amputations in technologically advanced countries, whereas trauma is still a major cause in the Third World countries. The percentage of amputations resulting from each of these causes, as shown in a large U.S. survey,[3] is approximately as follows: congenital, 3%; traumatic, 22%; neoplastic, 5%; and vascular/infectious, 70%.

LEVELS OF AMPUTATION

An amputation is commonly described according to the major joints that are intact or absent. Thus, in the lower limb, there are various levels of distal amputation, referring to pelvis, hip, and knee. More distal amputations have eponyms, such as Syme's amputation, which is essentially a disarticulation at the ankle (Fig. 5-1). Similarly, in the upper extremity, there are various levels of amputation referring to the wrist, elbow, and shoulder (Fig. 5-2). In general, the

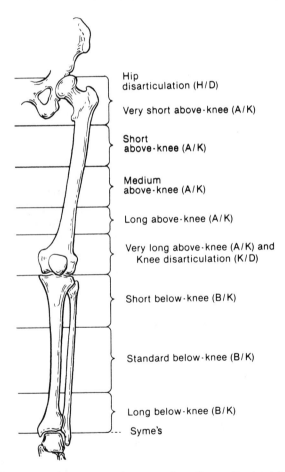

Hip
disarticulation (H/D)

Very short above-knee (A/K)

Short
above-knee (A/K)

Medium
above-knee (A/K)

Long above-knee (A/K)

Very long above-knee (A/K) and
Knee disarticulation (K/D)

Short below-knee (B/K)

Standard below-knee (B/K)

Long below-knee (B/K)

Syme's

Figure 5-1 Classification of lower extremity amputations. *Source:* Reprinted from *Handbook of Severe Disability* (p 179) by WS Stolov and MR Clowers (eds) with permission of the U.S. Department of Education RSA, © 1981.

surgeon performing an amputation strives to save as much length and as many joints as possible.

The most disabling of the lower extremity amputations is the hip disarticulation. It is fortunate that these amputations are relatively rare, as it is very difficult to fit with a prosthetic limb a patient who has undergone such an amputation. Most amputations in the lower limb are below-knee because saving the knee joint has been recognized as critical in rehabilitation. Foot amputations are less common and present relatively few problems in rehabilitation. When finger amputations are

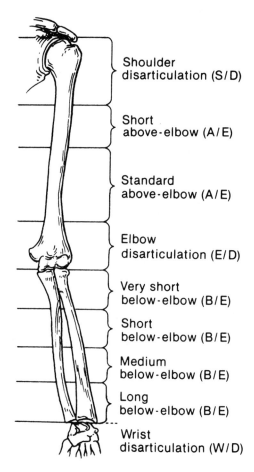

Shoulder
disarticulation (S/D)

Short
above-elbow (A/E)

Standard
above-elbow (A/E)

Elbow
disarticulation (E/D)

Very short
below-elbow (B/E)

Short
below-elbow (B/E)

Medium
below-elbow (B/E)

Long
below-elbow (B/E)

Wrist
disarticulation (W/D)

Figure 5-2 Classification of upper extremity amputations. *Source:* Reprinted from *Handbook of Severe Disability* (p 170) by WS Stolov and MR Clowers (eds) with permission of the U.S. Department of Education RSA, © 1981.

excluded, amputations in the upper limb are above-elbow or below-elbow in about equal proportion.

MANAGEMENT OF THE AMPUTEE

The goal of amputation surgery is generally twofold: removal of diseased or damaged parts and construction of a useful residual limb suitable for prosthetic restoration. The first goal is purely destructive, and the patient usually perceives it in just that way. Therefore, it is essential for the surgeon and others who will be involved in the patient's postoperative care and rehabilitation, such as the nurses and therapists, to counsel the patient preoperatively. They should explain the surgical procedure, the postoperative exercises required, and possibilities for wearing an artificial limb. The positive emphasis on the goal of functionally restoring the residual limb (a term preferred by many to "stump") will do much to ensure an untroubled emotional course for the anxious, depressed patient who is facing the prospect of losing a limb.

Surgery and Postoperative Care

The surgeon amputates a limb at the most distal level consistent with wound healing. That portion of the limb retained after amputation should have the maximum degree of painless sensory and motor capability. Amputations are generally performed only after there has been a careful clinical and laboratory assessment of blood supply, skin tolerance, joint and muscle mobility and after medical problems, such as severe infection or uncontrolled diabetes, have been brought under control.

Pain control, healng of the wound, and prevention of joint contracture are three primary considerations in the immediate postoperative period. Dressings of plaster or other rigid materials are widely advocated to control edema and to facilitate wound healing. This approach also helps to control pain in the first 4 or 5 days, which is important because stump pain or phantom pain sensations may linger if pain is poorly controlled during this period. Furthermore, such surgical dressings permit much earlier fitting of temporary or preparatory prostheses. Earlier fitting has a distinct psychologic advantage for the patient. Early touch perception and functional use of the restored limb ease the anxiety of the upper limb amputee, whereas early resumption of walking eases the anxiety of the lower limb amputee.[4]

Regardless of the dressing used, elastic sleeves or wraps are applied to control edema as soon as the wound has reasonable stability, and the patient actively exercises muscles and joints of the residual limb to prevent contractures.

Prosthetic Prescription

After the stump has healed well and the patient has been through a period of preliminary training with or without a temporary prosthesis, the patient is generally referred to an amputee clinic. Such clinics are headed by a physician or surgeon who is an expert in amputee care. Always in attendance are therapists, prosthetists, and a clinic coordinator. There may also be a nurse-clinician, a clinic administrator, a social worker, a vocational rehabilitation counselor, and other persons with special knowledge of amputees' problems.

The physician in charge reviews the patient's medical problems, together with information supplied by therapists, nurses, or others. The patient is examined, and prosthetic management is then discussed with particular attention to the desires of the patient. During this follow-up clinic visit, social and vocational plans are made and any further needs for therapy reviewed. Planning for social resettlement and prevocational assessment, which may have been started in the hospital, is developed further at this time. The clinic chief prescribes a prosthesis and discusses the rehabilitation plan with the patient, asking the patient to return to the clinic for a recheck after the prosthesis has been fitted and/or training is complete.

Successful rehabilitation with a prosthesis depends on many factors. By far the most important is the patient's motivation to function with a prosthetic device. Other factors, such as age, home, environment, cosmetic appeal, occupational status, and even the distance a patient needs to come for repair or service, must be considered in the prescription, however. The more sophisticated the device, the more it may need repair. Thus, it is unrealistic for patients in remote rural locations to be fitted with prostheses that are likely to require frequent repair.

COMPLICATIONS AFTER AMPUTATION

Unfortunately, prosthetic prescription and training do not always proceed in a smooth manner. Wearing a prosthesis comfortably for long periods depends on an accurate fit between the skin of the stump and the socket. The skin must adapt to a new environment with intermittent and varying degrees of applied pressure. This may cause excessive friction or sweating and may lead to infection, particularly if the surgical scar has not healed completely. Grinding out the offending areas in the socket may resolve simple skin pressure problems. In severe cases of infection or necrosis of the skin, however, the surgeon may need to revise the stump. Such a revision may delay the rehabilitation process by months.

Even long after amputation and prosthetic fitting, amputees must wrap their stumps at night or use "stump shrinkers," which are elastic sleeves or stockings that keep the stump compressed after the prosthesis has been removed. Otherwise, accumulating stump edema may make it impossible to don the prosthesis some morning. Edema is a particular problem in patients with a history of venous stasis or with cardiac or renal disorders. These patients may need diuretics or other medications to reduce edema.

An amputee may have trouble with skin disruption even after years of prosthetic wear and may have to stop wearing the prosthesis until the lesion heals or until a new, better-fitting socket is provided. Furthermore, amputees should be instructed to watch for any changes in the fit of their sockets, as a residual limb almost inevitably shrinks with time and prosthetic use. Amputees should return to a prosthetic clinic at least once a year for a checkup.

Persistent pain may be a major complication following amputation. Treating pain due to skin breakdown or infection is fairly easy; managing pain due to a scar or a painful neuroma (ie, a lump that forms at the end of a cut nerve) is more difficult. Sometimes these painful areas respond to physical treatment, such as desensitizing percussion or massage, ultrasound, or a local injection of an anesthetizing agent. Surgical removal of the painful tissue may be required, however.

By far the most difficult problem to manage after amputation is phantom pain. This must be distinguished from phantom sensation, which is a phenomenon characteristic of all acquired amputations and is so deceptive that a patient may try to walk on the missing leg or scratch the skin of a missing hand. The more unpleasant phantom pain after an amputation probably occurs in only 5% to 10% of cases. This pain is variously described as cramping, crushing, burning, or shooting. It may be intermittent or continuous, frequently waxing and waning in a cyclic manner. The pain is localized in the phantom area beyond the stump, although any contact with the stump, however innocuous, may precipitate it.

Phantom pain may persist in the limb if tissue damage had been extensive prior to amputation, but it generally disappears with time. Until then, various injections or drugs may be tried, but these patients often need personal counseling and behavior management techniques, as demonstrated in pain clinics, when usual treatment methods have failed.[5] The problem has recently been less evident with such improvements in amputation technique as careful handling of the residual tissues and early fitting of a prosthesis.

UPPER LIMB AMPUTATION

The problem of motivating a unilateral upper limb amputee to wear a prosthesis is vastly different from that of motivating a unilateral lower limb amputee. People can get through life quite well with only one arm, and many persons with upper limb amputations learn to do just that. Many quite good cosmetic replacements are on the market, and some amputees prefer such a replacement to an activated prothesis. The prostheses for arm amputees are largely mechanical devices. Major components of upper limb protheses include (1) terminal devices (eg, hands, hooks, or devices for discrete functions); (2) joints (eg, wrist, elbow, and shoulder); (3) sockets with various suspension straps; and (4) a harness with cables to activate the terminal device. They have no distinct sensation, an essential component of hand function, and even the electrically operated devices have very limited ranges of function. Amputees who do not need such a tool for everyday use or for their occupations may not want one.

Upper extremity amputees may have special environmental needs not only at work but also at home or in recreational activities, which cannot be met by prostheses alone. A number of special devices can replace the standard hooks for certain tasks, although even these devices may not meet all of a person's needs. This is particularly true for devices used to assist in driving. The occupational therapist should explore such special areas of need and introduce the amputee to the best choices that are available.[6]

Types of Upper Limb Prostheses

There are two major classes of artificial arms in present use: body-powered and electrically powered. The body-powered prostheses are operated by movements about the shoulder, mainly flexion and extension, that activate a cable attached to the terminal device. Electrically powered prostheses are operated by small battery-driven motors incorporated into the socket and controlled by switches that pick up electrical signals from the residual limb's functioning muscles (ie, myo-electronically).

Body-Powered Upper Limb Prostheses

Most upper limb amputees who really want to use a prosthesis prefer the versatility of the hook over the limited function of the hand. With the quick release or screw connection at the wrist unit, however, these terminal devices are interchangeable. Nearly all hooks in use today are opened voluntarily by a shoulder movement; the cable controls the width of the opening, but not the force of closure. Rubber bands or springs close the two "fingers" of these hooks after they have been opened. Simply adding rubber bands increases the tension between the "fingers." Various designs of terminal devices are available for specific tasks (including a whole series for various sporting or occupational needs), but the device most widely used in adults is the Dorrance #5 hook (Fig. 5-3).

These prostheses have various types of socket design and control.[7] Obviously, the shorter the stump, the more difficult the prosthetic fitting and control. As a

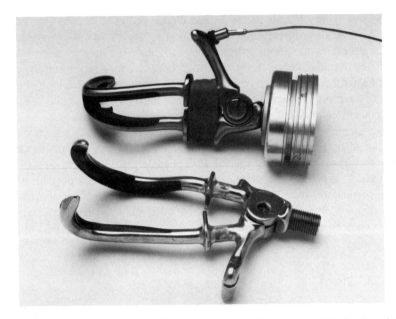

Figure 5-3 Dorrance #5 hook for upper limb prosthesis. *Top,* With wrist unit, rubber bands, and cable attached. *Bottom,* Without attachment.

patient with an above-elbow or shoulder amputation. Patients must have sufficient shoulder excursion and strength to operate the prosthesis. Furthermore, when the stump is short, the possible range of reach for the terminal device is less. Figure 5-4 shows a typical fitting of an above-elbow amputee with a body-powered prosthesis. Shoulder extension (pulling the arm down) locks the elbow by pulling the anterior cable; shoulder flexion (raising the arm) opens the terminal device.

Prostheses provided for bilateral amputees are the same as those provided for unilateral amputees, but a special wrist unit that permits wrist flexion at least on one side is generally prescribed. (Patients need such a device for toileting.) The harnesses for operating the prostheses are usually combined. Patients with bilateral shoulder disarticulations are extremely difficult to fit; because they have few remaining muscles with which to control prostheses, a unilateral device is all that is generally prescribed.

Electrically Powered Upper Limb

In the United States, the most widely used electrically operated terminal devices are those developed by the Otto Bock Company and the US Manufacturing

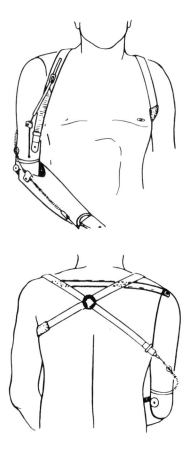

Figure 5-4 Above-elbow prosthesis with figure-of-eight harness behind and attached dual control system.

Company (VA-NU hand). These devices have a definite advantage over body-powered prostheses in that they provide a more cosmetic hand with better functional performance (Fig. 5-5). No elaborate harnessing is necessary in the below-elbow type. For the above-elbow amputee, a number of electric elbows have been developed; most are myoelectrically controlled, but some are controlled by mechanical switches operated by muscles in the residual limb.[7]

Despite many efforts to develop better electrically powered prostheses, progress has been slow. Justifying the expense of individual fittings with the rather limited gains provided by these devices had proved difficult. Except for specialized electrical prostheses for congenital amputees who can control switches mechanically by residual anomalous parts (for example, by the fingers attached to

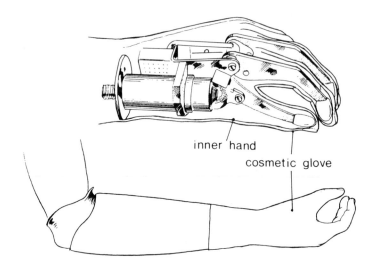

inner hand

cosmetic glove

Figure 5-5 Myoelectrically controlled prosthesis with electric hand. *Source:* Reprinted with *Krusen's Handbook of Physical Medicine and Rehabilitation,* ed 3 (p 918) by FJ Kottke, GK Stillwell and JF Lehman (eds) with permission of WB Saunders Co, © 1982.

the shoulder in patients with phocomelia), most switch controls have been operated by electromyographic signals sensed by external electrodes that are applied over limb muscles.

In amputee programs with well-organized approaches and skilled personnel to maintain myoelectrical fittings, electrically powered prostheses have been very satisfactory. Patients in white-collar occupations, particularly those who are concerned about cosmesis, are the most suitable candidates. Notable success has been achieved with congenital below-elbow amputees. According to Gibson,[2] the advantages of myoelectrical fittings compared with conventional fittings are

- elimination of harnessing
- increased gripping power
- improved appearance and freedom in clothing fashions
- improved function in awkward positions that make operating a cable control difficult
- less fatigue

Gibson also notes these disadvantages, however:

- high cost
- fewer available service facilities while more servicing is required

- malfunction of batteries in extremely cold weather
- slight motor noise
- loss of power in batteries
- weight of motor and batteries

Training in the Use of Upper Limb Prostheses

All patients with upper limb fittings require a period of training, generally by occupational therapists. During the period of training, the therapist checks the comfort and fit of the socket, and the prosthetist may need to make further adjustments. Below-elbow amputees need approximately 2 weeks or 5 to 6 hours of training; above-elbow amputees, 3 to 4 weeks or 10 to 15 hours. When the amputee can carry out a full day's program in complete comfort and demonstrates full functional use, a final check is necessary to ascertain that the prosthesis is providing full usefulness at that level.[6] If no further prosthetic alterations or training is needed and the prosthesis meets all standards, the patient need return to the clinic only for routine checkups—although vocational placement or training and other social and psychologic issues may still need attention.

Finally, all amputees must be taught to maintain their prostheses. This is particularly important for cosmetic gloves or bioelectric prostheses; the "hands" are easily stained, and the mechanism is delicate.

Vocational Considerations for the Upper Limb Amputee

Most unilateral upper limb amputees who held professional managerial, or other white-collar jobs before their amputations can return to their former employment. With proper training, an upper extremity amputee can return to work and resume household activities within 3 to 4 months after the amputation. Obviously, patients with bilateral arm amputations need a longer period of training before they can return to work, but even they can do well in white-collar jobs unless their jobs require considerable manual skills. The vocational disability is, of course, much more severe for those who were manual laborers prior to the amputation; the lower the amputee's educational level, the greater the problem. These patients not only need vocational guidance but also may require job training.

Work tolerance can be assessed by various job-simulated tasks. Before training, the counselor should analyze the previous job. Frequently, modifications of occupational tasks or specific environmental changes can be made, or a prosthesis can be designed especially for previous tasks or heavier stresses. Bilateral amputees may consider using their feet, if they can develop the dexterity.

Many unilateral amputees and all bilateral amputees find it difficult to use the prosthetic arms repetitively for long periods. Any extended use of the residual arm, even without a prosthesis, tires them quickly. Furthermore, the higher the amputation, the more easily the person's shoulder musculature will tire. Amputees who must rely almost entirely on the strength of the opposite shoulder girdle to control a prosthesis very often reject active prostheses; they prefer cosmetic limbs or shoulder caps to fill out the appearance of the shoulder. In recent years, electrically powered protheses have become available for such high-level amputees, although they are very expensive.

Any patient fitted with myoelectrical prosthesis needs much more training than does a patient fitted with a body-powered device. Training for electrical control involves learning about electrodes and the proper positions of electrical contacts, as well as practice in contracting muscles to generate the control signals. Because this is so complex, even amputees able to use electrical prostheses may prefer to work without a prosthesis or to use a body-powered prosthesis while on the job, especially in situations where cosmesis is not a serious consideration.

No prosthesis provides any real sensation, but there is some degree of sensory feedback from the shoulder in body-operated prostheses. This may account for the continued popularity of body-operated prostheses. Because of the lack of tactile and proprioceptive feedback, all amputees must use vision to coordinate prosthetic operations. Thus, it is virtually impossible to use a prosthesis effectively in subdued light or in a dark area.

In most job situations, unilateral amputees use a prosthesis primarily as a tool for gripping objects while they use the remaining hand for fine manipulation. An amputee who has lost the dominant arm needs training to shift dominance to the other side, but it is necessary to explain this switch of dominance carefully to the client. Patients with below-elbow amputations can quite readily learn to write using an adaptive device and may prefer to continue using the dominant hand. Partial hand amputees do not usually need to switch dominance.

Finally, the environment both at home and at work should be assessed. Hot and humid environments may cause skin breakdown, especially if there is friction between the stump and the socket. Also, a dusty environment may cause skin abrasions and damage the prosthesis. In the winter, exposure to cold during outdoor tasks may be a serious problem. Donning wool stump socks may be helpful, and the sockets of some prostheses may be heated.

An amputee's ability to use a prosthesis at work varies according to the level of amputation, the condition of the stump, and the amputee's general health. In considering employment and the level of amputation, the counselor or occupational therapist must examine the job demands. Distal level amputees have a much greater range of possible activities than do above-elbow amputees. For example, prostheses for shoulder disarticulation or forequarter amputations have such serious limitations that the amputee cannot really lift or gain much force in the terminal device. Therefore, employment requiring any significant manual labor is virtually impossible with these types of prostheses. The above-elbow amputee cannot lift anything above the shoulder level; actually such an amputee can lift very little at any level. Carrying capacity is much better, however. With the elbow locked, the amputee can carry up to 50 lb and may achieve approximately 3 to 4 lb of pinch in exceptional cases.

A long below-elbow (1 to 2 inches above the wrist) or wrist disarticulation amputee can lift loads that are 80% to 90% of premorbid capacity. Patients with very short stumps can lift no more than 1 to 2 lb. Strong patients can achieve up to 6 lb of force with their mechanical terminal devices; even stronger forces are possible with bioelectric arms.[8]

Patients with partial hands have the advantage of not needing a hook or terminal device. As long as they have good sensation in the parts that remain below the wrist, they can achieve an adequate and useful grasp. Their lifting capacity and grip strength ultimately depend on the length, mobility, and number of the residual parts of the hand.

In follow-up, patients with artificial upper limbs generally need less frequent changes of socket than do those with lower limb prostheses. Upper limb amputees should return at least annually for a clinical review, however, as the stump may change in dimension over time and new problems may arise. Furthermore, the patient may need continued encouragement to use the limb after leaving the training program.

Although a great many refinements have been introduced in body-powered systems in the past 20 years, the ideal upper limb prosthesis has not yet been developed. That perhaps will happen only when it is possible to replace the sensory components, as well as the mechanical or muscular actions, lost after amputation.

At the end of this chapter Table 5-1 lists vocational handicaps of upper extremity amputees.

LOWER LIMB AMPUTATION

The longer the stump of a lower limb amputee, the most muscle and bone available for strength and leverage—thus, the less energy needed to operate a prosthesis. An intact knee joint may reduce energy requirements another 50%. This difference is also reflected in impairment relating to age. For all lower limb amputees, the functional level of independence decreases with age, but there is also a significant correlation between aging and amputation level. The functional independence of above-knee amputees decreases more rapidly with age than does that of below-knee amputees.[9]

Most patients want to resume walking as soon as possible after a lower extremity amputation. Therefore, in contrast to the upper limb amputee who often must be persuaded to consider using a prosthesis, the lower limb amputee with severe medical complications may have to be dissuaded from trying a prosthesis. Severe medical problems or dementia that antedate the amputation may dramatically worsen the postopertive clinical picture. If the prognosis is uncertain, a trial after surgery of a temporary prosthesis or a plaster cast with a socket attached to a pylon (a substitute shank that has a bar with a rubber walking tip or foot) may be of definite value in establishing the possibility of prosthetic wear.[4]

When other extremities have already been amputated, the lower limb amputee's functional restoration may present particular problems. An amputee who did not use a prosthesis after the first amputation predictably will not use one after the second. Lower limb amputees who have also had upper limb amputations present a special problem, as they need to hold crutches or a walker to balance during the early training phase after a lower limb amputation. Even this can be overcome if the patient is fitted early with an arm prosthesis. A patient who has had bilateral below-knee amputations or even one above-knee and one below-knee amputation has a much better prospect of walking than does a person with two above-knee amputations.

Lower Limb Prostheses

Components of lower limb prostheses include a suspension system, socket, joint replacements, shank portion, and foot and ankle assembly.

The key to prosthetic wear for a lower limb amputee is a well-fitted socket. In the lower limb, except in the case of partial foot and Syme's (ankle) type amputations or the knee disarticulation, the skin or soft tissues do not tolerate much weight bearing over the end of the stump. Thus, sockets for the above-knee amputees are designed to take weight over the ischial tuberosities and adjacent soft tissues; sockets for below-knee amputees, the patellar tendon and the less sensitive tissues over the posterior and lateral aspects of the stump.

For the above-knee amputee, this weight-bearing concept is incorporated in the standard quadrilateral shaped socket with a keyholelike upper opening. The socket consists of a plastic shell derived from a plaster mold that mimics the contours of the stump as closely as possible. The older sockets are made of hard, unyielding plastic, but in the past few years, flexible plastic types that are much more comfortable have been introduced.[10]

Obviously, suspension is critical to ensure that the leg remains secure during walking; the amount of in-and-out slippage (pistoning) between the inside of the socket and the skin of the stump must be kept to a minimum. For the above-knee amputee, this is best achieved by a suction socket that has a one-way valve at the distal end through which air escapes when the socket is donned. Using a removable stump sock, the patient pulls the stump into the socket through a hole in the

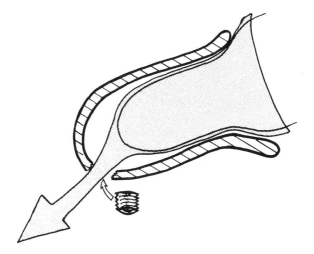

Figure 5-6 Above-knee suction socket. Soft tissues are drawn into the socket with a stocking through the valve opening, and the valve is then screwed into place in the socket wall.

distal end (Fig. 5-6). The vacuum thus created between the skin of the stump and the socket wall suspends the limb. Generally, suction sockets are used only in the young, as they are poorly tolerated in the elderly.

Fitting is difficult on any patient who has skin problems, however. Many patients rely on straps and belts that fit around the pelvis, the so-called Silesian bandage. An alternate and less desirable suspension is the single axis hinge joint, which is attached near the socket with a rigid pelvic band that is strapped to the waist. This arrangement is less comfortable than Silesian suspension; furthermore, because it restricts hip motion, particularly abduction, it limits the functional restoration of the amputee. All amputees without suction suspension wear stump socks to protect the skin and to absorb excess perspiration.

Below-Knee Prostheses

With the standard socket for the below-knee amputee, weight is borne primarily on the patellar (knee cap) tendon. This is a total contact socket molded directly from a cast of the stump, but provided with certain areas for pressure relief. It is essential that this socket be fitted skillfully, because excessive pressure points and skin breakdown are the greatest problems for below-knee amputees. Most older below-knee amputees use a standard suspension consisting of a supracondylar (above-knee) cuff or strap. Variations that achieve suspension without straps, including a socket that encloses the patella entirely, have been proposed, but they are best suited for younger patients. Most patellar tendon sockets used today have an elastic insert that prevents excessive pressure over critical areas, such as the distal tibia and the head of the fibula.

The shank portion of a prosthesis (including an above-knee prosthesis), is generally made of hard plastic laminated over a wood or foam underpart that is made as strong and as light as possible. Called an exoskeletal prosthesis, the shank is contoured in shape to match the opposite limb. All older limbs were made this way. There is also a type of fitting called an endoskeletal prosthesis, which resembles the normal limb. A ''bone'' of metal or plastic pipe is screwed or clamped at each end to the proximal knee assembly or socket and to the distal ankle-foot assembly. This shank can be permanently surrounded by foam or by a soft cosmetic cover (Fig. 5-7). Replacement of the shank and realignment are easier in these limbs than they are in the standard exoskeletal type, but the endoskeletal artificial limb is not as durable as is the exoskeletal artificial limb. Geriatric amputees have often used endoskeletal limbs; except for those who have undergone a hip disarticulation or other types of above-knee amputation, however, young amputees are less likely to use these as permanent limbs.

In the prosthesis prescribed following a Syme's or through-ankle amputation, the shank is contained in the socket. The suspension is usually achieved by a

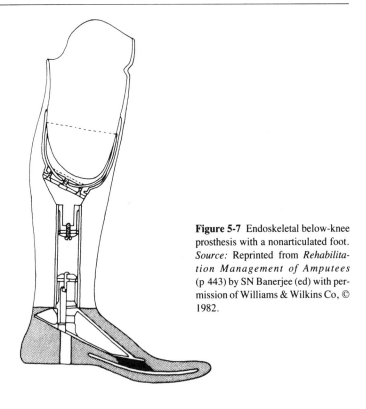

Figure 5-7 Endoskeletal below-knee prosthesis with a nonarticulated foot. *Source:* Reprinted from *Rehabilitation Management of Amputees* (p 443) by SN Banerjee (ed) with permission of Williams & Wilkins Co, © 1982.

bulbous socket end that grips the residual malleoli. Straps are rarely necessary. The socket is donned by using a hidden door. The solid ankle cushion heel foot attaches directly to this socket. Unlike patients who have undergone higher levels of amputation, these patients need little training in the use of the prosthesis; the weight-bearing end is used like a normal foot.

Hip Disarticulation Prostheses

The most elaborate socket used in the lower extremity is that prescribed for the hip disarticulation or hindquarter amputee. This socket is very extensive because it must completely enclose the pelvic area and attach to the opposite side. It has a broad hinge-like hip joint that allows 90° of flexion, but no extension or abduction. The joint is stabilized by setting the axis of rotation so far forward that, when standing erect, the patient has total stability in resting alignment (Fig. 5-8). The

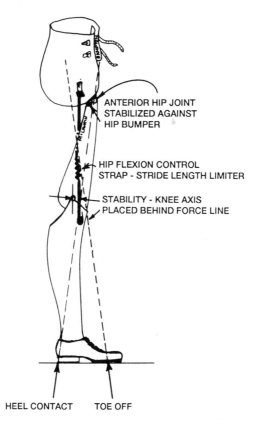

ANTERIOR HIP JOINT
STABILIZED AGAINST
HIP BUMPER

HIP FLEXION CONTROL
STRAP - STRIDE LENGTH LIMITER

STABILITY - KNEE AXIS
PLACED BEHIND FORCE LINE

HEEL CONTACT   TOE OFF

Figure 5-8 A hip disarticulation prosthesis. *Source:* Reprinted from *Rehabilitation Management of Amputees* (p 83) by SN Banerjee (ed) with permission of Williams & Wilkins Co, © 1982.

patient walks by tilting the pelvis; the inertia of the portion below the socket swings the limb forward. Because this manner of stepping is very limited, both in timing and length of stride, most patients find the energy required so overwhelming and the awkwardness of wearing such a prosthesis so cumbersome that they prefer to use crutches.

Joint Assemblies

The knee joint is the most critical of all the joints used in lower extremity prostheses. It must allow stability during the stance phase of gait and smooth action during the swing phase, without terminal impact or jarring when the heel strikes the ground. The type of knee joint that is simplest and needs the least repair is the single-axis constant friction type generally used in the elderly. Some other mechanical knees (eg, the Bock safety knee) give a little more control, as they provide increased stability during direct weight bearing.

For active young persons who need more precise knee control than the mechanical or friction types allow, there are prosthetic knee joints that, operating under hydraulic and pneumatic principles, adjust automatically with changes in cadence. Such knee units include those with the trade names of Dupaco, Hydraknee, and Henschke-Mauch. They provide a much more normal and functional gait than do the mechanical knee joints, but they are also considerably more expensive. Moreover, they are not as reliable or as easy to repair. Therefore, any patient who uses automatic knee units must have easy access to repair services.

Ankle and foot prostheses are available with or without articulated assemblies. The standard articulated foot has a single-axis ankle joint that allows no mediolateral motion. The multiaxis ankle-foot assembly, which is more complex, reduces torsional forces on the limb and allows mediolateral movements at the ankle. It is heavier, bulkier, and more likely to break down, but it is more useful for lower limb amputees who walk on uneven surfaces. The nonarticulated standard assembly is the solid ankle, cushion heel foot, which has no distinct ankle joint. It consists of a wooden heel bolted to the shank of the prosthesis and surrounded by molded polyurethane. Because this type of foot has no moving parts, it is a very light and very durable unit that can be easily unscrewed and replaced.

The greatest advance in lower limb prosthetics during the past few years has been the introduction of new types of artificial feet. A popular one is the Seattle foot, which stores energy during the weight-bearing phase of gait; this energy is then progressively released to propel the body forward as the foot toes off.[11] Not only is the Seattle foot lighter than conventional ones but also it is designed with better cosmesis. These feet are particularly useful for patients with bilateral below-knee amputations, but they can be used in all amputees. Although expensive, energy-storing feet have been in great demand by patients, especially below-knee amputees, who wish to engage in sports.

Training in the Use of Lower Limb Prostheses

Before fitting a patient with a lower extremity prosthesis, the physician must assess the strength and range of motion in the patient's trunk and upper extremities, as well as in the normal and residual lower limbs. Even before limb fitting, the patient is generally instructed to begin balancing in parallel bars and walking with crutches or a walker to improve general fitness and balance. At the same time, the patient practices transfer activities, performs strengthening exercises for the stump and other limbs, and adopts lying and sitting postures that prevent joint contractures. Wrapping the stump to control edema should start when the scar is considered stable and will continue until optimal function is achieved with the prosthesis.

Upon delivery, the permanent prosthesis must be checked for correct fit and alignment. Although the socket is completed, the shank of a new prosthesis is frequently in an unfinished form with an alignment device inserted between the socket and the foot. The alignment device is used to determine the correct position of the foot in relation to the upper portion of the limb. By asking the patient when he or she senses a correct fit and balance and by watching the patient's gait, the therapist can determine the ideal weight-bearing position and adjust the lower part of the prosthesis. After training with the temporary alignment device, the prosthesis can be completed in a final form, the so-called definitive prosthesis.

All patients begin standing with their prostheses in the parallel bars so that they can learn balance and control. They can then proceed under close supervision to develop good posture and walking patterns. Patients should have at least two training periods daily and should gradually increase the time that they wear the prosthesis. Patients must also learn about stump hygiene, sock wear, and stump wrapping to control edema. Young lower limb amputees can be trained in 2 to 3 weeks, although the higher the amputation, the longer the training period. Older unilateral amputees or bilateral amputees may require considerably more training, however. In addition, the process may be delayed if skin breakdown or other medical complications occur.

The amputee should be trained not only in walking on a level surface but also in walking on inclines, various floor surfaces, stairs and curbs, and rough ground outdoors. The trainee should also learn how to fall, kneel, and get up from the floor. Instruction in using public transportation, driving an automobile, or reviewing performance on the job may all follow after the patient has developed confidence in walking.

After the prosthesis has been checked thoroughly for fit, alignment, and comfort and the patient has been discharged, three to four monthly follow-up visits are arranged to assess the patient's performance with the limb and to evaluate any medical problems; for example, further ischemic problems in a dysvascular case or the presence of metastases after tumor removal. After 6 months, a new socket may be necessary, particularly for below-knee amputees, because the stump continues to shrink. After that, the prosthesis may need replacement only every 3 to 4 years, depending on individual use.

Vocational Considerations for the Lower Limb Amputee

As standing and walking are parts of almost any occupation, lower extremity amputees may have serious problems returning to work unless they are thoroughly practiced in the use of their prostheses. Persons in white-collar occupations have a relatively easy time in returning to their previous employment, but the experiences of blue-collar workers, particularly unskilled laborers, may be entirely different. They may need to change their occupations or alter their work environments. The problem of stump skin breakdown and subsequent time off may severely strain an employer-employee relationship. Because many older amputees have vascular disease, they may have to consider their medical condition, as well as the mechanical loss of a limb, in trying to arrange their return to employment.

The patient's prospects for future employment may affect the prosthetic prescription. For example, a below-knee amputee who may return to heavy lifting and carrying is likely to be better served by a prosthesis with an older type of design (ie, metal side bars and leather thigh corset) to reduce the load on the stump, rather than the standard patellar tendon suspension prosthesis.

As with the upper extremity amputee, vocational planning for the lower extremity amputee must take into account the employment environment. Excessive sweating of the stump in warm environments may lead to skin problems; stump size may also change. Dirt or sand may also cause stump problems or damage prosthetic components. No matter what the level of amputation, it is almost impossible for amputees to walk in swampy or muddy ground or sand without problems. Cold environments can also cause problems; there is no good way to warm the components of the prosthesis, and some of the automated knee joints work very poorly in cold weather.

A patient's abilities in walking, standing, climbing, pushing, pulling, and balancing must all be considered when matching a patient to an occupation. The least job-restricted patients are the below-knee amputees. Someone wearing a well-fitted below-knee prosthesis with a long stump uses only 10% more energy on level surfaces than does an unimpaired person.[12] Athletic records have been set by below-knee amputees; some have even engaged in mountain climbing or marathons. It was previously thought that running was a major problem for amputees, but the new energy-storing feet readily permit running. The only restrictions after a below-knee amputation in an otherwise healthy person may be heavy lifting, repeated heavy carrying, or working in situations where exceptional balance is required (eg, elevated construction jobs). The same applies to those with Syme's or partial foot amputations.

Job opportunities are much more limited for above-knee amputees. Such amputees who are fitted with automatic knee joints need less energy for standing and walking than do those who are fitted with a standard above-knee prosthesis, which may be an important consideration in prosthetic prescription. The above-knee amputee walking with a prosthesis may use more than three times the energy that the below-knee amputee uses, however.[12] Because older above-knee amputees have a lower total energy capacity, they may prefer an occupation that allows them to work in a wheelchair.

An above-knee amputee can only climb stairs one at a time and is at a particular disadvantage when walking over uneven surfaces or outdoors. Many require a cane or a crutch for walking, which restricts their abilities to carry anything. Even when they do not use a cane, limitations in carrying, balancing, and shifting loads from one side to the other are very evident because weight shifts throw an above-knee amputee off balance. Therefore, patients with above-knee amputations are best suited to seated occupations that require only minimal walking or standing.[8]

Patients who have undergone hemipelvectomy or hip disarticulation face similar difficulties. Even in young persons with good balance, the energy required to use a prosthesis is so great that they must perform most jobs from a wheelchair. As noted earlier, many such amputees find that using crutches is more practical and consumes less energy than wearing a limb. The bilateral use of crutches makes it impossible for the amputee to carry anything, however, and may eventually cause upper limb problems.

Driving is an essential aspect of many occupations. With automobile modifications, nearly all amputees can drive if they are in otherwise good health.

Table 5-1 lists vocational handicaps common to lower extremity amputees of a given residual limb length.

PSYCHOLOGIC PROBLEMS OF AMPUTEES

Much has been written about the psychologic effects of amputation; Friedmann, for example, has written a whole text on the subject.[13] As with all individuals with suddenly acquired disabilities, the adult amputee passes through a series of predictable phases: immediate shock, followed by anxiety and often anger, then depression, and eventually acceptance. The ways in which amputees progress through these various stages vary. Some patients deny the loss of the limb or internalize deep emotional feelings about the loss. In some, the process of adjustment is quite long. For example, those with tumors or advancing vascular disease are understandably more anxious than many who have experienced sudden trauma.

In congenital amputees, the problems are quite different. Many bilateral upper limb amputees may have been born without arms. Generally, those with limb deficiencies that occurred in childhood need much more psychologic and educational attention. Many children with amputations have had difficulties in upbringing and education, particularly if they required long periods of hospitalization during childhood.[2] A child who is born with an amputation or loses a limb at a very early age learns easily to manipulate the environment. Only later, usually at the time of school entry, does the child amputee become aware of the impairment through a comparison with normal peers. At this time, the child's emotional reactions to amputation may need special attention.

Two factors are very significant in helping child amputees make an emotional adjustment to their impairments: the attitude of their parents and a prosthetic fitting at such an early age that they accept the artificial limb as an integral part of the body. Referral to an amputee program at an early age permits those involved in amputee rehabilitation to foster accepting attitudes in the parents. The therapists in the amputee program can make the prosthesis an integral aspect of development by fitting it when the child begins to pull up to stand or, in the case of upper limb amputation, when the child starts to manipulate the environment, usually about 6 months of age.[14]

The loss of a limb has been compared with the loss of a spouse.[15] In both situations, the stress level is extremely high. According to Whylie, however, the amputee's level of anxiety drops rapidly during a stay in a rehabilitation unit.[16] She reported that, in detailed studies of 50 patients who entered such a unit, practical concerns such as "fear of falling," "phantom pain," and "financial problems" produced the greatest anxiety. On the other hand, "changes in body image," "reaction of family and friends," and "change in lifestyle" were the least anxiety-producing concerns, even though these are often cited as major problems in adjustment. The vast majority of amputees adjust well to their impairment when they undergo early rehabilitation with practical help from social services and psychologic support from a rehabilitation team. Special psychologic counseling should begin early if severe emotional problems appear to be developing.

After discharge from the rehabilitation unit, new amputees may benefit greatly from group support offered by amputee clubs or other organizations for the disabled. They may benefit particularly from the many recreational opportunities now available. Upon discharge, the patient should be directed not only to vocational or social agencies but also to self-help groups in the community and national organizations, such as the National Handicapped Sports and Recreation Association (1145 10th St., N.W., Suite 717, Washington, DC 20036) or the National Wheelchair Athletic Association (21007 Templeton Gap Rd., Suite C, Colorado Springs, CO 80907).[17,18]

Table 5-1 Vocational Handicaps

Impairment	Examples of Vocational Handicaps	Examples of Work Areas Affected
FOREQUARTER AMPUTATION	Restrictions on bimanual coordination, eye-hand coordination, arm-hand coordination, manual and finger dexterity, gross and fine manipulative skills, motor coordination, grip strength for grasping, use of small hand tools and power tools, lifting, carrying, pushing. Psychologic complications may significantly add to handicaps as well.	Craftsmanship and related work Precision working/manipulating Physical education, industrial training, typing and related recording Musical work, decorating and art work, handling, drafting and related work Investigating, protecting and related work
SHOULDER DISARTICULATION	Restrictions include all listed under Forequarter Amputation. Psychologic factors (in both types of amputation) may add limits on ability to relate to people and communicate ideas, ability to communicate ideas and influence others, ability to handle situational stress, ability to relate to people in a manner to win their confidence and establish rapport.	Same as above; additional examples: operating and controlling work, materials analysis and related work, medical, veterinary and related services, demonstration and sales work, beautician and barbering services, radio and television transmitting and receiving, transportation service work, news reporting and related work
ABOVE-ELBOW AMPUTATION	Restrictions include Forequarter and Shoulder Disarticulation examples. Physical and psychologic consequences may also include limits on ability to relate to people in order to motivate employees, attention to detail, concentration and ability to attend to tasks over sustained periods, climbing, balancing, work in awkward positions and work about unprotected heights.	Same as above; additional examples: Translating, editing and related work Flight and related training Delivery and service work Switchboard service Nursing x-ray and related services

continues

Table 5-1 continued

Impairment	Examples of Vocational Handicaps	Examples of Work Areas Affected
ELBOW DISARTICULATION	Restrictions remain much the same as earlier examples. Fewer psychologic complications may be seen although this must be judged on an individual case basis. In each type of amputation eliminating elbow joint function, prosthetic replacement produces less satisfactory results. The shorter the extremity stump above the elbow the less functional the prosthesis will be.	Same as above; additional examples: Transportation and test driving Surveying, prospecting and related work Creative entertaining High school, college, university and related education Sorting, inspecting, measuring and related work Cooking and related work
BELOW-ELBOW AMPUTATION	Restrictions remain similar to those previously listed but retention of elbow joint allows for more functional prosthetic device.	Same as above; additional examples: Costuming, tailoring, and dressmaking Computing and related recording Instructive work, fine arts, theater, music and related fields Account auditing and related work Paying and receiving
WRIST DISARTICULATION	Restrictions remain significant in dominant extremity (less so in nondominant extremity). Prosthetic function usually fair to good.	Same as above; additional examples: Child and adult care Photography and motion picture camera work Cashiering Vocational educational education

MIDCARPAL AMPUTATION OF HAND	Restrictions remain significant in dominant extremity, (less so in nondominant). Prosthesis is more cosmetic, function limited. Impact on vocational alternates still significant and psychologic complications can be severe.	Same as above; additional examples: Feeding/offbearing Amusement and entertainment work (physical) Cropping, animal farming, gardening and related work Animal care
FINGER(S) AMPUTATION	Restrictions may include eye-hand coordination, finger dexterity, grip strength for grasping, lifting or carrying, manual dexterity, some combination of manual dexterity and eye-hand coordination to use hand tools and manually controlled power tools, finger dexterity to give injections, use tweezers etc. Some limitations in lift, carry, push, pull. (No effective prosthetic replacement.)	Craftsmanship and related work Musical work (instrumental) Precision working Sorting, inspecting, measuring, and related work Nursing, x-ray and related services Surgery
THUMB AMPUTATION	Restrictions on grasping, grip strength, manual and finger dexterity, use of small hand tools, use of some power tools and equipment, fine manipulative skills, gross manipulative skills. (No effective prosthetic replacement.)	Craftsmanship and related work Precision working Secretarial and related work Operating-controlled work Surgery
HEMIPELVECTOMY	Restrictions on work about uneven terrain, climbing, balancing, work about unprotected heights, kneeling, stooping, crouching, standing, walking, pushing and pulling involved in pedal or equipment operation. Significant psychologic complications may be present, restricted ability to relate to others. (See forequarter, shoulder, above-elbow amputations.) Prosthetic device minimally functional.	Craftsmanship and related work Driving-operating Operating-controlling Surgery Investigating, protecting, and related work Photography and motion picture camera work

continues

Table 5-1 continued

Impairment	Examples of Vocational Handicaps	Examples of Work Areas Affected
HIP DISARTICULATION	Restrictions on (see hemipelvectomy) ability to work along with subordinates in difficult phases of a job, prolonged sitting, standing, walking, climbing. Psychologic complications and/or chronic pain may substantially increase handicaps. Operation of machinery, equipment, motorized vehicles severely hampered. (Prosthetic device awkward, minimally functional.)	Same as above Artistic restoration, decoration and related work Cashiering Inspecting and stock checking Classifying, filing and related work Craftsmanship and related work Driving-operating
ABOVE-KNEE	Restrictions remain consistent with hemipelvectomy and hip disarticulation although prosthetic device is less awkward and more functional (as stump lengthens).	Same as above—additional examples: Classifying, filing, and related work Cropping, animal farming, gardening, and related work Beautician and barbering services
KNEE DISARTICULATION	Restrictions remain consistent with hemipelvectomy, hip disarticulation and above-knee amputation. Loss of knee joint function is critical factor. Prosthetic function is fair. Prosthetic joint somewhat more difficult to develop due to stump length and partial presence of knee (distal third of femur).	Same as above—additional examples include: Therapeutic and related work Operating/controlling work Demonstration and sales work
BELOW-KNEE	Restrictions remain consistent with knee disarticulation but prosthetic function usually excellent. Capacity for sitting, standing, walking often good. Fewer handicaps although age, length of stump, education and work history will play a role.	Artistic restoration, decoration, and related work Investigating, protecting, and related work Typing and related recording Surveying, prospecting, and related work Transportation and test driving

ANKLE DISARTICULATION	Restrictions consistent with below-knee amputation. Prosthetic aid is functional. Walking and standing are restricted but less severely. Climb, balance, stoop, kneel, work about unprotected heights will be limited. Uneven terrain remains a problem.	Craftsmanship and related work Driving-operating Operating-controlling Precision working Beautician and barbering services
PARTIAL AMPUTATION OF THE FOOT	Restrictions may exist on prolonged standing and walking. Gait changes may cause some limitations. Psychologic and pain complications may also result in limitations. Prosthesis is by prescription and not always required. Overall limitations should not be severe.	Must be judged on individual case basis
AMPUTATION OF GREAT TOE	Restrictions consistent with partial amputation of the foot. Most serious concern is potential gait change. May result in some limits on lift, carry, and push for pedal operation.	Must be judged on individual case basis
TOE(S) AMPUTATIONS	Restrictions consistent with partial foot amputation.	Must be judged on individual case basis

Source: Copyright © 1985 by Matthew Bender & Co., Inc., and reprinted with permission from *A Guide to Rehabilitation* by Paul M. Deutsch and Horace Sawyer.

REFERENCES

1. Deutsch PM, Sawyer HW. Amputations. In: Deutsch PM, Sawyer HW, eds. *A Guide to Rehabilitation*. New York: Matthew Bender; 1985: section 18.01.

2. Gibson DA. Child and juvenile amputee. In: Banerjee SN, ed. *Rehabilitation Management of Amputees*. Baltimore: Williams & Wilkins; 1982:391–414.

3. Kay HW, Newman DJ. Relative incidences of new amputations; statistical comparisons of 6,000 new amputees. *Orthot Prosthet* 1977;29:3–16.

4. Burgess EM, Romano RL, Zettl JH. *The Management of Lower Extremity Amputations*. Washington, DC: US Government Printing Office; 1969.

5. Blankenbaker WL. The care of patients with phantom limb pain in a pain clinic. *Anesth Analg*. 1977;56:842–846.

6. Heger H. Adaptive devices for amputees and training for upper extremity amputees. In: Banerjee SN, ed. *Rehabilitation Management of Amputees*. Baltimore: Williams & Wilkins; 1982:255–329.

7. Wilson AB. Prosthetic fitting and components—upper extremity. In: Banerjee SN, ed. *Rehabilitation Management of Amputees*. Baltimore: Williams & Wilkins; 1982:99–149.

8. Friedmann LW. Amputation. In: Stolov WS, Clowers MR, eds. *Handbook of Severe Disability*. Washington, DC: US Department of Education RSA; 1981:169–188.

9. Goldberg RT. New trends in the rehabilitation of lower extremity amputees. *Rehabil Lit*. 1984;45:2–11.

10. Pritham CH, Fillauer K. Experience with the Scandinavian flexible socket. *Orthot Prosthet*. 1985;11:154–168.

11. Michael J. Energy storing feet: A clinical comparison. *Clin Prosthet Orthot*. 1987;11:154–168.

12. Gonzalez EG, Corcoran PF, Rodolfo LR. Energy expenditure in below knee amputee: correlation with stump length. *Arch Phys Med Rehabil*. 1974;55:111–119.

13. Friedmann LW. *The Psychological Rehabilitation of the Amputee*. Springfield, IL: Charles C Thomas; 1978.

14. Hubbard S. Social and psychological problems of the child amputee. In: Kostiuk JP, Gillespie R, eds. *Amputation Surgery and Rehabilitation*. New York: Churchill Livingstone; 1981:395–401.

15. Parkes CM. Psychosocial transition: comparison between reactions to loss of a limb and loss of a spouse. *J Psychol*. 1975;127:204–210.

16. Whylie B. Social and psychological problems of the adult amputee. In Kostiuk JP, Gillespie R, eds. *Amputation Surgery and Rehabilitation*. New York: Churchill Livingstone; 1981:387–393.

17. May BJ. Living with a prosthesis. In: Sanders GT, ed. *Lower Limb Amputations: A Guide to Rehabilitation*. Philadelphia: FA Davis; 1986:497–505.

18. Kegel B, Webster JC, Burgess EM. Recreational activities of lower extremity amputees: a survey. *Arch Phys Med Rehabil*. 1980;61:258–264.

chapter 6

Vocational Capacity with Cognitive Impairment

Bruce Caplan and Judith A. Shechter

A variety of conditions have cognitive consequences that can interfere with vocational competence. Among the most common are head trauma, stroke, dementing conditions, toxic encephalopathy, substance abuse, and depression. Some of these conditions have accompanying physical deficits, but impaired cognition, the final common pathway of numerous conditions, is generally the greater obstacle to the maintenance or resumption of productive work. For example, a significant proportion of patients experience difficulty or delay in returning to work following minor head trauma, despite essentially full physical recovery.[1] A stroke patient with Wernicke's aphasia may exhibit little motor disability, yet be unable to resume work because of the expressive language impairment. A patient with (early stage) Alzheimer's syndrome almost invariably reveals the condition in the cognitive sphere before it is apparent in the motor sphere.

Neuropsychologic evaluation can play a valuable role in the restoration of many cognitively impaired workers to competitive employment. In certain cases, the results of neuropsychologic testing suggest that an individual is likely to encounter significant difficulty if he or she attempts to take up a former position. That is, performance on formal tests may be so deficient as to be inconsistent with adequate vocational performance. Depending on the nature of the occupation, a deficiency that is rather small in absolute terms may be a significant vocational impairment. For example, a trial lawyer may be severely disabled by a mild degree of anomia; a ceramicist, by a subclinical degree of constructional apraxia. "Normal" test performance does not permit the sanguine assurance of vocational success, however. In their study of 98 severely head-injured patients, Brooks and associates found that, whereas the presence of a deficit was a very good predictor of failure to return to work, the absence of the deficit did not guarantee that the patient would return to work.[2] In other words, a clean bill of neuropsychologic health is a necessary, but not a sufficient, condition for vocational success. Thus, the best outcome is likely to be a finding that there is no evidence of a deficit sufficient to prevent a vocational trial.

NEUROPSYCHOLOGIC PREDICTORS OF VOCATIONAL STATUS: EMPIRIC FINDINGS

For patients with the kinds of conditions noted, a thorough delineation of neurobehavioral status is an efficient and cost-effective first step in the process of evaluating vocational potential. Nonetheless, neuropsychologic data constitute only one source of information in the determination of vocational competence. There is as yet sparse evidence documenting the predictive validity of neuropsychologic assessment for vocational success; indeed, the ecologic relevance of such testing has been seriously questioned,[3,4] and its association with various aspects of "practical intelligence" remains unknown.[5] As Heaton and Pendleton noted,[6] however, the tendency of many researchers to employ IQ as the primary (or only) index of neuropsychologic function has probably led to an underestimation of the predictive potential of neuropsychologic data. This assertion is supported by several studies in which the investigators used broader-based neuropsychologic measures and found significant differences between those subjects who achieved vocational rehabilitation and those who did not.

For example, Heaton, Chelune, and Lehman studied 381 subjects (excluding students and housewives) between the ages of 17 and 64.[7] At the time of evaluation, 45% were employed full-time, 10% were working part-time, and 45% were unemployed. Tests included an expanded Halstead-Reitan Neuropsychological Test Battery,[8] as well as additional measures of academic skills, new learning ability, and delayed recall. The general pattern of results was as predicted; full-time employees performed better than did part-time employees, who, in turn, performed better than did those in the unemployed group. Virtually all measures clearly distinguished between unemployed subjects and those working full-time; slightly more than one half of the contrasts between part-time workers and the unemployed subjects reached significance, but fewer than one third of the differences between the two employed groups were significant.

Dikmen and Morgan divided a group of 108 epileptic patients into those who had worked at least one half of the year preceding evaluation ("employed") and those who had not ("unemployed").[9] Neuropsychologic measures again included an expanded Halstead-Reitan Battery and supplementary measures of attention, memory, and cognitive flexibility. The employed group achieved higher scores on 33 of the 36 test variables, with the largest and most consistent differences on measures of flexibility of thinking, motor functions, and concentration/memory. According to Dikmen and Morgan, neuropsychologic measures (ie, those that reflect cerebral integrity) are superior to conventional intelligence and/or achievement tests in predicting employability because they provide a wider and more adequate sampling of job-related abilities.

Morris, Ryan, and Peterson studied 30 men (mean age = 36 years) who were undergoing vocational rehabilitation.[10] The group included 11 with drug dependence, 5 with affective disorders, 4 with schizophrenia, and another 4 with "miscellaneous medical" conditions. Morris and colleagues reported that two measures—the Category Test[8] and Trail Making Test (Part B)[11]—distinguished between those subjects who passed two sections of the Singer Vocational Evaluation System and those who failed. Their cut-off scores, however, were quite liberal (Category Test errors more than 66; Trail Making Test more than 106 seconds) for this relatively young sample.

Thus, the few extant published reports support the assertion of an association between neuropsychologic functioning and vocational status.

VOCATIONAL CONSEQUENCES OF STROKE AND HEAD TRAUMA

Two of the most common causes of cognitive impairment in working adults are stroke and head trauma. Both can have a profound vocational impact.

Stroke

Although stroke is primarily a disease of the elderly, recent surveys from comprehensive stroke center programs have shown that 20% of strokes occur in individuals under age 65.[12,13] Almost 25% of these young victims were working at the time the stroke occurred. Perhaps because of societal stereotypes and prejudices (ageism), there have been few studies of vocational function following stroke; researchers seem to have assumed that employment confers immunity from stroke or that resuming gainful employment rarely interests stroke survivors.

In an early study, Weisbroth, Esibill, and Zuger reported that more than one third of stroke patients under age 65 returned to competitive employment, although some did so at a lower level.[14] There were no differences in age or educational level between employed and unemployed subjects, but women were more likely than were men to return to work. Among patients with left hemisphere involvement, functional communication alone differentiated between employed and unemployed subjects. Among patients with right hemisphere involvement, two physical measures (ie, ambulation and the use of the affected upper extremity), as well as performance on the Wechsler Adult Intelligence Scale (WAIS) Block Design[15] subtest, discriminated between the two groups.

Gresham and associates reported "decreased vocational function" to be the most common functional deficit 6 months or more after a stroke.[16] When those disabilities attributable to a variety of comorbid conditions (eg, diabetes, arthritis, congestive heart failure) were removed, however, the incidence of decreased vocational function following stroke fell from 65% to 38%. Thus, stroke per se does not dictate vocational impairment.

An Australian study of stroke survivors 6 months after onset found that, of those subjects whose main prestroke activity was gainful employment, only about 60% of those without residual weakness or communication deficit were working at their premorbid level.[17] Interestingly, almost 40% of those with residual impairment were working at their premorbid skill level.

In order to determine the significance of two major socioeconomic variables—education and occupation—in poststroke employment, Smolkin and Cohen studied 74 hemiplegic individuals following vocational rehabilitation.[18] They found that those with fewer than 12 years of education were less likely to return to competitive employment, especially if they were women, than were high-school graduates. Prior occupation was the most powerful determinant of successful vocational rehabilitation. Professional, technical, and managerial workers were most likely to resume productive employment. Howard and associates reached similar conclusions in a follow-up study of 379 cerebral infarction patients who had been employed at the time that they were stricken.[19] They found that younger patients who had held professional-managerial positions were most likely to return to work than were older blue-collar or farm workers.

Carriero, Faglia, and Vignolo reported on 10 relatively young patients with moderate to severe aphasia who returned to jobs that required interpersonal communication.[20] Among the strategies employed were (1) reduction of working hours or territory covered (for salesmen), (2) selective interaction with customers or suppliers with whom the patient had dealt before the stroke, (3) reliance on overlearned behavior and language in the performance of new tasks, (4) initial help from a relative or close friend, and (5) delegation to others of certain aspects of the job. In addition to being younger than the average stroke patient, these individuals were all reported to be unusually well motivated. Nonetheless, these case studies demonstrate that meaningful employment is not necessarily an unrealistic goal in patients with a significant language deficit.

Head Trauma

Traumatic head injury is an extraordinarily common event, resulting in approximately 500,000 hospitalizations annually. Although most such injuries constitute relatively mild trauma, 5% to 10% of all head-injured individuals are unable to return to their preinjury level of function.[21] As the great majority are between the ages of 15 and 24[22] and are approaching or just beginning their careers, the economic costs of head injury are immense; in 1980, one estimate of the loss was $3.9 billion[23]

In reviewing studies of return to work after head injury, Humphrey and Oddy found rates that ranged from 50% to 99%.[24] According to the authors, however, their review provides "only a broad outline of occupational resettlement after head injury,"[24] as the studies varied widely with respect to age of subjects, severity of injury, duration of follow-up, and other pertinent variables. At least one group of experienced investigators has reported far more pessimistic results.[2] Furthermore, as Humphrey and Oddy themselves noted, there is no guarantee that a patient who returns to the same job will perform at the same intensity or level of excellence. Among the factors that seemed to predict successful resumption of work were younger age, superior intelligence, greater education, professional training, absence of premorbid psychopathology, and shorter duration of post-traumatic amnesia.

In an earlier study of head-injured patients (approximately 75% with penetrating injuries), Dresser and associates also found severity of injury (as indexed by depth of penetration) and duration of unconsciousness to be important predictors of a patient's return to work, although they were less predictive than preinjury cognitive ability.[25] Najenson and colleagues studied 147 patients with severe head injuries 6 months or more after their discharge from the hospital.[26] They reported negative prognostic factors to be the following: lengthy coma, aphasia, impaired cognition, low premorbid educational level, and "frontal behavior" (eg, loss of initiative, failure to recognize deficits). Of their subjects, 18% were engaged in skilled labor; 25%, in unskilled labor.

After a 10- to 15-year follow-up study of 40 patients with very severe head trauma, Thomsen reported that only three were employed full-time; another two were working part-time, seven were participating in sheltered workshops, and three subjects were able to manage housekeeping and shopping responsibilities.[27] Oddy, Humphrey, and Uttley found that 71% of patients with post-traumatic amnesia for less than 7 days had returned to work 6 months after their injuries, whereas only 27% of those with post-traumatic amnesia for more than 7 days had returned to work by that time.[28] Weddell, Oddy, and Jenkins found that only 11% of their severely head-injured patients (post-traumatic amnesia for at least 1 week) returned to work at roughly their preinjury level; another 14% were restored to less demanding positions.[29]

Van Zomeren and van den Burg also found the length of post-traumatic amnesia to be a potent predictor of return to work within 2 years after severe head injury.[30] Among their group of 57 patients, 58% had resumed their former work or educational program without alteration; 13% were working in the same job, but with reduced demands (eg, part-time); 5% were working at a lower level; 7% attended sheltered workshops; 16% were not working at all; and 1% could not be classified. The correlation between post-traumatic amnesia and return to work was .54 (P less than .001).

Brooks and colleagues conducted a long-term follow-up study of 134 patients with severe head injuries.[2] All patients had post-traumatic amnesia for at least 2 days, and 43% had post-traumatic amnesia for a period that exceeded 4 weeks. Patients were interviewed between 2 and 7 years following injury. Although 86% had been employed at the time of injury, only 29% had been working in the week prior to the interview. The proportion of employed subjects did not change between 2 and 5 years postinjury. Physical status was unrelated to return to work, but cognitive, communicative, or behavioral/emotional deficits were significantly associated with failure to resume employment.

In another study, Johnson found that 34% of 47 severely injured patients (average length of post-traumatic amnesia, 6 weeks), all of whom had been employed full-time at the time of injury, had made no attempt to return to work.[31] Twenty-eight percent returned to work, but failed to maintain employment for as long as 1 year; some of these individuals had held a series of different jobs. The remaining 38% had returned to work successfully and remained employed for at least 1 year. Twelve individuals had returned under "special conditions," however, including unpaid labor, simplified responsibilities, specific training targeted at ameliorating particular problems at work, and employer "tolerance."

Fraser and colleagues examined the vocational status of 48 survivors of head injury 1 year after injury.[32] In this group whose injuries varied a great deal in severity, 73% of subjects who were working at the time of injury had returned to employment at 1-year follow-up. Compared to the employed subjects, the unemployed subjects had sustained deeper and longer coma. Furthermore, neuropsychologic evaluation at 1 month after onset revealed significantly more impairment among unemployed subjects on the great majority of tasks; differences were especially pronounced on measures of motor speed, cognitive flexibility, visuospatial problem solving, and the Impairment Index, a summary measure computed from the core tests of the Halstead-Reitan Battery,[8] which is purported to be a reflection of general brain integrity. Average performance IQ among the unemployed group was 20 points below that of the employed group. It should be noted that, of those who had returned to work, 40% were reporting "head injury-related difficulties." This study provides additional evidence of the predictive value of neuropsychologic assessment.

Even comparatively mild head trauma can produce vocational disability. Rimel and associates studied patients who had been hospitalized fewer than 48 hours, who had not been unconscious more than 20 minutes, and whose score on the Glasgow Coma Scale had been at least 13.[1] Three months after discharge, one third of these patients had not yet returned to work. Involvement in litigation was not a factor; indeed, all patients who were involved in legal action had returned to work.

Wrightson and Gronwall followed 66 patients with minor head trauma, some for as long as 2 years.[33] All but three had experienced post-traumatic amnesia for 9 hours or less. All patients were back at work within 1 month. When questioned 90 days after the injury, 60% reported that they had experienced postconcussional symptoms (eg, headache, irritability, sensitivity to noise, impaired memory and/or concentration) upon return to work. Nearly one half reported that they were initially unable to work at their former capacity. The longer patients remained out of work, the less likely they were to exhibit symptoms upon their return. Although this may reflect the natural history of recovery from concussion, it may also be, as Wrightson and Gronwall suggested, that symptoms develop when patients return to work prematurely and overtax their reduced capacity. Whatever the explanation, clinicians working with patients who have sustained minor head trauma should urge caution and a phased resumption of work, if possible.

WORK-RELATED NEUROPSYCHOLOGIC ASSESSMENT

It is difficult to do more than sketch broad outlines for the content of a work-related neuropsychologic evaluation for at least two reasons. First, as noted by Heaton and Pendleton,[6] as well as by Chelune and Moehle,[34] the sizable variability in the cognitive demands of jobs dictates a flexible assessment approach. Thus, the appropriate content of an individual work-related neuropsychologic assessment depends on such factors as the nature of the job in question, the diagnostic entity, and tests that may have been previously administered by other clinicians.

Second, as Long, Gouvier, and Cole observed,[35] the content of a given assessment should be varied according to the phase of the particular patient's illness. At earlier stages, assessment of basic skills (eg, attention, visual tracking) may constitute the core of the evaluation, whereas later evaluations are likely to involve more complex problem-solving tasks (eg, Wisconsin Card Sorting Test).[36] Some degree of overlap is advisable, as it permits the clinician to draw inferences about the rate and extent of change, whether it be improvement (as typically happens with stroke or head trauma) or decline (as occurs in multi-infarct dementia or multiple sclerosis). Thus, even the earliest neuropsychologic assessment may be considered, in some sense, a "prevocational evaluation."

Preassessment Information Gathering

Before commencing formal assessment, the clinician is well advised to gather information regarding the patient's medical and psychiatric history, education level, occupational history (including specific duties and responsibilities), as well as possible exposure to toxic substances, avocational interests, personality, and social-emotional functioning. In this endeavor, such instruments as the General Health Questionnaire,[37] Minnesota Multiphasic Personality Inventory,[38] and Millon Behavioral Health Inventory[39] offer useful standardized measures with special applicability to medically ill individuals.

It is often revealing to have the patient and a close relative complete the same questionnaires and/or rating scales with respect to the patient's functioning. The Katz Adjustment Scale,[40] Cognitive Failures Questionnaire,[41] and the Patient Assessment of Own Functioning Inventory[42] have been found useful in this regard. The Sickness Impact Profile permits an assessment of the patient's (and/or family's) view of the effect of the patient's condition on his or her physical and psychosocial functioning.[43] Kay and Silver argued that the accuracy of the patient's perceptions regarding his or her own cognitive status can be an important predictor of vocational readiness.[4]

During the preassessment interview, the clinician should inquire about any emotional, physical, or other stressors that may affect the patient's ability to concentrate. Information should be obtained regarding the patient's current medications and alcohol usage because of their possible impact on test performance. It is often valuable to review potentially critical questionnaire items and to request elaboration. This discussion can also serve as a forum in which the clinician can explain the purpose of the evaluation more fully and can develop the needed rapport with the patient.

Neuropsychologic Test Procedures

In view of the relative paucity of studies relating neuropsychologic abilities to particular job performances, determining the vocational implications of test performance requires, at this time, some rather large inferential leaps. Furthermore, most neuropsychologic measures are multifactorial in nature; pure measures of hypothetical cognitive constructs simply do not exist.

Attention

Basic orientation is presumed to be intact in individuals who are referred for work-related evaluation. The global concept of attention has been divided into several models or schemata. For example, Sohlberg and Mateer described five varieties of attentional function: (1) focused attention, (2) sustained attention, (3) selective attention, (4) alternating attention, and (5) divided attention.[44] Van Zomeren, Brouwer, and Deelman distinguished among selective attention, alertness, and speed of information processing, observing that the latter was particularly susceptible to the effects of head injury.[45] Expanding on work by Weintraub and Mesulam on the ''attentional matrix,''[46,47] Auerbach posited five aspects of the ''mental control complex'': (1) arousal and alertness, (2) vigilance, (3) ability to shift set, (4) ability to inhibit inappropriate shifts, and (5) speed of processing.[48] Formal tests of attention frequently engage more than one of these processes.

Although simple measures of attention/concentration ability (eg, Digit Span,[15] Visual Cancellation[47]) may be administered during early examinations, more complex, lengthy, and cognitively demanding tasks are likely to give more vocationally relevant information. One such measure is Gronwall's Paced Auditory Serial Addition Task,[49] which requires the individual to listen to a series of 60 digits, presented at a rate of one every 1 to 2 seconds, and to add each adjacent pair of numbers. For instance, upon hearing the numbers 5-3-4-6, the subject should respond, ''8-7-10.'' The Trail Making Test, which requires the subject to connect numbers in sequence (part A) or to alternate between number and letter series (part B), demands sustained attention, as well as conceptual flexibility and psychomotor speed.[11] Vigilance tasks, such as that on the Continuous Performance Test, provide valuable information about the subject's sustained attention abilities.[50] This task requires the subject to monitor a changing display of letters and to respond only when a particular target appears; the complexity of the task may be increased by instructing the subject to respond only to a particular sequence of letters.

The clinician must be aware of the limitations of formal assessment of attentional capacity. Some patients may be able to attend adequately when confronted with a series of brief tasks in a quiet testing room, but reveal disabling distractibility when required to work in a more chaotic environment that approximates real world conditions. Certainly, however, patients who have difficulty with formal measures of attentional capacity administered under ideal conditions are unlikely to be good job candidates.

Verbal/Cognitive Ability

Included in the sphere of language function or, more broadly, verbal/cognitive ability are such skills as reading, vocabulary, verbal fluency, comprehension, repetition, verbal reasoning, and problem solving. It should not be assumed that aphasic patients, because of their verbal difficulties, are not viable vocational candidates.[20] The cognitive abilities of these individuals can be assessed meaningfully with measures that require responses of pointing (eg, Raven Matrices[51,52]), constructing (eg, Wechsler Adult Intelligence Scale-Revised [WAIS-R] Block Design[15]), arranging (eg, WAIS-R Picture Arrangement), or drawing (eg, Complex Figure Test[53]).

A relatively simple but often informative measure of verbal/cognitive ability is the verbal fluency (Controlled Oral Word Association) test, which requires the subject to produce within 1-minute periods as many words as possible that begin with a particular letter of the alphabet or belong to a given category (eg, four-legged animals).[54] This task provides information about the patient's speed of response, vocabulary, ability to initiate an activity and maintain the proper mental set, and semantic memory. It also gives some insight into the patient's strategy selection. For example, some patients give words with the same prefix (eg, *pro*fess, *pro*vide, *pro*test).

Expressive vocabulary may be measured by the vocabulary subtest of the WAIS-R, which requires the subject to generate definitions of words.[15] This test is often considered a fairly accurate index of premorbid ability in nonaphasic patients. For individuals with an expressive deficit, a more accurate appraisal of their vocabulary ability may be obtained with the multiple-choice vocabulary portion of the Shipley Institute of Living Scale.[55]

Clearly, an individual's vocabulary and reading skills are major determinants of vocational placement. Oral reading of single words can be measured with the Wide Range Achievement Test-Revised,[56] which has a large type edition available, or with the Reading Recognition subtest of the Peabody Individual Achievement Test.[57] Tests to measure reading at the sentence and paragraph levels include the Boston Diagnostic Aphasia Examination,[58] Gray Oral Reading Tests,[59] and the Gates-MacGinitie Reading Test.[60]

Many jobs require employees to fill orders or to take telephone messages. The clinician must evaluate the capacity of head-injured individuals interested in these jobs to repeat auditorially presented information. The repetition subtest of the Neurosensory Center Comprehensive Examination for Aphasia requires the patient to repeat sentences of gradually increasing length after they are spoken by the examiner.[61] The multilingual Aphasia Examination also has a repetition test.[62] The Minnesota Test for Differential Diagnosis of Aphasia contains a set of sentences to be read by the examiner and written by the patient.[63] The patient's ability to write—both spontaneously and in response to dictation—should be evaluated as well.

The WAIS-R contains several subtests that measure aspects of verbal reasoning ability. The Similarities subtest requires patients to detect conceptual relations between pairs of items; although they receive credit for correct concrete answers, they earn higher scores for more abstract responses. The Comprehension subtest evaluates social judgment and reasoning, as well as proverb interpretation. In interpreting the results of this test, the clinician is well advised to keep in mind Lezak's caveat. She pointed out the distinction between the ability

> to give reasonable-sounding responses to these structured questions dealing with single delimited issues and the judgment needed to handle complex, multi-dimensional real-life situations. In real life, the exercise of judgment typically involves defining, conceptualizing, structuring,

and delimiting the issue that requires judgment, as well as rendering an action-oriented decision about it. Thus, as demonstrated most vividly by many patients with right hemisphere lesions, high scores on Comprehension are no guarantee of practical common sense or reasonable behavior.[64]

More pertinent information may perhaps be garnered by asking patients personally relevant questions dealing with their awareness and understanding of their current condition, as well as their plans for avocational and vocational activity. In truth, there are no adequate, standardized, empirically validated measures of judgment, insight, and reasoning.[65,66]

Other useful measures of verbal/cognitive problem-solving ability include the Abstraction section of the Shipley Institute of Living Scale, which requires the subjects to determine the missing term in a series of letter and number sequences,[55] and the Verbal Concept Attainment Test, which is a verbal reasoning task composed of a set of cards, each containing several lines of printed words.[67] The subject must determine those words, one in each line, that are related in some way.

Visual-Perceptual and Visual-Constructional Ability

Integral to many jobs, both skilled and unskilled, are visual-perceptual and visual-constructional skills. The adequacy of the individual's visual scanning may be assessed by tests, such as visual cancellation,[46,68] reading,[69] or line bisection. Lateral attentional bias (ie, "visual neglect") may be revealed on visual problem-solving tasks, such as the Raven Matrices[51,52] or Matching Familiar Figures Test.[70] These tests, which require analysis and/or completion of patterns or objects, have a multiple-choice format, with the response alternatives arrayed in two rows of three items each. Patients with neglect tend to make their selections from the column ipsilateral to the hemisphere that has the lesion. Although these tasks require scanning, it is not the most salient skill involved, and some patients who compensate for neglect under less cognitively demanding conditions exhibit inattention on these measures. As the cognitive requirements of these tasks are more complex than are those of a cancellation task—thereby more nearly approximating real-world conditions—patients who manifest neglect on these tasks may be more likely to have difficulty with daily life activities in which scanning is an important, although secondary, consideration (eg, operating heavy machinery, driving a car).

Benton and colleagues developed two tasks that have potential vocational relevance.[71] The Line Orientation Test requires the subject to select the one item in an array of line segments that has the same angular inclination as the target line. The Face Recognition Test is a match-to-sample task in which the faces depicted in the response alternatives are presented from perspectives that differ from that of the target face. Clearly, this test taps a central skill for salespeople, many health care workers, and politicians!

Other visual-perceptual skills that ought to be evaluated include perception of detail (WAIS-R Picture Completion), figure-ground discrimination (Embedded Figures Test[72]), and visual organization and synthesis (Hooper Visual Organization Test[73]).

Individuals with a perceptual deficit may perform poorly on visual-constructional measures purely by virtue of their perceptual limitations. Although a constructional impairment may coexist with a perceptual impairment, the relative contributions of the two factors must be established. For example, the WAIS-R Block Design subtest, probably the most widely employed constructional measure, requires the subject to produce two-dimensional designs by assembling three-dimensional red and white blocks. Subjects who misperceive the designs create erroneous constructions. In order to isolate the impact of perceptual deficit, Bolla-Wilson and associates developed multiple-choice forms of the Block Design and Object Assembly subtests.[74] Individuals who perform well under this format, although exhibiting difficulty with the standard version, probably have a visual-constructional deficit that is not due to impaired perception. Other measures of constructional abilities include Benton's three-dimensional block construction task[71] and the Tinker Toy Test.[64]

Tests of drawing ability are usually classified as constructional tasks. The subject's performance on the copy administration of the Complex Figure Test,[73,75] which requires the subject to copy a complicated design, may be classified according to Osterrieth's typology of plans of action (eg, a carefully organized systematic approach, piecemeal reproduction of individual details with little overall structure).[75] Strub, Black, and Leventhal found that very simple designs lack clinical sensitivity, whereas more complex patterns were useful with patients of average premorbid intelligence.[76]

Memory

Of all cognitive processes, memory function is most commonly affected by head injury. Impaired memory is certainly the most disabling intellectual consequence of brain dysfunction, and much of the rehabilitation process for head-injured patients revolves around new learning or relearning. Given the multiplicity of processes involved in acquiring and retaining new information[77] and the several types of memory (eg, short-term, remote, echoic, procedural), a detailed analysis of this domain is warranted. Thus, an adequate neuropsychologic assessment not only should determine whether the patient has a memory impairment but also should clarify any defective aspect that is identified (eg, inattention, impaired comprehension or encoding, rapid decay, or retrieval failure). The effects of cueing (eg, providing the initial letter or category) should be examined, as well as the relative levels of impairment of free recall and recognition memory. As Caplan noted,

> If a patient cannot spontaneously recall a list of words, but can recognize them when they are embedded in a longer list, and can distinguish between material that was previously presented and that which was not, this pattern of performance suggests adequate attention, comprehension, encoding, and storage, but defective retrieval.[78]

If the clinician suspects that impaired attention is the primary determinant of the patient's poor performance on memory tasks, there are test paradigms that will negate the impact of this deficit by guaranteeing attention to, and processing of, the memoranda.[79–81] In Buschke's procedure, each target word is associated with a category, and the patient must identify specific items of the category (eg, color, food) in the list.[79] After the subject spontaneously recalls as many items as possible, categorical cues are provided for each item not retrieved. Warrington's two-part recognition memory test requires the individual to examine a series of 50 words or 50 faces and to state whether their associations with each item are pleasant or unpleasant.[81] No instruction is given to retain the information. A forced-choice paradigm is then administered in which 50 pairs of words or faces are displayed, and the individual must state which item was in the original list.

Serial Digit Learning requires the patient to learn an eight- or nine-digit series that is repeatedly read (to a maximum of 12 trials) by the examiner.[71] This task provides some information about the rate at which the subject learns, although its ecologic validity has yet to be demonstrated.

The Wechsler Memory Scale-Revised assesses the patient's immediate and delayed recall of both verbal and figural information, as well as paired associate learning procedures. Other measures of visual memory include the Benton Visual Retention Test[82] and the Complex Figure Test.[53,71] Remote memory is generally measured by the Information subtest of the WAIS-R, although there are other measures.[83–85] Intact remote memory may not affect rehabilitation, however, and historical recollection is often preserved in patients with severely defective learning ability.

The Randt Memory Battery is especially valuable in the rehabilitation setting.[86] Some subtests resemble those of the Wechsler Memory Scale, but there are five parallel forms of the Randt, which makes serial evaluation possible. Furthermore, because four subtests are readministered during the initial session and again following a 24-hour delay, the Randt provides recall measures over both brief and extended intervals. As successful rehabilitation requires the patient to carry over skills from one day to the next, these measures are quite important.

In discussing the ecologic validity of conventional memory tests, Sunderland, Harris, and Baddeley posed the question, "Do laboratory tests predict everyday memory?"[87] The answer appears to be, "We don't know." Three measures seem to possess at least surface ecologic validity. The Misplaced Objects Task was devised to study memory function in elderly patients.[88] The subject is instructed to place representations of 10 common objects in various locations on a schematic drawing of a seven-room house. Following an interval of 5 to 30 minutes, the individual is asked to recall the locations of the objects. The Rivermead Behavioural Memory Test measures a number of everyday memory functions, such as recall of names, faces, appointments, and routes.[89] This instrument appears to hold much promise, but large-scale, systematic investigations have not yet been reported. The California Verbal Learning Test is a carefully structured learning task comprising four shopping list items from each of four categories.[90] The clinician reads the list five times and then reads a parallel distractor list. Short-term recall for the original list is then tested, and the effects of cueing and a recognition paradigm are evaluated. Longer term memory (approximately 30 minutes) is also assessed via free recall, cueing, and recognition formats. Information may be derived on the subject's recall strategies, such as the extent to which items from the same category (eg, food, clothing) are clustered.

Executive Functions

The set of processes subsumed under the rubric of "metacognitive" skills include the abilities to formulate plans and intentions, to carry out activities in pursuit of a goal, to monitor one's own performance, to detect and correct one's errors, and to utilize existing knowledge effectively to guide behavior.[91,92] The self-structuring and organizational processes required by measures of executive functions may well be associated with an individual's ability to resume and maintain independent employment.[93]

Although it is admittedly difficult to obtain quantitative measures of executive functions, Lezak and others have suggested several measures that demand these skills—the Porteus Mazes, the Complex Figure Test, the Executive Functioning Route Finding Task, the Tinker Toy Test, and the Tower of Hanoi.[64,92,94,95] The Category Test, a visually presented concept formation task, requires mental flexibility, as well as the ability to formulate, test, and revise hypotheses after performance on the basis of feedback from the examiner.[8] This test is somewhat lengthy, but its complex, multifactorial character makes it especially valuable in the prediction of performance of multifaceted vocational tasks.[10] The Wisconsin Card Sorting Test demands many of the same cognitive skills as the Category Test, but it incorporates unannounced conceptual shifts that the subject must detect and that must prompt a new hypothesis.[36]

According to Kay and Silver, a qualitative evaluation of the patient's test-taking behavior may be the best source of information.[4] Even though actual test scores provide invaluable information, the skilled examiner can detect useful clues to ultimate vocational performance by carefully observing the patient during the test. The clinician should observe the patient's level of effort and persistence, capacity to detect and self-correct errors, frustration tolerance on more difficult items, strategy selection, and modifications, for example.

Limiting Factors

Extracting everyday implications from neuropsychologic test data is an art, not a science. A significant aspect of the neuropsychologist's art is the ability to integrate qualitative observations of the patient's test-taking behavior with the quantitative data.[4] Kay and Silver noted several factors that conspire to limit the vocational inferences that can be drawn from neuropsychologic testing, however: the higher structured, unambiguous, and nondistracting nature of the testing environment; the comparative lack of pressure; and the emphasis on overlearned, "crystallized" skills.[4]

The clinician must consider a number of factors when analyzing and interpreting test scores. Because of the problems in determining the ecologic validity of neuropsychologic test instruments and the dearth of criterion-related validation studies, clinicians must rely on common sense and clinical judgment in extrapolating predictions about on-the-job achievement from test performance—at least for the foreseeable future. As Heaton and Pendleton pointed out,[6] impairment of new learning may not be vocationally disabling for an individual who is required to execute only operations and procedures learned *prior to* the onset of brain dysfunction. Situations that require problem-solving ability in a new employee may evoke relatively automatic responses in an experienced employee.

Test results must be interpreted with reference to existing normative data. As certain demographic factors (eg, age, education, sex) affect neuropsychologic test performance,[96–98] normative data bases should include adjustments for the operation of these factors, singly or in combination. Regrettably, the existing data bases for most such tests do not possess this feature. Thus, in attempting to determine the (ab)normality of a given performance by an 80-year-old man with a sixth-grade education, the clinician must often extrapolate from the average score of a 60-year-old man with a high-school education; here again, experience and clinical judgment enter the equation.

Another current problem is the scarcity of parallel forms of most tests. In order to conduct valid serial evaluations, clinicians need equivalent, nonoverlapping forms that minimize learning effects. Although an increasing number of measures (eg, Serial Digit Learning, Randt Memory Battery, Verbal Fluency) have parallel forms available, most tests do not yet include parallel forms. Also, with some tasks (eg, WAIS-R Block Design), learning effects may be unavoidable; once the subject grasps certain strategies and maneuvers, the presentation of different patterns to be constructed does not, in itself, constitute a parallel form.

In attempting to determine whether a patient is likely to be able to maintain or to resume a former position, it would be helpful to know how the patient's current performance compares with his or her premorbid status. As most subjects have not been tested before the onset of brain dysfunction, the clinician must employ other methods, such as inferring premorbid level from current performance on tests felt to be lesion-resistant or deriving estimates from regression equations based on certain demographic variables.[64,99–101]

The possibility of malingering must occasionally be considered, especially when the test data do not make "neuropsychologic sense." It may be especially pertinent in workers' compensation or personal injury cases. The identification of malingering patients on the basis of test results can be quite difficult, however. Heaton and associates asked 10 experienced neuropsychologists to evaluate the test results of 60 volunteer malingerers and 16 head trauma patients.[102] The judges correctly classified 25% to 81% of malingerers and 44% to 81% of head trauma cases. These investigators stated that the profile characteristics of the two groups differed, with malingerers performing especially poorly on tests of motor and sensory function, but relatively well on several of the most lesion-sensitive tasks (eg, Category Test, Trail Making Test [Part B], Tactual Performance Test). Malingerers also obtained high scores on the F (validity) scale of the Minnesota Multiphasic Personality Inventory.

The lesson from recent research on the consequences of minor head injury is that clinicians must be quite cautious about invoking malingering as an explanation of deficient performance. Following a review of persisting symptoms after mild head trauma—symptoms that were formerly thought to be hysterical or intentional—Binder concluded that postinjury cognitive or behavioral pathology is often a direct consequence of neuroanatomic and/or neuropsychologic insult, rather than malingering.[103] If malingering is suspected, testing should be repeated and the patient's performance on the two occasions compared for gross discrepancies. Binder and Pankratz suggested a simple technique (Symptom Validity Testing) that may help the clinician to detect factitious disorders.[104] This procedure employs a two-choice forced response paradigm in which a 50% "hit rate" is expected by chance alone; significant negative deviations from chance suggest willful failure. Ultimately, however, the determination of malingering hinges on clinical judgment; as Binder observed, "There are no empirically validated objective criteria for the identification of malingering on neuropsychological testing."[103]

DISPOSITION OF RESULTS

Patient/Family Discussion

Findings from a work-oriented neuropsychologic assessment can form the basis for education of the patient and the family regarding the cognitive consequences of the patient's condition. Good clinical practice and common sense dictate a feedback session with the patient and family members in which the neuropsychologist describes the domains of spared and impaired function, with illustrative examples, and renders an informed professional opinion about the likely implications for daily life activities, including return to work. The importance of this aspect of the neuropsychologist's role cannot be overemphasized; the most comprehensive neuropsychologic evaluation is meaningless if the patient and the family leave the consultation room without the best possible understanding of the results of that evaluation. Furthermore, as Lezak noted, patients and families must be encouraged to make their own decision, as they are the ones who must live with the consequences of those decisions.[105] Although the neuropsychologist's data, impressions, and opinions should be taken into account, any suggestion that a neuropsychologist or other rehabilitation clinician should make such significant decisions for a patient reflects a hubris that is not warranted by the state of the neuropsychologic art.

Referral for Neuropsychologic Rehabilitation

Test results may offer clues to the appropriate individualized neuropsychologic rehabilitation program, which itself may be a prologue to a return to work. Neuropsychologic rehabilitation is an attempt to ameliorate acquired higher cortical dysfunctions through the use of specifically targeted interventions.[106] Techniques include rote drill, the learning of compensatory strategies, functional substitution, and "environmental prostheses," such as computer-based memory banks.[78]

Prigatano and associates defined "vocational successes" as those patients who had been productive (ie, gainfully employed at least part-time or enrolled in school) during at least 75% of the time since discharge from the rehabilitation program.[107] Of the 18 patients, 9 met this criterion. The successful group and the unsuccessful group did not differ significantly on any of the measures of neuropsychologic function; relatives' ratings of emotional and motivational state did, however, distinguish between the two groups. Subsequently, Prigatano described a modification of the neuropsychologic rehabilitation program in which work trials were instituted during the afternoon portions of the rehabilitation program.[108] He asserted that this modification has resulted in roughly a 70% return-to-work rate.

Similarly, Ben-Yishay and associates included occupational trials in their holistic neuropsychologic rehabilitation program for head trauma patients.[109] They reported that, 3 months after the start of these trials, 76% of their patients were rated as employable in the open market (25% of these were deemed to be employable in subsidized or part-time capacities), 11% were felt to be candidates for sheltered workshops, and 13% were considered unemployable. In a subsequent report, Ben-Yishay and colleagues described the regrettable dynamic character of employability ratings.[110] By the end of the occupational trials, only 6% were judged to be unemployable in any capacity; 18 months later, this figure had nearly tripled; by 36 months, 28% were rated unemployable. Thus, although the program initially appeared to be successful, a significant proportion of subjects failed to maintain their maximum levels of vocational capacity.

A practical approach to neuropsychologically based vocational rehabilitation may involve the teaching of domain-specific knowledge. This technique is best exemplified by the work of Glisky, Schacter, and Tulving, who demonstrated that head trauma patients with memory impairment were able to learn particular functions involved in the operation of a microcomputer.[111] This is an approach that warrants additional research.

Job Restructuring

The results of a neuropsychologic evaluation may be used as the basis for restructuring particular job functions in order to reduce the disability caused by persisting neuropsychologic dysfunction. For example, because of impaired memory, a clerk whose job was to handle telephone inquiries from customers had difficulty remembering which questions he was to ask in order to elicit the necessary information from the customer.[112] When he was provided with an outline to follow, the clerk was able to obtain pertinent information from customers in a systematic fashion. This strategy also allowed him to record and store (on paper) customers' responses until he was prepared to address their problems.

Raderstorf and colleagues described the case of a 30-year-old machinist who was able to return to his previous job after a head injury, despite severe aphasia and right hemiparesis.[113] Major factors in the patient's successful return were his high level of motivation and the coordinated effort by the rehabilitation team, the patient, and the employer; rehabilitation therapy structured with vocational return in mind, including a simulated work program during occupational therapy; employer accommodation (eg, initial return on a part-time basis to a related, but not identical job); and the encouragement of co-workers.

Test findings may also alert job coaches or supervisors to cognitive areas that may prove problematic for the patient upon return to work.

Disability Determination

Finally, the results of neuropsychologic assessment may help to establish the individual's eligibility for Social Security Disability payments. In brief, in order to qualify for disability payments, the claimant must exhibit ''loss of specific cognitive abilities or affective changes and the medically documented persistence"[114] of at least one of several specific psychologic or behavioral abnormalities associated with brain dysfunction (eg, disorientation, memory impairment, personality change, emotional lability, perceptual or thought disturbance). Furthermore, such impairment must disrupt at least two of the following: daily life activities, maintenance of social function, completion of tasks in a timely manner, and job performance. Puente made a strong case for the importance of the neuropsychologist's role in disability evaluation.[115]

SUMMARY

The traditional function of the neuropsychologist has been a diagnostic one. In recent years, however, increasing demands have been placed on neuropsychologists to make their data serve prescriptive, remedial, and predictive purposes. Given that this is still a nascent enterprise, extravagant claims for the predictive power of neuropsychologic tests must be avoided. Furthermore, in educating and advising patients and families, neuropsychologists must take into account the effects of situational factors on task performance, both in the testing room and in the real world.

Despite these caveats, neuropsychologic data can provide an objective basis for characterizing a head-injured patient's cognitive functioning, documenting the course of recovery, advising the patient and the family about the possible vocational implications of neuropsychologic deficits, and guiding the design of intervention programs. In these ways, neuropsychologic evaluation can make a valuable contribution to the assessment, treatment, and vocational rehabilitation of cognitively impaired workers.

REFERENCES

1. Rimel RW, Giordani B, Barth JR, et al. Disability caused by minor head injury. *Neurosurgery*. 1981;9:221–228.

2. Brooks N, McKinlay W, Symington S, et al. Return to work within the first seven years of severe head injury. *Brain Injury*. 1987;1:5–19.

3. Hart T, Hayden ME. The ecological validity of neuropsychological assessment and remediation. In: Uzzell B, Gross Y, eds. *Clinical Neuropsychology of Intervention*. Boston: Martinis Nijhoff Publishing; 1986:21–50.

4. Kay T, Silver SM. The contribution of the neuropsychological evaluation to the vocational rehabilitation of the head-injured adult. *J Head Trauma Rehabil* 1988;3:65–76.

5. Sternberg R, Wagner R. *Practical Intelligence*. New York: Cambridge University Press; 1986.

6. Heaton R, Pendleton M. Use of neuropsychological tests to predict adult patients' everyday functioning. *J Consult Clin Psychol*. 1981;49:807–821.

7. Heaton R, Chelune G, Lehman R. Using neuropsychological and personality tests to assess the likelihood of patient employment. *J Nerv Ment Dis*. 1978;166:408–416.

8. Reitan RM, Davison LA, eds. *Clinical Neuropsychology: Current Status and Applications.* New York: Winston/Wiley; 1974.

9. Dikmen S, Morgan S. Neuropsychological factors related to employability and occupational status in persons with epilepsy. *J Nerv Ment Dis.* 1980;168:236–240.

10. Morris J, Ryan JJ, Peterson RA. Neuropsychological predictors of vocational behavior. Presented at the American Psychological Association; 1982; Washington, DC.

11. Reitan RM. Validity of the Trail Making Test as an indicator of organic brain damage. *Percept Mot Skills.* 1958;8:271–275.

12. Becker C, Yatsu FM, Howard G, et al. Three comprehensive stroke center programs: demographic description of hospitalized stroke patients in North Carolina, Oregon, and New York. *Stroke.* 1986;17:285–293.

13. Yatsu FM, Becker C, McLeroy KR, et al. Community hospital-based stroke programs: North Carolina, Oregon, and New York: I. goals, objectives and data collection procedures. *Stroke.* 1986;17:276–284.

14. Weisbroth S, Esibill N, Zuger R. Factors in the vocational success of hemiplegic patients. *Arch Phys Med Rehabil.* 1971;52:441–446.

15. Wechsler D. *Wechsler Adult Intelligence Scale-Revised: Manual.* New York: Psychological Corp; 1981.

16. Gresham G, Phillips T, Wolf P, et al. Epidemiologic profile of long-term stroke disability: the Framingham study. *Arch Phys Med Rehabil.* 1979;60:487–491.

17. Christie D. Aftermath of stroke: an epidemiological study in Melbourne, Australia. *J Epidemiol Community Health.* 1982;36:123–162.

18. Smolkin C, Cohen S. Socioeconomic factors affecting the vocational success of stroke patients. *Arch Phys Med Rehabil.* 1974;55:269–271.

19. Howard G, Stanwood T, Toole JF, et al. Factors influencing return to work following cerebral infarction. *JAMA.* 1985;253:226–232.

20. Carriero MR, Faglia L, Vignolo LA. Resumption of gainful employment in aphasics: preliminary findings. *Cortex.* 1987;26:667–672.

21. US Department of Education, Office of Special Education and Rehabilitation Services. Head injury: The problem, the need. *Programs for the Handicapped.* 1982;6:1–3.

22. Rimel RW, Jane JL. Characteristics of the head-injured patient. In: Rosenthal M, Griffith E, Bond M, et al, eds. *Rehabilitation of the Head Injured Adult.* Philadelphia: FA Davis; 1983:9–21.

23. Lynch RT. Traumatic head injury: implications for rehabilitation counseling. *J Appl Rehabil Couns.* 1983;3:32–35.

24. Humphrey M, Oddy M. Return to work after head injury: a review of post-war studies. *Injury.* 1981;12:107–114.

25. Dresser A, Meirowsky A, Weiss G, et al. Gainful employment following head injury. *Arch Neurol.* 1973;29:111–116.

26. Najenson T, Groswasser J, Mendelson L, et al. Rehabilitation outcome of brain damaged patients after severe head injury. *Int Rehabil Med.* 1980;2:17–22.

27. Thomsen IV. Late outcome of very severe blunt head trauma: a 10–15 year second follow-up. *J Neurol Neurosurg Psychiatry.* 1984;47:260–268.

28. Oddy M, Humphrey M, Uttley D. Subjective impairment and social recovery after closed head injury. *J Neurol Neurosurg Psychiatry.* 1978;41:611–616.

29. Weddell R, Oddy M, Jenkins D. Social adjustment after rehabilitation: a two year follow-up of patients with severe head injury. *Psychol Med.* 1980;10:257–263.

30. van Zomeren AH, van den Burg, W. Residual complaints of patients two years after severe head injury. *J Neurol Neurosurg Psychiatry.* 1985;48:21–28.

31. Johnson R. Return to work after severe head injury. *Int Dis Stud.* 1987;9:49–54.

32. Fraser R, Dikmen S, McLean A, et al. Employability of head injury survivors: first year post injury. *Rehabil Counsel Bull.* In press.

33. Wrightson P, Gronwall D. Time off work and symptoms after minor head injury. *Injury.* 1981;12:445–454.

34. Chelune G, Moehle K. Neuropsychological assessment and everyday functioning. In: Wedding D, Horton A, Webster J, eds. *The Neuropsychology Handbook; Behavioral and Clinical Perspectives.* New York: Springer; 1986:489–525.

35. Long C, Gouvier W, Cole J. A model of recovery for the total rehabilitation of individuals with head trauma. *J Rehabil.* 1984;50:39–45.

36. Heaton R. *Wisconsin Card Sorting Test: Manual.* Odessa, FL: Psychological Assessment Resources; 1981:50.

37. Goldberg D: *Manual of the General Health Questionnaire.* London: NFER-Nelson; 1978.

38. Dahlstrom WG, Welsh GS, Dahlstrom LE. *An MMPI Handbook: I. Clinical Interpretation* (rev ed). Minneapolis: University of Minnesota Press; 1975.

39. Millon T, Green CJ. A new psychodiagnostic tool for clients in rehabilitation settings: the MBHI. *Rehabil Psychol.* 1982;27:23–35.

40. Katz MM, Lyerly SB. Methods for measuring adjustment and social behavior in the community: I. rationale, description, discriminative validity and scale development. *Psychol Rep.* 1963;13:503–535.

41. Broadbent DE, Cooper PF, FitzGerald P, et al. The Cognitive Failures Questionnaire (CFQ) and its correlates. *Br J Clin Psychol.* 1982;21:1–16.

42. Chelune GJ, Heaton RK, Lehman RAW. Neuropsychological and personality correlates of patients' complaints of disability. In: Golstein G, Tarter RE, eds. *Advances in Clinical Neuropsychology: III.* New York: Plenum Press; 1986:95–126.

43. Bergner M, Bobbitt RA, Pollard WE. The Sickness Impact Profile: validation of a health status measure. *Med Care.* 1976;14:57–67.

44. Sohlberg MM, Mateer CA. Effectiveness of an attention-training program. *J Clin Exp Neuropsychol.* 1987;9:117–130.

45. van Zomeren AH, Brouwer WH, Deelman BG. Attentional deficits: the riddles of selectivity, speed and alertness. In: Brooks N, ed. *Closed Head Injury: Psychological, Social and Family Consequences.* New York: Oxford University Press; 1984:74–107.

46. Mesulam M. Attention, confusional states, and neglect. In: Mesulam M, ed. *Principles of Behavioral Neurology.* Philadelphia: FA Davis; 1985:125–168.

47. Weintraub S, Mesulam MM. Mental state assessment of young and elderly adults in behavioral neurology. In: Mesulam, M, ed *Principles of Behavioral Neurology.* Philadelphia: FA Davis; 1985:71–124.

48. Auerbach SH. Neuroanatomical correlates of attention and memory disorders in traumatic brain injury: an application of neurobehavioral subtypes. *J Head Trauma Rehabil.* 1986;1:1–12.

49. Gronwall D. Paced Auditory Serial-Addition Task: a measure of recovery from concussion. *Percept Mot Skills.* 1977;44:367–373.

50. Rosvold H, Mirsky A, Sarason I, et al. A Continuous Performance Test of brain damage. *J Consult Psychol.* 1956;20:343–350.

51. Raven JC. *Guide to Standard Progressive Matrices.* London: HK Lewis; 1960.

52. Raven JC. *Guide to using the Coloured Progressive Matrices*. London: HK Lewis; 1965.

53. Visser RSH. *Manual of the Complex Figure Test*. Amsterdam: Swets & Zeitlinger BV; 1973.

54. Borkowski JD, Benton AL, Spreen O. Word fluency and brain damage. *Neuropsychologia*. 1967;5:135–140.

55. Zachary R. *Shipley Institute of Living Scale-Revised: Manual*. Los Angeles: Western Psychological Services; 1986.

56. Jastak S, Wilkinson G. *Wide Range Achievement Test: Manual*. Wilmington, DE: Jastak Associates; 1984.

57. Dunn LM, Markwardt FC Jr. *Peabody Individual Achievement Test—Manual*. Circle Pines, MN: American Guidance Service; 1970.

58. Goodglass H, Kaplan E. *The assessment of Aphasia and Related Disorders*, 2nd ed. Philadelphia: Lea & Febiger; 1983.

59. Wiederholt JL, Bryant B. *Gray Oral Reading Tests—Revised Manual*. Odessa, FL: Psychological Assessment Resources; 1986.

60. Gates AI, MacGinitie WH. *Gates-MacGinitie Reading Test*. New York: Teachers College Press; 1965/1969.

61. Spreen O, Benton AL. *Neurosensory Center Comprehensive Examination for Aphasia*. Victoria, British Columbia: Neuropsychology Laboratory, Department of Psychology, University of Victoria, 1969.

62. Benton A, Hamsher K. *Multilingual Aphasia Examination*. Iowa City: University of Iowa; 1978.

63. Schuell HM. *Minnesota Test for Differential Diagnosis of Aphasia* (rev ed). Minneapolis: University of Minnesota Press; 1972.

64. Lezak MD. *Neuropsychological Assessment*, 2nd ed. New York: Oxford University Press; 1983.

65. Kaplan KH. Assessing judgment. *Gen Hosp Psychiatry*. 1988;9:202–208.

66. Roca R. Bedside cognitive examination. *Psychosomatics*. 1987;28:71–76.

67. Bornstein RA. A factor analytic study of the construct validity of the Verbal Concept Attainment Test. *J Clin Neuropsychol*. 1982;4:43–50.

68. Weinberg J, Diller L, Gordon WA, et al. Visual scanning training: effect on reading-related tasks in acquired right brain damage. *Arch Phys Med Rehabil*. 1977;58:479–486.

69. Caplan B. Assessment of unilateral neglect: a new reading test. *J Clin Exp Neuropsychol*. 1987;9:359–364.

70. Kagan J, Rosman B, Day D, et al. Information processing in the child: significance of analytic and reflective attitudes. *Psychological Monographs* (Whole No. 578). 1964;1–78.

71. Benton A, Hamsher K, Varney N, et al. *Contributions to Neuropsychological Assessment*. New York: Oxford University Press; 1983.

72. Witkin HA, Oltman PK, Raskin E, et al. *A Manual for the Embedded Figures Test*. Palo Alto, CA: Consulting Psychologists Press; 1971.

73. Hooper HE. *The Hooper Visual Organization Test. Manual*. Los Angeles: Psychological Services; 1958.

74. Bolla-Wilson K, Robinson R, Price T, et al. *Visuoconstructional Assembly Difficulty-Influence of Site of Lesion and Task*. Presented at Annual Meeting of the International Neuropsychological Society; 1984; Houston.

75. Osterrieth PA. Le test de copie d'une figure complexe. *Archives of Psychologie*. 1944;30:206–365.

76. Strub RL, Black FW, Leventhal B. The clinical utility of reproduction drawing tests with low IQ patients. *J Clin Psychiatry.* 1979;40:386–388.

77. Shallice T. Neuropsychological research and the fractionation of memory systems. In: Nilsson LG, ed. *Perspectives on Memory Research.* Hillsdale, NJ: Erlbaum; 1979:257–277.

78. Caplan B. Neuropsychology in rehabilitation: its role in evaluation and intervention. *Arch Phys Med Rehabil.* 1982;63:362–366.

79. Buschke H. Cued recall in amnesia. *J Clin Neuropsychol.* 1984;6:433–440.

80. Fuld PA. Guaranteed stimulus-processing in the evaluation of memory and learning. *Cortex.* 1980;16:255–271.

81. Warrington EK. *Recognition Memory Test: Manual.* Odessa, FL: Psychological Assessment Resources; 1986.

82. Benton AL. *The Revised Visual Retention Test* (e 4). New York: Psychological Corporation; 1974.

83. Albert M, Butters N, Levin J. Temporal gradients in the retrograde amnesia of patients with alcoholic Korsakoff's disease. *Arch Neurol.* 1979;36:211–216.

84. Perlmutter M, Metzger R, Miller K, et al. Memory of historical events. *Exp Aging Res.* 1980;6:47–60.

85. Squire L, Slater PC. Forgetting in very long-term memory as assessed by an improved questionnaire technique. *J Exp Psychol (Hum Learn).* 1975;104:50–54.

86. Randt CT, Brown ER, Osborne DP. A memory test for longitudinal measurement of mild to moderate deficits. *Clin Neuropsychol.* 1980;2:184–194.

87. Sunderland A, Harris JE, Baddeley AD. Do laboratory tests predict everyday memory? A neuropsychological study. *J Verb Learning Verb Behav* 1983;1922:341–356.

88. Crook T, Ferris S, McCarthy M. The Misplaced Objects Task: a brief test for memory dysfunction in the aged. *J Am Geriatr Soc.* 1979;27:284–287.

89. Wilson B, Cockburn J, Baddeley A. *The Rivermead Behavioural Memory Test: Manual.* Reading, England: Thames Valley Test Co; 1985.

90. Delis DC, Freeland J, Kramer JH, et al. Integrating clinical assessment with cognitive neuroscience: construct validation of the California Verbal Learning Test. *J Consult Clin Psychol.* 1988;56:123–130.

91. Cicerone K, Tupper D. Cognitive assessment in the neuropsychological rehabilitation of head-injured adults. In: Uzzell B, Gross Y, eds. *Clinical Neuropsychology of Intervention.* Boston: Martinus Nijhoff; 1986:59–83.

92. Lezak MD. The problem of assessing executive functions. *Int J Psychol.* 1982;17:281–297.

93. Bayless JD, Varney NR. Executive functioning and return to work in head-injured persons: evaluation of an assessment technique. *J Clin Exp Neuropsychol.* 1988;10:42.

94. Sautter SW. Facilitating self-regulation in the head-injured adult. *Clin Biofeed Health.* 1986;9:116–123.

95. Shallice T. Specific impairments of planning. *Philos Trans Soc London.* 1982;B298:199–209.

96. Albert MS. Geriatric neuropsychology. *J Consult Clin Psychol.* 1981;49:835–850.

97. Heaton R, Grant I, Matthews C. Differences in neuropsychological test performance associated with age, education, and sex. In: Grant I, Adams K, eds. *Neuropsychological Assessment of Neuropsychiatric Disorders.* New York: Oxford University Press; 1986:100–120.

98. Parsons OA, Prigatano GP. Methodological considerations in clinical neuropsychological research. *J Consult Clin Psychol.* 1978;46:608–619.

99. Barona A, Reynolds CR, Chastain R. A demographically based index of premorbid intelligence for the WAIS-R. *J Consult Clin Psychol.* 1984;52:885–887.

100. Klesges R, Troster A. A review of premorbid indices of intellectual and neuropsychological functioning: what have we learned in the past five years? *Int J Clin Neuropsychol.* 1987;1:1–10.

101. Wilson R, Rosenbaum G, Brown G, et al. An index of premorbid intelligence. *J Consult Clin Psychol.* 1978;48:1554–1555.

102. Heaton R, Smith HH, Lehman R, et al. Prospects for faking believable deficits on neurosychological testing. *J Consult Clin Psychol.* 1978;46:892–900.

103. Binder L. Persisting symptoms after mild head injury: a review of the postconcussive syndrome. *J Clin Exp Neuropsychol* 1986;8:323–346.

104. Binder L, Pankratz L. Neuropsychological evidence of a factitious memory complaint. *J Clin Exp Neuropsychol* 1987;9;167–171.

105. Lezak MD. Living with the characterologically altered brain injured patient. *J Clin Psychiatry.* 1978;39:592–598.

106. Meier M, Benton A, Diller L. *Neuropsychological Rehabilitation.* New York: Guilford Press; 1987.

107. Prigatano G, Fordyce D, Zeiner H, et al. Neuropsychological rehabilitation after closed head injury in young adults. *J Neurol Neurosur Psychiatry.* 1984;47:505–513.

108. Prigatano G. Neuropsychological rehabilitation after brain injury: some further reflections. In: Williams J and Long C, eds. *The Rehabilitation of Cognitive Disabilities.* New York: Plenum Press; 1987:29–41.

109. Ben-Yishay Y, Rattok MA, Lakin P, et al. Neuropsychologic rehabilitation: quest for a holistic approach. *Semin Neurol.* 1985;5:252–259.

110. Ben-Yishay Y, Silver SM, Piasetsky E, et al. Relationship between employability and vocational outcome after intensive holistic cognitive rehabilitation. *J Head Trauma Rehabil.* 1987;2:35–48.

111. Glisky EL, Schacter DL, Tulving E. Computer learning by memory-impaired patients: acquisition and retention of complex knowledge. *Neuropsychologia.* 1986;24:313–328.

112. Miller E. *Recovery and Management of Neuropsychological Impairments.* New York: John Wiley & Sons; 1984.

113. Raderstorf M, Hine DM, Jencsen CS. A young stroke patient with severe aphasia returns to work: a team approach. *J Rehabil.* 1984;50:23–26.

114. Social Security Administration. *Disability Evaluation Under Social Security: A Handbook for Physicians.* Washington, DC: U.S. Government Printing Office; 1986.

115. Puente AE. Social Security disability and clinical neuropsychological assessment. *Clin Neuropsychologist.* 1987;1:353–363.

chapter 7

Vocational Capacity with Neuromuscular Impairment

Richard Gray, Pamela Brown, and F. Patrick Maloney

The vocational assessment of patients with neuromuscular disease presents a complicated and challenging array of problems because this disease category includes a wide range of clinical disorders with diverse symptoms and pathophysiology. When evaluating the vocational potential of a patient with a neuromuscular impairment, the clinician must consider prior work experience, vocational interests, and a number of factors intrinsic to the disease process itself: (1) the natural history of the disease, such as the age of onset and the rate of progression; (2) specific neurologic deficits; (3) limiting factors, such as fatigue and overwork weakness; (4) associated medical complications; and (5) available therapeutic interventions.

Although there are numerous types of neuromuscular disease (Table 7-1), muscular dystrophy and multiple sclerosis are specific and representative diseases from which it is possible to develop general principles that are applicable to other neuromuscular impairments.

According to the model of the World Health Organization,[1] the term *disease* refers to the active pathology/pathophysiology of the condition; *impairment* represents dysfunction at the organ level (eg, muscle weakness or sensory loss). *Disability* groups problems, such as gait abnormalities and self-care deficits (ie, dysfunction at the level of the person); and *handicap* signifies dysfunction at the level of society (ie, an altered ability to carry out "normal" or perceived normal roles, including vocational roles). This model provides not only a logical categorization of a specific clinical entity but also a framework on which to evaluate an individual's strengths.

MUSCULAR DYSTROPHY

Muscular Dystrophy as a Disease

The muscular dystrophies can be grouped into five main subgroups: (1) the pseudohypertrophic dystrophies (eg, Duchenne's and Becker's); (2) limb-girdle

Table 7-1 Types of Neuromuscular Disorders

Peripheral Nerve Disorders	Disorders of Muscle
Mononeuropathies (including entrapment neuropathies)	Muscular dystrophies X-linked (Duchenne, Becker)
Median (carpal tunnel)	Facioscapulohumeral
Ulnar (at elbow)	Scapuloperoneal
Radial (Saturday night palsy)	Limb girdle
Peroneal	Progressive external ophthalmoplegias
Posterior tibial	Myotonia congenita
Mononeuritis multiplex	Myotonic dystrophy
Plexopathies	Inflammatory myopathies
Acute brachial neuritis	Infectious (viral, bacterial, parasitic)
Lumbosacral plexitis	Immune mediated
Thoracic outlet syndrome	Polymyositis
Polyneuropathies	Dermatomyositis
Axonal neuropathies	Myositis associated with other
Diabetes	connective tissue disorders (systemic
Alcohol related	lupus polyarteritis nodosa, Sjogren's,
Uremia	rheumatoid arthritis, scleroderma)
Hypothyroidism	Endocrine myopathies
Sarcoidosis	Hyper-/hypothyroidism
Collagen vascular disease	Hyper-/hypocalcemia
Systemic lupus erythematosus	Hyper-/hypoadrenalism
Rheumatoid arthritis	Toxic myopathies
Wegener's granulomatosis	Alcohol
Paraproteinemias	Amphotericin B
Drugs	Vincristine
Isoniazid	Chloroquine
Hydralazine	Steroid
Nitrofurantoin	Inherited metabolic myopathies
Vincristine	Glycogen storage disorder (McArdle's,
Heavy Metals	phosphofructokinase and maltase
Lead	deficiency)
Arsenic	Lipid myopathies (carnitine and carnitine
Mercury	palmityl transferase deficiency)
Thallium	Periodic paralysis (hypo-/hyper-/
Industrial toxins	normokalemic)
N-Hexane	Malignant hyperthermia
N-butylketone	Congenital myopathies
Acrylamide	
Organophosphates	Neuromuscular Junction Disorders
Amyloidosis	Myasthenia gravis
Carcinoma (remote effect)	Botulism
Tick paralysis	Eaton-Lambert syndrome
Demyelinating neuropathies	Pseudocholinesterase deficiency
Guillain-Barré syndrome	Organophosphate intoxication
Chronic inflammatory polyradiculoneuropathy	
Diphtheria	
Porphyria	

Source: Data from *Interdisciplinary Rehabilitation of Multiple Sclerosis and Neuromuscular Disorders* (pp 176–183) by FP Maloney, JS Burks and SP Ringel (eds), JB Lippincott Co, © 1985.

dystrophy; (3) facioscapulohumeral dystrophy; (4) myotonic dystrophy; and (5) the ocular dystrophies. Although considerable variation is noted among and even within these groups, certain general principles hold true for all of them:

- The primary site of pathology is within the muscle.
- Most conditions are progressive.
- All are genetically determined.
- No cure exists at present.

Because both Duchenne's and Becker's dystrophies are inherited as X-linked recessive disorders, only men are clinically affected. Both conditions are characterized by pseudohypertrophy, with fatty infiltration of affected muscles (most commonly the calf muscles). In Duchenne's dystrophy, symptoms usually appear by age 3, and the disease then proceeds along a relentlessly progressive course. Death commonly occurs when the patient is in his early twenties. Becker's dystrophy, although commonly mimicking Duchenne's dystrophy in other aspects, usually does not become apparent until adolescence or the young adult years. The life span of a patient with Becker's dystrophy commonly extends into the fourth or fifth decade. In both diseases, the myocardium may be compromised. Central nervous system deficits, specifically mental retardation, can be seen in as many as one third of patients with Duchenne's dystrophy. Muscle biopsies show circular/atrophic fibers and extensive fibrosis.

The limb-girdle dystrophies, which are probably the result of autosomal recessive inheritance, affect men and women equally. On the average, each child has a one in four chance of inheriting the disease. Onset typically occurs when patients are in their twenties and thirties. The initial symptoms are usually noted in the muscles of the hip and shoulder girdles followed by the slow progression of weakness. The time of onset, as well as the extent and distribution of symptoms, varies greatly, however. Biopsies reveal atrophy with considerable variation in fiber size.

Facioscapulohumeral dystrophy commonly develops during adolescence. As with the limb-girdle dystrophies, men and women are affected equally, but facioscapulohumeral dystrophy results from autosomal dominant inheritance. Transmission is from generation to generation, affecting half of a pedigree on the average. Because the disease usually progresses slowly, a relatively normal life span is not uncommon. Some variants, particularly those with juvenile onset, may show a more rapid progression. Biopsies may at times show some degree of inflammation, and a trial of steroid therapy may be considered.[2]

Myotonic dystrophy is characterized by myotonia, believed to be secondary to a membrane abnormality. The disease is inherited as an autosomal dominant condition. It affects the distal musculature of the hands and feet earlier than it affects the proximal muscle groups. With an incidence of 3 to 5 per 100,000 population, myotonic dystrophy is one of the most common neuromuscular disorders. The disease usually appears first during the young adult years and progresses slowly. For example, patients commonly continue to ambulate into the adult years. Death usually occurs in the fifth or sixth decade. The abnormalities of myotonic dystrophy are not confined to the skeletal muscles. Both gastrointestinal smooth muscle and myocardium are affected, resulting in peristalsis and conduction abnormalities. The disease is associated with numerous endocrine abnormalities, as well as a predisposition to the development of cataracts, intellectual deficits, and changes in affect.

Of the ocular dystrophies, the oculopharyngeal subgroup is by far the most common. Inheritance is usually autosomal dominant. A high incidence has been noted among those of French-Canadian descent.[2] Onset typically occurs during the third or fourth decade, and the progression of the disease is generally slow. Although the disease affects primarily the facial and bulbar musculature, involvement can be more extensive. Biopsies reveal the presence of filamentous intranuclear inclusions.

In all the dystrophies, the levels of such muscle enzymes as creatine phosphokinase (CPK) may be elevated, although only in the X-linked disorders are the levels extremely high. Electromyograms typically show a myopathic picture with low amplitude/short duration motor unit action potentials and the presence of spontaneous activity and polyphasics.

Muscular Dystrophy as an Impairment/Disability

Weakness

The characteristic organ-specific impairment associated with the majority of the muscular dystrophies is weakness. Other than in myotonic dystrophy, in most cases, this weakness affects the proximal muscles of the hip and shoulder girdles during the initial phases of the disease. This symptom may first become apparent as difficulty in rising from a seated position or ascending/descending stairs. With upper extremity involvement, patients may report difficulty reaching above shoulder level (eg, for brushing the hair).

In myotonic dystrophy, the early involvement of the distal musculature may result in foot drop or fine motor problems of the hand. Patients may find it difficult to release objects that they have grasped and may have a sensation of stiffness. In facioscapulohumeral dystrophy, as well as in the myotonic and oculopharyngeal dystrophies, early involvement of the bulbar and facial muscles causes distinctive changes in appearance (eg, drawn or expressionless facies, bouche de tapir, swan neck, or hatchet-faced configurations).[2]

Weakness can be evaluated in a number of ways. By far the most common method used is the manual muscle test (MMT), in which the clinician ranks muscle strength on a scale of 0 to 5. This test requires no special equipment and can easily be performed at bedside or in the office. Although the MMT has the advantage of simplicity, it is not precise, particularly in the upper levels of strength. Beasley showed that this system is also insensitive to small increments of change.[3] Up to a 40% alteration in strength may be required before a change in grade is seen. Quantitative muscle testing by means of strain gauges or dynamometers provides more accurate and precise measurements of strength, but these methods require special equipment and therefore are less readily available. Moreover, this method measures primarily isometric maximums and only indirectly reflects isotonic and isokinetic capability. Functional muscle testing relies on the clinician's observation of the patient's strength in such activities as rising from a chair or climbing steps. Although this type of test closely parallels normal activities and reflects contributions from different types of muscle contractions, it is somewhat subjective in nature and monitors groups of muscles, rather than individual muscles. For purposes of vocational assessment, however, a job-specific functional capacity evaluation can be extremely useful (see Chapters 2 and 3).

When weakness is clinically evident, therapeutic exercise programs may be considered. Such programs must be prescribed with caution in cases of neuromuscular disease, however. Excessively vigorous bouts of muscle activity can result in an ''overwork weakness syndrome,'' with muscle breakdown and actual decline in functional status.[4] The exact cause of this syndrome remains somewhat unclear, but muscle fiber fatigue appears to play a role. At any rate, it is important to avoid both excessive eccentric work and activity sufficient to cause delayed onset muscle soreness.[5,6] The therapeutic window for exercises becomes progressively smaller with increasing muscle compromise (Fig. 7-1).

Weakness of the respiratory muscles requires special attention, as it may compromise functional activity. Both the inspiratory and expiratory muscles can be affected. Such respiratory weakness may eventually result in restrictive lung disease and may even become life threatening in some cases. Fatigue of the inspiratory muscles, in particular, may lead to acute respiratory failure.[7] Macklem advocated periodic measurements of vital capacity in all patients with neuromuscular disease to monitor for early signs of respiratory compromise.[8] Clinical changes in the form of tachypnea, dyspnea, paradoxical abdominal motion, and respiratory alternans are early evidence of respiratory compromise.[9] Such compensatory techniques as the provision of supplemental oxygen, the use of a rocker bed, and even periodic ventilatory assistance have been suggested for treatment. Although specific respiratory muscle exercise programs have been used successfully in patients with chronic obstructive lung disease and spinal cord injury, these programs require caution in patients with neuromuscular disorders because of the added risk of overwork weakness and fatigue.[10]

The onset of weakness directly affects a patient's mobility. Proximal involvement, as noted earlier, may lead to problems in rising from a chair or the floor. A

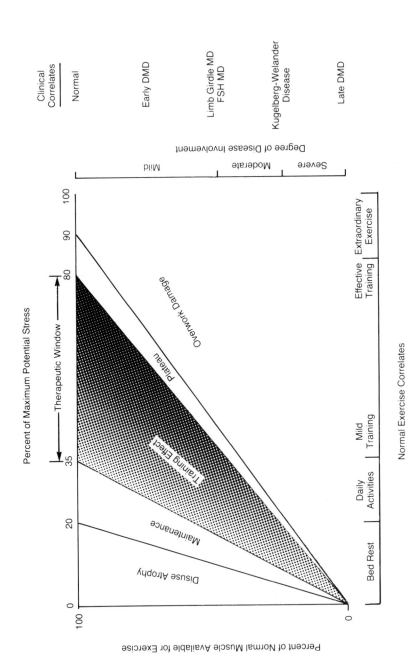

Figure 7-1 Idealized response of normal and impaired muscle to exercise. *Source:* Reprinted from *Interdisciplinary Rehabilitation of Multiple Sclerosis and Neuromuscular Disorders* (p 236) by FP Maloney, JS Burks and SP Ringel (eds) with permission of JB Lippincott, © 1985.

waddling-type gait pattern, with dropping of the hips during the swing phase, may also be noted. Weakness of the knee extensors can cause the knees to buckle, particularly while descending stairs, but also during level walking. Distal involvement may result in foot slap or foot drop. Gastrocnemius/soleus muscle involvement may result in decreased propulsion during the toe-off phase of the gait cycle.

The use of appropriate assistive devices, as well as gait training, may help the patient to maintain function. An ankle-foot orthosis not only helps to correct foot drop but also can increase knee stability. The roll-over effect of an ankle-foot orthosis during the toe-off phase may also increase propulsion during walking.[11] Long leg braces may be of value in selected patients. Other assistive devices, such as canes and walkers, are sometimes helpful in optimizing a patient's gait pattern.

At some point, the patient may need a wheelchair. Proper wheelchair prescription, with attention to such features as size, weight, arm/leg rest type, and accessories, is critical to successful wheelchair mobility. Similarly, training in proper transfer techniques is essential. In addition, it is important to place this phase of mobility in proper perspective. Many patients, as well as many health care professionals, view wheelchair use as a sign of defeat. Clinicians should emphasize to patients that a wheelchair does not confine them, but rather allows them to maintain their functional status.

Muscular dystrophy may compromise a patient's activities of daily living (ADL) skills. When the distal muscles are involved, the use of adaptive equipment (eg, buttonhooks, universal cuffs, built-up utensil handles) may help the patient to carry out daily tasks. Proximal weakness may make it necessary for the patient to use deltoid aids or ball-bearing feeding devices and to learn compensatory techniques for dressing and grooming. Bath benches, raised toilet seats, and other adaptive aids and modifications may also help those with neuromuscular disease to maintain their level of independence.

The maintenance of range of motion is critical. The development of contractures (eg, from muscle imbalance) not only limits functional motion at that joint but also may place the involved muscles at a mechanical disadvantage. The development of kyphosis and scoliosis may have far-reaching effects by further reducing an already compromised ventilatory capacity.[7] Proper instruction in range-of-motion techniques and appropriate positioning can ameliorate these complications.

Other Deficits in the Muscular Dystrophies

Intellectual deficits are associated with some of the muscular dystrophies, most commonly the X-linked recessive dystrophies and myotonic dystrophy.[2] Psychometric testing and clinical observation can help to quantify this factor and aid in the establishment of a treatment plan. (See Chapter 6 for a discussion of testing that is applicable to these patients.)

The progressive and often debilitating nature of these disorders can result in depression and other psychologic changes. Counseling, optimization of functional status, and the appropriate use of antidepressant medications may help to alleviate psychologic stress. Family counseling may be indicated as well.

Visual disturbances in the form of ptosis and ophthalmoplegia may occur. These are most common in the ocular and myotonic dystrophies. Modifications are required not only for activities, such as reading, but also for mobility and ADL.

The development of dysphagia is a common problem among patients with neuromuscular disease, particularly those with the oculopharyngeal and myotonic dystrophies. Abnormalities may develop in the oral, pharyngeal, or esophageal stages of the swallow. Detection requires careful history taking, as swallowing problems are commonly overlooked during routine examinations. Untreated dysphagia can lead to aspiration, dehydration, or malnutrition. Once clinical evidence of dysphagia has been established, a modified barium swallow, manometry, endoscopy, or electromyography may be used to determine the exact nature of the problem. Treatment programs are based on the specific findings and deficits; such programs may include compensatory positioning, modifications of diet, therapeutic exercises, or, perhaps, enteral feeding. During all phases of evaluation and treatment, protection of the airway and maintenance of adequate hydration and nutrition are of primary importance.

Outcome Measures

Functional outcome scales make it possible to quantify some of the deficits associated with neuromuscular disorders. These scales are commonly composed of various mobility, self-care, and medical categories, and the clinician assigns a numerical rating to reflect patients' abilities in each category. With such systems, a clinician can track patients' progress through their rehabilitation programs. The Barthel Index and PULSES Profile have been shown to be useful not only for quantifying functional outcome but also for predicting vocational status.[12,13] The Tufts Quantitative Neuromuscular Examination, introduced in 1986, may permit systematic tracking of specific neurologic deficits.[14] One of these functional outcome tools, the Uniform Data System for Medical Rehabilitation (Appendix 7-A), may serve as the basis for a national registry to evaluate disability/functional capacity.

Muscular Dystrophy as a Vocational Handicap

Any of the impairments and disabilities that result from muscular dystrophy can have an adverse impact on employability. Early vocational intervention can mitigate the detrimental effect of many of these problems.

Weakness decreases an individual's capacity to perform a job that requires heavy manual labor. As weakness progresses, even the more limited physical demands of clerical or other white-collar occupations may prove difficult for the person with muscular dystrophy. Job adaptations, therapeutic exercise, or the use of assistive devices may help an individual cope with these impairments more effectively.

Change in a person's mobility also have a direct effect on job performance. Even mild gait abnormalities limit the speed of an individual's walk and the distance that he or she can walk. Because of the increased energy demands secondary to these gait abnormalities, it may be preferable for the individual to use a wheelchair and conserve energy for other functional activities even when ambulation remains mechanically possible. Architectural barriers (eg, steps, curbings) must also be taken into consideration, particularly when dealing with a client who uses a wheelchair.

The clinician must assess the potential for overwork weakness syndromes during the evaluation and planning stages of a vocational program. The intensity, duration, and specific characteristics of all activities must be considered. Using a combination of manual, quantitative, and functional testing may help to determine a patient's exercise capacity. Sequential quantitative muscle assessments have been used successfully as a guide for modulating general vocational activities.[15]

Visual defects and other complicating medical problems can also affect job placement and performance. The development of intellectual deficits, in addition to physical impairments/disabilities, has a devastating effect on a person's vocational capabilities. Careful observation and testing may be required to define appropriate goals in these instances. Patients whose depression and lack of motivation interfere with their vocational planning may require counseling.

If symptoms of muscular dystrophy first appear in childhood or adolescence, the patient as an adult may have a poorly developed "vocational personality," those learned behavioral and social skills required for successful job adaptation.[16] Early intervention with the patient and the family can help to foster an environment that allows work identification to grow and mature.

In all cases, clinicians must remember the progressive nature of the muscular dystrophies. When progression is rapid, only short-term goals are practical. Even when the progression of the disease is relatively slow, periodic re-evaluation and a willingness to "readapt" are necessary. A comprehensive rehabilitation program that incorporates physical restoration and vocational modalities is essential for a successful outcome.[17]

MULTIPLE SCLEROSIS

Disease

Multiple sclerosis is the most common of all demyelinating diseases. The prevalence of multiple sclerosis at the time of a January 1976 study was 57.8 cases per 100,000 U.S. population.[18] Each year, 8,800 new cases are diagnosed,[18] and 90% of these cases develop in individuals between the ages of 15 and 50.[19] Multiple sclerosis most often affects women, whites, and young adults.[18]

The disease process causes a loss of myelin, but spares the axon. Lesions or plaques can occur throughout the nervous system, possibly involving the optic nerves, brainstem, dorsal spinal cord, cerebellar peduncles, and periventricular areas of the cerebrum. The distribution of these lesions determines the signs and symptoms that the patient experiences.

The course of this disease varies among patients, although there appear to be four major clinical courses[20]:

1. The benign course is characterized by few or no exacerbations, followed by complete recovery.
2. With the relapsing/remitting nonprogressive course, there is a complete return of function with each remission.
3. In the relapsing/remitting progressive course, neurologic deterioration may progress rapidly or slowly over weeks and months. Remissions of short duration usually signify a more aggressive course.
4. The progressive course is associated with deterioration of the neurologic function, either gradually or fairly rapidly after onset, without defined remissions and relapses.

When the course of multiple sclerosis is benign or relapsing/remitting nonprogressive, the patient may need no adjustments in the workplace. Progressive courses of any type may require adjustments in the workplace, however, if indeed the patient is to return to employment.

Multiple Sclerosis as an Impairment/Disability

Signs and Symptoms

As mentioned earlier, the signs and symptoms of multiple sclerosis are diverse. Involvement of the spinal cord can produce weakness, spasticity, paresthesias, and incontinence. When the cerebellum and brainstem are affected, the patient may have dysarthria, tremors, ataxia, incoordination, and nystagmus. Lesions to the optic nerve affect vision.

In the patient with multiple sclerosis, weakness can involve any or all limbs and the trunk. Initially, it is secondary to upper motor neuron lesions. If the disease progresses, however, inactivity may lead to disuse weakness; this type of weakness may improve with a supervised exercise program. The distribution of weakness is variable, with lower extremity paraparesis being the most common. Weakness is often more difficult to evaluate in the patient with concomitant spasticity.

Spasticity is believed to result from pathologically increased stretch reflex activity.[21] Because it limits the active range of motion of the extremities, spasticity may make mobility in transfers and ambulation difficult. The patient may also lose trunk control or balance in standing or sitting when a change in limb or trunk position activates stretch reflexes. It is important to ensure that therapeutic efforts to control spasticity have been adequate. Possible interventions include the provision of such medications as baclofen (Lioresal), diazepam (Valium), clonazepam (Clonopin), and dantrolene (Dantrium), as well as more permanent treatments, such as motor point blocks (spasticity treatment by local injection) and tendon releases. The drawback of these treatments is that a patient's mobility may actually decrease as spasticity is reduced if this muscle-tightening spasticity was used in lieu of willed motor function to stabilize joints during weight bearing.

When demyelination occurs in the cerebellum, the patient may have upper extremity tremors and incoordination, truncal instability, and a wide-based gait. The upper extremity tremor seen with multiple sclerosis is usually an intention tremor. Truncal ataxia may affect ambulation, standing, and dynamic sitting balance. Several drugs have been tried for ataxia, including isoniazide (INH), propranolol (Inderal), and clonazepam (Clonopin), with only modest results. A 4- to 6-week trial is necessary to determine their usefulness, however. The use of cuff weights on the upper extremities during activities improves coordination for some patients.

Dysarthria occurs when demyelination takes place in the neurologic pathways that control motor speech. Two types of dysarthria commonly associated with multiple sclerosis are spastic dysarthria, which is characterized by slow speech and imprecise consonant pronunciation, and ataxic dysarthria, which is characterized by hypotonia with inaccurate tonal range and timing of speech.[22] Fatigue of the speech and respiratory muscles magnifies the dysarthric features. Techniques of energy conservation may improve speech (see Chapter 8).

Visual problems that may develop in patients with multiple sclerosis include loss of vision in varying degrees and the inability to focus. Loss of vision accompanied by pain on movement of the eye is most often seen with an acute onset of optic neuritis; vision usually returns to normal in 3 to 6 weeks. An insidious onset of painless, progressive loss of vision is less common. Intranuclear ophthalmoplegia with weakness of the internal rectus extraocular muscle may limit medial movement of either or both eyes and may interfere with the ability to focus on objects. Patients with severe nystagmus, which may result in double vision, sometimes find an eye patch helpful. All these visual problems interfere with the patient's writing and fine work, and most are refractory to treatment.

An estimated 50% to 80% of patients with multiple sclerosis develop bladder dysfunction, such as frequency, urgency, retention, and incontinence.[23] These problems can best be evaluated by urodynamic studies. Treatment may include medication, intermittent catheterization, or drainage through an in-dwelling or condom catheter.

Easy fatigability is a common complaint among patients with multiple sclerosis. Vigorous physical activity, such as running or walking, may bring an unsteadiness or weakness. Warm temperatures or hot baths may also produce or exacerbate fatigue. In multiple sclerosis, fatigue tends to have a characteristic diurnal cyclic pattern. Most patients function better in the morning than in the afternoon, as fatigue develops later in the day, following their regular activities.

The most frequent psychiatric symptom associated with multiple sclerosis is a reactive depression, resulting from actual or anticipated disability. The euphoria sometimes associated with multiple sclerosis in the literature may actually be purposeful masking of an underlying depression. Treatment of these symptoms is important, as self-esteem, anxiety, and depression indirectly affect employment.

Medical Vocational Assessment

More than 75% of patients with multiple sclerosis see a physician regularly.[24] During these visits, the physician can determine a patient's physical limitations and capabilities. This evaluation should be thorough and individualized, with special attention given to the cognitive and neuromuscular aspects of the patient's condition.

The first step is to evaluate cranial nerves II through VII by checking the extra-ocular muscles and visual fields (cranial nerves II, III, IV, and VI). With an intra-nuclear ophthalmoplegia, a lesion in the medial longitudinal fasciculus of the brainstem decreases the ability of each eye to look medially. Visual acuity should be checked with a Snellen chart.

Sensation to pain, temperature, light touch, vibration, and proprioception should be tested in all four extremities. Loss of sensation in multiple sclerosis is often patchy in distribution and may not follow a dermatome or stocking-glove pattern.

Spasticity is first evaluated by noting any resistance to passive range of motion in the joints. Both proximal and distal joints should be evaluated in all four extremities. Deep tendon reflexes in the upper extremities (ie, biceps, triceps, brachioradialis) and lower extremities (ie, patellar, Achilles) should be tested. The presence of a Hoffman reflex in the upper extremity or a Babinski reflex in the lower extremity, as well as any sign of clonus, should be noted. The active range of motion in all four extremities should then be documented. Active range is tested by asking the patient to move each extremity against gravity with and without resistance applied by the examiner. If the patient is unable to move a joint against gravity, the examiner evaluates active range with gravity eliminated in the plane of movement.

Coordination should be evaluated in the upper and lower extremities. In the upper extremities, any past pointing should be noted as the patient attempts to touch his or her nose and the examiner's index fingers alternately several times. Slowness of the alternating movement when the patient attempts to turn a hand over and back as quickly as possible should be documented. In examining the lower extremities, the examiner watches for tremor as the patient places the heel of one foot on the skin of the other leg and lets it run down the other foot. Slowness in the patient's ability to tap the foot rapidly on the floor is also noted.

Finally, the patient's trunk balance in unsupported sitting and standing with the eyes open and closed is noted. A loss of balance with the eyes closed indicates a loss of position sense, rather than cerebellar disease. If possible, the examiner also observes the patient during gait. Problems common in patients with multiple sclerosis include a broad base (the width of the feet in stance), foot drop (toe pickup), foot equinus (no heel strike), and hip adductor muscle spasticity (scissoring of the legs).

A valuable part of the neurologic assessment is the Kurtzke Functional Systems (KFS), a grading system developed in 1979 by the International Federation of Multiple Sclerosis Societies.[25] The KFS scale contains eight categories of function (ie, pyramidal, cerebellar, brainstem, sensory, bowel/bladder, visual, cerebral, and other functions, including spasticity) that are graded on a 6- or 7-point scale (see Appendix 7-B). Patients who have variable function at different times of day should be examined at different times to determine their highest and lowest levels of function. The report of such an examination should include any specific suggestions for adaptations or limitations.

For the patient who wants to continue or return to employment, the KFS scale may have vocational use:

- A patient scoring a 3 on the pyramidal functions scale (having mild to moderate hemiparesis) may require a job that involves work at a desk, ambulation only for short distances, and no lifting.

- A patient scoring a 2 on cerebellar function (mild ataxia) may require testing to determine whether this ataxia will interfere with any fine motor work necessary for the job. The use of cuff weights on the upper extremities or adapted equipment (adapted typewriter) may also be suggested. Arranging for the patient to perform the majority of fine motor work in the morning when the patient is less fatigued may also be helpful.

- A patient with impaired sensation scoring a 4 on sensory function (marked decrease in pain and proprioception in two limbs) may be cautioned about working close to fast-moving or high-temperature machinery where the lack of sensation poses a danger to the patient.

- When bladder control is a problem, the patient should be allowed frequent breaks and should work near an accessible bathroom.

- For the patient with visual manifestations of multiple sclerosis, specific precautions for work around moving equipment or at heights should be taken. Cerebral dysfunction may warrant further psychologic or neuropsychologic testing.

The physician's report to the vocational counselor should include three categories of information. First, it should explain the manifestations of multiple sclerosis that may functionally limit the patient's ability to work and the physician's suggestions for ways to decrease these limitations. Second, it should describe the predicted course of the patient's disease, when possible. Finally, it should include documentation of any specific precautions necessary based on the patient's job description.

Multiple Sclerosis as a Vocational Handicap

The case for the employability of the patient with multiple sclerosis is strong. Although the patient may be expected to lose time during exacerbations of the disease, the time lost may not be excessive. Most of these patients are stricken during the most productive years of their lives; however, 85% have normal life spans after diagnosis, and intellectual function usually remains intact.[26] Disease stability may be more important than disease severity. Bauer, Firnhaber, and Winkler reported that the severely involved are as likely to be working 15 years after diagnosis as are the moderately and mildly affected.[27] Patients who experience relapses and remissions are reported to have the highest employment rates, whereas those with a progressive course of multiple sclerosis have the lowest.[27] Mitchell found a relationship between the age of onset and long-term employability.[24] The great majority of patients working 15 years after diagnosis had been under 35 years of age when the diagnosis was made.[24] This finding is also substantiated by the observation that disability develops more rapidly when patients are older at onset.[28]

In 1965, Bauer, Firnhaber, and Winkler found that 70% of individuals with multiple sclerosis were unemployed 20 years after onset.[27] Spastic paresis, incoordination, and disturbances of bowel and bladder function were the neurologic factors most commonly limiting continued employability. Scheinberg and associates studied 257 patients who had attended a Multiple Sclerosis Comprehensive Care Center and found that only 19.5% were working.[29] Of these workers, 80% were in white-collar managerial positions, and 78.4% had held the same job for more than 2 years. Of those patients not working, 18.3% were seeking employment, training, or education, and 21.4% could take care of their homes with little or no assistance. The most common reasons given for patients' unemployment were physical difficulty, visual difficulty, transportation difficulty, and fatigue. In their 1982 study, LaRocca and associates found mobility to have the most significant correlation with employment.[19]

Data from a National Multiple Sclerosis Survey conducted by the National Institute of Neurological and Communicative Disorders and Stroke and reported by Kornblith, LaRocca, and Baum[28] showed the largest drop in employment during the first 5 years of the disorder. Although approximately 60% of persons had been working at the onset of their disease, only 37.5% of those individuals were still working 5 years later. The authors speculated that some of these patients may have been so frightened by early exacerbations that they may have left their jobs prematurely.[28]

It usually takes approximately 5 years to determine what pattern of progression a particular patient's disease is taking. Basing judgments on this pattern, the physician may be able to predict the need for vocational re-evaluations in the future. The patient's functional status 5 years after diagnosis of multiple sclerosis is probably the best indicator of future performance. For example, patients who are ambulating 5 years after onset have a more favorable prognosis than do those restricted to a wheelchair. Patients with minimal cerebellar and motor signs at 5 years also have a better prognosis.

Patients with a relapsing/remitting nonprogressive course may be unable to work during exacerbations, but may return to their previous levels of function and be able to work without problems when these exacerbations resolve. In contrast, the patients with a relapsing/remitting progressive course may not return to their previous functional level after an exacerbation. These patients may need vocational re-evaluation to determine if modifications in the workplace or adaptive equipment may enable them to continue in their jobs. If this is not possible, the vocational counselor should seek other activities that the patients may perform at their new levels of function. Patients with a slowly progressive course of multiple sclerosis need periodic medical and vocational reassessments to determine if any deterioration of function has gone unnoticed in the absence of exacerbations.

Vocational counselors who work with patients who have multiple sclerosis should be familiar with the Kurtzke Expanded Disability Status Scale (Appendix 7-C), a compilation of the Kurtzke Functional Systems described earlier (see Appendix 7-B). The initial purpose of the Kurtzke Scale was to allow physicians to evaluate dysfunction objectively during clinical trials of therapy; however, the Kurtzke Expanded Disability Status Scale should be sensitive enough to indicate a neurologic or functional change in an individual that necessitates a vocational reassessment. For example, a patient whose functional ability decreases from a level of 6.0 to a level of 6.5 on this scale may now require bilateral assistive devices (eg, canes, crutches, or braces) to walk 20 meters without resting when he or she had formerly been ambulating with one assistive device for 100 meters without rest. The vocational reassessment can determine whether adaptive equipment can compensate for the patient's inability to ambulate long distances and carry things during ambulation or whether a change in the job requirements is necessary.

Finally, several specific precautions should be taken for almost all patients with multiple sclerosis who return to work. In general, the most important precaution concerns the temperature of the environment in which the individual works. The detrimental effects of increasing the core temperature of the patient with multiple sclerosis have been well documented.[30] For this reason, the workplace temperature should be controlled if possible to avoid temperatures that cause undue fatigue. Also, because physically vigorous work may raise the individual's core body temperature and cause symptoms, the individual should be allowed to pace work activity.

Workers who have multiple sclerosis should follow a program of energy conservation and should take frequent rest breaks during activities. The use of assistive devices, such as a three-wheeled, motorized scooter, may allow them to conserve energy for work, rather than exhausting themselves moving from parking lots to work or traveling from one place to another within the workplace. The most demanding work should be scheduled during a worker's most energetic hours, usually during the mornings. Employers and co-workers should be made aware of the reasons and needs for these measures, as they may be misunderstood by people unfamiliar with multiple sclerosis.

Returning the individual with multiple sclerosis to work requires the coordinated efforts of the physicians, the vocational counselor, the employer, and the patient. This effort is well spent, however, considering the potential productivity of these workers.

REFERENCES

1. World Health Organization. *International Classification of Impairments, Disabilities and Handicaps (ICIDH)*. Geneva: WHO; 1980.

2. Brooke MH. *A Clinician's View of Neuromuscular Disease*. Baltimore: Williams & Wilkins; 1985.

3. Beasley W. Quantitative muscle testing: principles and applications to research and clinical services. *Arch Phys Med Rehabil*. 1961;42:398–425.

4. Cobble ND, Maloney FP. Effects of exercise on neuromuscular disease. In: Maloney FP, Burks JS, Ringel SP, eds. *Interdisciplinary Rehabilitation of Multiple Sclerosis and Neuromuscular Disorders*. Philadelphia: JB Lippincott; 1985:228–238.

5. Armstrong R, Ogilvie R, Schwane J. Eccentric exercise-induced injury to rat skeletal muscle. *J Appl Physiol*. 1983;54:80–93.

6. Edwards R, Jones D, Newham D, et al. Role of mechanical damage in the pathogenesis of proximal myopathy in man. *Lancet*. 1984;1:548–552.

7. Smith PEM, Calverly PMA, Edwards RHT, et al. Practical problems in the respiratory care of patients with muscular dystrophy. *N Engl J Med*. 1986;316:1197–1205.

8. Macklem PT. Muscular weakness and respiratory function. *N Engl J Med*. 1986;314;775–776.

9. Cohen CA, Zagelbaum G, Gross D, et al. Clinical manifestations of inspiratory muscle fatigue. *Am J Med.* 1982;73:308–316.

10. Braun N, Faulkner J, Hughes R, et al. When should respiratory muscles be exercised? *Chest.* 1983;84:76–84.

11. Lehman JF. Lower limb orthotics. In: Redford JB, ed. *Orthotics Etcetera.* Baltimore: Williams & Wilkins; 1980:283–335.

12. Goldberg RT, Bernad M, Granger CV. Vocational status: prediction by the Barthel Index and PULSES Profile. *Arch Phys Med Rehabil.* 1980;61:580–583.

13. Granger CV, Albrecht GL, Hamilton BB. Outcome of comprehensive medical rehabilitation: measurement by PULSES Profile and the Barthel Index. *Arch Phys Med Rehabil.* 1979;60:145–154.

14. Andres P, Hedlun W, Finison L, et al. Quantitative motor assessment in amyotrophic lateral sclerosis. *Neurology.* 1986;36:937–941.

15. Wagner MB, Vignos PJ, Fonow DC. Serial isokinetic evaluations used for a patient with scapuloperoneal muscular dystrophy. *Phys Ther.* 1986;66:1110–1113.

16. Bolton B. Vocational adjustment and rehabilitation. In: Bolton B, ed. *Vocational Adjustment of Disabled Persons.* Baltimore: University Park Press; 1982:1–20.

17. Corcoran PJ. Neuromuscular diseases. In: Stolov WC, Clowers MR, eds. *Handbook of Severe Disability.* Washington, DC: US Government Printing Office; 1981:83–100.

18. National Analysts Division, Booz-Allen and Hamilton. *Prevalence, Incidence and Costs of Multiple Sclerosis—A National Study, Executive Summary.* Washington, DC: US DHEW; 1980. NIH-N07-NS-4-2335, NIH-N01-NS-0-2325.

19. LaRocca N, Kalb R, Kendall P, et al. The role of disease and demographic factors in the employment of patients with multiple sclerosis. *Arch Neurol.* 1982;39:256.

20. Maloney FP. Rehabilitation of the patient with multiple sclerosis. In: Maloney FP, Burks JS, Ringel SP, eds. *Interdisciplinary Rehabilitation of Multiple Sclerosis and Neuromuscular Disorders.* Philadelphia: JB Lippincott; 1985:75–82.

21. Burk D. A reassessment of the muscle spindle contribution to muscle tone in normal and spastic man. In: Feldman RG, Young RR, Koella WP, eds. *Spasticity: Disordered Motor Control.* Chicago: Year Book Medical Publishers; 1980:261–279.

22. Wertj RT. Neuropathologies of speech and language: an introduction to patient management. In: Johns DF, ed. *Clinical Management of Neurogenic Communicative Disorders.* Boston: Little, Brown and Co; 1985:1–96.

23. Auspurger RR. Bladder dysfunction in multiple sclerosis. In: Maloney FP, Burks JS, Ringel SP, eds. *Interdisciplinary Rehabilitation of Multiple Sclerosis and Neuromuscular Disorders.* Philadelphia: JB Lippincott; 1985:48–61.

24. Mitchell JN. Multiple sclerosis and the prospects for employment. *J Soc Occup Med.* 1981;31:134–138.

25. Maber A, LaRocca N, eds. *Minimal Record of Disability for Multiple Sclerosis.* New York: National Multiple Sclerosis Society; 1985.

26. Slater RJ, Yearwood AC. Facts, faith and hope. *Am J Nurs.* 1980;80:276–281.

27. Bauer HJ, Firnhaber, Winkler W. Prognostic criteria in multiple sclerosis. *Ann NY Acad Sci.* 1965;122:542–551.

28. Kornblith AB, LaRocca N, Baum HN. Employment in individuals with multiple sclerosis. *Int J Rehabil Res.* 1986;9:155–165.

29. Scheinberg L, Holland N, LaRocca N, et al. Vocational disability and rehabilitation in multiple sclerosis. *Int J Rehabil Res.* 1981;4:61–64.

30. Michael JA, Davis FA. Effects of induced hyperthermia in multiple sclerosis: differences in visual acuity during healing and recovery phases. *Acta Neurol Scand.* 1973;49:141–151.

Appendix 7-A

Uniform Data System for Medical Rehabilitation

Functional Independence Measure

FIM

L **E** **V** **E** **L** **S**	7 Complete Independence (Timely, Safely) 6 Modified Independence (Device)	NO HELPER
	Modified Dependence 5 Supervision 4 Minimal Assist (Subject = 75% +) 3 Moderate Assist (Subject = 50% +) Complete Dependence 2 Maximal Assist (Subject = 25% +) 1 Total Assist (Subject = 0% +)	HELPER

	ADMIT	DISCHG	FOL-UP
Self Care			
A. Eating			
B. Grooming			
C. Bathing			
D. Dressing-Upper Body			
E. Dressing-Lower Body			
F. Toileting			
Sphincter Control			
G. Bladder Management			
H. Bowel Management			
Mobility			
Transfer:			
I. Bed, Chair, Wheelchair			
J. Toilet			
K. Tub, Shower			
Locomotion			
L. Walk/wheel Chair	w/c	w/c	w/c
M. Stairs			
Communication			
N. Comprehension	a/v	a/v	a/v
O. Expression	v/n	v/n	v/n
Social Cognition			
P. Social Interaction			
Q. Problem Solving			
R. Memory			
Total FIM			

Note: Leave no blanks; enter 1 if patient is not testable due to risk.

Description of the Levels of Function and Their Scores

INDEPENDENT—Another person is not required for the activity (NO HELPER).

    7 **COMPLETE INDEPENDENCE**—All of the tasks described as making up the activity are typically performed safely, without modification, assistive devices, or aids, and within reasonable time.

    6 **MODIFIED INDEPENDENCE**—Activity requires any one or more than one of the following: An assistive device, more than reasonable time, or there are safety (risk) considerations.

DEPENDENT   —Another person is required for either supervision or physical assistance in order for the activity to be performed, or it is not performed (REQUIRES HELPER).

    MODIFIED DEPENDENCE—The subject expends half (50%) or more of the effort. The levels of assistance required are:

    5 **Supervision or setup**—Subject requires no more help than standby, cuing or coaxing, without physical contact. Or, helper sets up needed items or applies orthoses.

    4 **Minimal contact assistance**—With physical contact, the subject requires no more help than touching, and subject expends 75% or more of the effort.

    3 **Moderate assistance**—Subject requires more help than touching, or expends half (50%) or more (up to 75%) of the effort.

    COMPLETE DEPENDENCE—The subject expends *less* than half (*less* than 50%) of the effort. Maximal or total assistance is required, or the activity is not performed. The levels of assistance required are:

    2 **Maximal assistance**—Subject expends less than 50% of the effort, but at least 25%.

    1 **Total assistance**—Subject expends less than 25% of the effort.

Source: Reprinted from *Guide for Use of the Uniform Data Set for Medical Rehabilitation* by Data Management Service of the Uniform Data System for Medical Rehabilitation and The Center for Functional Assessment Research with permission of the Research Foundation, State University of New York, © 1990.

Appendix 7-B

Neurologic Assessment: Kurtzke Functional Systems (FS)

[Descriptors in brackets have been added to the Kurtzke items for additional clarification.]

1. Pyramidal Functions

   0 – Normal
   1 – Abnormal signs without disability
   2 – Minimal disability
   3 – Mild to moderate paraparesis or hemiparesis [detectable weakness, but most function sustained for short periods; fatigue a problem]; severe monoparesis [almost no function]
   4 – Marked paraparesis or hemiparesis [function difficult], moderate quadriparesis [function decreased, but can be sustained for short periods], or monoplegia
   5 – Paraplegia, hemiplegia, or marked quadriparesis
   6 – Quadriplegia
   9 – Unknown

2. Cerebellar Functions

   0 – Normal
   1 – Abnormal signs without disability
   2 – Mild ataxia [tremor or clumsy movements easily seen, minor interference with function]
   3 – Moderate truncal or limb ataxia [tremor or clumsy movements that interfere with function in all spheres]
   4 – Severe ataxia in all limbs [most function very difficult]
   5 – Unable to perform coordinated movements due to ataxia
   9 – Unknown
   Record #1 in small box when weakness (grade 3 or worse on pyramidal) interferes with testing.

193

3. Brain Stem Functions

    0 – Normal
    1 – Signs only
    2 – Moderate nystagmus or other mild disability
    3 – Severe nystagmus, marked extraocular weakness, or moderate disability of other cranial nerves
    4 – Marked dysarthria or other marked disability
    5 – Inability to swallow or speak
    9 – Unknown

4. Sensory Functions

    0 – Normal
    1 – Vibration or figure-writing decrease only in one or two limbs
    2 – Mild decrease in touch or pain or position sense, and/or moderate decrease in vibration in one or two limbs; or vibratory (c/s figure-writing) decrease alone in three or four limbs
    3 – Moderate decrease in touch or pain or position sense, and/or essentially lost vibration in one or two limbs; or mild decrease in touch or pain and/or moderate decrease in all proprioceptive tests in three or four limbs
    4 – Marked decrease in touch or pain or loss of proprioception, alone or combined, in one or two limbs; or moderate decrease in touch or pain and/or severe proprioceptive decrease in more than two limbs
    5 – Loss (essentially) of sensation in one or two limbs; or moderate decrease in touch or pain and/or loss of proprioception for most of the body below the head
    6 – Sensation essentially lost below the head
    9 – Unknown

5. Bowel and Bladder Functions
   (Rate on the basis of the worse function, either bowel or bladder.)

    0 – Normal
    1 – Mild urinary hesitancy, urgency, or retention
    2 – Moderate hesitancy, urgency, retention of bowel or bladder or rate urinary incontinence (intermittent self-catheterization, manual compression to evacuate bladder, or finger evacuation of stool)
    3 – Frequent urinary incontinence
    4 – In need of almost constant catheterization (and constant use of measures to evacuate stool)
    5 – Loss of bladder function
    6 – Loss of bowel and bladder function
    9 – Unknown

6. Visual (or Optic) Functions

   0 – Normal
   1 – Scotoma with visual acuity (corrected) better than 20/30
   2 – Worse eye with scotoma with maximal visual acuity (corrected) of 20/30 to 20/59
   3 – Worse eye with large scotoma, or moderate decrease in fields, but with maximal visual acuity (corrected) of 20/60 to 20/99
   4 – Worse eye with marked decrease of fields and maximal visual acuity (corrected) of 20/100 to 20/200; grade 3 plus maximal acuity of better eye of 20/60 or less
   5 – Worse eye with maximal visual acuity (corrected) less than 20/200; grade 4 plus maximal acuity of better eye of 20/60 or less
   6 – Grade 5 plus maximal visual acuity of better eye of 20/60 or less
   9 – Unknown
   Record #1 in small box for presence of temporal pallor.

7. Cerebral (or Mental) Functions

   0 – Normal
   1 – Mood Alteration only [no effect on Disability Status Scale]
   2 – Mild decrease in mentation
   3 – Moderate decrease in mentation
   4 – Marked decrease in mentation [chronic brain syndrome, moderate]
   5 – Dementia or chronic brain syndrome, severe or incompetent
   9 – Unknown

8. Other functions
   (Any other neurological findings attributable to MS)
   (a) Spasticity

      0 – None
      1 – Mild (detectable only)
      2 – Moderate (minor interference with function)
      3 – Severe (major interference with function)
      9 – Unknown

   (b) Others
      0 – None
      1 – Any other neurological findings attributed to MS:
         Specify _____
      9 – Unknown

Source: Reprinted from *Minimal Record of Disability for Multiple Sclerosis* (pp 16–18) by A Maber and N LaRocca (eds) with permission of the National Multiple Sclerosis Society, © 1985.

Appendix 7-C

Neurologic Assessment: Kurtzke Expanded Disability Status Scale (EDSS)

Note 1: EDSS steps 1.0 to 4.5 refer to patients who are fully ambulatory, and the precise step number is defined by the Functional System score(s). EDSS steps 5.0 to 9.5 are defined by the impairment to ambulation, and usual equivalents in Functional System scores are provided.

Note 2: EDSS should not change by 1.0 step unless there is a change in the same direction of at least one step in at least one FS. Each step (eg, 3.0 to 3.5) is still part of the DSS scale equivalent (ie, 3). Progression from 3.0 to 3.5 should be equivalent to the DSS score of 3.

0   Normal neurological exam (all grade 0 to FS*)

1.0   No disability, minimal signs in one FS* (ie, grade 1)

1.5   No disability, minimal signs in more than one FS* (more than one FS grade 1)

2.0   Minimal disability in one FS (one FS grade 2, others 0 or 1)

2.5   Minimal disability in two FS (two FS grade 2, others 0 or 1)

3.0   Moderate disability in one FS (one FS grade 3, others 0 or 1) or mild disability in three or four FS (three or four FS grade 2, others 0 or 1) though fully ambulatory

3.5   Fully ambulatory but with moderate disability in one FS (one grade 3) and one or two FS grade 2; or two FS grade 3; or five FS grade 2 (others 0 or 1)

4.0   Fully ambulatory without aid, self-sufficient, up and about some 12 hours a day despite relatively severe disability consisting of one FS grade 4 (others 0

---

*Excludes cerebral function grade 1

or 1), or combinations of lesser grades exceeding limits of previous steps; able to walk without aid or rest some 500 meters

4.5 Fully ambulatory without aid, up and about much of the day, able to work a full day, may otherwise have some limitation of full activity or require minimal assistance; characterized by relatively severe disability, usually consisting of one FS grade 4 (others 0 or 1) or combination of lesser grades exceeding limits of previous steps; able to walk without aid or rest some 300 meters

5.0 Ambulatory without aid or rest for about 200 meters; disability severe enough to impair full daily activities (eg, to work a full day without special provisions); (Usual FS equivalents are one grade 5 alone, others 0 or 1; or combinations of lesser grades usually exceeding specifications for step 4.0)

5.5 Ambulatory without aid or rest for about 100 meters; disability severe enough to preclude full daily activities; (Usual FS equivalents are one grade 5 alone, others 0 to 1; or combination of lesser grades usually exceeding those for step 4.0)

6.0 Intermittent or unilateral constant assistance (cane, crutch, brace) required to walk about 100 meters with or without resting; (Usual FS equivalents are combinations with more than two FS grade 3+)

6.5 Constant bilateral assistance (canes, crutches, braces) required to walk about 20 meters without resting; (Usual FS equivalents are combinations with more than two FS grade 3+)

7.0 Unable to walk beyond approximately 5 meters even with aid, essentially restricted to wheelchair; wheels self in standard wheelchair and transfers alone; up and about in wheelchair some 12 hours a day; (Usual FS equivalents are combinations with more than one FS grade 4+; very rarely pyramidal grade 5 alone)

7.5 Unable to take more than a few steps; restricted to wheelchair; may need aid in transfer; wheels self but cannot carry on in standard wheelchair a full day; may require motorized wheelchair; (Usual FS equivalents are combinations with more than one FS grade 4+)

8.0 Essentially restricted to bed or chair or perambulated in wheelchair, but may be out of bed itself much of the day; retains many self-care functions; generally has effective use of arms; (Usual FS equivalents are combinations, generally grade 4+ in several systems)

8.5 Essentially restricted to bed much of day; has some effective use of arm(s); retains some self-care functions; (Usual FS equivalents are combinations generally 4+ in several systems)

9.0 Helpless bed patient; can communicate and eat; (Usual FS equivalents are combinations, mostly grade 4 +)

9.5 Totally helpless bed patient; unable to communicate effectively or eat/swallow; (Usual FS equivalents are combinations, almost all grade 4 +)

10.0 Death due to multiple sclerosis

Source: Reprinted from *Minimal Record of Disability for Multiple Sclerosis* (pp 20–21) by A Maber and N LaRocca (eds) with permission of the National Multiple Sclerosis Society, © 1985.

chapter 8

Vocational Capacity with Communication Impairment

M. Drue Lehmann and Melanie A. Schleicher

> *"Nothing is more unaccountable than the spell that often lurks in a spoken word. A thought may be present to the mind and two minds conscious of the same thought, but as long as it remains unspoken, their familiar talk flows quietly over the hidden idea."*
>
> *Nathaniel Hawthorne*

An analysis of the specific abilities and behaviors necessary for vocational placement and successful adjustment makes it clear that communication is an essential skill for workers. In addition to actual work performance skills, prevocational skills (eg, fundamental reading and mathematics), job-seeking skills (eg, interpreting advertisements, completing job applications, preparing resumes), job interview skills (eg, giving information to and gaining information from an employer), and on-the-job social skills (eg, getting along with others, accepting criticism) involve various aspects of communication. As society has become more complex and technology has become more sophisticated, effective communication skills have become even more important for personal and professional gain.

DEFINITIONS

Communication is the interaction that occurs between living organisms, the means whereby humans solve the basic problems of coordinating and regulating society. It is most commonly described as oral and written exchanges between two or more individuals; however, communication behaviors may be not only oral and written but also verbal, tonal, postural, gestural, tactile, and contextual.[1,2]

A communication system consists of five divisions:

1. source, which generates and selects the message (eg, brain)
2. transmitter channel, which converts the message to a signal (eg, total speech mechanism, such as larynx, tongue, and lips)

199

3. channel, means by which the signal is sent from the transmitter to the receiver (eg, air)
4. receiver, which decodes the signal (eg, ear, cranial nerves, and circuits of the receiver)
5. destination, mechanism for which the original message is intended (eg, brain of the receiver)

A *communication impairment* exists when there is a malfunction in one or more elements of the communication system.

The components of the communication process that are critical for human interaction are speech, language, and voice. *Speech* refers to the actual physical production of speech sounds. The respiratory system, larynx, soft palate, tongue, and lips are all crucial components of the speech mechanism. Hence, when innervation to these areas is disrupted or when the muscles or structures in these areas are damaged, a disorder of speech, or articulation, may result.

Language refers to the set of symbols that humans use to communicate. Interpersonal communication involves the reception, or decoding, of language symbols (eg, understanding spoken language and reading) and the expression, or encoding, of language symbols (eg, verbal expression and writing). A few of the important components of language are syntax, which refers to the structural and grammatical rules of language; semantics, which refers to the meaning, or content, of language expression; and pragmatics, which refers to the function of language (eg, to question, direct, inform, greet). Pragmatics also refers to the nonverbal and social aspects of language, such as making eye contact, taking turns, and obeying basic conversational rules. Disorders of language may occur secondary to trauma, disease, or infection.

Voice refers to the sound produced by the vibration of the vocal cords. Several parameters are used to describe voice, such as quality, pitch, loudness, and resonance. The etiology of voice or phonation disorders includes both functional and organic causes.

In determining the degree of disability that results from a communication impairment, it is necessary to assess the impact of the impairment on functional abilities. Emerick maintained that a communication difference may be considered handicapping when[3]

- the transmission and/or perception of the message is faulty
- it places the person at an economic disadvantage
- it places the person at a learning disadvantage
- it has a negative impact on the emotional growth of the person
- the problem causes physical injury or endangers the health of the person

The personal, social, and economic consequences of communication impairments can be tremendous, as many such impairments occur during the person's most productive work years. Consequently, many individuals who had been leading active lives may be forced to withdraw prematurely from the work force.

PREVALENCE AND COSTS OF COMMUNICATION DISORDERS

It is estimated that 24 million U.S. citizens, or approximately 10% of the population, suffer from communication disorders.[4] More people suffer from speech, language, voice, and hearing impairments than from heart disease, paralysis, epilepsy, blindness, cerebral palsy, muscular dystrophy, and multiple sclerosis combined.

Of all U.S. citizens, 11,300,000, or roughly 5% of the population, demonstrate some degree of speech and language dysfunction.[4] One percent of persons aged 15 to 65 years have some difficulty in being understood.[5] The prevalence of voice disorders in adults is not as well determined. Laguaite found that, of 428 adults who underwent a multiphasic health screening, 7.2% of the men and 5% of the women had various types of laryngeal disorders that affected or could affect their voices.[6] The American Cancer Society estimated that, in 1987, there would be over 12,000 new cases of laryngeal cancer, 9,800 in men and 2,300 in women.[7] The 10 most frequently occurring laryngeal pathologies, according to a 1988 study, are listed in Table 8-1.[8]

Table 8-1 The 10 Most Frequently Occurring Laryngeal Pathologies in a Total Sample of 1,262 Reported Cases

Pathology	Number	Percentage
Nodules	272	21.6
Edema	179	14.1
Polyps	144	11.4
Cancer	122	9.7
Vocal fold paralysis	102	8.1
Dysphonia/no pathology	100	7.9
Laryngitis	53	4.2
Leukoplakia	52	4.1
Psychogenic disorders	34	2.6
Functional disorders	31	2.4

Source: From *Journal of Speech and Hearing Disorders* (1988;53:57), Copyright © 1988, American Speech-Language-Hearing Association.

Using data obtained from voluntary agencies and experts in relevant fields, the National Institute of Neurological and Communicative Disorders and Stroke has estimated that the costs of speech and language disorders total more than $16.5 billion.[9] This estimate reflects both the direct costs of health care and the indirect costs of income lost due to illness. Annual deficits in earning power among persons with speech and language disorders have been estimated to be at least $750 million.[4]

MEDICAL CONDITIONS AND CONCOMITANT COMMUNICATION IMPAIRMENTS

Speech, language, and voice impairments may result from cerebrovascular accidents, brain injury, neuromuscular disease, dementing conditions, cancer, and various functional conditions. Many of these disorders may occur during the individual's working lifetime.

Cerebrovascular Accidents

In 1987, it was estimated that there were 1.9 million people in the United States who had suffered a stroke.[9] Cerebrovascular accident is ranked as the third most common cause of death in the United States behind cancer and heart disease.[10] The incidence of stroke increases with age and is higher in blacks[11] and men.[10] In addition to residual physical impairments, stroke survivors may develop a multitude of communicative consequences, such as difficulty in the comprehension and expression of language; cognitive, behavioral, and affective changes; and speech planning, sequencing, and production disorders.

Aphasia

Described as a disorder of impaired decoding, or interpretation, and encoding, or formulation, of language,[12] aphasia may be further defined as a reduction and dysfunction in language content (meaning), form (structure), and use (function), along with a disruption of the underlying cognitive processes, such as recognition, comprehension, memory, and thinking.[13] Aphasia results from focal damage to the language specialization areas of the left cerebral hemisphere (Fig. 8-1) and may occur secondary to cerebrovascular accident, trauma, infectious processes, or tumor. It should not be confused with a speech problem, as it does not involve a disturbance in the mechanical processes of articulation or the execution of basic motor speech movements.[12] Rather, it involves impairments in listening, reading, speaking, gesturing, or writing skills. Symptoms vary in individuals as a function of the area and extent of brain damage.

Lateral depiction of the left cerebral hemisphere
with identification of language specialization areas

Approximate area of involvement in nonfluent
aphasia including Broca's area

Approximate area of involvement in fluent
aphasia including Wernicke's area

Figure 8-1 Focal damage to the language specialization areas of the left cerebral hemisphere.

Incidence of Aphasia. The total prevalence of aphasia from various causes is estimated to be 1 million cases,[14] with approximately 400,000 of these secondary to cerebrovascular accident.[15] It has been suggested that 20% to 30% of those who survive the initial insult of stroke will have aphasia at some point in their illness.[16] In a study of 976 patients who had experienced a stroke, Wade and associates reported that 24% were aphasic at 7 days and 12% demonstrated residual aphasia at 6 months.[17]

Several investigators have studied the relationship between age, sex, handedness, and aphasia type. The results of some studies have shown that patients with Wernicke's aphasia (posterior lesions) are typically older than those with other aphasia subtypes.[18–20] Patients with Broca's aphasia (anterior lesions) tend to constitute the youngest group in these investigations. Other studies, however, have not confirmed a definitive age-aphasia type relationship.[21] Several investigators have found no significant correlation between sex and the incidence of aphasia.[22,23] Kertesz and Sheppard have postulated that the greater incidence of aphasia in men follows the general incidence of stroke [22] (ie, there are more men than women with strokes, and thus more men are aphasic).

Although relationships between language representation and handedness are not completely understood, aphasia is typically associated with left hemispheric involvement. Code's review of the literature suggested that between 88% and 96% of the right-handed population have left hemispheric specialization for language.[24] Another study demonstrated that 4% of right handers and 15% of left handers have right hemispheric language specialization.[25] For the purposes of further discussion, the term "dominant" hemisphere will refer to the left hemisphere since, for the preponderant majority of people, the major speech center is on the left side.

Classification of Aphasia. The attempt to classify various aphasic disturbances has resulted in numerous descriptors over the past several years: expressive-receptive aphasia, afferent-efferent aphasia, and sensory-motor aphasia.[26–28] In addition, the presence or absence of repetition disorders and the distinction between oral and written language disorders have been suggested as important considerations in the classification of aphasia.[29] Most recently, however, increasing attention has been given to the fluency-nonfluency dichotomy in the assessment and classification of aphasias.[30,31]

Nonfluent aphasia, also known as expressive aphasia or motor aphasia, may be characterized by (1) a reduced verbal output, (2) increased effort in producing speech, (3) defective articulatory sequencing, (4) decreased phrase length, (5) agrammaticisms, (6) verbal stereotypic or automatic speech, and (7) awareness of the impairment and frustration.[32,33] The most common types of nonfluent aphasia include Broca's aphasia and global aphasia.[32,34–38]

Broca's aphasia is characterized by telegraphic and laborious speech, hesitancy, reduced vocabulary, misarticulations, and agrammaticisms. Auditory and reading comprehension are often relatively well preserved for simple material, but the impairment becomes more obvious as the grammatical complexity and length of the material increase. Writing and gesturing may mirror verbal performance. The main disturbance in Broca's aphasia appears to be in the processing and expression of grammatical or syntactic relationships, although the semantic aspects of communication remain intact.

Global aphasia consists of severe impairments in verbal expression, auditory and reading comprehension, writing, and gesturing. Speech is grossly nonfluent. The patient may have a limited ability to communicate and often may be able to produce only stereotypic or automatic words or phrases (eg, "OK," "oh yeah," "1,2,3"). The patient may be unable to repeat words, phrases, and sentences. Auditory comprehension may be severely compromised, as shown by the patient's inability to perform such simple tasks as identifying common objects and responding to simple, familiar questions. On occasion, the patient with global aphasia may appear to understand simple, contextually related verbal statements and to make appropriate nonverbal responses.

Fluent aphasia, also known as receptive aphasia or sensory aphasia, may be characterized by (1) increased verbal output, (2) effortless speech production,

(3) relatively normal articulation and prosody (stress and intonation), (4) seemingly normal grammatical structure, (5) meaningless or "empty" content, (6) paraphasias, and (7) lack of awareness of the impairment.[32,33] The most common types of fluent aphasia are Wernicke's aphasia and anomic aphasia.[32,34–38]

Auditory and reading comprehension are typically poor in Wernicke's aphasia. Verbal expression may be unmonitored and marked by fluent jargon, word substitutions, poor repetition, and severe naming difficulty. Despite the abundance of verbal utterances, speech may convey very little meaning. Patients with Wernicke's aphasia are typically unaware of their communicative difficulties.

The patient with anomic aphasia demonstrates fluent and well-articulated speech. Verbal production may be mildly paraphasic, but grammatically intact; however, speech may have very little content. A naming or word finding difficulty that may encompass any of the language modalities is common. Repetition skills are relatively well preserved.

Associated Problems. Because aphasia occurs in various forms, ranging from mild to severe, its impact on patients' abilities to understand and express thoughts, ideas, and desires varies. In addition to communication disturbances, a person with left hemispheric involvement may respond to new problems or situations in a slow, cautious, seemingly disorganized fashion, whether information is presented verbally or visually. The ability to learn new information may be compromised.[39] Depression is a common emotional response, although it may diminish when the patient learns to compensate for and adjust to residual impairments.

Verbal Apraxia

Apraxia of speech, or verbal apraxia, is an articulation disorder secondary to brain damage that affects a patient's ability to position and sequence muscle movements volitionally as necessary to produce speech sounds.[12] There is no significant weakness, slowness, or incoordination of the same musculature for automatic or reflexive actions, however.[40] For example, the patient may have difficulty volitionally positioning the tongue to produce a *t* sound, yet be able to perform the same movement automatically to clear peanut butter off the roof of the mouth. Linguistic and aphasic disturbances may accompany verbal apraxia.

The verbally apraxic patient makes more and more errors as the complexity of the speech task and the length of the word increases.[12] The patient transposes sounds, finding it difficult to sequence them in the correct order; for example, attempts to say "catastrophe" may result in "tastoprocaphe." The individual with apraxia has periods of fluent, well-articulated speech and may have minimal difficulty with automatic speech tasks (eg, "Good morning"). The same individual may have considerable difficulty in trying to convey a new idea, however.

Evidence suggests that the problem is not in word finding, as the apraxic patient may be able to write the word correctly or choose it from a group of other words.[12]

The differences between apraxia and aphasia are important both theoretically and clinically. Verbal apraxia may accompany aphasia; in this case, the aphasia is most often nonfluent. Verbal apraxia rarely occurs in isolation.[41]

Dysarthria

Patients develop dysarthria secondary to weakness, incoordination, or paralysis of any one or more of the motor components necessary for speech production (eg, diaphragm, abdomen, rib cage, larynx, veolpharynx, posterior tongue, anterior tongue, lips, and jaw).[42,43] Focal or diffuse damage to the central or peripheral nervous system caused by cerebrovascular accident, trauma, infection, or disease may result in dysarthria. Although clearly different from language or cognitive disorders, dysarthria may coexist with these conditions.[43] Studies of the prevalence of motor speech disorders in association with cerebrovascular accident are scarce, but at least one study has suggested that 15% of long-term stroke survivors may have residual dysarthria.[44]

Dysarthrias may be classified according to etiology; site and level of lesion; affected speech processes, speech valves, and events; and perceptual characteristics.[45] Darley and associates differentiated between six distinctive types of dysarthria based on perceptual speech and voice characteristics. They found the most commonly occurring dimensions of dysarthria to be imprecise articulation; hypernasality; slow rate; harsh, hoarse, or strained vocal quality; and poor control of pitch, loudness, and stress.[45]

In mild cases of dysarthria, the patient's speech may have a slightly slurred quality, although it is easily intelligible. In more severe cases, speech may be incomprehensible, or the patient may be nonvocal. In such instances, augmentative and alternative communication systems may be required.

Nondominant Hemispheric Communication Disturbances

It is well documented that damage to the right cerebral hemisphere may impair visual-perceptual and visual-spatial skills, attention, memory, facial recognition, emotional perception and expression, and pragmatic aspects of language.[46–49] Myers has proposed the following definition of right hemispheric communication deficits:

> Right hemispheric communication impairment is an acquired disorder in the expression and reception of complex, contextually based communicative events resulting from disturbance of the attentional and perceptual mechanisms underlying nonsymbolic, experiential processing.[50]

This definition suggests that, although the basic linguistic processes of phonology, syntax, and semantics are relatively preserved when the nondominant hemisphere is damaged, the ability to perceive and use contextual cues is not.

Patients with nondominant deficits may superficially perform relatively well in simple communication situations and conversations; however, affective presentation may appear somewhat dull, with little variation in pitch and facial expression. Responses in conversation may be delayed. These patients may demonstrate poor eye contact and may fail to adhere to other rules of social conversational interaction. There may be poor topic maintenance, redundancy, overfamiliarity, over-presupposition, egocentricity, and verbosity.[51] Verbal responses may appear impulsive, disorganized, and disinhibited. These individuals may fail to recognize nonverbal cues that they are losing the interest of their listeners. They may demonstrate difficulty with abstractions, and their interpretation may be concrete, or literal.[52] They may be unable to appreciate the gestalt or holistic aspects of linguistic and nonlinguistic information.[53]

Behaviorally, the patient with an injury to the right hemisphere may fail to attend to the left side of the body or the left side of the environment. This neglect may occur with verbal, visual, tactile, and olfactory information. For example, the patient may not notice food on the left side of the plate, may be unaware of people standing to the left, or may forget to bathe the left side of the body. In writing and reading activities, the left side of the page may be ignored. The patient may be unable to navigate or find routes in familiar (eg, home) and new environments.[50]

Even when neglect is not significant, the patient with damage in the nondominant hemisphere may find it difficult to pay selective attention to certain tasks and to maintain attention. The patient's expectations may be unrealistic. For example, an individual who is unable to walk or transfer independently may insist that he or she could return to a physically demanding vocation. In less extreme situations, the individual may act impulsively, failing to contemplate or anticipate the consequences of the action. In more severe cases, the individual may fail to recognize friends and family members and may confuse strangers with acquaintances.[54]

Brain Injury

Every year, 1 million people suffer brain injuries.[9] Such an injury can result from anoxia, toxemia, or brain tumor, but by far the most frequent cause is trauma. Motor vehicle accidents account for more than 50% of the incidents of head trauma. More than 400,000 head trauma victims of motor vehicle accidents require hospitalization, and possibly as many as 100,000 die each year.[9] Young men are twice as likely to sustain head injuries as are young women.[55] Most victims are between the ages of 15 and 24[55] and thus are beginning to develop their careers and to establish their social independence.

Brain injury may result in any combination of physical, psychologic, cognitive, and behavioral deficits. No two head injuries are identical in their long-term functional consequences. Health care professionals familiar with brain injury concur, however, that the cognitive and behavioral sequelae are the most lasting and disabling aspects of brain injury because they affect the patient's reintegration into society.[56,57]

Although brain injury can involve either focal or diffuse brain lesions, multifocal or diffuse brain lesions may have a more pervasive effect upon communication. Diffuse cortical lesions cause information-processing difficulties, cognitive and attention deficits, and memory disorders. Physical impairments, such as ataxia, dyskinesias, and spasticity, can produce dysarthria, aphonia, and prosody deficits. Brain injury can also render a person dyslexic and dysgraphic. Generally, open head injuries produce focal pathology,[58] whereas closed head injuries produce diffuse pathology.

Aphasia in Brain Injury

It is difficult to superimpose the traditional categories of aphasia on the language deficits that result from closed head injury. Heilman and colleagues[59] and later Thomsen[60] found that the most common type of aphasia in patients with a closed head injury was an anomic aphasia, which was generally associated with other deficits in higher-level cortical function. Wernicke's aphasia was the second most common type.[59]

Sarno used the term *subclinical aphasia* to describe the linguistic processing deficits that she found in patients with a closed head injury.[61] These deficits, which were unassociated with dementia, defied traditional aphasia classification. When Sarno and colleagues tested 125 patients who were 45 weeks postinjury on the average, they found that 70% demonstrated subclinical aphasia (Table 8-2).[62]

Table 8-2 Communication Impairment in 125 Closed Head Injured Patients

Impairment	Number	Percentage
Aphasia	37	30
Fluent	(19)	(15)
Nonfluent	(13)	(10)
Global	(5)	(5)
Dysarthria/subclinical aphasia	43	34
Subclinical aphasia	45	36

Source: From *Archives of Physical Medicine and Rehabilitation* (1986;67:402–403), Copyright © 1986, American College of Rehabilitation Medicine.

Cognition and Language in Brain Injury

Three particularly salient nonaphasic language disturbances seen in association with brain injury are talkativeness, tangentiality of thought in conversational speech, and use of peculiar words or phrases. Brain-injured persons who are restless and disinhibited are unable to halt their verbalization of thought. They are difficult to interrupt and do not observe conversational turn-taking. Prigatano and associates believed that this verbosity may be more emotional than cognitive.[63] With tangentiality, the syntax of language, both oral and written, is normal, but the patient demonstrates pragmatic dysfunction in maintaining a topic and in providing adequate connecting information. Weinstein and colleagues noted the tendency to use unusual expressions and word order in patients with closed head injuries who had amnesic disturbances.[64] They postulated that these patients were having difficulties with reality orientation.

Diffuse brain lesions have other pervasive adverse effects upon pragmatic language performance. Cognitive deficits of impaired attention, concentration, memory, problem-solving ability, analysis/synthesis of thought, organization, abstraction, and speed of processing are common after diffuse closed head injury.[65]

Speech and Voice in Brain Injury

Dysarthria, which may result from focal mass lesions to the left hemisphere[60] or diffuse brain injury,[61,62] is the most common speech defect following closed head injury. deMorsier[66] and Helm and colleagues[67] found a correlation between bilateral brain injury and acquired stuttering. Echolalia, the repetition of words spoken by others, and pallilalia, the repetition of one's own words, are infrequently seen in closed head injury.[68]

Closed head injury causes voice problems ranging from dysphonia due to tracheal intubation to aphonia secondary to bilateral vocal cord paralysis. Phonatory intensity may be insufficient or excessive because of poor self-monitoring skills.[56] Finally, the rare occurrence of spastic dysphonia, a disorder of vocal motor control, has been reported following head trauma.[69]

Neuromuscular Disease

Progressive neuromuscular diseases, such as multiple sclerosis, Parkinson's disease, amyotrophic lateral sclerosis, Huntington's chorea, and hereditary ataxia are known to affect the nervous system (see Chapter 7, Vocational Capacity with Neuromuscular Impairment). Such disease may result in an array of communication disturbances.

Multiple Sclerosis

Expressive communication deficits are typical, but not universal, in patients with multiple sclerosis. Dysarthria is the most commonly occurring[45]; aphasia is observed infrequently.[70]

Darby maintained that mixed dysarthria occurs in nearly 50% of patients with multiple sclerosis.[71] In a classic study of these patients, however, Darley and associates found that 59% of their subjects demonstrated "normal" speech performance in terms of its impact on a listener, 28% demonstrated minimal impairment, and 13% demonstrated more severe impairment.[45] The most frequently reported deviation was impairment of loudness control. Approximately one quarter of the patients demonstrated hypernasality. Also frequently reported were harshness of voice; defective articulation; inappropriate phrasing; and impaired use of rate, pitch, and loudness for emphasis. In general, the more severe the neurologic involvement, the more severe the speech disturbance.

In an attempt to assess the presence and severity of expressive disturbances in patients with multiple sclerosis, Beukelman and associates surveyed 656 patients.[70] Of the total sample, 23% reported that a speech or communication impairment was a symptom of their disease; however, 96% of those communicatively impaired reported that strangers could understand them. Of those 4% who responded that strangers could not understand them, 28% reported using an augmentative or alternative means of communication.

Reading and writing disturbances are common in patients with multiple sclerosis; these disturbances are secondary to visual and motor deficits. Cognitively based linguistic disturbances are also frequently reported.[72–74]

Parkinson's Disease

Although Parkinson's disease does not typically involve patients before the age of 65, a small number of patients develop symptoms earlier, even in the fourth and fifth decades of life.[75] Nonverbal and verbal speech disturbances are often associated with the disease.[76] In fact, approximately 50% of the patients with Parkinson's disease demonstrate some type of speech disturbance.[77] Most common speech difficulties of the 32 patients whom Darley and colleagues described were monotony of pitch and loudness, articulation imprecision, inappropriate silences, short rushes of speech, and breathy vocal quality.[45] All patients demonstrated an articulatory problem, with reduced intelligibility in 78% of the speakers.

Reduced facial expression secondary to rigidity of facial muscles; rigidity of muscles in the hand and arm, which may impair writing and gesturing; and slower speed of eye movements, which impairs the individual's ability to switch eye gaze quickly, may also decrease the communicative effectiveness of patients with Parkinson's disease.[78] Thirty to 39% of patients are estimated to have dementia, with difficulty in new learning and slowed information processing.[79] Although vocabulary and general facility with language may be preserved, perseveration, reduced initiative in speech, and naming difficulties may be present.

Amyotrophic Lateral Sclerosis

Occurring in the middle to later working years, amyotrophic lateral sclerosis may cause progressive difficulty in speaking and swallowing.[80] Patients generally succumb to the disease when respiratory processes are involved, unless ventilatory assistance by machine is provided.

Most patients with amyotrophic lateral sclerosis retain their normal intellectual function, remaining alert and aware despite the progressive decline in motoric function. Investigators have found the predominant speech characteristic to be consistent with mixed dysarthria, including grossly defective articulation of consonants and vowels, slow rate of speech, impaired phrasing, marked hypernasality, severe harshness of vocal quality, and a strained-strangled vocal quality.[45]

Huntington's Chorea

A progressive degenerative disorder, Huntington's chorea may result in motor speech and language disturbances.[81] Speech in the individual who has this disease may be characterized by imprecise articulation and impaired prosody.[45] Dementia also occurs in a large percentage of patients with Huntington's chorea.[79] Language difficulties may vary from mild word-finding problems and reduced perception of subtleties in the early stage of the disease to severe anomia, restricted vocabulary, poor comprehension, bizarre or empty speech, and echolalia in the later stages.

Hereditary Ataxias

Dysarthric communication disturbances commonly occur in association with hereditary ataxias. Most frequently reported speech symptoms include imprecise articulation, impaired use of stress, and a harsh or strained vocal quality.[45]

Voice Disorders

Either disease or emotion can lead to a voice disorder, defined as any aberration in quality, pitch, or loudness. The exact prevalence of adult voice disorders is not well documented. The most frequently occurring laryngeal pathologic conditions (see Table 8-1) can be divided into functional voice disorders (eg, nodules, edema, polyps, laryngitis, dysphonia with no pathology, and psychogenic disorders) and organic voice disorders (eg, vocal cord paralysis, leukoplakia, and laryngeal carcinoma).

Functional Voice Disorders

Vocal nodules, probably the most common functional disorder, are caused by vocal abuse and misuse. The initial stage of nodule development is usually evidenced by edema and a localized submucous hemorrhage. If the abuse ceases, the edema and hemorrhage disappear; if the abuse continues, the edema and hemorrhage may produce a nodule. The symptoms of vocal nodules, which are usually bilateral, include hoarseness, breathiness, and increased laryngeal tension.

Vocal polyps are cystic sacs commonly caused by a single episode of vocal strain. The polyps may evolve, after long standing abuse, into a more diffuse polypoid degeneration. Symptoms of a vocal polyp range from intermittent dysphonia to severe hoarseness and breathiness.

Chronic laryngitis may follow repeated bouts of acute laryngitis, prolonged vocal abuse, excessive smoking or alcohol abuse, or continued irritation by allergies. The voice tires easily, and the patient may cough and clear the throat nonproductively.

Dysphonia without laryngeal pathology is not uncommon.[8,82] The patient complains of chronic vocal fatigue, and voice quality is compromised. The condition is usually secondary to vocal misuse and a generalized weakness of the laryngeal musculature.

Psychogenic voice disorders occur nearly six times as often in women as in men; they are most prevalent in individuals between the ages of 25 and 44 years.[8] The two most common conditions are conversion aphonia and dysphonia. The symptoms range from total loss of the speaking voice to a dysphonia. Onset is usually sudden and may be coincident with flu-like symptoms. The vocal cords are not paralyzed, as movements are normal on coughing, throat clearing, and, frequently, laughing. The disorder is thought to be due to the patient's unconscious psychologic need to avoid a stressful communicative situation.

Organic Voice Disorders

Peripheral damage to the recurrent laryngeal or superior laryngeal nerves as a result of surgical trauma (eg, thyroidectomy), cardiovascular and neurologic diseases, trauma, or intubation and bronchoscopy may result in vocal cord paralysis. In 36% of cases, the cause of the vocal cord paralysis is unknown, however.[83] The voice quality and vocal functionality vary greatly, depending on whether one or both vocal cords are affected and what the static position of the paralyzed cord(s) is. The closer the lesion to the midline of the glottis, the better the quality and functional use of the voice.

Leukoplakia, a potentially precancerous vocal cord epithelial thickening, results from focal abuse, habitual throat clearing and coughing, and smoking. It is estimated that 80% of laryngeal tumors are malignant.[84] The ratio of occurrence in men to women is 71:4.[7] The age of onset is generally between 50 and 70 years.[84]

Etiologic factors include tobacco smoking, heavy alcohol consumption, and previous radiation therapy treatment.[85] Hoarseness is the first noticeable manifestation of the disease. In later stages, the patient may notice a lump in the neck or throat pain.

Dementia and Language Disturbances

Dementia is a condition of progressive deterioration of the intellect, memory, and communicative function owing to organic disease of the cerebral hemispheres. This deterioration leads to a reduction in the level of a patient's social and occupational abilities. Although dementia is generally associated with old age, the symptoms of early onset Alzheimer's disease, for example, appear in the prime of midlife.[86] In a study of 1,225 cases of dementing diseases, Malamud cited three other conditions with onset in the prime of midlife: Pick's disease, Creutzfeldt-Jakob disease, and multi-infarct dementia.[87]

Communication deficits have been recognized in dementia patients regardless of the stage of their disease. In the early stages, language impairment is subtle because cognition is only mildly affected. In fact, language impairment may be unnoticeable in casual conversation. Generally, the more routine a particular communicative function is, the less it is affected in the early stages. Linguistic processes that require conscious attention, memory, and perception are more likely to be impaired,[88] and patients who recognize their subtle difficulties may try to avoid mentally or linguistically challenging situations or dismiss them as trivial.[79] In conversation, they may demonstrate disinhibition or difficulty with topic maintenance and may digress at length. Their ability to detect humor and sarcasm may be impaired. Expressively, they may be less able to show creativity in description and depend more on cliches.[79] Anomia and perseveration or inability to change a particular response style is not uncommon in dementia. Patients repeat ideas, phrases, or words long after the verbal response is appropriate. In the later stages of dementia, patients produce jargon or semantic neologisms.[82] Circumlocution, talking around an idea while failing to cite the idea explicitly, is another symptom of dementia.[79]

Hearing Impairment

Acquired hearing loss may be due to injury, disease, toxic effects of drugs, noise exposure, or the aging process. In the United States, hearing loss is the most common chronic disability.[89] The later in life that hearing loss occurs, the less severe the consequences. Once speech is established, it can usually be maintained even after the development of a hearing impairment.

Hearing loss not only affects sound perception and discrimination but also can cause speech and voice deficits secondary to the hearing-impaired person's inability to self-monitor via auditory feedback. Thus, the adult who has a severe to profound hearing loss that results in speech discrimination difficulties is likely to demonstrate problems in voice quality and articulation.

A hearing loss that is severe and of long duration can affect the individual's voice quality, as well as the use of pitch variation. The first speech sounds that deteriorate with severe hearing loss seem to be those that require the most precision in articulation and the greatest amount of auditory monitoring; for example, *s, r, l, sh,* and *ch.*

COMMUNICATION ASSESSMENT

The physician who suspects that a patient has a communication disturbance should refer that patient to a speech pathologist for a communication evaluation. The primary purpose of such an evaluation is to identify the presence and severity of alterations in communicative function. Of equal importance is the identification of the patient's residual abilities and areas of strength that the patient may use to compensate and overcome limitations imposed by the communication disturbance. Also essential in the evaluation process is the determination of whether, in fact, the identified impairment presents a true handicap in the patient's social, personal, and professional interactions. For example, the vocational impact of a mild verbal communication disturbance is greater for an individual whose job requires effective oral communication skills than is the impact of a more severe disturbance in an individual whose job requires manual labor. Finally, the evaluation procedure makes it possible for the clinician to determine the prognosis for recovery, to recommend interventions, and to delineate appropriate treatment goals.

The determination of the ability of the worker with a communication impairment to return to previous employment or to pursue new vocational goals requires the collaboration of a dedicated, well-trained team of professionals. The contributions of the speech pathologist to this process include assessment of communicative effectiveness, remediation of identified disorders, patient and family counseling, education of fellow professionals regarding the patient's communication ability, and provision of specific recommendations regarding vocational capacity.

Initial Assessment

The communication evaluation should begin as soon as possible after the onset of the impairment. If possible, the assessment should be conducted as soon as the patient's medical condition is stable and the process can be tolerated. Various studies have indicated that those individuals who receive early intervention perform better in the long run than do those in whom intervention was postponed.[90,91] In the more acute phase of illness, specific concerns may be focused on the patient's immediate ability to convey basic needs and wants; early intervention goals, however, indirectly establish the framework for more long-range, vocationally related goals. In other conditions, such as neuromuscular disorders and dementias, early assessment can provide baseline data to which subsequent performance levels can be quantitatively compared. In the case of vocal dysfunction, particularly with prolonged hoarseness or other sound aberration lasting more than 6 weeks, immediate referral to an otolaryngologist is crucial. As previously discussed, hoarseness and progressive deterioration of vocal quality may be indicative of more serious conditions, such as laryngeal cancer.

Assessment Procedures

Assessment of vocational capacity in the communicatively impaired individual is a special application of the usual assessment format. The process should include evaluation of the work environment, specific job responsibilities, and the needs and expectations of the worker and employer.

Testing tasks should be as functionally relevant as possible, reflecting the patient's home and work environment. The patient's performance during a speech, language, or voice assessment may be influenced by many factors that should be taken into account in test interpretation. Formal tests are standardized means of assessing a patient's performance, but the results can be influenced by patient fatigue or medication. Cultural differences or first language differences must also be considered in the interpretation of test results.

Language Assessment

In a language assessment, the clinician focuses on the patient's linguistic, communicative, and linguistically related cognitive systems.[13] Of important consideration is the individual's psychosocial history, premorbid levels of language (eg, educational level, vocational activities, interests), and personality characteristics. A major component of a language assessment is the differentiation of aphasia from other linguistic disturbances.

Evaluation of linguistic skills involves specific assessment of the individual's ability to recognize, recall, and process auditory and visual information, as well as the ability to integrate this information and to formulate and express language symbols through verbal, written, and gestural modes. Also assessed through a variety of unstructured and structured measures are motivation, ability to attend, awareness of errors, ability to self-correct mistakes, and ability to learn and generalize information.

Aphasia. A number of tests are available for the assessment of aphasia. The most frequently used aphasia tests are

- Boston Diagnostic Aphasia Examination[92]
- Western Aphasia Battery[93]
- Porch Index of Communicative Ability[90]
- Minnesota Test for Differential Diagnosis of Aphasia[91]

Most of the tests used in aphasia provide information on specific functioning in the modalities of auditory, visual, verbal, and written language by means of a hierarchy of test stimuli that range from the simple to the more complex.

Assessing auditory comprehension may require the individual to identify common objects, follow directions of increasing complexity, and respond to familiar and novel questions. The processing of higher-level linguistic material may be assessed by the clinician's reading a paragraph orally to the patient and asking him or her to respond to questions regarding its content, conversational exchanges, humor, and other subtleties of language. The patient may respond by pointing, gesturing, and expressing affirmation/negation if he or she has difficulty with verbal expression.

The clinician may assess visual reception by having the patient match forms and pictures, identify alphabet letters, match single words to pictures, and follow short written instructions. Assessing higher-level skills may involve having the patient read lengthy paragraphs, identify the main idea, draw conclusions, and make inferences from the written test. Functional reading skills, such as the ability to read a newspaper, locate material in a telephone book, follow recipes, and read a menu, may also be evaluated.

Assessment of verbal expression involves the analysis of grammatical structure, word retrieval, sentence formulation, fluency, and imitative skills in a variety of tasks. The clinician may ask the patient to count or to recite the days of the week and months of the year in an effort to evaluate automatic production, which is often preserved in the aphasic patient. In assessing verbal repetition skills, the clinician may have the patient repeat words, phrases, and sentences of increasing length and complexity. Naming skills may be assessed by asking the patient to name objects on confrontation and by analyzing word retrieval facility in conversation. Higher level language skills may be evaluated by asking the patient to define words, express opinions, solve problems, and sequence ideas.

The clinician may evaluate writing skills by asking the patient to write biographical data, letters and words to dictation, short sentences, and paragraphs. Functional writing skills, such as writing a letter, making lists, filling out applications, and writing checks, may also be assessed. Spelling, grammatical structure, organization, and general composition skills in any graphic production are evaluated. Supplemental language tests that are modality-specific include

- Reading Comprehension Battery for Aphasia[94]
- Auditory Compensation Test for Sentences[95]
- Revised Token Test[96]

In addition to the administration of formal test batteries, observation of the patient's ability to communicate in a variety of settings is important. Such observations allow the clinician to determine how the patient's language skills may vary within different contexts (eg, home, clinic, work) and how different situations may affect the length, complexity, responsiveness, and fluency of interaction.

One of the drawbacks of test batteries designed specifically for aphasics is their failure to differentiate aphasia from other linguistic disturbances. It is often necessary to administer other tests in order to distinguish neurogenic from cognitively based linguistic deficits.

Cognitively Based Communication Disorders. It is obvious that a language impairment will result in a communication disorder, but a cognitive impairment will also result in a communication disorder. Cognition refers to the manner in which an individual acquires knowledge and processes that knowledge. Language is an interrelated and integrated component of that knowledge. The breakdown that occurs in association with brain injury, lesions of the right hemisphere, and dementia results in a multidimensional complex of cognitively based communication disorders. Thorough assessment of the patient with cognitive communication disorders involves neuropsychology, as well as speech pathology.

Intrinsic to competent communication is a knowledge of appropriate ways to speak with different partners in different contexts,[97] as well as a knowledge of the obligations, rights, and expectations that support and maintain conversation.[98] Thus, competent communication implies a knowledge of who can say what to whom, in what manner, when and where, and by what means.[99]

No formal tests that address specifically the complex of cognitive communication disorders in the adult population have yet been validated. The best assessment method to date is careful observation of the patient in a variety of environments where physical contexts and communication partners can be varied and where communication intent and turn-taking can be noted.[100] Varying the physical context makes it possible to determine whether the patient is flexible in complying with the rules of communication. Does the patient adjust to different communication partners appropriately? Can the patient convey or interpret intent?[101] Does the patient initiate, maintain, and conclude the communication exchange reasonably? Here again, identification of the limitations and strengths suggests methods of compensation and the likely vocational ramifications.

Apraxia. The assessment of apraxia should include a general measure of language, an oral-verbal apraxia battery, and a speech sample.[40] Language should always be assessed in view of the fact that apraxia often accompanies aphasia. In tests of oral-verbal apraxia, the patient's ability to make voluntary nonspeech movements of the musculature (eg, pucker lips) is compared with the patient's ability to approximate similar postures in speech production (eg, lip rounding in the production of "oo"). The examiner may assess the articulatory integrity of the patient's speech by asking the patient to repeat sounds, syllables, words, and sentences of increasing complexity and length. A speech sample allows the examiner to analyze articulatory errors during such tasks as counting, describing pictures, reading aloud, and conversing.

There are few formal tests for apraxia. In the Apraxia Battery for Adults,[102] the patient performs diadochokinetic tasks (rapid repetition of a sound or sequence of sounds), repeats words of increased length, names pictures, reads orally, and produces both automatic and spontaneous speech. Similarly, Wertz, LaPointe, and Rosenbek evaluate motor speech through such tasks as conversation, prolongation of vowels, repetition of syllables and words, counting, picture description, and oral reading.[103]

In assessing the vocational capacity of the apraxic speaker, the examiner must consider the level of auditory and visual comprehension. Also, the patient's ability to compensate for verbal expressive deficits by writing, gesturing, or other augmentative means should be investigated.

Dysarthria. The examiner may appraise dysarthria through either perceptual or instrumental measures. In a perceptual assessment, a trained speech pathologist listens to the patient's speech and voice, making judgments about the type of abnormality demonstrated. Because speech is a dynamic process, it is difficult to isolate and judge one particular aspect, however. In addition, the patient may be attempting to compensate for speech difficulty by such components of speech as altering the rate or manner of articulation; in this case, it may be difficult to differentiate between the speech problem itself and the patient's compensatory strategies. It is also difficult to standardize perceptual judgments over time and in different settings, which contributes to problems in inter- and intrarater reliability. Despite the pitfalls of perceptual assessment, it remains the most widely used method of appraising dysarthria. It provides a comprehensive evaluation of the processes of respiration, phonation, articulation, resonance, and prosody.

The Assessment of Intelligibility of Dysarthric Speech is a perceptual tool that allows the examiner to make a quantitative assessment of the single word intelligibility, sentence intelligibility, and speaking rate of dysarthric speakers.[104] The severity of dysarthria is established by measures of speech intelligibility and speaking rate. Another perceptual tool, the Frenchay Dysarthria Assessment, involves the assessment of various speech components and dimensions.[105] The patient performs designated tasks, such as prolonging a sound or counting, and the examiner assesses such factors as muscle function, intelligibility, and rate. Scoring is based on the patient's second attempt at each task.

In an instrumental evaluation of dysarthria, a speech pathologist interprets data received from instruments that are sensitive to the aerodynamics, neural events, and movements associated with speaking. Rosenbek and LaPointe cautioned, "Alone, instrumental evaluation is far from a panacea"[42]; together with a complete history and clinical observation, however, instrumentation can provide important information on the type and nature of dysarthric symptoms. Sound spectrograms can provide useful data on acoustic variables of speech, such as pitch contours, loudness of segments, pause time, and articulation time. Electromyographic tests can provide information on the activity of articulatory musculature, intraoral and subglottal air pressure, nasal airflow, and speaking rate. Regardless of the specific measure used in dysarthria assessment, the examiner makes judgments on the type and severity of the motor speech disorders, their impact on speech intelligibility, and appropriate treatment.

The vocational implications of dysarthria vary with each individual. For example, mildly impaired speech intelligibility may be of little importance to a painter, computer programmer, or truck driver, but may present a significant vocational obstacle for a receptionist, waitress, educator, or entertainer. Some patients with severely impaired speech intelligibility may require an augmentative or alternative method of communicating in order to perform communicative tasks in the work environment.

Voice Assessment

The patient who requires a voice assessment must first see an otolaryngologist for an evaluation of the involved physical structures. Ideally, the speech pathologist is present during the examination so that he or she can better appreciate the type and degree of laryngeal pathology associated with the patient's voice problems.

A voice assessment has several objectives. The speech pathologist educates the patient in the anatomy and physiology of normal voice production to give the patient a greater insight into the voice problems and a greater sense of control in the remedial process. In addition, the speech pathologist tries to ascertain the precipitating and maintaining causes of the voice problem from hearing the patient's report, listening to the voice, observing the patient during voice production, and obtaining objective voice measurements. The speech pathologist describes the vocal properties and the deleterious effect of disease or abuse/misuse on the vocal mechanism. The final objective of the voice assessment is to develop an individualized management plan that may involve voice therapy, retraining, and/or modification of the patient's environment, either at work or at home.

Functional Voice Disorders. By far the most common cause of functional voice disorders is vocal abuse/misuse. Several studies have identified occupations that place the voice at high risk.[8,82,106] Given prolonged use of the voice in these occupations, individuals who would probably have no difficulty in conversational situations may develop voice problems. Teachers, factory workers, homemakers, salespeople, supervisors, secretaries, telephone operators, lawyers, nurses, and social worke:: psychologists fall into this category. People who depend on their voices for then livelihood can develop voice problems when they are forced to use their voices in an adverse environment or to carry out job duties with a cold or laryngitis. The singer, actor, or orator who must project to an audience in a dusty, dry air theater or the preacher who must deliver the Sunday sermon despite a bout with allergies falls into this second category. Nodules, edema, polyps, and dysphonia are common within these professions.

Organic Voice Disorders. For patients with laryngeal carcinoma, the speech pathologist ideally conducts both preoperative and postoperative consultations, the latter until the patient has acquired some form of alaryngeal communication. There are currently three successful methods of alaryngeal speech habilitation: (1) use of an artificial larynx, (2) esophageal speech, and (3) tradheosophageal speech produced via surgical prosthetics. All three methods have advantages and disadvantages. The most appropriate method for a particular patient depends on the patient's vocational needs.

Assessment of Communication Skills in the Hearing Impaired

The assessment of the receptive and expressive communication skills of the hearing-impaired worker is multifold. Regardless of the extent of the hearing loss or the possibility that the worker can benefit from amplification, the speech pathologist should assess and refine the patient's speech-reading ability. This process involves an appraisal of the patient's ability to receive a visual message, to store its content in short-term memory, and to transfer the information into long-term memory for retrieval purposes.

The test of the need for auditory training is the person's ability to understand and discriminate speech sounds with or without amplication. The person who has difficulty understanding speech, regardless of hearing acuity, is likely to benefit from auditory training. Assessment generally involves examination of the individual's ability to discriminate high-frequency, low-powered, voiceless speech consonants, such as *h*, *s*, *sh*, and *ch*.

PROGNOSIS FOR RECOVERY AND RETURN TO WORK

The communicatively impaired patient's prognosis for recovery of communication skills and return to work is typically contingent on a number of factors, including age, etiology of impairment, severity of deficits, and motivation.

Cerebrovascular Accidents

Aphasia

Several authors have outlined important considerations in determining the prognosis for improvement in the aphasic individual.[12,103,107,108] They consist of the following:

- Generally, the younger the patient, the better the prospects for recovery.
- Individuals whose speech rehabilitation is initiated early after onset of cerebrovascular accident or injury have a better chance for improvement.
- If a patient is aware of errors and is able to self-correct, there is a better prognosis for improvement.
- The individual who has a flexible personality and accepts the impairment with little anxiety has a better prognosis.
- Aphasia in the traumatically brain-injured individual has a generally better recovery than aphasia secondary to degenerative vascular diseases.
- The less severe the initial aphasia involvement, the better the chances of recovery.
- The presence of other health, sensory, and motor deficits tends to be a negative prognostic indicator.

The influence of premorbid intelligence and social milieu on the prognosis of the aphasic patient remains undetermined.[107] Some investigators argue that, because more highly educated individuals have more language to lose, aphasia is a greater relative impairment for them than for those with less education. Prognosis for residual function is generally more favorable in more intelligent and more highly educated individuals, however.

Over the past several years, authorities have been debating whether language rehabilitation results in measurable improvement beyond that which can be expected from spontaneous recovery in aphasic patients. The spontaneous recovery curve is steepest during the first month after onset, flattens at 2 to 3 months, but continues to rise at 6 to 9 months and even longer.[12] For all practical purposes, the period of spontaneous recovery appears to be 6 months. Although the results of research are not totally conclusive, several studies have demonstrated that language therapy is beneficial beyond spontaneous recovery.[109–112]

Speech pathologists have hundreds of treatment techniques available to them. The two principles that dominate the selection of treatment methods to be used with aphasic patients reflect contrasting views: (1) aphasia is a problem of impaired "access" to language, and (2) aphasia is a "loss" of language.[113] Whatever the methods used, some experts believe that roughly 50% to 70% of all stroke patients with language problems will be able to communicate adequately for expressing their basic needs.[114]

There are studies that specifically address aphasia and occupational resettlement. Clearly, the individual with aphasia may have appreciable difficulty returning to a vocation that requires verbal and written communication. Furthermore, the ability to carry out necessary job responsibilities may be hampered by the individual's difficulty in understanding verbal and visual information and by compromised verbal and written communication. When Hatfield and Zangwill studied two aphasic men with primarily receptive involvement and two aphasic men with primarily expressive involvement, however, they found that all four were able to return to work (ie, assistant chef, storekeeper, ranch manager, and laboratory technician) and all received excellent reviews of job performance from their superiors.[115] In all cases, the men performed job responsibilities adequately, despite their significant difficulty in describing what their duties actually were. Hatfield and Zangwill suggested that a patient's personality is crucial to vocational integration, particularly the patient's acceptance of disabilities and determination to communicate.[115]

Raderstorf and colleagues described the return to work of a young machinist 18 months after the onset of aphasia.[116] Here, the rehabilitation team collaborated with the patient's employer, visiting the patient's workplace prior to his return and structuring therapeutic goals toward job responsibilities. After the patient successfully returned to work, there was a positive change in his disposition. He began assuming responsibility for other activities related to home (eg, yardwork, shopping, babysitting) that he had previously neglected. A few other, similar case studies have been cited in the literature.[117–119]

In another study, Carriero and associates outlined specific job restructuring strategies employed with 10 moderate to severe aphasics who returned to work.[120] Strategies that enabled the patients to return to work included

- reducing the number of hours worked and the size of territory
- reducing the number of verbal interactions necessary by the number of new and different individuals with whom the patient had to interact
- allowing the patient to use overlearned language and behaviors when confronting new and unfamiliar tasks
- seeking initial assistance from friends or relatives, particularly when interaction with new customers was required

The returning workers also delegated problematic job responsibilities to other workers. These authors postulated that the capacity to return to work is often greater than the findings of a formal language assessment would suggest, particularly with younger, more motivated aphasic patients. Socially, the self-employed patients, who had the capacity to modify their own jobs, appeared to have a distinct advantage over those employees whose jobs were regulated by employers.

Apraxia

Although there are no definitive signs of the prognosis for verbally apraxic speakers, some factors suggest a more favorable prognosis than do others[103]:

- Given identical degrees of apraxia of speech, the patient who is less than 1 month postonset has a better prognosis than the patient in later stages of recovery.
- The smaller the lesion, the better the prospects for improvement.
- The patient with minimal coexisting aphasia is more likely to recover than is a patient with more severe language disturbances.
- The absence of other medical and sensory deficits is a positive prognostic sign.
- The combination of education, counseling, and drills, together with the patient's motivation and ability to learn—and generate—new information, enhances improvement.

The prognosis for functional improvement in the untreated apraxic speaker is poor. On the other hand, the prognosis for the patient with severe apraxia is considered fair if treatment is provided; the prognosis for the patient with mild to moderate apraxia is good with speech rehabilitation.[103]

Therapy for the apraxic speaker generally involves hierarchies of stimuli through which the clinician attempts to help patients progress from a level of limited automatic speech to volitional communication.[121] Auditory and visual modalities are emphasized as they appear to be therapeutically effective with apraxics. Therapeutic methods include the use of compensation, increased control of volitional speech movements, self-monitoring, early intervention, and encouragement of self-confidence and motivation.[45]

Dysarthria

Several variables appear to influence the prognosis for dysarthric speakers.[122]

- Patients with bilateral subcortical or brainstem lesions or degenerative diseases that result in dysarthria tend to have the poorest prognosis; patients with less massive cortical lesions (or even bilateral lesions that spare subcortical areas) tend to have a better prognosis.
- The younger the patient, the better the prognosis for recovery.
- The patient's incorporation of ''automatic'' adjustments to the lesion may be a positive indicator of outcome (eg, slowing speech rate to facilitate intelligibility).

- Certain personality characteristics, such as premorbid optimism and goal-directed behaviors, tend to be positive prognostic indicators.
- The presence of supportive individuals with realistic expectations tends to enhance ongoing treatment and promote the carryover of skills, the maintenance of intelligible speech, and the use of augmentative and alternative means of communication.

The management of the dysarthric patient may require medical, behavioral, instrumental, and/or prosthetic techniques. Medical management may involve surgery or drug therapy. Behavioral methods include traditional speech therapy techniques with the ultimate goal of "compensated intelligibility."[42] The speech pathologist can increase the patient's confidence in his or her ability to overcome speech problems by using various exercises that improve the strength, speed, precision, and range of movements of speech musculatures, as well as teaching the patient how best to use residual abilities. Instrumental methods involve the use of equipment that provides visual and auditory feedback to the speaker. Prosthetic interventions, such as a palatal lift to decrease hypernasality, vocal fold injections, or surgical procedures that involve realignment of the affected vocal fold to decrease hoarseness or breathiness, may be appropriate for severely dysarthric patients. Augmentative and alternative means of communication, such as the use of communication boards and electronic devices, may be used with the severely impaired patient.

Return-to-work statistics for patients with motor speech disorders secondary to cerebrovascular accident are scarce. In general, vocational success appears to be related largely to an individual's ability to produce intelligible language expression, whether it be through verbal communication, writing, or gesturing, or through the use of augmentative or alternative means of communication. The prognosis for a return to work may be more optimistic in the patient without a significant coexisting language or cognitive disturbance.

Nondominant Hemispheric Disturbances

Information regarding the prognosis for patients with right hemispheric communicative disturbances is limited. In comparison to patients with left hemispheric damage, those with right hemispheric injury have persisting self-care disability.[123] Also, those with right-sided brain involvement demonstrate persistence in communication impairments.[124]

In one study of several variables that may affect the return to work of patients who have right hemispheric damage, it was found that age and education offered little predictive information.[125] Sex, ability to walk, use of the affected arm, and cognition (tested by block design performance) all had prognostic significance, however. More women than men returned to work. Those who could walk and had some use of their affected extremity were more apt to return to work. Of the total sample, only 37% with right hemispheric involvement returned to work; the average length of time between the onset of the disability and the return to work was 19 months.

Visuospatial and perceptual deficits, with their consequent effects on reading, writing, and other visual skills, most certainly hold predictive value in determining the ability of these patients to return to work. Those patients whose jobs are of a more verbal than visual nature may find it easier to return to work.

Brain Injury

The prognostic indicators useful in predicting the outcome of rehabilitative efforts with brain-injured patients include duration of coma and post-traumatic amnesia, age, and the extent of other medical/physical complications.[56] Premorbid personality and behaviors also affect recovery; persons who are self-driven and highly motivated have a better prognosis. Indicators of a poor prognosis are a history of drug or alcohol abuse, mental/emotional instability, poor work or academic record, and poor motivation.[56] Other factors that reduce the probability of a patient's return to work are nonsupportive family and employers; a premorbid job that required speed, efficiency, and safety precautions; and patient dissatisfaction with simpler or nondemanding jobs.[126] Ben-Yishay and associates reported that professionals at a workshop on the employment of head-injured individuals most often cited the following reasons for the failure of these individuals to return to work[127]:

- deficits in memory, attention, persistence, and executive skills
- deficits in initiation (adynamia) and/or disinhibition
- poor interpersonal skills, which would encompass cognitively based communication skills
- poor insight into the implications of the injury
- unrealistic expectations as to employment capacity

The process of recovery from brain injury varies. LeMay and Geschwind reported that people aged 20 to 40 years continue to improve for 5 to 6 years postinjury and people aged 40 to 60 years improved for 2 years postinjury.[128] Groher suggested that the most dramatic improvement following brain injury occurs in the first month, the first 2 months, or the first 6 months and that improvement is much slower beyond these periods of spontaneous recovery.[129]

The recovery of communication skills following closed head injury is generally faster than is the recovery of these skills following cerebrovascular accident. The recovery of expressive communication skills tends to parallel the recovery of receptive communication skills; both begin to plateau at 6 months. The deficits that remain are likely to be in more cognitively based communication skills and in reading and writing.[130] Hagen and colleagues found that the recovery of communication skills in 2,000 head trauma patients closely paralleled and was dependent on cognitive recovery; furthermore, the process was hierarchical.[131] Other researchers found that recovery in communication paralleled recovery in locomotion and activities of daily living (ADL).[132]

Many studies have shown that mildly to moderately impaired patients recover from aphasia or are not "typically" aphasic 6 months postinjury, but continue to have residual difficulties that interfere with higher level ADL, interpersonal communication skills, and return to work.[60,132–135] Communication dysfunction after 6 months may be characterized by deficits in verbal memory, learning, and problem solving (see Cognitively Based Communication Disorders).

The general principles of treatment for residual communication deficits follow the therapeutic design of a successful cognitive rehabilitative approach. Tasks are designed to promote the patient's success and are systematically graduated in difficulty to provide challenges and to encourage learning. Tasks are practiced repeatedly in a variety of environments to allow for generalization across situations. The patient is given increasing responsibility in goal setting, treatment planning, and problem solving to increase independence and motivation. Treatment approaches are made consistent with family, employer, and treatment team expectations so that demands on the patients are similar. Communication tasks are planned according to the patient's chronological and developmental age, as well as premorbid social, educational, and vocational status. Group therapy not only allows for practice of social/interpersonal skills but also, by sharing of experiences, provides the patient with greater insight into the consequences of the injury.[136] (See Chapter 6, "Vocational Capacity with Cognitive Impairment, for data concerning the return to work of brain-injured patients).

Neuromuscular Disease

Multiple Sclerosis

One of the major problems in determining the vocational potential of patients with multiple sclerosis is the uncertainty of the future course of the disease (see Chapter 7, Vocational Capacity with Neuromuscular Impairment). As the disease progresses, communication skills may be impaired by reduced speech intelligibility, poor vision, compromised writing skills, and mental decline.

In managing the patient with multiple sclerosis, a speech pathologist focuses on problems with speech production that interfere with intelligibility and overall functional communication. The speech pathologist often works with the patient during the period of remission, when the patient's condition is more stable.[42] Treatment is designed to improve physiologic support for speech by means of exercises to increase muscle strength and function. In addition, as with dysarthria secondary to cerebrovascular accident or trauma, a primary goal of therapy is to help the patient compensate for impairments and make the best use of residual abilities. More severely affected patients may require augmentative communication systems.

Beukelman and associates surveyed 656 patients with multiple sclerosis in an attempt to assess the presence and severity of expressive communication disturbances and their impact on employability.[70] The employment patterns of the communicatively impaired group (23% of the sample) were decidedly different from those of the total sample. A smaller percentage (7%) were employed full-time as compared to the percentage of the total sample (17%), whereas a larger percentage of communicatively impaired were in the "disabled" category. Yet, when asked if communication disorders interfered with employment, only 3% of respondents reported this as a problem.

Parkinson's Disease

Many individuals with Parkinson's disease have excellent potential to resume everyday activities after diagnosis because of the gradual onset and relatively slow progression of the disease. Many symptoms may not interfere with the patient's functional abilities until after the age of 65 years. As the disease progresses, however, impaired verbal and nonverbal communication skills may interfere with the patient's social, personal, and professional interactions. In the later stages, patients may occasionally demonstrate mental decline, confusion, reduced initiative, and impaired judgment.

Some authorities have advocated early speech intervention as a means of slowing the degeneration of functional skills.[45] In addition to therapy, various drugs have been observed to improve speech intelligibility. Carbidopa-levodopa (Sinemet), for example, may improve the clarity of articulation, nasal resonance, volume, phrasing, vocal quality, and pitch variation.[137] Calne suggested that speech therapy may be most effective in patients whose conditions are medically stable and in those whose speech has improved secondary to medication.[138] Speech therapy may focus on improving vocal function, increasing loudness, improving prosody and nonverbal communication, altering pitch, and reducing speaking rate.

Literature on the return to work of patients with communication deficits as a result of Parkinson's disease is scarce. Some individuals with the disease can perform their job responsibilities adequately until the condition is relatively well advanced. If the position requires a great deal of talking and interpersonal interaction, however, reduced speech intelligibility, compromised affect, and difficulty managing saliva may necessitate job restructuring. Periodic follow-up of the patient with Parkinson's disease is necessary to monitor any deterioration in interpersonal skills on the job.

Amyotrophic Lateral Sclerosis

At the present time, no medical treatment has proved effective in treating amyotrophic lateral sclerosis. Long-term prognosis is poor due to the steady deterioration of the patient's condition as the disease progresses. It is uncommon, but not rare, for the patient with amyotrophic lateral sclerosis to live more than 6 to 10 years after diagnosis.[80] Because the patient's functional limitations depend on the muscles that are affected at any given time, the disease may or may not affect communication skills. The residual effects on speech may be mild initially, but often worsen during the course of the disease.

Speech therapy may focus on improving or maintaining physiologic support for speech, educating the patient and family on communicative consequences, and training the patient in the use of augmentative and alternative communication systems (eg, gesturing, communication boards, and electronic devices). Many individuals are able to return to work after diagnosis, but it may be necessary to modify any job responsibilities that require interpersonal contact as the ability to speak begins to decline. It is important to remember that amyotrophic lateral sclerosis does not generally affect intelligence. Productive work and pursuit of other interests should be encouraged, as long as the individual is physically and emotionally able to tolerate participation in such activities.

Huntington's Chorea

The short-term vocational prognosis may be good for patients in the initial stages of Huntington's chorea. Many years may pass before the patient becomes completely incapacitated or is unable to continue with work. The long-term prognosis is poor, however, as there are no known treatments that slow the steady progression of the disease. The disease may eventually compromise speech intelligibility and may lead to obvious limitations in the patient's intellectual abilities, verbal expression, learning ability, and memory.

Speech therapy with the patient who has Huntington's chorea may focus on the identification of the best input and output channels; that is, determining the modality through which the individual best processes and communicates information (eg, verbal vs. visual, talking vs. writing). In addition, the speech pathologist may advise the patient and family on the best ways to structure or simplify the environment in order to facilitate successful interactions. The ultimate goal of therapy is to maintain the patient's residual speech and intellectual abilities. When necessary, therapy may also address means of augmentative or alternative communication.

Friedreich's Ataxia

Although Friedreich's ataxia is a rare disease, its vocational implications are important because it affects a young age group. The disease results in a steady deterioration of the patient's condition; some patients may be physically incapacitated by the time that they are in their mid-twenties. There are no known medications or treatment that slow the progression of the disease. Intelligence and learning ability typically remain unimpaired. Speech, however, may be characterized by impaired articulation with reduced intelligibility. Job reintegration should take into consideration the interpersonal demands of the position, and appropriate modifications should be made, as necessary.

Voice Disorders

Prognostic indicators of the voice-disordered patient's successful return to work include (1) early recognition and accurate diagnosis of the voice disorder, which entails the identification of precipitating and maintaining causes; (2) immediate initiation of an appropriate treatment regimen, which may entail voice therapy, surgery, medical treatment, and/or psychologic intervention; (3) adequate cognitive abilities and motivation; and (4) some flexibility in restructuring or adjusting vocal usage in the work environment, if necessary.

Intrinsic to the successful treatment of functional voice disorders (eg, nodules, polyps, laryngitis) is the modification or elimination of etiologic factors. When misuse of respiration, phonation, resonation, pitch, loudness, rate, and decreased laryngeal muscle strength and tone have produced the vocal disorder, direct symptom modification is employed.[85]

Several organic voice disorders caused by medical conditions or surgery are amenable to modification through voice therapy.[85] For the laryngectomee, successful alaryngeal voice selection is crucial for a return to work. Speech rehabilitation through the use of the artificial larynx, esophageal speech, tracheoesophageal speech, or any combination of these modalities becomes particularly important in view of the fact that the current 5-year survival rate following laryngectomy is 66%. If the lesion is localized, the 5-year survival rate is 80%.[139] Thus, although the incidence of laryngeal carcinoma has increased in recent years, the mortality rate has decreased.

Past attitudes toward the use of an artificial larynx have not always been positive. In some circles of professionals and laryngectomees, the artificial larynx has been regarded as the patient's ''scarlet letter'' of failure to develop his or her own alaryngeal voice. Furthermore, despite pitch and volume controls, it has a mechanical or robot-like sound, which distracts the naive listener from the speaker's communicative content. In addition, speech intelligibility is slightly compromised because all voiceless speech sounds (for example, *p, t, k,* and *ch*) are perceived as their voiced speech sound cognates (*b, d, g,* and *j*).[140] Finally, the most frequently used models require manual operation, which affects the return to work of laryngectomees who must use their hands in their jobs.

The most outstanding advantages of the artificial larynx are its ready availability and its ease of use. It is also the least expensive of the three methods.[85] Several investigators who have compared the speech intelligibility of the three methods concluded that the intelligibility of artificial larynx speech compares favorably to that of the other two methods in a quiet environment and is consistently the best of the three in a noisy environment.[141–144] Thus, the artificial larynx is at least the initial choice for the laryngectomee who wishes to return to work quickly or in a noisy environment.

Traditionally, rehabilitative efforts to restore speech in laryngectomized patients have centered on the acquisition of esophageal speech. This "voice" is produced by the laryngectomee's remaining anatomic structures. With self-injected air, the person sets the muscles of the upper esophagus and pharynx into vibration, generating sound. This voice, viewed as the person's "natural" voice, gives the laryngectomee a greater sense of indendence. A good esophageal speaker's voice sounds similar to a slightly hoarse, laryngeally produced voice.

In the past, the proportion of laryngectomees able to communicate effectively by means of esophageal speech was reported to be as high as 86%.[145] In the 1980s, however, the reported proportion was approximately 26%.[146] Today's laryngectomee is older, has more advanced disease and is more apt to be receiving post-operative radiation therapy, all of which may impede the development of esophageal speech.[146] The major disadvantage of functional esophageal speech is that learning fluent and functional esophageal speech requires a minimum of 6 months to a year of arduous dedication in treatment.

The newest form of speech rehabilitation for laryngectomees is tracheoesophageal speech produced via surgical prosthetics. In 1979, Dr. Mark Singer, an otolaryngologist, and Dr. Mark Blom, a speech pathologist, reported a new surgical procedure, describing it as the "tracheoesophageal puncture."[147] In order to provide lung air for esophageal speech, a small fistula is created in the wall between the esophagus and the trachea; the fistula is maintained by a silicone prosthesis that acts as a one-way valve. When the stoma to the trachea is occluded, the prosthesis allows lung air to pass into the esophagus.

There are many advantages in having more than 2,000 ml of lung air available for esophageal speech production. Compared to that in regular esophageal speech production, the loudness range in tracheoesophageal speech production is much more spontaneous. There is also an increase in pitch variation and an extension of the sound duration.[148] In addition, the average time that it takes a speech pathologist to evaluate the patient's ability to manage the prosthesis, fit the prosthesis, and train the patient in its care and use is ony 10 hours.[85] Finally, the success rate with the prosthesis has been estimated to be as high as 85%.[85]

On the other hand, the creation of a tracheoesophageal fistula does require a surgical procedure (which may be performed at the time of the laryngectomy or as a later procedure). Although the success rate is high, most studies have involved a carefully selected sample. Patients must have good mentation, motivation, manual dexterity, and good vision for the proper use and care of the prosthesis. Esophageal dysfunctions that preclude the acquisition of regular esophageal speech also preclude the acquisition of tracheoesophageal speech; furthermore, the trachea must be in good condition for tracheoesophageal speech, and pulmonary function must be adequate to support sound generation. The tracheoesophageal puncture requires the use of the hand to occlude the stoma for voice production, which is a vocational disadvantage. A tracheostoma breathing valve that would free the hand has been developed, but to date, its functional usefulness has been limited.[147]

Regarding the return to work of these patients, Richardson found that laryngectomees have more problems in retaining jobs or finding new jobs than do other cancer patients.[149] She found that 67% of 46 subjects under the age of 64 were retired or unemployed on an average of 2 years after surgery. The laryngectomees themselves commonly decided not to work after surgery, and their decisions were not correlated significantly to a failure in speech and social rehabilitation. Richardson's survey and clinical experience suggested that successful vocational rehabilitation of the laryngectomee depends not only on speech acquisition and physical health but also on psychologic and emotional well-being.

MODIFICATION OF THE WORK ENVIRONMENT

The vocational rehabilitation and placement of the speech-language-voice-disordered individual are best orchestrated by an interdisciplinary team. Most communicatively impaired persons who need work adjustment services also have other physical/cognitive disabilities that must be taken into account.

The return to work of the communicatively disabled person demands very careful evaluation of (1) the job setting; (2) the nature of the residual communicative impairment; (3) the complexity of the job's speech, interpersonal, language, and voice requirements; and (4) the extent of new learning necessitated.[150] It is also essential to evaluate the employer's expectations. In a survey of 142 employers who had hired disabled students, Burton and colleagues found that interpersonal skills, ability to communicate with the public, basic reading and mathematics skills, and ability to fill out a job application ranked in the top 13 of 22 skills that employers desired.[151] The remaining 9 skills in the top 13 could be interpreted as cognitively based skills with less direct emphasis on communication per se, such as punctuality, dependability, pride in work, respect for authority, enthusiasm, good grooming, ability to accept on-the-job training, ability to find a job, and ability to use transportation.[151]

The purpose of job modification for the communicatively impaired individual is twofold: to compensate for deficits and to enhance performance. Factors that frequently interfere with the work performance of patients who have experienced a brain injury or a cerebrovascular accident include[152]

- language impairments that affect the ability to understand instructions and explanations
- language processing problems that are accentuated by the quantity of information, the complexity of information, or the rate of presentation
- cognitive deficits in the areas of attention and concentration, memory, organization, problem solving, and self-monitoring
- emotional lability and impulsivity
- perceptual difficulties
- behavioral problems
- fatigue or endurance problems that exacerbate the communication difficulty
- general slowness of response

Factors that frequently interfere with the work performance of vocally impaired persons include

- vocal fatigue
- difficulty competing in noisy environments
- environmental irritants to the vocal or respiratory mechanism or laryngectomees

If employers can limit the impact of these factors, their communicatively impaired employees are more likely to be successful.[152]

Most job accommodations that employers have to make for speech-impaired workers are reasonable, minimal, and of little or no expense. When Berkeley Planning Associates surveyed 2,000 federal contractors concerning compliance with the Rehabilitation Act of 1973, 54% of the contractors reported zero costs, whereas 21% reported costs ranging from $100 to $499.[153] The single most frequently reported job accommodation was orientation of co-workers and supervisors (67.9%). The next most frequent job accommodation was additional training for the speech-impaired worker (18.9%).

The orientation of co-workers and supervisors is essential to the successful return to work of a communicatively impaired person. Such an orientation should range in scope from pointers on basic courtesies to insights into the impaired person's communicative strengths, weaknesses, and best learning style. Basic information should include the fact that communicatively impaired individuals are not necessarily hearing impaired, so shouting does not enhance comprehension. Also, co-workers should understand that an impaired person's comprehension may be quite good, despite expressive difficulties, so they should not exclude the person from conversation. More specific orientation may relate to a communicatively impaired worker's need for an augmentative means of receiving and retaining instructions; the worker may need not only verbal instructions but also written or even printed instructions that are shorter in length and simpler in language. Most workers benefit from a familiar job routine. In fact, variance in job duties may decrease their job capacity appreciatively. Some workers may benefit from secretarial assistance in taking telephone calls, typing out instructions, or making appointment schedules. The use of calculators, tape recorders, or computers may help to reduce the possibility of errors in taking and writing orders.

AUGMENTATIVE AND ALTERNATIVE COMMUNICATION SYSTEMS

Individuals whose speech does not meet their communication needs may require augmentative and alternative means of communication. Augmentative systems supplement the individual's remaining vocal abilities.[154] Alternative systems are used when the individual's physical problems are so extensive that speech production is deemed improbable. Augmentative and alternative communication systems may be used with individuals who have dysarthria or language disorders secondary to stroke, trauma, or other neurologic disease or with individuals who have voice disorders secondary to trauma, dysfunction, or anatomic anomalies.

Two different communication techniques are typically used in augmentative and alternative communication.[155] Unaided communication techniques require only the individual's body; such techniques include speech, sign language, gestures, and facial expressions. Aided communication techniques require an object or device, such as a notebook, board, or electronic device. Language symbols used in communication may include pictures, alphabet letters, printed or verbalized words, and manual signs.

Determination of the most effective augmentative or alternative communication system for a particular patient requires careful consideration of several factors, including the relationships among the individual, vocation, communication system, and the environment. Panton recommended that the following factors be evaluated[156]:

- personal factors (eg, age, sex, medical diagnosis, educational achievement, motivation, prognosis)
- equipment factors (eg, size, color, age, portability)
- workspace factors (eg, work, home, school, community)
- environmental factors (eg, physical and psychosocial)
- system factors (eg, general acceptability, necessity to train others)

The expectations and concerns of the communicatively impaired user, along with those of family, friends, educators, and employers, must always be considered when selecting an appropriate communication system.

The person with a voice disorder, whether it is secondary to a tracheostomy, vocal cord paralysis, laryngectomy, or other vocal condition, may benefit from any number of augmentative systems. Initially, the speech pathologist may encourage the patient to use writing or an artificial larynx until speech proficiency improves. Self-activated pneumatic voicing systems are available for physically dependent individuals who are unable to phonate because of interrupted airflow to the larynx. Voice amplifiers can be used to make the voice louder if reduced volume is the primary defective component of speech.

Although the advantage of an alternative means of communication for the non-vocal person are obvious, there are also disadvantages.[157] Vocal language users may be reluctant to accept the use of such a communication system, as they may have difficulty understanding the message or may not be willing to take the time necessary to receive the message. Also, such systems may be expensive, not only because of the actual equipment costs but also because of the training required for individuals to use the system.

The cognitively impaired individual may benefit from nonalphabetic communication systems, such as pictorial boards or devices. Alphabetic systems, which require higher level cognitive and language skills, are most often used with electronic aids. Many electronic devices have both a printer and a speech synthesizer. Although many synthesizers have a somewhat "mechanical" sound, technology has made it possible to modify the pitch and rate of speech in these devices. Some systems allow the user to produce verbal messages by recording another individual's voice on tape. Many electronic systems can be programmed around the user's vocabulary needs and have the capacity to store and retrieve hundreds of words, phrases, and sentences. Sophisticated microcomputer-based devices are now available; in addition to communication functions, these devices may have drawing, educational, and entertainment features. If the individual using the system is physically unable to point to the required symbols, a number of other selection modes allow access to the system by virtually any other physical movement (eg, head pointing, eye gazing, blinking).

Determining the effectiveness of augmentative and alternative communication systems in the workplace involves assessment of several parameters, such as the speed and accuracy of the message transmission; spontaneous usage and initiation of messages; frequency of use; adequacy of vocabulary; length of utterance; acceptance by user and communication partners; and ability to use the system with confidence, independence, motivation, and minimal frustration.[158]

CONCLUSION

Communication impairments are often a debilitating consequence of disease or trauma and may interfere with an individual's ability to return to work or pursue new vocational goals. The prognosis for recovery of many communicatively impaired individuals who demonstrate difficulty understanding and using language, as well as physically producing speech, is favorable with early identification and intervention, however.

REFERENCES

1. Brooks WD. *Speech Communication*. Dubuque, IA: William C Brown; 1971.

2. Irwin JV. Communication. In: Weston AJ, ed. *Communicative Disorders: An Appraisal*. Springfield, IL: Charles C Thomas; 1972.

3. Emerick LL. *Speaking for Ourselves: Self Portraits of the Speech or Hearing Handicapped*. Danville, IL: Interstate Printers and Publishers; 1984.

4. American Speech and Hearing Association. Media resource center. Rockville, MD: ASHA; 1985.

5. US Bureau of the Census. *Disability, Functional Limitation, and Health Insurance Coverage: 1984/85*. Washington, DC: Current Population Reports; 1986. Series P-70 No. 8.

6. Laguaite JK. Adult voice screening. *J Speech Hear Disord*. 1972;37:147–151.

7. Division of Cancer Prevention and Control, Division of Cancer Treatment. *Annual Cancer Statistics Review*. Bethesda, MD: National Cancer Institute; 1988.

8. Herrington-Hall BL, Lee L, Stemple JC, et al. Description of laryngeal pathologies by age, sex, and occupation in a treatment-seeking sample. *J Speech Hear Disord*. 1988;53:57–64.

9. The National Institute of Neurological and Communicative Disorders and Stroke. *Profile*. Bethesda, MD; 1987.

10. Sahs A, Hartman EC, eds. *Fundamentals of Stroke Care*. Washington, DC: US Department of Health, Education, Welfare; 1976.

11. Soltero I, Kiv K, Cooper R, et al. Trends in mortality from cerebrovascular diseases in the United States, 1960–75. *Stroke*. 1978;9:549–558.

12. Darley FL. *Aphasia*. Philadelphia: WB Saunders; 1982.

13. Chapey R. The assessment of language disorders in adults. In: Chapey R, ed. *Language Intervention Strategies in Adult Aphasia*, 2nd ed. Baltimore: Williams & Wilkins; 1986:81–140.

14. National Institutes of Health. *Aphasia*. Bethesda, MD: NIH; 1979. NIH Pub No 80-391.

15. Kertesz A, Black SE. Cerebrovascular disease and aphasia. In: Darby JK, ed. *Speech and Language Evaluation in Neurology: Adult Disorders*. Orlando, FL: Grune & Stratton; 1985:83–122.

16. Leske MC. Prevalence estimates of communicative disorders in the US: language, hearing and vestibular disorders. *ASHA*. 1981;23:229–237.

17. Wade DT, Hewer RL, David RM, et al. Aphasia after stroke: national history and associated deficits. *J Neurol Neurosurg Psychiatry*. 1986;49:11–16.

18. Obier LK, Albert ML, Goodglass H, et al. Aphasia type and aging. *Brain Language*. 1978; 6:318.

19. Miceli G, Caltanirone C, Gainotta G, et al. Influence of age, sex, literacy and pathologic lesion on incidence, severity and type of aphasia. *Acta Neurol Scand*. 1981;64:370.

20. Steinvil Y, Ring H, Luz Y. Type of aphasia: relationship to age, sex, previous risk factors, and outcome of rehabilitation. *Scand J Rehabil Med*. 1985;12:68–71.

21. Habib M, Ali-Cherif A, Poncet M. Age-related changes in aphasia type and stroke location. *Brain Language*. 1987;31:245–251.

22. Kertesz E, Sheppard A. The epidemiology of aphasia and cognitive impairment in stroke. *Brain*. 1981;104:117–128.

23. Schechter I, Schechter M, Abarbanel R. Sex and aphasia syndromes. *Scand J Rehabil Med*. 1985;12:64–67.

24. Code C. *Language, Aphasia and the Right Hemisphere*. Chichester, Great Britain: John Wiley & Sons; 1987.

25. Rasmussen T, Milner B. The role of early left-brain injury in determining lateralization of cerebral brain functions. *Ann NY Acad Sci*. 1977;299:355–369.

26. Weisenberg T, McBride KE. *Aphasia*. New York: Commonwealth Fund; 1935.

27. Luria A. Factors and forms of aphasia. In: DeReuck A, O'Connor M, eds. *Disorders of Language*. London: J&A Churchill; 1964:143–167.

28. Luria AR, Hutton JT. A modern assessment of basic forms of aphasia. *Brain Language*. 1977; 4:129–151.

29. Albert ML, Goodglass H, Helm N, et al. *Clinical Aspects of Dysphasia*. Vienna: Springer-Verlag; 1981.

30. Geschwind N. Problems in the anatomical understanding of the aphasias. In: Benton AL, ed. *Contribution to Clinical Neuropsychology*. Chicago: Aldine; 1969:107–128.

31. Geschwind N. Aphasia. *N Engl J Med*. 1971;284:654–656.

32. Benson DF. *Aphasia Alexia, Agraphia*. New York: Churchill Livingstone; 1979.

33. Davis G. *A Survey of Adult Aphasia*. Englewood Cliffs, NJ: Prentice-Hall; 1983.

34. Goodglass H, Kaplan E. *The Assessment of Aphasia and Related Disorders*, 2nd ed. Philadelphia: Lea & Febiger; 1983.

35. Kertesz A. *Aphasia and Associated Disorders*. New York: Grune & Stratton; 1979.

36. Sarno MT, ed. *Acquired Aphasia*. New York: Academic Press; 1981.

37. Roch LeCours A, Lhermitte F, Bryans B. *Aphasiology*. London: Balliere Tindall; 1983.

38. Holland A, ed. *Language Disorders in Adults*. San Diego: College-Hill Press; 1984.

39. Carson DH, Carson FE, Tikofsky RS. On learning characteristics of the adult aphasic. *Cortex*. 1968;4:92–112.

40. Wertz RT. Neuropathologies of speech and language: an introduction to patient management. In: Johns DF, ed. *Clinical Management of Neurogenic Communicative Disorders*. Boston: Little Brown & Co; 1978:1–101.

41. Wertz RT, Rosenbek JC, Deal JL. A review of 228 cases of apraxia of speech: classification, etiology, and localization. Presented at the Annual Convention of the American Speech and Hearing Association; 1970; New York.

42. Rosenbek JC, LaPointe LL. The dysarthrias: description, diagnosis, and treatment. In: Johns DF, ed. *Clinical Management of Neurogenic Communicative Disorders*. Boston: Little Brown and Co; 1978:251–310.

43. Netsell R, Rosenbek J. Treating the dysarthrias. In: Darby JK, ed. *Speech and Language Evaluation in Neurology: Adult Disorders*. Orlando, FL: Grune & Stratton; 1985:363–392.

44. Gresham GE, Philips TF, Wolf PA, et al. Epidemiologic profile of long-term stroke disability: the Framingham Study. *Arch Phys Med Rehabil*. 1979;60:487–491.

45. Darley FL, Aronson AE, Brown JR. *Motor Speech Disorders*. Philadelphia: WB Saunders; 1975.

46. Joynt R, Goldstein M. The minor hemisphere. *Adv Neurol*. 1975;7:147–183.

47. Riege W, Metter EJ, Hanson WR. Verbal and nonverbal recognition memory in aphasic and non-aphasic patients. *Brain Language*. 1980;10:60–70.

48. Cicone M, Wapner W, Gardner H. Sensitivity to emotional expressions and situations in organic patients. *Cortex*. 1980;16:145–158.

49. Gardner H, Brownell HH, Wapner W. Missing the point: the role of the right hemisphere in the processing of complex linguistic materials. In: Perecman E, ed. *Cognitive Processing in the Right Hemisphere*. London: Academic Press; 1983:169–191.

50. Myers PS. Right hemispheric communication impairment. In: Chapey R, ed. *Language Intervention Strategies in Aphasia*, 2nd ed. Baltimore: Williams & Wilkins; 1986:446.

51. Myers PS. Right hemispheric involvement. In: Holland A, ed. *Language Disorders in Adults*. San Diego: College-Hill Press; 1984:177–208.

52. Winner E, Gardner H. The comprehension of metaphor in brain-damaged patients. *Brain*. 1977;100:719–727.

53. Brookshire RH, Nicholas LE. Comprehension of directly and indirectly stated main ideas and details by brain-damaged and nonbrain-damaged listeners. *Brain Language*. 1984;21:21–36.

54. Meadows JC. The anatomical basis of prosopagnosia. *J Neurol Neurosurg Psychiatry*. 1974; 37:489–501.

55. Annegers JF, Grabow JD, Kurland LT, et al. Incidence, causes, and secular trends of head trauma in Olmstead County, Minnesota, 1935–1974. *Neurology*. 1980;30:912–919.

56. Adamovich BB, Henderson JA, Auerbach S. *Cognitive Rehabilitation of Closed Head Injured Patients*. San Diego: College-Hill Press; 1985.

57. Brooks N, Campsie L, Symington C, et al. The five year outcome of severe blunt head injury: a relative's view. *J Neurol Neurosurg Psychiatry*. 1986;49:764–770.

58. Dresser AC, Meirowsky AM, Weiss GH, et al. Gainful employment following head injury. *Arch Neurol*. 1973;29:111–116.

59. Heilman KM, Safran A, Geschwind N. Closed head trauma and aphasia. *J Neurol Neurosurg Psychiatry*. 1971;34:265–269.

60. Thomsen IV. Evaluation and outcome of aphasia in patients with severe closed head trauma. *J Neurol Neurosurg Psychiatry*. 1975;38:713–718.

61. Sarno MT. The nature of verbal impairment after closed head injury. *J Nerv Ment Dis*. 1980; 168:685–692.

62. Sarno MT, Buonaguro A, Levita E. Characteristics of verbal impairment in closed head injured patients. *Arch Phys Med Rehabil*. 1986;67:400–405.

63. Prigatano GP, Roueche JR, Fordyce DJ. Nonaphasic language disturbances after brain injury. In: Prigatano GP, Fordyce DJ, Zeiner HK, et al , eds. *Neuropsychological Rehabilitation after Brain Injury.* Baltimore: The Johns Hopkins University Press; 1986:18–28.

64. Weinstein EA, Martin SL, Keller NA. Amnesia as a language pattern. *Arch Gen Psychiatry.* 1962;6:259–270.

65. Hagen C. Language disorders in head trauma. In: Holland A, ed. *Language Disorders in Adults.* San Diego: College-Hill Press; 1984:245–281.

66. deMorsier G. Sur 23 cas d'asphasie traumatique. *Psychiatria Clinica.* 1973;6:226–239.

67. Helm NA, Butler RB, Benson DF. Acquired stuttering. *Neurology.* 1978;1159–1165.

68. Thomsen IV. Evaluation and outcome of traumatic aphasia in patients with severe verified focal lesions. *Folia Phoniatrica.* 1976;28:362–377.

69. Finitzo T, Pool KD, Freeman FJ, et al. Spastic dysphonia subsequent to head trauma. *Arch Otolaryngol Head Neck Surg.* 1987;113:1107–1111.

70. Beukelman DR, Kraft GH, Freal J. Expressive communication disorders in persons with multiple sclerosis: a survey. *Arch Phys Med Rehabil.* 1985;66:675–677.

71. Darby JK. Epidemiology of neurologic diseases that produce communication disorders. In: Darby JK, ed. *Speech and Language Evaluation in Neurology: Adult Disorders.* Orlando, FL: Grune & Stratton; 1985:29–41.

72. Peyser JM, Edwards KL, Poser CM, et al. Cognitive functioning in patients with multiple sclerosis. *Arch Neurol.* 1980;37:557–579.

73. Grant J, McDonald WI, Trimble MR. Deficient learning and memory in early and middle phases of multiple sclerosis. *J Neurol Neurosurg Psychiatry.* 1984;47:250–255.

74. Jennekens-Schinkel A, Sanders EA. Decline of cognition in multiple sclerosis: dissociable deficits. *J Neurol Neurosurg Psychiatry.* 1986;49:1354–1360.

75. National Institutes of Health. *Parkinson's Disease: Hope through Research.* Bethesda, MD: NIH; 1983. NIH Pub No 83-139.

76. Scott S, Caird FI, Williams BO. *Communication in Parkinson's Disease.* Rockville, MD: Aspen Publishers, 1985.

77. Oxtoby M. *Parkinson's Disease Patients and Their Social Needs.* London: Parkinson's Disease Society; 1982.

78. LePatourel J. Communication aids for the progressively ill. In: Enderby P, ed. *Assistive Communication Aids for the Speech Impaired.* Edinburgh: Churchill Livingstone; 1987:79–86.

79. Bayles KA. Language and dementia. In: Holland A, ed. *Language Disorders in Adults.* San Diego: College-Hill Press; 1984:209–244.

80. National Institutes of Health. *Amyotrophic Lateral Sclerosis: Hope through Research.* Bethesda, MD: NIH; 1984. NIH Pub No 84-916.

81. National Institutes of Health. *National Research Strategy for Neurological and Communicative Disorders.* Bethesda, MD: NIH; 1979. NIH Pub No 79-1910.

82. Stemple JC, Lehmann MD. Throat clearing: the unconscious habit of vocal hyperfunction. Poster session presented at the American Speech, Language and Hearing Association convention; 1980; Detroit.

83. Williams RG. Idiopathic recurrent laryngeal nerve paralysis. *J Laryngol Otol.* 1959;73:161–166.

84. English GM. *Otolaryngology.* New York: Harper & Row; 1976.

85. Stemple JC. *Clinical Voice Pathology, Theory and Management.* Columbus, OH: Charles E Merrill; 1984.

86. National Institutes of Health. *The Dementias: Hope through Research*. Bethesda, MD: NIH; 1983. NIH Pub No 83–2252.

87. Malamud N. Neuropathology of organic brain syndromes associated with aging. In: Gaitz CM, ed. *Aging and the Brain*. New York: Plenum Press; 1972:63–87.

88. Bayles KA. Management of neurogenic communication disorders associated with dementia. In: Chapey R, ed. *Language Intervention Strategies in Adult Aphasia*, 2nd ed. Baltimore: Williams & Wilkins; 1986:462–473.

89. Schein JD. Hearing impairments and deafness. In: Stolov W, Clowers M, eds. *Handbook of Severe Disability*. Washington, DC: US Department of Education, Rehabilitation Services Administration; 1981:395–407.

90. Porch BE. *Porch Index of Communicative Ability*. Palo Alto, CA: Consulting Psychologists Press; 1971.

91. Schuell H. *The Minnesota Test for Differential Diagnosis of Aphasia*. Minneapolis, MN: University of Minnesota Press; 1965.

92. Goodglass H, Kaplan E. Boston Diagnostic Aphasia Examination. In: Goodglass H, Kaplan E, eds. *The Assessment of Aphasia and Related Disorders*. Philadelphia: Lea & Febiger; 1972: 74–100.

93. Kertesz A. *Western Aphasia Battery*. New York: Grune & Stratton; 1982.

94. LaPointe L, Horner J. *Reading Comprehension Battery for Aphasia*. Tigard, OR: CC Publications; 1979.

95. Shewan CM. *Auditory Comprehension Test for Sentences*. Chicago: Biolinguistics Clinical Institutes; 1979.

96. McNeil MR, Prescott TE. *Revised Token Test*. Baltimore: University Park Press; 1978.

97. Craig H. Application of pragmatic language models for intervention. In: Gallagher TM, Prutting CA, eds. *Pragmatic Assessment and Intervention Issues in Language*. San Diego: College-Hill Press; 1983:101–127.

98. Ochs E, Schieffelin B, eds. *Developmental Pragmatics*. New York: Academic Press; 1979.

99. Prutting C. Process/pra/,ses/n: the action of moving forward progressively from one point to another on the way to completion. *J Speech Hear Disord*. 1979;44:3–30.

100. Chapey R. Cognitive intervention: stimulation of cognition, memory, convergent thinking, divergent thinking, and evaluative thinking. In: Chapey R, ed. *Language Intervention Strategies in Adult Aphasia*, 2nd ed. Baltimore: Williams & Wilkins; 1986:215–238.

101. Dore J. A pragmatic description of early language development. *J Psycholinguist Res*. 1974; 3:343–350.

102. Dabul B. *Apraxia Battery for Adults*. Tigard, OR: CC Publications, 1979.

103. Wertz R, LaPointe L, Rosenbek J. *Apraxia of Speech in Adults*. New York: Grune & Stratton; 1984:98–103.

104. Yorkston K, Beukelman D. *Assessment of Intelligibility of Dysarthric Speech*. Tigard, OR: CC Publications; 1981.

105. Enderby P. *Frenchay Dysarthria Assessment*. San Diego: College-Hill Press; 1983.

106. Cooper M. *Modern Techniques of Vocal Rehabilitation*. Springfield, IL: Charles C Thomas; 1973.

107. Eisenson J. *Adult Aphasia*. Englewood Cliffs, NJ: Prentice-Hall; 1984.

108. Sarno J. Emotional aspects of aphasia. In: Sarno M, ed. *Acquired Aphasia*. New York: Academic Press; 1981:465–484.

109. Vignolo LA. Evolution of aphasia and language rehabilitation: A retrospective exploratory study. *Cortex*. 1964;1:344–367.

110. Marks M, Taylor ML, Rusk H. Rehabilitation of the aphasic patient: a survey of three years experience in a rehabilitation setting. *Neurology*. 1975;7:837–843.

111. Hagen C. Communication abilities in hemiplegia: effect of speech therapy. *Arch Phys Med Rehabil*. 1973;54:454–463.

112. Shewan C, Kertesz A. Effects of speech and language treatment on recovery from aphasia. *Brain Lang*. 1984;23:272–299.

113. Sarno MT. Recovery and rehabilitation in aphasia. In: Sarno M, ed. *Acquired Aphasia*. New York: Academic Press; 1981:485–529.

114. Fowler RS. Stroke and cerebral trauma: psychosocial and vocational aspects. In: Stolov WC, Clowers MR, eds. *Handbook of Severe Disability*. Washington, DC: US Department of Education, Rehabilitation Services Administration; 1981:127–135.

115. Hatfield FM, Zangwill OL. Occupational resettlement in aphasia. *Scand J Rehabil Med*. 1975; 7:57–60.

116. Raderstorf M, Hein DM, Jenesen CS. A young stroke patient with severe aphasia returns to work: a team approach. *J Rehabil*. 1984;50:23–26.

117. Rau MT. Beyond our usual treatment goals: treatment of a high level aphasic person. In: Marshall RC, ed. *Case Studies in Aphasia Rehabilitation*. Austin, TX: Pro-Ed; 1986:31–44.

118. Wertz RT. Response to treatment: a case of chronic aphasia. In: Marshall RC, ed. *Case Studies in Aphasia Rehabilitation*. Austin, TX: Pro-Ed; 1986:59–73.

119. VanDemark A. Aphasia treatment: intensive and residential. In: Marshall RC, ed. *Case Studies in Aphasia Rehabilitation*. Austin, TX: Pro-Ed; 1986:75–88.

120. Carriero MR, Faglia L, Vignolo LA. Resumption of gainful employment in aphasics: preliminary findings. *Cortex*. 1987;26:667–672.

121. Rosenbek JC, Lemme ML, Ahern MB, et al. A treatment for apraxia of speech in adults. *J Speech Hear Disord*. 1973;38:462–472.

122. Netsell R. A neurobiologic view of the dysarthrias. In: McNeil JM, Rosenbek J, Aronson A, eds. *The Dysarthrias: Physiology, Acoustics, Perception, Management*. San Diego: College-Hill Press; 1984:1–36.

123. Forer S, Miller L. Rehabilitation outcome: comparative analysis of different patient types. *Arch Phys Med Rehabil*. 1980;61:359–365.

124. Golper LA. A study of verbal behavior in recovery of aphasic and nonaphasic persons. In: Brookshire RH, ed. *Clinical Aphasiology: Proceedings of the Conference*. Minneapolis: BRK Publishers; 1980:28–38.

125. Weisbroth S, Esibill N, Zuger RR. Factors in the vocational success of hemiplegic patients. *Arch Phys Med Rehabil*. 1971;52:441–446.

126. Heiskanen O, Sepponen P. Prognosis of severe brain injury. *Acta Neurol Scand*. 1970;46:343.

127. Ben-Yishay Y, Silver SM, Piasetsky E. Relationship between employability and vocational outcome after intensive holistic cognitive rehabilitation. *J Head Trauma Rehabil*. 1987;2:35–48.

128. LeMay M, Geschwind N. Asymmetries of the human cerebral hemispheres. In: Caramazza A, Zurif E, eds. *Language Acquisition and Language Breakdown*. Baltimore: Johns Hopkins Press; 1982: 311–328.

129. Groher M. Language and memory disorders following closed head trauma. *J Speech Hear Res*. 1977;20:212–223.

130. Groher M. Communication disorders. In: Rosenthal M, Griffith ER, Bond MR, et al , eds. *Rehabilitation of the Head Injured Adult*. Philadelphia: FA Davis; 1983:155–165.

131. Hagen C, Malkmus D, Burditt G. Intervention strategies for language disorders secondary to head trauma. Short courses presented at the American Speech, Language and Hearing Association convention; 1979; Atlanta.

132. Hajenson T, Saxbon L, Fiselzon J, et al. Recovery of communicative functions after prolonged traumatic coma. *Scand J Rehabil Med*. 1978;10:15–21.

133. Groher M. Language and memory disorders following closed head trauma. *J Speech Hear Res*. 1977;20:212–221.

134. Groswasser Z, Mendelson L, Stern MJ, et al. Re-evaluation of prognostic factors in rehabilitation after severe head injury. *Scand J Rehabil Med*. 1977;9:147–149.

135. Levin HS, Grossman RG, Sawwar M, et al. Linguistic recovery after closed head injury. *Brain Lang*. 1981;12:360–374.

136. Szekers SF, Ylvisaker M, Cohen SB. A framework for cognitive rehabilitation therapy. In: Ylvisaker M, Gobble EM, eds. *Community Re-Entry for Head-Injured Adults*. Boston: Little Brown and Co; 1987:87–136.

137. Rigrodsky S, Morrison EB. Speech changes in Parkinsonism during L-dopa therapy; preliminary findings. *J Am Geriatr Soc*. 1970;18:142–151.

138. Calne DB. *Parkinsonism: Physiology, Pharmacology, and Treatment*. London: Edward Arnold; 1970.

139. American Cancer Society. *Annual Cancer Statistics Review*. New York: ACS; 1988.

140. Weiss MS, Basili AG. Electrolaryngeal speech produced by laryngectomized subjects: perceptual characteristics. *J Speech Hear Res*. 1985;28:294–300.

141. Kalb MB, Carpenter MA. Individual speaker influence on relative intelligibility of esophageal speech and artificial laryngeal speech. *J Speech Hear Dis*. 1981;46:77–80.

142. Clark JG, Stemple JC. Assessment of three modes of alaryngeal speech with a synthetic sentence identification (SSI) task in varying message-to-competition ratios. *J Speech Hear Res*. 1982; 25:333–338.

143. Clark JG. Alaryngeal speech intelligibility and the older listener. *J Speech Hear Disord*. 1985; 50:60–65.

144. Williams SE, Watson JB. Differences in speaking proficiencies in three laryngectomee groups. *Arch Otolaryngol*. 1985;111:246–219.

145. Hunt RB. Rehabilitation of the laryngectomee. *Laryngoscope*. 1964;74:382–395.

146. Gates GA, Hearne EM III. Predicting esophageal speech. *Ann Otol Rhinol Laryngol*. 1982;91: 454–457.

147. Singer M, Blom E. An endoscopic technique for restoration of voice after laryngectomy. *Ann Otol Rhinol Laryngol*. 1980;89:529–532.

148. Robbins J, Fisher HB, Blom ED, et al. A comparative acoustic study of normal, esophageal, and tracheoesophageal speech production. *J Speech Hear Disord*. 1984;49:202–210.

149. Richardson JL. Vocational adjustment after total laryngectomy. *Arch Phys Med Rehabil*. 1983;64:172–175.

150. Anderson TP. Stroke and cerebral trauma: medical aspects. In: Stolov WC, Clowers MR, eds. *Handbook of Severe Disability*. Washington, DC: US Department of Education, Rehabilitation Services Administration; 1981:119–126.

151. Burton LF, Chavez JA, Kokaska CJ. Employability skills: survey of employers opinions. *J Rehabil*. 1987;53:71–74.

152. Gobble EM, Henry K, Pfahl JC, et al. Work adjustment services. In: Ylvisaker M, Gobble EM, eds. *Community Re-Entry for Head-Injured Adults.* Boston: Little Brown, and Co; 1987: 221–257.

153. Berkeley Planning Associates. *Analysis of Policies of Private Employers toward the Disabled.* Washington, DC: US Department of Health and Human Services; 1981. Contract HEW-100-79-0180.

154. Harris D, Vanderheiden GC. Augmentative communication techniques. In: Schiefelbusch RL, ed. *Nonspeech Language and Communication: Analysis and Intervention.* Austin, TX: Pro-Ed; 1980:259–302.

155. Shane HC, Sauer M. *Augmentative and Alternative Communication.* Austin, TX: Pro-Ed; 1986.

156. Panton L. Speech, language, cognitive and physical assessment for a communication aid. In: Enderby P, ed. *Assistive Communication Aids for the Speech Impaired.* Edinburgh: Churchill Livingstone; 1987:12–26.

157. Musselwhite CR, St Louis KW. *Communication Programming for the Severely Handicapped.* San Diego: College-Hill Press; 1982.

158. Easton J. Developing effective communication in aid users. In: Enderby P, ed. *Assistive Communication Aids for the Speech Impaired.* Edinburgh: Churchill Livingstone; 1987:87–111.

chapter 9

Vocational Capacity with Psychiatric Disability

*Arthur T. Meyerson, Karen Danley, William Anthony, and
Theodora Fine*

The concept of a psychiatric disability as the functional limitation of a mentally ill person in the conduct of life activities is defined and made operational in radically different ways by clinicians, by epidemiologists, and by the panoply of federal and state programs intended to benefit those so severely limited in activity that they are unable to work. As noted by Goldman and Manderscheid, the only common theme is that of functional incapacity.[1] This definitional ambiguity gives rise to confusion in determining who is mentally disabled and in providing for them within social benefit programs.

In the realm of private practice, clinicians and patients alike are confounded by the disparate determination requirements of federal Society Security Disability Insurance (SSDI), Veterans Administration disability programs, and state workers' compensation programs. For example, the 1987 edition of the *Diagnostic and Statistical Manual of Mental Disorders* requires evidence of "disability" as a prerequisite for some diagnoses (eg, schizophrenia).[2] In contrast, the Social Security Act defines disability under Titles II and XVI as "a medically determinable physical or mental impairment . . . which has lasted or can be expected to last for a continuous period of not less than 12 months" and which results in an inability to perform "substantial gainful activity."[3] Under this definition, disability does not lead to, but rather follows from, diagnosis.

Adding still further to this confusion is the nature of psychiatric illness itself. Kaufmann and Weinberger pointed out that the functional limitations imposed by disease are most frequently perceived as incapacities in mobility, language, or learning that result from a physical disorder (eg, stroke, multiple sclerosis, trauma).[4] Many patients with psychiatric illnesses are equally limited, however, particularly in their capacities for self-direction and self-care. Indeed, the limitations may be so severe that these patients require considerable support for community living—if they can live outside a hospital at all.

DEFINING THE POPULATION

Although it is widely agreed that psychiatric illness ranks fifth among those disease categories that limit activities,[5] estimates of the population of the psychiatrically disabled range widely. Goldman has suggested that as many as 900,000 of the most severely chronically mentally ill reside in institutions and that an additional 350,000 to 800,000 severely disabled and 700,000 moderately disabled individuals reside in the community.[6] In contrast, using its own definition of disability, the Social Security Administration estimated that, in 1983, there were approximately 827,000 chronically mentally ill adults between the ages of 18 to 64 years.[7] This figure is based on the number of mentally ill on the rolls of the federal SSDI or Supplemental Income Security (SSI) programs, the two benefit programs under which the Department of Health and Human Services provides income maintenance for those unable to work—disabled—as the result of a physical or mental impairment.

The lack of a generally accepted definition of either disability or chronic mental illness itself is partly responsible for the imprecision in counting the mentally disabled.[8] Indeed, even if such definitions existed, counting would be difficult. Many of the mentally ill, among them the most severely disabled, remain hidden in our communities, unseen and untreated, partially because of the stigma and fear that still surround the very concept of mental illness. Furthermore, major mental illnesses tend to become exacerbated at one time and go into remission at another, causing those who would count the mentally disabled or chronically mentally ill to "miss" a significant portion of the population at a particular moment in time.

Epidemiologic studies have demonstrated that psychiatric illness—and in some cases, consequent psychiatric disability—knows no age, no culture, and no economic boundaries. Ashbaugh and associates found that as many as 3 million children in the United States are seriously emotionally disturbed.[9] In an epidemiologic study of 2,500 persons over 65 years of age, Weissman and associates found a psychiatric impairment rate of 6.7%, with 3.4% suffering from severe cognitive impairment.[10] Bachrach reported that the mentally ill homeless are not only in large sectors of major cities but also in rural and suburban areas.[8]

Moreover, psychiatric disability has both biologic and socioenvironmental determinants. It cuts across a variety of diagnostic categories, as well as a variety of social characteristics. Among all of those diagnosed as (or suspected to be) mentally ill, the psychiatrically disabled generally represent the "sickest of the sick." Kaufmann and Weinberger characterized the population most succinctly: "The psychiatrically disabled are a group of patients with varied diagnoses but a shared pathogenesis. They suffer from behavioral and cognitive deficits that are relatively irreversible and that are correlated with chronicity and poor outcome."[4] The shared pathogenesis is neurobiologic in nature and potentially demonstrable through imaging, neurochemical, neurophysiologic, and/or neuropsychologic techniques. This possibility holds the promise for more clearly objective assessments of psychiatric disability in the future.

The population of the mentally disabled may include the autistic child and the adolescent schizophrenic with not only the traditional flagrant positive symptoms (eg, hallucinations and threatening behavior) but also the negative symptoms (eg, affective flattening or withdrawal) that are now postulated to be closely related to predictors of chronicity.[4] Also counted among the psychiatrically disabled are the manic-depressive who is resistant to usually effective pharmacologic treatment and the aging Alzheimer's disease patient who is becoming increasingly impaired. In addition, the population of the mentally disabled may include as many as 50% of the homeless who wander the nation's streets.[11] A number of chronically physically impaired persons have such severe limitations as to precipitate disabling clinical depression.[12] At the heart of a benefit program controversy today are two other diagnostically distinct groups, perhaps the largest within the working-age population—those whose disability results from substance abuse disorders and those whose disability results from chronic psychogenic pain.

The social, medical, economic, and rehabilitative needs of the mentally disabled are as varied as the composition of the population. The environmental, educational, and social needs of a child who suffers from infantile autism or a schizophrenic disorder are substantially different from those of a mentally impaired street person, for whom immediate medical care, food, and housing are of foremost concern.[13] Unfortunately, our willingness to provide for the needs of these mentally disabled varies as a product of our social mores and state and federal budgets.

Public and private health insurance programs established to pay for at least a portion of the medical needs of this population may provide only for minimal health care needs, excluding from coverage the costs of rehabilitation, psychotropic medications, and respite care for family caregivers. Programs initially designed to provide income during the process of rehabilitation from disability have become ends in themselves, providing limited income and little more.

MAJOR DISABILITY PROGRAMS

Social Security Disability Insurance and Supplemental Security Income

The Social Security Act provides for disability benefits under two major sections: Title II (SSDI) for disabled workers who have worked and contributed through the FICA tax for a statutorily established period of time and Title XVI for the financially indigent disabled who have not previously contributed sufficiently through the FICA tax.[3] The Social Security Administration has developed a

Listing of Impairments that catalogues physical and mental impairments by body system.[14] Within each listing are specific examples of the signs, symptoms, and laboratory findings that the Social Security Administration considers sufficient to justify a designation of a claimant as disabled under that category. Section 12.00 Categories of Impairment—Mental contains eight broad categories: (1) organic mental disorders; (2) schizophrenic, paranoid, and other psychotic disorders; (3) affective disorders; (4) mental retardation and autism; (5) anxiety-related disorders; (6) somatoform disorders; (7) personality disorders; and (8) substance addiction disorders. (Although substance addiction disorders are included in the Listing of Impairments, they do not qualify per se as disabling conditions.)

The descriptions of the signs and symptoms of these disorders focus on such areas as restrictions of activities of daily living, inability to maintain appropriate social functioning, the deficiencies of concentration and task persistence, and inability to tolerate the increased mental demands associated with competitive work. These descriptions are so constructed that an individual who falls within one of the categories could not reasonably be expected to engage in any "substantial gainful activity."

Using these functional definitions, the examiner reviews the claimant's record to determine whether there is an impairment of such severity that it "meets or equals" a particular disorder identified in the Listing of Impairments. If so, the claimant is determined to be disabled. If not, the examiner looks to work capacity. Given the age, education, and work history of a claimant, the examiner evaluates the "residual functional capacity" of the claimant to determine whether the severe impairment precludes the capacity to engage in any work. A finding that a severely impaired individual cannot work again permits a finding of disability.

Because the SSDI adjudication procedure is essentially a paper process and because it places the burden of proof on the claimant, the importance of a patient's records—medical, vocational, educational, and social—cannot be taken lightly. Clinicians who develop the medical records of severely and chronically mentally ill patients should be aware that these records may become central to a disability determination, particularly since the patients/claimants may be unable to work on their own behalf as effectively as do those with severe physical impairments. Careful attention should be given, therefore, to issues of functional capacity.

Episodes of transient remission from an otherwise chronic psychiatric condition must be explained with precision, as should the effect of medication on the patient. Since 1985, the Social Security Administration has recognized in its Listing of Impairments that many psychiatric disorders fluctuate in severity, especially under stress, and that, although they may control the signs and symptoms of psychiatric disorders, many medications have their own impairing effects.

At the heart of this program is the need for clinicians to document in a plain, but detailed, fashion not only the existence of an impairment but also the way in which it interferes with the claimant's conduct of life and work. An extensive, longitudinal, nonjudgmental history developed with knowledge and understanding of the structure and requirements of the SSDI program is perhaps the best tool that clinicians can use on behalf of their severely mentally impaired patients.

Veterans Administration Programs

Like the Social Security Administration, the Veterans Administration has established a disability program of substantial complexity. In 1985, the Veterans Administration found that the mentally impaired constituted the largest single category among the more than 2.9 million veteran beneficiaries who were receiving either service-connected or non-service-connected disability benefits from the Veterans Administration.[15] As is the Social Security program, the Veterans Administration disability system is a costly one; therefore, public policy makers have struggled to achieve a balance between responsiveness and caution. Unlike the SSDI and SSI programs, however, the Veterans Administration disability program is not based entirely on inability to perform work. Rather, it pays *compensation* to those with service-connected impairments and *pensions* to those with non-service-connected impairments.

Because one of the key questions in the area of service-connected disability adjudication is the precise link between active service and the onset of the impairing illness, the role of the clinician is of considerable importance. The establishment of a causal relationship often spells the difference between approval and denial of benefits. A clinician who undertakes a medical evaluation of a patient who is applying for benefits, therefore, should take considerable time to develop a complete medical history, including not only a thorough clinical evaluation but also a review of previous examinations, earlier treatment, and military records. This review is of particular salience in cases of post-traumatic stress disorder (PTSD) and other psychiatric disorders that manifest themselves after military service. As Lipkin cautioned, "The VA requires careful documentation. . . . Any details and corroborative materials which can be provided during the examination will facilitate this determination."[16] Clinicians unfamiliar with military service and wartime conditions are urged to consult with colleagues who may have performed similar evaluation in the past.

Workers' Compensation

Markedly different from the federal programs, workers' compensation programs frequently involve active rehabilitation efforts to return a worker to full or partial employment. Furthermore, unlike SSDI or SSI, which may be perceived as "the dole" or is otherwise stigmatized, workers' compensation is more likely to be perceived by recipients and those around them as appropriate remuneration for a job-related injury until rehabilitation is successful or permanent disability established.

The role of the psychiatrist in the determination of disability for the purpose of workers' compensation is also markedly different from that under either the Social Security Administration or the Veterans Administration programs. Whereas the patient's teaching clinician acts as an advocate under the latter programs, he or she may be consulted only for records under the former. The treating professional does not conduct the disability examination. Rather, the employer or the employer's agent usually contracts for an independent psychiatric assessment when there is a dispute regarding the legitimacy of a claimant's complaint or a question regarding the efficacy of rehabilitation efforts. The contracting psychiatrist is often presented only with a list of specific questions relevant to the case for response following a full evaluation of the claimant.

Brodsky cautioned that, upon accepting such a contract, a psychiatrist is well advised to maintain a detachment from patient and employer alike and to work from both existing records and the substance of the evaluation alone.[17] Indeed, Brodsky posited that the evaluation should be conducted in a manner not unlike the traditional psychiatric history taking and examination, although perhaps with somewhat closer attention to the substance of occupational issues. Many psychiatric textbooks contain formats for such an evaluation.

Because workers' compensation programs vary from state to state, definitions of permanent, severe, and slight disability also vary. It is incumbent upon the evaluating clinician to be familiar with his or her state's requirements as the evaluation report often forms the basis for a legal decision to award or continue workers' compensation income maintenance, health insurance, and rehabilitation benefits. Moreover, because the determination process is legal, not medical, the report must be written in simple, accurate language that conveys not qualitative, but quantitative, estimates of the level of disability, its potential duration, and the likely outcome of rehabilitation. Substantial discursive description of the reasoning behind conclusions often weighs heavily in the determination process.[18]

REHABILITATION: INCENTIVES AND DISINCENTIVES

Notwithstanding the lip service paid to rehabilitation under the SSDI and Veterans Administration programs, only the workers' compensation program appears to have specific concern about and engagement with the rehabilitation process. This poses a dilemma, because the degree to which a patient's impairment may be made less disabling and the degree to which a patient is willing to try to reduce such an impairment are products of the competence and creativity of a rehabilitation program and the patient's own desire to retreat from what Brodsky described as "disabling behavior."[17] Unfortunately, as Lamb noted, mentally disabled SSI or SSDI beneficiaries often receive a message of support for continued disability behavior.[19] Lamb and Goertel reported that, among the psychiatrically disabled on the SSI or SSDI roles, their very status as beneficiaries sets them above others designated as chronically mentally ill.[20] The impetus thus is toward continued dependence and regression, ironically through the attainment of a level of self-esteem comparable to that attributed to successful entry into the job market (rehabilitation).

If a psychiatrically disabled patient is able to break away from the spiral of dependence and enter a rehabilitation program, several innovative and apparently successful models are available. In the main, each encompasses what Liberman and associates have described as "three interlocking strategies for professional intervention,"[21] including the use of appropriate psychotropic agents, the introduction of training to foster the development or reacquisition of social and work-related skills, and the modification or manipulation of both the physical and social environments to support the patient's current level of functioning and to encourage progression to a still higher level of capacity.

In the past 15 years, the field of psychiatric rehabilitation has grown exponentially. In 1985 the national directory of organizations providing psychosocial rehabilitation services identified 985 individual U.S. programs that provide comprehensive rehabilitation care to severely mentally ill adults.[22] Such programs encompass vocational services, residential services, educational and social/recreational services, traditional health care services, case management, and medication monitoring among their services. Moreover, the program modalities vary widely, ranging from the clubhouse model (with Fountain House as its foremost example); the high-expectancy model, as exemplified by Thresholds in Chicago and described by Dincin[23]; and the intensive case management model developed by Stein and Test[24] to the consumer-guided model, such as the Lodge program, which sets its roots in the soil of the self-help movement.

In the clubhouse model, membership rather than patient hood is stressed. Work activities that are essential to the operation of the clubhouse serve as prevocational opportunities for the members. Transitional employment can assist members to enter other supported or competitive employment. A return to an independent, productive life is the ultimate goal.

The high-expectancy model exemplifies a more traditional rehabilitation program. A team of professionals develop the treatment plan with the goal of steady improvement and return to productive life. The intensive case management model adds an element that could be viewed as a "parenting" role to either of the models that have been described. Adopting a holistic approach, clinicians address the housing, transportation, financial support, and other context-specific problems of patient participants. Finally, in the consumer-guided model, patients with or without family support come together to develop self-help programs with their peers.

Although these programs may generally be successful for particular subsets of the mentally disabled, no one program "works" for all individuals. Optimally, rehabilitation teaches patients to overcome the disabilities that may accompany severe mental impairment. Realistically, however, many patients need rehabilitation to learn to live with disability.

CATEGORIES OF PSYCHIATRIC IMPAIRMENT*

Psychiatric disabilities carry separable and distinct risks of vocational handicap, depending on the pathophysiology, clinical presentation, and pharmacologic control of symptoms and signs of the individual suffering from the specific disorder. Although substance abuse, organic brain disorders, and somatoform disorders also involve the genesis of specific symptoms and behavioral abnormalities that can lead to social and/or work-related disability, the following conditions are more commonly seen.

Schizophrenia

Often considered the prototypically disabling psychiatric illness, schizophrenia may cause a thought disorder that renders patients incapable of understanding simple conceptualizations and instructions necessary to perform even unskilled labor. These patients may also suffer from affective instability and lability, which makes them disruptive in the workplace. Delusions or hallucinations and intense suspiciousness may render them terrified and terrifying to the public, co-workers, and supervisors. These well-known features of schizophrenia may be accompanied by equally devastating clinical phenomena, termed "negative symptoms," including the constellation of flat affect, apathy, and withdrawal. Unfortunately, this less dramatic presentation is often misconstrued as a stubborn resistance to societally imposed tasks, such as work. Such negative symptoms may be associated with a neurobiologic, genetically determined pathophysiology, as indicated by recent findings of abnormal neuropsychologic assessments, cerebral regional blood flow studies, computed tomography (CT) scans, and response to medication.[4]

Affective Disorders

Conventional thought in psychiatry held that the affective disorders, unlike schizophrenia, do not usually lead to social or vocational disability. More recent

---

*Specific definition and the diagnostic criteria may be found in the *Diagnostic and Statistical Manual of Mental Disorders*, Third Edition—Revised (Washington, D.C.: American Psychological Association, 1987).

studies, however, indicate that a significant percentage (20% to 40%) of patients with affective disorder (particularly, bipolar depressive illness) suffer from such disabilities.[4] These disabilities may be secondary to frequent recurrences of illness, but a small percentage of patients with bipolar disorders appear to suffer identifiable pathophysiology of a neurobiologic sort.

Anxiety Disorders

A variety of anxiety disorders, including specific phobias and panic disorder, as well as general anxiety disorder, may be associated with an inability to function in the workplace. Patients with a panic disorder, for example, may be terrified to leave home, and patients with a phobic disorder may be unable to take public transportation to reach the work setting. Disabilities are less frequently associated with anxiety disorders than with the major psychotic disorders, yet they do occur. Recent advances in the biologic treatment of such disorders with the benzodiazepines, monamine oxidase inhibitors, and tricyclics, as well as psychosocial intervention, offer hope to many, but not all, individuals with anxiety disorders.

Character and Personality Disorders

Individuals suffering from a borderline personality disorder may have such interpersonal sensitivity and self-destructive behaviors (including substance abuse) that they are functionally disabled. Patients with an obsessive/compulsive personality disorder, a narcissitic personality, or a sociopathic personality may be unable to function successfully in the workplace because of their severe maladaptive behaviors.

ASSESSMENT OF VOCATIONAL CAPACITY

In many cases, the variety of symptoms present makes it extraordinarily difficult to determine the extent of psychiatric disability by means of a typical interview-based assessment in the office. A flagrantly delusional patient whose delusions are restricted to the area of religion, for example, may be able to work. In ironic contrast, a nonpsychotic patient with agoraphobia may be unable to leave the house even to apply for a job. Of course, many cases of psychiatric disability are readily apparent and relatively easy to assess. Even a casual observer can see that a patient with schizophrenia or an affective disorder who has had multiple hospitalizations and broad-based disturbance of social and cognitive functions is disabled for employment.

Variables once thought to be useful in predicting a patient's vocational capacity (eg, diagnosis, severity of impairment, and other demographic characteristics) do not appear to be reliable indicators of vocational outcome for the psychiatrically disabled individual.[25–27] The patient's performance in nonvocational settings does not predict vocational outcome either.[28–31] In fact, Strauss and Carpenter concluded that such dimensions as work, psychiatric symptoms, social relationships, and recidivism are largely independent factors.[32,33]

In a national survey of vocational rehabilitation practitioners, Hursh determined that these professionals rated most traditional forms of psychometric testing, both psychologic and vocational, as nonpredictive of vocational outcome.[34] The three factors that these practitioners rated most useful were (1) knowledge of the person over time, (2) a situational assessment, and (3) knowledge of past work history. Following an extensive review of the literature, Anthony and Jansen concluded[25]:

- The best demographic predictor of work performance is the person's prior employment history.
- The best clinical predictors of future work performance are ratings of a person's work adjustment skills made in a workshop setting or sheltered job site.
- A significant predictor of future work performance is a person's ability to function socially with others.
- The best paper-and-pencil test predictors of future vocational performance are tests that measure a person's adaptive (ego) strengths and self-concept in the role of worker.

Danley, Anthony, and MacDonald-Wilson have proposed three core sets of factors that practitioners can use to determine and enhance the probability of a psychiatrically impaired person's vocational success.[35] These factors include (1) the person's skills, (2) the quantity and quality of available supports, and (3) the person's "vocational maturity." Skills are the behaviors that can be used where, when, and as often as needed to gain success and/or satisfaction from a specific environment. Supports are the places, objects, and/or activities that other people are willing and able to provide so that the person can use existing skills or compensate for those skills that are lacking. Vocational maturity, a term borrowed from the vocational development literature,[36–40] refers to the ability to use information about oneself and about work to select, obtain, and retain employment that is both successful and satisfying. Because vocational maturity for all persons, including persons with disabilities, is a product of successful work experiences, it might be expected that persons whose vocational development has been delayed, interrupted, or disrupted by a disability need assistance to acquire work experiences that help them to gain vocational maturity. Power and Hershenson concluded:

It is not the disability itself that often hinders a disabled person from career maturity or renewed career options. There are a host of other factors that restrict career development and opportunities, such as the attitudes in the home, school, or workplace that reflect lowered career expectations, exclusive attention to the disability itself that overshadows an appreciation of a person's strengths and residual capability, or the conviction from parents, teachers, and employers that for persons with disability, career alternatives are very limited.[41]

Functional Approach to Vocational Assessment*[42–45]

Knowledge of the variables that correlate with vocational outcome, coupled with experience in effective rehabilitation practices, suggests new directions in vocational assessment procedures for persons with psychiatric disabilities.[25,38–39]

The Center for Psychiatric Rehabilitation at Boston University has developed a functional assessment approach that offers promise as a methodology for conducting vocational assessment with persons who have psychiatric disabilities. This approach, grounded in psychiatric rehabilitation research, is designed around the concept of environmental specificity and based on the observation that, for most disabled persons, the ability to transfer skills between dissimilar environmental settings is minimal. The implication for vocational rehabilitation practitioners is that, in order to maximize both their predictive and their prescriptive potential, assessments should be conducted in relation to the environment in which a disabled person chooses to function. Defined by the person with the practitioner, this environment is identified as the overall rehabilitation goal.[29] All assessment then proceeds directly from an understanding of the demands of the setting and/or the expectations that the person has for him- or herself in relation to the setting.

This prescriptive approach, although requiring an initial heavy investment of practitioner time in the mutual selection of a specific work setting, increases the long-range efficiency of the assessment process. Only these factors that are relevant to performance in a particular setting become the focus of the assessment process. The early extensive involvement of the person in this process also enhances the practitioner's ability to determine vocational maturity and to provide additional work experiences to increase the level of vocational self-awareness and competence.

Source: Excerpted from Anthony WA, *Principles of Psychiatric Rehabilitation*, PRO-ED, © 1980; Anthony WA, Cohen MR, Cohen BF, "Psychiatric Rehabilitation" in *The Chronic Mental Patient: Five Years Later*, J Talbot (ed.), Allyn & Bacon, © 1984; Anthony WA, Cohen MR, Danley KS, "The Psychiatric Rehabilitation Approach as Applied to Vocational Rehabilitation" in *Vocational Rehabilitation of Persons with Prolonged Mental Illness*, J Ciardello and M Bell (eds.), Johns Hopkins University Press, in press; and Anthony WA, Cohen MR, Nemec P, "Assessment in Psychiatric Rehabilitation" in *Handbook of Measurement and Evaluating in Rehabilitation*, B Bolton (ed.), Paul H. Brookes Publishers, © 1987. Reprinted with permission.

Because skills and resources are both deemed essential to success, both factors are assessed. In contrast to the traditional psychiatric focus on pathology and symptoms, this approach identifies the unique skills and resources required to achieve success and satisfaction in a particular setting.

Assessment Interview

Vocational assessment of a person with a psychiatric disability is conducted during a series of interviews. Many severely psychiatrically disabled persons do not know how to participate in an interview, however; they may be accustomed to psychiatric interviews that focus on their symptoms, maladaptive behaviors, and probable causes of impairment, with minimal attempts to involve them. The psychiatric rehabilitation assessment interview is based on two principles[45,46]:

1. The practitioner attempts to maximize the involvement of the disabled person in the interview process.
2. The information collected during the interview is recorded in a way that maximizes the person's understanding of the assessment result.

Involvement of the Disabled Person

Involving the patient in the interview means facilitating the patient's active participation in completing each of the tasks that is part of a rehabilitation assessment. This involvement increases the person's ownership of the rehabilitation assessment. The practitioner involves the individual in the assessment by (1) orienting, (2) giving instructions, (3) requesting information, and (4) demonstrating understanding throughout the interview.

Orienting means describing the task, its goal, and the roles of both the practitioner and the disabled person in the task. The way in which the practitioner orients the individual is important. The practitioner must use language that the individual is likely to understand and continually check the individual's understanding of what has been said.

Giving instructions is similar to orienting in that both give direction. Giving instructions, however, specifically directs the person to perform a particular action or set of actions. The instructions include the specific steps that the person should follow.

Requesting information encourages the disabled person to participate actively in the interview process. The practitioner asks for facts, opinions, and feelings, leading to a discussion of a particular topic.

Demonstrating understanding is capturing in words what the disabled person is feeling or thinking. It shows the person that the practitioner is listening and trying to see the person's situation from his or her perspective.

These four ways of involving the disabled person in the assessment require the practitioner to be proficient in interpersonal skills, such as paraphrasing, responding to feelings, asking questions, and giving direction.

Recording Information to Promote Understanding

Assessment records vary in the number of details included and in the format. The assessment recorded in the individual's file, regardless of the particular agency's record-keeping format, should be clear, brief, and environmentally specific.

Minimally, the final results of the assessment interview—the overall rehabilitation goal, a functional assessment, and a resource assessment—are recorded. Each of these three parts of the assessment has specific characteristics. For example, the overall rehabilitation goal is stated in a simple sentence that indicates a specific environment (or type of environment) and a date by which the goal should be achieved. The functional assessment is skill-focused, behavioral, observable, and measurable. The record of the functional assessment includes the critical skills, the use of these skills needed in a specific environment, and the person's present and needed use of the skill (Table 9-1).

The resource assessment has many of the same record-keeping characteristics as the functional assessment (ie, observable, measurable, environmentally specific, clear, and brief). The recorded resource assessment includes names of the critical supports, the needed use of the supports, and the present and needed or planned use of these supports (Table 9-2).

Use of Vocational Assessment Instruments

If used at all with psychiatrically disabled persons, vocational assessment instruments should be used to supplement and validate information gathered during the interview process. Ideally, an instrument provides information that is not available through direct experience or observation. Standard vocational assessment tools offer the practitioner and the disabled person the opportunity to compare the disabled person's performance with that of others or with his or her own performance at other times.

Because each psychiatrically disabled person has unique assessment needs, it is not possible to recommend specific instruments or batteries. It is possible, however, to provide some guidelines for instrument selection. Useful instruments increase the quantity and quality of information about skills and supports. In addition, instruments that provide descriptive data about vocational maturation and career development may affect the person's vocational choice. Vocational assessment instruments should be clear and brief. As most instruments are com-

Table 9-1 Functional Assessment Chart

Name: Eddie
Goal: To work at the Comet Supermarket Warehouse through January 1987

+/−	Critical Skill	Skill Use Description	Skill Functioning*					
			Spontaneous Use		Prompted Use		Performance	
			Present	Needed	Yes	No	Yes	No
+	Dressing	Number of days per week Eddie puts on clothing that matches the requirements of his work task in his apartment between 7:00 A.M. and 7:30 A.M. weekdays before leaving for work	5	5				
−	Clarifying directions	Percent of times per week Eddie requests additional information when he is confused by instructions given by the work supervisor at the job site	0	80%	Yes			
−	Requesting social contact	Percent of time per week Eddie asks someone to spend time with him when he is doing nothing during breaks or after work	0	75%		No		No

*The client skills level is evaluated in three different ways. The Spontaneous Use column indicates the client's highest present level of use of the skill in the particular environment as compared to the needed level of skill use. The Prompted Use column indicates whether the client can (Yes) or cannot (No) perform the skills when asked to in the particular environment. The Performance column indicates whether the client can (Yes) or cannot (No) perform the skill outside of the particular environment. If the client's present (P) level of spontaneous skill use is zero, then prompted use is evaluated. Similarly, if the client has been evaluated as unable to use the skill when prompted (No), then skill performance is evaluated.

Source: Reprinted from Vocational Rehabilitation of Persons with Prolonged Mental Illness, (p 70) by J Ciardello and M Bell (eds) with permission of Johns Hopkins University Press, © 1988.

Table 9-2 Resource Assessment Chart

Name: Eddie

Goal: To work at the Comet Supermarket Warehouse through January 1987

+/−	Critical Skill	Resource Use Description	Use	
			Present	Needed
−	Supportive supervisor	Number of times per week job-site supervisor praises Eddie for completing tasks	0	1
+	Recreational facility	Number of days per weekend staff open the Recreational Center between 10:00 A.M. and 10:00 P.M.	2	2
−	Social contact	Number of days per week friends phone Eddie to talk for 10 minutes or more	1	5

Source: Reprinted from *Vocational Rehabilitation of Persons with Prolonged Mental Illness,* (p 70) by J Ciardello and M Bell (eds.), with permission of Johns Hopkins University Press, © 1988.

prehensive, it may be necessary to select those items with particular relevance to the rehabilitation goal.

Skills-Oriented Instruments

Many states have developed forms for measuring the functional levels of persons in community support programs. These forms often include ratings of client skills. The CSS-100, which is used by many community support programs, has separate scales that measure both adjustment to the environment (eg, using public transportation, managing funds, dressing self) and behavior problems or symptoms (eg, hospitalization, employment-related services, community living programs, socialization activities).[47] Similarly, the Multifunction Needs Assessment used in Rhode Island and Connecticut includes assessment of functioning (eg, self-maintenance, environmental interaction), psychiatric symptoms, and current use of services.[48] Other forms, developed along the same lines, are in use in New Jersey[49] and Michigan.[50]

The Katz Adjustment Scale was developed many years before the Community Support Program,[51] but it is still in use in a variety of settings. The wide use of this scale is probably related to the considerable data available on its reliability, validity, sensitivity, and norms, as well as to the usefulness of the materials available for training staff to administer the scale.[52] Although many items measure psychiatric symptoms (eg, trouble sleeping, suicide attempts) and behavioral excess (eg, periods of constant movement, temper tantrums), this scale also includes items that measure community adjustment skills. It provides for an assessment of physical skills (eg, helps with household chores), emotion/interpersonal skills (eg, gets along with neighbors), and intellectual skills (eg, helps with the family budgeting). The skills are often phrased positively (ie, "the client does this") and are rated on a frequency scale (ie, "is not doing, is doing some, is doing regularly"). The measurement provides a picture of skill strengths, as well as skill deficits.

Designed to measure vocational skills of psychiatrically disabled persons, the Standardized Assessment of Work Behavior records a broad range of skills (eg, uses tool/equipment, communicates spontaneously, grasps instructions quickly).[53-56] Items are rated on a continuum from skill strength (eg, looks for more work) to skill deficit (eg, waits to be given work). Reliability and validity data are available for this scale.

The Functional Assessment Inventory, a new scale with a vocational focus, has been developed for use with all disability groups.[57] It focuses on eight major functional dimensions: (1) personality and behavior, (2) motor functioning, (3) cognitive functioning, (4) medical condition, (5) vision, (6) hearing, (7) vocational qualifications, and (8) economic disincentives. The scale does not measure skills in all of these areas and where it does, the emphasis is on assessing deficiencies. Some items focus on strengths, but these are considered "moderator variables," rather than items of equal weight to the limitations (ie, they are meant to account for positive attributes or abilities that appear to override limitations). Both reliability and validity data are available.

Resources-Oriented Scales

Few scales that focus on resource assessment are in use. Other types of supports (eg, income, mental health services) are assessed as a part of some checklists, but such checklists are not widely used. The Uniform Client Data Instrument, developed for use in Community Support Programs nationwide, includes checklists on family members who are living, earnings and financial benefits received, and services currently being received.[58,59] Similarly, the Multifunction Needs Assessment includes a Current Services Profile on which those services received during the previous month and the approximate amount of service (in hours per week) are listed.[48] Although there is no indication of the needed services that are not being received, the Current Services Profile does encompass a broad range of resources: people (eg, a friendly visitor), places (eg, a child day care center program), things (eg, prosthetics, medication), and activities (eg, recreational therapy).

Another community support program instrument is the Alabama Mental Health Services Utilization and Needs Assessment.[60] Quite comprehensive, this instrument includes service needs, service providers (ie, if service need is being met), and barriers to service (if service need is unmet). Types of resources assessed include people (eg, crisis service provider, advocate), places (eg, nutrition center), things (eg, transportation, medication), and activities (eg, training, planned recreational activities). Reliability and validity data are not yet available.

In the area of social supports, the Pattison Psychosocial Kinship Inventory offers a systematic method for assessing the social system of a psychiatrically impaired individual.[61] The instructions specify which people to list on the instrument:

> anyone important in your life; anyone important not listed below, but who is significant to you. . . . They may be persons who you see every day or only occasionally, persons who are strategically important to you; or those who are important because you specifically don't like them or they cause you difficulty.

Thus, the instrument includes resources and people who provide support and those who may cause distress.

Environmentally Specific Scales

It is necessary to identify the environment in which the person is expected to function in order to assess the level of functioning meaningfully. Ideally, then, an assessment instrument determines the person's performance within a particular environment. A standardized instrument, by definition, cannot provide adequate specificity; it may have been developed for use in a particular type of environment, such as a rooming house or transitional employment program, but it still misses some of the environmental requirements of a particular rooming house or a specific transitional employment placement.

An instrument can be developed for an environment by tailoring it to the requirements of that setting. In a treatment program, for example, an assessment instrument can be based on the entrance and exit criteria for the program. A skills-oriented assessment form may list the skills that a person must demonstrate to be admitted to the program and the skills that a person must acquire before being discharged as a "successful graduate." Such an instrument should be reliable and have construct face validity, thus permitting program evaluation and clinical assessment.

The Standardized Assessment of Work Behavior mentioned earlier is probably the most environmentally specific assessment instrument in use.[53] It was developed in the hospital workshops and clerical units of the Rehabilitation Unit of Maudsley Hospital (England), and it can be adapted for use in other work settings.

Vocational Maturation

Comprehensive vocational instruments that are self-administered offer the promise of identifying overall vocational potential. Danley and associates have developed a self-directed vocational assessment process that involves a self-administered instrument derived from several existing occupational sources[62] (including *Exploring Career Decision Making*,[63] *Guide to Occupational Information*,[64] *Classification of Jobs* handbook,[65] *The Skills of Career Development*,[66] and the *Dictionary of Occupational Titles*.[67] When used with careful instruction and with focused assessment interviews, these materials proved to be extremely helpful to disabled persons in establishing a vocational perspective that facilitated vocational choice.[68] Standard instruments for measuring career maturity may also be useful if administered according to the principles of maximizing client involvement and understanding.[69–71] Power and Hershenson cautioned, however, that practitioners who use these instruments with disabled persons must be aware of the lack of norms for adult disabled populations.[41]

General Considerations

Any chosen instrument, the process of administration, and the results all must be comprehensible to the affected individual. The instrument selected must be clearly relevant to the patient's situation, and the practitioner should explain the reason for the choice. The practitioner should also give an explanation of the process and purpose of the instrument, along with clear instructions. Of the instruments previously mentioned, three have been used as self-report forms with some success: (1) Griffith's Standardized Assessment of Work Behavior,[53] (2) the Katz Adjustment Scale,[51] and (3) Pattison's Psychosocial Kinship Inventory.[61]

Brevity and simplicity in administration facilitate an instrument's utility within the assessment interview. A brief instrument is easier to integrate into the assessment process and less likely to change the interview from individualized exploration to rote and mechanical measurement than is a longer form.

The clinician should treat a completed instrument as but one source of information. At this time, psychiatric rehabilitation assessment instruments are more valuable in research and program evaluation than in clinical applications. In clinical situations, the assessment process itself must "begin" and "end" with the affected person. Before instruments are used, the practitioner attempts to obtain the psychiatrically disabled person's perspective on his or her skills and resources (strengths and deficits). The assessment then should proceed to include information from significant others, testing, and/or observations in simulated environments. Once the data have been gathered, the information is recorded and reorganized in such a way that the disabled person understands the completed assessment. In order to accomplish all this in a psychiatric rehabilitation and assessment, a practitioner must be able to establish a trust-based relationship.[72]

Frey noted the limitations of assessment instruments.[73] The focus and conduct of the process, rather than the instruments, are the foundation of a valid vocational assessment.

The Boston University Center for Rehabilitation Research and Training in Mental Health has recently developed and field tested a training package designed to teach practitioners how to conduct a functional assessment.[74] The package includes trainer guides, trainee reference handbooks, and videotaped case studies. A systematic follow-up with ongoing supervised practice and study groups is employed to help practitioners learn to use the skills in their own agency settings. The use of the package has been shown to increase practitioners' ability to perform a functional assessment.

CONCLUSION

To what extent should society seek to develop programs that meet the multifold needs of the psychiatrically disabled, particularly since the outcome of rehabilitation is so much in doubt? The response varies according to the particular population and the resources—both programmatic and economic—necessary to meet the needs. For example, rehabilitation experts have found that, with careful intervention, some severely mentally ill patients may experience total remission of symptomatology. In contrast, many patients remain in fragile balance, requiring substantial medical and psychosocial support. Others have lifelong residual disability with incomplete remission of clinical symptoms, requiring ongoing medical treatment. We are beginning to identify those for whom dollars and programs can be marshalled effectively.

REFERENCES

1. Goldman HH, Manderscheid RW. The epidemiology of psychiatric disability. In: Meyerson AT, Fine T, eds. *Psychiatric Disability: Clinical, Legal and Administrative Dimensions*. Washington, DC: American Psychiatric Press; 1987:13–22.

2. American Psychiatric Association. *Diagnostic and Statistical Manual of Mental Disorders*, 3rd rev ed. Washington, DC: American Psychiatric Press; 1987.

3. 20 C.F.S. §404.1050.

4. Kaufmann CA, Weinberger DR. The neurobiological basis of psychiatric disability. In Meyerson AT, Fine T, eds. *Psychiatric Disability: Clinical, Legal and Administrative Dimensions*. Washington, DC: American Psychiatric Press; 1987:23–48.

5. Kottke FJ, Lehmann JF, Stillwell GK. Preface. In: Kottke FJ, Stillwell GK, Lehmann JF, eds. *Krusen's Handbook of Physical Medicine and Rehabilitation*. Philadelphia: WB Saunders: 1982.

6. Goldman HH. Epidemiology. In Talbot JC, ed. *The Chronic Mental Patient: Five Years Later.* Orlando, FL: Grune & Stratton; 1984.

7. Social Security Administration. Unpublished data. In Ashbaugh JW, Leaf PJ, Manderscheid RW, et al. Estimates of the size and selected characteristics of the adult chronically mentally ill population in U.S. households. In Greenley JR, ed. *Research in Community and Mental Health*, Vol 3. Greenwich, CT: JAI Press; 1983.

8. Bachrach LL. Disability among the homeless mentally ill. In: Meyerson AT, Fine T, eds. *Psychiatric Disability: Clinical, Legal and Administrative Dimensions.* Washington, DC: American Psychiatric Press; 1987:183–195.

9. Ashbaugh JW, Leaf PJ, Manderscheid RW, et al. Estimates of the size and selected characteristics of the adult chronically mentally ill population in U.S. households. In Greenley JR, ed. *Research in Community and Mental Health*, Vol 3. Greenwich, CT: JAI Press; 1983.

10. Weissman MM, Myers JK, Tischler GL, et al. Psychiatric disorders (DSM-III) and cognitive impairment among the elderly in a U.S. urban community. *Acta Psychiatric Scand.* 1985;71:366–379.

11. Lamb HR, ed. *The Homeless Mentally Ill.* Washington, DC: American Psychiatric Association; 1984.

12. Gallagher RM, Stewart F. Psychiatric rehabilitation and chronic physical illness. In: Meyerson AT, Fine T, eds. *Psychiatric Disability: Clinical, Legal and Administrative Dimensions.* Washington, DC: American Psychiatric Press; 1987:143–182.

13. Knitzer J. *Unclaimed Children: The Failure of Public Responsibility to Children and Adolescents in Need of Mental Health Services.* Washington, DC: Children's Defense Fund; 1982.

14. Social Security Administration. Federal Old-Age, Survivors and Disability Insurance: Listing of Impairments-Mental Disorders; final rule. *Fed Reg.* 1985;20:35038–35070.

15. Office of Information Management and Statistics. *Disability Compensation Data, RCS 20-0223.* Washington, DC: Veterans Administration; 1985.

16. Lipkin JO. *Psychiatric disability: The Veterans Administration.* In: Meyerson AT, Fine T, eds. *Psychiatric Disability: Clinical, Legal and Administrative Dimensions.* Washington, DC: American Psychiatric Press; 1987:333–342.

17. Brodsky CM. The psychiatric evaluation in workers' compensation. In: Meyerson AT, Fine T, eds. *Psychiatric Disability: Clinical, Legal and Administrative Dimensions.* Washington, DC: American Psychiatric Press; 1987:313–332.

18. Pollack S, Gross BH, Weinberger LE. Principles of forensic psychiatry for reaching psychiatric-legal opinions: application. In: Gross BH, Weinberger LE, eds. *The Mental Health Professional and the Legal System.* San Francisco: Jossey-Bass; 1982.

19. Lamb HR. Incentives and disincentives of disability insurance for the chronically mentally ill. In: Meyerson AT, Fine T, eds. *Psychiatric Disability: Clinical, Legal and Administrative Dimensions.* Washington, DC: American Psychiatric Press; 1987:343–350.

20. Lamb HR, Goertel V. The long-term patient in the era of community treatment. *Arch Gen Psychiatry.* 1977;34:670–682.

21. Liberman RP, Jacobs HE, Blackwell GA, et al. Overcoming psychiatric disability through skills retraining. In: Meyerson AT, Fine T, eds. *Psychiatric Disability: Clinical, Legal and Administrative Dimensions.* Washington, DC: American Psychiatric Press; 1987:221–250.

22. International Association of Psychosocial Rehabilitation Services. *Organizations Providing Psychosocial Rehabilitation and Related Community Support Services in the United States: 1985.* McLean, VA: IAPRS; 1985.

23. Dincin J. A community agency model. In: Talbot JA, ed. *The Chronically Mentally Ill: Treatment Programs and Systems.* New York: Human Sciences Press; 1981.

24. Stein LI, Test MA. The community as the treatment arena in caring for the chronic psychiatric patient. In: Barofsky I, Budson RD, eds. *The Chronic Psychiatric Patient in the Community*. New York: SP Medical and Scientific Books; 1983.

25. Anthony WA, Jansen M. Predicting the vocational capacity of the chronically mentally ill: research and policy implications. *Am Psychologist*. 1984;39:537–542.

26. Freeman HE, Simmons OC. *The Mental Patient Comes Home*. New York: John Wiley & Sons; 1963.

27. Gurel L, Lorei TW. Hospital and community ratings of psychopathology as predictors of employment and readmission. *J Consult Clin Psychol*. 1972;39:286–291.

28. Ellsworth RB, Foster L, Childres B, et al. Hospital and community adjustment as perceived by psychiatric patients, their families, and staff. *J Consult Clin Psychol Monographs*. 1968;32 (3, pt. 2).

29. Cohen MR, Farkas M, Unger K. *Setting the Overall Rehabilitation Goal: Psychiatric Rehabilitation Trainer Package*. Boston: Boston University Center for Psychiatric Rehabilitation. (In press.)

30. Summers F. The effects of aftercare after one year. *J Psychiatric Treat Eval*. 1981;3:405–409.

31. Tessler R, Manderscheid R. Factors affecting adjustment to community living. *Hosp Commun Psychiatry*. 1982;33:203–207.

32. Strauss J, Carpenter W. The prediction of outcome in schizophrenia. *Arch Gen Psychiatry*. 1972;27:739–746.

33. Strauss J, Carpenter W. The prediction of outcome in schizophrenia: 2. *Arch Gen Psychiatry*. 1974;31:37–42.

34. Hursh N. Diagnostic vocational rehabilitation with psychiatrically disabled individuals: a national survey. Presented at the American Psychological Association Convention; 1983; Anaheim, CA.

35. Danley KS, Anthony WA, MacDonald-Wilson K. *Psychiatric Vocational Rehabilitation Approach: A Workshop Guide for Vocational and Rehabilitation Counselors*. Boston: Boston University Center for Psychiatric Rehabilitation; 1988.

36. Super D. A theory of vocational development. *Am Psychologist*. 1953;8:185–190.

37. Super D. The dimensions of vocational maturity. *Teachers College Rec*. 1955;57:151–163.

38. Super D. *The Psychology of Careers*. New York: Harper & Row; 1957.

39. Super D, Overstreet P. *The Vocational Maturity of Ninth Grade Boys*. New York: Teachers College, Columbia University; 1960.

40. Tiedeman D. Decision and vocational development: a paradigm and its implications. *Personnel Guid J*. 1961;40:15–20.

41. Power P, Hershenson D. Assessment of career development and maturity. In: Bolton B, ed. *Handbook of Measurement and Evaluation in Rehabilitation*. Baltimore: Paul H. Brookes; 1987:219–233.

42. Anthony WA. *Principles of Psychiatric Rehabilitation*. Austin, TX: Pro-Ed; 1980.

43. Anthony WA, Cohen MR, Cohen BF. Psychiatric rehabilitation. In: Talbot J, ed. *The Chronic Mental Patient: Five Years Later*. New York: Grune & Stratton; 1984:137–157.

44. Anthony WA, Cohen MR, Danley KS. The psychiatric rehabilitation approach as applied to vocational rehabilitation. In: Ciardiello J, Bell M, eds. *Vocational Rehabilitation of Persons with Prolonged Mental Illness*. Baltimore: Johns Hopkins University Press; 1988.

45. Anthony WA, Cohen MR, Nemec P. Assessment in psychiatric rehabilitation. In: Bolton B, ed. *Handbook of Measurement and Evaluating in Rehabilitation*. Baltimore: Paul H Brookes; 1987:309–312.

46. Cohen BF, Anthony WA. Functional assessment in psychiatric rehabilitation. In: Halpern A, Fuhrer M, eds. *Functional Assessment in Rehabilitation*. Baltimore: Paul H Brookes; 1984:79–99.

47. New York State Office of Mental Health. *CSS-100, Community Support Systems NIMH Client Assessment*. Albany, NY; unpublished manuscript, 1979.

48. Angelini D, Potthof, Goldblatt R. *Multifunction Needs Assessment Instrument*. Cranston, RI: Rhode Island Department of Mental Health; 1980.

49. New Jersey Division of Mental Health and Hospitals. *Level of Functioning Assessment*. Trenton, NJ: NJ Division of Mental Health; 1979.

50. Cornhill Associates. *Michigan Needs Assessment Instrument*. Watertown, MA; Author, 1980.

51. Katz NM, Lyerly SB. Methods of measuring adjustment and social behavior in the community. *Psychol Rep*. 1963;13:503–535.

52. Weissman NN. The assessment of social adjustment. *Arch Gen Psychiatry*. 1982;32:357–365.

53. Griffiths RDP. A standardized assessment of the work behavior of psychiatric patients. *Br J Psychiatry*. 1973;123:403–408.

54. Griffiths RDP. The accuracy and correlates of the psychiatric patients' self assessment of their work behavior. *Br J Soc Clin Psychol*. 1975;14:181–189.

55. Griffiths RDP. The prediction of psychiatric patients' work behavior in the community. *Br J Soc Clin Psychol*. 1977;16:165–173.

56. Watts FN. A study of work behavior in a psychiatric rehabilitation unit. *Br J Soc Clin Psychol*. 1978;17:85–92.

57. Crewe NM, Athelstan GT. *Functional Assessment Inventory*. Menomonie, WI: Materials Development Center, Stout Vocational Rehabilitation Institute, University of Wisconsin-Stout; 1984.

58. Market Facts. *Collaborative Data Collection and Analysis for Community Support Program Demonstration Projects*. Rockville, MD: National Institute of Mental Health; 1980.

59. Stroul BA. *Toward Community Support Systems for the Mentally Disabled: The NIMH Community Support Program*. Boston: Boston University Center for Rehabilitation Research and Training in Mental Health; 1984.

60. State of Alabama Department of Mental Health Services. *Utilization and Needs Assessment*. Birmingham, AL: AL Department of Mental Health Services; 1984.

61. Pattison EM, De Francisco D, Wood P, et al. A psychosocial kinship model for family therapy. *Am J Psychiatry*. 1975;132:1246–1251.

62. Danley KS, Kohn L, Hutchinson D, et al. *Career Development Curriculum for Continuing Education Program*. Boston: Boston University Center for Psychiatric Rehabilitation; 1987.

63. Appalachian Educational Laboratory. *Exploring Career Decision Making*. Bloomington, IL: McKnight; 1978.

64. Harrington TF, O'Shea AJ, eds. *Guide to Occupational Information*. Bloomington, IL: American Guidance Service; 1984.

65. Field T, Field J. *Classification of Jobs According to Worker Trait Groups*. Roswell, GA: VDARE Services, Inc.; 1980.

66. Pierce R, Cohen M, Anthony W, et al. *The Skills of Career Development*. Baltimore: University Park Press; 1980.

67. US Department of Labor. *Dictionary of Occupational Titles*. Washington, DC: US Government Printing Office; 1983.

68. Unger K. *A University-based Rehabilitation Center for Severely Psychiatrically Disabled Young Adults*. Boston: Boston University Center for Psychiatric Rehabilitation; 1988.

69. Crites J. *Theory and Research Handbook for the Career Maturity Inventory*. Monterey, CA: CTB/McGraw-Hill; 1978.

70. Super D, Thompson A. A six scale, two factor measure of adolescent career and vocational maturity. *Vocat Guid Q*. 1979;28:6–15.

71. Westbrook B, Mastie M. The measure of vocational maturity: a beginning to know about. *Measurement Eval Guid*. 1973;6:8–16.

72. Anthony WA, Pierce R, Cohen MR. *The Skills of Diagnostic Planning*. Baltimore: University Park Press; 1980.

73. Frey WD. Functional assessment in the 80s: a conceptual enigma, a technical challenge. In: Halpern AS, Fuhrer MJ, eds. *Functional Assessment in Rehabilitation*. Baltimore: Paul H. Brookes; 1984:11–43.

74. Cohen MR, Farkas M, Nemec P. *Functional Assessment Trainer Package*. Boston: Boston University Center for Psychiatric Rehabilitation; 1985.

chapter 10

Vocational Capacity with Alcohol or Other Substance Abuse

William Frankenstein

Substance abuse has proved to be a ubiquitous phenomenon of increasing national concern. Often, it is in reference to the occupational sphere that the widespread prevalence of substance abuse and its consequences become known. All too common is the phenomenon of the professional athlete, the transportation worker, the entertainer, the politician, the physician, or other newsworthy individual who is injured, injures others, enters treatment, or is prevented from working because of substance abuse. Moreover, the impact of substance abuse on the less visible worker is undoubtedly even more damaging to productivity, safety, and the quality of goods and services.

Abuse denotes the range of possible situations within which substance use may present problems in working. This definition is broadly inclusive. Therefore, a typically light-drinking electrician who has a few beers at lunch, returns to work, falls and hurts his back may be considered a substance abuser. So, too, is the Demerol-addicted dentist whose finances and marriage are in disarray, yet whose professional practice is unaffected.

Substance abuse, once treated, should not preclude a return to work as soon as is feasible. The concomitants, correlates, or secondary effects of substance abuse are probably more likely to influence return-to-work decisions. For return-to-work assessment with substance abusers, there are five basic objectives:

1. to identify the pre-existing conditions, correlates, concomitants, and effects of substance abuse and to provide recommendations, referrals, or treatment
2. to identify conditions that support ongoing sobriety and to provide treatment, when indicated
3. to monitor compliance with treatment planning
4. to use an assessment strategy that can detect relapse
5. to contract for the protocol to be followed in the event of relapse

Although it may be necessary to assess and treat the correlates and consequences of substance abuse independently, a substance abuser is most likely to return to work successfully in a supportive environment that has a built-in capacity for the detection of relapse.

OCCUPATIONAL SUBSTANCE ABUSE

Recent data suggest that an estimated 18 million adults in the United States experience problems as a result of alcohol abuse.[1] Depending on the age of the sample, between 35% and 80% of this population have problems with other drugs as well,[2] and many millions of others have primary drug problems.

Of the total costs to society attributed to substance abuse, estimated in 1983 to be $176.4 billion,[3] $104 billion (approximately 59%) was related to reduced productivity and lost employment. To place this in perspective, the occupational costs of substance abuse are seven times the costs for treatment of substance abuse and its health consequences.

It is estimated that between 5% and 10% of the work force abuses alcohol and is dependent on it and that another 3% to 7% of the employed abuse illicit drugs.[4] Overall, the data show that the substance-abusing employee has a higher incidence of job-related accidents, is absent from work more often for sickness or disability, makes more workers' compensation claims, loses more working years over a lifetime, and, in general, performs more poorly than do members of the work force who are not impaired by alcohol or drug abuse.[4-8]

Workplace variables influence substance use and abuse on the job; however, there are as yet no theories that satisfactorily explain how and why substance abuse is tolerated, condoned, encouraged, or unrecognized on the job.[9,10] Therefore, in determining work suitability, job or workplace analysis is less relevant than are the individual characteristics of a substance abuser.

Those in business, industry, and the professions have established many programs that address substance use, abuse prevention, and intervention in the workplace. Generally, a substance abuser, once identified, is remanded for education or treatment or faces some disciplinary action. The decision in each instance is based on a complex equation that includes the company policy regarding substance use on and/or off the job; the evaluation of a personnel, employee assistance, or health care professional; and the identified worker's response to having been identified.

For example, a crew foreman, whose job is to manage emergency cleanups of toxic waste spills, is screened for drug use as part of an annual physical. Although the test result is positive, an evaluation shows that he does not meet diagnostic criteria for a substance use disorder. It turns out that he smokes marijuana only infrequently and only at social gatherings or parties. Company policy forbids any use of drugs by employees, however. Therefore, the company gave the employee a reprimand, warned him, and provided education on company policy and company concern over the effects of drug use on employee and public safety. Following a brief period of reassignment, during which the evaluation, feedback, and education took place, the employee returned to his former position—on the condition that he provide periodic samples taken randomly to test for violation of company policy.

In a comparison example, an airplane pilot's supervisor refers him to an employee assistance counselor for evaluation because of a documented deterioration in the pilot's work performance (eg, in the area of paperwork and reliability, personal appearance) and because of concerns expressed by co-workers. Evaluation indicates that the pilot meets diagnostic criteria for alcohol dependence. As a condition for keeping his job without prejudice, the pilot agrees to commit himself to an inpatient alcoholism treatment facility. It is decided that he may return to work following his discharge from treatment on the conditions that he attend an aftercare program for a specified period of time; that he attend a certain number of Alcoholics Anonymous (AA) meetings per week, with his attendance verified objectively; and that he submit to periodic and random breath alcohol tests.

In both examples, the return-to-work decisions were based upon the employee's actual substance use and/or abuse problem, the intervention provided and its outcome, and the nature of the work performed. Those who make such decisions must have a basic understanding of the dimensions of substance use and the diagnostic criteria of substance use disorders, their course, treatment, and outcome.

Our society particularly disapproves of substance use, even casual or recreational substance use, in the occupational sphere. Undoubtedly, this value reflects many influences. Certainly, the work transaction in which an employee receives a wage for his or her services or the professional sells his or her services for a fee is predicated upon an understanding that the wage or fee entitles the purchaser to competent performance. If even occasional use of substances may compromise performance, the transaction between seller and buyer is sullied. In extreme cases, there may be an increased threat or risk to the public safety. Societal standards, in contrast, are more permissive regarding substance use if such use is private and relatively free from generalized risk.

In the United States, most of the adult population drinks alcohol; many others use drugs obtained illicitly or by prescription.[11] Most alcohol and many other drug users experience no personal or social sanctions against their practices. Yet, it is estimated that between 10% and 23% of all workers use dangerous drugs on the job.[12] Some currently unknown proportion of substance users will be sanctioned within the occupational sphere for detection of use, either on or off the job, yet will be free of other consequences or pathologic use. Another segment of the population will develop a substance use disorder. Because treatment differs for these two groups, it is important to differentiate accurately between individuals who are occupational substance abusers and those who have diagnosed substance use disorders.

Etiology and Maintaining Variables of Addictive Disorders

It is the common belief today that addictive disorders result from the interactions of environment and heredity. Although the respective contributions of environment and heredity have yet to be determined, the currently accepted view is that the equation differs for different classes of abused drugs and for different individuals.[13-16] For the purposes of making return-to-work decisions, however, determining the precise cause of an individual's substance abuse provides essentially no help. It is more useful to identify the variables that maintain rather than cause an addictive disorder.

Maintaining variables are those classes of conditions, situations, personal factors, or social factors, the presence of which tends to increase the likelihood of substance use. They are categorized as environmental or intrapersonal. Environmental variables include the following categories (with some examples):

- familial
    1. physical, sexual, or emotional abuse/neglect of children
    2. child psychiatric or behavioral problems
    3. adult children at home
    4. disorganized family structure
- marital
    1. discord or dissatisfaction
    2. separation or divorce
    3. no marriage
    4. spouse abuse
- financial
    1. gambling debts or erosion of savings
    2. costs of child support or maintenance
    3. indebtedness
    4. legal costs or fines
- social system
    1. substance-abusing peers or friends
    2. lack of alternative social support
    3. people who enable substance abuse
- occupational
    1. workplace that tolerates, condones, or encourages use
    2. high-stress environment

    3. boredom or tedium
    4. unpleasant work or working conditions
    5. lack of supervision or accountability
    6. substance taking as "part of the job"
- legal
    1. restraining orders
    2. revocation of driving privileges
    3. involvement in social agency cases (eg, youth services)
- situational
    1. residence near a tavern
    2. exposure to alcohol advertising
    3. expectations or norms in a situation that promotes use
    4. unpleasant tasks
    5. celebrations

Intrapersonal variables include the following categories:

- emotional
    1. relaxation or tension reduction
    2. soothing of psychiatric symptoms
    3. mood improvement
- cognitive
    1. belief in improved thinking or social ability
    2. increased assertiveness
    3. escape from unpleasant situation
    4. low self-esteem or poor self-efficacy
- physiologic
    1. relief of craving or withdrawal symptoms
    2. relief of pain
- health
    1. gastrointestinal disorders
    2. cognitive dysfunction or head injury
    3. other health problems
- psychiatric
    1. affective disorder
    2. anxiety disorder
    3. borderline, antisocial, or compulsive personality disorder

Some combination of these variables maintains substance-taking behavior. Maintaining variables differ not only for different individuals but also for users and abusers.

For example, if a warehouse worker knows that drinking is commonplace during his shift and believes that his group of work friends expect him to drink, the social interaction at work is likely to be a potent variable that increases the worker's risk of alcohol abuse. Similarly, if an alcohol-dependent schoolteacher in recovery subsequently believes that she can have one or two drinks a night, her prognosis for a return to an alcoholic drinking pattern is increased. In this example, the teacher's beliefs about her ability to resume controlled alcohol use reflects the distorted thinking that maintains her drinking behavior.

It is necessary to evaluate the unique maintaining variables on a case-by-case basis. The most common method for assessing maintaining variables is behavioral assessment.[17,18]

Substance Abuse as a Disease

Often, substance abuse is regarded as a disease. Although the search for a particular pathogen has had negative results, the evolution of the societal view of substance abuse from being a weakness to the more current disease perspective enlightens those who believe that the cure is a simple cessation of substance use. Substance abuse disorders are extremely resistant to treatment, and recovery rates do not differ appreciably from those seen for many cancers.

The disease concept permits a more productive view of substance abuse as beyond the control of the afflicted individual. It promotes the need for treatment, rather than incarceration. It permits those around the substance abuser to recognize that the abuser is sick and needs help, and it promotes the notion that an abuser can recover.

Diagnosis

In the 1987 edition of the *Diagnostic and Statistical Manual of Mental Disorders*,[19] substance use disorders are categorized as either psychoactive substance-induced organic mental disorders or as psychoactive substance use disorders. The hallmark of substance-induced organic mental disorders is an impairment in mental, emotional, and behavioral function that results directly from the effects of the substance on the nervous system. The impairment may be transient or permanent. The 11 classes of substances and the organic mental disorders associated with them are listed in Table 10-1.

The substance use disorders reflect more or less regular substance use in a pattern of pathologic consumption coupled with the presence of significant consequences of use in major life areas. Substance use disorders focus on the maladaptive behavior caused by regular use and its accompanying symptoms. Pathologic use is diagnosed as either dependence or abuse.

Table 10-1 Psychoactive Substance-Induced Organic Mental Disorders

Alcohol
- intoxication
- idiosyncratic intoxication
- uncomplicated withdrawal
- withdrawal delirium
- hallucinosis
- amnesic disorder
- dementia associated with alcoholism

Amphetamine or similarly acting sympathomimetics
- intoxication
- withdrawal
- delirium
- delusional disorder

Caffeine
- intoxication

Cannabis
- intoxication
- delusional disorder

Cocaine
- intoxication
- withdrawal
- delirium
- delusional disorder

Hallucinogen
- hallucinosis
- delusional disorder
- mood disorder
- posthallucinogen perception disorder

Inhalant
- intoxication

Nicotine
- withdrawal

Opioid
- intoxication
- withdrawal

continues

Table 10-1 continued

Phencyclidine (PCP) or similarly acting arylcyclohexylamines
- intoxication
- delirium
- delusional disorder
- mood disorder
- organic mental disorder not otherwise specified

Sedatives, hypnotics, or anxiolytics
- intoxication
- uncomplicated withdrawal
- withdrawal delirium
- amnesic disorder

Other or unspecified psychoactive substance may cause
- intoxication
- withdrawal
- delirium
- dementia
- amnesic disorder
- delusional disorder
- hallucinosis
- mood disorder
- anxiety disorder
- personality disorder
- organic mental disorder not otherwise specified

In substance dependence, the individual is unable to control his or her use of a substance and continues to use it despite the consequences. Although the severity of substance dependence varies from mild to severe, some combination of the following symptoms is inevitably present:

- greater consumption or longer period of use than intended
- persistent desire to use or failed attempts to control use
- extended periods of time spent in acquiring, using, or recovering from the substance use
- frequent intoxication or withdrawal that interferes with competent functioning in life areas
- sacrifice of important activities because of use
- continued use despite knowledge of a problem caused or exacerbated by use

- marked tolerance
- characteristic withdrawal symptoms
- use of substance to avoid withdrawal symptoms

Psychoactive substance abuse is a maladaptive pattern of substance use indicated by continued use despite the knowledge that it exacerbates a persistent problem or by recurrent use in situations that are physically hazardous. The symptoms must persist for 1 month or must have recurred over a longer period of time.

Polysubstance dependence is diagnosed when a person repeatedly uses at least three substances (not nicotine or caffeine) over a 6-month period. No single substance predominates in the use pattern, but all other criteria for substance dependence are met. This category is particularly important, as there is an increasing trend toward polysubstance dependence or abuse in younger adults with addictive disorders.

Course

Alcoholism and drug dependence have been described as chronic, progressive disease processes. In other words, unless the abuser recovers by natural means, through self-help, or through formal treatment, a substance use disorder manifests itself in progressive deterioration and death.

There are vast individual differences in the age of onset of a substance use disorder. Most substance abusers begin to use substances in mid-adolescence, but so do most nonproblem substance users. A clear abuse pattern often does not become apparent until a person has reached the mid-twenties. Typically, substance abusers remain in the characteristic pattern of occasional excessive use, experimentation with a range of substances, and mild negative consequences of use after their age peers have lost interest in it.

It is not unusual for substance abusers to experience periods of abstinence prior to full recovery. In other words, "slips" (ie, brief, isolated incidents of substance use) and "relapses" (ie, prolonged return to an abuse pattern) are commonplace. Therefore, the substance abuser's recovery is often discontinuous.

Treatment

Substance abuse is unique in its capacity for deluding the substance abuser into believing that he or she does *not* have a substance abuse problem. Often called "diseases of denial," substance use disorders are difficult to treat partly because the substance abuser absolutely denies the presence of a problem. The denial is not actually a conscious misrepresentation; rather, it reflects the unconscious wish of the substance abuser not to have to relinquish the substance and admit to out-of-control use.

Because treatment for substance abuse disorders is still evolving, there is no treatment of choice. It is widely agreed, however, that the outcome of treatment is superior to the outcome of no treatment. Specific therapies that have been used include individual, marital, family, and group counseling; pharmacotherapy; education; and self-help. These therapies are practiced in inpatient, outpatient, and partial settings (eg, intensive outpatient, day treatment, and halfway houses).[11,20,21] Complicating the research on the efficacy of treatment is the presence of Alcoholics Anonymous (AA) and Narcotics Anonymous (NA), large self-help groups that, because they are based on the principle of members' anonymity and because they do not view themselves as treatment programs per se, do not lend themselves to empiric evaluation. Overall, there is merit to the position that there are several clinical presentations of substance abuse disorders and that each case requires a degree of individualized treatment planning.[22]

ASSESSMENT OF VOCATIONAL IMPAIRMENT IN SUBSTANCE ABUSERS

Assessment of substance use disorders is complex, especially in an evaluative context such as that required when a treated worker wants to return to work. First, denial and resistance to acknowledging the problem, admitting a lack of control over the substance, and obtaining help contaminate a substance abuser's self-report. For those in the substance abuse field, the experience of interviewing a patently intoxicated person who has alcohol on the breath, who shows all the behavioral signs of intoxication—and who steadfastly denies drinking—leaves a lasting impression as to the potency of denial processes. Second, substance abusers are prone to "blackouts" and "brownouts"; they have head injuries and other nonmotivational reasons for impaired recall and report of substance use. Although substance abusers routinely evidence denial and resistance, the evaluative context increases their motivation to present themselves as abstinent. They perceive the substance abuse assessor as holding the key to their return to work. Therefore, it is critical that the actual substance abuse assessment in the return-to-work evaluation be sensitive to both unconscious and conscious biases in reporting.

As mentioned earlier, most substance abusers resume their substance use for occasional periods during the recovery process. Therefore, the return-to-work substance abuse assessment must include provisions for long-term follow-up and an agreed-upon contract for the protocol to be followed in the event of slips or relapse.[23]

Pre-Existing Conditions and Concomitant Impairments

Substance abuse both accompanies and results in other work-relevant disorders; it is the hidden dimension of vocational impairment. Because of their history of substance use, substance abusers have increased rates of head injuries, seizure disorders, traumatic injuries, gastrointestinal disorders, poor medical health, and malnutrition. In addition, substance abusers are more likely than nonabusers to suffer significant mental illness (eg, affective disorders) or characteriologic disorders (eg, antisocial personality disorder).

As substance abuse is so highly correlated with so many other putative causes of work disability, it seems prudent to incorporate a substance abuse screen in most return-to-work evaluations. Among the conditions that may signal some increased likelihood of an undiagnosed substance use disorder are the following:

- accidental injury
    1. bruises, especially at furniture height or of unknown origin
    2. burns, especially third-degree burns
    3. cigarette burns on hands and clothes
    4. injury from falls
    5. injury from fights
    6. frostbite or exposure
    7. injury from motor vehicle or machine accident
- cardiac and circulatory system disease
    1. alcohol cardiomyopathy
    2. angina/myocardial infarction
    3. cardiac arrhythmias
    4. clotting disorders
    5. congestive heart failure
    6. coronary artery disease
    7. hematopoietic complications
    8. hypertension
    9. spider angiomas
    10. tachycardia
    11. vascular engorgement of the face
- gastrointestinal disease
    1. colitis
    2. esophageal varices, other gastrointestinal bleeding
    3. esophagitis
    4. gastritis
    5. pancreatitis
    6. ulcers

- infection, especially with increased incidence of
  1. abscesses
  2. acquired immunodeficiency syndrome (AIDS)
  3. bacterial endocarditis
  4. cellulitis
  5. opportunistic infections
  6. repeated upper respiratory/bronchial infection
  7. tuberculosis
  8. ulceration of the extremities
- liver disease and concomitants
  1. alcoholic hepatitis
  2. ascites
  3. cirrhosis
  4. fatty liver
  5. hepatitis
  6. hepatorenal disease
  7. portal hypertension
- metabolic disease
  1. diabetes
  2. gout, repeated episodes
  3. hypoglycemia
  4. thyroid disease
- musculoskeletal disease or disorder
  1. alcohol myopathy
  2. flaccid muscles
  3. joint pain or inflammation
  4. radiographic evidence of past breaks or fractures
- neurologic disease or neuropsychologic deficit
  1. alcohol cerebellar degeneration
  2. cerebral degeneration without apparent cause
  3. memory deficits, "blackouts"
  4. optic neuropathy
  5. past or present psychoactive substance-induced organic mental disorder
  6. peripheral neuropathy
  7. problem-solving or novel learning deficit
  8. seizure disorder
  9. subdural hematoma
  10. toxic amblyopia
  11. visuospatial deficits
  12. Wernicke-Korsakoff syndrome

- nutritional disorder
  1. beriberi
  2. chronic malnutrition, vitamin or mineral deficiency
  3. hypokalemia
  4. pellagra
- psychiatric or psychologic disorder or symptoms
  1. affective disorder
  2. anxiety disorder
  3. impotence without organic cause
  4. personality disorder, especially antisocial, borderline, or obsessive-compulsive disorder
  5. post-traumatic stress disorder
  6. repeated family crises
  7. schizophrenic or schizophreniform disorder
  8. sleep disorder
  9. suicidal ideation or intent, past attempts

The failure to diagnose substance abuse when it is masked by one of these conditions increases the likelihood of poor adjustment in the resumption of work.

Assessment Methods

There is no single assessment method that the examiner can use with confidence to confirm the presence of current substance abuse or, for that matter, to rule out the absence of substance abuse. To correct for the lack of sensitivity in any one method, the best approach to take in a return-to-work substance abuse evaluation is to incorporate multiple methods. These methods include both subjective measures (eg, questionnaires, structured interview schedules, unstructured self-report, and the report of collaterals) and objective measures (eg, blood alcohol level, the presence of drug metabolites in body fluids, indirect clinical laboratory measures, and documentary evidence). The most commonly used measures are listed in Appendix 10-A.

A battery of measures is desirable. The battery optimally includes measures that screen for the broad range of substance abuse behaviors and consequences, make it possible to evaluate specific individual case concerns, and are capable of yielding positive findings despite a biased self-report. The results obtained on these measures may not routinely converge; however, a positive result on one measure (eg, metabolites of methamphetamine in a urine drug screen) may expose as invalid another result (eg, self and collateral report of abstinence coupled with verified regular AA and NA attendance).

Moreover, abstinence must be reassessed periodically. One reason for these reassessments is to establish a baseline data point, which is critical in determining the meaning of a subsequent positive value. For example, a chronic alcoholic may show continued elevations on alcohol-sensitive clinical laboratory measures (eg, SGOT, SGPT, serum gamma-glutamyltransferase) even after a period of abstinence. Elevated liver function tests may persist because the recovery of liver function may follow a slower course or may not occur. Comparison to a baseline data point may reveal whether these elevations reflect a return to drinking or a slow recovery of function with abstinence.

As discussed earlier, recovery from a substance use disorder is not a linear process. Slips are common not only for the newly abstinent but also for those who have been abstinent for years. Repeated screening increases the possibility of intervention to prevent full-blown relapse and the consequences of relapse for the employer, employees, consumers, the substance abuser, and his or her family and friends. Furthermore, repeated negative results can be used in advocacy efforts for a recovering substance abuser.

Assessment of current substance use alone is not sufficient to convey the status of a substance abuser's recovery. Assessment should be broad-based and should focus on all significant life areas, including general health, family and marital, social, legal, financial, and occupational variables. Improved status in particular life areas coincident with recovery is further evidence of continued abstinence, whereas no change or a deterioration may signal increased risk of relapse or actual relapse.

Subjective Assessment Methods

All subjective methods for assessing substance abuse are compromised by their dependence on the verbal report of the substance abuser or a collateral informant. Like the self-report of the substance abuser, the reports of others may be inaccurate or misleading. To compensate for the bias inherent in self-report methods, interview schedules or questionnaires are used to structure the self-report process. Although some aspect of the assessment process must remain unstructured so as to permit the assessor to pursue important details, many semistructured or structured interview protocols permit necessary digression.

Interview Schedules. The advantage of interview schedules is that they are comprehensive and adaptable. They cover a broad range of variables related to the individual's history, substance use pattern, progression of the substance use disorder, negative consequences in significant life areas, treatment efforts, current recovery, and involvement in treatment or self-help supports. In addition to giving the assessor a comprehensive understanding of the person's substance abuse history and recovery, the broad coverage suggests areas for further investigation.

Some interview schedules provide a structure for recalling substance use over a stipulated period of time. Substance use data obtained by this method, called the time-line follow-back procedure, are more accurate than data obtained by unstructured free recall (eg, "Have you had anything to drink over the last 6 months?"). The time-line follow-back procedure uses current events, personal event dating, and specific questioning techniques for improving data quality.[24]

The disadvantage of interview schedules is that they do not yield standardized data that can be used for comparison, either with a norm or with a person's own baseline. Moreover, administering them requires a relatively long period of time.

Questionnaires. As mechanisms for evaluating substance abuse and its consequences, questionnaires are relatively cost-efficient. Furthermore, questionnaires are available for the assessment of specific substance abuse domains, such as the extent of alcohol dependence syndrome symptomatology. Because administration is standard and an instrument's psychometric properties can be developed, the data obtained from questionnaire responses can be compared to norms for a reference population.

Some questionnaires yield information on the quality of a subject's response set. For example, some yield validity scale scores that are measures of the degree to which a respondent may be "faking good" (ie, answering in a socially desirable manner) or otherwise distorting responses. Other questionnaires assess subtle concomitants of substance abuse that, when present in sufficient number, suggest undetected substance abuse. For example, a history of certain types of trauma in adulthood is highly suggestive of a substance abuse problem.[25]

Still other questionnaires include criterion-keyed responses to questions that have no surface relationship to substance abuse. On the MacAndrew Alcoholism Scale of the Minnesota Multiphasic Personality Inventory,[26] for example, the item "I like to cook" is significantly more frequently endorsed by alcoholics than by nonalcoholics. The essence of the criterion-keyed approach is to establish empirically those items that are functionally unrelated to substance abuse, but nevertheless correlate highly with its presence.

Questionnaires have several drawbacks. First, respondents may misinterpret the nature of the queries. In this case, the questionnaire produces a poor representation of the subject's actual situation or status. Second, because the administration is standardized, the assessor has less opportunity to investigate individual responses and misunderstandings. Finally, many questionnaires are not time-sensitive. In other words, the questions fail to take into account the time period within which particular behaviors occurred. For example, on the Michigan Alcoholism Screening Test,[27] a commonly used questionnaire, an affirmative response to the item "I have gotten into physical fights while drinking" would yield the same score for an alcoholic who is experiencing a relapse and an alcoholic who has been sober for 15 years, but had engaged in the behavior as a young adult. The lack of time sensitivity makes questionnaires relatively useless for repeat screening.

Collateral Reports. Especially when there has been a slip or relapse that the substance abuser has denied, collateral reports are extremely useful adjuncts to the self-report of a substance abuser. They can provide specific observations of the times, dates, places, and circumstances of a return to substance use. Of course, the report of collaterals is generally subject to the same constraints as a self-report.

Overall, self-report of substance abusers and collateral informants represents the cornerstone of the valuation process. Although there are considerable contaminants in self-report data, the presence of multiple methods and measures that make it possible to assess the quality and validity of self-report makes self-report a key souce of data on which to base return-to-work decisions. The subjective methods, however, can be well supplemented by the incorporation of objective methods.

Objective Assessment Methods

All objective assessment methods are independent of the substance abuser's self-report. A positive value on an objective measure can sometimes provide indisputable evidence of substance use. Some objective measures lack sensitivity, however; they do not detect substance use when it has occurred. For example, documentary records that fail to show a connection between substance use and driving violations do not establish abstinence. Other objective measures lack specificity, so that factors other than substance use may produce a falsely positive value. For example, an elevated level of SGOT may reflect liver damage unrelated to alcohol or other drug use.

Direct Serum Measurement. In practice, direct serum measurement is routinely used for the detection of alcohol, but except in emergency medicine, it is rarely used for the detection of other drugs. A person's blood alcohol concentration is rarely obtained directly from a blood sample; because alcohol is essentially equally distributed through body tissues, a blood alcohol concentration obtained via breath sample is essentially the same as an actual blood alcohol concentration.

A positive blood alcohol concentration indicates relatively recent consumption only. Although the blood alcohol concentration ascends rapidly and peaks within an hour or so after the last drink, it falls more slowly. Once metabolized, alcohol does not leave metabolites that can be reliably assessed, for example, by urinalysis. Thus, for assessment purposes, a blood alcohol concentration test detects drinking only for a relatively short time period. A positive blood alcohol concentration in an ostensibly recovered alcoholic is the sine qua non for detection, however.

Direct serum measures of other psychoactive substances are supplanted by indirect measurement of metabolites, which are detectable for varying periods of time (depending on the substance) and are easily obtained via urine drug screens.

Indirect Measures of Drug Metabolites. For drugs other than alcohol, indirect measurement of body fluids (and more recently hair samples) has become the standard objective assessment of recent drug consumption. Although attacked for a variety of legal and moral reasons, urine drug screens are reliable and valid when the testing is done properly. The accuracy of urine drug screening for drug consumption is directly proportional to the procedure used, the frequency and randomness of testing, the procedure used for follow-up to initial positive findings, and the conditions under which the urine sample was obtained.

Standards for the conduct of urine drug screens have been published, and the most legally defensible methods of sample analysis have been determined.[28–32] Clearly, drug testing has advantages over other methods insofar as detecting recent use is concerned. In general, however, urine drug screens must be used frequently to ensure abstinence. The detection limits for drugs of abuse vary according to the specific substance and the method of analysis. Most substances can be detected for between 2 and 5 days after the last use, and some (eg, marijuana) can be detected for longer periods.[28]

Practical constraints of cost and yield limit the use of regular widespread testing. In practice, the frequency and scheduling of drug testing for a recovering worker are proportional to the degree that the worker's undetected substance abuse has implications for the individual and public safety.

Indirect Clinical Laboratory Measures. Indirect objective measures of recent substance consumption may be obtained by analysis of certain blood chemistry values that are sensitive to the regular consumption of certain substances. The measures most sensitive to alcohol dependence are serum gamma-glutamyl-transferase; red blood cell mean corpuscular volume; and liver enzyme studies, such as measures of SGOT or SGPT. Each of these measures may be elevated in alcoholism, but serum gamma-glutamyltransferase is probably the most sensitive to current consumption. The finding of abnormal values in these markers increases the likelihood of a substance use disorder, but they lack both sensitivity and specificity.

Documentary Evidence. There are many sources of documentary evidence that may relate to a worker's drug-taking behavior: checks or credit card slips that reveal purchases made at liquor stores, bars, or restaurants; driving records that reveal drug-related motor vehicle infractions; attendance slips from AA or NA meetings, signed by the group secretary; or work attendance or physician records.

Documentary evidence may sometimes be the only data source that establishes substance use. For example, a drunk driving arrest that occurs after the date of return to work and is discovered in follow-up procedures establishes alcohol consumption during a period of presumed abstinence. Examination of cancelled checks leads to the discovery of expenditures at a local liquor store during the time in which an individual professes abstinence. Conversely, documentary evidence can establish compliance with a recovery program. For example, if an individual's return to work is conditioned on his compliance with the employer's demand that he remain involved with AA or NA, an attendance slip verifies that compliance.

In addition, documentary evidence may reveal some "soft signs" that a worker is at an increased risk for relapse. Often, an individual's involvement in self-help programs decreases prior to a relapse. Recorded attendance provides a validity check on a recovering individual's relative risk for "falling off the wagon."

CONCLUSION

It should be clear that the assessment of substance use in a treated worker who wants to return to work is complicated. No single measurement methodology is sufficient to identify all cases of relapse or to document work suitability. To a degree, all methods are necessary. Practical considerations dictate just what measures are selected, how frequently they are administered, and who bears the costs of the evaluation.

A generic assessment strategy that represents the range of practical assessment protocols available is presented in Appendix 10-B. The best protocol for a vocational assessment prior to the return to work of an employee who has been a substance abuser should take into consideration the impact of the employee's relapse for productivity, employability, and the health and safety of the employee and the public.

REFERENCES

1. *Sixth Special Report to the US Congress on Alcohol and Health*. Washington, DC: US Department of Health and Human Services, National Institute on Alcohol Abuse and Alcoholism; 1987.

2. *Fifth Special Report to the US Congress on Alcohol and Health*. Washington, DC: US Department of Health and Human Services, National Institute on Alcohol Abuse and Alcoholism; 1983.

3. Harwood HJ, Napolitano DM, Kristiansen PL, et al. *Economic Costs to Society of Alcohol and Drug Abuse and Mental Illness: Special Report to the Alcoholism, Drug Abuse and Mental Health Administration*. Research Triangle Park, NC: Research Triangle Institute; 1984.

4. Quayle D. American productivity: the devastating effect of alcoholism and drug abuse. *Am Psychol*. 1983;38:454–458.

5. McDonnell R, Maynard A. Estimation of life years lost from alcohol-related premature death. *Alcohol Alcsm*. 1985;20:435–443.

6. Lings S, Jensen J, Christensen S, et al. Occupational accidents and alcohol. *Int Arch Occup Environ Health*. 1984;53:321–329.

7. Pell S, D'Alonzo CA. Sickness absenteeism of alcoholics. *J Occup Med*. 1970;12:198–210.

8. Hingson RW, Lederman RI, Walsh DC. Employee drinking patterns and accidental injury: a study of four New England states. *J Stud Alcohol*. 1985;46:298–303.

9. Fillmore D, Caetano R. Epidemiology of alcohol abuse and alcoholism in the professions. In *Occupational Alcoholism: A Review of Research Issues*. Washington, DC: US Government Printing Office, 1982. National Institute on Alcohol Abuse and Alcoholism Research Monograph No. 8.

10. Parker DA, Brody JA. Risk factors for alcoholism and alcohol problems among employed women and men. In: *Occupational Alcoholism: A Review of Research Issues*. Washington, DC: US Government Printing Office; 1982. National Institute on Alcohol Abuse and Alcoholism Research Monograph No. 8.

11. *Drug Abuse and Drug Abuse Research: The Second Triennial Report to Congress from the Secretary, Department of Health and Human Services*, Rockville, MD: US Department of Health and Human Services, National Institute on Drug Abuse: 1987.

12. Backer TD. *Strategic planning for workplace drug abuse programs*. Rockville, MD: National Institute of Drug Abuse; 1987. US Department of Health and Human Services publication No. (ADM) 87-1538.

13. Goodwin DW. The genetic determinants of alcoholism. In: Mendelson JH, Mello NK, eds. *The Diagnosis and Treatment of Alcoholism*, 2nd ed. New York: McGraw-Hill; 1985: chap 3.

14. Jones CL, Battjes RJ. *Etiology of Drug Abuse: Implications for Prevention*. Rockville, MD: National Institute of Drug Abuse; 1984. US Department of Health and Human Services, Research Monograph No. 56.

15. Murray RM, Stabaneau JR. Genetic factors in alcoholism predisposition. In: Pattison EM, Kaufman E, eds. *Encyclopedic Handbook of Alcoholism*. New York: Gardner Press; 1982, chap 9.

16. Gottheil E, Druley KA, Skoloda TE, et al. *Etiologic Aspects of Alcohol and Drug Abuse*. Springfield, IL: Charles C Thomas; 1983.

17. Miller PM. Assessment of alcohol abuse. In: Barlow DH, ed. *Behavioral Assessment of Adult Disorders*. New York: Guilford Press, 1981; chap 9.

18. McCrady BS. Alcoholism. In: Barlow DH, ed. *Clinical Handbook of Psychological Disorders*. New York: Guilford Press; 1985, chap. 5.

19. American Psychiatric Association. *Diagnostic and Statistical Manual of Mental Disorders*, 3rd ed, revised. Washington, DC: APA; 1987.

20. Mendelson JH, Mello NK, eds. *The Diagnosis and Treatment of Alcoholism*. New York: McGraw-Hill; 1985.

21. Nace EP. *The Treatment of Alcoholism*. New York: Brunner/Mazel; 1987.

22. McCrady BS, Noel NE, Nirenberg TD, eds. *Future Directions in Alcohol Abuse Treatment Research*. Rockville, MD: US Department of Health and Human Services; 1985. National Institute on Alcohol Abuse and Alcoholism Research Monograph No. 15, DHHS publication No. (ADM) 85-1322.

23. Marlatt GA, Gordon JR, eds. *Relapse Prevention: Maintenance Strategies in the Treatment of Addictive Disorders*. New York: Guilford Press; 1985.

24. Sobell MB, Maisto SA, Sobell LC, et al. Developing a prototype for evaluating alcohol treatment effectiveness. In: Sobell LC, Sobell MB, Ward E, eds. *Evaluating Alcohol and Drug Abuse Treatment Effectiveness: Recent Advances*. New York: Pergamon Press; 1980:129–150.

25. Skinner HA, Holt S, Schuller R, et al. Identification of alcohol abuse using laboratory tests and a history of trauma. *Ann Intern Med*. 1984;101:847–851.

26. MacAndrew C. The differentiation of male alcoholic outpatients from nonalcoholic psychiatric outpatients by means of the MMPI. *J Stud Alcoholism*. 1965;26:238–246.

27. Selzer ML. The Michigan Alcoholism Screening Test: the quest for a new diagnostic instrument. *J Psychiatry*. 1971;127:1653–1658.

28. American Medical Society on Alcoholism and Other Drug Dependencies. *Review Course Syllabus*. New York: AMSAODD; 1987.

29. Lehrer M. Drug screening in the workplace. *Clin Lab Med*. 1987;7:389–400.

30. Hoyt DW, Finnigan RE, Nee T, et al. Drug testing in the workplace—are methods legally defensible? *JAMA*. 1987;258:504–509.

31. Hawks RL, Chiang CN. *Urine Testing for Drugs of Abuse*. Rockville, MD: US Department of Health and Human Services; 1987. US Department of Health and Human Services, National Institute of Drug Abuse Research Monograph No. 73, DHHS publication No. (ADM) 87-1481.

32. US Department of Health and Human Services. Scientific and technical guidelines for federal drug testing programs; standards for certifications of laboratories engaged in urine drug testing for federal agencies. *Fed Reg*. 1987;52:30638–30652.

Appendix 10-A

Subjective and Objective Measures for Assessing the Vocational Capacity of Substance Abusers

DIAGNOSTIC OVERVIEWS

The Alcohol Clinical Index (A-1)*
A Diagnostic Algorithm (A-2)
National Council on Alcoholism Diagnostic Criteria (A-3)

SUBJECTIVE MEASURES

INTERVIEWS
  Intake and Follow-Up Interviews (A-4) +
  Client Follow-Up Interview (A-5) +
  Comprehensive Drinker Profile (A-6)* +
  Baseline and Follow-Up Interviews (A-7)* +
  Addiction Severity Index (A-8)* +
  Client Interview (A-9) +
  Lifetime Drinking History (A-10)* +
  Time-Line Follow-Back Assessment Method (A-11)* +
  Assessment Interviewing Guide (A-12)
QUESTIONNAIRES
  General Questionnaires
    CAGE Questionnaire (A-13)*
    Michigan Alcoholism Screening Test (A-14)* +
    Drug Abuse Screening Test (A-15)*
    Alcohol Dependence Scale (A-16)*
    Alcohol Use Inventory (A-17)* +
    Severity of Alcohol Dependence Scale (A-18) +
    Alcohol Expectancy Questionnaire (A-19)*

Questionnaires That Assess Concomitants or Subtle Indicators
Skinner Trauma Scale (A-20)*
MacAndrew Addictions Scale (A-21)* +
Questionnaires That Provide Information on Quality of Report
Minnesota Multiphasic Personality Inventory (MMPI)—Validity Scales
(A-22)
Basic Personality Inventory—Denial, Social Desirability, and Infrequency
Scales (A-23)*

OBJECTIVE METHODS

INDIRECT CLINICAL LABORATORY MEASURES
Abuse Associated with Elevated Values (A-24)
Serum gamma-glutamyltransferase (GGT)*
Red blood cell mean corpuscular volume (MCV)*
Serum glutonic oxalacetic transaminase (SGOT)*
Serum glutonic pyruvic transaminase (SGPT)
Alkaline phosphatase (Alk Phos)
Prothrombin time
Partial thromboplastin time
Urinary ketones, protein, or myoglobin
Total bilirubin (T bili)
Serum amylase
Abuse Associated with Decreased Values
Platelets
Serum magnesium
Calcium, phosphorus, potassium
Blood glucose
White blood count
Hemoglobin/Hematocrit

*Most useful measures or those with greater empirical support.

+ Available in Lettieri DJ, Nelson JE, Sayers MA, eds. *Alcoholism Treatment Assessment Research Instruments.* Rockville, MD: US Department of Health and Human Services; 1985. National Institute on Alcohol Abuse and Alcoholism Treatment Handbook Series No. 2, DHHS publication No. (ADM) 85-1380.

REFERENCES

A-1   Skinner HL, Holt S. *The Alcohol Clinical Index: Strategies for Identifying Patients With Alcohol Problems.* Toronto: Addiction Research Foundation; 1987.

A-2   Whitfield CL, Liepman MR, eds. *The Patient with Alcoholism and Other Drug Problems.* Baltimore: University of Maryland; 1980.

A-3 National Council on Alcoholism. Criteria for the diagnosis of alcoholism. *Am J Psychiatry.* 1972;129:127–135.

A-4 Annis HM. A basic assessment package. In: Glaser FB, Skinner HA, Pearlman S, et al, eds. *A System of Health Care Delivery.* Toronto: Addiction Research Foundation; 1984.

A-5 Kelso D, Fillmore KM. *Overview: Alcoholism Treatment and Client Functioning in Alaska.* Anchorage: Center for Alcohol and Addiction Studies, University of Alaska; 1984.

A-6 Marlatt GA, Miller WR. Comprehensive drinker profile. In: Mash EJ, Terdal L, eds. *Behavior Therapy Assessment.* New York: Springer Press; 1976.

A-7 McCrady BS. *Alcoholic Couples Treatment Interviews.* New Brunswick, NJ: Center of Alcohol Studies, Rutgers University; 1985.

A-8 McLellan AT, Luborsky L, Woody GE, et al. An improved diagnostic instrument for substance abuse patients: the Addiction Severity Index. *J Nerv Ment Dis.* 1980;168:26–33.

A-9 Polich JM, Armor DJ, Braiker HB. *The Course of Alcoholism: Four Years After Treatment.* New York: John Wiley & Sons; 1981.

A-10 Skinner HA. *Lifetime Drinking History.* Toronto: Addiction Research Foundation; 1984.

A-11 Sobell MB, Maisto SA, Sobell LC, et al. Developing a prototype for evaluating alcohol treatment effectiveness. In: Sobell LC, Sobell MB, Ward E, eds. *Evaluating Alcohol and Drug Abuse Treatment Effectiveness: Recent Advances.* New York: Pergamon Press; 1980:129–150.

A-12 Cohen S, Callahan JF. *The Diagnosis and Treatment of Drug and Alcohol Abuse.* New York: Haworth Press; 1986.

A-13 Ewing JA. Detecting alcoholism: the CAGE Questionnaire. *JAMA.* 1984;252:1905–1907.

A-14 Selzer ML. The Michigan Alcoholism Screening Test: the quest for a new diagnostic instrument. *Am J Psychiatry.* 1971;127:1653–1658.

A-15 Skinner HA. The Drug Abuse Screening Test. *Addict Behav.* 1982;7:363–371.

A-16 Horn JL, Skinner HA, Wanberg K, et al. *The Alcohol Dependence Scale.* Toronto: Addiction Research Foundation; 1984.

A-17 Horn JL, Wanberg K, Foster FM. A differential assessment model for alcoholism: the scales of the Alcohol Use Inventory. *J Stud Alcohol.* 1977;38:512–543.

A-18 Stockwell TR, Hodgson RJ, Murphy R. The Severity of Alcohol Dependence Questionnaire: its use, reliability and validity. *Br J Addict.* 1983;78:145–155.

A-19 Brown SA, Goldman MS, Inn A, et al. Expectations of reinforcement from alcohol: their domain and relation to drinking patterns. *J Consult Clin Psychol.* 1980;48:419–426.

A-20 Skinner HA, Holt S, Schuller R, et al. Identification of alcohol abuse using laboratory tests and a history of trauma. *Ann Intern Med.* 1984;101:847–851.

A-21 MacAndrew C. The differentiation of male alcoholic outpatients from nonalcoholic psychiatric outpatients by means of the MMPI. *Q J Stud Alcohol.* 1965;26:238–246.

A-22 Lachar D. *The MMPI: Clinical Assessment and Automated Interpretation.* Los Angeles: Western Psychological Services; 1974.

A-23 Jackson DN. *Basic Personality Inventory.* London, Canada: Author, 1976.

A-24 American Medical Society on Alcoholism and Other Drug Dependencies. *Review Course Syllabus.* New York: AMSAODD; 1987.

Generic Protocol for Assessing the Vocational Capacity of the Substance Abuser

1. DEMOGRAPHICS
   - Name
   - Age
   - Dates of evaluation
   - Date of report
   - Referral source
2. NATURE OF THE ASSESSMENT
   - Source of the referral
   - Reason for the referral
   - Purpose of the evaluation
     1. provide a substance use diagnosis
     2. describe the prognosis given the diagnosis, any correlates, and present risk factors
     3. describe functional limitations imposed by the substance abuse and its correlates
     4. describe suitable work environments
     5. make recommendations for ongoing evaluation, treatment, or aftercare
3. TESTS ADMINISTERED
   - Subjective measures listed
   - Objective measures listed
   - Ancillary measures listed
4. MENTAL STATUS, APPEARANCE, AND BEHAVIOR
   - Cooperation and compliance with the requirements
     1. cancellations, ''forgetfulness,'' inability to provide urine sample, lateness, guardedness

- Appearance, grooming, and self-care
  1. appropriate dress, disheveled, burns in clothing, poor grooming, cutaneous signs, decayed teeth
- Mood and affect
  1. "stoned"; affect inappropriate to mood; unusually depressed, anxious, or euphoric mood
- Thought process and content
- Speech quality
- Estimated intellectual capacity
  1. signs of substance-induced cognitive dysfunction
- Judgment and insight
- Estimate of quality or self-report
  1. signs of denial, distortion, memory failure, concentration problems

5. HISTORY OF SUBSTANCE USE
   - Current report of substance use for each category of substances (alcohol, illicit drugs, prescription drugs)
     1. quantity, frequency, variability of use for each substance used
   - Past history of use
     1. age of onset of use
     2. pattern of use over time
     3. progression of use over time
   - Consequences of use in particular life areas, by each substance
   - Signs and symptoms of abuse and dependence
   - Prior efforts to cut down or stop
   - Past efforts at treatment
   - Current status, length of abstinent period, involvement in treatment or aftercare, compliance with substance abuse treatment plan

6. TEST RESULTS
   - General screening questionnaires: results and interpretation
   - Specific data questionnaires: results and interpretation
   - Subtle correlates or criterion-keyed questionnaires: results and interpretation
   - Quality of self-report questionnaires: results, interpretation, and relevance to overall data quality
   - Reports of collaterals, reliability of client or patient data
   - Objective measures of blood or body fluids for evidence of recent consumption: results and interpretation
   - Documentary evidence: results and interpretation

7. SUMMARY
  - Overall statement of compliance and cooperation
  - Internal consistency of data
  - Diagnostic impression according to *Diagnostic and Statistical Manual of Mental Disorders*, 3rd edition, revised
    1. use versus abuse
  - Prognosis
    1. description of involvement in treatment or aftercare, risk for relapse, quality of recovery and abstinence, risk factors that compromise recovery, relevance of past history to current attempt at abstinence, relevant correlates of substance abuse, motivation and attitude of worker
  - Functional limitations imposed by the substance use, abuse, or dependence
  - Appropriateness of current treatment plan or aftercare plan of the worker

8. RECOMMENDATIONS
  - Statement on need for ongoing monitoring of substance use
    1. frequency of monitoring, conditions of monitoring, what is to be monitored, who bears the cost of monitoring, contingencies for failure to comply with monitoring agreement
  - Statement on need for education, treatment, or aftercare in addition to that currently received
  - Statement on the protocol to be followed in the event of a relapse, if detected
  - Statement on protocol to be followed if worker reports relapse and requests help
  - Statement on work environments or occupations that are contraindicated
    1. worksites that condone, tolerate, or encourage substance use; worksites in which substance use is undetected; occupations in which undetected substance use presents safety risks for self or others
  - Statement on policy regarding substance use on the job or off the job.

chapter 11

Vocational Capacity with Epilepsy

Michael D. Privitera and Steven J. Scheer

Many employers continue to harbor unjustified prejudice against job applicants with epilepsy. This problem may relate to the misconceptions that the general public holds about epilepsy. Contrary to some generally held beliefs, persons with epilepsy do not usually suffer from other neurologic impairments, uncontrolled tonic-clonic (grand mal) seizures, mental illness, or mental retardation. In the majority, seizures can be completely controlled with appropriate therapy, which may include antiepileptic drug treatment and counseling. In persons for whom such therapy is not entirely successful, seizures vary considerably in form, frequency, and severity. Any assessment of the vocational capacity of a person with epilepsy must take into account the seizure type and the degree of control.

DEFINITION AND CLASSIFICATION

In the nineteenth century, the eminent neurologist, Hughlings Jackson, postulated that a seizure was a sudden, excessive, disorderly discharge of cerebral neurons.[1] This description remains accurate, and the location, number, and degree of spread of these discharging neurons determine the clinical manifestation of seizures. Causes of seizures may include structural lesions of the brain (eg, tumor, vascular malformation, stroke), genetic factors, toxic/metabolic factors (eg, hypoglycemia, anoxia), or combinations of these.

The number of persons who have had a seizure in their lifetimes is higher than might be expected. One study in Great Britain revealed that an individual's risk of having a seizure at some point in life is approximately 4%.[2] Goodridge and Shorvon found that 1.7% of the patients in their general practice had experienced two or more nonfebrile seizures.[3] In another cumulative study, Hauser and associates reported that 3.2% of their patients up to the age of 80 years had experienced a seizure.[4]

Because of the insignificance of short-lived febrile seizures in earlier life, an operational definition of epilepsy is the occurrence of more than one nonfebrile seizure at any time.[5] Thus, although the incidence of a single seizure in a person's lifetime is 3% to 4%, the prevalence of active epilepsy is closer to 0.5% to 1%.[6] Many studies have confirmed that approximately 50% of epilepsy patients achieve lasting remission within the first few years after onset.[3,7] Other studies, however, have shown a higher recurrence rate.[7] The nature of the sample population, the use of anticonvulsants, and the time interval for following the patients will variably affect the rate of seizure occurrence after a single nonfebrile seizure.

An understanding of the modern classifications of epileptic seizures and epileptic syndromes is important in determining the prognosis, etiology, and treatment of seizures, as well as the capabilities of those affected. In 1981, the International League Against Epilepsy (ILAE) published a classification of epileptic seizures so that a common language could be used in describing seizures[8]:

   I. Partial Seizures (seizures beginning locally)
     A. Simple partial seizures
       (with no impairment of consciousness)
       1. With motor symptoms
       2. With somatosensory or special sensory symptoms
       3. With autonomic symptoms
       4. With psychic symptoms
     B. Complex partial seizures
       (with impairment of consciousness)
       1. Beginning as simple partial seizures and progressing to impairment of consciousness
       2. With impairment of consciousness at onset
         a. With impairment of consciousness only
         b. With automatisms
     C. Partial seizures secondarily generalized
       1. Secondary to simple partial seizures
       2. Secondary to complex partial seizures
  II. Generalized Seizures (bilaterally symmetrical and without local onset)
     A. Absence seizures
     B. Myoclonic seizures
     C. Clonic seizures
     D. Tonic seizures
     E. Tonic-clonic seizures
     F. Atonic seizures
 III. Unclassified Epileptic Seizures
      (due to incomplete data)

The first distinction to be made is whether the seizures are of partial onset (ie, arise from a specific brain region, then spread) or primary generalized (ie, arise from the entire brain at once). Partial seizures may be simple partial (no impairment of consciousness), complex partial (impairment of consciousness), or secondarily generalized. Primary generalized seizures also have a variety of manifestations.

Tonic-clonic seizures or staring spells may have either a partial or primary generalized origin. This distinction must be made from details of the history, physical examination, EEG, and imaging studies. Partial onset and primary generalized seizures may differ in the prognosis, medical treatment, and extent of evaluation necessary. For example, a patient with presumed focal onset seizures should have an imaging study of the brain (computerized tomography or magnetic resonance scan) to determine whether a structural lesion is present, whereas a patient with true primary generalized seizures rarely has an underlying abnormality of brain structure.

The EEG may provide information that helps the physician to distinguish among different seizure types. An EEG performed when a clinical seizure is not occurring (interictal) may show epileptiform discharges in the form of sharp waves, spikes, or spike and wave complexes. In patients with partial onset seizures, these epileptiform discharges are usually focal and may occur near the region of the brain where the seizures begin. In patients with primary generalized seizures, spike and wave discharges occur over the entire cortex at once. Interpretation of an EEG performed during an actual seizure (ictal) is more complex, but may show a similar distinction between focal and generalized seizure origin. Ictal EEG recordings are most useful when there is a simultaneous video recording so that the time sequence of the clinical behavioral changes can be correlated with the EEG changes.

Many persons have two or more types of seizures, and these can frequently be grouped into syndromes. The ILAE has recently revised its classification of epileptic syndromes, and identifying a particular epileptic syndrome may have important implications for prognosis and etiology.[9] For example, juvenile myoclonic epilepsy is a primary generalized epileptic syndrome that first appears between the ages of 10 and 18 years; may occur in several members of a family; and typically consists of a combination of myoclonic jerks, absence (staring spells), and generalized tonic-clonic seizures. The true syndrome is never caused by a structural lesion, and the prognosis is excellent. Approximately 90% of patients obtain complete seizure control on valproic acid therapy. In contrast, complex partial seizures of temporal lobe origin (a partial onset seizure type) may become refractory to medication in up to 40% of cases. For patients in this latter group, surgical excision of the epileptogenic focus (even when there is no obvious structural lesion) is becoming more widely used and can result in freedom from seizures or major improvement at prolonged follow-up in up to 80% of selected patients.[10]

Although primary generalized seizures make up the majority of childhood epilepsy cases, only about 10% of adults with epilepsy have true primary generalized seizures of idiopathic causation. Many partial onset seizures in adults have no obvious cause, but newer imaging techniques, such as magnetic resonance scanning and study of surgically resected specimens, show that many patients have mesial temporal sclerosis, low-grade tumors, vascular malformations, or a variety of congenital brain lesions. In persons whose seizure diagnosis is unclear or who are being considered for surgery, simultaneous video and EEG monitoring of seizures in an inpatient unit may be necessary.

TREATMENT OPTIONS

Antiepileptic drugs may produce a variety of unwanted side effects. If prescribed properly, however, these medications should not produce any side effects that have a noticeable effect on work performance. Standardized testing has shown that phenobarbital and phenytoin may cause a mild cognitive impairment when used in the recommended therapeutic range; however, Dodrill and Temkin have suggested that, although phenytoin does mildly slow motor speed, the reported cognitive impairments due to phenytoin may not be significant when the effect of motor slowing on tests is considered.[11] Recent studies also show that higher doses of a single antiepileptic drug produce fewer side effects and are usually associated with equal or better seizure control when compared to antiepileptic drug combinations.[12,13] Depression among persons with epilepsy appeared to be multifactorial, but was most severe in those taking phenobarbital and least severe in those taking carbamazepine in the study done by Robertson and colleagues.[14] Other dose-related effects of antiepileptic drugs that may affect work performance to some degree include tremor with valproic acid and diplopia or dizziness at high serum concentrations of carbamazepine.

One group of persons with epilepsy who may be entering the work force for the first time or seeking a change in employment as a result of improved seizure control are those who have undergone surgical treatment of epilepsy. A larger number of centers are now providing the facilities for the extensive preoperative evaluation necessary (the Epilepsy Foundation of America has a listing of medical centers with specialized epilepsy units). The majority of patients have no substantial postoperative neuropsychologic impairment, and many patients enjoy improvement in cognitive function, presumably because of improved seizure control.[15]

Although some studies have shown substantial problems in psychologic and social adjustment among persons with epilepsy, Trostle and colleagues showed that the majority of these individuals in a community-based sample were well adjusted.[16] These authors felt that previous studies may have been biased because their samples were drawn from those who were seeking specialty clinics or services from social service agencies and thus were more likely to have clinical, psychologic, or social problems.

Alcohol is a particularly potent precipitant in those predisposed to seizures. A variety of other medications are reported to lower the threshold for seizures; however, the relative risk must be weighed against the potential benefit of a second medication in the individual patient.

VOCATIONAL CONSIDERATIONS

Many studies have focused on the employment capabilities of persons with epilepsy. More than 40 years ago, the Department of Labor conducted a landmark study of the performance of physically impaired workers within the manufacturing industries.[17] The epilepsy group showed no differences in absenteeism compared to matched controls. Although the incidence of work injury was slightly higher in the persons with epilepsy, the group was otherwise entirely capable of normal work performance. The study conducted by Dasgupta and associates within the British Steel Corporation revealed no significant difference between epileptic persons and controls in sickness, absence, accident records, and overall job performance.[18] Numerous other studies in the United States and abroad have supported these findings.[19–23]

Employers may argue that it is because they have screened out persons with epilepsy who pose a serious risk that the statistics for work safety and performance are reassuring. There are undoubtedly a considerable number of employees who do not disclose that they have epilepsy and are not considered in the count, however.[24] Inevitably, it must be concluded that some of the prejudices faced by workers with epilepsy are irrational and thus cannot be overcome by mere employer education.[21]

An occupational physician who is aware that a patient with epilepsy wants to apply for work should have a frank discussion with the patient about seizure type and degree of control. Once these factors have been assessed, the job site and job tasks can be chosen to minimize the risks to the patient and co-workers. Frequently, employees fear that the revelation of their epilepsy will restrict their opportunities for finding a job or for being promoted once they are employed. Furthermore, they fear that fellow workers will ridicule or avoid them. A survey in London revealed that more than half of the persons with epilepsy who held full-time jobs had never disclosed their conditions to their employers.[25]

Where possible, factors that precipitate seizures should be considered in the selection of a job. Varying shift work, for example, can disturb patterns of sleep, thus increasing the chance of a seizure even in those with well-controlled epilepsy.[18] Stress has been reported to cause seizures in those predisposed to the condition, although stress is a difficult entity to quantify and the mechanism of its effect on seizures is not clear.[26] Photosensitivity is an unusual cause of seizures, but it does occur.[27] Those with photosensitive epilepsy usually have primary generalized seizures, demonstrate sensitivity before age 22, and typically demonstrate a photoconvulsive response on EEG. Rarely, watching television, especially close to the set, can be a provocative stimulus for a person with photosensitive epilepsy.

In the United States, it is illegal to deny employment to an otherwise qualified applicant so long as the disability does not pose a health and safety risk for the employee or co-workers. In a 1978 survey of U.S. employers, however, Hicks and Hicks found that few would employ persons known to have had a tonic-clonic seizure in the previous year.[28] Other seizure types may be more tolerated because they are less disruptive.

In regard to job restrictions that may be necessary for the workers with epilepsy, the guidelines of the Employment Commission of the International Bureau for Epilepsy state the following[29]:

> When medical advice is sought about the suitability of particular jobs for people with epilepsy, the guidance given should take into account the requirements of the job and the known facts about epilepsy and seizures. Blanket prohibitions should be avoided.
>
> In those jobs known to carry a high degree of physical risk to the individual worker or to others, the organization of work practice should be examined to reduce this potential risk to an acceptable level. Only in those situations in which this cannot be achieved are restrictions on the employment of people with epilepsy justified.

It may be necessary to assess the safety of the performance of the following activities by a worker with epilepsy:

- climbing and working unprotected at heights
- driving or operating construction vehicles
- doing transportation jobs
- working around unguarded machinery
- working near fire or water
- working for long periods in an isolated situation
- using hand-held power tools fixed in the on position

Jobs in transport (eg, train, truck, airline, or boating pilots) and in commercial diving are all at high risk because one seizure can cause a catastrophe. If any job restrictions are needed, there should be clearly stated policies about their implementation, their review, and set time periods in which the restrictions may be removed.

Workers with epilepsy should be reminded that their intentional failure to abide by any restrictions may put not only their lives but also those of colleagues and friends at risk. Furthermore, it may be impossible for them or their families to collect compensation from their insurance companies for injuries sustained as a result of their evasion of restrictions. Work restrictions should be reassessed for any employee with epilepsy who becomes seizure-free or has a substantial change in seizure frequency for a prolonged period. The employee should be told to report any changes in seizure activity to the occupational physician or safety manager. Any change in anticonvulsant medication may require closer monitoring at work or a temporary reintroduction of safety restrictions.

Thus, to assess the employability of a person with epilepsy appropriately, the occupational physician must be familiar with the particular seizure manifestations and degree of control in that person. In only a minority of people do seizures occur at work or prescribed antiepileptic drugs impair work performance. In such cases, assessment by a physician expert in epilepsy often improves seizure control and reduces these side effects. Any necessary work restrictions must be matched to the abilities and limitations of the individual person, and they should be stated clearly and reviewed periodically.

REFERENCES

1. Jackson JH. On the anatomical, physiological, and pathological investigation of the epilepsies. *The West Riding Lunatic Asylum Medical Reports* 1873;3.

2. Research Committee of the Royal College of General Practitioners. A survey of the epilepsies in general practice. *Br Med J*. 1960;2:416–422.

3. Goodridge DMG, Shorvon SD. Epileptic seizures in a population of 6000. *Br Med J*. 1983; 287:641–644.

4. Hauser WA, Annegers JF, Anderson VE. Epidemiology and the genetics of epilepsy. In: Ward AA, Penry JK, Purpura D, eds. *Epilepsy*. New York; Raven Press; 1983.

5. Brown I, Hopkins AP. Epilepsy. In: Edwards FC, McCallum RI, Taylor PJ, eds. *Fitness for Work*. Oxford: Oxford University Press; 1988:210–232.

6. Kurtzke JF. The current neurologic burden of illness and injury in the United States. *Neurology*. 1982;32:1207–1214.

7. Elwes RD, Johnson AL, Shorvon SD, et al. The prognosis for seizure control in newly diagnosed epilepsy. *N Engl J Med*. 1984;311:944–947.

8. Commission on Classification and Terminology of the International League Against Epilepsy. Proposal for revised clinical and electroencephalographic classification of epileptic seizures. *Epilepsia*. 1981;22:489–501.

9. Commission on Classification and Terminology of the International League Against Epilepsy. Proposal for revised classification of epilepsies and epileptic syndromes. *Epilepsia*. 1989;30:389–399.

10. Engel J. Outcome with respect to epileptic seizures. In: Engel J, ed. *Surgical Treatment of the Epilepsies*. New York: Raven Press; 1987:553–571.

11. Dodrill CB, Temkin NR. Motor speed as a contaminating variable in the measurement of "cognitive" effects of phenytoin. *Epilepsia*. 1987;28:587.

12. Lesser RP, Pippinger CE, Lueders H, et al. High-dose monotherapy in treatment of intractable seizures. *Neurology*. 1984;34:707–711.

13. Schmidt D, Einicke I, Haenel F. The influence of seizure type on the efficacy of plasma concentration of phenytoin, phenobarbital, and carbamazepine. *Arch. Neurol.* 1986;43:263–265.

14. Robertson MM, Trimble MR, Townsend HRA. Phenomenology of depression in epilepsy. *Epilepsia*. 1987;28:364–372.

15. Novelly RA, Augustine EA, Mattson RH, et al. Selective memory improvement and impairment in temporal lobectomy for epilepsy. *Ann Neurol.* 1984;15:64–67.

16. Trostle JA, Hauser WA, Sharbrough FW. Psychologic and social adjustment to epilepsy in Rochester, Minnesota. *Neurology*. 1989;39:633–637.

17. *The Performance of Physically Impaired Workers in Manufacturing Industries*. Washington, DC: US Dept of Labor Bulletin No. 293; 1948.

18. Dasgupta AK, Saunders M, Dick DJ. Epilepsy in the British Steel Corporation: an evaluation of sickness, accident, and work records. *Br J Indust Med.* 1982;39:146–148.

19. Udell MM. The work performance of epileptics in industry. *Arch Environ Health.* 1960;1:257–264.

20. Lennox W, Cobb S. Employment of epileptics. *Indust Med Surg.* 1972;2:571–575.

21. MacIntyre I. Epilepsy and employment. *Comm Health.* 1976;7:195–204.

22. Kettle M. Disabled people and accidents. *J Occup Accidents.* 1984;6:277–293.

23. Sands H, Salkind S. Effects of an educational campaign to change employer attitudes toward hiring epileptics. *Epilepsia*. 1972;13:87–96.

24. Edwards F, Espir M, Oxley J. *Epilepsy and Employment*, International Congress Symposium Series #86. London: Royal Society of Medical Service Publishers; 1986.

25. Scambler G, Hopkins AP. Social class, epileptic activity and disadvantage at work. *J Epidemiol Community Health.* 1980;34:129–133.

26. Temkin NR, David GR. Stress as a risk factor of seizure among adults with epilepsy. *Epilepsia*. 1984;25:450–456.

27. Jeavone PM, Harding GFA. Photosensitive epilepsy: a review of the literature and a study of 460 patients. *Clinics in Developmental Medicine*, Spastics International Publications, No. 56. London: Heinemann; 1975.

28. Hicks RA, Hicks MJ. The attitudes of major companies towards the employment of epileptics: an assessment of 2 decades of change. *Am Correct Ther J.* 1978;32:180–182.

29. The Employment Commission of the International Bureau for Eipilepsy. Employing people with epilepsy: principles for good practice. *Epilepsia*. 1989;30:411–412.

chapter 12

Vocational Capacity with Cardiac Impairment

Charles A. Dennis

Cardiac impairment is common and causes significant vocational disability. More than 5 million U.S. citizens have symptomatic coronary artery disease. More than 800,000 survive myocardial infarction, and nearly 240,000 undergo coronary artery bypass graft surgery annually. An additional 2 million U.S. citizens have symptomatic valvular heart disease.[1] Other disorders, such as idiopathic cardiomyopathy, congenital heart disease in adults, supraventricular and ventricular arrhythmias, and pericardial disease, are less common, but potentially significant causes of disability.

The direct costs of medical care for cardiac disease are high, estimated at $64 billion in 1986.[1] These direct costs are related to hospital services, medications, diagnostic tests, and physician fees. As high as the direct costs are, the indirect costs are staggering. Indirect costs represent economic products—goods and services—that are not produced because of disability. For coronary artery disease, which is the most common cause of cardiac impairment, indirect costs are estimated to be 4.5 times direct costs.[2]

The economic costs represent only one aspect of the burden borne by individual patients and society. Pain and suffering, loss of leisure-time activities, and psychologic harm to patients and families are immeasurable losses of unquestioned importance. In many cases, the economic and noneconomic costs of disability from cardiac disease are unavoidable. Many factors can intereact to cause unnecessary disability in patients who have the potential to continue working, however. Patient and physician perceptions of prognosis, perceived liability of employers and health care providers, and the lack of objective standards to assess vocational capacity can all delay or prevent re-employment in a patient with cardiac disease.

A clinical and pathophysiologic approach to the vocational assessment of the patient with myocardial infarction, the most common cardiac cause of interrupted employment, is the focus of this chapter. Rehabilitation after myocardial infarction has progressed significantly in the past 15 years.[3] The average duration of hospitalization has been shortened from 3 weeks to 10 days or less. Early exercise testing as the basis for prognostic assessment and prescription of exercise training has become common practice.[4] Exercise training in supervised gymnasium programs or at home has been demonstrated to be safe and efficacious.[5]

Despite early mobilization and exercise training, the timing of re-employment after myocardial infarction has not improved. The majority of employed patients recovering from myocardial infarction return to work within 6 months. Sedentary patients return to work at an average of 60 to 80 days after myocardial infarction, a convalescent period that has not changed since 1970.[6,7] Employees who perform physical work return to work at an average of 90 to 110 days.[6,7] Similar delays are common in patients recovering from coronary artery bypass graft surgery. Decisions regarding vocational rehabilitation remain based in subjective judgments; few objective data are available to assist the clinician.

The list of factors that can influence the success and timing of return to work after an acute cardiac illness is long. Symptoms, physical capacity, patient perceptions regarding health and work, physican perceptions of prognosis and functional capacity, employer and family influences, economic necessity, and the availability of compensation and disability insurance are only some of these factors. The relative importance of each of these factors varies with each patient, physician, and employer. No single method for improving re-employment after a cardiac illness has been found.

The fact that there are no standard guidelines for the assessment of vocational ability in cardiac patients reflects, in part, the complex role that nonmedical and medical factors play in re-employment decisions. More important, data regarding the prognosis and physical capacity of patients recovering from an acute cardiac illness are limited. These two factors are the major concerns of clinicians who care for cardiac patients. Only recently have techniques for the assessment of prognosis and physical capacity been more broadly applied to patients recovering from acute cardiac illnesses, such as myocardial infarction and unstable angina. These techniques can play a paramount role in the assessment of vocational ability.

PATHOPHYSIOLOGY AND PATHOGENESIS OF CARDIAC DISEASE

The pathophysiology of cardiac disease is closely linked to symptoms, physical capacity, and prognosis. In most cardiac diseases, one or more of three major pathophysiologic processes influence the patient's clinical status: ventricular dysfunction, myocardial ischemia, and electrical instability. These processes may operate individually or in concert in a variety of cardiac disease states. All three processes are important in coronary artery disease, which is used as a model for the pathogenesis of impairment.

Ventricular Dysfunction

Of the three processes that affect symptoms, physical capacity, and prognosis, ventricular function is paramount. Left ventricular dysfunction is more common than right ventricular dysfunction, although they may exist in combination. Left ventricular dysfunction may be acute or chronic. The most common cause of acute left ventricular dysfunction is myocardial infarction; chronic left ventricular dysfunction is most commonly a late sequela of myocardial infarction, but may also be caused by cardiomyopathies from various causes, valvular disease, pericardial disease, and congenital abnormalities.

The pathophysiology of chronic left ventricular dysfunction results from the combination of a loss of contractile function of the myocardium, the compensatory mechanisms that occur to maintain cardiac output, and the drug therapy provided to the patient. Compensatory mechanisms intrinsic to the cardiovascular system are often sufficient to maintain cardiac output when contractile function is only mildly diminished; however, severe ventricular dysfunction generally overwhelms normal compensatory mechanisms, and medication is required to optimize cardiac output. Drug therapy is directed at optimizing ventricular filling pressures, reducing blood pressure (which reduces cardiac work), and improving salt and water balance.

Myocardial Ischemia

An imbalance between myocardial oxygen demand and supply causes myocardial ischemia. In patients with coronary artery disease, this imbalance is caused primarily by atherosclerotic obstructions, with other mechanisms playing variable roles. Increased coronary vasomotor tone may transiently reduce the amount of oxygen delivered to the myocardium, thereby constricting arteries generally or focally. This reduction is especially critical if coronary spasm occurs at the site of significant atherosclerotic narrowing. Platelets may collect in areas of endothelial damage, which is especially common at atherosclerotic plaques. This aggregation may lead to thrombosis and subtotal obstruction of a coronary artery, causing more severe manifestations of myocardial ischemia. Other less common causes of decreased oxygen supply include coronary embolus, coronary vasculitis, anemia, hypotension, and congenital anatomic abnormalities. Increased myocardial oxygen demand as a result of exercise or psychologic stress may also lead to myocardial ischemia, most commonly in association with obstructive atherosclerosis.

The degree of myocardial ischemia is therefore related to a combination of factors: coronary obstruction, coronary tone, platelet aggregation, and relative demand. In addition, the location of coronary lesions plays a role in the degree of ischemia. Proximal lesions reduce oxygen delivery to a greater area of the myocardium than do more distal lesions. The involvement of two or three coronary vessels generally imposes a greater ischemic burden than does the involvement of a single vessel.

Ischemia alters the myocardial repolarization process, as evidenced by transient displacement of the ST segment on an ECG. This electrical abnormality is generally associated with contractile dysfunction in the ischemic area. The primary compensatory mechanism for ischemia is coronary vasodilation. Coronary vascular resistance is mediated through coronary arterioles that dilate in response to decreased flow through obstructed epicardial arteries. As coronary atherosclerosis progresses, coronary vasodilatory reserve is progressively diminished, until the arterioles become permanently dilated. At this critical juncture, minor changes in coronary supply or demand can have major ischemic consequences. The most severe clinical consequence of myocardial ischemia is acute myocardial infarction, in which prolonged myocardial ischemia leads to myocardial necrosis in the distribution of the affected artery.

Electrical Abnormalities

Abnormalities in the automaticity of cardiac tissue and disturbances in the conduction of the action potential through cardiac tissue are the basis for the majority of clinically significant dysrhythmias. Although some dysrhythmias may occur in the absence of demonstrable structural heart disease, most are associated with organic heart disease. The clinically significant dysrhythmias are (1) ventricular dysrhythmias, such as ventricular tachycardia and fibrillation; (2) arterial dysrhythmias, such as atrial flutter and fibrillation; and (3) conduction system abnormalities, such as second- and third-degree heart block and bundle branch block. The type of cardiac dysrhythmia that occurs in a particular patient is determined by a complex interaction between the location of abnormalities of conduction and automaticity and the capacity of different cardiac tissues to assume the role of dominant pacemaker of the heart.

Cardiac dysrhythmias exert their clinical effects through nonphysiologic tachycardic and bradycardic responses. Bradycardia may diminish cardiac output, causing fatigue, dizziness, or frank syncope. Prolonged bradycardia may exacerbate left ventricular dysfunction. Tachycardic rhythms shorten the length of the diastolic filling period. When left ventricular function is depressed, however, ventricular filling is an important compensatory mechanism for diminished contractile function. Thus, the decreased ventricular filling that results from tachycardic rhythms can cause cardiac output to fall.

Other Mechanisms

Other pathophysiologic processes may contribute to the effects of ventricular dysfunction, myocardial ischemia, and electrical abnormalities. These processes include stenosis or incompetence of cardiac valves, inflammation or infection of cardiac valves, inflammatory disease of the myocardium, pulmonary embolism, cardiomyopathies, pericardial disease, cardiac tumors, and other rare forms of heart disease. Data regarding vocational rehabilitation of patients with coronary heart disease are limited; in these less common cardiac disorders, data are rare or nonexistent.

HISTORY, PHYSICAL EXAMINATION, AND TESTING

The clinician should direct the history taking, physical examination, and specialized testing of patients with cardiac disease toward the assessment of the underlying pathophysiology.

Assessment of Ventricular Dysfunction

The earliest manifestation of left ventricular dysfunction is dyspnea (shortness of breath). As left ventricular filling pressures increase, so do pulmonary capillary pressures; as a result, pulmonary venous congestion and impaired oxygen exchange may occur. In mild left ventricular dysfunction, dyspena is associated primarily with exertion. As left ventricular dysfunction becomes more severe, dyspnea occurs with less physical activity and may even occur at rest. Complaints of peripheral edema, paroxysmal nocturnal dyspnea, and orthopnea signal more severe left ventricular dysfunction.

Findings on physical examination may also range from subtle to overt. A passive diastolic filling sound, the S_3, may be the earliest sign of left ventricular dysfunction. Other physical signs are variable and depend on the severity of ventricular dysfunction, the compensatory mechanisms that have come into play, and medical therapy. Blood pressure may vary, but in severe left ventricular dysfunction, the blood pressure is low, the pulse pressure narrow, and the pulse rapid. The jugular venous pressure is elevated to a level higher than 10 cm H_2O. Venous pulsations are evident when the patient's thorax and head are elevated at 45°. Pulmonary examination reveals dullness to percussion at the bases if pleural effusions are present. Rales are present at one or both bases in moderate left ventricular dysfunction and at higher levels in more severe cases.

On precordial inspection and palpation, the point of maximal impulse (PMI) is generally found to be displaced lateral to the midclavicular line and inferior to the sixth intercostal space. The PMI is diffuse and sustained. On auscultation, the first and second heart sounds may be normal, but the second heart sound may vary in cases of severe left ventricular dysfunction. For example, a paradoxically split second sound when other causes (eg, left bundle branch block, right ventricular pacing, left ventricular outflow obstruction) have been ruled out is generally a sign of severe left ventricular dysfunction. A fourth heart sound is common, and a third heart sound is often present. Cardiac murmurs are variable and also dependent on the specific etiology of the left ventricular dysfunction. Other physical findings that may be present with severe left and right ventricular dysfunction include hepatomegaly, hepatojugular reflux, ascites, and peripheral edema.

Laboratory test results may be abnormal, depending on the severity of left ventricular dysfunction. A chest roentgenogram generally demonstrates cardiomegaly with a cardiothoracic ratio of greater than 0.50. The pulmonary vasculature is usually abnormal, ranging from only upper zone redistribution in mild and moderate left ventricular dysfunction to pulmonary edema with pleural effusions in severe left ventricular dsyfunction. Electrocardiographic abnormalities are common and may reflect the etiology of left ventricular dysfunction, such as myocardial infarction or long-standing left ventricular hypertrophy. It is common for the results of blood tests to be abnormal, reflecting the consequences of diminished cardiac output. The concentrations of urea nitrogen and creatinine may be elevated as a result of diminished renal perfusion. Hyponatremia occurs secondary to stimulation of antidiuretic hormone release and retention of free water.

Specialized cardiovascular tests can confirm the diagnosis of left ventricular dysfunction, provide evidence concerning etiology, and quantitate the degree of left ventricular dysfunction. The resting radionuclide ventriculogram is a noninvasive method to quantitate the ejection fraction and to determine the presence of wall motion abnormalities. Echocardiography can provide semiquantitative measures of the ejection fraction and can document wall motion abnormalities that may reflect underlying coronary artery disease. Cardiac catheterization can also document increased intracardiac pressures and decreased cardiac output. A left ventricular angiogram obtained as part of the cardiac catheterization can help to quantitate the ejection fraction and document wall motion abnormalities. The specialized test chosen for individual patients must be related to their clinical circumstances, and the guidance of a cardiologist is often necessary.

Assessment of Myocardial Ischemia

The clinical evaluation of myocardial ischemia relies heavily on the history and diagnostic tests; there are few physical findings that are specific for ischemia. Most patients with myocardial ischemia have chest discomfort. Some describe classic exertional angina, which is a substernal pressure associated with exertion and relieved by rest. The discomfort is commonly described as pressure, heaviness, tightness, squeezing, or cramping. The discomfort may remain substernal or radiate to either shoulder or arm, the neck, or the jaw. Less commonly, the discomfort radiates to the epigastrium or back. There may be associated symptoms of dyspnea, diaphoresis, and fatigue. Prolonged angina may lead to nausea, vomiting, and dizziness.

Unfortunately, many patients with myocardial ischemia have either atypical symptoms or no symptoms at all. Atypical presentations include chest discomfort that is sharp, stabbing, or burning and is located in other areas of the precordium or epigastrium than the substernal area. Symptoms may predominate at rest or with emotional stress. Atypical exertional symptoms, such as cough or excessive fatigue, may also be manifestations of myocardial ischemia. When symptoms are atypical, the clinical response to sublingual nitroglycerin often provides helpful information. If nitroglycerin relieves the symptoms within 1 to 2 minutes, the problem is more likely to be ischemia. The only major exception is the discomfort of esophageal spasm, which is also responsive to nitroglycerin.

Physical examination is usually unrevealing in patients with myocardial ischemia. There may be evidence of left ventricular dysfunction if the patient has previously had a myocardial infarction. Clinical evidence of antecedents to coronary heart disease, such as diabetes mellitus, hypertension, and hypercholesterolemia, may be obvious from the physical examination.

A variety of diagnostic tests, both routine and specialized, are available for evaluating myocardial ischemia. The resting ECG may be normal, reveal a prior myocardial infarction, or show evidence of myocardial ischemia at rest. Myocardial ischemia is usually diagnosed by means of a depression of the ST segment of at least 0.1 mV (1 mmeter) at 80 ms beyond the J point. A flat or down-sloping ST depression is more significant than an up-sloping ST depression. Other causes of such ST changes include left ventricular hypertrophy with strain and digitalis administration. Evidence of myocardial ischemia on a resting ECG is unusual in the absence of symptoms and should prompt the clinician to look for other causes of an ST depression.

Treadmill exercise testing is the most widely available and least costly provocative test for myocardial ischemia. The physiologic basis of exercise testing is the creation of an imbalance between myocardial oxygen supply and demand. The ischemic response is most commonly defined as an ST segment depression of 0.1 mV or more. Other test-related responses that may indicate ischemia include angina, exercise-induced hypotension, ventricular arrhythmias, and a diminished exercise capacity.

The rest and exercise radionuclide ventriculogram is a sensitive test for myocardial ischemia. In general, the left ventricular ejection fraction rises with exercise, even in the presence of resting left ventricular dysfunction. Exercise-induced ischemia may be manifested by the development of wall motion abnormalities and a decrement in the ejection fraction with exercise. A failure of the ejection fraction to rise by at least 5% or an actual fall in the ejection fraction is abnormal.

Thallium perfusion scintigraphy performed in conjunction with exercise is an extremely sensitive test for myocardial ischemia. Thallium is a potassium analog, the distribution of which in myocardial cells depends on the amount of coronary flow and the activity of cellular sodium-potassium ATPase. Thallium is injected just prior to peak exercise, and imaging is performed. Areas of ischemia and/or infarction show lower thallium uptakes. These two types of low uptakes at peak exercise are distinguished by scanning 4 hours following exercise. Normal thallium activity in a previously low uptake area suggests ischemia. Fixed thallium defects generally represent a myocardial scar, consistent with a prior myocardial infarction.

Although coronary arteriography is the best method for documenting the presence of coronary atherosclerosis, it does not actually demonstrate myocardial ischemia. Coronary artery stenoses of 50% or greater are generally considered markers for myocardial ischemia, but the degree of ischemia on functional testing is only moderately correlated with anatomic coronary disease. Other specialized tests that can demonstrate myocardial ischemia include thallium scintigraphy performed in conjunction with atrial pacing or following high-dose dipyridamole administration, positron emission tomography, and ST segment analysis on ambulatory monitoring. The general availability and utility of these tests are limited, however, and they should be performed with the guidance of a cardiologist.

Assessment of Dysrhythmias

The clinical evaluation of dysrhythmias relies on the history, physical examination, and specialized testing. Symptoms are variable. Some high-grade arrhythmias, such as ventricular tachycardia and complete heart block, may be completely asymptomatic, whereas more benign dysrhythmias, such as isolated ventricular premature beats and second-degree atrioventricular block of the Wenckebach variety, may cause symptoms in individual patients. Clinically significant symptoms are generally related to tachycardic or bradycardic rhythms that affect cardiac output.

Patients with dysrhythmias most commonly complain of palpitations, which may be described as a pounding in the chest or as an occasional extra or skipped beat. The pattern of palpitations is sometimes helpful in determining the cause. Rapid, regular palpitations are generally caused by ventricular tachycardia or atrial flutter. Rapid, irregular palpitations are more likely to represent atrial fibrillation, but the history is not always reliable. Skipped or missed beats may represent isolated ventricular or atrial premature beats. Syncope, a more severe manifestation of dysrhythmias, results from an inadequate cardiac output. Syncope may be caused by either tachycardic or bradycardic dysrhythmias.

When the history or physical examination suggests a dysrhythmia, a variety of tests may be useful to identify the specific dysrhythmia present. The resting ECG is often abnormal and documents the presence of most chronic dysrhythmias, including atrial flutter and fibrillation, atrioventricular block, and intraventricular conduction abnormalities. The ECG may demonstrate transient dysrhythmias, if obtained at the opportune time.

Many patients have intermittent dysrhythmias, and the choice of test is dictated by the potential severity of the dysrhythmias. Ambulatory ECG monitoring by means of portable Holter recorders is the most widely available and useful tool for patients with daily dysrhythmias. For patients with less frequent symptoms, portable monitors are available for them to use while having symptoms. These monitors can transmit ECG signals over the telephone to stations that can record, print, and analyze the ECG for dysrhythmias. Patients who have more severe symptoms, such as frequent syncope, or who have been resuscitated from sudden cardiac death may require invasive electrophysiologic testing both for diagnosis and evaluation of therapy. A cardiologist should direct the management of these patients.

PROGNOSIS

The history, physical examination, routine tests, and specialized examinations all have prognostic value. As might be expected, more symptomatic patients are at a higher risk for cardiac events than are less symptomatic patients. Specialized testing has a limited prognostic role in symptomatic patients. For example, an exact measurement of the ejection fraction in a patient with dyspnea, rales, and a third heart sound offers little useful information regarding the clinical status or prognosis. Most minimally symptomatic patients have an excellent prognosis. In these patients, specialized testing is best used to identify prognostically important pathophysiology that is not obvious by history or physical examination.

Medical versus Surgical Therapy

Once the diagnosis of coronary artery disease has been established, decisions regarding therapy and employment are best based on prognosis and physical capacity. Traditionally, the demonstration of the extent and severity of coronary atherosclerosis by arteriography has been the gold standard of diagnosis and prognosis. Recent studies suggest a more limited role for coronary arteriography and a more important role for exercise-related functional tests, however. This change in roles is especially important in vocational rehabilitation.

The history of modern therapy for coronary disease sheds light on the reasons why tests of coronary anatomy are now of less importance in vocational assessment. The increasingly widespread availability of coronary arteriography and coronary surgery in the early 1970s combined a compelling diagnostic test with a powerful therapy. Coronary artery bypass graft surgery relieved symptoms and improved functional capacity to a far greater extent than did the limited medical therapy available at the time. It was assumed that, because most patients with two- and three-vessel coronary disease had such obvious clinical benefit from this surgery, the definition of coronary anatomy is the key to therapeutic decision making. Noninvasive tests were judged primarily on their ability to predict two- and three-vessel coronary disease.

In the past decade, several factors have changed this perspective of coronary disease. New drugs and improved drug delivery systems (eg, calcium channel blocking drugs, receptor-specific beta-blocking drugs, cutaneous patches, and long-acting oral preparations) provide better control of symptoms by medical therapy than was previously possible. At the same time, the value of coronary surgery for improving prognosis is being challenged. Three large cooperative studies of medical versus surgical therapy for stable coronary artery disease have demonstrated that surgery improves the prognosis in only limited anatomic subsets. The Veterans Administration Cooperative Study (VACS) and the Coronary Artery Surgery Study (CASS) demonstrated that only patients with left main coronary artery disease or three-vessel coronary disease in combination with left ventricular dysfunction had improved survival with surgical therapy as compared to medical therapy.[8,9] The European Cooperative Group Study (ECGS) demonstrated improved survival with surgical therapy in patients with three-vessel coronary disease and two-vessel coronary disease that involved the proximal left anterior descending artery.[10] No patient in that study had left ventricular dysfunction. The primary reason that patients with less extensive anatomic disease in the ECGS benefited from surgery was that the ECGS enrolled patients with more severe angina and more treadmill-induced ischemia. Both the VACS and the CASS enrolled only mildly symptomatic patients.

Prognosis Associated with Left Ventricular Dysfunction

Of the three major pathophysiologic processes, left ventricular dysfunction has the greatest effect on prognosis. Patients with moderate to severe symptoms or signs have a poor prognosis, with mortality rates of 30% or more each year.[11] These patients also have a limited physical capacity. In patients with mild symptoms or signs of left ventricular dysfunction, the resting radionuclide ventriculogram is a valuable prognostic test. Ejection fractions of less than 40% are associated with higher mortality rates.[12] One study has shown a linear relationship between survival and ejection fraction at peak exercise.[13] Treadmill exercise testing can also identify patients with left ventricular dysfunction at higher risk for cardiac events. A low peak treadmill workload may be a sign of left ventricular dysfunction and indicates a poor prognosis.[14,15]

Decisions regarding therapy in patients with left ventricular dysfunction are difficult. Coronary surgery improves survival in patients with three-vessel coronary disease and ejection fractions of 35% to 50%.[8,9] Medical therapy with preload and afterload reduction appears to improve survival and functional capacity in patients with moderate and severe left ventricular dysfunction.[16,17]

Prognosis Associated with Cardiac Dysrhythmias

The type of dysrhythmia, the symptoms, and the associated pathophysiology determine the prognosis for patients with cardiac dysrhythmias. Ventricular arrhythmias and complete heart block have the most prognostic significance. The prognosis for patients with ventricular arrhythmias is not completely defined, although certain characteristics are associated with a poor outcome: sustained ventricular tachycardia, high-grade ventricular ectopy following myocardial infarction, resuscitated sudden death, ventricular ectopy in association with left ventricular dysfunction, and failure of arrhythmias to respond to therapy guided by electrophysiologic testing.[18,19] Complete heart block with coronary artery disease is usually associated with significant left ventricular dysfunction. Although permanent cardiac pacing has been shown to improve survival, mortality rates may still average 10% per year because of the underlying left ventricular dysfunction.[20] The evaluation and treatment of significant dysrhythmias are changing rapidly; an experienced cardiac electrophysiologist should assist in the care of these patients.

Prognosis Associated with Myocardial Ischemia

The prognosis for patients with myocardial ischemia is related to symptoms and to the results of specialized testing. Severe ischemia, manifested by symptoms of angina at rest that are uncontrolled by medical therapy, is associated with a high risk of myocardial infarction.[21] Provocative tests for ischemia have prognostic value in patients with mild symptoms, in patients with stable angina or unstable angina controlled with medical therapy, and in patients who have had a myocardial infarction.

Treadmill Testing for Prognostic Information

Peak treadmill workload and the ST segment response provide most of the prognostic information during treadmill testing. The CASS illustrated the prognostic power of treadmill testing in patients with stable angina. In patients treated medically, the degree of functional impairment and of myocardial ischemia were important predictors of long-term survival. Those patients able to achieve more vigorous levels of Stage 3 or higher on the Bruce protocol (see Table 12-2) had a 99% 1-year and 91% 7-year survival. Patients able to achieve only Stage 1 or less had 1- and 7-year survivals of 96% and 80%, respectively, whereas those with an ST depression of more than 0.2 mV had survival rates of 97% and 79%, respectively. Patients with both low workloads and ST depression had 1- and 7-year survival rates of 95% and 72%, respectively. In patients with both abnormalities, the survival rate was improved with surgical therapy over the rate obtained with medical therapy alone.[22]

Similar prognostic results have been reported in patients hospitalized with unstable angina. In those patients whose symptoms are controlled with medical therapy, treadmill test responses separate high- and low-risk subsets. Approximately half of such patients have no ST segment depression on treadmill testing 2 to 3 days after their symptoms have been stabilized. These patients have a 2% to 12% rate of recurrent myocardial infarction or death in the succeeding year. In the patients with a low peak treadmill workload or an ST depression of more than 0.1 mV, 1-year event rates range from 35% to 50%.[23,24]

Patients recovering from myocardial infarction can also be stratified into high- and low-risk subsets. Approximately 30% to 40% of patients have symptoms of left ventricular dysfunction or myocardial ischemia that preclude treadmill testing. Of the remaining patients, one-fourth have a low peak treadmill workload or an ST segment depression. These patients have cardiac event rates of 8% to 15% in the succeeding year. The 50% of patients with mild or no symptoms following myocardial infarction and a normal treadmill response have excellent prognoses, with recurrent myocardial infarction or death occurring in less than 4% in the succeeding year.[4]

Treadmill exercise testing may play an important role in the vocational assessment of patients with left ventricular dysfunction, myocardial ischemia, and arrhythmias. The safety of exercise testing is directly related to the experience of the supervising personnel, including the physician, and the selection of patients. Patients with symptoms at rest related to any of the three pathophysiologic processes described are not candidates for exercise testing, as they are at high risk for cardiac events. For patients with well-controlled symptoms, however, exercise testing may be appropriate. A physician experienced in exercise testing must evaluate each case independently to avoid potential adverse events during the test.

WORK CAPACITY ASSESSMENT

Several natural history studies of employment in patients with coronary disease have been published. The results of 15 of these studies are summarized in Table 12-1.

Assessment of Risk Factors

Substantial progress has been made in the identification of patients at high and low risk for cardiac events after myocardial infarction. Early risk stratification is important because most second events occur early; 60% of first-year events occur within 3 months, and 85% occur within 6 months.[40] A risk stratification model was developed retrospectively in patients recovering from myocardial infarction in six community hospitals. In the retrospective derivation, 665 patients underwent a clinical assessment consisting of a history, physical examination, and a review of routine test results and complications during hospitalization. Fifty percent of these patients had no contraindications to symptom-limited treadmill testing; these patients were tested at 3 weeks after myocardial infarction.[41]

All patients were followed for an average of 33 months for medical events (eg, death, recurrent myocardial infarction, unstable angina, and congestive heart failure). These medical events were related retrospectively to historical, clinical, and treadmill test data to define high- and low-risk subsets of patients. The medical event rate of patients with historical or clinical risks was found to be twice the rate of those without these risks: 8.6% vs. 4.4% over the first 6 months. Historical risks included two or three of the following: a history of previous myocardial infarction; a history of angina pectoris for more than 3 months before the index infarction; and recurrent ischemic chest pain at rest more than 24 hours after admission, but before hospital discharge. Clinical risks were primarily contraindications to symptom-limited treadmill testing, such as rest angina or angina not controlled by medical therapy; congestive heart failure; or severe vascular, cerebrovascular, pulmonary, or orthopedic disease.[41]

Of the 50% of patients who performed treadmill testing, medical events occurred in 4.4% at 6 months. High- and low-risk subsets were defined retrospectively on the basis of severe exercise-induced myocardial ischemia. The best predictor of medical events was the development of an ST depression of 0.2 mV or more at a heart rate less than 135 beats/min. The 10% of patients with this abnormality had a medical event rate of 9.7% over 6 months. The 90% of patients without severe treadmill ischemia had a medical event rate of 3.9%.[41]

Decisions regarding diagnostic testing and therapy in high-risk patients remain controversial. As discussed earlier, aggressive therapy of left ventricular dysfunction and myocardial ischemia in high-risk patients appears warranted. The diag-

Table 12-1 Return to Work after Cardiac Events

Author	Population	Cardiac Condition	Factors Influencing Return to Work
Shapiro, Winblatt, and Frank[25]	470 men	Survived MI	Of employed men surviving MI, 79% return to work; younger men with white-collar jobs and less severe MIs return to work sooner.
Wigle, Symington, Lewis, et al.[26]	97 patients	Survived MI	Medical advice to retire and availability of pensions predicted failure to return to work.
Garrity[27]	58 patients	Survived MI	Patients' perception of health, social class, and sense of control over fate predicted return to work.
Kushnir, Fox, Tomlinson, et al.[28]	98 patients	Survived MI	Early consultation by a cardiologist hastened return to work.
Dennis, Houston-Miller, Schwartz, et al.[29]	201 men	Survived uncomplicated MI	Early treadmill test and advice to patients and primary physicians shortened return-to-work time from 75 to 51 days in a randomized trial.
Kjoller[30]	644 patients	Survived MI	Age < 60; lack of symptoms and sedentary work predicted return to work; 80% of previously employed patients returned to work.
Hammermeister, DeRouen, English, et al.[31]	1,567 patients	Patients undergoing arteriography (n equals 238) or CABG (n equals 1333)	Employment before procedure, more years of education, age < 55, better functional class prior to procedure predicted return to work; CABG did not improve re-employment rates.
Dimsdale, Hackett, Hutter, et al.[32]	182 men	Underwent arteriography for suspected CAD	Lower age, absence of cardiac morbidity or prior MI, and more optimistic mood predicted return to work.
Misra, Kazanchi, Davies, et al.[33]	113 men 7 women	CAD, CABG	Working immediately prior to CABG and age < 45 years predicted return to work; left ventricular function and extent of CAD not predictive of postoperative work status.
Danchin, David, and Bourassa[34]	100 patients subset of CASS	CAD, randomly assigned to medical (n equals 49) or CABG (n equals 51) therapy	Work status similar at 1 year in both groups, despite better symptom control in CABG group.

Bruce, Kusumi, Bruce, et al.[35]	77 patients	CAD, CABG	Age and functional aerobic impairment predicted patients who did not return to work.
Barnes, Ray, Oberman, et al.[36]	350 patients	CAD, CABG	Higher educational level, degree of improvement of angina or CHF symptoms, and greater extent of CAD predicted patients more likely to return to work.
Love[37]	99 patients	CAD, CABG	Self-employed patients age < 55, without left ventricular dysfunction were more likely to return to work.
Anderson, Barboriak, Hoffman, et al.[38]	564 men	CAD, CABG	Age < 55, employment prior to CABG, sedentary work, relief of symptoms by CABG predicted return to work.
Rimm, Barboriak, Anderson, et al.[39]	893 men	CAD, CABG	Age < 60, lack of symptoms, and sedentary work predicted return to work; 80% of previously employed patients returned to work.

Note: MI, myocardial infarction; CABG, coronary artery bypass graft; CAD, coronary artery disease; CASS, Coronary Artery Surgery Study; CHF, congestive heart failure.

nostic and therapeutic approach to low-risk patients should be less controversial. When medical event rates are less than 5%, as demonstrated in half of all survivors of myocardial infarction, it is doubtful that any medical or surgical interventions will be shown to improve that prognosis. These low-risk patients are also excellent candidates for early and rapid rehabilitation, including return to work.

Performance of Treadmill Testing

A risk stratification approach that uses treadmill testing has the concomitant advantage of measuring physical capacity. At least half of the patients who recover from myocardial infarction in a hospital are eligible for symptom-limited treadmill testing within 3 weeks of the infarction because they have no evidence of congestive heart failure or severe ischemia. Low-level treadmill testing of patients with compensated left ventricular dysfunction has been shown to be safe with careful patient selection and supervision.[15] Patients with myocardial ischemia may be safely tested after their symptoms have been ameliorated by medical or revascularization therapy. In general, higher risk, symptomatic patients are tested later than are low-risk patients, but most can be tested within 6 to 8 weeks of myocardial infarction.

Early treadmill testing of more than 1,000 low-risk patients resulted in no significant complications, such as unstable angina, myocardial infarction, or death.[5,41,42] Cardioactive medications should be tapered and stopped prior to testing, especially in asymptomatic patients. Testing while patients are not taking medications enhances the prognostic power of the test and may allow the physician to discontinue unnecessary medical therapy in patients with normal treadmill tests after myocardial infarctions. The need for medical therapy, such as prophylactic beta blockade, is controversial in such patients.[43]

Physical capacity is usually defined in METs, or multiples of resting oxygen consumption. Laying quietly awake requires 1 MET (metabolic cost), or approximately 3.5 ml O_2/kg body weight/min. Total body oxygen requirements are directly related to myocardial oxygen consumption and are therefore a reasonable measure of cardiac performance.

Several treadmill testing protocols are available and vary in the rate at which speed and incline are changed at each stage. Although the Bruce protocol is more commonly used, the modified Naughton protocol is recommended for patients tested within 4 weeks of myocardial infarction or coronary bypass surgery because it begins at a low workload of 3 METs and progresses at one-MET increments in each stage (Table 12-2). This approach provides a more accurate estimate of exercise capacity and allows patients to exercise longer, which increases their confidence in their physical capacity.[44]

Table 12-2 Comparison of Bruce and Modified Naughton Treadmill Protocols

Modified Naughton					Bruce				
Stage	Speed (mph)	Grade %	Minutes	METs	Stage	Speed (mph)	Grade %	Minutes	METs
1	2.0	3.5	3	3	1	1.7	10	3	4-5
2	2.0	7.0	3	4					
3	2.0	16.5	3	5					
4	2.0	14.0	3	6					
5	2.0	17.5	3	7	2	2.5	12	3	6-7
6	3.0	12.5	3	8					
7	3.0	15.0	3	9	3	3.4	14	3	9-10
8	3.0	17.5	3	10					
					4	4.2	16	3	13-14

The progressive stages of either protocol require greater and greater exercise capacity as shown by the increasing METs (total body oxygen consumption). Speed of the treadmill and/or angle of treadmill inclination compared to the ground is raised to increase the exercise level.

Before treadmill testing, a brief medical history and physical examination should be performed to ensure that no complications have developed. A resting 12-lead ECG should be recorded and compared to the predischarge ECG. Patients performing symptom-limited treadmill testing should be instructed to exercise to near-maximal capacity.

Experienced personnel, including a cardiologist, should supervise treadmill testing after myocardial infarction. The ECG should be continuously monitored for arrhythmias and ischemia. Three leads, which reflect anterior, inferior, and lateral distributions (II, aV_F, V_5), should be printed each minute, and a 12-lead tracing should be printed at the end of each stage. Blood pressure should be taken during the last minute of each stage. Automated treadmills are currently available to assist with these tasks.

Endpoints of exercise may be symptoms, clinical signs, or blood pressure and ECG readings. Fatigue and dyspnea are the most common endpoints. Moderate angina, such as 6 on a scale of 10, should be an endpoint. Other symptomatic endpoints include leg cramps and dizziness. Failure of the systolic blood pressure to increase by 10 mm Hg on two successive stages or a fall in systolic blood pressure of 10 mm Hg or more on successive stages is abnormal and is an endpoint. An abnormal blood pressure response may be a sign of ischemia, an indication of left ventricular dysfunction, or the result of cardioactive medications.

Isolated ventricular premature beats are common in patients with coronary disease and alone are not a reason for stopping an exercise test. High-grade ectopy, especially three or more ventricular beats in a row (ventricular tachycardia), is a reason for stopping the test, however. Atrial fibrillation, second- or third-degree heart block, and rate-related bundle branch block are uncommon dysrhythmias with exercise testing, but are reasons for discontinuing a test. Dysrhythmias are most common immediately following exercise, so ECG monitoring should be maintained for at least a 5-minute recovery period.

The interpretation of an exercise test should focus on symptoms and signs that develop with exercise, the peak workload achieved, the blood pressure response, and any ischemic or arrhythmic abnormalities that develop during the test. Angina is common on treadmill testing after myocardial infarction, occurring in 10% to 25% of patients, depending on the eligibility criteria for testing. Exercise-induced angina is most strongly predictive of angina during the months of follow-up, but is not necessarily predictive of cardiac death or recurrent myocardial infarction.[41] The average low-risk patient performs 7 to 8 METs on a symptom-limited treadmill test 3 weeks after myocardial infarction, which is well above the average MET load of virtually all usual activities and sedentary jobs (Table 12-3). Some manual labor jobs require higher MET capacities, but these jobs are rarely performed by men in their forties and fifties, the ages when myocardial infarction is most common. It is estimated that work can be sustained for long periods at 40%

Table 12-3 Approximate Metabolic Costs of Occupational Activities

MET Requirement	Occupational Activity
1.5-2	Desk work, sales clerk, automobile driving
2-3	Light janitorial work, applicance repair, light assembly
3-4	Plastering, bricklaying, welding, cleaning windows
4-5	Painting, masonry work, light carpentry
5-6	Light shoveling, digging
6-7	Moderate shoveling (10 lb at 10 strokes/min)
7-8	Carrying 80 lb, manual sawing
8-9	Heavy shoveling (14 lb at 10 strokes/min)
10 +	Very heavy shoveling (16 lb at 10 strokes/min)

One MET is defined as the amount of oxygen consumed by the resting but wakeful person.

Source: Adapted with permission from *Modern Concepts of Cardiovascular Disease* (1972;41:6), copyright © 1972, American Heart Association.

to 50% of peak MET capacity.[45] Thus, the average low-risk patient should have the capacity to perform virtually all sedentary jobs and most jobs involving moderate physical work.

Physical Conditioning

Patients recovering from myocardial infarction have a lower exercise capacity than do age-matched controls. Their lower functional capacity is related not only to a diminished cardiac reserve as a result of the myocardial infarction but also to a loss of physical conditioning as a result of the bedrest and restriction of activity commonly imposed as part of their treatment.[46,47] Other factors also influence functional capacity in the early recovery period. The enforced bedrest of care after myocardial infarction leads to intravascular volume depletion, which can reduce exercise capacity transiently. Following hospitalization, resumption of a normal diet and the maintenance of an upright posture for 8 to 12 hours daily normalize volume status.[48] Chronotropic incompetence, or an inability to achieve the peak predicted heart rate estimated for age, is common in these patients. It resolves gradually over 6 to 8 weeks after myocardial infarction.[49]

Exercise training is commonly prescribed for patients after myocardial infarction. Aerobic exercises, such as walking, jogging, swimming, or bicycling, have been shown to improve the functional capacity of these patients. The safety of exercise training depends on the medical status of the patients. Low-risk patients can exercise at home after learning to monitor their pulse rates. High-risk patients with left ventricular dysfunction or ischemia who are not candidates for revascularization should receive appropriate medical therapy and an exercise evaluation before beginning an exercise program. Group exercise programs with appropriate surveillance are recommended for these patients.[50]

Exercise training after myocardial infarction has not been shown to prolong life or to reduce the risk of cardiac events.[51,52] When patients undergoing moderate intensity exercise training are compared to those not receiving exercise training at 6 months, the functional capacities are similar and significantly better than at 3 weeks following myocardial infarction. These findings suggest that exercise training is of limited benefit for patients after myocardial infarction if only late changes in functional capacity are considered.[5]

There are benefits to exercise training, however. The rate of recovery of functional capacity is significantly accelerated with early exercise training. Patients undergoing exercise training in the early recovery period after myocardial infarction achieve a normal functional capacity in 8 to 11 weeks, whereas those not receiving formal exercise training require 11 to 26 weeks to achieve a normal functional capacity.[5] Exercise promotes weight loss and can improve lipid profiles. In patients with glucose intolerance, exercise can improve glucose metabolism. Finally, an unquantifiable, but real, psychologic benefit is obvious in patients undergoing exercise training soon after myocardial infarction.[53] Exercise enhances patients' confidence in their abilities to perform physical activity, accelerating the recovery of their functional abilities in other areas, such as vocation.[44]

Exercise need not be intensive to be beneficial. Longer duration, lower intensity aerobic exercise has been demonstrated to augment functional capacity.[54] Most patients with mild or no symptoms after myocardial infarction are candidates for at least low-intensity exercise training. The exercise prescription can be based upon the symptom-limited treadmill test.

Work Simultation

Although work simulation is an important tool in occupational therapy, questions have been raised concerning the need for work simulation after acute myocardial infarction. The crucial issue regarding vocational assessment in the patient who has had a myocardial infarction is whether the standard clinical assessment is sufficient to simulate the physical and psychologic stress of work. This question was addressed in a series of studies that used physical capacity, myocardial ischemia, and ventricular arrhythmias as the primary physiologic endpoints in comparing treadmill testing to more complex work simulation. The studies were designed to determine if work simulation was superior to more widely available treadmill testing for eliciting abnormalities.

In those studies, dynamic treadmill exercise was compared with several physiologic and psychologic stresses. These stresses included upper extremity static work, dynamic leg exercise in combination with upper extremity static work, and static and dynamic effort in the postprandial state.[55–59] Psychologic stress testing involved a variety of standard psychologic stressors.[60,61] The outcome measures included functional capacity in METs, rate pressure product (ie, peak heart rate times peak systolic blood pressure), angina, ECG evidence of ischemia, left ventricular ejection fraction as determined by radionuclide angiography, and severity of ventricular arrhythmias.

In low-risk patients, dynamic exercise testing on the treadmill was found to be equivalent or superior to static, static-dynamic, and postprandial exercise testing for eliciting a maximal cardiovascular response and evidence of left ventricular dysfunction, myocardial ischemia, and ventricular arrhythmias.[56–59] Although job stress is a major concern for patients after myocardial infarction, none of a variety of psychologic stress tests was nearly as effective as dynamic treadmill testing for eliciting physiologically significant abnormalities.[60,61] For the majority of low-risk patients, work simulation offers no added benefit over a standard clinical assessment by means of treadmill testing. For higher risk patients with left ventricular dysfunction or myocardial ischemia, more sophisticated job simulation testing may be necessary to evaluate work capacity fully. Such patients should also undergo treadmill testing as an initial screening test before work simulation is performed.

NONMEDICAL FACTORS THAT AFFECT RE-EMPLOYMENT

Nonmedical factors are at least as influential as medical factors are in decisions regarding the return to work of cardiac patients. Physicians and vocational specialists can influence some of these factors, but not all of them. These factors are variable and must be considered within the context of individual cases.

Unchangeable factors that influence the success and timing of return to work include age, employment status before the acute illness, job type, and company policies. Education is a factor that is difficult to change. Older patients, especially those workers aged 55 to 65 years, are significantly less likely to return to work after myocardial infarction or coronary artery bypass graft surgery than are younger patients,[25] especially when disability and retirement policies are favorable to them. Patients unemployed for 3 or more months before their illnesses are less likely to be employed following their illnesses. This high unemployment rate reflects the poorer health status of such patients and a pattern of vocational disability that is difficult to interrupt.[31] Blue-collar workers and those with less than 12 years of education are less likely to return to work than are white-collar workers or those with at least a high-school education. In general, these patients do not return to work because their low-skill jobs are easily filled by others.[25]

The perception that blue-collar workers with cardiac disease cannot return to work because of the physical requirements of their jobs is incorrect.[62] Heavy physical labor is performed by less than 20% of the U.S. work force, and most of those who do such work are in their twenties and thirties. Less than 10% of the 45- to 65-year-old workers in whom symptomatic coronary disease is common perform heavy physical labor.[63] Even in patients with minimal cardiac impairment, re-employment may be difficult, however.

Perceptions of Patients and Physicians

Patients perceptions regarding health, prognosis, and physical capacity can profoundly influence their return to work. Several misconceptions perpetuate cardiac disability. Many people believe that heart disease almost invariably carries a poor prognosis. They also believe that physical stress is harmful for cardiac patients, especially those recovering from myocardial infarction.[27] In reality, only a small minority of cardiac patients have a poor prognosis. Carefully prescribed exercise programs are safe and can improve physical capacity.

The relationship between symptoms and return to work is not simple. For example, the presence or absence of angina in one study of patients after myocardial infarction had no influence on the success of their return to work.[64] Patients' perceptions of their symptoms, however, especially as they relate to prognosis and physical capacity, are very influential in decisions regarding a return to work. Pessimistic perceptions regarding prognosis and a lack of confidence regarding physical capability have been shown to delay the return to work after myocardial infarction. Patients who believe that their work contributed to the development of myocardial infarction are more likely to delay the return to work than are patients who do not have that belief.[27]

The advice that physicians give patients regarding a return to work is the most important determinant of the success and timing of re-employment after myocardial infarction.[28] For that reason, physicians' perceptions regarding prognosis and physical capacity play a critical role in the return-to-work process. These perceptions have traditionally been based on subjective judgments,[6,7] which are often incorrect. For example, in a prospective follow-up study of patients who had no evidence of angina at rest or congestive heart failure after myocardial infarction, physicians and patients were asked to estimate the probability of cardiac death or recurrent myocardial infarction within 6 months. Physicians estimated a probability of 20%; patients, a probability of 25%. The actual cardiac event rate was 3.5%.[29]

If physicians have pessimistic perceptions of their patients' prognosis and physical capacity, the patients will adopt those perceptions. Failure of the physician to provide explicit advice about physical activity, prognosis, and resmption of customary activities, including work, will perpetuate the misconceptions that patients harbor already. Patients who do not receive explicit advice after myocardial infarction rarely resume their normal activities quickly. Instead, they adopt a trial-and-error approach to build their confidence gradually in returning to usual activities and exercise. Therefore, correcting basic misconceptions of patients concerning cardiac disease is an important first step in facilitating both medical and vocational recovery. Using an objective evaluation of prognosis and physical capacity may allow physicians to tailor their advice to individual patients.

Psychosocial Considerations

The psychologic impact of myocardial infarction is often far more significant than clinicians realize and must be evaluated and treated as carefully as the cardiac illness. Patients' confidence in their abilities to perform their usual activities may be significantly reduced.[44] "Bandura[65] has developed a psychologic concept called self-efficacy. Self-efficacy is used to describe how a patient's perception of his or her capacity to do a task predicts actual success or failure for that action. Several self-efficacy scales have been validated for physical activities of cardiac patients. In a series of studies, patients' rated their self-efficacy for activities similar to treadmill walking, such as walking and jogging, and for activities dissimilar to treadmill walking, such as lifting and sexual activity. These ratings were performed before and after treadmill testing and again following a counseling session. The counseling session emphasized the generic nature of treadmill testing for predicting the cardiac response to physical and psychologic stress.[44] On pre-treadmill test ratings, self-efficacy was low for all activities. Following exercise testing, but before counseling, self-efficacy ratings improved significantly for activities similar to treadmill walking, but not for dissimilar activities. Following counseling, self-efficacy for all activities rose significantly.

In a related study, patients' exercise patterns were measured by means of a portable heart rate and activity monitor in the days before and after treadmill testing and counseling. Despite the fact that exercise prescriptions were not given as part of counseling, the duration and intensity of voluntary exercise performed by patients increased significantly following treadmill testing and counseling.[44]

The spouse and family can influence dramatically the psychologic and physical recovery of patients after myocardial infarction. Spouses tend to be overly protective of patients, shielding them from physical and psychologic stress.[66] This overprotective attitude results from spousal misperceptions regarding the prognosis and physical activity for patients with cardiac disease and from the spouse's low self-efficacy ratings of the patient's physical activity. A trial to change spousal self-efficacy was performed with three groups of low-risk patients who were undergoing treadmill testing after myocardial infarction. Spouses completed scales of their perceived self-efficacy for patients' activities before and after treadmill testing and after counseling. In the first group, the spouse was not allowed to watch the treadmill test, but did participate in counseling. In the second group, the spouse watched the treadmill test and participated in counseling. In the third group, the spouse watched the treadmill test and then walked on the treadmill at the highest stage achieved by the patient. The spouse then participated in counseling.[67]

Spousal self-efficacy scores for patients' activities were significantly lower than the patients' own scores before treadmill testing. Spousal self-efficacy scores following treadmill testing did not increase in the first group, but did increase in the second and third groups. The third group had the largest increase. Self-efficacy scores increased significantly in all groups following counseling, but were again highest in the third group. A more realistic understanding of the patient's prognosis and physical capacity by the spouse can play an important role in the patient's recovery.[67]

Counseling after myocardial infarction should be comprehensive; it should address the pathophysiology of myocardial infarction, the prognosis, physical capacity, the resumption of usual activities, and secondary prevention. Pathophysiology is best discussed in terms of ventricular function and the consequences of myocardial necrosis or ischemia. A simple discussion of the pathogenesis of coronary atherosclerosis is helpful for later discussions of risk factor modification. Patients understand and appreciate an explicit definition of prognosis, especially if it is linked with a treatment plan. In low-risk patients, such a plan should include physical reconditioning; risk factor evaluation; treatment; and guidelines for resuming household activities, sexual relations, driving, and work. In high-risk patients, a plan for the medical evaluation and treatment required should preface specific activity guidelines while the medical condition is being stabilized. The patient's physical capacity should be defined and a specific exercise prescription given. Finally, coronary risk factors of hypertension, diabetes, hypercholesterolemia, smoking, and type A behavior should be specifically addressed and evaluated.[68]

Such comprehensive counseling can be performed by health care professionals other than physicians. Nurses trained in cardiac rehabilitation are especially qualified to provide such counseling initially and to follow patients in the context of rehabilitation programs. The psychologic and social benefits of counseling and follow-up cannot be overestimated.

THE STANFORD CARDIAC REHABILITATION
PROGRAM RETURN-TO-WORK STUDY

As an initial step to test whether decisions regarding the timing of a patient's return to work after myocardial infarction can be based upon prognosis and physical capacity, a randomized clinical trial was performed at the Stanford Cardiac Rehabilitation Program.[29] Employed men, aged 60 years or less, who were at low risk for a cardiac event in the months following myocardial infarction were studied. Low-risk status was defined as the absence of rest angina or congestive heart failure at the time of hospital discharge. In a consecutive series of patients, 39% met all eligibility criteria; 201 patients and their physicians were randomized to an early re-employment intervention (*n* equals 99) or to usual care (*n* equals 102).

The 99 intervention patients underwent symptom-limited treadmill testing in a Naughton protocol at 23 days after myocardial infarction when they were taking no cardiac medications. The physicians based their recommendations regarding return to work on the treadmill test results. In the 70 patients with a normal treadmill response without ischemia, a 5% risk of cardiac death or recurrent myocardial infarction was predicted, and return to work was recommended at 35 days from the date of myocardial infarction. In the 24 patients with mild ischemia, a 10% risk was predicted, and return to work was recommended at 42 days after myocardial infarction. Mild ischemia was defined as angia and an ST depression of less than 2 mm (= 0.2 mV). Antianginal medications were recommended in these patients. In the 6 patients with severe ischemia, coronary arteriography was recommended prior to decisions regarding return to work. Four of these patients had coronary artery bypass graft surgery, one had a recurrent myocardial infarction, and the other had no cardiac event within 6 months.

During the 6-month follow-up period, medical events of death and recurrent myocardial infarction were rare. One intervention and two usual care patients died (1.5%), and one intervention and three usual care patients suffered nonfatal myocardial infarction (2%) for a total medical event rate of 3.5%. Revascularization procedures were performed in 23 patients (11%) without differences between the groups. The risk stratification model was accurate, predicting cardiac death or recurrent myocardial infarction in 5% of patients; the actual rate was 3.5%.

At 6 months, the large majority of patients in both the intervention and usual care groups—92% and 86%, respectively—had returned to work. More than 90% returned to the same jobs. The timing of return to work was significantly different between the groups, however. Usual care patients returned to work at a median of 75 days (range 5 to 180), whereas intervention patients returned a median of 51 days (range 9 to 183). This 33% reduction in return-to-work time was not associated with a higher rate of cardiac events.

The economic benefits of an early return to work were measured by changes in costs and benefits between intervention and usual care patients.[69] Intervention patients earned more than $2,000 more per patient than did usual care patients in the 6 months following myocardial infarction. Medical care costs were more than $500 lower per patient in the intervention group in these 6 months. The lower medical care costs were due primarily to lower rates of rehospitalization in intervention patients for diagnostic testing and treatment related to angina. It appeared that the physicians who were treating intervention patients were reassured by their excellent prognosis, as predicted by the early treadmill test, and were less likely to perform further testing. In addition, in those patients who did develop angina, hospitalization was more common than outpatient treatment in the usual care group.

By many measures, the early return to work of low-risk patients after myocardial infarction was associated with improved outcome. Income was higher; medical care costs were lower. Perceptions of health were improved. Unexpected cardiac event rates of death and recurrent myocardial infarction were low. Treatment of myocardial ischemia was initiated early as the result of early symptom-limited treadmill testing.

CLINICAL APPLICATION OF RE-EMPLOYMENT GUIDELINES

The objective evaluation of vocational disability associated with cardiac illness remains clouded by strongly held perceptions regarding the prognosis and the capacity for physical and psychologic stress of these patients. Other factors, such as today's litigious environment, dissuade employers and health care professionals from encouraging an early return to work after an acute cardiac illness. Even though employers have much to gain, such as improved productivity from an experienced worker and lower costs for disability payments, retraining, and temporary help, they remain fearful of potential liability. Physicians have little to gain and a potentially large liability if they recommend an early return to work for a patient who subsequently suffers a cardiac event at work.

Although a significant proportion of employed men who suffer myocardial infarction can return to work safely as soon as 35 days after the event, a conservative interpretation of the Stanford study would limit the findings to low-risk men under the age of 60. Because a work evaluation following myocardial infarction has its basis in a prognostic assessment and an objective evaluation of physical capacity, the results can probably be extended to include low-risk men up to age 70 years and low-risk employed women as well.

The results of the Stanford study cannot be extended to higher risk subsets of patients with left ventricular dysfunction or myocardial ischemia, but the same concepts of risk stratification and physical capacity assessment should be applied in the management of these patients. An alternative approach would be to use the findings from exercise training studies, which have demonstrated that supervised exercise training programs can increase physical capacity and raise the ischemic threshold. Coupled with other methods of cardiac rehabilitation, exercise training may allow higher risk patients to develop the physical capacity necessary for a return to work. Table 12-4 provides some general guidelines regarding the return to work of patients with left ventricular dysfunction, myocardial ischemia, and ventricular arrhythmias. Until better data are available, however, each case must be evaluated individually.

Patients with other cardiac disorders, such as those who are undergoing valve replacement[70,71] and those who have cardiomyopathic disease, have shown improvements in physical capacity with exercise training.[72] Prognostic assessment has not been as clearly developed in these patients as in those with coronary disease. Each of these patients requires a thorough evaluation by a cardiologist and a thoughtful assessment by the primary care physician regarding the risks and benefits of work. Occupational therapy with work simulation and cardiac monitoring may have a distinct role in returning a motivated patient to work.

In some instances, insurmountable obstacles prevent patients from returning to the same or similar work after an acute cardiac illness. For example, severely ill patients may lack the physical capacity for their former jobs. The law limits or prohibits the re-employment of those whose occupations involve public safety, such as police officers and airline pilots. In these and other circumstances, the vocational counselor is an invaluable aid in the re-employment of the patient with cardiac disease. The development of other skills and interests with directed retraining of individuals can improve vocational outcomes for these patients.

CONCLUSION

Progress in the vocational rehabilitation of patients with cardiac disease will require more objective evaluation of prognosis and physical capacity. Physicians and other health care providers concerned about vocational rehabilitation must be educated in the techniques of risk stratification and measurement of physical capacity. More comprehensive rehabilitation services that include both physical reconditioning and patient education about vocational rehabilitation must be developed. The physical and psychologic benefits of such services to patients are obvious. The social and economic benefits to society are equally important.

Table 12-4 Re-employment Guidelines for Patients with Three Major Pathophysiologic Processes

Syndrome	Clinical Manifestations	Vocational Potential	Therapeutic Options	Comments
Left ventricular dysfunction			Medical therapy titrated to symptoms and treadmill capacity (eg, diuretics, nitrates, afterload reducers, digitalis)	Sedentary or light physical work is possible. Moderate to heavy physical work is contraindicated.
Mild	Dyspnea with high-level exertion	Good		
Moderate	Dyspnea with low-level exertion ± edema	Marginal		
Severe	Dyspnea with minimal exertion ± edema ± orthopnea ± paroxysmal nocturnal dyspnea	Poor		
Myocardial ischemia			Medical therapy with mild to moderate ischemia (eg, beta blockers, nitrates, calcium channel blockers)	Both medical and revascularization therapy are beneficial. A good symptomatic response coupled with a good treadmill workload in the absence of ischemia identifies patients with excellent vocational potential.
Mild	Angina, ST depression at high-level exertion (> 8 METs)	Excellent		
Moderate	Angina, ST depression at moderate-level exertion (5-8 METs)	Good	Revascularization therapy with moderate to severe ischemia or incomplete response to medical therapy (eg, coronary angioplasty, CABG)	
Severe	Angina, ST depression at low-level exertion (<5 METs)	Marginal		

Ventricular arrhythmias				
Mild	Isolated ventricular beats, no symptoms	Excellent	Medical therapy to abolish higher grade arrhythmias and eliminate symptoms	Ventricular arrhythmias are commonly associated with left ventricular dysfunction. Patients with high-grade arrhythmias and/or symptoms usually require specialized evaluation.
Moderate	Ventricular couplets, rare triplets with symptoms	Good	Other therapies, such as implantable defibrillators guided by a cardiac electrophysiologist	
Severe	Ventricular tachycardia with or without symptoms	Marginal to poor		

Note: Patients with moderate or severe manifestations usually require evaluation by a cardiac specialist. CABG, coronary artery bypass graft.

REFERENCES

1. *Heart Facts*. New York: American Heart Association; 1986.

2. Hartunian NS, Smart CN, Thompson MS. The incidence and economic costs of cancer, motor vehicle injuries, coronary heart disease, and stroke: a comparative analysis. *Am J Public Health.* 1980;70:1249–1260.

3. Stewart MJ, Gregor FM. Early discharge and return to work following myocardial infarction. *Soc Sci Med.* 1984;18:1027–1036.

4. DeBusk RF, Blomquist CG, Kouchoukos NT, et al. Identification and treatment of low-risk patients after acute myocardial infarction and coronary-artery bypass graft surgery. *N Engl J Med.* 1986;314:161–166.

5. Miller NH, Haskell WL, Berra K, et al: Home versus group exercise training for increasing functional capacity after myocardial infarction. *Circulation.* 1984;70:645–649.

6. Wenger NK, Hellerstein HK, Blackburn H, et al. Uncomplicated myocardial infarction. *JAMA.* 1973;224:511–514.

7. Wenger NK, Hellerstein HK, Blackburn H, et al. Physician practice in the management of patients with uncomplicated myocardial infarction: changes in the past decade. *Circulation.* 1982;65:421–427.

8. The Veterans Administration Coronary Artery Bypass Surgery Cooperative Study Group. Eleven-year survival in the Veterans Administration randomized trial of coronary bypass surgery for stable angina. *N Engl J Med.* 1984;311:1333–1339.

9. CASS Principal Investigators and Their Associates. Coronary Artery Surgery Study (CASS): a randomized trial of coronary artery bypass surgery. Survival data. *Circulation.* 1983;5:939–950.

10. European Coronary Surgery Study Group. Long-term results of prospective randomized study of coronary artery bypass surgery in stable angina pectoris. *Lancet* 1982;2:1173–1180.

11. Franciosa JA, Wilen M, Ziesche S. Survival in men with severe chronic left ventricular failure due to either coronary heart disease or idiopathic dilated cardiomyopathy. *Am J Cardiol.* 1983;51:831–836.

12. Engler R, Ray R, Higgins CB, et al. Clinical assessment and follow-up of functional capacity in patients with chronic congestive cardiomyopathy. *Am J Cardiol.* 1982;49:1832–1837.

13. Pryor D, Harrell FE, Lee KL. Prognostic indicators from radionuclide angiography in medically treated patients with coronary artery disease. *Am J Cardiol.* 1984;53:18–24.

14. Ehsani AA, Biello D, Seals DR, et al. The effect of left ventricular systolic function on maximal aerobic exercise capacity in asymptomatic patients with coronary artery disease. *Circulation.* 1984;4:552–560.

15. Weber KT, Janicki JS. Cardiopulmonary exercise testing for evaluation of chronic cardiac failure. *Am J Cardiol.* 1985;55:22A–31A.

16. Cohn JN, Archibald DG, Ziesche S, et al. Effect of vasodilator therapy on mortality in chronic congestive heart failure: results of a Veterans Administration Cooperative Study. *N Engl J Med.* 1986;314:1547–1552.

17. CONSENSUS Trial Study Group. Effects of evalapril on mortality in severe congestive heart failure. *N Engl J Med.* 1987;316:1429–1434.

18. Swerdlow CD, Winkle RA, Mason JW. Prognostic significance of the number of induced ventricular complexes during assessment of therapy for ventricular tachyarrhythmias. *Circulation.* 1983;68:400–405.

19. Swerdlow CD, Winkle RA, Mason JW. Determinants of survival in patients with ventricular tachyarrhythmias. *N Engl J Med.* 1983;308:1436–1442.

20. Hindman MC, Wagner GS, Jaro M, et al. The clinical significance of bundle branch block complicating acute myocardial infarction: 2. indications for temporary and permanent pacemaker insertion. *Circulation*. 1978;58:689–698.

21. Mulcahy R, Al Awadhi AH, De Buitleor M, et al. Natural history and prognosis of unstable angina. *Am Heart J*. 1985;109:753–758.

22. Weiner DA, Ryan TJ, McCabe CH, et al. The role of exercise testing in identifying patients with improved survival after coronary artery bypass surgery. *J Am Coll Cardiol*. 1986;8:741–748.

23. Butman SM, Olson HG, Gardin JM, et al. Submaximal exercise testing after stabilization of unstable angina pectoris. *J Am Coll Cardiol*. 1984;4:667–673.

24. Swahn E, Areskog M, Berglund U, et al. Predictive importance of clinical findings and a predischarge exercise test in patients with suspected unstable coronary artery disease. *Am J Cardiol*. 1987;59:208–214.

25. Shapiro S, Winblatt E, Frank CW. Return to work after first myocardial infarction. *Arch Environ Health*. 1972;24:17–26.

26. Wigle RD, Symington DC, Lewis M, et al. Return to work after myocardial infarction. *Can Med Assoc J*. 1971;104:210–212.

27. Garrity TF. Vocational adjustment after first myocardial infarction. Comparative assessment of several variables suggested in the literature. *Soc Sci Med*. 1973;7:705–717.

28. Kushnir B, Fox KM, Tomlinson IW, et al. The effect of a predischarge consultation on the resumption of work, sexual activity, and driving following acute myocardial infarction. *Scand J Rehabil Med*. 1976;8:155–159.

29. Dennis C, Houston-Miller N, Schwartz RG, et al. Early return to work after uncomplicated myocardial infarction: results of a randomized trial. *JAMA*. 1988;260:214.

30. Kjoller E. Resumption of work after myocardial infarction. *Acta Med Scand*. 1976; 199:379–385.

31. Hammermeister KE, DeRouen TA, English MT, et al. Effect of surgical versus medical therapy on return to work in patients with coronary artery disease. *Am J Cardiol*. 1979;44:105–111.

32. Dimsdale JE, Hackett TP, Hutter AM, et al. The association of clinical, psychosocial and angiographic variables with work status in patients with coronary artery disease. *J Psychosom Res*. 1982;26:215–221.

33. Misra KK, Kazanchi BN, Davies GJ, et al. Determinants of work capability and employment after coronary artery surgery. *Eur Heart J*. 1985;6:176–180.

34. Danchin N, David P, Bourassa MG. Coronary artery surgery as a measure of vocational rehabilitation: an analysis of the working status of patients with mild angina randomly assigned to medical or surgical treatment. *Eur Heart J*. 1983;4:687–690.

35. Bruce RA, Kusumi F, Bruce EH, et al. Relationships of working status and cardiac capacity to functional age before and after coronary bypass surgery. *Int J Cardiol*. 1985;8:193–204.

36. Barnes GK, Ray MJ, Oberman A, et al. Changes in working status of patients following coronary bypass surgery. *JAMA*. 1977;238:1259–1262.

37. Love JW. Employment status after coronary bypass operations and some cost considerations. *J Thorac Cardiovasc Surg*. 1980;80:68–72.

38. Anderson AJ, Barboriak JJ, Hoffman RG, et al. Retention or resumption of employment after aortocoronary bypass operations. *JAMA*. 1980;243:543–545.

39. Rimm AA, Barboriak JJ, Anderson AJ, et al. Changes in occupation after aortocoronary vein-bypass operation. *JAMA*. 1976;236:361–364.

40. The Multicenter Post-Infarction Research Group. Risk stratification and survival after myocardial infarction. *N Engl J Med*. 1983;309:331–336.

41. DeBusk RF, Kraemer HC, Nash E. Stepwise risk stratification soon after acute myocardial infarction. *Am J Cardiol*. 1983;52:1161–1166.

42. DeBusk RF, Haskell W. Symptom-limited vs. heart rate-limited exercise testing soon after myocardial infarction. *Circulation*. 1980;61:738–743.

43. Griggs TR, Wagner GS, Gettes LS. Beta-adrenergic blocking agents after myocardial infarction: an undocumented need in patients at lowest risk. *J Am Coll Cardiol*. 1983;1:1530–1533.

44. Ewart CK, Taylor CB, Reese LB, et al. The effects of early post infarction exercise testing on self perception and subsequent physical activity. *Am J Cardiol*. 1983;51:1076–1080.

45. Fox SM, Naughton JP, Gorman PA. Physical activity and cardiovascular health. *Mod Concepts Cardiovasc Dis*. 1972;41:6.

46. Savin WM, Haskell WL, Houston-Miller N, et al. Improvement in aerobic capacity soon after myocardial infarction. *J Cardiac Rehabil*. 1981;1:337–342.

47. Hung J, Goldwater D, Convertino VA, et al. Mechanisms for decreased exercise capacity following bed rest in normal middle-aged men. *Am J Cardiol*. 1983;51:344–348.

48. Convertino V, Hung J, Goldwater D, et al. Cardiovascular responses to exercise in middle-aged men following ten days of bed rest. *Circulation*. 1982;65:134–140.

49. Haskell W, DeBusk R. Cardiovascular responses to repeated treadmill exercise testing soon after myocardial infarction. *Circulation*. 1979;60:1247–1251.

50. Van Camp SP, Peterson RA. Cardiovascular complications of outpatient cardiac rehabilitation programs. *JAMA*. 1986;256:1160–1163.

51. May PA, Nagle FJ. Changes in rate-pressure product with physical training of individuals with coronary artery disease. *Phys Ther*. 1984;64:1361–1366.

52. Ehsani AA, Martin WH III, Heath GW, et al. Cardiac effects of prolonged and intense exercise training in patients with coronary artery disease. *Am J Cardiol*. 1982;50:246–254.

53. Taylor CB, Houston-Miller N, Ahn DK, et al. The effects of exercise training programs on psychosocial improvement in uncomplicated post-myocardial infarction patients. *J Psychosom Res*. 1986;30:581–586.

54. Gossard D, Haskell WL, Taylor CB, et al. Effects of low and high intensity home exercise training on functional capacity in healthy middle-aged men. *Am J Cardiol*. 1986;57:446–449.

55. DeBusk RF, Valdez R, Houston N, et al. Cardiovascular responses to dynamic and static effort soon after myocardial infarction: application to occupational work assessment. *Circulation*. 1978;58:368–375.

56. DeBusk RF. Effect of glucose administration on the ECG stress test. *JAMA*. 1978;239:1321.

57. DeBusk RF, Pitts W, Haskell WL, et al. A comparison of cardiovascular responses to combined static-dynamic and dynamic effort alone in patients with chronic ischemic heart disease. *Circulation*. 1979;59:977–984.

58. Markiewicz W, Houston N, DeBusk R. A comparsion of static and dynamic exercise soon after myocardial infarction. *Israeli J Med Sci*. 1979;15:894–897.

59. Hung J, McKillop J, Savin W, et al. Comparison of cardiovascular response to combined static-dynamic effort, to post-prandial dynamic effort and to dynamic effort alone in patients with chronic ischemic heart disease. *Circulation*. 1982;65:1411–1419.

60. DeBusk R, Taylor CB, Agras S. A comparison of exercise testing and psychological stress testing soon after myocardial infarction. *Am J Cardiol*. 1979;43:907–912.

61. Taylor CB, Davidson DM, Houston N, et al. The effect of a standardized psychological stressor on the cardiovascular response to physical effort soon after uncomplicated myocardial infarction. *J Psychosom Res*. 1982;26:263–268.

62. Weinblatt E, Shapiro S, Frank CW, et al. Return to work and work status following first myocardial infarction. *Am J Public Health*. 1966;56:169–185.

63. US Department of Labor. *Handbook of Labor Statistics*. Washington, DC: Bureau of Labor Statistics; 1985.

64. Nagle R, Gangola R, Picton-Robinson I. Factors influencing return to work after myocardial infarction. *Lancet*. 1971;2:454–456.

65. Bandura A. Self-efficacy mechanism in human agency. *Am Psychol*. 1982;37:122.

66. Wishnie HA, Hackett TP, Cassem NH: Psychological hazards of convalescence following myocardial infarction. *JAMA*. 1971;215:1292–1296.

67. Taylor CB, Bandura A, Ewart CK, et al. Exercise testing to enhance wives' confidence in their husbands' capability soon after clinically uncomplicated myocardial infarction. *Am J Cardiol*. 1985;55:635–638.

68. Dennis C. Care and rehabilitation after myocardial infarction. In: Rakel RE, ed. *Conn's Current Therapy*. Philadelphia: WB Saunders; 1985.

69. Picard MH, Dennis C, Schwartz RG, et al. Cost-benefit of early return to work after uncomplicated myocardial infarction. *Am J Cardiol*. 1989;63:1308.

70. Landry F, Habel C, Desaulniers D, et al. Vigorous physical training after aortic valve replacement: analysis of 10 patients. *Am J Cardiol*. 1984;53:562–566.

71. Newell JP, Kappagoda CT, Stoker JB, et al. Physical training after heart valve replacement. *Br Heart J*. 1980;44:638–649.

72. Conn EH, Williams RS, Wallace AG. Exercise responses before and after physical conditioning in patients with severely depressed left ventricular function. *Am J Cardiol*. 1982;49:296–300.

chapter 13

Vocational Capacity with Respiratory Impairment

Brian Boehlecke

The chronic obstructive pulmonary diseases, emphysema and chronic bronchitis, are by far the most common respiratory cause of reduced work capacity. The disease process has been researched extensively, and the principles derived from these investigations can be applied to the assessment of the vocational capacity of persons with other conditions that limit ventilation. The basic approach is to measure the remaining functional capacity objectively and determine if it is sufficient to meet the demands of work. If it is not, the person is considered disabled. As in other impairments, an individual with respiratory impairment can have significant functional disability and yet not be vocationally handicapped. Alternatively, a person requiring much respiratory reserve for work can have minimal measured pulmonary dysfunction and yet be handicapped for his or her job.

SCOPE OF THE PROBLEM

Chronic respiratory diseases impose a heavy burden of morbidity and mortality on society. The National Health Survey showed a prevalence of chronic bronchitis and emphysema of 3.9% and 2.2%, respectively, for persons aged 45 to 64 years, and underreporting is likely to occur in a survey of this type.[1] A study in a Michigan community indicated that approximately 14% of the adult men and 8% of the adult women had chronic bronchitis, obstructive airways disease, or both.[2] Even the lower estimates suggest that almost 8 million U.S. citizens have chronic bronchitis, and more than 2 million have emphysema.

In the Michigan study, nearly 50% of men with emphysema stated that it limited their major daily activities.[2] Disability days averaged 32 per year for persons with emphysema and 9 for persons with chronic bronchitis. Asthma, reported by 3.2% of respondents, resulted on the average in 16 days of restricted activity per year.

Asthmatics lost an average of 1.4 days of work per year owing to their respiratory disease. Together, the chronic obstructive lung diseases have been estimated to result in an annual loss of $2.4 billion because of reduced productivity and $2.7 billion because of premature deaths.[3]

Data from a major long-term disability insurance carrier showed that chronic respiratory diseases accounted for 5.6% of all claims.[4] The median age of claimants with pulmonary disease was 57 years, and 45% did not return to work before reaching age 65. Thus, chronic respiratory diseases are major causes of disability and lost productivity in the United States today.

PATHOPHYSIOLOGY OF CHRONIC RESPIRATORY DISEASE

The primary diseases of the lungs can be grouped into three broad categories: those with airways obstruction as a major feature, those with diffuse inflammation or fibrosis of the lung parenchyma, and those with a primary disorder involving the pulmonary vasculature. Abnormalities outside the lungs and airways (eg, neuromuscular defects) can also reduce ventilatory capacity.

Disorders with Airways Obstruction as a Major Feature

Emphysema

Permanent dilation and destruction of air spaces distal to the terminal bronchioles characterize emphysema.[5] Because their walls are damaged, the respiratory bronchioles (which have direct communication with alveoli), alveolar ducts, and alveoli have a tendency to collapse during expiration, when they are dynamically compressed.[6]

The destruction of elastic and other tissue in alveolar walls decreases lung recoil forces, leads to hyperinflation, and causes a loss of driving pressure during expiration, which further limits the rate of airflow. Furthermore, it reduces the surface area available for the diffusion of oxygen from alveolar gas into the pulmonary capillary blood and the transfer of carbon dioxide in the opposite direction. As a result, ventilation becomes inefficient, and total ventilation must be greater than normal to maintain adequate gas exchange. If the loss of vascular cross-sectional area is sufficient to increase pulmonary vascular resistance significantly, the workload on the right ventricle is increased, and heart disease secondary to lung disease (cor pulmonale) may result. Reversible constriction of pulmonary arterioles associated with a decrease in alveolar oxygen tension in lung units that are underventilated also contributes to pulmonary hypertension and right ventricular strain.

Chronic Bronchitis

Epidemiologically, chronic bronchitis is defined as excessive mucous production for at least 3 months a year for 2 years or more.[7] Pathologic correlates of the usual symptoms of cough and phlegm are an increased thickness of the bronchial walls in large and intermediate-sized airways due to hyperplasia and hypertrophy of the mucous glands and increased numbers of mucous-secreting goblet cells in smaller airways.[5] The airway mucosa and submucosa are edematous and infiltrated with inflammatory cells. There may be increased smooth muscle mass in airway walls and peribronchial fibrosis. Airway lumina are partially or totally occluded with mucus plugs.

Because cigarette smoking is closely associated with both chronic bronchitis and emphysema, most patients who smoke have an element of both conditions. The label COPD is used to describe the functional nature of the abnormality without specifying the exact underlying pathologic process. Chronic bronchitis may have abnormal gas exchange and seem prone to hypoventilation with carbon dioxide retention and hypoxemia.[8] Voluntary increases in ventilation can reverse the blood gas abnormalities, however, which may be related to both the increased work of breathing and a disturbance of respiratory drive.

Asthma

Although asthma has proved difficult to define, it is clinically manifested by a variable obstruction to airflow due to diffuse narrowing of the airways that remits spontaneously or with treatment.[9] Constriction of hypertrophied airway smooth muscle is the major cause of the rapidly reversible obstruction to airflow during an acute attack. Edema of the bronchial walls and infiltration with eosinophils are usually present to some degree, however.[10] The more prolonged the attack, the more likely that it will not respond well to smooth muscle relaxants. The airway wall changes described earlier and mucous plugging of the airway lumina appear to produce this less readily reversible obstruction. Hypertrophy of mucous glands in airway walls may also be a contributing factor; like smooth muscle hypertrophy, mucous gland hypertrophy persists between acute attacks of bronchospasm.

The term *occupational asthma* describes the condition of a patient whose respiratory symptoms occur primarily in the workplace. Triggering agents for acute attacks may include antigens to which the asthmatic has developed specific immunologic sensitization or nonspecific irritants (eg, cold air, smoke, dust). Antigen-antibody binding on the surface of airway mast cells results in the release of chemical mediators of bronchoconstriction and airway inflammation when an antigen is inhaled. Reflex arcs initiated by irritant receptors in the airway epithelium may be responsible for the bronchoconstriction associated with nonantigenic materials. Between attacks, ventilatory function may be normal or nearly so, but bronchoprovocation with an antigen to which the asthmatic is sensitized or with a nonspecific agent, such as methacholine, reveals airway hyper-responsiveness. This heightened response to even nonspecific stimuli may produce recurrent attacks precipitated or aggravated by concentrations of airborne irritants in the workplace that are not bothersome to others.

Disorders with Diffuse Inflammation and/or Fibrosis of the Lung Parenchyma

Diffuse inflammation of the lung parenchyma occurs as a response to various insults. In some instances, the inciting agent is well characterized (eg, inhaled fungal spores [actinomycetes] in "farmer's lung," inhaled asbestos fibers in asbestosis). In other cases, the cause is not known (eg, sarcoidosis, idiopathic diffuse pulmonary fibrosis).[11] The lung may also be but one organ affected by a systemic disorder, such as rheumatoid arthritis or progressive systemic sclerosis. Although the pathologic changes and clinical pictures of these conditions may be distinctive, they are all associated with a decrease in lung compliance and abnormalities in gas transfer that worsen with exercise.

Diffuse inflammation in the alveolar walls with or without deposition of collagenous fibrous tissue increases the elastic recoil of the lungs so that more force is required to inflate them. This decreases the volume of gas that can be inhaled with a maximal effort and increases the work of breathing. The term *restrictive lung disease* is used for this type of abnormality.

Nonuniform regional alveolar compliance results in uneven distribution of ventilation and inefficient gas transfer. During exercise, an increased cardiac output traversing a pulmonary capillary bed with a reduced cross-sectional area results in a more rapid transit of red blood cells through the lung, and the oxygen tension between alveolar gas and pulmonary end-capillary blood may not reach an equilibrium. Thus, significant arterial hypoxemia may develop during exercise, even though the arterial blood oxygen tension at rest is normal or nearly normal.

Disorders with Primary Abnormality of the Pulmonary Vasculature

Obstruction of the pulmonary vascular tree may result from recurrent pulmonary thromboemboli (circulating "blood clots") or may develop insidiously without a recognized cause in the condition called primary pulmonary hypertension.[12] Involvement of the pulmonary vasculature is also prominent in some of the collagen-vascular disorders that produce restrictive lung disease, such as progressive systemic sclerosis.

In these conditions, mechanical ventilatory function is essentially normal. Because the distribution of blood flow is uneven, however, perfusion is insufficient relative to ventilation in some lung units and excessive in others. The underperfusion contributes to an increase in wasted or "dead space" ventilation, and the overperfusion results in inadequate oxygenation of pulmonary capillary blood. Again, exercise shortens red cell transit time through the lung, heightening the effect of any incomplete equilibration in oxygen tension between alveolar gas and pulmonary capillary blood. Much of the excessive ventilation that occurs during exercise goes to the underperfused units and therefore does not increase gas exchange.

If the cross-sectional area of the pulmonary vasculature is sufficiently reduced, whatever the cause, pulmonary hypertension develops. It is accentuated during exercise, as there are reduced pulmonary vessels that can be recruited to accommodate the increased cardiac output. Right ventricular work is increased, and cor pulmonale with limitation of cardiac output may result. Fatigue and shortness of breath with exertion are often prominent clinical symptoms in patients with pulmonary hypertension.

Other Disorders That Affect Ventilatory Function

Neuromuscular

Any neuromuscular disorder that affects the neural input to or the strength of the respiratory musculature can compromise the mechanical bellows function of the respiratory system. For example, the motor neuron diseases reduce efferent neural input, whereas the muscular dystrophies affect muscles directly[13,14]; both types of diseases can affect the respiratory system. Although different disorders may involve specific muscle groups preferentially, the important physiologic consequence to all these conditions is a decreased ability to expand the thoracic cage/lung system. A reduction in the volume of air that can be inhaled causes abnormalities in gas exchange during exercise, when demand for ventilation is increased. Insufficient ventilation is associated with a rise in arterial carbon dioxide tension and a fall in oxygen tension. Eventually, ventilatory capacity is inadequate to maintain normal gas exchange even at rest. Diminished effectiveness of coughing may lead to retention of secretions and recurrent infections that further compromise the ventilatory and gas-exchanging functions.

Skeletal

Abnormalities that limit chest wall motion also decrease vital capacity. Kyphoscoliosis, for example, is associated with a reduction in vital capacity proportional to the angle of scoliosis.[15]

Obesity reduces the compliance of the chest wall and thus the resting end-expiratory volume of the lung.[16] This reduction in volume is associated with airway closure in the dependent portions of the lung and impaired gas exchange, leading to hypoxemia. It is especially pronounced when the patient is in the supine position. Voluntary deep breaths usually reverse the hypoxemia. If obesity is massive, vital capacity may be reduced despite normal muscle strength and normal lungs.

Obesity is also a risk factor for sleep apnea syndromes in which the airflow ceases periodically during sleep.[17] The apnea may be obstructive, in which the upper airway is completely occluded, but respiratory efforts continue; central, in which all respiratory efforts cease; or mixed. Hypoxemia may be severe during apneic episodes. Interestingly, some patients with sleep apnea may also have hypoxemia and hypercapnia when they are awake, even though the results of pulmonary function tests are normal. The usual sequelae of severe hypoxemia, including right-sided congestive heart failure, may occur. The physiologic mechanisms responsible for the sleep apnea syndromes are not completely understood at present, but the abnormalities in gas exchange and the excessive daytime drowsiness associated with the periodic arousals from sleep in patients with obstructive apnea can be reversed by tracheostomy. Limitation of work capacity may be more directly related to the excessive somnolence associated with these syndromes than to the derangement of gas exchange.

Cardiac

Even with normal lungs, congestive heart failure can compromise ventilatory function by leading to interstitial edema. Limitation of cardiac output also complicates obstructive and fibrotic lung conditions of long-standing duration. Typically, a low cardiac output is accompanied by a high heart rate with development of lactic acidosis at a low workload.

ASSESSMENT OF RESPIRATORY IMPAIRMENT

Impairment is defined as a loss or abnormality of structure or function.[18–20] Generally, in pulmonary disease, impairment refers to reduced airflow due to bronchial narrowing, increased elastance secondary to pulmonary or pleural fibrosis, and gas exchange abnormalities from abnormal distribution of ventilation and perfusion and/or from reduced diffusing capacity.

To determine if an individual's functional capacity is normal, it must be measured or estimated in some way and then compared to the functional capacity expected for healthy individuals. For the respiratory system, objective measurements of ventilatory and gas-exchanging functions can be made at rest and during exercise. Because the correlation of these objective measures with symptoms and with the individual's ability to perform the activities of daily life and work is not perfect, a clinical assessment must take into account subjective sensations (eg, pain, dyspnea, fatigue) and the impact of multisystem impairments in order to arrive at a valid determination of the functional capacity of an individual with respiratory disease.

History

The most common manifestation of respiratory system impairment is the sensation of shortness of breath or dyspnea. Although the pathophysiologic mechanisms of dyspnea are not clearly understood, an awareness of a greater than expected amount of respiratory work for the amount of activity (ventilatory and/or total exertion) is a basic feature.[21] This awareness may be due to an excessive neural outflow from respiratory centers that reaches the cortical level of the brain.

The clinician should quantify the severity of dyspnea by determining the level of exertion or the types of activities that provoke the sensation (eg, distance walked or number of stairs climbed before stopping for breath) and the types of activities now foregone because they cause intolerable dyspnea. The severity of dyspnea can then be related to the degree of impairment found on objective tests of respiratory function. If there is a major discrepancy between the severity of symptoms and objective tests of function made at rest, exercise testing may be useful to distinguish between organic and functional impairment.[22] Some guidelines for the evaluation of impairment/disability include specific descriptions of dyspnea severity in each category of impairment.[20,23]

Clinical evaluations of functional status that are based on subjective information alone are not reliable. Agreement beyond chance between two physicians who classified patients into three broad functional categories (ie, normal, able to work, or able to care for self) was only 50% in one study.[24] Furthermore, the physicians agreed with the patient's own assessment less than one third of the time.

Patients appear to have difficulty in quantifying their exercise capacity accurately.[25] Disability claimants tend to underestimate their capacity and to have more severe symptoms at a given level of ventilatory function, as measured by spirometry, than do nonclaimants.[26–28] Disability claimants are not necessarily exaggerating their symptoms, however. They may have other medical problems that contribute to their overall functional impairment. They may also have more physically demanding jobs that provoke more severe symptoms. Thus, dyspnea out of proportion to objective impairment of ventilatory function suggests the need for more careful evaluation of other factors that may be contributing to the individual's loss of overall functional capacity.

Wheezing, a sign of airways obstruction, can be heard in COPD, as well as in asthma. An asthmatic's lack of wheezing at the time of examination is not a reliable predictor that the condition is mild; recurrent episodes of bronchospasm may still produce severe functional impairment.[29] Thus, the physician should obtain a precise history of the frequency, severity, and provoking circumstances for episodes of bronchospasm. Also, the medication requirements, both chronic and episodic, should be documented.

Wheezing due to diffuse airways obstruction should be carefully differentiated from stridor due to upper airway obstruction caused by such conditions as tracheal tumors, thyroid enlargement, or vocal cord paralysis. These lesions have obvious differences in management and implications for long-term vocational ability. The physical examination and laboratory tests of airflow are essential in making a diagnosis of upper airway obstruction.

Chronic cough may be produced by airway inflammation; fibrosis or cellular infiltration of the lung interstitium, resulting in decreased lung compliance; or by direct impingement of intrinsic or extrinsic masses on the airways. In certain circumstances, a severe and persistent cough can preclude adequate performance of the patient's vocation. This is certainly true when the cough produces sputum and the job requires continuous use of ventilatory protective equipment to prevent a harmful environmental exposure. The amount and character of sputum produced are therefore important not only in the determination of the reason for the cough but also in the assessment of the cough's contribution to a vocational impairment.

The history of the use of tobacco products is important both for determining the cause of the current ventilatory impairment and for assessing the potential for functional improvement. Smoking cessation can improve ventilatory function significantly in persons with chronic bronchitis and certainly reduces the risk for development of bronchogenic lung cancer.[30,31]

A detailed occupational history is an essential component of an assessment of a respiratory impairment, as workplace exposures may have caused or contributed to the impairment. Continued exposure at current levels may be medically contraindicated, given the patient's present condition, even if the workplace exposure is not found to be a primary cause of that condition. The physical activity required on the job should be documented carefully. The average and peak levels of exertion, the ability of the worker to determine the pace of work, and the timing and duration of breaks should be assessed. These factors are important in determining whether a given degree of respiratory impairment is likely to preclude the patient from performing the job without undue distress.

Physical Examination

The physician forms an overall clinical impression of the patient's condition through the physical examination. Naturally, special attention should be given to the respiratory system and to specific findings that may suggest an etiologic diagnosis for the respiratory impairment. Abnormalities of other organ systems that may contribute to the overall functional impairment must not be overlooked, however.

The patient's general nutritional status should be documented. Cachexia suggests severe respiratory impairment or other significant chronic illness. Loss of muscle mass from whatever cause may itself limit the capacity for exertion. Because obesity places additional demands on the cardiopulmonary system, it reduces the amount of external work that an individual with a given level of cardiopulmonary function can do. The general chest shape should be noted. Significant deformities of the rib cage or kyphoscoliosis may cause a restrictive ventilatory impairment. An increased anteroposterior diameter ("barrel chest") is often considered to indicate airways obstruction and hyperinflation, but this finding was not confirmed when investigated on a population-based sample.[32] The respiratory pattern, including rate and apparent depth of breathing, should be noted. The use of accessory muscles of respiration, intercostal space or supraclavicular fossae retractions, or pursed lip breathing suggest significant airways obstruction.

Palpation of the chest may reveal tenderness over the ribs or costochondral junctions that may contribute to a reduction in vital capacity because of pain on deep inspiration. Deviation of the trachea suggests loss of lung volume due to collapse or fibrosis. A lag or decrease in motion of one side of the chest on inspiration may result from large airway obstruction, hemidiaphragmatic weakness, or unilateral air space or pleural disease. Transmission of vibration is increased in consolidation with filling of air spaces when airways are patent, whereas pleural effusions produce damping. Diaphragmatic motion should be assessed by percussion.

Auscultation may reveal an abnormal decrease in breath sound intensity, which indicates a reduction in airflow.[33] The major source of sound is turbulent airflow in large airways, and the reduction in flow rate that occurs with significant airways obstruction (eg, as seen in emphysema) may result in a virtual absence of normal inspiratory breath sounds. Abnormal (adventitious) lung sounds are classified as continuous wheezes or rhonchi and discontinuous crackles or rales.[34] Wheezes are musical sounds produced by airway vibration when air flows through narrowed segments. Bronchospasm in asthmatics is characterized by wheezing in different airways that is random in onset and cessation; it may occur in inspiration, as well as in expiration. Wheezes can also be heard in expiration in patients with significant COPD due to dynamic compression of the airways. Unlike those heard in asthmatics, these wheezes tend to begin at the same point of expiration. Such expiratory wheezing may also be heard in normal persons near the end of a maximal expiratory effort.

Crackles are repetitive sounds due to the sudden opening of collapsed air spaces and small airways. Showers of fine crackles late in inspiration are characteristic of interstitial infiltration with inflammatory cells or fibrosis. Coarser late inspiratory crackles can at times be heard in chronic bronchitis or emphysema. Coarse, low-pitched crackles early in inspiration, and sometimes late in expiration, can also be heard in chronic bronchitis.

Clubbing of the fingers or toes is characteristic of certain pulmonary diseases. Signs of true clubbing are softness of the nail bed, an increase in the hyponychial angle with curvature of the nails, and an increase in soft tissue of the fingertips. Its presence suggests lung cancer; interstitial lung disease; or chronic infections, including bronchiectasis or lung abscess. Absence of clubbing does not rule out these conditions. True clubbing is not usually associated with COPD. Cyanosis of the extremities due to desaturated hemoglobin may occur if the resting arterial oxygen tension is reduced significantly; cyanosis may also result from a reduction in local blood flow due to peripheral vascular disease, however.

Signs of cardiovascular impairment should be sought carefully. Cor pulmonale may further decrease the patient's functional capacity and has a poor prognosis. Signs of right ventricular failure include elevated venous pressure, hepatic congestion, peripheral edema, and a right ventricular diastolic gallop that increases during inspiration. A loud second pulmonic component of the second heart sound may indicate pulmonary hypertension; because a physical examination is not sensitive for increased pulmonary artery pressure, more extensive laboratory testing (eg, echocardiography) should be done if this diagnosis is suspected. Primary cardiac or vascular impairments may contribute to the patient's exercise intolerance; shortness of breath out of proportion to measured ventilatory impairment suggests cardiovascular compromise.

Radiography

Radiographic examination of the chest is helpful in making an etiologic diagnosis of respiratory impairments and in assessing the cardiac size and pulmonary vasculature. Hyperinflation, a loss of pulmonary vascular marking, an increase in retrosternal air space, and a low or flattened diaphragm are consistent with emphysema, although these radiographic findings are not pathognomonic of this diagnosis. The presence of bullae is a more definitive sign. The correlation between radiographic signs and ventilatory function is poor for the obstructive lung diseases, however. Fibrotic lung diseases are more readily identified radiographically, but a physiologically significant amount of interstitial infiltration can be present without detectable radiographic abnormality.[35] Again, functional impairment is only poorly correlated with the severity of radiographic involvement, even in more advanced disease. The system of the International Labor Organization (ILO) for classifying pneumoconioses is useful in standardizing interpretation of films with diffuse opacities, but should not be considered a scale for impairment.[36]

Pulmonary Function Laboratory Testing

Most laboratory tests for pulmonary capacity are measures of anatomic and physiologic function; thus, they are also indicators of impairment.

Spirometry

Because it is simple, inexpensive, and reproducible, spirometry is the most widely used measure of pulmonary function. Most diseases that produce clinically important impairment of the respiratory system at some point affect ventilatory function as measured by spirometry. The American Thoracic Society has recommended a standard technique for obtaining accurate measurements.[37,38] Basically, patients are asked to inhale as deeply as possible and then to exhale into the spirometer as fast and as hard as they can. They are instructed to continue exhaling as long as possible. Measurements made from this maneuver include the forced vital capacity (FVC), which is the total volume of gas exhaled; the forced expiratory volume in the first second of expiration (FEV_1); and flow rates at various points during the expiration.

The accuracy of the results obtained from a spirometry test depends on the patient's ability to understand the maneuver and to cooperate in making a maximal effort. If coaching is adequate and the equipment accurate, most persons can quickly perform three acceptable maneuvers with the largest FVC and FEV_1 within 5% of the second largest. There is little to be gained from additional maneuvers after this criterion is met.[39,40] If spirometry is repeated several times over a period of days to weeks, the coefficient of variation for the FVC and FEV_1 is 2.5% to 3% for healthy persons and approximately twice that for persons with clinically significant ventilatory impairment.[41,42]

An individual's measured values for FVC and FEV_1 can be compared to predicted values derived from epidemiologic studies of asymptomatic nonsmokers who report no history of serious respiratory illness or exposure to respiratory hazards at work.[43–45] When attempting to determine whether a patient has a ventilatory impairment, however, the clinician must consider several factors that affect normal function.[46,47] Such variables as age, height, and gender account for much of the observed variability in the FVC and FEV_1 among healthy persons, and these variables are used in the prediction equations derived from the epidemiologic data.

Race has also been shown to be a factor that must be considered in the prediction of ventilatory function.[48–50] Healthy black men in the United States have been shown to have 10% to 15% lower values for the FVC and FEV_1 than do their white counterparts. This is felt to be due primarily to a difference in body habitus; the trunk length and thus the lung size of a black man of a given height are less than that of a Caucasian man of the same height. The large epidemiologic studies done in the United States to determine predicted values on spirometry have included only Caucasians. This omission has prompted some federal programs in which spirometric testing is mandated to require that the predicted values be adjusted by 0.85 before they are compared to observed values in blacks.[51] The American Medical Association recommends a 10% decrement (0.90 adjustment factor) for blacks when rating their impairment of ventilatory function.[20]

Even after all these factors have been considered, variability in the FVC and FEV_1 among healthy persons remains. The predicted values are essentially averages for persons of the same age, height, gender, and race. Because some healthy persons have values below those predicted, a lower limit of normal (LLN) is usually established for clinical purposes. Traditionally, the LLN has been set at a specific percentage of the predicted value; for the FVC and FEV_1, this has usually been 80%. Because the FVC and FEV_1 normally decrease with age after the age of 25 to 30 years, however, a fixed percentage decrement below the predicted value becomes smaller in absolute value for older persons. As the variability in the FVC and FEV_1 among persons does not appear to decrease with age, this method of setting the LLN classifies the FVC and FEV_1 as abnormal in a greater proportion of healthy older persons than in healthy younger persons. Similarly, the FVC and FEV_1 in shorter persons are more likely to be below the LLN than are those in taller persons. In view of this phenomenon, it has been recommended that the percentile rank of an individual's values in the distribution of values of the healthy population studies to be used as a measure of the probability that the individual has abnormal ventilatory function.[52]

Subtracting a fixed absolute value from the predicted value to establish the LLN for all ages and heights has also been recommended.[44] It is more statistically accurate for the distribution of values for the FVC and FEV_1 found in healthy adults of varying ages and heights. For rating impairment, however, most classification systems continue to use the percentage of the predicted value as the variable that defines the severity of the impairment.

A reduction in the FVC is the spirometric hallmark of the restrictive pattern of ventilatory impairment. Such a reduction can result from a loss of lung compliance (eg, the interstitial lung diseases), a loss of lung substance (eg, surgical removal of lung tissue), compromise of lung tissue due to pneumonia or pleural fluid, neuromuscular or skeletal abnormalities that reduce chest wall motion, or failure to give a maximal effort for whatever reason (eg, pain, inability to understand, malingering).

An obstructive ventilatory impairment, commonly due to emphysema, chronic bronchitis, or asthma, results in a reduction of the FEV_1. Because the FEV_1 may also be reduced in a restrictive impairment, the FEV_1:FVC ratio is used to determine whether there is obstruction. In restrictive conditions, the FEV_1, is reduced in proportion to the FVC, so the ratio remains normal. In diffuse fibrotic lung diseases, such as idiopathic interstitial pulmonary fibrosis, the airways tend to be held open by the surrounding scar tissue, and the FEV_1:FVC ratio may even be increased. Predicted values for the FEV_1:FVC ratio are approximately 75% for middle-aged men and women, with a slight decrease with age.[53] There is some decrease with height for men.

Flow rates at various points during expiration, especially after the first 25% of the vital capacity has been expelled, have been investigated as possible effort-independent measures of small airways function. Despite the theoretical potential for increased sensitivity to abnormality in small airway function, such measures as the forced expiratory flow from 25% to 75% of the vital capacity have not been shown to correlate as closely as does the FEV_1 with the overall clinical impairment of the individual.[54,55] Therefore, although these measures may be useful to detect subtle abnormalities and, in some instances, to assist in the diagnosis of various lung disorders, they are generally not considered useful measures of impairment for vocational assessment. For persons with a significant obstructive impairment, spirometry should be repeated after the administration of an inhaled bronchodilator to determine if significant acute reversible bronchospasm is present. If so, optimal medical management may alter the individual's level of impairment.

Bronchoprovocation Testing

For patients who have symptoms consistent with bronchospasm, but for whom routine spirometry shows no significant obstructive impairment, bronchial challenge testing may reveal airway hyper-responsiveness.[56] A series of graded doses of methacholine, histamine, or carbachol are given by inhalation, and pulmonary function is measured after each dose.[57–59] A significant decrease in a measured variable (eg, a 20% decrement in the FEV_1) is the criterion for response. The cumulative dose of the provocative agent inhaled at the point of response is then compared to the dose that produces a response in asymptomatic healthy persons without a history of asthma or any other atopic condition. Asthmatics may show a response at a dose less than 1% of the dose that causes a response in those who are healthy.[60] The degree of bronchial hyper-responsiveness may be correlated with the severity of symptoms caused by exposure to irritants or sensitizers and thus with the difficulty of working in environments that contain such agents.[61]

Respiratory Muscle Strength Testing

For patients with neuromuscular disorders, measurements of maximal inspiratory and expiratory pressures may reveal an impairment not readily apparent from spirometry alone.[62] A reduction in the force generated by respiratory muscles has only a small effect on the FVC and FEV_1 measured from individual forced expiratory maneuvers until the muscle weakness is quite severe. Exercise tolerance may be reduced by the patient's inability to sustain an increased ventilatory effort, however. Although maximal pressure testing is more difficult for the patient and less reproducible than spirometry, it does provide a quantitative estimate of impairment of the bellows function of the respiratory system that other tests done at rest do not necessarily reflect.

Lung Volumes

Spirometry measures only the amount of gas that can be expelled from the lungs (vital capacity). A reduction in vital capacity signifies a change in the relationship between total lung capacity (ie, the volume of gas in the lung when maximally inflated) and residual volume (ie, the amount of gas remaining in the lung at the end of a maximal expiratory effort). It is not possible to distinguish among the various combinations of alterations in total lung capacity and residual volume that may reduce vital capacity by means of spirometry alone, however.

Lung volume determination is primarily useful to clarify the underlying pathophysiologic basis for a reduction in vital capacity. Methods to measure absolute lung volumes include inert gas dilution or nitrogen washout breathing pure oxygen, body plethysmography, and estimation from measurements made on chest radiographs. Restrictive lung diseases, such as idiopathic pulmonary fibrosis, are associated with a reduction in total lung capacity, residual volume, and the resting end-expiratory volume (ie, functional residual capacity). Emphysema is associated with an increase in total lung capacity and functional residual capacity, as well as a large increase in residual volume with a consequent reduction in vital capacity. Muscle weakness may reduce a patient's total lung capacity and vital capacity because of the inability to stretch normally compliant lungs, but the functional residual capacity is unaffected.

Lung volumes are not generally considered in the quantification of impairment for evaluation of vocational capacity. Lung volume measurements may allow a more precise characterization of the pathophysiologic process producing the overall respiratory impairment, however, and may also permit an accurate diagnosis. Together, these are important benefits, as adequate management and prognostic assessment depend on the accuracy of the diagnosis.

Diffusing Capacity

The lung's diffusing capacity is operationally defined as the volume of gas transferred from the alveoli to the pulmonary capillary blood per unit time per unit pressure gradient. The diffusing capacity for oxygen is of most concern, but is difficult to measure directly; a functional test can be done more easily with a low concentration of carbon monoxide.[63,64]

In such a test, the subject inhales from residual volume to total lung capacity from a bag containing low concentrations of carbon monoxide and helium. After holding the breath at total lung capacity for 10 seconds, the subject exhales; a sample of the exhalate is taken for analysis, after discarding the initial portion (the dead space gas from larger airways in which no gas exchange occurs). The volume of gas in the lungs at the start of inhalation determines the reduction in the concentration of helium in the exhalate relative to that inhaled, as helium is quite insoluble and little is absorbed during the breathhold. This dilution factor can then be applied to the observed exhaled concentration of carbon monoxide to determine the amount absorbed during the breathhold and thus the diffusing capacity of the lung.

Many technical factors, including the duration of breath-holding, the length of time of collection, and the volume of exhaled gas collected for analysis, affect the test results. Meaningful comparison of an individual's results with predicted values depends on the comparability of the technique used to that used when the predicted values were obtained. The American Thoracic Society maintains that interlaboratory variability is too great for any single set of predicted values to be universally applicable.[64] The Society recommends that each laboratory conduct tests on a group of healthy individuals to determine which set of published reference values produces the least overall divergence of observed from predicted values and proceed to use those values in its testing. The lack of agreement between laboratories makes it difficult to establish criteria that indicate the severity of impairment of the diffusing capacity. As with spirometry, 80% of the appropriate predicted value has been suggested as the LLN for the diffusing capacity.[65] The results of repeated tests on an individual should agree within 10% before the results are considered valid and reliable.[65]

The lung's diffusing capacity is impaired whenever the surface area of the interface between alveolar gas and pulmonary capillary blood is decreased. Therefore, it may be decreased in emphysema, interstitial lung disease, and pulmonary vascular disorders, including chronic pulmonary emboli. The diffusing capacity may be clearly abnormal in the interstitial lung diseases, even when ventilatory function is nearly normal by spirometry. A reduction in gas transfer capacity may be more evident during exercise, which increases the demands placed on gas exchange and reduces red blood cell transit time through the lungs. A reduction in diffusing capacity may also be due to anemia with an approximately 25% decrement for a drop in hemoglobin from 15 to 10 g/dl.[64] Cigarette smoking may cause difficulty in interpretation. The presence in the blood of carboxyhemoglobin at the start of the test may reduce the measured value by approximately 1% for each percent of carboxyhemoglobin. Smokers may have carboxyhemoglobin levels of 5% or more.[66,67]

Arterial Blood Gases

The measurement of arterial blood gas levels is extremely valuable in the overall clinical assessment of patients with respiratory impairment. It is less useful in the evaluation of vocational capacity, except when combined with exercise testing.

Although a reduction in arterial oxygen tension implies abnormal gas exchange, the nature of the impairment is critical in determining the overall significance of such a reduction for vocational capacity. Obesity, which reduces the functional residual capacity and causes abnormalities in ventilation-perfusion matching with relative underventilation of the bases of the lungs, may be associated with significant arterial hypoxemia without underlying lung abnormality.[68] Taking deeper breaths voluntarily or in response to the stimulus of exercise usually reverses the hypoxemia completely, however.

Resting arterial blood gas levels have also not been predictive of the ability to exercise or the clinical degree of disability in patients with obstructive ventilatory impairment.[69-71] This is consistent with the finding of a ventilatory limit to exercise in these patients and the usual lack of significant falls in arterial oxygen tension at the exercise limit, even in those with severe obstruction.[72] In fact, some patients, especially those with chronic bronchitis, may show improvement in oxygenation during exercise.[73]

Emphysema is sometimes characterized by relatively well-maintained arterial blood gas levels at rest (ie, normal or nearly normal arterial oxygen tension and arterial carbon dioxide tension) at the expense of an increased total ventilation. The patient's ability to exercise may be limited, however, because of the need for excessive ventilation at all workloads.

For persons with interstitial lung disease, gas exchange may worsen with exertion; the arterial oxygen tension may fall in association with the limit of exercise.[74] The inability of a person with neuromuscular disease to increase ventilation in proportion to carbon dioxide production may result in a rising arterial carbon dioxide tension during exercise, despite near-normal resting measures of ventilatory function and gas exchange. Thus, arterial blood gas measurements are most informative when performed during an exercise test protocol.[75]

ASSESSMENT OF RESPIRATORY DISABILITY

A respiratory disability involves a reduced capacity to exercise as a result of pulmonary impairment. The cardiovascular and respiratory systems normally respond to the demand for increased oxygen delivery during exercise with an increase in cardiac output and an increase in ventilation. The ability to sustain physical exertion is dependent on the capacity to provide working muscles with an adequate quantity of oxygen to produce the required energy through oxidative metabolism.[76] Work can be performed for brief periods at rates that exceed the body's aerobic capacity, but doing so depletes muscle metabolic substrates and causes a build-up of the products of anaerobic metabolism, such as lactic acid, in the tissues and blood. The sensation of fatigue then develops, and the person cannot maintain work at this rate.

Normal Physiologic Responses to Exercise

Additional oxygenated blood is delivered to working muscles through an increase in cardiac output and a dilation of muscle arterioles to increase local blood flow. The rise in cardiac output is due partly to a modest increase in the volume of blood ejected per heart beat (stroke volume), which occurs at low levels of exercise, and partly to an increase in heart rate. As the energy output rises, the heart rate rises in direct proportion to oxygen consumption; stroke volume changes little, however. Maximum oxygen delivery is determined by maximum cardiac output, which occurs when the maximum heart rate is reached. The maximum heart rate is age-dependent, with a predicted value of [210-.65 (age)] beats/min.[77] A reduction in either stroke volume or peak heart rate achievable decreases the maximum cardiac output possible and thereby the individual's ability to sustain aerobic work.

The oxygen available to exercising muscles may also be increased by a greater extraction of oxygen per unit of blood passing through muscle capillaries. This increases the arterial-venous oxygen content difference. There is a limit to the amount of oxygen that can be extracted, however, because the partial pressure of oxygen in the tissue must be sufficient to allow diffusion to the mitochondrial membrane sites where oxidative metabolism occurs. One effect of exercise training is an increase in muscle capillary density, which improves the body's capacity to extract oxygen from blood. This increases oxygen availability for a given level of arterial oxygen content and blood flow.

During exercise, the amount of air breathed per minute increases in direct proportion to the amount of oxygen consumed and the amount of carbon dioxide produced during low to moderate levels of exertion. The increase in the amount of air breathed per minute is due to an increase in tidal volume and respiratory rate, with the former providing most of the change. At higher levels of exertion, the tidal volume may reach 50% to 60% of the vital capacity; the respiratory rate increase accounts for the continued rise in minute ventilation. As energy output is increased above one half of the maximum oxygen consumption for the individual, the amount of air breathed rises more rapidly relative to oxygen consumption than it does during less strenuous exertion.[78] At maximal exertion, a sensation of intolerable shortness of breath occurs, and exercise cannot be sustained at that level.

For healthy persons, the highest level of ventilation reached is generally less than 70% of the maximum voluntary ventilation measured at rest during a brief period (usually 15 seconds) of maximum effort breathing.[79] Arterial blood gas measurements at peak exertion show no drop in oxygen tension from resting levels, although carbon dioxide tension is decreased and pH may be slightly reduced from resting levels. Arterial blood gas levels should always be measured during a steady state after at least 4 minutes of exercise at a given workload.

Otherwise, the transient decrements in Pa_{O_2} that occur prior to completion of the adjustment in ventilation and cardiac output for the workload may be misinterpreted as indications of abnormalities in gas exchange. Even healthy persons show significant transient drops in Pa_{O_2} at the initiation of exercise.[80]

The mechanism that produces dyspnea at maximal exertion in healthy persons is not fully understood. It appears to involve the amount of ventilation reached relative to that achievable with a maximum ventilatory effort. Therefore, any respiratory impairment that either limits the maximum achievable ventilation or increases the amount of ventilation required at a given level of exertion will reduce the capacity for muscular work.

Maximum Exercise Capacity

A patient's maximum exercise capacity can be measured directly by means of a progressively increasing workload study in the laboratory. Energy output is systematically increased on a cycle ergometer or treadmill until the patient reaches a symptomatic limit or medical criteria require termination of the study. These criteria may include reaching target heart rate (eg, 85% of the predicted maximum) or signs or symptoms of inadequate organ perfusion (eg, dizziness, muscle cramps, arrhythmias, ST segment depression on ECG, angina). The exercise level at which the arterial oxygenation may decrease enough to become a stimulus for additional ventilation and thereby contribute to shortness of breath and limitation of exertion cannot be predicted accurately from measurement of arterial blood gases at rest, however. Thus, relatively normal blood gases at rest do not rule out exercise limitation in patients with interstitial lung diseases. Likewise, other abnormalities at rest, although likely to worsen with exercise, do not define the level of exertion that can be tolerated.

Oxygen consumption should be measured during the test, as it is the most direct indication of the stress placed on the cardiovascular and respiratory systems. Estimates of oxygen consumption calculated indirectly from the external workload imposed may be inaccurate. For example, obese persons perform additional work in moving heavy extremities, and static muscle tension (eg, gripping the handlebars of a cycle ergometer) requires an energy expenditure not measured by external work.[81] Heart rate, respiratory frequency, tidal volume, and minute ventilation are also monitored and their values related to oxygen consumption. The pattern of increase in cardiovascular and respiratory variables, as well as the maximum values achieved, can provide information concerning the cause and severity of any impairment of exercise capacity. The considerations discussed earlier in determining the LLN for resting tests of ventilatory function also apply in interpreting exercise test results (see Spirometry).

The major disadvantages of performing maximum exercise testing on all persons with a potentially disabling respiratory impairment are cost and patient discomfort. There is also some risk in tests of maximum exertion, especially in older individuals who may have undocumented cardiac abnormalities. Therefore, attempts have been made to estimate maximum exercise capacity from submaximal exertion. Wright developed an equation to predict maximum oxygen consumption from the maximum voluntary ventilation (MVV) and the ventilatory equivalent for oxygen, which is the number of liters of air breathed for each liter of oxygen consumed.[82] The assumption underlying the equation is that ventilation at high levels of exertion can be predicted from the observed ventilatory equivalent at lower levels of exertion.

Armstrong and co-workers applied this equation using the ventilatory equivalent for oxygen measured during submaximal exercise and the MVV measured at rest.[83,84] Although they found a reasonable correlation between observed maximum oxygen consumption and that predicted, this technique has major limitations. The presence of a cardiovascular limitation is likely to result in an overestimation of the exercise capacity. Also, the ventilatory equivalent depends on the level of exercise at which it is measured; at low levels of exertion, voluntary increases in ventilation can raise it. There is also a normal decrease of the ventilatory equivalent for oxygen with increasing energy output until levels above 50% to 60% of the maximum oxygen consumption are reached. Thus, the predicted oxygen consumption depends on the level of submaximal exertion used to measure the ventilatory equivalent. Other factors, such as the development of hypoxemia, may also lead to increases in ventilation during exertion that are not predicted from the ventilatory equivalent found at lower levels of exercise. As a result, the ventilatory limit may be reached at a lower-than-predicted oxygen uptake.

Others have used the normally linear relationship between heart rate and oxygen consumption to estimate maximum oxygen consumption by extrapolating the observed plot of heart rate against oxygen consumption for submaximal exercise to the predicted maximum heart rate.[85–87] Factors that alter the linearity of the heart rate-oxygen consumption relationship (eg, cardiac ischemia) cause inaccuracies, however. Also, individuals may not be able to reach their predicted maximum heart rates due to intrinsic cardiac disease or medications that suppress the chronotropic response. Again, this leads to an overestimation of the exercise capacity. Overall, these methods, although of research interest, have not been found to be sufficiently accurate for individuals to warrant their general use in the evaluation of work capacity.

Limitation of Exercise Capacity

Exercise capacity is reduced in the presence of three types of respiratory impairments: those that limit ventilatory capacity, those that increase the demand for ventilation at a given level of exertion, and those that limit cardiac output.

Many of the respiratory system disorders that have been described early in this chapter diminish exercise capacity through combinations of these mechanisms.

Obstructive Airways Disease

Individuals with significant airways obstruction have a reduced maximum ventilatory capacity and may also have increased wasted ("dead space") ventilation. Thus, they reach a ventilatory limit at a lower-than-expected level of exertion. In these individuals, the minute ventilation at maximal exertion is often equal to or even greater than their MVV measured at rest.[72]

In patients with airways obstruction, shortness of breath on exertion has been shown to be related to the proportion of the MVV used during the exercise.[26,88] If minute ventilation during exercise is less than 35% of the MVV, subjects rarely complain of dyspnea; shortness of breath is usually reported when ventilation exceeds 50% of the MVV, however. Because the FEV_1 has generally been found to correlate closely with the MVV in patients with obstructive impairment, prediction of exercise capacity from the FEV_1 has a logical basis. The subjective severity of dyspnea reported during a standard exercise of walking 2 mph for 4 minutes was found to be closely correlated with the FEV_1 as a percent of the predicted value for patients with airways obstruction, but no other recognized cause for shortness of breath.[89] Maximum exercise tolerance on a treadmill was found to correlate better with the absolute value of FEV_1 than with the FEV_1 expressed as a percent of the predicted value,[90] although exercise tolerance does vary widely for a given level of the FEV_1.

The findings of a less-than-maximum heart rate, no significant lactic acidosis, and a high level of ventilation are indications that individuals with severe airways obstruction have reached a true mechanical limit to ventilation at maximal exertion. Some patients with emphysema may have significant pulmonary vascular compromise, which increases the workload of the right ventricle and thereby limits cardiac output. This vascular compromise also contributes to a limitation of exercise capacity.

When patients with obstructive lung disease and no other disabling conditions were separated into six functional classes based on a detailed history of actual activities, the overall correlation between functional category and the FEV_1 was high. Variability was great enough, however, that some individuals judged clinically as class 3 were placed in classes 2 through 5 by a prediction equation that considered FEV_1, MVV, age, and vital capacity.[91] Thus, disability cannot always be predicted by a measurement of physiologic impairment.

Interstitial Lung Disease

For patients with interstitial lung disease, symptoms during exercise are even less closely related to resting tests of ventilatory function than for patients with obstructive impairment. Correlation between the FVC or the FEV_1 and severity of dyspnea on standard exercise was only 0.4.[89] The highest correlation was found between symptoms and the lung's diffusing capacity, but even this relationship was weak (r equals 0.5). Although a previous study had shown a correlation between the diffusing capacity and both the distance walked in a 12-minute walking test and the patient's estimate of the stress of the exercise,[25] prediction of clinical incapacity from an equation based on the diffusing capacity was only moderately accurate.[92]

More recent studies have also indicated that resting tests of function are relatively poor predictors of directly measured maximum oxygen consumption. The abnormality of maximum oxygen consumption was underestimated in 23 of 61 pneumoconiosis disability claimants by resting tests and overestimated in 12 of 61.[93] When the work capacities of asbestos-exposed workers were classified into normal, low, or indeterminate categories independently using resting tests of pulmonary function and results of a progressive workload cycle ergometer exercise test, agreement was poor between the ratings.[94] Of workers whose capacity was judged normal by resting tests, 31% had a low exercise capacity. Many of these workers were felt to have cardiovascular limitations, however. Interestingly, 33% of those predicted to have low exercise capacity from resting tests actually had normal exercise tolerance.

If exercise precipitates a significant decrease in arterial oxygen tension in a patient with interstitial lung disease, ventilation may be increased via carotid body receptors. Usually exercise is terminated by the patient due to shortness of breath or fatigue. Table 13-1 compares findings at maximal tolerated exertion for cardiac and ventilatory limitations, pulmonary vascular disease, and malingering.

The decrease in pulmonary compliance associated with interstitial lung disease increases the work of breathing and perhaps heightens the patient's awareness of the high level of ventilation. Pulmonary vascular compromise may limit cardiac output, as it does in patients with emphysema. Therefore, exercise tolerance is limited by a complex interaction that causes both excessive ventilation for the level of energy output and an unpleasant awareness of that ventilation.

NATURAL HISTORY AND THE EFFECTS OF TREATMENT/ REHABILITATION

The major objectives of the medical management of patients with COPD are (1) the maximization of ventilatory function, with emphasis on the reduction of obstruction to airflow and (2) the prevention and treatment of complications, such as respiratory infections and cor pulmonale. Psychosocial adjustment is also important. Finally, because vocational capacity is often a major factor in determining patient self-image, preservation or re-establishment of the ability to work is an extremely important objective.

Table 13-1 Findings at Maximum Tolerated Exertion

	Cardiac Limitation	Ventilatory Limitation	Pulmonary Vascular Disease	Malingering
Heart rate	Near predicted maximum	Less than predicted maximum	Usually high, but may not be at predicted maximum	Normal for level of $\dot{V}_{O_2}$
Oxygen consumption as percent of predicted maximum	Decreased	Decreased	Decreased	Decreased
Ventilation	Usually less than 50%–60% of MVV	Usually at or above 70% of MVV, $\geq$ 100% of MVV	May be high, but usually not above 70% of MVV	Normal for level of $\dot{V}_{O_2}$
Lactic acidosis	Present	Usually absent	May be present	Absent
Symptoms	Fatigue predominates; dyspnea often present	Dyspnea predominates; fatigue may be present	Fatigue, dyspnea	Variable
Recovery	Slow	Rapid	Slow	Variable

Note: MVV, maximum voluntary ventilation; $\dot{V}_{O_2}$, minute oxygen consumption.

The course of COPD is a progressive reduction in ventilatory capacity with superimposed exacerbations in obstruction due to infections or bronchospasm without explicit causes.[95,96] Bronchodilating medications may ameliorate bronchospasm and are considered a standard part of management; their use should be guided both by objective measurement of ventilatory function on spirometry and by the subjective response of the patient, including reported cough frequency, ability to raise secretions, exercise tolerance, and general feeling of well-being. The administration of steroids by mouth or inhalation may reduce airway inflammation and decrease obstruction in some patients who appear to have a fixed (ie, nonbronchospastic) obstruction.[97] Because of the possible complications associated with chronic steroid treatment, dosage should be maintained as low as possible.

Newer atropine-like agents, such as ipratropium bromide, have been demonstrated to be useful in the management of chronic bronchitis, with only minor side effects presently recognized.[98] Prompt treatment of respiratory infections with antibiotics lessens the duration of symptoms and the period of reduced activity, even though many exacerbations of bronchitis may be primarily viral in origin.[99] When cardiovascular complications are present, standard diuretic therapy may relieve edema, but digitalis is probably helpful only when left ventricular failure is present in addition to right ventricular congestion.[100]

Oxygen administration in patients with demonstrated hypoxemia has proven efficacious in preventing secondary complications and reducing mortality.[101] Patients with an arterial oxygen tension of 55 mm Hg or less while breathing room air should receive continuous supplemental oxygen. Patients who have complications of hypoxemia (eg, cor pulmonale, increased red blood cell mass, pulmonary hypertension) and whose arterial oxygen tension is less than 60 mm Hg should also receive oxygen therapy.[75,88] Exercise performance is improved by the administration of supplemental oxygen when hypoxemia is present or occurs during exertion.[102] Because not all patients with COPD show worsening of gas exchange with exercise, documentation of a significant exercise-induced reduction in arterial oxygen tension is necessary to justify the use of supplemental oxygen in those who are not hypoxemic at rest.

The patient's psychosocial adaptations to the illness should be assessed. Reactive depression is quite common and may exacerbate the functional limitation.[103] The inability to participate in exercise programs and other rehabilitation activities because of depression may impede progress toward maximizing working capacity. Educational programs that stress the integration of therapeutic maneuvers into daily life may help to resolve this problem and may also increase patient compliance with prescribed treatments.[104] Patients may be able to overcome the feeling of helplessness if they understand the goals of treatment and have reasonable expectations of the progress that they can make during rehabilitation. No program for those who continue to smoke would be complete without counseling and assistance for smoking cessation. Not only does quitting give these patients a sense of accomplishment and control but also it improves their short-term ventilatory function and reduces their long-term decline in FEV_1.[31,105,106]

Pulmonary rehabilitation programs generally encompass a range of therapies aimed at maximizing functional capacity by reducing symptoms and increasing tolerance for physical exertion. A nutritional assessment and plan for correcting any deficiencies should be carried out prior to the institution of a progressive exercise program. Inadequate nutrition can contribute to functional limitation through generalized weakness, and it can reduce ventilatory capacity by impairing respiratory muscle function.[107] Breathing retraining, including diaphragmatic breathing and pursed lip exhalation, may lessen airways obstruction due to dynamic compression. Increased tidal volume with decreased respiratory rate may reduce symptoms and improve gas exchange.[108] Energy conservation and relaxation techniques may be helpful in decreasing oxygen consumption and thus reducing the demand for ventilation. An occupational therapist may be able to assist the patient in making accommodations that reduce physiologic stress in the activities of daily life and work.

Exercise training has been shown to increase exertional capacity, even if it does not improve ventilatory function.[109] Increased endurance for a given task may require specific training for that task, however.[110] Inspiratory muscle training seeks to increase ventilatory endurance by reducing respiratory muscle fatigue. Despite some documented success, improvement in overall functional capacity has not always followed such training.[111]

The overall effectiveness of rehabilitation programs for patients with COPD is controversial.[112] Symptomatic improvement has been observed in many structured programs, but until the physical impairment is quite severe, functional improvement may depend more on psychosocial factors than on physical limitations.[113,114] Patients who participate in comprehensive rehabilitation programs are more likely to work after discharge than are those who do not receive these services, but maintaining employment appears to be a more realistic goal of pulmonary rehabilitation than a return to work after a significant hiatus.[115,116]

ASSESSMENT OF WORK HANDICAP

The World Health Organization (WHO) specifically distinguishes an impairment, an abnormality in function, from a disability, the resulting lack of ability to perform an activity in the same manner as those without the impairment. The extent to which the impairment and disability results in a limitation or inability to fulfill a normal vocational role in society constitutes the individual's handicap.[117] The degree of handicap depends on a comparison of job demands and the patient's functional skills. A person who is very disabled by poor exercise tolerance may experience little handicap if his or her daily vocational tasks require only slight physical exertion. In contrast, a person employed in a heavy industrial occupation may be very handicapped by a small disability in terms of exercise capacity.

The capacity to participate in gainful employment depends then on the ability to meet the intellectual, psychologic, and physical demands of the jobs currently available in the workplace. Therefore, the social and economic environment in which the individual functions affects the vocational impact of a respiratory impairment that reduces the individual's physiologic capacity for physical exertion. The American Thoracic Society maintains that medical practitioners are unable to determine the handicap caused by a respiratory impairment because of the nonmedical factors that must be considered.[65,75] Others, however, have recommended greater participation by physicians in the process of determining handicap.[118] The physician is, after all, best qualified to assess the risk to well-being that a given level of exertion poses for an individual with respiratory and/or other impairment. When multisystem impairment is present, medical understanding of the relationship between various symptoms and physiologic abnormalities is essential for vocational assessment.

In fact, there is a need for both medical and administrative professionals to collaborate in vocational capacity determinations. Some personal characteristics not always apparent to the physician, however, such as education, training, and prior work experience, also play an important role in determining what jobs are available to an individual with a respiratory impairment. Failure to recognize the complex interaction between the medical impairment and these nonmedical factors may lead to an unrealistic assessment of the vocational capacity of the individual. Health care professionals and administrators involved in the assessment of a patient's capacity for work must recognize the less-than-direct relationship between an abnormality in a specific physiologic function and the inability to fulfill successfully the necessary role in a work situation.

Assessing the Vocational Capacity of Workers

Clearly, measurement of functional capacity in the impaired individual for the specific tasks of the work to be done is necessary for the most accurate assessment of handicap. The energy requirements of given tasks vary, depending on such factors as the individual's training and experience in performing the tasks, the pacing of the tasks, and adaptations made to accommodate a given impairment. Unfortunately, except in special instances, laboratory measures of ventilatory function and exercise capacity must be used for assessing an individual's capacity to function in the workplace. Nevertheless, even though laboratory studies of exercise capacity are often used, the conditions of the workplace should be simulated to the extent possible.

A major consideration is whether the exertion required involves predominantly the upper or the lower extremities. Work with the arms requires a higher level of ventilation at a given level of oxygen consumption.[119] Some jobs may require isometric exertion (ie, maintaining static forces) that is known to produce a greater cardiovascular response than does dynamic work at the same metabolic rate.[120] Therefore, a generalization of exercise capacity measured on a treadmill to the energy requirements of a given task in the workplace may not be valid.

Assessing the Energy Demands of Jobs

Measured Job Energy Requirements

There are several methodologies to be considered in assessment of physiologic and psychologic capacity of the worker to handle the job.

Biomechanical Approach. The mechanical work that must be performed in a job can be estimated by summing the change in position in body parts and loads over time during typical job activities. Detailed time-motion studies and models of dynamic characteristics for all component actions may be necessary to arrive at reasonably accurate estimates. These methods are suitable for intense investigation of a few types of work, but they cannot be applied to all the activities in which persons with a respiratory impairment may be involved.

Behavioral Approach. Scales, such as Borg's relative perceived exertion, can be used to rank subjective assessments of the strenuousness of various activities.[121] This approach may be useful for classifying large numbers of jobs into major categories of exertional levels and for studying the factors that affect the perception of the stress imposed by a given activity. The perception of stress correlates with the energy demand as measured by oxygen consumption, but the relationship varies with the intensity of work.[122] Light work tends to be underestimated and heavy work overestimated. This finding suggests that factors other than metabolic demand contribute to the relative perceived exertion.

Physiologic Approach. Oxygen consumption per unit time may be measured and the result used to calculate total energy expenditure during an activity. Oxygen consumption can be measured directly by collecting expired gas while the subject performs the activity, but this requires the subject to wear a relatively bulky collection device. The device may interfere with the activity under study and may significantly increase the energy required over that in the unencumbered state. A less intrusive method is to measure the heart rate during the activity and then to estimate oxygen consumption based on the direct relationship between the heart rate and oxygen consumption, which can be determined by means of a standard progressive exercise test using a cycle ergometer or treadmill in the laboratory. To characterize a given job activity, the energy expended by several individuals can be averaged. The average energy expenditure may not be a valid estimate for an individual who has either special training that increases efficiency or an impairment that reduces efficiency, however.

If it is difficult to measure oxygen consumption under actual working conditions, as often happens, the job can be simulated in the laboratory. Doing so has the advantages of lower costs, ease of testing multiple individuals, and fewer technical difficulties, although it is difficult to simulate all aspects of the work situation so that the energy demands in the laboratory are equivalent to those on the job. After establishing heart rate-oxygen consumption relationships in the laboratory during cycling on an ergometer, treadmill walking, and treadmill walking with a load, Oja and colleagues estimated the energy output of mail carriers under various working conditions from the measured heart rate.[123] The estimated oxygen consumption was consistently higher than that found from direct measurement, sometimes by as much as 66%. The correlation between predicted and observed values for walking mail delivery using a hand cart was very low (*r* equals 0.1 to 0.3). The authors concluded that energy expenditure estimates made from heart rate measurements on the job using the heart-oxygen consumption relationship determined in the laboratory were useful only if the laboratory exercise closely simulated the actual conditions of work.

Several factors may alter the heart rate-oxygen consumption relationship.[124–131] For example, high temperatures, dehydration, food or alcohol ingestion, and anxiety may increase the heart rate for a given level of oxygen consumption. When work is done in the supine position, cardiac stroke volume is essentially at its maximum value initially and does not increase significantly as energy output increases. Therefore, heart rate may be lower, but it increases more rapidly at low levels of exertion than for work done while upright. Certain drugs (eg, the beta blockers) may also decrease the heart rate response to exercise. Thus, estimates of energy requirements of specific activities arrived at by this methodology are not necessarily accurate for a given impaired individual under the actual work conditions that he or she may face.

The physiologic approach has several advantages, however. It measures all the energy expended during an activity, including internal metabolic and static (isometric) work not easily estimated by biomechanical modeling. It avoids the potential biases of subjective assessments and provides measures of absolute energy requirements for each activity, not just a relative ranking. Conceptually, in spite of its limitations, it seems the most appropriate method to use in estimating the overall stress that a job imposes on the respiratory system.

Although specific types of work have received intensive study, there have been no general surveys or reviews of the energy requirements of a variety of jobs since that of Passmore and Durnin in 1955 (Table 13-2).[132] In addition to these average results, they also presented information on an individual miner observed over a

Table 13-2 Average Energy Requirements of Various Activities

Activity	Oxygen Consumption (liter/min)	METS
Resting	0.25*	1*
Washing and dressing	0.65	2.6
Walking 3 mph	0.875	3.5
Clerical work		
Sitting	0.375	1.5
Standing	0.425	1.7
Light industry		
Light	0.4 (0.3–0.5)	1.6
Medium	0.7 (0.4–0.8)	2.8
Heavy	1.0 (0.7–1.35)	4.0
Mining		
Loading	1.4 (1–1.8)	5.6
Drilling	1.1 (0.75–1.75)	4.4

*For a 70-kg man, 1 MET equals the amount of oxygen consumed while resting and awake.

Source: Adapted with permission from *Physiological Reviews* (1955;35:801–840), Copyright © 1955, American Physiological Society.

1-week period. His energy expenditure varied from 0.32 liter/min or 1.7 METS (basal equals 1 MET) while sitting during a break to 1.34 liter/min or 7.1 METS during walking and hewing. Taking into account the percentage of time spent at each type of activity, his average energy expenditure was 0.89 liter/min (4.7 METS); approximately 40% of his time was spent at an exertion level of 2 METS or less. This illustrates the difficulty of characterizing the energy required in a given type of work by means of a single value.

Harber and co-workers studied 12 underground coal miners using the method of indirect estimation of oxygen consumption from heart rate after determining the heart rate-oxygen consumption relationship for each individual from a limited laboratory exercise test.[133] They found that the average load was quite different from the peak demand; for example, three track workers spent 50% of their time at energy expenditure levels below 3.5 METS, but had peak requirements of up to 7.65 METS. Furthermore, workers with the same job title had widely divergent average and peak energy outputs. For roof workers, the 50% percentile exertion level ranged from 1.38 to 6.42 METS, whereas the 90% percentile or peak load ranged from 4.24 to 9.4 METS. Again, it is clear that a single estimate of average energy requirement does not adequately characterize a given job.

Naturally, the mental and psychologic demands of the job play an important role in the worker's perception of the stress imposed by the work. If the overall level of stress is beyond the tolerance of the worker, the physical requirements may be perceived as unacceptably high and the unpleasant physiologic sensations increased. This factor must be considered in the overall assessment of the relationship between a worker's physiologic capacity and the demands of the job.

Factors That Affect Energy Demands

Several factors affect the energy required to accomplish the same amount of measurable external work and thus to fulfill job requirements. The use of devices to change the amount of static work can alter the energy demand significantly. For example, carrying a load with a yoke rather than under the arm can reduce the energy expended by 30%.[134] Training can also increase the efficiency with which a worker accomplishes a specific task. Patients with severe ventilatory impairments were able to achieve significantly higher levels of external work on a treadmill after specific training, even though resting tests of their respiratory function and exercise tolerance on a cycle ergometer did not improve.[110]

Pacing of tasks also alters the stress imposed on workers. Heavy work results in less cumulative fatigue and demands less cardiac work and ventilation if workers take their rest time in frequent short pauses, rather than in longer, but less frequent, breaks.[135] Blood lactate levels are higher for the same average power output when work periods and rest periods are longer.[129] If workers are allowed to set their own pace, they may accomplish the same amount of work with less physiologic strain.[136]

The use of the upper extremity muscles appears less energy-efficient than is the use of the lower extremity muscles. The same external work required a 40% to 55% higher oxygen consumption when done with the arms on an ergometer than when done with the legs.[119,137] Of special importance for persons with a respiratory impairment was the finding that ventilation relative to the energy expended was also higher for arm work. At a given level of oxygen consumption, ventilation was approximately 25% greater when the work was performed with the arms. Thus, the demand for ventilation in two jobs that require the same total energy output is significantly different if one involves primarily arm work while the other involves predominantly leg work. Isometric work is also associated with a higher heart rate, a higher level of ventilation, and a greater relative perceived exertion than is dynamic exercise.

Determining the Individual's Ability to Work

It is generally assumed that a respiratory impairment limits a person's work capacity by reducing the maximum exertion attainable before symptoms develop. Once the patient's maximum capacity for exertion has been measured or estimated and the energy requirements of the job have been determined, an index of the stress of a given job can be calculated by comparing the individual's capacity to the energy requirements. When Michael and associates investigated the relationship between the proportion of an individual's maximum capacity used and the development of unpleasant symptoms (eg, excessive fatigue) in sustained work, they found that, with only short periodic breaks, healthy subjects could maintain an energy output of up to 35% of their maximum for 8 hours without developing undue fatigue.[138] If the individual can set the pace of work, an average exertion of up to 40% of maximum oxygen consumption can be sustained.[139] For shorter periods, exertion of 50% of maximum exertion capacity can be sustained comfortably. On the basis of these findings, it can be assumed that an individual can perform a job without experiencing unacceptable stress if the average energy requirements of the job are less than 40% of the individual's maximum capacity for exertion.[75]

In establishing criteria for disability in coal miners with respiratory impairment, the Social Security Administration attempted to validate this assumption. Roemmich and co-workers estimated that an energy expenditure of 7.5 METS (1 MET [the resting level] equals 3.5 mL/kg/min of oxygen consumption or approximately 0.25 liter/min for a 70-kg individual) would exceed the demands of the majority of jobs in the general labor market.[140] They reasoned that a worker who could achieve an oxygen consumption of 1.75 liter/min or approximately 7.5 times the basal consumption rate could perform moderately strenuous work. In support of this conclusion, they found that 26% of the active coal miners whom they studied in the laboratory achieved a maximum oxygen consumption of less than 1.75 liter/min, yet were tolerating work without difficulty.

Criteria were then established for the level of the FEV_1 that was believed to be disabling for men of a given height by using an empirically derived relationship between the FEV_1 and maximum oxygen consumption. The FEV_1 values so derived are absolute values, not percentages of the predicted values for healthy persons. This approach emphasizes the amount of ventilatory function that remains (ability), rather than the amount that has been lost (impairment). It assumes that, if a certain ventilatory capacity is needed for exertion of a given intensity without unacceptable discomfort, persons with that capacity can be expected to perform at that intensity—regardless of how much ventilatory function they may have lost.

The calculations were based on an age of 50 years and were adjusted only for height. This may be construed as favoring older individuals, as a greater loss in function from the expected value must occur before a younger individual reaches the absolute value of the FEV_1 that is considered disabling. Because the ventilatory capacity needed to sustain work of a given intensity may be greater for older individuals,[137] the bias may be less than expected, however. This approach has been supported by some[28,141] and criticized by others.[89] It is still used by the Social Security Administration.[142]

The American Medical Association and the American Thoracic Society base their recommendations for rating respiratory impairment on the reduction from the expected normal value for tests of ventilatory and gas exchange capacity, but use absolute values for maximum oxygen consumption (Table 13-3).[20,65] The criterion for severe impairment of an FEV_1, which is less than 40% of the predicted value, is actually quite similar to that established by Roemmich and co-workers.[140] The absolute values that they derived are approximately 50% of the predicted value for persons aged 50 years and are therefore a smaller percentage of the predicted value for younger persons. The American Thoracic Society notes that a mild impairment is usually not associated with a diminished ability to perform most jobs, whereas a severe impairment is associated with an inability "to meet the physical demands of most jobs, including travel to work."[65] Thus, it is recognized that preparing for and getting to and from work may require more exertion than do the job-related activities of a sedentary job. Under these circumstances, the demands of the job may not be the limiting factor in determining the stress on the individual.

The American Thoracic Society recommends exercise testing only when there is a clinical suspicion that routine tests of function done at rest have underestimated the overall impairment; for example, when the reported severity of dyspnea is out of proportion to that usually associated with the level of function shown on the tests. This is more likely when the patient has multisystem abnormalities, interstitial lung disease, or pulmonary vascular disorders. It is quite unlikely that a severe impairment of exercise capacity will be uncovered in a person with completely normal resting tests, chest radiograph, ECG, and physical findings. For persons with some degree of abnormality on one or more of these examinations, however, the judgment is more difficult. Formal exercise testing may clarify the patient's condition and prevent needless repetitions of routine examinations and tests. The physician must still apply clinical judgment to the interpretation of all test results in making an assessment of the degree of impairment or, more important, the amount of remaining functional capacity.

Assessing Impairments in Special Situations

The limitations produced by some respiratory disorders cannot be characterized by the approach that has been described. In asthma, for example, airways obstruction may be markedly variable, and it is not possible to determine the impairment by routine spirometry at a given time. Because the limitation for working may be a function of the frequency and severity of bronchospastic episodes, the American Thoracic Society has suggested that severe impairment is present when asthmatic attacks require hospital or emergency room treatment approximately six times per year and wheezing is present between attacks despite

Table 13-3 Recommendations for Rating of Impairment

	American Medical Association[20]	American Thoracic Society[65]
None	Dyspnea consistent with activity OR FVC, FEV₁, and FEV₁/FVC above 95% lower confidence limit for predicted value OR $\dot{V}_{O2}$ max >25 mL/(kg min)	Dyspnea not specifically used FVC, FEV₁ and D_LCO ≥80% of predicted value $\dot{V}_{O2}$ max >25 mL (kg min) qualifies for continuous heavy exertion
Mild	Dyspnea walking uphill or fast on the level OR FVC, FEV₁, or FEV₁/FVC below 95% confidence limit but >60% of predicted value OR $\dot{V}_{O2}$ max = 20 to 25 mL/(kg min)	FVC or FEV₁, or D_LCO = 60% to 79% of predicted or FEV₁/FVC = 0.6 to 0.74 N/A $\dot{V}_{O2}$ max = 15 to 25 mL(kg min) qualifies for work requiring less than 40% of $\dot{V}_{O2}$ max
Moderate	Dyspnea on one flight of stairs OR FVC 51% to 59% of predicted value or FEV₁ 41% to 59% of predicted value or FEV₁/FVC >0.4 absolute value, but <60% of predicted value OR $\dot{V}_{O2}$ max = 15 to 20 mL/(kg min)	FVC = 51% to 59% of predicted value or FEV₁ or D_LCO = 41% to 59% of predicted value or FEV₁/FVC = 0.41 to 0.59 N/A $\dot{V}_{O2}$ max same as mild
Severe	Dyspnea after 100 meters on level at own pace OR FVC <50% of predicted value or FEV₁ or D_LCO <40% predicted value or FEV₁/FVC <0.4 OR $\dot{V}_{O2}$ max <15 mL/(kg min)	FVC <50% of predicted value or FEV₁, or D_LCO <40% of predicted value or FEV₁/FVC <0.4 N/A $\dot{V}_{O2}$ max ≤15 mL(kg min) makes unable to perform most jobs or get to work

FVC, forced vital capacity; FEV₁, forced expiratory volume in the first second of expiration; D_LCO, lung oxygen diffusing capacity; $\dot{V}_{O2}$ max, maximum oxygen consumption.

optimal medical treatment.[65] These criteria have been criticized for failing to recognize severe impairment in individuals who require large doses of medication, possibly including steroids, to suppress bronchospasm, however.[29]

Persons with bronchial hyper-responsiveness may be unable to tolerate their usual workplace environment because of the presence of irritants, including cold air, or materials to which they are sensitized, despite relatively normal spirometry test results when not exposed. Therefore, the degree of bronchial hyper-responsiveness and the amount of medication required to control symptoms should be considered in the assessment of impairment for these individuals. In occupational asthma, bronchial hyper-responsiveness may decrease or disappear after exposure to the sensitizing agent ceases, but recur after an inhalation challenge in the laboratory or re-exposure in the workplace.[61] Spirometry performed before and after workplace exposure may document acute decrements in FEV_1, but severe late phase responses that do not begin until 4 to 6 hours after exposure may be missed if studies are not continued for 12 to 24 hours. Thus, determination of the impairment of an individual with bronchial hyper-responsiveness requires an assessment of the potential for the induction of a bronchospasm by the work environment.

The presence of other conditions induced or aggravated by exposures in the workplace may require job modification or complete avoidance of the responsible agent. Pneumoconioses, regardless of the severity of ventilatory impairment at the time, are considered relative contraindications for further exposure. A judgment of the risks of further exposure at the levels likely to be present in the workplace requires both a consideration of the current level of impairment and an understanding of the natural history of the condition.

NEEDS FOR FURTHER RESEARCH

It has been assumed that the severity of unpleasant ventilatory symptoms and signs of physiologic adverse consequences during work are related in some systematic way to the proportion of the worker's remaining functional capacity used at work. An improved understanding of the mechanisms for dyspnea is necessary to find better predictors of the level of exertion or types of tasks that are likely to cause intolerable symptoms in an individual with a respiratory impairment. Prediction of exercise limitation is especially uncertain when multiple impairments are present. For patients with abnormalities that produce gas exchange impairments exacerbated by exercise, simplified exercise test protocols to predict exertional capacity must be validated. Although the influence of psychologic factors, such as motivation and tolerance for unpleasant sensations, on working capacity has been studied in patients with respiratory impairment, further work on the interaction among psychologic, emotional, and physical factors is needed. The discrepancy between the symptoms reported by claimants in benefit programs who have a given level of impairment and those reported by non-claimants with comparable objective severity of impairment has not been addressed adequately.

The energy requirements of jobs in the workplace today have not been documented adequately. The changing nature of manual tasks as a result of the increasing use of mechanical devices that potentially produce more static loads and reduce flexibility in pacing makes previous estimates of energy requirements inadequate. The causes for the large observed differences in energy use by persons apparently doing the same job successfully need further clarification. Job modifications that may lower energy demands have been applied more extensively for persons with musculoskeletal impairments than for those with respiratory disorders. The proportion of maximum capacity for exertion that can be sustained comfortably for long periods without undue distress may differ between the impaired and the healthy. Studies of sustained exertion in the impaired are needed to establish realistic expectations under varying conditions of work. Efforts should be made to determine whether job simulation in laboratories can be used to develop standardized models applicable to a variety of jobs grouped by such features as arm versus leg work, static versus dynamic loading, and paced versus unpaced work.

The role of subjective clinical impressions and judgments in the evaluation of work capacity has not been investigated systematically. The goal of future work in all these areas is to improve the objective assessment of impairment while maintaining fairness based on sound clinical judgment.

REFERENCES

1. *Prevalence of Selected Chronic Conditions, United States*. Washington, DC: National Health Survey, Series 10, No. 155; 1979–1981. DHHS publication No. (PHS) 86-1583.

2. Higgins MW, Keller JB, Becker M, et al. An index of risk for obstructive airways disease. *Am Rev Respir Dis*. 1982;125:144–151.

3. National Heart, Lung, and Blood Institute. *Fact Book, Fiscal Year 1985*. Washington, DC: U.S. Government Printing Office; 1985.

4. Hester EJ, Decelles PG. *The Worker Who Becomes Physically Disabled: A Handbook of Incidence and Outcomes*. Topeka, KS: The Menninger Foundation; 1985:68–71.

5. Thurlbeck WM. A pathologist's approach to chronic bronchitis and emphysema. In: Fishman AP, ed. *Update: Pulmonary Diseases and Disorders*. New York: McGraw-Hill; 1982:137–148.

6. Mead J, Turner JM, Macklem PT, et al. Significance of the relationship between lung recoil and maximum expiratory flow. *J Appl Physiol*. 1967;22:95–108.

7. Medical Research Council, Committee on the Aetiology of Chronic Bronchitis. Standardized questionnaires on respiratory symptoms. *Br Med J*. 1960;2:1665.

8. Thurlbeck WM, Henderson JA, Fraser RG, et al. Chronic obstructive lung disease: a comparison between clinical, roentgenologic, functional and morphologic criteria in chronic bronchitis, emphysema, asthma and bronchiectasis. *Medicine*. 1970;49:81–145.

9. Meneely GR, Renzetti AD Jr, Steele JD, et al. Definitions and classification of chronic bronchitis, asthma and pulmonary emphysema. A statement by the American Thoracic Society, Committee on Diagnostic Standards for Nontuberculous Respiratory Diseases. *Am Rev Respir Dis.* 1962;85:762–768.

10. Dunnill MS. The morphology of the airways in bronchial asthma. In: Stein M, ed. *New Directions in Asthma.* Park Ridge, IL: American College of Chest Physicians; 1975:213.

11. Winterbauer RH, Hammar SP. Sarcoidosis and idiopathic pulmonary fibrosis. In: Simmons DH, ed. *Current Pulmonology*, vol 7. Chicago: Year Book Medical Publishers; 1985:117–164.

12. Hughes JD, Rubin LJ. Primary pulmonary hypertension: an analysis of 28 cases and a review of the literature. *Medicine.* 1986;65:56–72.

13. Kilburn KH, Eagan JT, Sieker HO, et al. Cardiopulmonary insufficiency in myotonic and progressive muscular dystrophy. *N Engl J Med.* 1959;261:1089–1096.

14. Kreitzer SM, Saunders NA, Tyler HR, et al. Respiratory muscle function in amyotrophic lateral sclerosis. *Am Rev Respir Dis.* 1978;117:437–447.

15. Kafer ER. Idiopathic scoliosis. *J Clin Invest.* 1975;55:1153–1163.

16. Naimark A, Cherniack RM. Compliance of the respiratory system and its components in health and obesity. *J Appl Physiol.* 1960;15:377–383.

17. Dempsey JA, Skatrud JB. Fundamental effects of sleep state on breathing. In: Simmons DH, ed. *Current Pulmonology*, vol. 9. Chicago: Year Book Medical Publishers; 1988:267–304.

18. Gaensler EA, Wright GW. Evaluation of respiratory impairment. *Arch Environ Health.* 1966;12:146–189.

19. Richman SI. Meanings of impairment and disability: the conflicting social objectives underlying the confusion. *Chest.* 1980;78(suppl):367–371.

20. American Medical Association. The respiratory system. In: *Guides to the Evaluation of Permanent Impairment*, 2nd ed. Chicago: AMA; 1984:85–102.

21. Altose MD. Psychophysics—an approach to the study of respiratory sensation and the assessment of dyspnea. *Am Rev Respir Dis.* 1987;135:1227–1228. Editorial.

22. Becklake MR. Organic or functional impairment. *Am Rev Respir Dis.* 1984;129 (suppl):s96–s100.

23. Veterans Administration. *Physician's Guide: Disability Evaluation Examinations.* Washington, DC: Veterans Administration; 1976.

24. Hutchinson TA, Boyd NF, Feinstein AR, et al. Scientific problems in clinical scales, as demonstrated in the Karnofsky index of performance status. *J Chronic Dis.* 1979;32:661–666.

25. McGarvin CR, Artvinli M, Naco H, et al. Dyspnoea, disability and distance walked: comparison of estimates of exercise performance in respiratory disease. *Br Med J.* 1978;2:241–243.

26. Lindgren I, Muller B, Gaensler EA. Pulmonary impairment and disability claims. *JAMA.* 1965;194:111–118.

27. Coates EO. Disability evaluation in dyspneic applicants for Social Security benefits. *Ninth Aspen Emphysema Conference*; 1968:379–389.

28. Cotes JE. II. Assessment of disability due to impaired respiratory function. *Bull Physiopathol Resp.* 1975;11:210–217.

29. Chan-Yeung M. Evaluation of impairment/disability in patients with occupational asthma. *Am Rev Respir Dis.* 1987;135:950–951.

30. Doll R, Peto R. Mortality in relation to smoking: 20 years' observations on male British doctors. *Br Med J.* 1976;2:1525–1536.

31. Tashkin DP, Clark VA, Coulson AH, et al. The UCLA population studies of chronic obstructive respiratory disease: VIII. effects of smoking cessation on lung function: a prospective study of a free living population. *Am Rev Respir Dis*. 1984;130:707–715.

32. Kilburn KH, Asmundsson T. Anteroposterior chest diameter in emphysema. *Arch Intern Med*. 1969;123:379–382.

33. Banaszak EF, Kory RC, Snider GL. Phonopnuemography. *Am Rev Respir Dis*. 1973; 107:449–455.

34. Robertson AJ, Coop R. Rales, rhonchi and Laennec. *Lancet*. 1957;2:417–423.

35. Epler GR, McLoud TC, Gaensler EA, et al. Normal chest roentgenogram in chronic diffuse infiltrative lung disease. *N Engl J Med*. 1978;298:934–939.

36. International Labor Organization. *Guidelines for the Use of ILO International Classification of Radiographs of Pneumoconioses*. Geneva: International Office of ILO; 1980.

37. American Thoracic Society. Standardization of spirometry. *Am Rev Respir Dis*. 1979; 119:831–838.

38. American Thoracic Society. Standardization of spirometry—1987 update. *Am Rev Respir Dis*. 1987;136:1285–1298.

39. Ferris BG Jr, Speizer FE, Bishop Y, et al. Spirometry for an epidemiologic study: deriving optimum summary statistics for each subject. *Bull Eur Physiopathol Respir*. 1978;14:145–166.

40. Tager I, Speizer FE, Rosner B, et al. A comparison between the three largest and three last of five forced expiratory maneuvers in a population study. *Am Rev Respir Dis*. 1976;114:1201–1203.

41. Cochrane GM, Prieto F, Clark TJH. Intrasubject variability of maximal expiratory flow volume curve. *Thorax*. 1977;32:171–176.

42. Hruby J, Butler J. Variability of routine pulmonary function tests. *Thorax*. 1975;30:548–553.

43. Morris JF, Koski A, Johnson LC. Spirometric standards for healthy nonsmoking adults. *Am Rev Respir Dis*. 1971;103:57–67.

44. Crapo RO, Morris AH, Gardner RM. Reference spirometric values using techniques and equipment that meet ATS recommendations. *Am Rev Respir Dis*. 1981;123:659–664.

45. Knudson RJ, Lebowitz MD, Holberg CJ, et al. Changes in the normal maximal expiratory flow-volume curve with growth and aging. *Am Rev Respir Dis*. 1983;127:725–734.

46. Buist AS. Evaluation of lung function: Concepts of normality. In: Simmons DH, ed. *Current Pulmonology*, vol 4. New York: John Wiley & Sons; 1982:141–165.

47. Harber P, Schnur R, Emery J, et al. Statistical "biases" in respiratory disability determinations. *Am Rev Respir Dis*. 1983;127:413–418.

48. Lapp NL, Amandus HE, Hall R, et al. Lung volumes and flow rates in black and white subjects. *Thorax*. 1974;29:185–188.

49. Rossiter CE, Weill H. Ethnic differences in lung functions: evidence for proportional differences. *Int J Epidemiol*. 1974;3:55–61.

50. Schoenberg JB, Becker GJ, Bouhuys A. Growth and decay of pulmonary function in healthy blacks and whites. *Respir Physiol*. 1978;33:367–393.

51. Occupational exposure to cotton dust. Final mandatory occupational safety and health standards, CFR 1910.1043. *Fed Reg*. Dec. 5, 1978; 56893.

52. Elveback LR, Guillier CL, Keating FR. Health, normality and the ghost of Gauss. *JAMA*. 1970;211:69–75.

53. Morris JF, Temple WP, Koski A. Normal values for the ratio of one-second forced expiratory volume to forced vital capacity. *Am Rev Respir Dis*. 1973;108:1000–1003.

54. Becklake MR, Permutt S. Evaluation of tests of lung function for "screening" for early detection of chronic obstructive lung disease. In: Macklem PT, Permutt S, eds. *The Lung in Transition between Health and Disease.* New York: Marcel Dekker; 1978:345–387.

55. Soloman DA. Are small airways tests helpful in the detection of early airflow obstruction? *Chest.* 1978;74:567–569.

56. Parker CD, Bilbo RE, Reed CE. Methacholine aerosol as test for bronchial asthma. *Arch Intern Med.* 1965;115:452–458.

57. Chai H, Farr RS, Froehlich LA, et al. Standardization of bronchial inhalation challenge procedures. *J Allergy Clin Immunol.* 1975;56:323–327.

58. Guidelines for bronchial inhalation challenges with pharmacologic and antigenic agents. *American Thoracic Society News.* 1980:11–19.

59. Ryan G, Dolovich MB, Roberts RS, et al. Standardization of inhalation provocation tests: two techniques of aerosol generation and inhalation compared. *Am Rev Respir Dis.* 1981;123:195–199.

60. Cockroft DW, Killian DN, Mellon JJ, et al. Bronchial reactivity to inhaled histamine: a method and clinical survey. *Clin Allergy.* 1977;7:235–243.

61. Chan-Yeung M, Lam S, Koerner S. Clinical features and natural history of occupational asthma due to western red cedar (*Thuja plicata*). *Am J Med.* 1982;72:411–415.

62. Black LF, Hyatt RE. Maximal static respiratory pressures in generalized neuromuscular disease. *Am Rev Respir Dis.* 1971;103:641–650.

63. Ferris BG. Epidemiology standardization project. *Am Rev Respir Dis.* 1978;118 (part 2):7–113.

64. American Thoracic Society. Single breath carbon monoxide diffusing capacity (transfer factor). *Am Rev Respir Dis.* 1987;136:1299–1307.

65. American Thoracic Society. Evaluation of impairment/disability secondary to respiratory disorders. *Am Rev Respir Dis.* 1986;133:1205–1209.

66. Forster RE, Roughton JW, Cander L, et al. Apparent pulmonary diffusing capacity for CO at varying alveolar O_2 tensions. *J Appl Physiol.* 1957;11:277–289.

67. Chevalier RB, Krumholz RE, Ross JC. Reaction of nonsmokers to carbon monoxide inhalation. *JAMA.* 1966;198:1061–1064.

68. Said SI. Abnormalities of pulmonary gas exchange in obesity. *Ann Intern Med.* 1960; 53:1121–1129.

69. Miller RD, Fowler WS, Helmholtz HF. The relationship of arterial hypoxemia to disability and to cor pulmonale with congestive failure in patients with chronic pulmonary emphysema. *Proc Staff Meeting Mayo Clinic.* 1953;28:737–743.

70. Syner JC. Relation of disability to hypoxemia and congestive failure in pulmonary emphysema. *US Armed Forces Med J.* 1957;8:1577–1586.

71. Tammivaara-Hilty R. Physical working capacity in severe chronic obstructive lung disease. *Ups J Med Sci.* 1972;77:189–201.

72. Spiro SG, Hahn HL, Edwards RHT, et al. An analysis of the physiological strain of submaximal exercise in patients with chronic obstructive bronchitis. *Thorax.* 1975;30:415–425.

73. Morgan WKC, Lapp NL, Seaton D. Respiratory disability in coal miners. *JAMA.* 1980; 243:2401–2404.

74. Fulmer JD, Roberst WC, Von Gal ER, et al. Morphologic-physiologic correlates of the severity of fibrosis and degree of cellularity in idiopathic pulmonary fibrosis. *J Clin Invest.* 1979; 63:665–676.

75. American Thoracic Society. Evaluation of impairment/disability secondary to respiratory disease. *Am Rev Respir Dis.* 1982;126:945–951.

76. Wasserman K, Whipp BJ. Exercise physiology in health and disease. *Am Rev Respir Dis.* 1975;112:219–249.

77. Jones NL, Campbell EJM. *Clinical Exercise Testing,* 2nd ed. Philadelphia: WB Saunders; 1982.

78. Wasserman K, Whipp BJ, Koyal SN, et al. Anaerobic threshold and respiratory gas exchange during exercise. *J Appl Physiol.* 1973;35:236–243.

79. Spiro SG. Exercise testing in clinical medicine. *Br J Dis Chest.* 1977;71:145–172.

80. Young IH, Woolcock AJ. Changes in arterial blood gas tensions during unsteady-state exercise. *J Appl Physiol.* 1978;44:93–96.

81. Goodwin G, Shephard RJ. Body weight and the energy cost of activity. *Arch Environ Health.* 1973;27:289–293.

82. Wright GW. Maximum achievable oxygen uptake during physical exercise of six minutes duration correlated with other measurements of respiratory function in normal and pathological subjects. *Fed Proc.* 1953;12:160–161.

83. Armstrong BW, Workman JN, Hurt HH, et al. Clinico-physiologic evaluation of physical working capacity in persons with pulmonary disease: part I. *Am Rev Respir Dis.* 1966;93:90–99.

84. Armstrong BW, Workman JN, Hurt HH, et al. Clinico-physiologic evaluation of physical working capacity in persons with pulmonary disease: part II. *Am Rev Respir Dis.* 1966;223–233.

85. Astrand PO, Rhyming I. A nomogram for calculation of aerobic capacity (physical fitness) from pulse rate during submaximal work. *J Appl Physiol.* 1954;2:218–221.

86. Moritz JS, Morrison JF, Peter J, et al. A practical method of estimating an individual's maximum oxygen intake. *Ergonomics.* 1961;4:97–122.

87. Margaria R, Aghemo P, Rovelli E. Indirect determination of maximal O_2 consumption in man. *J Appl Physiol.* 1965;20:1070–1073.

88. Gilson JC, Hugh-Jones P. Lung function in coal worker's pneumoconiosis. *Medical Research Council Special Report,* 1955: Series #290.

89. Epler GR, Saber FA, Gaensler EA. Determination of severe impairment (disability) in interstitial lung disease. *Am Rev Respir Dis.* 1980;121:647–659.

90. Gilbert R, Keighley J, Auchincloss JH. Disability in patients with obstructive pulmonary disease. *Am Rev Respir Dis.* 1964;90:383–394.

91. Wilson RH, Hargis BJ, Horn RL, et al. A clinical and laboratory method of determining the degree of pulmonary disability with a proposed classification. *Am J Med.* 1964;37:251–262.

92. Wilson R. Clinical application of the single breath diffusion test as an independent variable in the prediction of degree of pulmonary disability. *Lancet.* 1968;88:71–77.

93. Vedal S, Lee-Chuy E, Abboud RT. Exercise testing in the determination of impairment in pneumoconiosis. *Am Rev Respir Dis.* 1986;133:A264. Abstract.

94. Oren A, Sue DY, Hansen JE, et al. The role of exercise testing in impairment evaluation. *Am Rev Respir Dis.* 1987;135:230–235.

95. Diener CF, Burrows B. Further observations on the course and prognosis of chronic obstructive lung disease. *Am Rev Respir Dis.* 1975;111:719–724.

96. Fletcher C, Peto R, Tinker C, et al. *The Natural History of Chronic Bronchitis and Emphysema.* Oxford: Oxford University Press; 1976.

97. Mendella LA, Manfreda J, Warren CPW, et al. Steroid response in stable chronic obstructive pulmonary disease. *Ann Intern Med.* 1982;96:17–21.

98. Gross NJ, Skorodin MS. Anticholinergic, antimuscarinic bronchodilators. *Am Rev Respir Dis.* 1984;129:856–870.

99. Anthonisen NR, Manfreda J, Warren CPW, et al. Early antibiotic therapy of exacerbations of COPD. *Am Rev Respir Dis.* 1986;133:A127. Abstract.

100. Brown SE, Pakron FJ, Milne N, et al. Effects of digoxin on exercise capacity and right ventricular function during exercise in chronic airflow obstruction. *Chest.* 1984;85:187–191.

101. Nocturnal Oxygen Therapy Trial Group. Continuous or nocturnal oxygen therapy in hypoxemic chronic obstructive lung disease: a clinical trial. *Ann Intern Med.* 1980;93:391–398.

102. Stein DA, Bradley BL, Miller WC. Mechanisms of oxygen effects on exercise in patients with chronic obstructive pulmonary disease. *Chest.* 1982;81:6–10.

103. McSweeney J, Grant I, Heaton RK, et al. Life quality of patients with chronic obstructive pulmonary disease. *Ann Intern Med.* 1982;142:473–478.

104. Mazzuca SA. Does patient education in chronic disease have therapeutic value? *J Chronic Dis.* 1982;35:521–529.

105. Buist AS, Nagy JM, Sexton GL. The effect of smoking cessation on pulmonary function: a 30-month follow-up of two smoking cessation clinics. *Am Rev Respir Dis.* 1979;120:953–957.

106. Bosse R, Sparrow D, Rose CL, et al. Longitudinal effect of age and smoking cessation on pulmonary function. *Am Rev Respir Dis.* 1981;123:378–381.

107. Wilson DO, Rogers RM, Hoffman RM. Nutrition and chronic lung disease. *Am Rev Respir Dis.* 1985;132:1347–1365.

108. Mueller RE, Petty TL, Filey GF. Ventilation and arterial blood gas changes induced by pursed lip breathing. *J Appl Physiol.* 1970;28:784–789.

109. Chester EH, Belman MJ, Gahler RC, et al. Multidiscipline treatment of chronic pulmonary insufficiency: III. the effect of physical training on cardio-pulmonary performance in patients with chronic obstructive disease. *Chest.* 1977;72:695–702.

110. Paez PN, Phillipson EA, Masangkay M, et al. The physiologic basis of training patients with emphysema. *Am Rev Respir Dis.* 1967;95:944–953.

111. Levine S, Weiser P, Guillen J. Evaluation of a ventilatory muscle endurance training program in the rehabilitation of patients with chronic obstructive pulmonary disease. *Am Rev Respir Dis.* 1986;133:400–406.

112. Make BJ. Pulmonary rehabilitation: myth or reality? *Clin Chest Med.* 1986;7:519–540.

113. Kass I, Dyksterhuis JE, Rubin H, et al. Correlation of psychophysiologic variables with vocational rehabilitation outcome in patients with chronic obstructive pulmonary disease. *Chest.* 1975;67:433–440.

114. Dudley DL, Glaser EM, Jorgenson BN, et al. Psychosocial concomitants to rehabilitation in chronic obstructive pulmonary disease. *Chest.* 1980;77:413–420, 544–551, 677–684.

115. Haas A, Cardon H. Rehabilitation in chronic obstructive pulmonary disease. *Med Clin North Am.* 1969;53:593–606.

116. Petty TL, MacIlroy ER, Swigert MA, et al. Chronic airway obstruction, respiratory insufficiency, and gainful employment. *Arch Environ Health.* 1970;21:71–78.

117. World Health Organization. *International Classification of Impairment, Disabilities and Handicaps.* Geneva: WHO; 1980.

118. Harber P, Rothenberg LS. Controversial aspects of respiratory disability determination. *Semin Respir Med.* 1986;7:257–269.

119. Vokac Z, Bell H, Bautz-Holter E, et al. Oxygen uptake/heart rate relationships in leg and arm exercise, sitting and standing. *J Appl Physiol.* 1975;39:54–59.

120. Ilmarinen J. Physical loads on the cardiovascular system in different work tasks. *Scand J Work Environ Health*. 1984;10:403–418.

121. Borg G. Psychophysical bases of perceived exertion. *Med Sci Sports Exercise*. 1982; 14:377–381.

122. Asfour SS, Ayoub MM, Mital A, et al. Perceived exertion of physical effort for various manual handling tasks. *Am Indust Hyg Assoc J*. 1983;44:223–228.

123. Oja P, Ilmarinen J, Loukevaara V. Heart rate as an estimator of oxygen consumption during postal delivery. *Scand J Work Environ Health*. 1982;8:29–36.

124. Hermansen L, Ekblom B, Saltin B. Cardiac output during submaximal and maximal treadmill and bicycle exercise. *J Appl Physiol*. 1970;29:82–86.

125. Wasserman K, VanKessel AL, Burton G. Interaction of physiological mechanisms during exercise. *J Appl Physiol*. 1967;22:71–85.

126. Astrand PO, Ekblom B, Saltin B, et al. Intra-arterial blood pressure during exercise with different muscle groups. *J Appl Physiol*. 1965;20:253–256.

127. Astrand PO, Rodahl K. *Textbook of Work Physiology: Physiological Bases of Exercise*, 2nd ed. New York: McGraw-Hill; 1977.

128. Stenberg J, Astrand PO, Ekblom B, et al. Hemodynamic response to work with different muscle groups, sitting and supine. *J Appl Physiol*. 1967;22:61–70.

129. Blomquist G, Saltin B, Mitchell JH. Acute effects of ethanol ingestion on the response to submaximal and maximal exercise in man. *Circulation*. 1970;42:463–470.

130. Smith HPR. Heart rate of pilots flying aircraft on scheduled airline routes. *Aerospace Med*. 1967;38:1117–1119.

131. Saltin B. Aerobic work capacity and circulation at exercise in man. *Acta Physiol Scand*. 1964; 62(suppl 230):6–51.

132. Passmore R, Durnin JVGA. Human energy expenditure. *Physiol Rev*. 1955;35:801–840.

133. Harber P, Tamimie J, Emory J. Estimation of the exertion requirements of coal mine work. *Chest*. 1984;85:226–231.

134. Randle IPM, Legg SJ. A comparison of the effects of mixed static and dynamic work with mainly dynamic work in hot conditions. *European J Appl Physiol*. 1985;54:201–206.

135. Christensen EH. Speed of work. *Ergonomics*. 1962;5:7–13.

136. Oja P, Loukevaara V, Korhonen O. Age and sex as determinants of the relative aerobic strain of non-motorized mail delivery. *Scand J Work Environ Health*. 1977;3:225–233.

137. Norris AH, Shock NW, Yiengst MJ. Age differences in ventilatory and gas exchange responses to graded exercise in males. *J Gerontol*. 1955;10:145–155.

138. Michael ED, Hutton KE, Horvath SM. Cardiorespiratory responses during prolonged exercise. *J Appl Physiol*. 1961;16:997–1000.

139. Astrand PO. Quantification of exercise capability and evaluation of physical capacity in man. *Prog Cardiovasc Dis*. 1976;19:51–67.

140. Roemmich W, Blumenfeld HL, Moritz H. Evaluating remaining capacity to work in miner applicants with simple pneumoconiosis under 65 years of age under Title IV of public law 91-173. *Ann NY Acad Sci*. 1972;200:608–616.

141. Morgan WKC. Clinical significance of pulmonary function tests: disability or disinclination? *Chest*. 1979;75:712–715.

142. US Department of Health and Human Services. Social Security Administration. *Disability Evaluation under Social Security*. Baltimore, MD: SSA; 1986. SSA publication No. 05-10089.

chapter 14

Vocational Capacity in Spite of Medical Impairments

Dianne M. Parrotte

When evaluating the work capacity of an individual with medical impairment, the physician must consider disease-specific, patient-specific, job-specific, and employer-specific variables. When job requirements and employer specifications are known, the worker's performance on such functional tests as the forced vital capacity, exercise tolerance tests, and lifting capacity may provide useful guidelines. Disease-specific diagnostic testing is generally not as useful in predicting vocational capacity. Although people with diabetes, renal failure, or cancer are all impaired, there are no definitive blood levels of glucose, creatinine, or carcinoembryonic antigen that indicate a mild, moderate, or severe disability. Furthermore, the symptoms caused by many of these diseases often include such poorly measurable complaints as fatigue, weakness, poor concentration, loss of mental acuity, and nausea. Rather than quantitate a symptom such as fatigue directly, a physician may derive more useful information by assessing the individual's residual capacity to function.

There are many instruments that measure function by assessing the ability to carry out the activities of daily living.[1] Some instruments are quite detailed; for example, the Klein-Bell activities of daily living scale evaluates 170 tasks as specific as "put right hand through right arm hole."[2] Others are specific to an age group[3,4] or to a disease.[5–7] In some situations, the evaluator may conduct a general overview of the patient's ability to perform self-care (ie, feeding, dressing, toileting), mobility, household activities, and/or social interactions. Unfortunately, none of these techniques has been consistently shown to be more useful than the others.[8]

Most people who are able to perform all the activities of daily living can do some type of compensable work, though in many cases with some specific restrictions upon the type and extent of activity. People who require extensive assistance for the minimal activities of daily living are likely to be disabled in the workplace as

375

well. Striking exceptions exist, however, even to this general rule. Rochlin described a severely impaired C1 quadriplegic who was able to move his eyes and speak, but was obviously dependent on assistance for all activities of daily living. In spite of his severe impairment and associated disability, he was employed as a computer programmer with a voice-activated terminal.[9]

More common than the patient who is able to perform compensable employment in spite of striking physical limitations is the patient who appears unable to work or to perform the routine activities of daily living when little physical impairment is observable. In this situation, the physician must consider psychologic impairment and nonmedical causes.

The phrase *cardiac cripple* has been used to describe the patient in whom observed disability far exceeds that expected as a result of measurable impairment. The term describes the cardiac patient who believes that physical activity will be harmful to the heart, even though cardiac rehabilitation has been successful and an exercise tolerance test and ejection fraction studies suggest that normal activity could be resumed easily. The same syndrome can be observed in patients with many other medical diseases who believe that certain activities will be harmful to their health, although there is no medical evidence to support this belief.

Once patients begin to perceive themselves as "sick" or disabled, both vocational assessment and possible return to employment become more difficult. These patients are not malingering, but believe that they are much more limited than their physical exam or laboratory data suggest. They are often supported in this belief by the behavior of family and friends. At times, the "secondary gains" of the sick role are so great that the patient is unwilling or unable to give them up. These secondary gains may be in the form of emotional, physical, or financial support that the patient would not otherwise receive. A newly diagnosed diabetic or hypertensive man may suddenly receive much more attention at home than previously when his wife needs to learn to prepare salt-free or diabetic diets. A woman with inflammatory bowel disease may be relieved of distasteful household chores while she is "sick," but would be expected to resume them if she became well enough to return to her usual employment.

Many people gain a sense of self-worth from work. The workplace may also fulfill some of their social needs. For others work is considered a dull, tedious necessity performed only for the financial reward it provides. For these people, disability insurance or workers' compensation payments may create a disincentive to wellness by relieving the financial necessity to work. Other patients will freely admit they do not wish to return to work because they dislike the boss, a co-worker, or the job or because there are social or home-related problems that complicate the ready return to work.

Most vocational capacity evaluations, however, involve a patient whose displayed disability is commensurate with expected disability based on disease state. In this case, the physician must consider the job description. A well-controlled diabetic may easily return to a 9 A.M. to 5 P.M. clerical job, but be unable to return to a swing-shift job on a loading dock that requires great variations in energy expenditure and makes the regulation of insulin difficult or impossible. If a job description is not available, the physician should make a specific statement regarding the patient's capabilities and inabilities. Returning a patient to work with a note to the employer to place the worker on ''light duty'' is fraught with peril. One supervisor's perception of ''light duty'' may differ considerably from that of another supervisor, company physician, or worker. It is more helpful to both management and employee if the physician makes specific recommendations, such as ''may return to work 4 hours daily for 2 weeks, then 8 hours daily; no lifting more than 25 lb; no repetitive lifting.'' Such declarations should be supported by objective evidence of performance.

Finally, in setting a return-to-work date, the physician may need to know the policies of the company for which the patient works. Some corporations require employees to be 100% capable of performing their previous jobs on a full-time basis before they return to work. Other companies allow employees to return to part-time work, possibly at different jobs, or are willing to modify the employees' previous jobs to suit their new physical requirements. The union may have similar policies allowing for or precluding a return to light duty.

Thus, a disability evaluation involves variables relating to the patient, the illness or injury, the job, and the employer. Such evaluations are often difficult. Although general guidelines may be developed for any given illness or injury, each case must be decided individually.

METABOLIC ILLNESS: CHRONIC RENAL FAILURE

More than 22,800 U.S. citizens develop end-stage renal failure yearly.[10] Not all of these individuals were in the work force before they developed disease, however. The Menninger Foundation has estimated that 14,800 people leave the work force and go into the long-term disability system yearly because of renal and urologic disorders.[11] Many of these workers suffer from chronic renal failure. Once established, chronic renal failure generally progresses to end-stage renal failure.[12] Regardless of the initial cause of renal failure, the disabilities that result from it are often the same. The patient may suffer from fatigue, loss of mental acuity, nausea, and vomiting.

The extent of disability that the patient suffers as a result of this condition may depend in part on the therapy that is used to treat it. Milder cases of uremia may be controlled by means of diet therapy alone, whereas more advanced cases may require dialysis or transplant. The type of dialysis chosen (ie, continuous peritoneal dialysis versus hemodialysis) may further affect the degree of disability. Diet therapy alone may not only help to relieve symptoms but also may slow progression to end-stage renal failure. Patients on this therapy may be able to maintain most, if not all, activities of daily living and will therefore have high ratings on any functional index. Although many continue to work, fatigue may cause some disability. In fact, the most common work restriction required by chronic renal failure is limitation of the number of hours worked weekly.

> *Case Study.* L.M. is a 40-year-old white man who had asymptomatic proteinuria at the age of 18 years. It was evaluated by intravenous pyelogram (IVP), cystoscopy, and renal biopsy. The biopsy results were consistent with glomerulonephritis. No treatment was given. On a pre-employment physical examination at the age of 20 years, pro-teinuria (1 +) was again noted. He was hired as a mechanic without restriction at that time. He continued to work without restriction as a mechanic for several years. When he was 30 years old, his creatinine level was 2.1 (normal up to 1.0); his blood urea nitrogen (BUN), 29 (normal up to 20). Over the next 7 years, the creatinine level rose to 4.0; the BUN, to 46. At this point, diet therapy was begun. The creatinine level continued to increase, reaching 6.8 with a BUN level of 97 in the 4 ensuing years while the patient was on diet therapy. During the last 2 years, the patient has become symptomatic with fatigue. He continues to work as a mechanic without restriction, however, and also to request overtime routinely.

Patients with more severe renal failure may require more extensive treatment than diet therapy alone. Treatment may include hemodialysis, hemofiltration, or hemoprofusion. Maintenance therapy consists of three treatments weekly of 4 to 6 hours each. These treatments may be performed at a hospital, at a free-standing dialysis center, or at home. Initially, dialysis was developed as a maintenance therapy to sustain patients until transplantation could be performed. As more equipment, personnel, and government economic support have become available, dialysis is now a therapy for all patients with kidney failure, even for those patients deemed unsuitable for transplant.

The goal of chronic hemodialysis has always been ''near-normal health and productive life.''[12] The number of patients who could be treated was limited, however, compared to the number who could benefit from the therapy. One of the criteria for selection was that the patient show potential for complete rehabilitation and full-time gainful employment.[13] Some investigators predicted that 40% of dialysis patients could return to work without any re-education or retraining. The remaining 60% would require some re-education, but would eventually return to work.[14] Other investigators suggested that more than 80% of dialysis patients would be vocationally rehabilitated.[15,16] Remmers and associates indicated that 65% of their group were working full-time.[17] More recent studies have suggested that the rate of return to full-time work is less than 50%,[18] and some have suggested that it is closer to 20%.[19–22] Youth, higher level of education, and employment prior to dialysis have all been correlated with the likelihood of a full return to employment.[20,23] Although the more recent studies do not bear out the optimistic early hopes of a 100% return to work, they do suggest that only 30% of patients on dialysis will be totally disabled and approximately 50% will be able to return at least to part-time work.[20] Tews and colleagues, after reviewing the cases of 612 patients below 60 years of age, concluded that "most dialysis patients were able to work part-time, but unable to work full-time."[23]

> *Case Study.* B.L. is a 52-year-old white man who had proteinuria on a pre-employment physical examination. At that time, his BUN and creatinine were normal. He was hired as a senior engineer without work restrictions. By 1978, his renal function had deteriorated; his BUN was 89, and his creatinine was 5.9. Berger's disease was diagnosed by renal biopsy. Home hemodialysis was begun three times per week in 1980. For the following 3.5 years, he continued to work full-time on dialysis. In 1983, a kidney transplant was performed, but the new kidney was rejected. He returned to work at that time, but was restricted to working 3 days weekly because of fatigue. He continued on dialysis and remained working on this part-time schedule until 1986, when a second transplant was performed. Complications eventually made it necessary to remove this transplant. The patient returned to dialysis. He was able to arrange for night dialysis, however, and he began working 5 days weekly without restriction of his work activities.

Renal failure may be treated with peritoneal dialysis, rather than hemodialysis. At first, peritoneal dialysis was performed as an inpatient procedure in patients whose hemodynamic status did not permit hemodialysis. As a result of advances in catheter technology, including the development of collapsible plastic containers for dialysate and appropriate tubing, continuous ambulatory peritoneal dialysis (CAPD) is now possible. Not only is CAPD less likely to cause anemia than is hemodialysis but also it frees the patient from machinery and electrical outlets.[24] Because of its convenience and simplicity, CAPD is expected to increase patient independence and improve patient mobility.[25] These advantages may lead to a greater degree of rehabilitation through CAPD than can be achieved through chronic hemodialysis, but this has not yet been demonstrated.[26]

Definitive therapy for end-stage renal failure is transplantation. The patient's rehabilitation potential is highest with this treatment. Evans and associates indicated that 74% of patients who receive a renal transplant are able to work.[22,27] This finding agrees with earlier predictions that 70% of nondiabetic renal transplant patients would be able to return to full-time work.[28]

NEOPLASTIC ILLNESSES

Each year, a million new cases of cancer occur in the United States. Thirty-three percent of American citizens will have some type of cancer other than skin cancer in their lifetimes, and 20% of these people will die of cancer.[29] Approximately 51,800 cancer patients leave the work force each year to enter the long-term disability system.[11] As newer techniques of detection and treatment evolve, more types of cancer are being cured or put into long-term remission. Survival rates for cancer have increased from 39% in the 1960–1966 period to 50% in the 1977–1983 period for white U.S. citizens and from 27% to 38% in the same time periods for black U.S. citizens.[30] As a result, greater numbers of cancer patients have been able to return to the workplace.

Statistics indicate that most people who have been treated for cancer do return to the labor force.[31] Approximately 71% of men and 79% of women with cancer returned to work in 1977.[32] At Bell Telephone Company, 88% of patients treated for genital cancer and 85% of women treated for breast cancer returned to work.[33] Of the people employed prior to the diagnosis of head and neck cancer, 62% returned to employment after treatment.[34] Sixty-four percent of patients returned to employment with their previous employer after treatment for Hodgkin's disease.[35]

The challenges of returning to work are both physical and psychologic. Some physical effects are unique to the specific cancer and to the degree of resolution obtained (ie, remission versus cure). Other effects, such as fatigue, weight loss, appetite loss, weakness, depression, and fear of recurrence, are common to all types of cancer.

When assessing a cancer patient's ability to return to work, the physician should consider the possibility that the disease or the therapy has induced a low white blood cell count, a low platelet count, or a low hematocrit. If the patient's susceptibility to infection is increased because of a low white blood cell count, it is advisable for the patient to avoid areas of possible high bacterial load (eg, working as a technician in a bacteriology laboratory, cleaning septic systems). If the patient is likely to bleed profusely, it is reasonable to avoid placing the patient in a job where the risk of trauma is increased (eg, cutting sheets of glass to handmill as lenses). If anemia is marked, it may be necessary for the patient to avoid heavy physical labor. Any patient with a history of cancer may be proscribed from working with known carcinogens due to this susceptibility. Other restrictions are unique to the specific cancer and its treatment. Thus, work limitations must be made on a patient-by-patient basis.

Breast Cancer

The most common malignancy among women is breast cancer, with approximately 130,000 new cases each year.[30] Although the risk of developing breast cancer is approximately 9%, the risk of dying of breast cancer is only 3.6%.[36] As a result, many women treated for this disease are able to return to the work force. The initial treatment of breast cancer may involve a modified radical mastectomy or a segmental mastectomy (lumpectomy) with radiation. Radical mastectomies are no longer commonly performed. Modified radical mastectomies eliminate the need for radiation therapy, but the cosmetic result is worse. Either therapy may result in some loss of shoulder motion, edema in the arm, and shoulder pain. Edema and reduced circulation may slow the healing in the ipsilateral arm if burns, infections, or trauma occur. Although most of these patients are able to return to work after they have recovered from surgery, they may need restrictions against heavy lifting or excessive pushing and pulling with that arm. Many of these women return to work at least part-time during radiation or chemotherapy.

> *Case Study.* D.J. is a 56-year-old white woman who was employed as the coordinator of an assembly team in a light manufacturing plant. She noted a lump under her left arm in August of 1984 and underwent a modified radical mastectomy for breast cancer in September of 1984. This procedure was followed by chemotherapy. She returned to work in January of 1985 while undergoing chemotherapy. She experienced extreme fatigue on chemotherapy and was restricted to working 4 hours daily.
>
> Her job required a high degree of manual dexterity and an ability not only to do the assembly work but also to teach it to others. Because her work did not routinely entail heavy lifting, her only restriction was the limitation in the number of hours that she worked. She continued to increase the number of hours worked daily over the ensuing months and has worked full-time at her original job since July of 1985.

Women with metastatic disease may be treated with chemotherapy, hormone therapy, or palliative radiation. They may suffer from weakness, nausea, or fatigue, either because of the disease process or because of the treatment. Fatigue and weakness may be accommodated by part-time work. Metastatic disease, particularly in the bone, usually requires restrictions on the patient's work. Such restrictions may include limitations in standing, walking, and lifting if the metastatic disease is in the long bones of the leg or in the spine.

Most women with breast cancer are away from work only a short time, usually from 2 to 6 weeks after surgery.[34] Sixty to eighty-five percent return to their previous employment. Those who work in traditional female roles that do not require physically intensive labor have few restrictions. As women seek more diversified, less traditional jobs, restrictions may be needed to accommodate their successful return to work.

Colorectal Cancer

More than 140,000 cases of colorectal cancer occur annually in the United States.[30] The cause of the disease remains unknown. Dietary factors are strongly implicated. A family history of bowel cancer and the presence of certain polyp syndromes increase the likelihood of this disease. Survival depends largely on the stage of disease at diagnosis.

The symptoms and treatment of colorectal cancer depend to some extent on the location of the lesion. Neoplasms in the right side of the colon classically produce iron-deficiency anemia, with few if any symptoms. Neoplasms of the left side of the colon and of the rectum are more likely to cause obvious symptoms (eg, rectal bleeding, obstruction, or pain) and thus are more likely to be diagnosed at an earlier stage.

Primary treatment is surgical. The anatomic location of the lesion dictates the selection of colectomy with anastomosis or colostomy. If the tumor has penetrated the bowel wall or if there is lymph node involvement, radiation may be used in addition to surgery. Both radiation and chemotherapy, mainly with 5 fluoro-Uracil, have been used as palliation, but chemotherapy has been only minimally successful in colorectal cancer.

The degree of disability depends in part on the therapy. Of the patients with colorectal cancer in the Rosewell Park Tumor Registry, 64% felt that they were fully capable of all normal activity.[37] If a colectomy alone has been performed, lifting restrictions may be necessary in the postoperative period to ensure that the incision heals properly. If a colostomy has been performed, there may be some physical disability, but the psychologic disability may be more serious.[38] Depending on the location of the ostomy and the type of ostomy appliance used, ostomy care may be necessary every 4 hours. Appropriate facilities must be available to the employee to perform this care. Most ostomy patients can return to work however, if their jobs do not require excessive physical movement.[39]

Case Study. D.F. is a 65-year-old woman employed as a security guard who underwent sigmoid resection for carcinoma in December 1983, followed by radiation treatment. In early 1984, she returned to her work as a security guard, which required her to lift 25 to 35 lb on a routine basis. She was restricted to lifting less than 10 lb and to working only 4 hours daily. She was able to continue her job with these restrictions until July 1984, when she developed a small bowel obstruction that required surgical resection with anastomosis of the ileum to the transverse colon. After this surgery, she developed multiple fistulas with moderate drainage. She continued to have severe diarrhea as well. After several surgical procedures to repair these fistulas, she returned to work in September 1985. She was again given a restriction against lifting and placed on a 4-hour daily rehabilitation program. She did well at work until January 1986 when she again developed multiple fistulas to the abdominal wall and one vesicocutaneous fistula. It was unclear whether these fistulas were related to the radiation treatment or cancer recurrence. After multiple surgical procedures for these fistulas, she returned to work in September 1986 with a restriction against lifting more than 20 lb and a restriction against working more than 4 hours daily. At this point, the employee requested an increase in work hours. She has continued to do well while working 6 hours daily with a restriction against lifting more than 20 lb.

Head and Neck Cancer

Forty-four thousand cases of head and neck cancer occur yearly in the United States, and approximately one third of those afflicted die of the disease.[40] Most head and neck cancer is related to tobacco and alcohol use. Early detection of small lesions may result in high cure rates, but the prognosis for patients with advanced lesions is quite poor.

Treatment for most head and neck cancers has been surgery. In the past, this surgery has often involved extensive procedures that leave marked cosmetic defects. With the newer surgical reconstructive techniques, however, the deformity is less, and the remaining function is greater. Both radiation and chemotherapy may be used in addition to surgery. Some early studies suggest that chemotherapy alone may be curative in selected cases.[41]

In spite of the newer surgical techniques, rehabilitation may be extremely difficult. In one group, 62% of patients had been unemployed prior to treatment, and these patients were considered unlikely to seek employment after surgery. Only 28% of patients who had undergone a laryngectomy returned to work; only 13% of patients who had undergone a glossectomy or pharyngectomy returned to work.[34] Because of the difficulty of relearning speech, the psychologic problems caused by deformity, and the decreased strength with limitation of movement in the upper extremities (secondary to radical neck dissection), patients with head and neck cancer are among the least likely of cancer patients to return to work.

Urogenital Cancers

Prostate Cancer

There are 96,000 cases of prostate cancer every year.[30] Because this type of cancer most commonly occurs in men who are in their sixties and seventies, it is an unusual cause of work disability. Treatment may be a combination of surgery (orchiectomy), radiation, and hormone therapy, depending on the state of the disease and the overall health of the patient.

When employment is affected, the dysfunction is more likely to result from painful metastatic disease or pathologic fracture than from the primary lesion. Disability may also result from depression about impotence or from concerns about body image after orchiectomy. Most patients without metastatic disease are able to return to work. If there are metastatic lesions to bone, restrictions against heavy lifting may be desirable.

Testicular Cancer

Although cancer of the testicle is relatively rare (5,500 cases occurring yearly), most cases occur in the working-age population (ie, 25 to 30 years old).[30] Testicular cancer most commonly appears as a painless scrotal mass. It can be extremely aggressive, but it is often curable. Treatment depends on the germ cell type involved and the state of the disease. Inguinal orchiectomy may be followed by retroperitoneal lymph node dissection removal, depending on whether or not the tumor is radiosensitive. Cure rates of 95% to 100% have been achieved in stage 1 and stage 2, with slightly lower rates of 80% to 90% in stage 2B and stage 3.[42]

The greatest disability caused by testicular cancer may be psychiatric in nature. The physician should refer the patient for appropriate treatment in this case. If metastatic disease is present, some work restrictions may be needed.

> *Case Study.* H.B. is a 28-year-old white man who developed pain in the left testicle in May of 1981 and, after his condition had been diagnosed as testicular cancer, underwent left radical orchiectomy followed by retroperitoneal node dissection in June of 1981. He developed a local recurrence in the scrotal area in November of 1981, and a regimen of chemotherapy with radiation was started. He later underwent thoracotomy for possible metastatic disease in the lungs.
>
> He eventually returned to work in October of 1982, approximately 1½ years after the lesion was first discovered. He worked as a general operator in a light manufacturing facility. Because of incisional pain in the chest wall, which was exacerbated by lifting, he was given two restrictions: no lifting more than 10 lb and no repetitive reaching. He was also limited to working 4 hours daily for several months because of fatigue. Eventually, he returned to full-time work at his previous job without restriction.

Genital Cancer in Women

There are approximately 12,000 new cases of cervical cancer in the United States each year. The highest incidence occurs among women who are in their early forties to late fifties. Uterine cancer occurs more frequently, with 35,000 new cases yearly. The highest incidence of uterine cancer is among women in their fifties to late sixties, so some of these women have left the workplace prior to diagnosis. Ovarian cancers occur at a rate of approximately 19,000 new cases yearly, with most cases occurring in a slightly older age group (ie, the late fifties to the late seventies). Many of these women will have retired from the work force before the disease is detected.[30]

Treatment of the cervical neoplasia may include hysterectomy or a combination of intracavitary and external radiation. Pelvic exenteration may be required if the disease recurs. The state of uterine cancer also dictates treatment. Abdominal hysterectomy and salpingo-oophorectomy may be used alone or in combination with intracavitary and external radiation. Hormone therapy may be useful for palliation. Therapy of ovarian cancer consists of surgery and chemotherapy, plus radiation as determined by cell type and anatomic involvement.

The type and degree of disability depend on the stage of disease at diagnosis and the type of therapy. Again, some of the symptoms may arise from either the disease process or the therapy. Weakness, weight loss, low back discomfort, and leg swelling are not uncommon. If surgery has been extensive, bladder or bowel ostomies may be necessary. If treatment included radiation or the tumor was large, enterocutaneous or vesicocutaneous fistulas may occur. Many women with genital cancer may be able to return to work after therapy, but they may need restrictions against heavy lifting, pushing, or pulling. If an ostomy has been performed, facilities appropriate for ostomy care must be available to the employee.

> *Case Study.* J.S. is a 57-year-old woman who had a total abdominal hysterectomy and bilateral salpingo-oophorectomy in August of 1980 for fibroids and endometriosis. The pathology report showed superficial papillary adenocarcinoma of the right fallopian tube. No further therapy was pursued. After the hysterectomy, she returned to her work as a laboratory technician without restriction in December of 1980. She did well until September of 1984 when she noticed vaginal bleeding. Cancer was diagnosed. She then underwent a radical vaginectomy and partial resection of the bladder. This was followed by a course of chemotherapy. She returned to work as a laboratory technician in June of 1985 without restriction of physical activity, although she was absent from work for approximately 3 days every 3 weeks for chemotherapy over the ensuing 6 months. During the time of chemotherapy, she also required multiple blood transfusions. In spite of the fatigue associated with chemotherapy and anemia, she was able to continue to work without restriction.

Bladder Cancer

Each year, there are 45,400 new cases of bladder cancer, generally in patients between 50 and 70 years old.[30] Most of these cancers originate in the transitional epithelial cells that line the bladder. Cigarette smoking, food preservatives, chronic inflammation, and certain industrial compounds have all been implicated in the causation of bladder cancer.

Superficial bladder cancer appears to be a relatively benign tumor. Ninety percent of patients with this disease survive more than 5 years. There is a much lower likelihood of metastatic disease with superficial than with invasive bladder cancer. Superficial bladder cancer can often be treated without cystectomy. Endoscopic resection or intravesical chemotherapy is commonly used. Laser therapy or radiation may also be appropriate.

Therapy for invasive bladder cancer may be radiation alone or preoperative radiation followed by radical cystectomy. If cystectomy is used, a urinary diversion (ileal loop procedure or ureterostomy) must also be created. Systemic chemotherapy is available only as a protocol for advanced metastatic disease.

As with other types of cancer, disability may arise from either the disease or the treatment. If the cancer is not cured, weakness and fatigue may prevent the patient from working full-time. If radiation has been used in treatment, the bladder may be contracted so that it requires frequent emptying. Radiation may also cause bowel irritability. These problems are chronic in less than 10% of cases. However, when they are chronic, they may limit the patient to working only in areas with close access to toilet facilities. If an ostomy has been created, heavy lifting, bending, or twisting may cause leakage. It is essential that employees with an ostomy have appropriate facilities and adequate time for proper ostomy care while they are in the workplace.[39]

Renal Carcinoma

There are 21,900 new cases of renal cancer each year,[30] generally in the 40- to 50-year-old age group. Unlike bladder cancer, which has a distinct association with exposures to various chemicals, renal cell carcinoma has not been associated with chemical exposures or with viral or hormonal etiologies.

Unless the disease is advanced, the symptoms of renal carcinoma may be subtle and variable, as is the course of the disease. Fever, hematuria, weight loss, pain, and a palpable mass in the abdomen are common. The red blood cell count may be elevated. Although an occasional patient lives for years without treatment, the natural history of the disease suggests that less than 4% of untreated patients survive as long as 3 years.

The treatment of renal carcinoma is radical nephrectomy with aggressive surgical pursuit of solitary metastatic lesions. Radiation is rarely useful because renal carcinoma is highly radioresistant. It has been even more resistant to chemotherapy. Immunotherapy with interferon may yield better results. If surgery cures the disease, the patient has no long-term disability. If the disease has metastasized, however, disability may be extensive. Restrictions on the patient's return to work depend on the location of metastasis and symptoms.

Leukemia

More than 26,000 cases of leukemia occurred in the United States in 1987.[30] Cases of leukemia are divided evenly between acute and chronic disease. The cause of leukemia is not clear, but appears to be multifactorial. Not only is there evidence of a genetic factor but also chemical exposures, particularly to hydrocarbons and alkylating agents, and radiation exposures have been implicated in the disease. Certain viral exposures may also play a role.

Although the etiologic agents may differ, the pathophysiology is similar in the acute leukemias. Stem or precursor cells proliferate, but fail to differentiate and mature normally. The end result is a decreased production of normal cells, resulting in anemia, thrombocytopenia, and granulocytopenia.

Most cases of childhood leukemia are acute lymphocytic; most cases of adult leukemia are myelogenous. The therapy for both types of acute leukemia has dramatically increased cure rates and prolonged disease-free intervals.[43]

Chemotherapy is the basic treatment for both the lymphocytic and the myelogenous leukemias. There are multiple drug combinations used in the induction phase of therapy; the second phase consists of a maintenance regimen that may last for several months and can often be administered on an outpatient basis. In patients who remain in remission, the final phase of therapy may consist of a short course of consolidation or intensification therapy.

Therapy for the chronic leukemias has not produced dramatic changes in the survival rate of patients. Both chronic lymphocytic leukemia and chronic myelogenous leukemia can be treated with chemotherapy at certain stages of the disease. Therapy in both types is aimed at alleviation of symptoms and avoidance or control of complications, rather than cure.

Leukemia may cause weakness, fatigue, fever, and weight loss. Pancytopenia, caused either by the disease or by the therapy, may result in increased bleeding and/or increased susceptibility to infection. Because induction therapy is usually administered as an inpatient procedure, few, if any, people are in the workplace at the time of diagnosis and initiation of therapy. Many patients on maintenance therapy are able to work, however. They may have absences of 2 to 3 days if maintenance therapy is provided as an inpatient procedure or is complicated by nausea or vomiting.[35] Care should be taken to place these patients in jobs where the likelihood of trauma is low (because of the possibly increased bleeding) and where heavy physical labor is not necessary (because of the possibly decreased stamina associated with anemia). If the patient's white blood cell count is depressed, it is prudent to avoid placing the patient in jobs where there is a higher than normal likelihood of exposure to infectious agents (eg, technician in a bacteriology laboratory, sanitation worker who cleans septic systems).

Lymphoma

More than 37,000 cases of lymphoma occurred in the United States in 1987.[30] Approximately 20% of patients with lymphoma have Hodgkin's disease. The etiology of lymphoma is unclear, although viruses, particularly the Epstein-Barr virus, and genetic variations expressed as chromosomal abnormalities have been implicated.

Treatment of both Hodgkin's disease and other lymphomas depends on the stage of the disease. In Hodgkin's disease, either chemotherapy or radiation therapy can be curative. If both are used, the incidence of subsequent leukemias is high. Because approximately 50% of patients with Hodgkin's disease can now be cured and the 10-year disease-free interval may be as high as 90%, many patients with this disease are able to return to the work force. Feldman's study indicated that approximately 54% of lymphoma patients return to full-time work after treatment and another 18% return to part-time work.[35] Patients treated for lymphoma may require restrictions similar to those needed by patients who return to work after leukemia treatment.

> *Case Study.* T.C. is a 45-year-old white woman who found a mass in her neck in June of 1981. Biopsy revealed Hodgkin's disease. A splenectomy and staging laparotomy were performed in July of 1981. Radiation therapy was begun in August of 1981. The employee returned to her job as a personnel administrator in September of 1981. She has continued to function well in that capacity without further loss of time from work.

HEMATOLOGIC ILLNESS: HEMOPHILIA

Hemophilia is an inherited disorder of bleeding. The severity of the disease depends on the degree of deficiency of the blood-clotting factors VIII (Type A hemophilia) or IX (Type B hemophilia). If the activity of factor VIII in the plasma is less than 1% of normal, bleeding and hemorrhage may occur spontaneously. With activity levels of 1% to 5%, bleeding occurs after only minor trauma. Hemophilia is considered severe in persons with 5% factor VIII activity or less. With plasma activity levels of 5% to 25%, bleeding occurs with trauma, surgery, or dental procedures, but spontaneous hemorrhage does not occur. Hemophilia is considered moderate in these patients. With activity levels of 25% to 50%, bleeding is severe only after major trauma, and hemophilia is considered mild. Patients with activity levels higher than 50% generally have no abnormal bleeding.

In approximately 10% of those with hemophilia A and approximately 1% of those with hemophilia B, the disease is further complicated by the presence of inhibitors to factors VIII or IX. These inhibitors do not increase the number of bleeding episodes; however, they do decrease the effectiveness of transfusions of factors VIII or IX.

The incidence of hemophilia in the United States is 1.7 per 10,000 male births.[44] Because of better diagnostic techniques, better treatment, and thus a longer life expectancy, the prevalence of hemophilia is an estimated 6 to 10 cases per 100,000.[45] The introduction of new therapy in the 1970s lengthened life expectancy dramatically. In the years 1900 to 1942, the minimal age of death for severe hemophiliacs in a Swedish population was 16.5 years; for those with moderate disease, 19.9 years; and for those with mild disease, 29.6 years.[46] This age increased in the years 1969 to 1980 to ages of 45.8, 55.6, and 66.6 years respectively.[47] As a result, there are more people with hemophilia in the workplace than ever before. Similar shifts have been shown in the U.S. population.[48,49] Prior to the AIDS epidemic, some investigators predicted a near-normal life span for patients with hemophilia.[50]

Initially, therapy consisted of whole blood transfusions when bleeding occurred. When plasma was found to be the source of the defect, plasma transfusions replaced whole blood transfusions. After the development of cryoprecipitation techniques, concentrates of factor VIII and IX became readily available.

Although extremely effective, concentrate therapy is not entirely benign. One vial of concentrate contains material obtained from between 2,500 and 25,000 blood or plasma donors.[51] Thus, there is a high risk of exposure to infectious agents, such as hepatitis and human immunodeficiency virus (HIV). Although 90% of hemophiliacs are hepatitis B antigen-positive and have mild elevations of transaminases, they do not have clinical hepatitis. More than 90% of hemophilia A patients are HIV positive, although only 1% actually have the disease.[52,53]

Factor concentrate has changed therapy from an inpatient to an outpatient procedure. Training patients in the prophylactic self-administration of cryoprecipitate has resulted in a marked reduction in the number of days in the hospital and the number of visits to the emergency room, coincidentally decreasing the number of days that these patients are away from the workplace.[54] Various studies prior to the development of this therapy showed that 18% to 35% of hemophiliacs were unemployed.[55,56] This figure had dropped to 12.8% by 1984 in a group of 4,742 adult patients.[57]

Of 368 employed hemophiliacs, 90% reported no difficulty with work and required no special restriction in their work. Of this same group, however, 25% felt that their work was not suitable for a person with a bleeding disorder because it required heavy physical labor that could precipitate hemarthrosis or carried a high risk of cuts or bruises.[58] This group averaged one bleed per month at work, usually from bumping furniture, slips, or trips, rather than from injuries related to equipment or from strains caused by lifting. Hemophiliacs in a Pennsylvania study similarly reported little need for job modification or restriction in workplace activities.[59]

Most people with hemophilia who can learn to inject themselves with factor concentrate should be able to perform compensable work. Although many report being able to perform without restrictions at work, it is reasonable to place these people in positions in which cuts and bruises are unlikely. Restriction against heavy lifting may decrease the likelihood of hemarthrosis. It is also necessary for an employee to have an appropriate area for the storage of the medical equipment (eg, vials of concentrate, syringes) needed in the self-administration of factor concentrate while at work.

DERMATOLOGIC ILLNESS

Skin is a multifunctional organ that provides protection from the environment; assists in temperature control; aids in sensation perception; prevents loss of internal fluid; and provides some metabolic function in cholesterol, steroid, and vitamin synthesis. When the skin is damaged, any or all of these functions may be impaired. Because the skin repairs itself, skin conditions are only infrequently associated with chronic disability; when they do cause disability, the period of disability is generally shorter than that associated with other diseases. Even so, approximately 10,200 people leave the work force yearly because of skin-related conditions and remain approximately 1.5 years in the long-term disability system as a result of these conditions.[11]

Many skin disorders are intermittent and cause little or no disability when in remission. Because skin is a highly visible organ, some disorders (eg, severe facial acne) may be associated with depression and lack of social acceptance. These patients should be referred for appropriate psychologic evaluation and counseling. Among the diseases likely to cause long-term disability are psoriasis and hidradenitis suppurativa.

Psoriasis

Caused by abnormalities in the keratinizing process of the skin and changes in the vascular system of the skin, psoriasis has a hereditary component as well. The disease is common, occurring in the United States with a prevalence of 0.5% to 2.8%.[60,61] It is a disease of the working-age group in that it is rarely seen before the age of 10 years.[62] The increased cellular proliferation results in an erythematous plaque covered with thick, silver-white, flaking scales. Lesions are common on the bony prominences, but may also occur in intertriginous areas. In severe cases, all of the skin may be involved.

Treatment depends on the extent and severity of the disease. Topical glucocorticoids may be used with or without occlusive dressings. Ultraviolet therapy may be used alone or in conjunction with psoralens. Methotrexate has been used in severe cases, but the liver toxicity of this drug limits its usefulness. Severe episodes may require hospitalization, not only for treatment of the psoriasis but also for management of metabolic abnormalities as a result of fluid and electrolyte loss from damaged skin or secondary infection.

Most patients with mild to moderate forms of psoriasis are able to maintain all activities of daily living, although they may need protective clothing for some activities (eg, gloves to wash dishes). Forty-four percent of psoriasis patients report functional difficulties at work.[63] At least some of these difficulties may be overcome by the use of protective clothing and appropriate work placements, however.

> *Case Study.* D.P. is a 61-year-old white woman who developed mild psoriasis in her early forties. The disease began as small patches, but eventually affected the entire body. She was hospitalized and treated with methotrexate. When elevations in liver enzymes developed, the methotrexate was discontinued. Therapy with topical steroids and antihistamines was started.
>
> She returned to work as a quality control inspector. Her work required continuous handling of small piece parts. Initially, this contact exacerbated the psoriasis on her hands, but she found that wearing cotton gloves allowed her to perform inspection work without irritating her skin. She began to receive ultraviolet therapy as an outpatient. One year later, she developed a skin cancer that was believed to be secondary to the ultraviolet therapy. The cancer was treated with an excisional biopsy.
>
> A second attempt at therapy with methotrexate again resulted in elevations of liver function that made it necessary to discontinue the drug. Most recently therapy with etretinate has been started. The patient continues to function well in her quality control job as long as she is able to use the appropriate protective clothing.

Hidradenitis Suppurativa

Although hidradenitis suppurativa is a rare disease, it may cause disability and even death when it is severe.[64] Inflammation of the apocrine glands in the groin and axilla occurs after keratin plugging has occluded these glands.[65] Repeated episodes result in fibrotic scarring and occasional sinus tract formation. Suppuration with marked drainage may occur.

Treatment includes the administration of topical and systemic antibiotics, as well as incision and drainage of localized areas. More severe cases may require surgical excision and, occasionally, the creation of skin flaps.[66] More recently, Accutane has been used. In extreme cases, steroids and radiation have been used in treatment.[67]

Disability may arise from pain caused by the lesions. Excessive drainage from these lesions requires frequent dressing changes, which may make it difficult for the patient with hidradenitis suppurativa to work. Fibrosis may limit the range of motion in the upper extremities.

> *Case Study.* W.L. is a 32-year-old man with hidradenitis suppurativa who developed carbuncles on his neck at the age of 16 years. These carbuncles required surgical incision and drainage.
>
> At the age of 22 years, he developed extensive carbuncles on the buttocks; these were treated with incision and drainage in conjunction with oral antibiotics. This eventually led to surgical resection, with a flap repair of the buttocks. Multiple draining sinus tracts developed in this area. At the age of 28 years, he started taking antibiotics and Accutane. The lesions spread to the groin and the axillary area. Pain from the lesions prevented him from sleeping without analgesics. He was out of work for a time during this period because of pain and excessive drainage. Cortisone injections were utilized in the buttocks, and a 10% benzoyl peroxide solution was applied topically.
>
> At the age of 31 years, he was working as an operator in a light piece parts factory, where the job required him to sit on a moving belt line. He experienced a flare-up of his hidradenitis suppurativa in the buttocks, and sitting became painful. Prolonged sitting also led to an accumulation of malodorous drainage. He was out of work for several months as a result.
>
> The patient was eventually asked to seek an independent evaluation from a third physician who, because of W.L.'s sitting difficulties, declared him ''100% disabled for performing a useful occupation, even on a part-time basis.''
>
> The patient elected to return to work within 4 weeks of this evaluation, despite receiving full pay while he was out of work. He was given restrictions against working more than 4 hours/day and against sitting for more than 10 minutes. He returned to work full-time within 6 months with a restriction against sitting for more than 10 minutes. He also has a restriction against excessive reaching with his right arm, because scarring and fibrosis have reduced the range of motion in that extremity.

ENDOCRINE ILLNESS: DIABETES MELLITUS

More than 5% of the total U.S. population has diabetes mellitus, and the diabetic population is expected to double in the next 15 years. The economic cost of diabetes is more than $10 billion yearly.[68]

Diabetes is not a single disease.[69] This fact was recognized in the early terminology, under which the disease in each patient was classified as either of juvenile onset or of adult (maturity) onset. Terminology has frequently changed to reflect the various pathophysiologies (eg, ketosis-prone, ketosis-resistant) or to reflect the various treatment strategies (eg, insulin-dependent, non-insulin-dependent).

Both juvenile and adult forms of diabetes are believed to result from a combination of environmental and genetic factors. Insulin-dependent diabetes may result from damage to the pancreatic beta cells caused by a virus. A genetic factor is also involved, but alone is not sufficient for the development of disease. Studies have shown only 40% concordance in the development of insulin-dependent diabetes in identical twins; in contrast, there is 100% concordance in the development of non-insulin-dependent diabetes in identical twins.[70-72] Although genetic factors clearly play a role in non-insulin-dependent diabetes, other factors, including obesity, are also important. The patient with insulin-dependent diabetes has an absolute insulin deficiency compared to the relative insulin deficiency in the patient with non-insulin-dependent diabetes mellitus. In addition, many patients with non-insulin-dependent diabetes, especially the obese, demonstrate resistance to the effects of insulin. This difference of absolute versus relative deficiency dictates treatment.

Treatment of diabetes mellitus ranges from diet alone, diet plus oral agents, to diet plus insulin. In patients with mild, non-insulin-dependent diabetes, weight reduction and diet alone may control the disease. If not, oral agents (ie, sulfonylureas) may be used in addition to diet. The mechanism of action is not clear; however, these agents stimulate beta cells to release more insulin. Because a functioning beta cell must be present before these drugs can be effective, they are useful in non-insulin-dependent diabetes, but not in insulin-dependent diabetes. Although it is possible to have hypoglycemic episodes on longer acting oral agents (eg, chlorpropamide), such an occurrence is rare. Insulin may be needed for the patient with non-insulin-dependent diabetes that cannot be controlled with oral agents. Insulin is necessary for patients whose pancreatic beta cells cannot be stimulated to produce insulin.

Although the types of insulin and the methods of administration have changed,[73] much of the regimen for insulin therapy remains the same. Patients take insulin in single or multiple bolus doses or by continuous infusion pump. The risk of hypoglycemic episodes (insulin reactions) does not decrease when the patient receives the insulin by continuous administration pump, rather than by multiple daily injections.[74]

Complications of diabetes may be severe. The likelihood of blindness in a diabetic is 25 times that in the nondiabetic population; that of renal disease, 17 times greater; and that of cardiovascular disease, 2 times greater.[75] It remains unclear at this time whether stricter control of blood sugar will prevent some of these complications.[76]

According to most studies, the ability of diabetics to perform compensable work is related to the type of treatment and the severity of complications. For those who have suffered blindness, renal failure, or myocardial infarction, the ability to work depends not only on the diabetes but also on any disability caused by complications. Diabetics who have no complications and are able to control their disease by diet alone should be able to work without restriction.[77–79] Those able to control their disease with oral agents should be able to perform most types of employment, although in some countries, they may not be allowed to join the armed services, police or fire brigades, or merchant navy, or to fly commercial airlines because of concern over possible hypoglycemic reactions. There is no good documentation, however, that diabetic persons who take oral agents have harmed themselves during hypoglycemic episodes.[80]

The frequency and severity of hypoglycemic reactions are greater in patients with insulin-dependent diabetes than in those with non-insulin-dependent diabetes. To help avoid these reactions, the worker with insulin-dependent diabetes should avoid frequent shift changes. Employment that requires a relatively even level of physical activity rather than having intense peaks and lulls is also preferable. Diabetic employees may need access to appropriate facilities for storing and administering insulin.

Decisions concerning restrictions for diabetic workers must be made on a patient-by-patient basis. For example, a patient who has had multiple hypoglycemic episodes may risk injury by working around any mechanical equipment. A restriction against driving motor vehicles seems reasonable in an insulin-dependent diabetic who experiences multiple hypoglycemic reactions weekly. Such a restriction, however, may be excessive for a worker with insulin-dependent diabetes who has not had such an episode in several years. In spite of the possible need for restrictions in the workplace, at least one study has shown little difference in employment rate between diabetics and the general population.[81] Furthermore, the overall work record of diabetics shows no excessive employer bias against hiring diabetics.

Case Study. M.O. is a 46-year-old white man who developed insulin-dependent diabetes at the age of 11 years. During a pre-employment physical at the age of 26 years, he was noted to be on 18 units of regular insulin and 25 units of Lente daily. It was believed that his disease was under control, and he was designated ''fit for any work.'' He was hired without restriction as an engineer. Over the ensuing years, he had several insulin reactions. One of these resulted in a motor vehicle accident, resulting in a subdural hematoma that required surgical removal. Another occurred while he was cleaning his auditory canal, resulting in a ruptured eardrum. Because his work did not require him to use company automobiles or power equipment (eg, a fork truck), or to work on any moving belt operations, no restriction concerning these activities was written. In the early 1980s, he began to use home blood monitoring procedures, resulting in better control of his diabetes and fewer insulin reactions. He continues to be employed as an engineer without restriction.

DIGESTIVE DISEASE: INFLAMMATORY BOWEL DISEASES

Inflammatory bowel disease is a group of heterogeneous disorders with similar symptomatology. The two most common diseases in this group are ulcerative colitis and Crohn's disease (regional enteritis). The incidence of these diseases ranges between 5 to 15 new cases per 100,000.[82] Onset of both diseases most commonly occurs between the ages of 15 and 25 years.[83] Mortality rates in the United States range from 1 per million in the 20- to 29-year-old age group to 3 to 4 per million in the 50- to 59-year-old age group.[84] The death rate for both seems to be declining in the United States.[85] The disease itself, complications of medical or surgical treatment, or the late development of colon cancer may be the cause of death.[86]

The etiology of inflammatory bowel disease is unclear. Multiple genetic and environmental factors have been cited in many different studies.[87,88] Although the pathophysiology of ulcerative colitis differs from that of Crohn's disease, the symptoms may initially be similar. Ulcerative colitis may begin with constipation, rectal urgency, and the passage of mucus-containing stools. Eventually, diarrhea and constitutional symptoms, such as fever, fatigue, and weight loss, begin. Antidiarrheal agents may be used to treat mild cases. Sulfasalazine may maintain the patient in remission. Topical steroids by enema may be useful in acute episodes; systemic steroids may also be necessary. Even with full medical treatment, recurrence is common. Surgery may be necessary to handle complications, such as perforation, stricture, or cancer.

The incidence of colon cancer increases markedly with the number of years that a patient has ulcerative colitis; many of these patients eventually undergo total colectomy with ileostomy. This surgery effectively controls the disease, and the patient can experience a normal life span. Strictures, especially in the rectosigmoid area, also may require surgery. The disease may be complicated by skin lesions and arthritis.

Patients with Crohn's disease experience abdominal pain, diarrhea, fatigue, and weight loss. They frequently develop fistulas from the colon to the bladder or to the skin. The treatment for mild cases may be antidiarrheals, sulfasalazine, or systemic steroids. Surgery may be needed for fistulas and stricture, but the surgery is rarely curative. In spite of this, the mortality rate of patients with Crohn's disease remains considerably lower than that of patients with ulcerative colitis.

Because of frequent attacks, occasional hospitalizations, and the occasional need for surgery, patients with inflammatory bowel disease may have a high rate of absenteeism from work. In one study, 20% of ulcerative colitis patients felt that their earning capacity was limited by their disease.[89] In a group of patients with Crohn's disease, 6% no longer worked because of the disease, 13% worked part-time, and the remaining 81% were able to maintain their full-time employment.[90] Because toilet facilities must be nearby, both for diarrhea and for ostomy care, special restrictions may be needed upon return to work. Other restrictions depend on the degree of fatigue due to anorexia and/or anemia.

> *Case Study.* J.S. was a 34-year-old white man who developed bloody diarrhea in 1971. Workup at that time revealed Crohn's disease involving the colon, rectum, and distal ileum. In October of 1973, he underwent an ileostomy. In June of 1974, a flare-up resulted in a total colectomy. In July of that year, proctectomy was also performed. He was able to avoid further surgery until February of 1977 when a revision of his ostomy was done after a bowel obstruction.
>
> In August of 1977, he applied for a job as a material specialist. The job description indicated that the requirements were mathematic ability, reading ability, driving a forklift, and handling materials weighing up to 50 lb. After a preplacement physical, he was hired for this position without restriction. He did well from 1977 until 1983, when he was out of work for several months for a resection of the small bowel and a revision of the ileostomy secondary to torsion. He returned to work after the surgery with a restriction against lifting more than 20 lb and against lifting any weight repetitively. He continued to do well at work until April of 1986, when he again entered the hospital for a gastroenterostomy for relief of a gastric outlet obstruction. He returned to work 2 months after this surgery, but was restricted to working 4 hours daily for the initial 2 to 3 weeks. He was restricted during the ensuing months from lifting more than 15 lb or from lifting any weight repetitively, but continues in his job as a material specialist by using driver-operated equipment for lifting heavier loads.

CARDIOVASCULAR ILLNESS: HYPERTENSION

Approximately 60 million U.S. citizens have hypertension.[91] More than half of these are in the workplace. Slightly more than 7,000 workers leave the work force yearly to enter the long-term disability system.[11] Many of these employees are disabled by complications of hypertension, rather than by the hypertension itself. Medical care costs due to hypertension are estimated to be between $12 and $16 billion each year, with industry paying more than half of the bill.[92]

Ninety percent of people with high blood pressure suffer from essential hypertension. Although the etiology is unknown, it is believed to be multifactorial. Alterations in the sympathetic nervous system, changes in the renin-angiotensin system, deficiencies of vasodilators, and hereditary sensitivity to sodium intake have all been causally implicated. In the remaining 10% of cases, hypertension is caused by renal, vascular, or endocrine disease.

Hypertension generally has no symptoms, but if it remains untreated, it can lead to stroke, myocardial infarction, renal failure, congestive heart failure, and sudden death. Treatment depends in part on cause. Nonpharmacologic measures in the treatment of essential hypertension include weight reduction, low-sodium diets, aerobic exercise programs, relaxation, and stress reduction techniques. If these measures do not adequately reduce the patient's blood pressure, a stepped-care drug regimen is instituted.

The introduction of angiotensin-converting enzyme inhibitors, beta blockers, calcium channel blockers, and select vasodilators has revolutionized the pharmacologic treatment of hypertension. Several excellent reviews detail specifics of treatments and possible side effects of these medicines.[93–95]

In secondary forms of hypertension, correction of the primary abnormality may normalize the blood pressure. Diseases that damage renal parenchymal tissue may result in hypertension; therefore, pyelonephritis, glomerulonephritis, connective tissue disease, and diabetes should be controlled promptly to avoid this complication. Hypertension secondary to vascular disease, such as renal artery stenosis and coarctation of the aorta, can be corrected surgically. Surgery can also correct hypertension caused by pheochromocytomas and hyperparathyroidism.

Since uncomplicated hypertension generally causes no symptoms, it might be anticipated that this condition is seldom associated with disability. Although the disease does not cause symptoms, the hypertensive "label" does appear to adversely affect life quality.[96] In one study, 75% of hypertensive patients reported at least one symptom that they attributed to the disease.[97] Furthermore, several studies have demonstrated that absenteeism from work increases after a diagnosis of hypertension has been made.[98–100] In a Canadian study, it was found that absenteeism not only increased, but also remained high over a 4-year follow-up period.[101] In some studies, investigators found increased absenteeism among workers who were mistakenly labeled as hypertensive.[102,103] These studies suggest that this increase in absenteeism is not due to the disease process or even to side effects of treatment, but is due to the patients' new perception of themselves as "sick."[104] Treatments that include extensive patient teaching and frequent support with follow-up visits help to decrease absenteeism in newly diagnosed hypertensives.[105]

If hypertension is mild and treatment is dietary, there is little need for restriction in the workplace. If hypertension is moderate or severe and requires drug therapy, the side effects of the therapy may result in disability. Many antihypertensive drugs cause drowsiness or orthostatic hypotension. If the medical regimen cannot be altered to avoid these side effects, the patient should be restricted from working with hazardous equipment, or in any other job that requires alertness to avoid injury. The employee whose blood pressure is not yet controlled should be restricted from heavy lifting or pushing that can cause acute, dangerous elevation of blood pressure. Because sudden death is known to be associated with untreated hypertension, the uncontrolled hypertensive should be restricted from working in jobs in which an acute hypertensive episode or sudden death would endanger others (eg, commercial airline pilot, public bus driver).

Emotional stress may exacerbate hypertension. Physicians may therefore advise patients to avoid stressful situations. Following this advice may, however, be difficult in the workplace. Although one employee may find the boredom of working in a low-production area stressful, another employee may find working in a fast-moving conveyor belt operation stressful. Creating a stress-free workplace is not a realistic goal. Relaxation exercises or meditation may be useful for the worker susceptible to stress. As a last resort, referring such a patient to an employment counselor or a personnel administrator for counseling, retraining, or reassignment to another position may be necessary.

Chronic exposure to some heavy metals (ie, lead, mercury, cadmium) can result in hypertension. Other potential worksite causes of hypertension include carbon disulphide, vinyl chloride, pesticide, herbicide, and phthalate plasticizer exposures.[106] The hypertensive patient should be advised to avoid such an exposure, either by avoiding work that involves these materials or by using appropriate personal protective equipment when working with such substances. The same advice applies to working with any agent that can interact adversely with a patient's antihypertensive medications.

Patients who have suffered complications of hypertension, such as stroke, myocardial infarction, or renal failure, are generally more likely to have a vocational disability than are those with uncomplicated hypertension. Their ability to return to work depends on the severity of damage to end-organ systems. All well-controlled, uncomplicated hypertensives should be able to return to full-time employment. At least one study has suggested that unemployment itself is a risk factor for hypertension: diastolic hypertension was present in 27% of the unemployed population, but in only 12% of those employed.[107] Furthermore, if a hypertensive employee is returning to employment at a company with a worksite screening and follow-up hypertension program, the likelihood of good blood pressure control is greater for that employee than for a patient who is followed by a private physician or by a hospital clinic. In this case, a return to work may not be only safe, but also medically beneficial to the hypertensive patient.[108-112]

Case Study. D.G. is a 40-year-old man who works as an air-conditioning maintenance repairman. At his pre-employment physical examination approximately 18 years ago, he was noted to be in good health and was hired without restriction. He received several citations for perfect attendance in the 1970s and 1980s.

In early 1986, he developed a persistent cough, for which he saw a physician. An elevation of blood pressure was noted. Readings remained high. Therapy with a beta-blocking agent was initiated, and the dosage was slowly increased to obtain good control of blood pressure. During the next 12 months, his rate of absenteeism rose from 0% to 20%. He experienced headaches and episodes of flushing, which he felt were caused by his hypertension. He had never been ill prior to the diagnosis of hypertension. He stated that, since he turned 40 and developed hypertension, his "body was falling apart." Even though he was still physically capable of performing all job-related duties, he expressed concern that his body would "betray him" and he would no longer be able to earn enough to support his family. A chance inquiry by the company physician revealed that a great deal of his anxiety was due to a loss of sexual potency secondary to the medication, and an alternative treatment was chosen.

Follow-up appointments with this physician had initially been scheduled every 1 to 2 weeks to regulate blood pressure medication, but it was felt that the frequency of these visits might be adding to the patient's altered view of himself as a "sick person." The frequency of physician visits was decreased, while a reassuring, supportive atmosphere was maintained during each visit. The physician emphasized that his blood pressure was under excellent control and that there were likely to be no complications of high blood pressure. The patient was also referred to a supportive and insightful clinical social worker. By late 1987, his absenteeism had dropped from 20% per month to 3%, the norm for the company.

AN ACTUAL RETURN-TO-WORK PROGRAM IN INDUSTRY

The Polaroid Corporation is self-insured for its "sick pay" or short-term disability system. If an employee is absent from work because of illness or injury for more than 5 days, he or she must submit to the corporate benefits system a form from the private physician with a diagnosis and the estimated length of disability. Employees who are 100% disabled continue to receive 100% of their pay for up to 52 weeks.

The corporate medical director reviews all forms submitted. If, upon reviewing a diagnosis and the estimated length of disability, the corporate medical director feels that the patient is not 100% disabled or that the estimated length of disability seems greater than expected for the specific diagnosis, there are three options. First, the medical director may call the private physician and explain Polaroid's disability policy. The private physician who indicated, for example, that a loading dock worker with a fractured tibia would be disabled for 3 months may allow the patient to return to work sooner when informed that Polaroid will provide medical parking immediately adjacent to the building, a sit-down job with leg elevated, and other accommodations.

Second, the medical director may request that the employee see one of the Polaroid physicians. After examining the employee and any relevant records, the Polaroid physician may agree that the employee is, in fact, temporarily 100% disabled. Alternatively, the Polaroid physician may determine the patient is only partially disabled. The physician will then offer the employee an opportunity to return to work under circumstances modified to suit his or her medical condition. If the employee decides not to return to modified work, a specialist is chosen to perform an independent medical evaluation (see Chapter 1). The result of that evaluation is binding on both the employee and the company. If the independent physician states that the employee is 100% disabled, the employee continues to receive 100% of pay until he or she is well or has exhausted 52 weeks of disability pay. (At that point, the employee is eligible for the long-term disability program.) If the independent physician finds the employee less than 100% disabled, the employee must return to modified work or the sick pay will be discontinued.

The employee returning to modified work is re-examined by a Polaroid physician and given a temporary restriction form for his or her supervisor. This form does not indicate the diagnosis, but does indicate the number of hours per week that the employee should work and the types of activities that the employee is medically restricted from performing. Specific restrictions may be to work only 4 hours daily, to lift no more than a certain number of pounds, or to avoid repetitive pushing with the left hand. Corporate policy specificaliy requires supervisors to make all reasonable effort to modify jobs, when possible, to be consistent with these restrictions.

Temporary restrictions may be written for as long as 3 months. If the employee's condition has not resolved by this time, an indefinite medical restriction is written. These are reviewed once each year and modified as necessary. Copies of indefinite medical restrictions are given to the employee, to the supervisor, to the personnel administrator, and to the union representative, if the employee requests that the union representative have a copy.

Once an indefinite medical restriction has been issued, the personnel administrator aids management in altering the job or finding a different placement for the employee. Job alterations generally consist of simple changes, such as lowering the height of a work station so that a job previously done in the standing position can be done in the sitting position. Expensive alterations are usually avoided by placing the employee in a different job. For example, if a dusty packaging area meets the air quality requirements of the federal government, but is still dusty enough to aggravate an employee's asthma, the company is unlikely to install a different ventilation system. Instead, an effort would be made to place the employee in an area free of dust or chemical fumes.

Several restrictions are not considered appropriate in Polaroid's short-term disability system. These include restrictions to specific shifts or to specific work sites. Although certain medical problems (eg, insulin-dependent diabetes) make it unwise for an employee to change shifts frequently, there are few, if any, medical conditions that require an employee to work a specific shift. An employee may prefer working at a location close to home rather than at one more distant, and his or her physical condition may make long automobile drives difficult. Rather than regulating this type of problem with medical restrictions, responsibility of obtaining appropriate transportation to work (eg, public transportation versus driving, or company-sponsored car pools) is left to the employee.

It is clearly in the best interests of management and personnel to make any reasonable adjustment that allows impaired employees to return to modified work. The system of restrictions has been developed to assist them in doing so. When the problem cannot be dealt with appropriately by a medical restriction, the patient is referred to the personnel department for further assistance in resolving the issue. The medical department may participate in negotiations between management and the employee to ensure an appropriate placement.

CONCLUSION

Most patients with medical illnesses can perform some type of employment. Obviously, during an acute flare-up of disease, they may be absent from work. Many are able to return to their previous work without restriction once a flare-up has subsided; others require restrictions of work hours, weights lifted, or environmental exposures in order to return to work successfully. Assessments of work capacity and restrictions must be made on a case-by-case basis, since no single standardized instrument has yet been developed to evaluate these patients adequately or efficiently.

REFERENCES

1. Feinstein AR, Josephy BR, Wells CK. Scientific and clinical problems in indexes of functional disability. *Ann Intern Med.* 1986;105:413–420.

2. Klein RM, Bell B. Self-care skills: behavioral measurement with Klein-Bell ADL Scale. *Arch Phys Med Rehabil.* 1982;63:335–338.

3. Kane RA, Kane RL. *Assessing the Elderly: A Practical Guide to Measurement.* Lexington, MA: Lexington Books, DC Health; 1981.

4. Moskowitz E, McCann CB. Classification of disability in the chronically ill and aging. *J Chronic Dis.* 1957;5:342–346.

5. Feigenson J, Polkow L, Meikle R, Ferguson W. Burke Stroke Time-Oriented Profile (BUSTOP): an overview of patient function. *Arch Phys Med Rehabil.* 1979;60:508–511.

6. Lee P, Jasani MK, Dick WC, Buchanan WW. Evaluation of a functional index in rheumatoid arthritis. *Scand J Rheumatol.* 1973;2:71–77.

7. Colville PL. An assessment of IFMSS 1982 minimal disability rating system. *Acta Neurol Scand.* 1984;101(suppl):58–64.

8. Sheikh K. Diability scales: assessment of reliability. *Arch Phys Med Rehabil.* 1986;67:245–249.

9. Rochlin JF. Retention of workers: a challenge for American business and industry. In: Woods DE, ed. *Employer Initiatives in the Employment Re-employment of People with Disabilities: Views from Abroad.* New York: World Rehabilitation Fund; 1985:123–126.

10. Hakim RM, Lazanis JM. Medical aspects of hemodialysis. In Brenner JM, ed. *The Kidney.* Philadelphia: WB Saunders; 1986:1824.

11. Hester EG, Decelles PG. *The Worker Who Becomes Physically Disabled: A Handbook of Incidence and Outcomes.* Topeka, KS: The Menninger Foundation; 1985.

12. Murray JS, Pendras JP, Lindholm DD, Erickson RV. Twenty-five months experience in the treatment of chronic uremia at an out-patient community hemodialysis center. *Trans Am Soc Artif Intern Organs.* 1964;10:191–199.

13. Scribner BH, Fergus EB, Boen ST, Thomas ED. Some therapeutic approaches to chronic renal insufficiency. *Annv Rev Med.* 1965;16:285–300.

14. Rettig RA. End stage renal disease and the "cost" of medical technology. In: Blandon R, Altman S, eds. *Medical Technologies—The Culprit behind Health Care Costs?* Santa Monica, CA: Rand Corp; 1977:190–191.

15. Blagg CR, Hickman RO, Eschbach JN, et al. Home hemodialysis: six years experience. *N Engl J Med.* 1970;283:1126–1131.

16. Bryan FA Jr. *The National Dialysis Registry: Fifth Annual Report.* Bethesda, MD: National Institute for Arthritis, Metabolism and Digestive Diseases; 1972.

17. Remmers AR, Lindley JD, Cotton DL, et al. Home dialysis: a 6-year experience with 107 consecutive patients. *Trans Am Soc Artif Intern Organs.* 1974;20:184–187.

18. Roberts JL. Analysis and outcome of 1063 patients trained for home hemodialysis. *Kidney Int.* 1976;9:363–374.

19. Bonney S, Finkelstein FO, Lytton B, et al. Treatment of end stage renal failure in a defined geographic area. *Arch Intern Med.* 1978;138:1510–1513.

20. Gutman RA, Amara AH. Outcome of therapy for end-stage uremia. *Postgrad Med.* 1978;64:183–194.

21. Gutman RA, Stead WW, Robinson RR. Physical activity and employment status of patients on maintenance dialysis. *N Engl J Med.* 1981;304:309–313.

22. Evans RW, Manninen DL, Garrison, LD, et al. The quality of life of patients with end stage renal disease. *N Engl J Med.* 1985;312:553–559.

23. Tews HP, Schreiber WK, Huber W, et al. Vocational rehabilitation in dialyzed patients. *Nephron.* 1980;26:130–136.

24. Oreopoulos DG, Khanna R, William P. Continuous ambulatory peritoneal dialysis—1981. *Nephron.* 1982;30:295–303.

25. Beasley CRW, Smith DA, Neale TJ. Exercise capacity in chronic renal failure patients managed by continuous ambulatory peritoneal dialysis. *Aust NZ J Med.* 1986;16:5–10.

26. Charytan C, Spinowitz BS, Galler M. A comparative study of continuous ambulatory peritoneal dialysis and center hemodialysis. *Arch Intern Med.* 1986;146:1138–1143.

27. Evans RW. Cost-effectiveness analysis of transplantation. *Surg Clin North Am.* 1986; 66:603–616.

28. Simmons RG, Schilling KJ. Social and psychological rehabilitation of the diabetic transplant patient. *Kidney Int.* 1974;6:152–158.

29. Costanza ME, Li FP, Greene HL, Patterson WB. Cancer prevention and detection: strategies for practice. In: Cady B, ed. *Cancer Manual.* Boston: American Cancer Society, Massachusetts Division; 1986.

30. Silverberg E, Lubera J. Cancer statistics, 1987. *Cancer.* 1987;37:12–19.

31. Holland J. Special problems of cancer patients returning to work. *Trans Assoc Life Ins Med Dir Am.* 1985;69:87–94.

32. Bond MD. Employability of cancer patients. *Rocky Mt Med J.* 1977;74:153–156.

33. Steve RW. Employing the recovered cancer patient. *Cancer.* 1975;36:285–286.

34. Mellette SJ. The cancer patient at work. *Cancer.* 1985;35:360–373.

35. Feldman FL. *Work Expectations and Cancer Health Histories: Experiences of Youth Ages (13–23) with Cancer Histories.* San Francisco: American Cancer Society, California Division; 1980.

36. Seidman H, Mushinski MH, Gelb SK, Silverberg E. Probability of eventually developing or dying of cancer—United States, 1985. *Cancer.* 1985;36:36–56.

37. Mettlin C, Cookfair DL, Lane W, et al. The quality of life in patients with cancer. A survey at one treatment center. *NY State J Med.* 1983;83:187–193.

38. Druss RG, O'Connor JF, Prudden JF, Steen O. Psychologic response to colostomy. *Arch Gen Psych.* 1968;18:53–59.

39. Logigian MK. Oncological rehabilitation. In: Logigian MK, ed. *Adult Rehabilitation: A Team Approach for Therapists.* Boston: Little Brown and Co; 1982.

40. Strong MS, Wang CC, Clark JR. Cancer of the head and neck. In Blake C, ed. *Cancer Manual.* Boston: American Cancer Society, Massachusetts Division; 1986:132–140.

41. Mead G, Jacobs C. Changing role of chemotherapy in treatment of head and neck cancer. *Am J Med.* 1982;73:582–595.

42. Garnick MD, Scully RE, Weber ET, Krane RJ. Cancer of the testis. In: Cady B, ed. *Cancer Manual.* Boston: American Cancer Society, Massachusetts Division; 1986:268–277.

43. Schottenfeld D, Zauber A, Kerner J, Warshaver MA. Recent trends in cancer survival. *Trans Assoc Life Ins Med Dir Am.* 1985;69:66–86.

44. Smiley RK. Prognosis in hemophilia and related disorders. *Trans Assoc Life Ins Med Dir Am.* 1986;70:63–71.

45. Larsson SA, Nilsson IM, Blombäck M. Current status of Swedish hemophiliacs. *Acta Med Scand.* 1982;212:195–200.

46. Ramgren O. Hemophilia in Sweden. *Acta Med Scand.* 1962;379:37–41.

47. Larsson SA, Wiechel B. Death in Swedish hemophiliacs, 1975–80. *Acta Med Scand* 1983;214:199–206.

48. *Summary Report: NHLI's Blood Resource Studies.* Bethesda, MD: National Heart and Lung Institute; 1972. DHEW publication No. (NIH) 73-416.

49. Johnson RE, Lawrence DN, Evatt BL, et al. AIDS among patients attending hemophilia treatment centers and mortality experience of US hemophiliacs (1968 to 1979). *Am J Epidemiol.* 1985;121:797–810.

50. Ikkala E, Helske T, Myllyla G, et al. Changes in the life expectancy of patients with hemophilia A in Finland in 1930–79. *Br J Haemotol.* 1982;52:7–12.

51. Levine PH. The acquired immunodeficiency syndrome in persons with hemophilia. *Ann Intern Med.* 1985;103:723–726.

52. Kitchen LW, Barin F, Sullivan JL. Aetiology of AIDS—antibodies to human T-cell leukemia virus (type III) in hemophiliacs. *Nature.* 1984;312:367–369.

53. Goedert JJ, Sarngadharan MG, Eyster ME. Antibodies reactive with human T cell leukemia viruses in the serum of hemophilias receiving factor VIII concentrate. *Blood.* 1985;65:492–495.

54. Levine PH, Britten AM. Supervised patient-management of hemophilia. *Ann Intern Med.* 1973;78:195.

55. Prothero J. *Hemophilia Society Survey.* London: Hemophilia Society; 1977.

56. Markova I, Lockyer R, Forbes CD. Hemophilia: a survey on social issues. *Health Bull.* 1977;35:177–182.

57. Smith PS, Levine PH, Directors of Eleven Participating Hemophilia Centers. The benefits of comprehensive care of hemophilia: a five-year study of outcomes. *Am J Pub Health.* 1984;74:616–617.

58. Stuart J, Forbes CD, Jones P, et al. Improving prospects for employment of the hemophilia. *Br Med J.* 1980;280:1169–1172.

59. Nimorivicy P, Tannebaum J. Educational and vocation achievement among hemophilias: the Pennsylvania experience. *Chronic Dis.* 1986;39:743–750.

60. Hellgren L. *Psoriasis: The Prevalence in Sex, Age and Occupation Groups in Total Populations in Sweden: Morphology, Inheritance and Association with Other Skin and Rheumatologic Diseases.* Stockholm: Almquist & Wiksell; 1967.

61. Lomholt G. *Psoriasis: Prevalence, Spontaneous Course and Genetics: A Census Study on the Prevalence of Skin Disease in the Faroe Islands.* Copenhagen: GEC Gad; 1963.

62. Stewart WD, Danto JL, Madden S. *Psoriasis in Dermatology Diagnosis and Treatment of Cutaneous Disorders.* St. Louis: CV Mosby Co; 1978.

63. Jowett S, Ryan T. Skin disease and handicap: an analysis of the impact of skin conditions. *Soc Med.* 1985;20:425–429.

64. Moschella SL. Hidradenitis suppurativa: complications resulting in death. *JAMA.* 1966;198:201–203.

65. Shelley WB, Cahn MM. Pathogenesis of hidradenitis suppurativa in man: experimental and histologic observations. *Arch Dermatol.* 1955;72:562–565.

66. Mullins JF, McCash WB, Boudreau RF. Treatment of chronic hidradenitis suppurativa: surgical modification. *Postgrad Med.* 1959;26:805–808.

67. Zeligman I. Temporary X-ray epilation therapy of chronic axillary hidradenitis suppurativa. *Arch Dermatol.* 1965;92:690–694.

68. Friis R, Nanjundappa G. Diabetes, depression and employment status. *Soc Sci Med.* 1986;23:471–475.

69. Ganda OP, Sveldner SS. Genetic, acquired and related factors in the etiology of diabetes mellitus. *Arch Intern Med.* 1977;173:461–469.

70. Gottlieb MS, Rovt HF. Diabetes mellitus in twins. *Diabetes.* 1968;17:693–704.

71. Tattersoll RB, Pyhe DA. Diabetes in identical twins. *Lancet*. 1972;2:1120–1125.

72. Rotter JI, Rimoin DL. The genetics of the glucose intolerance disorders. *Am J Med*. 1981;70:116.

73. Felig P, Bergman M. Intensive ambulatory treatment of insulin-dependent diabetes. *Ann Intern Med*. 1982;97:225–230.

74. Rizza RA. New modes of insulin administration: do they have a role in clinical diabetes? *Ann Intern Med*. 1986;105:126–128.

75. Davidson MB. *Diabetes Mellitus: Diagnosis and Treatment*. New York: John Wiley & Sons; 1981.

76. Raskin P, Rosenstock J. Blood glucose control and diabetic complications. *Ann Intern Med*. 1986;105:254–263.

77. Welch RA. Employment of diabetes in a post office-region. *J Soc Occup Med*. 1986;36:80–85.

78. Lister J. The employment of diabetics. *J Soc Occup Med*. 1982;32:153–158.

79. Lister J. The employment of diabetics. *Br Med J*. 1983;287:1087–1088.

80. Sonksen PH. The employment of diabetics. *Br Med J*. 1984;288:239.

81. Hutchinson SJ; Kesson CM, Slater SD. Does diabetes affect employment prospects? *Br Med J*. 1983;287:946–947.

82. Calkins BM, Mendeloff AI. Epidemiology of inflammatory bowel disease. *Epidemiol Rev*. 1986;8:60–91.

83. Alkins BM, Calkins BM, Lilienfeld AM, Garland CF, et al. Trends in the incidence rates of ulcerative colitis and Crohn's disease. *Dig Dis Sci*. 1984;29:913–920.

84. National Center for Health. *Statistics: Vital Statistics of the United States, 1971*. Rockville, MD: Department of Health, Education and Welfare, Public Health Service; 1974.

85. Sonnenberg A. Mortality from Crohn's disease and ulcerative colitis in England—Wales and the US from 1950-1983. *Dis Colon Rectum*. 1986;29:624–629.

86. Smart HL, Mayberry JF. Epidemiologic studies of mortality in patients with ulcerative colitis. *Arch Intern Med*. 1986;146:651–652.

87. Morson BC. Pathology of ulcerative colitis. In: Kirsner JB, Shunter RG, eds. *Inflammatory Bowel Disease*. Philadelphia: Lea & Febiger; 1980:293–307.

88. Whitehead R. Pathology of Crohn's. In: Kirsner JB, Shunter RG, eds. *Inflammatory Bowel Disease*. Philadelphia: Lea & Febiger; 1980:281–295.

89. Lennard-Jones JE. The clinical outcome of ulcerative colitis depends on how much of the colonic mucosa is involved. *Scand J Gastroenterol*. 1983;18(suppl 88):48–53.

90. Gazzard BG, Price HL, Libby GW, et al. The social role of Crohn's disease. *Br Med J*. 1978;2:1117–1119.

91. *The 1984 Report of the Joint National Committee on Detection, Evaluation, and Treatment of High Blood Pressure*. Bethesda, MD: US Department of Health and Human Services; 1984.

92. *Cardiovascular Primer for the Workplace*. Washington, DC: National Institutes of Health; 1986. NIH publication No. 81-2210.

93. Cutler JA, Horan MJ, Roccilla EJ, Zusman RM, eds. The National Heart, Lung and Blood Institute workshop on antihypertensive drug treatment. *Hypertension*. 1989;13:I1–I157.

94. Gifford RW. Mild hypertension: critical analysis of different therapeutic approaches. *Clev Clin J Med*. 1989;56:337–456.

95. Dzau VJ. Evolution of the clinical management of hypertension: emerging role of "specific" vasodilators as initial therapy. *Am J Med*. 1987;82(suppl A):36–43.

96. Wenger NK. Quality of life issues in hypertension: consequences of diagnosis and considerations in management. *Amer Heart J*. 1988;116:628–632.

97. Carroll C. Ascription of symptoms to hypertension by a rural population. *Prev Med*. 1978;7:49.

98. Haynes RB, Sackett DL, Taylor DW, Gibson ES, Johnson AL. Increased absenteeism from work after detection and labeling of hypertensive patients. *NEJM*. 1978;299:741–744.

99. MacDonald LA, Sackett DL, Haynes RB, Taylor DW. Labelling in hypertension: a review of the behavioral and psychological consequences. *J Chronic Dis*. 1984;37:933–942.

100. Rudd P, Price MG, Graham LE, et al. Consequences of worksite hypertension screening: differential changes in psychosocial function. *Am J Med*. 1986;80:853–859.

101. Johnston ME, Gibson ES, Terry CW, et al. Effects of labelling in income, work and social function among hypertensive employees. *J Chronic Dis*. 1984;37:417–423.

102. Bloom JR, Monterosa S. Hypertension labeling and sense of well-being. *Am J Pub Heal*. 1981;71:1228–1232.

103. Wagner EH, Strogatz DS. Hypertensive labeling and well-being: alternative explanations in cross-sectional data. *J Chronic Dis*. 1984;37:943–947.

104. Milne BJ, Logan AG, Flanagan PT. Alterations in health perception and life style in treated hypertensives. *J Chronic Dis*. 1985;38:37–45.

105. Charlson ME, Alderman M, Melcher L. Absenteeism and labelling in hypertensive subjects. Prevention of an adverse impact in those at high risk. *Am J Med*. 1982;73:165–170.

106. Hatch LL. Occupational environment as an etiology of hypertension. *Prev Med*. 1978;7:85.

107. Franti CE. Trends in high blood pressure control related to employment status. *Prev Med*. 1978;7:73.

108. Alderman MH, Davis T. Hypertension control at the work site. *J Occup Med*. 1976;18:793–796.

109. Alderman MH, Ochs OS. Treatment of hypertension at the university medical clinic. *Arch Intern Med*. 1977;137:1707–1710.

110. Engelland AL, Alderman MH, Powell HB. Blood pressure control in private practice: a case report. *Am J Public Health*. 1979;69:25–29.

111. Foote A, Erfurt JC. Hypertension control at the work site: comparison of screening and referral alone, referral and follow-up, and on-site treatment. *N Engl J Med*. 1983;308:809–813.

112. Littenberg B, Garber AM, Sox HC. Screening for hypertension. *Ann Int Med*. 1990;112:192–202.

chapter 15

The Law-Medicine Interface in Assessing Vocational Capacity

Mark A. Rothstein

The vocational capacity of an impaired worker has legal significance for two main reasons. First, several public and private forms of income replacement and benefits, such as Social Security Disability Insurance, workers' compensation, and long-term disability insurance, are based on the impaired individual's lost earning capacity. Thus, the focus is on the *disability* that results from the impairment. Second, a variety of state and federal laws prohibit discrimination in employment against otherwise qualified handicapped individuals. In this context, the focus is on the *ability* of the individual, despite some degree of impairment.

The legal definitions of the terms *impairment, disability*, and *handicap* differ slightly from those popularized by the World Health Organization, as described in Chapter 1. According to the American Medical Association (AMA):

> It is particularly important to understand the distinction between a patient's *medical impairment*, which is an alteration of health status assessed by medical means, and the patient's *disability*, which is an alteration of the patient's capacity to meet personal, social, or occupational demands, or to meet statutory or regulatory requirements, which is assessed by nonmedical means. In a particular case, the existence of permanent medical impairment does not automatically support the presumption that there is disability as well. Rather, disability results when medical impairment leads to the individual's inability to meet demands that pertain to nonmedical fields and activities.[1]

In other words, impairment refers to an individual's medical condition; disability refers to the administrative or legal conclusion regarding the effects of the impairment on the individual. Handicap is a legislative classification based on the presence of certain enumerated impairments. Therefore, to be disabled, an individual

407

must have an impairment; to be handicapped (under many statutes), an individual must have an impairment, have a history of impairment, or be perceived to have an impairment. An individual may be disabled, but not handicapped (eg, an alcoholic who is unable to work, but is excluded from coverage under a law protecting the handicapped); handicapped, but not disabled (eg, an orthopedically impaired individual who has a sedentary job); or both disabled and handicapped (eg, a stroke victim who is unable to work).

VOCATIONAL CAPACITY AND ELIGIBILITY FOR BENEFITS

Eligibility requirements vary from one disability support system to another. Systems in common use in the United States include Social Security Disability Insurance, veterans' benefits, workers' compensation, and long-term and personal injury insurance.

Social Security Disability Insurance

The Social Security Act provides for two separate programs of disability income benefits.[2] Title II of the Social Security Act provides for disability insurance benefit payments to individuals who have not reached 65 years, are insured for disability insurance benefits, and are disabled. Title XVI of the Social Security Act provides for Supplemental Security Income (SSI) to the aged, blind, and disabled. In order to be eligible for SSI, the individual must have limited income and resources. Although disability insurance benefits are funded by Social Security taxes paid by employers, employees, and the self-employed, the SSI program is financed from general funds of the U.S. Treasury.

Under Social Security, the finding of disability is an all-or-nothing proposition. Unlike workers' compensation, there are no Social Security benefits for partial disability. The statute defines disability as the

> inability to engage in any substantial gainful activity by reason of any medically determinable physical or mental impairment . . . [lasting at least a year and] of such severity that [the claimant] . . . is not only unable to do his previous work but cannot, considering his age, education, and work experience, engage in any other kind of substantial gainful work which exists in the immediate area in which he lives, or whether a specific job vacancy exists for him or whether he would be hired if he applied for such work.[3]

Regulations promulgated by the Social Security Administration prescribe a five-step test to determine whether a claimant is disabled. The claimant has the burden of proof for the initial four steps:

1. The claimant must not be working at any "substantial gainful activity."
2. The claimant must have a severe impairment that significantly limits the claimant's "physical or mental ability to do basic work activities" (ie, the abilities and aptitudes necessary to do most jobs).
3. If the claimant meets the duration requirements (12 months) and has an impairment that is specifically listed in the regulations or that is equal to one of the listed impairments, the claimant will be deemed disabled without any consideration of nonmedical factors.
4. If the claimant's impairment is not listed in the regulations, the claimant must be unable to perform his or her previous work.[4]

Four factors are considered in determining whether the claimant has satisfied this initial burden: (1) objective medical facts or clinical findings; (2) diagnoses of examining physicians; (3) subjective evidence of pain and disability (eg, the testimony of the claimant and the claimant's family); and (4) the claimant's age, education, and work history. These factors are considered both singly and in combination.

Once the claimant has proved the existence of an impairment that meets or equals the listed criteria or that prevents the performance of past relevant work, the burden shifts to the Secretary of Health and Human Services for the fifth step of the test. The Secretary must prove that the claimant is able to perform other work. The Secretary must evaluate the claimant's disabilities and determine whether they are of such severity that the claimant cannot engage in any substantial gainful work; this is a two-part process. First, the Secretary must consider the claimant's physical ability, age, education, and work experience. Second, the Secretary must consider whether there are jobs in the national economy that a person with the claimant's qualifications can perform.

Prior to 1978, the Secretary relied on vocational experts to establish the existence of jobs suitable for impaired workers. In order to improve the uniformity and efficiency of this determination, the Secretary promulgated medical-vocational guidelines as part of the 1978 regulations. These guidelines involve a grid system that contains three tables: one for sedentary work, one for light work, and one for medium work. A claimant's age, education, and previous work experience are considered in each table and ultimately plotted on the grid. For each combination of these three factors, there is a prior determination of job availability and, consequently, of the claimant's ability or disability.[5]

The grid system has been criticized as arbitrary, inaccurate, oversimplified, and inflexible. In *Heckler v Campbell*,[6] however, the Supreme Court unanimously upheld the medical-vocational guidelines. According to the Court, the Social Security Act's requirement for individualized determinations does not preclude the Secretary from using rule-making authority to determine issues that do not require case-by-case consideration. Moreover, even though there may be a tendency to use the grid in an inflexible manner, the grid is only a "framework" for disability determination. Nonexertional environmental limitations that restrict a claimant's ability to tolerate certain work settings, such as dust, fumes, or heat, may establish disability when the mechanical use of the grid system indicates no disability.

Veterans' Benefits

The Veterans' Benefits Act provides for disability compensation for personal injuries suffered and diseases contracted while on active duty in the military service, whether in time of war or peace.[7] Veterans are ineligible for compensation if they were dishonorably discharged or if their disability is the result of their own willful misconduct, but they are eligible for benefits if their disability results from the aggravation of a pre-existing injury or disease.

Under the Veterans' Benefits Act, disability payments vary according to the disability rating, which ranges from 10% to 100% in 10% increments. Congress sets the monthly benefits levels for each disability rating and has specified the payment levels for various service-connected disabilities involving anatomic losses, blindness, deafness, and similar conditions. In addition, the Veterans Administration has promulgated a detailed schedule for rating other disabilities. Employability plays a major role in the disability rating.

Workers' Compensation

The workers' compensation system consists of a series of state and federal laws designed to provide individuals disabled by work-related injury or illness with a replacement income, as well as financial assistance in meeting the expenses associated with medical care and rehabilitation services. Each state has its own workers' compensation laws, and federal laws provide additional coverage for federal civilian employees, longshoring and harbor workers, sailors, railroad workers, and coal miners.

Essentially, workers' compensation is a form of employer-provided life and disability insurance for work-related injury, illness, and death. With only a few exceptions, such as domestic household employees, all employees are covered. Employers pay premiums into an insurance fund from which worker claims are paid. Work-related injuries and illnesses are compensable without regard to the fault of the employer, the employee, or any third person. Common law defenses, such as contributory negligence, assumption of the risk, and the fellow servant rule (disqualifying employees whose injury or illness was due to the fault of a co-employee), are inapplicable. Because resort to the workers' compensation system is an exclusive remedy, an employee who receives benefits from the system loses the common law right to bring a negligence action against the employer.

Each state law sets the eligibility requirements, benefit levels, and claims procedures for its own workers' compensation system, but most state laws are quite similar. Virtually all workers' compensation systems are based on a four-way classification of disabilities: (1) temporary partial, (2) permanent partial, (3) temporary total, and (4) permanent total. A temporary partial or permanent partial disability makes it impossible for the claimant to perform at his or her regular job, but allows the claimant to engage in some other gainful employment. Compensation under these circumstances is based on wage loss, but it also includes medical and hospital expenses. The disability of a claimant who is unable to work at all for a limited period of time is a temporary total disability. All states have waiting periods (from 3 to 7 days) before a claimant with a temporary total disability is eligible for wage replacement benefits. The purpose of such a provision is to discourage workers from malingering. There are usually no waiting periods for medical benefits, however.

From a medical standpoint, it may be difficult to determine when a temporary total disability either has ended or has become a permanent partial disability. The dates most frequently used as the basis for such decisions are the date on which the claimant has reached maximum medical improvement, the date on which the impairment has become stable, or the date on which the claimant is able to return to work.

Awards for permanent partial disability may be scheduled or unscheduled. State legislatures establish scheduled benefits for such conditions as total loss or loss of the use of specific body members, where wage loss is presumed. The claimant may receive these scheduled benefits in addition to benefits received for temporary total disability; furthermore, the claimant is entitled to a scheduled payment regardless of the economic consequences of the impairment. In other words, the basis of the award is medical impairment, rather than wage loss. In contrast, unscheduled permanent partial disability benefits are generally based on the wage loss principle. The degree of disability is calculated by comparing a worker's earnings before the injury or illness with the worker's earning capacity after the injury or illness. This latter estimate, of course, depends on the medical determination of impairment, as well as on nonmedical factors relative to the claimant's employment opportunities.

Many workers' compensation laws and regulations are vague about the method that examining physicians are to use in calculating a claimant's level of impairment. Some states, such as Florida, use the American Medical Association's *Guides to the Evaluation of Physical Impairment*.[1] Other states, such as Washington, have their own systems. Commonly, the physician first determines the degree of anatomic impairment caused by an injury or illness to a specific organ system or body part and then, using a set of provided tables, calculates the degree of impairment to the body as a whole.

It is not necessary for a worker to be totally impaired to be considered totally disabled. In West Virginia, for example, a worker is considered totally disabled whenever the impairment rating is 85% or more. Even with a percentage of impairment below the statutory total disability level, a claimant may be considered totally disabled if the impairment, in combination with nonmedical factors, precludes the claimant from gainful employment. According to the Supreme Court of Tennessee, "In determining what may constitute permanent total disability, the concepts embodied in Workmen's Compensation take into account many pertinent factors, including skill, education, training, duration and job opportunity for the disabled."[8]

Perhaps the best demonstration of the fact that medical impairment is only one factor in determining disability is the "odd lot" doctrine. The case of *Turner v American Mutual Insurance Co*,[9] for example, involved a mentally retarded wood cutter whose right foot had been crushed in a work-related accident. Although the man was only partially impaired, the Supreme Court of Louisiana held that he was entitled to a rating of permanent total disability by applying the odd lot doctrine:

> An injured employee is entitled to total, permanent disability compensation if he can perform no services other than those which are so limited in quality, dependability, or quantity that a reasonably stable market for them does not exist. This determination is made after scrutiny of the evidence of the worker's physical impairment as well as his mental capacity, education, and training. If the worker establishes that he falls into the odd-lot category, he is entitled to total, permanent disability compensation unless the employer or his insurer is able to show that some form of suitable work is regularly and continuously available to the employee within reasonable proximity to the worker's residence.[10]

Some workers' compensation statutes call for the use of presumptions in determining whether a claimant is totally disabled. Under the Black Lung Benefits Act,[11] for example, a coal miner with at least 10 years of work in the mines can establish a presumption of total disability by demonstrating the presence of pneumoconiosis through positive roentgenographic findings, abnormal results of blood gas studies, or other medical evidence, including the documented opinion of a physician that the miner has a totally disabling respiratory or pulmonary impairment. This presumption can be rebutted, however, if it can be shown that the miner is performing or is able to perform usual coal mine work or comparable work, that the disability did not arise in whole or in part from coal mine employment, or that the disability is not pneumoconiosis.

Insurance

Provisions in many insurance policies require a medical examination of the insured before the payment of a claim. These provisions are generally upheld by the courts, although the insurer may not be entitled to repeated examinations. An insured's refusal to submit to an examination may preclude recovery under the policy, even where the insured's religious beliefs do not recognize the efficacy of physicians. For disability insurance policies, the issue to be determined is whether the insured is able to continue performing in the same job or in any job.

Personal Injury Litigation

In a lawsuit involving personal injury, the vocational capacity of the individual following the injury greatly affects the amount of compensatory damages recoverable in the lawsuit. Rule 35 of the Federal Rules of Civil Procedure provides that the court may order the physical or mental examination of a party to a lawsuit. There is a similar provision in the rules of civil procedure in all but three states. In most instances, the party to be examined is the plaintiff, but defendants are also subject to rule 35.

Under rule 35, the condition of the party to be examined must be "in controversy," and there must be "good cause" for the examination. The good cause requirement has been interpreted to mean that the information cannot be obtained by other means (eg, medical records). If these requirements are met, the court may order any examinations deemed necessary. The court will not order an examination, however, if there is evidence that the party to be examined will be subject to unreasonable annoyance, embarrassment, oppression, or undue burden or expense. In addition, the court will consider the health, comfort, and safety of the individual to be examined. Blood tests and radiologic studies are permitted, but an individual generally need not submit to painful or invasive procedures.

Because rule 35 is silent about the choice of physician, the courts have developed guidelines for selecting a physician. The usual course is for the parties to agree on the physician by stipulation. If the parties cannot agree on a physician, however, the court will choose one. Nothing in the rule precludes an examination by several physicians or specialists where necessary. The courts are divided on the question of whether the patient's personal physician has a right to be present at the examination.

ASSESSMENT OF VOCATIONAL CAPACITY

Pain

The degree of pain caused by the impairment often affects an impaired individual's ability to work, but the difficulty of verifying and quantifying pain has sometimes presented problems in assessing such an individual's vocational capacity for the purposes of determining benefits. In workers' compensation and Social Security cases, the existence of pain is considered additional medical evidence of impairment and thus is used to establish the disability. Once it has been established, the disability (ie, the inability to work) rather than the pain is the basis for the compensation. In personal injury litigation, on the other hand, the presence of pain not only establishes disability and therefore lost income but also may be an independent basis for the award of damages.

Medical testimony may be used in an attempt to prove the presence or absence of pain or that alleged pain is not genuine. Although ultimate determinations of credibility rest with the trier of fact, courts often presume, perhaps unrealistically, that medical experts are capable of distinguishing between real and imagined or feigned pain.

Conflicting Medical Evidence

The determination of eligibility for benefits is often an adversarial process, and it is common for medical experts employed by opposing parties to have vastly different opinions about an individual's vocational capacity. The court or other body making a determination of disability must then decide which physician's assessment of medical impairment should be the basis for its ruling.

Under Social Security, the administrative law judge is required to resolve conflicting medical opinions. Although this judge is not bound to accept the conclusions of the claimant's personal physician, there is considerable support for the proposition that the expert opinion of a claimant's treating physician is entitled to extra weight and, unless there is substantial contradictory evidence, is conclusive. This is so even when the treating physician's opinions are unaccompanied by particular clinical tests or findings.

Under workers' compensation law, there is less agreement on the appropriate way to resolve conflicts in medical evidence. As in the Social Security system, the administrative body—the industrial commission or workers' compensation board—is charged with determining which medical testimony is to be accepted. In workers' compensation, however, the opinions of the treating physician are not necessarily given deference. Even in those jurisdictions that do follow such a policy, only the opinion of the physician who has actually treated the worker merits this deference. The opinion of a new physician chosen by the claimant solely in anticipation of the workers' compensation hearing receives no special deference.

The rationale for giving greater weight to the testimony of treating physicians is that a treating physician is more familiar with the health status of a specific patient than is an examining physician. Although it can be argued that the testimony of some treating physicians may be colored by undue sympathy for their regular patients, it can also be argued that some examining physicians may be unduly sympathetic to the financial interests of the parties who have retained their services.

Change of Condition

Under the workers' compensation laws or the Veterans' Benefits Act, a case can be reopened if the claimant's physical or mental condition has changed since a prior disability determination. The most relevant evidence of a change in vocational capacity subsequent to an initial determination of vocational incapacity is evidence of actual gainful employment. This evidence is generally admissible and given credence. Other evidence proffered in an attempt to prove vocational capacity, however, may be considered less probative. In *Pinellas Ambulance Service, Inc v Gettinger*,[12] the employer contended that a paraplegic former employee was not totally disabled for the purposes of workers' compensation because she was able to compete in wheelchair athletics and had earned a 2-year college degree after her injury. The Florida statute contains a presumption that an individual who is paraplegic is permanently totally disabled, and the Florida Court of Appeals held that "mere ability to excel in other nonemploymnent-related endeavors is legally insufficient" to overcome that presumption.[12]

VOCATIONAL CAPACITY AND EMPLOYABILITY

The vocational capacity of workers is a source of continuing concern for all employers. Although employers vary widely in their medical examination policies, they may require assessments of vocational capacity before employment, before placement, at regular intervals, or after an injury or illness (ie, before an employee returns to work). In general, large companies and those in hazardous industries are more likely than are other companies to require examinations, to schedule them often, and to make them comprehensive.

Some medical examinations are required by collective bargaining agreements. Some federal health standards, such as those involving exposure to asbestos, lead, and ethylene oxide, require preplacement and periodic medical testing.[13] Fitness examinations are also mandated by the government for airline pilots, truck drivers, and other employees whose performance has a direct bearing on public safety. The vast majority of employer-provided medical examinations are not legally required, however, but are used in an attempt to select and maintain a healthy and productive work force. There are virtually no restrictions on the number or nature of procedures that can be made a valid condition of employment. The main limitations on performing tests are state laws prohibiting certain tests, such as genetic tests or HIV antibody tests. The main limitations on the use of test results are laws that prohibit discrimination in employment and common law and statutory protections for the privacy of medical information.

Handicap Discrimination Law

The Rehabilitation Act of 1973 was the first comprehensive federal effort to bring handicapped individuals into the mainstream of American life.[14] The act seeks, among other things, to extend ''the guarantee of equal opportunity'' to the handicapped. Section 501 prohibits employment discrimination on the basis of handicap by the federal government, and Sections 503 and 504 extend protections to certain employees in the private sector. (The proposed Americans with Disabilities Act, if enacted, would extend protection to most private sector employees as well.)

Section 503 provides that any contract involving an amount in excess of $2,500 entered into with any federal department or agency shall contain a provision requiring that the contracting party take affirmative action to employ and promote qualified individuals with handicaps. The term *individual with handicaps* is defined in the Rehabilitation Act as ''any person who (A) has a physical or mental impairment which substantially limits one or more of such person's major life activities, (B) has a record of such an impairment, or (C) is regarded as having such an impairment.''[15] Under this broad statutory definition and the definition contained in the implementing regulations, as many as 40 to 68 million handicapped persons are covered by the statute.

Section 504 provides that no otherwise qualified individual with handicaps shall, solely by reason of handicap, be excluded from participation in, be denied the benefits of, or be subjected to discrimination under any program or activity receiving federal financial assistance. Unlike Section 503, Section 504 applies to all federal programs, regardless of the amount of financial assistance received. Three million firms—approximately half the businesses in the United States—

may be covered by the act. Section 504 incorporates the same broad statutory definition of handicap as Section 503 does.

Forty-eight states and the District of Columbia have enacted laws that prohibit discrimination based on handicap in public and private employment. The two remaining states (Alabama and Mississippi) prohibit discrimination based on handicap only in public employment. The state laws usually have wider coverage than does the federal law, but they vary widely in coverage, procedures, and remedies.

A number of legal issues have arisen under state and federal handicap discrimination laws. Often, the first question is whether an individual's medical condition qualifies as a handicap within the statutory definition. In *School Board v Arline*[16] the Supreme Court held that tuberculosis and other contagious diseases are handicaps under the Rehabilitation Act, indicating that the term *handicap* should be construed broadly. On the other hand, *Arline* is not likely to alter the body of state and federal case law in which it has been ruled that minor physical conditions, such as varicose veins,[17] small stature,[18] and left-handedness,[19] are not handicaps.

Although handicap discrimination laws thus are intended to cover only serious conditions, they do not require that an individual with such a condition be hired, retained, or re-employed if the individual is not otherwise qualified and capable of performing essential job functions. The criteria by which the determination of vocational capacity is made, however, must be job-related. In *Western Weighing Bureau v Wisconsin Department of Industry, Labor and Human Relations*,[20] a former employee brought suit against his employer because he was seeking re-employment after his discharge from the Army. The employer was a company that handled rail cargo, and the individual applied for the job of inspector. Although the job involved some climbing and getting down on his hands and knees, it did not involve lifting or strenuous work; in fact, it was less strenuous than the job that the individual had performed satisfactorily before he joined the Army. The individual was hired as an inspector, but was discharged after only 1½ days. A roentgenogram of his back that had been taken at a required physical examination revealed spondylolisthesis, a congenital condition in which the last lumbar vertebra slips forward. Solely because of this radiologic finding, the company physician recommended that the individual not be employed as an inspector. Neither the state human relations commission nor the Wisconsin Circuit Court had much difficulty in finding that the employer had violated the state fair employment act. As the inspector's job did not involve lifting or strenuous work, disqualification on the basis of spondylolisthesis was simply not job-related.

The Rehabilitation Act and several state laws not only prohibit discrimination against otherwise qualified individuals who have handicaps but also require "reasonable accommodations" (ie, supportive measures) that will permit the handicapped individuals to perform the job. It is impossible to predict in the abstract what reasonable accommodations will be required. According to one court, the factors that must be considered are the size of the employer, the type of operation, the composition of the work force, and the cost of the necessary accommodations.[21] Employers have been required to make facilities accessible by adding ramps and widening doors[22]; to attempt to transfer a newly impaired employee to a more suitable position[23]; and to allow the use of lead dogs, orthopedic aids, and mechanized equipment to help the employee perform the job.[24] On the other hand, accommodations are not considered reasonable and thus are not required if they would result in undue hardship to the employer, including excessive expense. Thus, employers have not been required to rewrite job descriptions materially to accommodate a single employee,[25] to modify equipment being used if doing so would be burdensome,[26] or to reassign personnel and alter workloads to accommodate a single applicant.[27]

Some employers have tried to justify the refusal to employ an otherwise qualified handicapped person on the grounds of increased health insurance costs. The case of *State Division of Human Rights v Xerox Corp* concerned a woman who was hired as a systems consultant, provided that she passed a pre-employment medical examination.[28] Although there were no remarkable clinical or laboratory findings, she was 5 ft, 6 in tall and weighed 249 lb. She was denied employment because of the physician's finding of "active gross obesity." The New York Court of Appeals held that obesity was a handicap under New York law, that the woman was otherwise qualified, and that she could not be denied employment on the ground that she posed a risk to disability and life insurance programs administered by the company.

It also may be illegal, under Section 510 of the Employee Retirement Income Security Act (ERISA),[29] for an employer to discharge a current employee who develops an illness. A provision in the federal pension law prohibits the discharge of an employee to deprive that employee of any benefit protected by ERISA, including health and disability insurance benefits. The case of *Folz v Marriott Corp* involved a hotel manager who was terminated from his job when his employer learned that he suffered from multiple sclerosis.[30] The court held that the employer's action had violated Section 510 of ERISA.

The defense most likely to succeed against a claim of handicap discrimination is safety—particularly public safety. Such a defense requires proof that a job-related handicap poses an appreciable risk to safety and that reasonable accommodation is not possible. Furthermore, there must be an individualized determination of whether the handicapped person is able to perform the job safely. Even with this standard, the courts have issued different opinions. For example, one court held that a police officer candidate could not be disqualified on the basis of asymptomatic spondylolisthesis,[31] but another court held that a lifeguard at risk of back spasm because of mild scoliosis could be denied a job.[32] Where the risk is only to the handicapped worker, the courts perform a similar analysis, and the results also vary. For instance, it was lawful for an employer to refuse to hire an individual with a heart condition for the arduous job of park technician[33] and a taxi driver who was congenitally absent a right hand and forearm.[34] It was improper, however, to discharge a woman with a mild case of spondylolysis from her job as an airport operations officer[35] and to discharge a railroad employee whose epilepsy was controlled.[36]

These cases are generally instructive, but they do not provide any assurances of the way in which courts will rule in the future. The two most important factors remain the nature of the individual's impairment and the demands of the job. Any disqualification from employment must be based on the individual's inability to perform the job.[37]

Re-Employment of Workers Following Injury or Illness

In virtually every jurisdiction, it is unlawful to discharge or otherwise discriminate against an employee because the employee has filed a workers' compensation claim. Nevertheless, if the employee misses time from work while recovering from a work-related (or non-work-related) injury or illness, the employer is permitted to discharge the individual or to hire a permanent replacement; the employer has no duty to re-employ the original worker after recovery is complete.[38] The only protection afforded the ill or injured employee is that, at the time the employee seeks re-employment, the employer may not discriminate on the basis of handicap.[39]

Four states have enacted laws that give limited re-employment rights to employees who have sustained a job-related injury. Oregon requires that the worker be reinstated if the position is available.[40] Hawaii and Massachusetts give first preference to the injured employee for any available position that the employee is capable of performing.[41,42] Wisconsin provides that an employer who, without reasonable cause, refuses to rehire an employee who has been injured in the course of employment—where suitable employment is available—may be liable to the employee for back wages.[43,44]

TESTIFYING AS AN EXPERT WITNESS

There are two main forums in which physicians and vocational rehabilitation counselors are called upon to testify about an individual's physical impairment: judicial proceedings and administrative proceedings. Judicial proceedings (or courtroom trials) are formal and adversarial; a judge presides over them, and there may or may not be a jury. Witnesses testify under oath, there is a verbatim transcript, and the lawyers for the opposing party cross-examine witnesses. A personal injury case resulting from an automobile accident is such a proceeding.

Administrative proceedings (or administrative hearings) are less formal. They may be adversarial (eg, a contested workers' compensation claim) or nonadversarial (eg, clarification of Social Security or veterans' benefits). There is never a jury. An administrative law judge, a hearing officer, or a panel of similar officials may preside. Witnesses testify under oath, but there is not always a transcript. Cross-examination takes place only in the adversarial type proceedings. The rules of evidence and other procedural matters are not as strictly enforced.

In judicial proceedings and, occasionally, in administrative proceedings, a potential witness may be asked to make a full statement, under oath, before the trial. This is known as a deposition. Such a statement is less formal in the sense that it is taken outside the court (eg, in a law office), but the questions are quite similar to those that will be asked at the trial. Depositions are very important to a lawsuit, and statements that are inconsistent with later testimony at a trial may be used to discredit a witness. Therefore, a witness should prepare for a deposition as he or she would prepare for judicial and administrative testimony.

Regardless of the nature of the proceedings, the first part of an expert's testimony is devoted to establishing his or her credentials and qualifications. In many cases, one or more experts testify for each side, and the case may become a "battle of the experts." Therefore, it is extremely important to develop the credibility of witnesses through their qualifications. The usual areas of inquiry for an expert witness are (1) basic formal education, (2) licensing boards, (3) specialized training, (4) professional boards, (5) teaching positions, (6) professional writings, (7) memberships in professional organizations, and (8) awards received.

After qualification, the expert is asked a series of questions pertaining to the impairment at issue. The expert is expected to review the file (and perhaps the reports of other experts) before the trial and to confer with the lawyers about the areas to be discussed in testimony. In answering questions on direct examination, the witness should attempt to (1) be professional and objective, (2) minimize the use of medical jargon, (3) avoid unduly qualifying answers, and (4) acknowledge the existence of a contrary viewpoint.

After direct examination, in which the witness is questioned by the lawyer for the party who has called the witness, the lawyer for the opposing party conducts a cross-examination. Physicians often view cross-examination as the most irritating and least civilized part of a trial or hearing; they may perceive lawyers as clever, sometimes ruthless, persons who ask trick questions, attempt to manipulate answers, and seek to discredit them.

Cross-examination is important in testing the truthfulness and credibility of all witnesses. The cross-examination of an expert witness is especially important, however, and the expert witness is especially vulnerable. Expert witnesses who understand the goals and strategies of cross-examination are much better witnesses. The four main goals of cross-examination are (1) to induce the expert to modify the conclusions expressed on direct examination, (2) to discredit the conclusions that the expert expressed on direct examination, (3) to discredit the expert personally, and (4) to create an impression in the jury that the cross-examination was successful.

Knowing these goals, the expert witness should be prepared to answer questions about prior inconsistent statements and about the contrary conclusions of other experts. Sometimes cross-examinations focus on the credentials and objectivity of the witness. Questions may be asked about the expert's qualifications, testimony in other cases, or fee for testifying. The expert should listen to the questions carefully and attempt to be responsive. In answering, the witness should not be sarcastic or condescending and should not display bias against any party or irritation at the cross-examiner. The judge and jury are likely to view a witness who is in command of the facts, knows what to expect, and can remain composed as a credible witness.

CONCLUSION

Although assessing vocational capacity is a medical responsibility, important legal consequences often result from the assessment. The two most common legal consequences involve (1) the eligibility for income replacement and other benefits and (2) the eligibility for employment. In each of these main areas, there is some variation among programs and statutes in the methods, procedures, and legal criteria used to determine vocational capacity. Physicians seem to be given greater leeway in making their determinations of impairment in the benefits area than in the employment area, where handicap discrimination laws require assessors to use job-related medical criteria and may also require employers to make reasonable accommodation for otherwise qualified handicapped workers.

REFERENCES

1. American Medical Association. *Guides to the Evaluation of Permanent Impairment*, 2nd ed. Chicago: AMA; 1984.

2. 42 USC §§ 401-433 (1982).

3. 42 USC § 423(d) (1982).

4. 20 CFR § 404.1520 (1987).

5. 20 CFR § 404, subpart P., app. II (1987).

6. 461 US 458 (1983).

7. 38 USC §§ 101-5228 (1982).

8. *Pulaski Rubber Co v Rolin*, 481 SW2d 369, 371 (Tenn 1972).

9. 390 So2d 1330 (La 1980).

10. *Id.*, at 1331.

11. 30 USC §§ 901-945 (1982).

12. 504 So2d 1386 (Fla App 1987).

13. Rothstein MA. *Medical Screening of Workers*. Washington, DC: BNA Books; 1984;19–22.

14. 29 USC §§ 701-796 (1982).

15. 29 USC § 706(7)(B) (1982).

16. 107 S Ct 1123 (1987).

17. *Oesterling v Walters*, 760 F2d 859 (8th Cir 1985).

18. *American Motors Corp v Labor & Industry Review Commission*, 119 Wis 2d 706, 350 NW2d 120 (1984).

19. *de la Torres v Bolger*, 781 F2d 1134 (5th Cir 1986).

20. 21 FEP Cases 1733 (Wis Cir Ct 1977).

21. *Nelson v Thornburgh*, 567 F Supp 369 (ED Pa 1983), *aff'd*, 732 F2d 146 (3d Cir 1984), *cert denied*, 469 US 1188 (1985).

22. See *Alderson v Postmaster General*, 598 F Supp 49 (WD Okla 1984).

23. *Dean v Municipality of Metropolitan Seattle-Metro*, 104 Wash 2d 627, 708 P2d 393 (1985).

24. See *Jenks v Avco Corp*, 340 Pa Super 542, 490 A2d 912 (1985).

25. *Bento v ITD Corp*, 599 F Supp 731 (DRI 1984).

26. *Jesany v United States Postal Service*, 755 F2d 1244 (6th Cir 1984).

27. *Treadwell v Alexander*, 707 F2d 473 (11th Cir 1983).

28. 65 NY2d 213, 480 NE2d 695, 491 NYS2d 106 (1985).

29. 29 USC § 1140 (1982).

30. 594 F Supp 1007 (WD Mo 1984).

31. *City of New York v State Division of Human Rights (Granelle)*, 70 NY2d 100, 510 NE2d 799, 517 NYS2d 715 (1987).

32. *Dauten v City of Muskegon*, 128 Mich App 435, 340 NW2d 117 (1983).

33. See *supra* note 27.

34. *Boynton Cab Co v Department of Industry, Labor, and Human Relations*, 96 Wis2d 396, 291 NW2d 850 (1980).

35. *Salt Lake City Corp v Confer*, 674 P2d 632 (Utah 1983).

36. *Higgins v Maine Central Railroad*, 471 A2d 288 (Me 1984).

37. Rothstein MA. *Medical Screening and the Employee Health Cost Crisis*. Washington, DC: BNA Books; 1989:125–159.

38. See *Leamon v Workers' Compensation Appeals Board*, 190 Cal App 3d 1409, 235 Cal Rptr 912 (1987).

39. See *Kenall Manufacturing Co v Illinois Human Rights Commission*, 152 Ill App 3d 695, 504 NE2d 805 (1987).

40. Or Rev Stat § 659.415 (Supp 1987).

41. Hawaii Rev Stat § 386.142 (1985).

42. Mass Gen Laws Ann ch 152, § 75A (West 1988).

43. Wash Rev Code Ann § 51.32.250 (Supp 1988).

44. Rothstein MA. A Proposed Model Act for the Reinstatement of Employees Upon Recovery from Work-Related Injury or Illness. *Harv J on Legis*. 1989;26:263.

Glossary of Terms

AA/NA: Alcoholics Anonymous, Narcotics Anonymous—self-help groups run solely by members and unaffiliated with any other organizations, in which members are united by a common desire to recover from alcohol or other drug problems, respectively.

activities of daily living (ADL): Such commonplace tasks as orofacial hygiene, dressing, and eating performed daily by independent persons.

adrenergic nervous system: Portion of the nervous system that releases adrenalin, which increases blood pressure and contraction of the heart.

aerobic capacity: Maximum intensity at which a person can exercise continuously without excessive cardiorespiratory fatigue.

affirmative action: Policy or program for correcting effects of past discrimination or for preventing future discrimination.

aggrieved individual: A person whose legal right has been invaded.

agrammaticism: Impairment or difficulty with grammar or syntax.

Alzheimer's disease: Presenile dementia beginning at middle age and characterized by cortical atrophy and secondary ventricular dilation.

anaerobic threshold: The level of oxygen consumption above which anaerobic mechanisms begin to supply a significant fraction of the energy demands.

angina pectoris: A syndrome of chest discomfort related to an imbalance between oxygen demand and oxygen delivery to the heart muscle.

angioplasty: The dilation of partially blocked coronary vessels using specialized catheters during a cardiac catheterization.

ankylosing spondylitis: A form of spinal arthritis in which the spine slowly assumes a flexed forward posture and becomes one rigid mass of bone.

anomia: Word-finding difficulty, most easily detected by object-naming tasks.

anoxia: A deficiency of oxygen of such severity as to result in permanent brain damage.

423

aphasia: A communication disorder characterized by a complete or partial impairment of language comprehension, use, and/or expression. Aphasia may result from stroke, trauma, infection, or tumor. See also Broca's and Wernicke's aphasias.

aphonia: Whispered speech that results from the failure of the vocal cords to approximate.

apraxia of speech (verbal apraxia): A communication disorder, as a result of brain damage, which results in the impaired capacity to plan and sequence articulatory movements for voluntary speech production; occurs in the absence of significant weakness or incoordination of the speech musculature, with voluntary movements of the same apparatus reasonably intact.

artificial larynx: A mechanical sound generator used by laryngectomees to produce voice.

assumption of risk: A defense to a negligence or other tort action in which the plaintiff knowingly assumes the risk of potential injury through the fault of no one or of someone else.

ataxia: An inability to coordinate voluntary muscular movements.

atherosclerosis: The process of deposition of lipids in arterial walls leading to stenosis, thrombus formation, and aneurysmal dilation.

auscultation: Listening to cardiac sounds with a stethoscope.

automaticity: Intrinsic periodic release of electrical activity in the heart muscle leading to heart muscle contraction.

BFOQ: Bona fide occupational qualification; statutory defense to Title VII case permitting employers to differentiate on the basis of religion, sex, or national origin when necessary to the normal operation of the business.

beta blockade: Treatment with a class of medications known as beta blockers, which block stimulation of the heart by catecholamines, such as adrenalin.

bioelectric prostheses: Any prosthetic device that uses electrical signals or electrical motors as a part of its operating principles.

bradycardia: A slow heart rate, usually less than 50 beats per minute.

Broca's aphasia: Language disorder primarily affecting expressive capabilities. Speech is nonfluent, effortful, and agrammatic. Comprehension is relatively preserved.

bronchoscopy: Examination of the bronchi through a bronchoscope.

business necessity: A defense to an employment discrimination case; a legitimate business purpose so compelling as to override any adverse impact resulting from such practice.

cable: A flexible wire surrounded by a nonremovable metal covering used in upper limb prostheses; sometimes called a Bowden cable. Tension on the flexible wire running through the covering moves the joints or terminal device in a prosthesis.

cardiac catheterization: A technique in which catheters are placed in and around the heart to measure pressures and image the coronary arteries and ventricles with injection of contrast material.

cardiomyopathy: Disease of myocardial muscle due to various causes that results in ventricular dysfunction.

cauda equina syndrome: Usually from central disc herniation, it is responsible for ongoing and severe neurologic deficits affecting bowel/bladder function, perianal sensation, and lower extremity muscles; usually a neurosurgical emergency.

chronotropic: Refers to changes in heart rate. Chronotropic incompetence refers to an inability of the heart rate to rise to predicted levels with exercise.

circumlocution: Talking around an idea while failing to cite the idea explicitly.

cognitive flexibility: Capacity to shift back and forth between and among different concepts and/or mental processes.

common law: Body of rules and principles established over time by usage and custom or from the judgments or decrees of the courts.

communication: Interaction or exchange of ideas, knowledge, experiences, and emotions by speech, writing, reading, and gesturing.

compensatory damages: Money judgment to replace the loss suffered by the plaintiff.

congestive heart failure: A syndrome of shortness of breath due to inadequate pumping of the heart, resulting in fluid accumulation in the lungs.

constructional apraxia: Impairment of drawing and/or assembly skills; not attributable to weakness or poor comprehension.

contracture: Refers to decreased active and passive range of motion of a joint secondary to stiffening/tightening of the connective tissue.

contralateral: On the opposite side.

contributory negligence: A defense to a negligence or other tort action; act or omission on the part of the complaining party that amounts to lack of ordinary care.

COPD (chronic obstructive pulmonary disease): A condition in which there is chronic obstruction of airflow; generally refers to emphysema and chronic bronchitis.

cor pulmonale: Hypertrophy or failure of the right ventricle resulting from lung disease.

coronary artery bypass graft (CABG): A cardiac operation in which veins taken from the legs are used to bypass significant obstructions in coronary arteries in order to improve blood flow to cardiac muscle.

coronary vasomotor tone: Relative constriction or relaxation of the coronary arteries due to intrinsic nervous control and circulating hormones.

covenant: Agreement, convention, or promise; may be expressed or implied by law.

Creutzfeldt-Jakob disease: A rare, usually fatal transmissible viral encephalopathy occurring in midlife associated with progressive dementia.

dead space ventilation: Ventilation that goes to areas of the lung that receive little or no blood flow and therefore is ''wasted'' because it does not contribute to the exchange of oxygen and carbon dioxide.

deltoid aid: An assistive device utilizing counterbalanced pulleys to compensate for weakness of shoulder abduction.

diffusing capacity of the lung: The capacity of the lung to transfer gas to the capillary blood; usually measured for carbon monoxide and reported as the volume of CO transferred per minute per unit of driving pressure.

disability: According to the WHO, a personal dysfunction or inability to perform an activity; generally follows from the presence of disease or impairment (eg, inability to walk following paralysis or inability to carry following low back pain).

disarticulation: Separation of two bones at a joint, the result of an injury or performed surgically in the course of an amputation.

discogenic: Of or relating to pathology of the intervertebral disc.

distal end: The end of an extremity or stump that is furthest from the body.

diuretic: A drug that increases the volume of urine produced by promoting excretion of salt and water from the kidney.

dolorimeters: Machines that *attempt* to measure pain.

dysarthria: Collective term for motor speech disorders resulting from brain damage that may cause weakness, incoordination, or paralysis of the muscles involved in respiration, phonation, articulation, resonation, and/or prosody.

dysgraphia: An inability to write properly; may be part of a language disorder.

dyskinesia: An impairment of the power of voluntary movement, resulting in fragmentary or incomplete movements.

dyslexia: An inability to read with understanding, due to a central lesion.

dysphonia: A disorder in vocal quality that results from the aperiodic vibration of the vocal cords.

dyspnea: Shortness of breath.

dysrhythmias: Abnormal rhythms of the heart.

echocardiography: A technique using ultrasound to image the heart structures and observe its contraction pattern.

echoic memory: Immediate recall process; usually tested by digit repetition.

echolalia: The repetition of words spoken by others.

ecological relevance: Extent to which a test relates to "real-world" performance.

ecological validity: Extent to which a test predicts "real-world" performance.

edema: The presence of abnormally large amounts of fluid in the intercellular tissue spaces of the body (eg, muscles).

EEOC: Equal Employment Opportunity Commission; federal agency charged with administering Title VII of the Civil Rights Act of 1964 and the Age Discrimination in Employment Act.

ejection fraction: The percent of blood inside the heart ejected on each beat, generally 50% or greater.

electrophysiologic testing: A technique of programmed stimulation of the heart muscle using pacemaker wires to diagnose and treat cardiac dysrhythmias.

encoding: Translation of information from one form to another prior to storage in memory.

environmental prosthesis: Modification of surroundings for the purpose of facilitating adaptive behavior.

ergonomics: Application of a body of knowledge dealing with the interactions between man and his total working environment, as well as all tools and equipment of the workplace.

esophageal speech: Voice produced by the laryngectomee with self-injected air that sets the muscles of the upper esophagus and pharynx into vibration.

executive functions: "Meta-cognitive" abilities including planning, self-monitoring, self-correcting, initiating, and using feedback.

facet arthropathy: Intervertebral joint disease in the posterior spinal elements.

fellow servant rule: Common law rule that the employer is not liable for injuries to an employee caused by the negligence of a fellow employee.

FEV$_1$ (forced expiratory volume in 1 second): The volume of gas exhaled in the first second of a maximal exhalation.

fibrillation: A disorganized electrical rhythm of the heart. Atrial fibrillation leads to rapid heart rates and disorganized pumping function. Ventricular fibrillation leads to cardiac arrest and death if not treated.

figure-ground discrimination: Ability to separate a salient item from its context.

flail knee: Refers to a knee joint so lax it seems to swing around like a weight on the end of a string.

Frank-Starling mechanism: Compensatory mechanism of damaged heart muscle whereby increased stretching of the muscle leads to increased contraction.

functional capacity: A term that designates the capacity to work or exercise, generally measured in energy expended (METs), anthropometric limits (eg, reach), or physical prowess (eg, lifting capacity).

Glasgow Coma Scale: Clinical tool for measuring depth of unconsciousness; uses measures of motor, verbal, and oculomotor function.

glomerulonephritis: Inflammatory changes in the kidneys that may be acute or chronic.

handicap: An environmental or societal problem in resettling of a disabled person trying to pursue a position.

harness: The straps, retainers, clips, etc., that are used to suspend an upper extremity prosthesis from the body. Activating cables are attached to the harness.

hemodialysis: Removal and filtration of a person's blood by way of a vascular shunt.

hypercapnia: An increase in carbon dioxide in the blood.

hypesthesia: Diminished sensation to pain or temperature.

hypoxemia: A reduction in the oxygenation of the blood, as measured in arterial blood oxygen tension (PaO_2).

impairment: According to the WHO, an organ defect, with abnormality of structure, appearance, or function (eg, coronary artery disease, blindness, peripheral nerve injury, etc.); generally synonymous with diagnosis.

impairment rating: Rating by a physician of the permanent degree of anatomic or physiologic loss of function; measured in percentage of whole body (eg, amputation of arm at the elbow = 57% of whole body; continued angina pectoris and ventricular failure after coronary bypass surgery, low ejection fraction = 90% of whole body impairment).

inotropic effect: Refers to the contractile function of the heart. Certain drugs that stimulate the contraction of heart muscle have a positive inotropic effect.

intoxication: Recent ingestion of a psychoactive substance coupled with mal-adaptive behavioral change and substance-specific physiologic or psychologic signs.

intubation: The insertion of a tube into a body canal or hollow organ, as into the trachea.

invasion of privacy: Tort of unreasonable interference with a person's solitude or personality; includes intrusion into seclusion or affairs, public disclosure of private facts, appropriation of name or likeness, and placing a person in a false light.

ipsilateral: On the same side.

ischial tuberosity: The large rounded protuberance on the lower end of the pelvic bone; the point on which one sits.

isokinetic strength tests: Technique to measure muscle group strength at constant speed of motion throughout the joint range.

jargon: Communication impairment characterized by continuous speech that may be unintelligible or lack meaning.

job-relatedness: Defense to Title VII cases; use of selection criteria significantly correlated with essential elements of the job.

kyphosis: An increased convexity of the curvature of the thoracic spine.

language: Symbols through which thoughts, ideas, and desires are communicated. Linguistic symbols may include pictures, words, or gestures.

laryngitis: Inflammation of the larynx.

lesion: Pathologic change of tissue due to injury or disease.

leukoplakia: White patches on the vocal folds that can be premalignant.

METs: The energy expended during any activity compared to that expended under resting conditions (eg, 2 METs is a work rate twice that of the resting level).

meta-cognitive functions: Those abilities involving simultaneous and coordinated use of multiple cognitive skills. See *executive functions.*

minute ventilation (V_E): The volume exhaled in 1 minute; may be measured at rest or during exercise.

modality: Sensory mode through which information is received, such as visual, auditory, olfactory, tactile, and taste.

motor point block: A technique to decrease spasticity in a muscle by injecting a caustic substance, such as phenol, into the area of intramuscular nerve branches resulting in their sclerosis (also referred to as intramuscular neurolysis).

multiple myeloma: Malignant neoplasm of plasma cells with multiple bone marrow tumor cell foci and widespread bony lytic lesions appearing punched out on x-ray.

MVV (maximum voluntary ventilation): The volume exhaled in 1 minute with a maximal effort, usually measured over 15 seconds and extrapolated to 1 minute.

myocardial infarction (MI): Damage to heart muscle secondary to acute closure of a coronary artery.

myocardial ischemia: Imbalance between the oxygen demands and oxygen supplies to the heart muscle generally resulting in angina pectoris.

myocardial necrosis: Death of a portion of heart muscle and replacement by scar tissue; usually secondary to myocardial infarction.

myoelectric: A term referring to the use of electrical signals that arise in muscles, when nerve impulses pass through the muscle, for controlling prostheses. By detecting these nerve signals, it is possible to activate electric motors in the socket of the prosthesis and thus simulate human motion more closely.

neuroma: A benign tumor arising from the fibrous coverings of a peripheral nerve often after the nerve is cut. It is usually symptomless unless pressure is applied to it.

neuropsychological evaluation: Series of psychological test and procedures used to evaluate the integrity of brain functions.

NIOSH: National Institute for Occupational Safety and Health; part of U.S. Department of Health and Human Services responsible for research on job safety and health matters.

obstructive ventilatory impairment: A reduction in the rate at which gas can be expelled from the lungs due to obstruction of the airways.

OSHA: Occupational Safety and Health Administration; federal agency charged with administering the Occupational Safety and Health Act of 1970.

OSHA standard: Regulation specifying required methods of eliminating workplace safety or health hazard.

osteoarthritis: A condition common in any vertebrate creature. In humans, one or more joints may become painful, weak, and unstable; bony spurs called osteophytes form at joint margins. The cartilage in the affected joints is destroyed slowly. It is not generally considered a systemic disease. Although the causes are not fully known or understood, overuse, trauma, obesity, or aging may be jointly responsible.

osteophytosis: A sign of degenerating disc disease, it is demonstrated as bony overgrowth of the vertebral segments.

oxygen consumption ($\dot{V}O_2$): The volume of oxygen consumed per unit time; a measure of the rate of energy expenditure (ie, the work rate).

pain clinic: A clinic organized to treat intractable pain. Usually a group of specialists work as a team. Typically the clinic will be staffed by one or more physicians, a nurse, several therapists, and a psychologist with a background in behavioral management.

paired associate learning: Memory test requiring the individual to supply the second member of a word pair when the first word is presented by the examiner.

palilalia: The repetition of one's own words.

paraphasia: Word substitution.

pars interarticularis: Interlocking bone connecting adjacent vertebral segments.

patellar tendon: The tough, whitish cord consisting of numerous parallel bundles of collagen fibers that attaches the lower end of the knee cap to the upper end of the tibia or shin bone. In kneeling, one bears weight on the patellar tendons.

pelvic band: A molded strap of metal (usually covered with leather or plastic) designed to suspend a lower limb prosthesis as one would suspend a pair of pants with a belt.

peripheral arthritis: A nonspecific term for pain, stiffening, inflammation, or deformation in the joints of the upper or lower extremities, rather than the joints of the spine, including the neck.

peripheral vascular disease: Disease involving any part of the arteries or veins.

peritoneal dialysis: In the absence of kidney function, removal of a person's liquid waste material by administration of fluid into the abdomen, and later removal of the fluid.

perseveration: Persistent repetition of the same verbal or motor response to varied stimuli.

phantom pain: Pain that seems to come from the amputated part and believed to arise from stimulation of the severed nerves that formerly carried messages from the removed portion.

phantom sensation: The sensation that an arm or leg or part of an arm or leg is still attached to the body after an amputation.

phocomelia: Absence of the proximal portion of a limb or limbs so that the hands or feet are attached to the trunk by a single small bone.

phonation (voice): Physiologic process of producing voice within the larynx.

Pick's disease: Lobar atrophy of the brain.

post-traumatic amnesia (PTA): Period of clouded consciousness following the onset of brain dysfunction. PTA begins with emergence from coma and ends with the return of continuous day-to-day memory.

practical intelligence: Capacity to deal effectively in real-world settings, including occupational, community, and home environments.

pragmatics: In communication, the rules underlying the use or function of language.

procedural memory: Ability to learn and remember skills or techniques; contrasts with memory for facts or events.

prosody: The variation in stress, pitch, and rhythm of speech by which different shades of meaning are conveyed.

prosthesis: Artificial limb.

psoriatic arthritis: A spondyloarthropathy in patients who have psoriasis; the spine may be affected similar to involvement in ankylosing spondylitis. Other small joints may also be involved.

psychomotor speed: Rate at which cognitively mediated motor behavior occurs.

quadrilateral socket: A socket for the above-knee amputee that has an opening with four sides; the anterior and lateral sides are higher than the posterior ones so that the stump can be better stabilized inside the socket.

radicular effects: Patient's complaints on exam findings related to nerve root impingement.

radionuclide ventriculogram: An imaging technique that uses radioactive tracers to demonstrate the contraction pattern of the ventricles.

reasonable accommodation: Affirmative obligation imposed by handicap discrimination laws to accommodate the physical and mental limitations of employees and applicants unless it would impose an undue burden on the conduct of the business.

Reiter's disease: A spondyloarthropathy in which parts of the spine are similar to those with ankylosing spondylitis and parts are normal. The tendency to get this condition seems to be inherited.

remote memory: Very long-term memory; historical recollection.

residual volume: The volume of gas remaining in the lung at the end of a maximal exhalation.

restrictive ventilatory impairment: A reduction in the total amount of gas that can be expelled from the lungs with a maximal breath. This reduction may be due to abnormalities of the lung or of the chest wall that reduce the volume of the lung at maximal inspiration.

revascularization: The restoration of blood flow to an area of heart muscle either by coronary angioplasty or coronary artery bypass graft surgery.

rheumatoid arthritis (RA): A disease in which the tissue that lines the joints (synovial tissue) becomes inflamed. Usually both sides of the body are affected similarly. It cripples by deforming and destroying the joints, and even eroding the bones; it may fuse the joints into an unmovable mass (ankylosis) or make them so loose they do not work (laxity). RA is also a systemic disease that may affect the eyes, nervous system, lungs, blood, lymph system, and skin (subcutaneous nodules). The cause is not fully known or understood. RA is rarely fatal.

SACH: An abbreviation referring to a special type of replacement for a foot-and-ankle assembly that has no joints and instead consists of a wooden heel surrounded by a firm foam material; hence, a Solid Ankle Cushion Heel.

Scheuermann's disease: Juvenile-onset disease of the spinal growth centers.

scoliosis: Lateral curvature of the spine.

semantic memory: Organized knowledge about words, verbal symbols, and facts.

semantic neologisms: Newly coined words, the meaning of which may be known only to the person using it.

semantics: The meaning or content of language.

sensory feedback: Feedback refers to the coupling of the output of a process to the input. The term ''sensory feedback'' is used in prosthetics to mean the sensory signals experienced by the amputee in detecting the position and function of his or her prosthesis.

short-term memory: Limited-capacity working memory. Contents are in conscious awareness.

shoulder extension: Backward movement of the upper arm on the trunk at the shoulder.

shoulder flexion: Forward movement of the upper arm away from the trunk at the shoulder.

socket: In strict medical definition, the hollow or depression of the prosthesis applied to fit the residual limb.

spastic dysphonia: Hyperadduction or hyperabduction of the vocal cords of neurogenic origin.

speech: Physical production of speech sounds through the sequenced articulatory movements of the tongue, palate, and lips.

speech pathologist: A certified health care professional trained in the diagnosis and management of speech, language, voice, and fluency disorders.

spina bifida occulta: Defect in bony spinal canal without spinal cord protrusion.

spinal segmentation abnormality: Instability of spinal structure noted especially with trunk movement.

spirometry: Technique used to measure vital capacity of lungs; exhaled breath measured for total amount and rate of flow.

spondyloarthropathies: Forms of arthritis similar to rheumatoid arthritis except that not only the synovial tissue but also the tissue that fastens ligaments and muscular tendons to bones—the enthesis—become inflamed and turn to bone. Finally, one bone is immovably linked to another. Asymmetric involvement may occur. These diseases may run in families.

spondyloarthropathy: Disease of joint(s) of the spine.

spondylolisthesis: Forward displacement of one vertebra over another, usually of the L5 segment over the sacrum, or the L4 segment over L5, after a pars interarticularis defect.

stasis: Stagnation or cessation of flow; for example, venous stasis refers to inability of the veins to carry blood effectively from the limbs toward the heart.

stump shrinker: A knitted or elastic sleeve of adjustable design to cover and compress the stump so as to reduce or prevent excessive swelling.

subluxation: Partial dislocation of a joint.

supracondylar cuff: The strap in a below-knee prosthesis that suspends the prosthesis by encircling the lower end of the thigh above the prominent bony ends of the femur or the condyles.

suspension: A general term used to describe how a prosthesis is held on to the remaining limb. Generally, suspension is achieved by straps or belts, but it can also be built into the socket itself through suction.

syncope: Fainting spell due to decreased blood output of the heart or low blood pressure.

synovitis: Inflammation of the synovium, or lining of a joint. Inside the synovium is the synovial fluid, which normally looks almost clear; it becomes cloudy when the joint is inflamed.

syntax: The structure of grammatical aspects of language.

tachycardia: A fast heart rate, usually greater than 100 beats per minute.

tangentiality: Divergence, digression; a state of abrupt change in the course of conversation.

tendon angulation: A measurement of the geometric relationship between a tendon and a bone.

terminal device: The operating end of any upper extremity prosthesis, generally classified into hooks or hands, but can include special tools, such as hammers, wrenches, etc.

thallium perfusion scintigraphy: An imaging technique using radioactive tracers to evaluate distribution of blood flow to the heart muscle.

Title VII: Part of the Civil Rights Act of 1964 prohibiting discrimination in employment based on race, color, religion, sex, or national origin.

tort: A private or civil wrong, independent of a contract, arising from a violation of a duty.

total lung capacity: The total volume of gas in the lung at maximal inspiration.

toxemia: An abnormal condition associated with the presence of poisonous substances in the blood.

tracheoesophageal speech: Voice produced by the laryngectomee. Lung air is diverted into the esophagus via a prosthesis allowing esophageal speech to be produced.

transfer activities: A general term referring to all actions in which a person changes from one posture to another; for example, turning from one side to another, coming from lying to sitting, moving from one surface to another as from a bed to a wheelchair.

unilateral neglect: Failure to notice or respond to stimuli from the side of space opposite the lesioned hemisphere, despite adequate sensation and comprehension; may occur in any sensory modality, but is primarily observed in the visual sphere.

universal cuff: An assistive device consisting of a leather cuff or mitt worn over a paretic hand. Various utensils used for ADLs can be attached to the cuff resulting in improved function in an individual unable to grasp them otherwise.

unstable angina: The syndrome of increasing frequency or severity of angina pectoris usually associated with severe coronary artery disease.

valgus: A deformity in which a joint is bent so that the more distant part of it leans away from the center of the body.

varus: A deformity in which part of the body is bent inward, as, for example, in bow legs. It is the opposite of valgus.

ventilation: See *dead space ventilation; MVV; minute ventilation.*

ventricular dysfunction: Abnormal contraction or relaxation of the right or left ventricles.

ventricular tachycardia: Three or more ventricular premature beats in a row; a rhythm associated with a high likelihood of syncope or sudden cardiac death.

verbal reasoning: The drawing of inferences or conclusions via linguistically mediated thought processes.

visual memory: Recall of information presented through the visual modality; usually involves spatial or figural material.

visual organization: Mentally arranging the elements of a visual display.

visual synthesis: Mentally integrating and combining fragmented elements into a whole.

vital capacity: See *FVC*.

$\dot{V}O_2$ max (maximum oxygen consumption): The maximum rate of oxygen use that can be reached during exercise; a measure of the maximum work rate.

vocal abuse: Condition in which the vocal cords are forced to adduct in a hyperfunctional manner.

vocal nodules: Small white protuberance on the free margin of the vocal cord at the junction of the anterior and middle third.

vocal polyps: Smooth rounded, sessile, or pedunculated swellings, occurring on the true vocal cords.

Wernicke's aphasia: Language disorder characterized by fluent, but paraphasic speech output; comprehension is severely impaired.

Whipple's disease: A spondyloarthropathy (spine arthritis) in combination with a disease of the bowel.

withdrawal: A syndrome that develops in a substance-dependent individual coincident with the reduction or cessation of substance use, which has substance-specific physical and psychological effects.

wrist flexion: Flexion of the wrist toward the palmar side.

Index